Dave's Book of Top 10 Lists for

Great Windows Programming

Dave Edson

M&T BOOKS

M&T Books
A Division of MIS:Press, Inc.
A Subsidiary of Henry Holt and Company, Inc.
115 West 18th Street
New York, New York 10011

© 1995 by Dave Edson/Chapters 17-22 © by Bob Schmidt

Printed in the United States of America

All rights reserved. No part of this book may be reproduced or transmitted in any form or by any means, electronic or mechanical, including photocopying, recording, or by any information storage and retrieval system, without prior written permission from the Publisher. Contact the Publisher for information on foreign rights.

Limits of Liability and Disclaimer of Warranty

The Author and Publisher of this book have used their best efforts in preparing the book and the programs contained in it. These efforts include the development, research, and testing of the theories and programs to determine their effectiveness.

The Author and Publisher make no warranty of any kind, expressed or implied, with regard to these programs or the documentation contained in this book. The Author and Publisher shall not be liable in any event for incidental or consequential damages in connection with, or arising out of, the furnishing, performance, or use of these programs.

All products, names and services are trademarks or registered trademarks of their respective companies.

Edson, Dave.
    Great Windows Programming : Dave's Book of Top Ten Lists/Dave Edson.
        p.   cm.
    Includes Index
    ISBN 1-55851-388-4
    1. Windows (Computer programs) 2. Daytona (Computer file)
    I. Title.
    QA76.76.W56E26   1994   94-24153
    005.265—dc20   CIP

Editor-in-Chief: Paul Farrell   Technical Editor: Bob Schmidt
Project Editor: Michael Sprague   Production Editor: Anne Alessi
Development Editor: Kevin Shafer   Assoc. Production Editor: Erika Putre

Dedication

This book is dedicated to my wife, Kate, who actually let me write this book almost immediately after finishing my last one.

Hats Off...

To Eric Maffei, Gretchen Bilson, and Laura Euler at the Microsoft Systems Journal for letting me get away with so much goofiness in my articles. To the Premier Developer Support Team for knowing so much. To Brian Scott for getting me up to speed on MFC and making sure I wrote good MFC tips. To Brian Staples for bailing me out of NT Kernel issues. To Don Hasson, Randy Morgan, and Mark Bader for coming up with ideas for lists that unfortunately had to be nixed (but thanks for playing!). To Greg Keyser for saving my Windows 95 butt on D-Day (more than once). Hey Greg, I finally installed SLM! To Chris Guzak for answering all those stupid questions about the Common Controls DLL. To Kyle Sparks for knowing about the bowels of NT. To Bob Schmidt for writing the last section of this book, for making sure I write better C code, and for providing dry, callous remarks every time I say the word "WinCheck." (LoseCheck?) To Kate for dealing with me through this and supplying additional doses of inspiration. To Joe Rzepiejewski for showing me something cool about SendMessage and deadlock under Windows NT. To Pogo, Roxy, and Hannah for keeping the LaserJet's corona wires furry. To the Late Gene Roddenberry for creating *Star Trek*. And, to the U.S. Media, which blows everything out of proportion, giving me an excellent source for my weird sense of humor.

Foreword

The Pacific Northwest is home to a Very Big Software Company that develops and sells incredible amounts of the most popular software on earth. To try and keep the purchasers of all that software happy,

the Very Big Software Company provides phone support. Callers who are especially lucky (those whose employers have paid the extra fee for "premier tier support") and don't hang up during the occasional music-on-hold (usually the latest Pacific Northwest grunge band) will end up getting routed to Dave Edson. Dave is somewhat of a black belt, having mastered the entire family of Microsoft Windows operating systems.

Dave has been programming for over fifteen years, almost since the first day that micro-based systems were readily available. It all started back in 1978, on the outskirts of Boise, Idaho, when a plucky thirteen-year old got his hands on his first micro—an Ohio Scientific Superboard II. Since then he's followed a twisty little maze that led him from BASIC-In-ROM through assembler to his current status as a C and C++ Windows guru and author of the book you're now holding.

Too many of the Windows programming books currently available are repetitious, superfluous, and irrelevant. Dozens mindlessly regurgitate baseline information already covered by the SDK, pore over internal Windows vestiges such as the Bunny_351 call, or posit conspiracy theories concerning undocumented functions. This book is different. It's a pragmatic guide to all variants of Windows, including 16-bit Windows 3.x, Windows for Workgroups, Windows 95 (formerly codenamed Chicago), as well as Windows NT Workstation and Windows NT Advanced Server (formerly codenamed Daytona). Dave puts heavy emphasis on the Win32 API—the future arena for all Windows programmers—and all the subtle and not so subtle ways its implementation varies from Win32s to Windows 95 and Windows NT.

Both beginning Windows programmers and seasoned pros alike will profit from Dave's Top Ten Lists. If you're a novice, you'll become familiar with the myriad gotchas you should be aware of in advance of writing your first line of code. You'll be able to anticipate and avoid typical Windows programming headaches, and avail yourself of the kind of programming insights that are gained only after many long nights spent coding and drinking many cups of coffee (OK, latte, if you too are in the Pacific Northwest).

If you're a veteran, you'll find this book chock full of practical information that's immediately applicable to your day-to-day coding tasks. Dave's lists can be put to work as checklists of do's and don't for yourself as well as your entire development team. Dave's sample code will greatly aid not only programmers working with Visual C++ and the MFC Class library, but those pedal to the metal programmers who are sticking to coding with straight C and the Windows API.

Each hour spent perusing the lists of tips, tricks, and pitfalls that Dave supplies in these pages can help shave days off your development cycle. If you're in the bookstore right now asking yourself whether this book is worth your while (and your $39.95), my answer is an unqualified yes. Head straight to the cashier. Then go back to your PC, fire up your compiler, put Dave's ideas to work, and write some great Windows code.

Eric J. Maffei
Editor-in-Chief, Microsoft Systems Journal
New York, October 1994

About Windows 95

The programming information in this book is based on information for developing applications for Windows 95 made public by Microsoft in their 6.4 beta release in October. Since this information was made public before the final release of the product, there may have been changes to some of the programming interfaces by the time the product is finally released. We encourage you to check the updated development information that should be part of your development system for resolving issues that might arise.

The end user information in this book is based on information on Windows 95 made public by Microsoft with their 6.4 beta released in October. Since this information was made public before the release of the product, we encourage you to visit your local bookstore at that time for updated books on Windows 95.

If you have a modem or access to the Internet, you can always get up-to-the-minute information on Windows 95 direct from Microsoft on WinNews:

On CompuServe:	GO WINNEWS
On the Internet:	ftp://ftp.microsoft.com/PerOpSys/Win_News/Chicago
	http://www.microsoft.com
On AOL:	keyword WINNEWS
On Prodigy	jumpword WINNEWS
On Genie	WINNEWS file area on Windows RTC

You can also subscribe to Microsoft's WinNews electronic Newsletter by sending Internet email to enews@microsoft.nwnet.com and putting the words SUBSCRIBE WINNEWS in the text of the email.

TABLE OF CONTENTS

INTRODUCTION

This is a book of answers. Answers to programming questions. As a Windows Programming Support Engineer, I spend all day, every day, helping fellow programmers get out of binds. That is the inspiration for this book. Before you call your techie support person, check here. You may find the answer you need without having to wait for a response on CompuServe, the phone, or the Internet. And even if you don't find the answer, you may stumble across a tip that makes your programming day a little more pleasant.

With Windows NT, Windows 95, MFC, and OLE, Windows programming has become a task too huge for any one person to master. This book does not contain only my knowlege. It brings in the talents of many of my programming buddies who excel in areas that I don't. The end result is that this book covers a vast array of topics about Windows programming. With the exception of Part 4 ("Programming in C"), I did actually write all the words in the first three sections of this book; so don't worry about wading through a bunch of different people's writing styles. The lists that were devised by my pals were handed to me in a nice technobabble rough "Here it is Dave!" form. However, Part 4 was written completely by Bob Schmidt. Bob is almost *Mr. C.* His credentials include schooling from one of the people on the ANSI C Standards Committee, and his code is extremely consistent, portable, and well-designed. He has written six lists of great information about programming with the C language (and C++); I will expunge on that later in this introduction.

Something you won't find much of in this book is 16-bit Windows programming. Windows 95 (code named "Chicago") and Windows NT ("Daytona") will completely dominate the Windows Desktop by the end of 1995. The information in this book is almost exclusively 32-bit, and therefore, the information is equally valid for Windows 95 and Windows NT. Of course, as of the writing of this material, Windows 95 hasn't shipped yet. This book was completed at the "M7" beta timeframe, and I have been assured that the API's and programming techniques won't (read: shouldn't) change any more in the future. Still, if you find that one of my Windows 95 tips seems to work a little strange (or maybe won't even compile), check the latest docs from Microsoft, especially once Windows 95 ships.

Some of the material in this book you may have read in the Microsoft Systems Journal (MSJ). I have taken the original material from these lists, and updated them to correct errors, and to be valid for Windows 95 and Windows NT. This means that some of the tips have changed a little, and some tips have even been completely replaced with new tips that are more relevant for the new versions of Windows. So they are not a total "recycling" job, consider them new, up-to-date material.

Most of the material, however, is brand new, and I am sure that at least one of your programming questions will be solved somewhere in one of my lists. Let's take a look at how this book is organized:

Part 1: General Windows Stuff

This part of the book covers your basic windows programming questions, with no binding to a particular operating system. These tips work for Windows 95, Windows NT, and even Windows 16-bit. Quite a bit of these lists are oriented towards user interface programming, as you can see in the lists:

Chapter 1, "Things You Might Want to Know About USER" is a hodgepodge of facts I have discovered about USER, along with a couple tricks to get some nice stuff done. For example, I cover dialogs, the new Menu messages, and the Common Dialogs.

Chapter 2, "Things You Might Want to Know About Windows KERNEL" is Brian Staple's list of the most common questions and answers he hears about dealing with the low-level system services of Kernel.

Chapter 3, "Party Phrases to Ensure that You Maintain Your Computer Nerd Status" is required reading for my disciples.

Chapter 4, "Ways to Lose, Waste, Track, or Ration System Resources" applies as much to Win32 programming as it does Win16. Even though Windows 95 provides you with a 4MB USER Heap, it is still no excuse to waste system resources. No matter how much memory is available, keep in mind that software will find ways to eat it all up. This chapter provides some techniques (mainly for C programmers) to manage these resources, and includes a tool to try and make life easier for Win16 programmers.

Chapter 5, "Common Headaches Encountered by Windows Programmers" covers those common roadblocks that so many of the programmers I support run into. These headaches range from improper initialization of fields to strange behavior by Windows controls.

Chapter 6, "Very Bad Things to Do While Writing Windows Code" is a laundry list of the things that make products like Windows 95 take so long to develop. This list came from a developer at Microsoft who loves to point out "bad apps" that force them to write compatibility hacks. If you don't do any of the things on this list, your program has a much much better chance of requiring nothing more than a recompile to run on the next flavor of the operating system.

Chapter 7, "Tricks, Hints, and Techniques for Programming in Windows" is an updated version of an MSJ article I wrote. These are ten of my very favorite cool things to do while writing Windows programs, everything here is documented and legal. I cover topics such as messing around with WM_NCHITTEST to make Windows obey your every wish and using invisible windows to prevent the users from spazzing out with mouse clicking fits.

Part 2: Windows NT and Windows 95 Specialties

This part of the book focuses on particular aspects of 32 bit Windows programming, for both Windows NT and Windows 95. I cover some of the major new concepts that mess with our heads about Win32, as well as the new goodies in Windows 95.

Chapter 8, "Migrating to Win32" is an updated version of the MSJ article I wrote. This list is a must for programmers who are moving their 16-bit code to Windows 95 or Windows NT. These porting "beasties" range from integer size conversion to file layouts.

Chapter 9, "Questions About Win32" comes from Kyle Sparks; he told me of those nasty problems that befuddle us at 3am when writing our 32-bit code. Topics range from special issues involved with subclassing to how SendMessage between threads and processes can cause deadlock (along with a solution to deadlock from Joe Rzepiejewski).

Chapter 10, "Windows 95 Road Signs" is a very modified version of the "Seventeen Techniques" MSJ article. This list is aimed more at program managers and program designers than it is aimed at programmers. The technical details are fairly soft, while the overall concept and guidelines, such as new tools and paradigms are dicussed.

Chapter 11, "Windows 95 User Interface Goodies" is for the programmers. This MondoList is a combination of the three-part MSJ series I did (six goodies), along with four more goodies that did not make it into the series. And, since so much changed after those articles came out, you should re-read this list in its entirety to see how API's and interfaces changed. This list covers goodies such as the RichEdit control, the Toolbar Control, the ListView control, the Header Control, the Image List, and five other goodies.

Chapter 12, "Names of Pets Owned by Windows Programmers" was written with Pogo, Roxy, and Hannah keeping me at gunpoint in front of my computer.

Part 3: MFC

Hopefully everyone who starts writing new applications will use C++ and the Microsoft Foundation Classes (MFC). It's so much nicer, more convienient, and powerful. Of course, it's also much more to learn. And, the way this industry works, we find ourselves learning new concepts such as MFC by... writing a new program that's due in a month. So, we find ourselves diving into a huge mess, and only asking for help when we need it. Of course, there are those lucky few who had the time and resources to learn MFC before they needed to write that Killer App. Brian Scott is one of them. He gave me a trio of lists that really made it a lot easier for me to get my MFC programming in order. And, since Brian answers MFC questions all day at his job, he has put the really good ones here.

Chapter 13, "MFC Gotchas" is a list of all those mistakes we make while writing our first (and probably second) MFC program. This list covers the real answers for issues such as object lists, the Document/View architecture, and CDialogs.

Chapter 14, "Cool MFC Ideas" covers the tricks Brian uses to make his programming life easier under MFC. Although MFC provides a lot of really great features, there is always room for more. Topics of this list include things such as getting at global data easily, subclassing, dealing with the CFormViews, and message maps.

Chapter 15, "Pre-IBM PC Trivia" should bring a tear to your nostalgic eye.

Chapter 16, "MFC Programming Checklist" provides you with advice to decide the *strategy* of your MFC application *before* you write even one line of code. You should read this list before running AppWizard: It will make life easier for you in the long run. Topics include debugging facilities, class design and interopability, and some OLE considerations.

Part 4: Programming à la C

This is a mini-book within a book. You will find an introduction and an in-depth explanation for the chapters, as well as his rules and conventions all at the start of this section.

In brief, this part contains three lists for C programmers, and three lists for C++ programmers. Topics include enumerations, constants, conversion from C to C++, ANSI C, and unexpected behavior of C compilers.

Since I didn't write a single word of this part, I can review it without beating my own drum: It's excellent. Bob's knowledge of C and C++ is through and very textbook. If we all write code like this, we would have a lot better programs floating around. And, Bob's writing style makes this a truly enjoyable experience.

About the Code Listings and the Disk

All of the code written in the first three parts is designed to compile using Microsoft Visual C++ Version 2.0. If the code is for Windows NT, you can use the compiler "out of the box". If the code is for Windows 95, you will (during the beta) need to install VC++ 2.0 first, then install the Windows 95 SDK. I'm sure Microsoft will release a integrated Windows 95/VC++ programming environment as soon as possible.

The enclosed disk has all of the listings in this book, as well as makefiles and other giblets associated with them. The files may be compressed, the PKUNZIP utility will be supplied in that case. If you need to unzip any files, be sure to use the -d switch:

```
PKUNZIP -d MYFILE.ZIP
```

in order to preserve directory names.

About Some of the People Who Helped (they helped me write these Bio's)

Brian Scott works for a large software company in the Pacific Northwest in the Premier Developer Support Team, helping big companies fix their code. He has been working with C++ and MFC for 3 years. He has a BS in Physics and Math from University in Texas, and a Masters in Physics from University of California, at Santa Barbara. After studying physics for so long, he decided playing with computers is more fun. Brian likes hiking, wierd fringe theater movies, and coffee. Brian lives in the House of Grapes with his wife Carla.

Kyle Sparks is a programmer for a large software company in the Pacific Northwest who has spent most of the last six and a half years supporting everything from the Xenix Cobol compiler to the Windows DDK. He spent a brief two years wearing his software engineer hat on two successive versions of Microsoft Test for Windows. From time to time, he enjoys doing what got him started in computers: freelance vertical-market programming on everything from silly Macintosh apps to contract Windows device drivers. He resides in rural Maple Valley, Washington with his wife, Loretta.

Brian Staples (a.k.a. "Brain Staples") is yet another programmer for a large software company in the Pacific Northwest who also works in Premier Developer Support Team. He has a BS in Computer Information Sciences from Ohio State. He enjoys everyting about the Pacific Northwest and recently climbed almost to the top of Mount Rainer.

Part 1

General Windows Stuff

CHAPTER 1

Things You Might Want to Know About USER

USER is a core component of the Windows operating system. It handles the user interface, which is comprised of window management, message handling, controls, menus, and high-level input (such as the keyboard and mouse messages). If you check out the "User Functions" part of the help file, you can see the enormous amount of responsibility that USER has.

These ten things about USER range from tips to traps to simple information about Windows. They all have USER in common, and the example listings should help you out in some way during your Windows programming ventures. Remember first and foremost that USER is nothing but a DLL, and anything they do, you can do as well.

10. Popup Menus Are Windows

Not only are popup menus windows, but they are really a type of control. You can't create one by using **CreateWindow** (well, I guess you can, but that's undocumented, and you will probably end up hosing yourself). So, even though you use **CreateMenu** or some other menu API, you will still end up getting a window. The catch is: How to get the window handle to that menu? Well, Microsoft has made the classname "#32768" the official classname of the popup menu (the menu bar on your top-level windows are not really menus—they are just a nice paint job by USER). Therefore, if you use **FindWindow** with "#32768" as the **szClassname**, you will get back the handle to the currently displayed popup menu. Once you have this handle, you can send it messages. These messages are freshly documented in Windows 95.

Now, before I go into these messages, please keep in mind that you are fooling around with Mother Nature here. Don't just arbitrarily do funky stuff to these menus. Use these messages wisely, and don't even consider changing the menu of any app except your own app.

MN_SETHMENU (WM_USER+1)

```
wParam:       HMENU handle to set
lParam:       Not used, set to zero
Return value:   n/a
```

This message sets the menu to use the new hMenu indicated in *wParam* (handy for changing the contents of the menu on the fly).

MN_GETHMENU (WM_USER+2)

```
wParam:       Not used, set to zero
lParam:       Not used, set to zero
Return Value:   HMENU handle
```

This message gets the HMENU handle of the menu window receiving this message.

MN_SIZEWINDOW (WM_USER+3)

```
wParam:        Not used, set to zero
lParam:        Not used, set to zero
Return Value:    Loword: cx, Hiword: cy
```

This message forces a menu to resize itself to a "comfortable" size. The WM_MEASUREITEM message is forced for owner-draw menus in response to this message. This is usually used after MN_SETHMENU.

MN_OPENHEIRARCHY (WM_USER+4)

```
wParam:        Not used, set to zero
lParam:        Not used, set to zero
Return Value:    hWnd of new Popup cascading menu
```

This message forces a nested popup menu to "pop out." The current menu selection must be over the popout menu's title with the arrow for this message to work.

MN_CLOSEHEIRARCHY (WM_USER+5)

```
wParam:        Not used, set to zero
lParam:        Not used, set to zero
Return Value:    n/a
```

This message is the opposite of the MN_OPENHEIRARCHY message.

MN_SELECTITEM (WM_USER+6)

```
wParam:       Zero-based MF_BYPOSITION index of menu item to select, -1 for none
lParam:       Not used, set to zero
Return Value:  MF_* flags of item
```

This message selects an item in the menu (if possible), forcing a WM_MENUSELECT message to be sent to the menu's owner. This is useful for automation.

MN_CANCELMENUS (WM_USER+7)

```
wParam: Command ID to send (ID of menu item)
lParam: LOWORD: TRUE to choose the item (and send a WM_COMMAND), FALSE to cancel and
        just close the menus
Return Value:    n/a
```

This message is used to either choose a menu and cause a WM_COMMAND to be sent if the LOWORD of *lParam* is set to TRUE. If the LOWORD of *lParam* is sent to FALSE, the entire menu hierarchy is closed up. This is helpful to cancel "menu mode."

MN_SELECTFIRSTVALIDITEM (WM_USER+8)

```
wParam: Not used, set to zero
lParam: Not used, set to zero
Return Value:    Zero-based index of first valid item selected
```

This message selects the first valid item in the menu, skipping any disabled menus.

These messages are a very powerful (and dangerous) means to get those menus to do what you want them to do. However, keep in mind that you are playing with a loaded Stiletto and that you may get yourself knee-deep in trouble with other applications and future versions of Windows if you aren't careful.

When a popup menu is displayed on the screen, quite simply the "display popup menu" call inside Windows is akin to **CreateWindow** or **ShowWindow** (or both). If you think about how a menu would be implemented, it is quite similar to a list box control. Each menu item is an item in a list box, and selecting the items has a similar effect. There is no real magic involved, although some very interesting hacks are implemented in the menu code to ensure that everything works.

A complete discussion of these hacks can be found in Matt Pietrek's January 1994 *Microsoft Systems Journal* "Questions and Answers" column, under the question from Stephen Johnson. Here's a summary of that column. Just as the **DialogBox** API has its own private little message loop, the same happens when menus are displayed. Therefore, while you have a menu up, it is not a good idea to go into your own **PeekMessage** loop. Doing so will disable menu functionality, since the **IsMenuMessage** type function deep inside USER is starved from execution until your own **PeekMessage** loop returns control. Therefore, don't do **PeekMessage** loops in response to WM_INITMENUPOPUP or WM_MENUSELECT messages, and don't set timers to yank away control (such as the sample program in Pietrek's column did).

9. Dialogs Are Just Windows and Message Boxes Are Just Dialogs

Dialog boxes are critical to the Windows user interface. However, they are essentially the exact same thing as any other window. Take a look at the following pseudocode involved for the **CreateDialogIndirectParam** API:

```
READ Window Caption, styles, and size of dialog box from template
CREATE Window with that handle
WHILE There are child controls to read in template
  CREATE child control with styles and sizes and parent them to main dialog window
```

```
END WHILE
RETURN handle to main dialog
```

Now, take a look at the following pseudocode involved for the **DialogBox** API:

```
READ Template from Program's Resource File
CALL CreateDialogIndirectParam
DISABLE Dialogs' Parent
ENTER PeekMessage Loop Using IsDialogMessage Until Dialog Box is Closed
ENABLE Dialog's Parent
RETURN Exit Code from Dialog
```

This pseudocode is inside USER, and, as you can see, it contains a **PeekMessage** loop that seizes control of program execution until the dialog box is closed.

Listing 1.1 contains a function that emulates the **DialogBox** API. This approach is sometimes desirable because the **PeekMessage** loop in the **DialogBox** API keeps program control down inside the USER DLL until the dialog box is closed. This characteristic of USER may be displeasing, especially if modal and modeless dialogs are mixed up. (In fact, multimodal-mixing algorithms don't work. Microsoft has confirmed this in their Knowledge Base. The reason for this is because a modeless dialog expects the **IsDialogMessage** API to be called from your application, yet, if you have a modal dialog displayed, the program control is inside USER, not your application).

LISTING 1.1 FAKING A MODAL DIALOG BOX WITH A MODELESS DIALOG BOX

```
/***********************************************************************
*                                                                     *
* This function fakes a call to DialogBox, but uses CreateDialog      *
* instead. This keeps the message loop inside your code, not USER's   *
*                                                                     *
***********************************************************************/

BOOL MY_ModalDialog (  LPSTR   szTemplate,
                       FARPROC FunctionName,
                       HWND    hWndParent,
                       LPARAM  lParam
                    )
{
  HWND    hDlg;
  MSG     msg;
```

```
FARPROC  lpfnDlg;

// ghInst is the hInstance of the module that has the resource
// for the dialog.
lpfnDlg = MakeProcInstance ( FunctionName, ghInst );


// Create the dialog ala modeless. You can make your own
// custom window with lits of kiddie controls here if you want,
// the IsDialogMessage API down below will make the keyboard
// accelerators work just fine.
hDlg = CreateDialog ( ghInst, szTemplate, hWndParent, lpfnDlg, lParam );


if (!IsWindow(hDlg)) return FALSE;


// Disable the parent to make the dialog act more modal.
// *** NOTE: Enable the parent BEFORE calling DestroyWindow
// in the Dialog callback procedure, otherwise Windows wont
// know where to set focus to, and most likely it will be
// Program Manager.
EnableWindow ( hWndParent, FALSE );


// Message loop central
do
   {
   if (PeekMessage ( &msg, NULL, 0, 0, PM_REMOVE ))
     if (!IsDialogMessage (hDlg, &msg))
       {
       TranslateMessage ( &msg );
       DispatchMessage  ( &msg );
       }
   }
while (IsWindow(hDlg));


return TRUE;
}
```

The **MY_ModalDialog** function allows for more control, since a modeless dialog is faked to look like a modal dialog. This allows you to put any desired extra code inside the message loop (such as checking a state variable to abnormally shut down or notify the open dialog). Keep in mind that this dialog is a modeless dialog. So, instead of ending the dialog with the **EndDialog** API, close it with the **DestroyWindow** API. It is especially important to use the **EnableWindow** API to re-enable the dialog's parent *before* you destroy the dialog window. If you do no re-enable the parent, Windows will not know where to set focus, and will take a guess. Usually, Program Manager is the Windows guess in Windows 3.1. Therefore, if you close a dialog, and Program Manager pops up front, chances indeed are good that the dialog's parent is disabled.

Since a dialog is just a window, you can do anything to a dialog handle that you can do to a regular window handle. One common operation done by programmers is to use properties in a dialog box. This way, extra information can be stored along with a dialog box. However, dialog properties are slow.

Instead, just do the same thing you would do with any other window—use extra window bytes. In fact, 4 extra bytes are reserved in a standard dialog already! **Set/GetWindowLong (hDlg, DWL_USER,...)** will let you access enough memory to manage a pointer to a structure that contains all the information you may need. See Listing 1.2 for a dialog box function that stores a pointer to an *ITEM* data structure in the extra bytes instead of using a static variable. By using extra bytes instead of a static variable (which usually lives in your DS unless you take advantage of some compiler directives), your program uses less space in your DS. Your function thus remains instanced, which allows for multiple dialogs using the same dialog procedure to be displayed on the screen at the same time.

LISTING 1.2 USING THE DWL_USER EXTRA BYTES TO YOUR ADVANTAGE

```
/*
 * This code comes from the source code to HomeWorks, which
 * is in the book "Writing Windows Applications from Start To
 * Finish".
 *
 * This is just one example of how the DWL_USER extra byte
 * fields can be used. In this sample, a long pointer to
 * the structure below is stored in those extra bytes.
 *
 * At WM_INITDIALOG, the strucutre's pointer is saved in the
 * extra bytes, and the fields on the dialog are filled in with
 * the information in the structure (the code to do this has
 * been pared down for this example).
 *
 * At IDOK time, the pointer to the strucutre is fetched from
 * the dialog, and then the information can be placed back into
```

```
* the data structure.
*
* Applications can have multiple modeless dialogs for different
* items, and all use this same dialog procedure, provided that
* lpItem points to different chunks of memory for each dialog.
*
*/


// This is an ITEM data structure, loaded with all sorts of fields.

typedef struct tagITEM
   {
   LONG    lRecordNumber;
   LONG    lFlags;
   char    szFilterName[MAXFILTERNAMEv100FINAL];
   char    szDescription[MAXDESCLENv100FINAL];
   LONG    lRankDesc ;
   WORD    wProductType;
   LONG    lActualValue;
   LONG    lActualValueTopRange;
   LONG    lInsuredValue;
   LONG    lInsuredValueTopRange;
   WORD    wWarrantyDescription[MAXITEMWARRANTIESv100FINAL];
   WORD    wWarrantyUnit[MAXITEMWARRANTIESv100FINAL];
   LONG    lWarrantyDuration[MAXITEMWARRANTIESv100FINAL];
   WORD    wYearPurchased;
   WORD    wMonthPurchased;
   WORD    wDayPurchased;
   WORD    wYearAppraised;
   WORD    wMonthAppraised;
   WORD    wDayAppraised;
   char    szLocationPurchased[MAXITEMLOCPURCHLENv100FINAL];
   LONG    lRankStore;
   char    szReceiptInformation[MAXITEMRCPINFOLENv100FINAL];
   WORD    wLocationInHome;
   WORD    wCatalogMethod;
   WORD    wSortKey;
   char    szComments[MAXITEMCOMMENTLENv100FINAL];
   COLUMN  ViewColumns[MAXSLIDERCOLUMNSv100FINAL];
   }
ITEM;


/***********************************************************************
*                                                                    *
* This is the dialog box procedure that stores the pointer to an     *
* item in the DWL_USER extra bytes                                   *
```

```
 *                                                                 *
 * Code not relevant to this example has been deleted, therefore   *
 * this is not a complete dialog box procedure.                    *
 *                                                                 *
 ******************************************************************/

DLGPROC ITEM_ItemDlgProc ( DIALOG_PARAMS )
{
  LPITEM lpItem;

  switch ( msg )
    {
    case WM_INITDIALOG: // The pointer to the item comes in lParam

        SetWindowLong ( hDlg, DWL_USER, lParam ); // Sets pointer to ITEM

        lpItem = (LPITEM)lParam;

        /* ... deleted lots of code for this sample */

        SetDlgItemText ( hDlg, IDD_DESCRIPTION,   lpItem->szDescription );
        return TRUE;

    case WM_MYCOMMAND:
    case WM_COMMAND:

      return WM_COMMAND_ItemDlgProcHandler ( hDlg, msg, wParam, lParam );

    default:

      break;
    }

  return FALSE;
}

/******************************************************************
 *                                                                 *
 *                                                                 *
 *                                                                 *
 ******************************************************************/

BOOL WM_COMMAND_ItemDlgProcHandler ( DIALOG_PARAMS )
```

```
{
  LPITEM lpItem;
  WORD   i;

  CRACKER_VARS
  CRACK_MESSAGEsc

  FLOATING_HELP_TRIGGER

  switch ( CRACKER_wID )
    {
    /* Plenty of extra code deleted for this sample */

    case IDOK:

      // This call passes hDlg to FillItemDataStructure so that
      // FillItemDataStructure can also get to the lpItem pointer.

      if (!FillItemDataStructure ( hDlg )) return FALSE;

      // Here we get the pointer to the ITEM

      lpItem = (LPITEM)GetWindowLong ( hDlg, DWL_USER );

      // Dink with it

      lpItem->lFlags |= ITEMFLAG_GETSFOCUS;

      // Update the database

      DBMS_ModifyItem ( ghDBFile, lpItem );

      EndDialog ( hDlg, IDOK );
      return TRUE;

    default:

      break;
    }

  return FALSE;
}
```

If you need more than 4 extra bytes (which should *never* be the case, since you can store a pointer to any-sized structure in 4 bytes), or if you need to change some of the class properties of the dialog at creation time, you can take one of two routes. You can create a custom dialog class, or you can make your own window and use the **IsDialogMessage** trick from Chapter 7, "Tricks, Hints, and Techniques for Programming in Windows."

A message box is nothing more than a dialog box. In fact, if you take the code from Listing 1.1 and modify it to use predefined templates, you could emulate the **MessageBox()** API very easily. You would need to pass the *MB_** flags and your message text in a structure to the dialog box's WM_INITDIALOG message. See Listing 1.3 for a baby **MY_MessageBox** function. I leave it as an exercise to the reader to "smarten up" the algorithm in order to fix up the text placement and message box sizing.

LISTING 1.3 HOME-BREW MESSAGE BOX

```
//=============================================================
//
// MYMSGBOX.H
//
//=============================================================

#define IDD_ICON        1000
#define IDD_TEXT        1001
#define IDD_MSGBUTTON1  1002
#define IDD_MSGBUTTON2  1003
#define IDD_MSGBUTTON3  1004
#define IDD_MSGBUTTON4  1005
#define IDD_MSGBUTTON5  1006

typedef struct tagMSGBOXSTRUCT
    {
    HWND    hWndParent;
    LPSTR   szText   ;
    LPSTR   szCaption ;
    UINT    uiFlags  ;
    }
MSGBOXSTRUCT;

typedef MSGBOXSTRUCT FAR * LPMSGBOXSTRUCT;
```

```
MYMSGBOX_MyMessageBox ( HWND   hParent,
                        LPSTR  szText,
                        LPSTR  szCaption,
                        UINT   uiFlags
                      );


//=============================================================
//
// MYMSGBOX.DLG
//
//=============================================================

MYMSGBOX DIALOG 37, 70, 160, 72
STYLE DS_MODALFRAME | WS_POPUP | WS_VISIBLE | WS_CAPTION | WS_SYSMENU
CAPTION "Messagebox Title"
FONT 8, "MS Sans Serif"
BEGIN
  CONTROL "(icon)", IDD_ICON      , "Static", SS_LEFT,
        6,  9,   0,  0
  CONTROL "",          IDD_TEXT    , "Static", WS_GROUP,
        34,  7, 112, 22
  CONTROL "1",         IDD_MSGBUTTON1, "Button", BS_DEFPUSHBUTTON|WS_TABSTOP,
        19, 39,  40, 14
  CONTROL "2",         IDD_MSGBUTTON2, "Button", BS_PUSHBUTTON  |WS_TABSTOP,
        62, 39,  40, 14
  CONTROL "3",         IDD_MSGBUTTON3, "Button", BS_PUSHBUTTON  |WS_TABSTOP,
        106, 39,  40, 14
  CONTROL "4",         IDD_MSGBUTTON4, "Button", BS_PUSHBUTTON  |WS_TABSTOP,
        41, 39,  40, 14
  CONTROL "5",         IDD_MSGBUTTON5, "Button", BS_PUSHBUTTON  |WS_TABSTOP,
        84, 39,  40, 14
END


//=============================================================
//
// MYMSGBOX.C - A sample my messagebox function
//
//=============================================================


#include <windows.h>

#include "base1.h"  // For the BASE1_ModalDialog function,
                    // This automatically include basedefs.h
#include "mymsgbox.h"
```

```
static BOOL NEAR DlgProc_WM_COMMAND ( DIALOG_PARAMS );

        void      SetupMessageBox    ( HWND            hDlg,
                                       LPMSGBOXSTRUCT lpMsgBox
                                     );


// Adventuresome programmers will put these values in a stringtable
// for easy internationalization

static char szOK[]      = "&OK";
static char szCancel[]  = "&Cancel";
static char szAbort[]   = "&Abort";
static char szRetry[]   = "&Retry";
static char szIgnore[]  = "&Ignore";
static char szYes[]     = "&Yes";
static char szNo[]      = "&No";


/***********************************************************************
 *                                                                   *
 *                 Vanilla Dialog Box Procedure                      *
 *                                                                   *
 ***********************************************************************/

DLGPROC MYMSGBOX_DlgProc ( DIALOG_PARAMS )
{
  HDC    hDC;
  HICON  hIcon;
  DWORD  dwValue;
  POINT  pt;

  switch (msg)
    {
    case WM_PAINT:

      // For dialog boxes, you don't want to do any painting
      // here. Instead, let the dialog do its own painting,
      // and post yourself a message to paint your icon later.

      PostMessage ( hDlg, WM_MYCOMMAND, 0, 0L );
      return FALSE;


    case WM_MYCOMMAND:

      // This message comes after the WM_PAINT message above
```

```
// has been painted by the standard dialog window procedure
// that lives somewhere in USER.

// Grab the ID of the icon to draw
dwValue = GetWindowLong ( hDlg, DWL_USER );

if (dwValue)  // If draw an icon
   {
   // Get the icon from Windows' internal resources
   hIcon = LoadIcon ( NULL, (LPSTR)dwValue );

   // Get the DC of the dialog for drawing the icon
   hDC   = GetDC ( hDlg );

   // Use the location of the placeholder static control
   // that sez "(icon)". Convert it to client coordinates
   // of the dialog by converting the client coordinates
   // of theicon to screen coordinates, and then convert
   // those screenn coordinates to dialog client coorindates

   pt.x = pt.y = 0;
   ClientToScreen ( GetDlgItem ( hDlg, IDD_ICON ), &pt );
   ScreenToClient ( hDlg, &pt );

   // Do the dirty job of drawing the icon
   DrawIcon ( hDC, pt.x, pt.y, hIcon );

   // Release the DC to avoid crashing Windows
   ReleaseDC ( hDlg, hDC );
   }
  break;

case WM_INITDIALOG:

  SetupMessageBox ( hDlg, (LPMSGBOXSTRUCT)lParam );
  return FALSE;

case WM_COMMAND:

  return DlgProc_WM_COMMAND ( hDlg, msg, wParam, lParam );

default:

  return FALSE;
```

```
    }

  return TRUE;
}


/***********************************************************************
*                                                                     *
* Command Handler for dialog procedure                                *
*                                                                     *
***********************************************************************/

static BOOL NEAR DlgProc_WM_COMMAND ( DIALOG_PARAMS )
{
  CRACKER_VARS
  CRACK_MESSAGEsc

  switch ( CRACKER_wID )
    {
    case IDOK        :
    case IDCANCEL :
    case IDABORT  :
    case IDRETRY  :
    case IDIGNORE :
    case IDYES       :
     case IDNO            :

       // If the user clicks on a button, be sure to
       // send the ID of that back to the function that
       // called the DialogBox() API.

       if ( BN_CLICKED == CRACKER_wNotification )
         EndDialog ( hDlg, CRACKER_wID );
       return TRUE;

    default:

       return FALSE;
    }
}


/***********************************************************************
*                                                                     *
* This function does all the "dirty" work for setting up a message    *
* box wannabe dialog. The original template cna be found in           *
* MYMSGBOX.DLG, which contains all five buttons. These five buttons   *
```

```
*   can be trimmed down to show 1, 2 or 3 buttons, centered on the    *
*   screen. Adventuresome programmers can either create these buttons *
*   dynamically, or they can move buttons around. However, this       *
*   requires pixel-wise manipulation of the dialog, which is a bit    *
*   of a pain in the programming butt.                                *
*                                                                     *
*   This function does the following tasks:                           *
*                                                                     *
*   0. Sets the text of the dialogs' caption and message              *
*   1. Figures out how many buttons to display                        *
*   2. Hides the extra buttons, leaving only the buttons              *
*      that the user should see.                                      *
*   3. Changes the text and ID of the buttons to match               *
*      what the user expects to see.                                  *
*   4. Sets the default pushbutton                                    *
*   5. Sets which icon to use, if any. The ID ofthe icon is          *
*      stored in the DWL_USER extra byte field.                       *
*                                                                     *
*   This function is a bit on the brute force level, sassy            *
*   programmers can put a lot of this information into arrays         *
*   and twiddle the flags to reference information in arrays.         *
*   That, however, would rely on Windows constants staying            *
*   linear, which would be an unwise idea.                            *
*                                                                     *
***********************************************************************/


// These are some macros to make the actual code easier to read,
// and these are called redundantly. They can easily be placed in
// mini-functions if code size is a critical issue.

#define HIDEBUTTON(iNum) ShowWindow ( GetDlgItem(hDlg,iNum), SW_HIDE )

#define SETDEFBUTTON(iNewDefID)                                      \
  {                                                                  \
  SendMessage ( hDlg,                                                \
             DM_SETDEFID,                                            \
             (WPARAM)iNewDefID,                                      \
             0L                                                      \
           );                                                        \
  SendDlgItemMessage                                                 \
           (                                                         \
           hDlg,                                                     \
           iButton1,                                                 \
           BM_SETSTYLE,                                              \
           (WPARAM)BS_PUSHBUTTON,                                    \
           TRUE                                                      \
```

```
                    );                                          \
    SendDlgItemMessage                                          \
            (                                                   \
            hDlg,                                               \
            iNewDefID,                                          \
            BM_SETSTYLE,                                        \
            (WPARAM)BS_DEFPUSHBUTTON,                           \
            TRUE                                                \
            );                                                  \
    SetFocus (GetDlgItem (hDlg, iNewDefID));                    \
    }


#ifdef WIN_DOS
#define SETBUTTONID(iOldID,iNewID)                             \
    {                                                          \
    SetWindowWord (GetDlgItem(hDlg, iOldID), GWW_ID, (WORD)iNewID); \
    iOldID = iNewID;                                           \
    }
#endif
#ifdef WIN_NT
#define SETBUTTONID(iOldID,iNewID)                             \
    {                                                          \
    SetWindowLong (GetDlgItem(hDlg, iOldID), GWL_ID, (LONG)iNewID); \
    iOldID = iNewID;                                           \
    }
#endif

//————— The actual function —————-

void SetupMessageBox ( HWND hDlg, LPMSGBOXSTRUCT lpMsgBox )
{
    int    iNumButtons;
    int    iButton1;
    int    iButton2;
    int    iButton3;
    LPSTR  iIcon;


    // Step 0: Set the text, hide the "(icon)" static text

    SetDlgItemText ( hDlg, IDD_TEXT, lpMsgBox->szText    );
    SetWindowText  ( hDlg,           lpMsgBox->szCaption );
    HIDEBUTTON ( IDD_ICON );

    // Step 1: Count the buttons

    switch ( lpMsgBox->uiFlags & MB_TYPEMASK )
```

```
  {
  case MB_OK                  : iNumButtons = 1; break;
  case MB_RETRYCANCEL    :
  case MB_YESNO              :
  case MB_OKCANCEL        : iNumButtons = 2; break;
  case MB_ABORTRETRYIGNORE:
  case MB_YESNOCANCEL       : iNumButtons = 3; break;
  }

// Step 2: Hide the extra butons
//        Place into iButton1, iButton2, and iButton3 the
//        ID's of the buttons to be used. These values
//        will be used later to set the default button

switch ( iNumButtons )
  {
  case 1: HIDEBUTTON ( IDD_MSGBUTTON1 );
          HIDEBUTTON ( IDD_MSGBUTTON3 );
          HIDEBUTTON ( IDD_MSGBUTTON4 );
          HIDEBUTTON ( IDD_MSGBUTTON5 );

          iButton1 =
          iButton2 =
          iButton3 = IDD_MSGBUTTON2;
          break;

    case 2: HIDEBUTTON ( IDD_MSGBUTTON1 );
          HIDEBUTTON ( IDD_MSGBUTTON2 );
          HIDEBUTTON ( IDD_MSGBUTTON3 );
          iButton1 = IDD_MSGBUTTON4;
          iButton2 =
          iButton3 = IDD_MSGBUTTON5;
          break;

    case 3: HIDEBUTTON ( IDD_MSGBUTTON4 );
          HIDEBUTTON ( IDD_MSGBUTTON5 );
          iButton1 = IDD_MSGBUTTON1;
          iButton2 = IDD_MSGBUTTON2;
          iButton3 = IDD_MSGBUTTON3;
          break;
  }

// Step 3: Change the text (this can be combined with step 1 if you like)
//        Change the ID of the buttons

switch ( lpMsgBox->uiFlags & MB_TYPEMASK )
```

29

```
{
case MB_OK                      :

  SetDlgItemText ( hDlg, iButton1, szOK );
  SETBUTTONID ( iButton1, IDOK       );
  break;

case MB_RETRYCANCEL         :

  SetDlgItemText ( hDlg, iButton1, szRetry  );
  SetDlgItemText ( hDlg, iButton2, szCancel );
  SETBUTTONID ( iButton1, IDRETRY   );
  SETBUTTONID ( iButton2, IDCANCEL  );
  break;

case MB_YESNO               :

  SetDlgItemText ( hDlg, iButton1, szYes    );
  SetDlgItemText ( hDlg, iButton2, szNo     );
  SETBUTTONID ( iButton1, IDYES     );
  SETBUTTONID ( iButton2, IDNO      );
  break;

case MB_OKCANCEL            :

  SetDlgItemText ( hDlg, iButton1, szOK     );
  SetDlgItemText ( hDlg, iButton2, szCancel );
  SETBUTTONID ( iButton1, IDOK      );
  SETBUTTONID ( iButton2, IDCANCEL  );
  break;

case MB_ABORTRETRYIGNORE:

  SetDlgItemText ( hDlg, iButton1, szAbort  );
  SetDlgItemText ( hDlg, iButton2, szRetry  );
  SetDlgItemText ( hDlg, iButton3, szIgnore );
  SETBUTTONID ( iButton1, IDABORT   );
  SETBUTTONID ( iButton2, IDRETRY   );
  SETBUTTONID ( iButton3, IDIGNORE  );
  break;

case MB_YESNOCANCEL         :

  SetDlgItemText ( hDlg, iButton1, szYes    );
```

```
      SetDlgItemText ( hDlg, iButton2, szNo     );
      SetDlgItemText ( hDlg, iButton3, szCancel );
      SETBUTTONID ( iButton1, IDYES    );
      SETBUTTONID ( iButton2, IDNO     );
      SETBUTTONID ( iButton3, IDCANCEL );
      break;


    }


  // Step 4: Set the default pushbutton

  switch ( lpMsgBox->uiFlags & MB_DEFMASK )
    {
    case MB_DEFBUTTON1: SETDEFBUTTON(iButton1); break;
    case MB_DEFBUTTON2: SETDEFBUTTON(iButton2); break;
    case MB_DEFBUTTON3: SETDEFBUTTON(iButton3); break;
    }


  // Step 5: Determine the icon to ue

  switch ( lpMsgBox->uiFlags & MB_ICONMASK )
    {
    case MB_ICONHAND       : iIcon = (LPSTR)IDI_HAND        ; break;
    case MB_ICONQUESTION   : iIcon = (LPSTR)IDI_QUESTION    ; break;
    case MB_ICONEXCLAMATION: iIcon = (LPSTR)IDI_EXCLAMATION; break;
    case MB_ICONASTERISK   : iIcon = (LPSTR)IDI_ASTERISK    ; break;
    default                : iIcon = (LPSTR)NULL            ; break;
    }


  SetWindowLong ( hDlg, DWL_USER, (LONG)iIcon );
}


/**********************************************************************
*                                                                   *
*  The Public function, which takes idential arguments as the       *
*  MessageBox API.                                                  *
*                                                                   *
*  The BAS1_ModalDialog function can be replaced with the          *
*  standard code to display a dialog box using the                  *
*  DialogBoxParam() API if you do not want to use the               *
*  BASE1_ModalDialog function.                                      *
*                                                                   *
**********************************************************************/


MYMSGBOX_MyMessageBox ( HWND  hParent,
```

```
                        LPSTR szText,
                        LPSTR szCaption,
                        UINT  uiFlags
                     )
{
  MSGBOXSTRUCT MsgBoxStruct;

  MsgBoxStruct.hWndParent = hParent  ;
  MsgBoxStruct.szText     = szText   ;
  MsgBoxStruct.szCaption  = szCaption;
  MsgBoxStruct.uiFlags    = uiFlags  ;

  return BASE1_ModalDialog ( "MYMSGBOX",
                              MYMSGBOX_DlgProc,
                              (LONG)(LPMSGBOXSTRUCT)&MsgBoxStruct
                            );
}
```

8. WM_SETTEXT Versus SetWindowText (or SetDlgItemText)

If you want to go around setting the text of window captions (or edit controls), you normally use the **SetWindowText** API. Inside USER, this code translates to a call to WM_SETTEXT. However, one particularly nasty difference between the API and the message is that the API will only work with windows belonging to your application. If you use **SetWindowText** on a window that belongs to another application, it will fail. However, WM_SETTEXT will work just fine (unless you are running under Windows 95 or NT, where the separate-address-space-issue alligator will come and bite your butt). However, if you are still running Windows 3.1, use WM_SETTEXT to do your dirty work.

7. Controls and Style Bits

Windows controls cache away their style bits. For example, if you create an edit control by using the ES_MULTILINE style bit, it will not be possible to use the **SetWindowLong (GWL_STYLE)** API to change these style bits to a single-line edit control. This is because when an edit control is created, a chunk of memory is allocated for an internal data structure. The style bits are translated into easier (and quicker to) read fields inside this internal data structure. For the lifetime of the edit control, this internal data structure is used instead of the style bits.

What can you do? Not much, really. The best solution is to create a second edit control with your new style bits, and then transfer your text from the old edit control to the new one. Then you can destroy the old edit control.

This method of caching away style bits is employed by virtually every built-in control in Windows. In addition to style bits, the handle to the parent window is also cached away (see Chapter 5, "Common Headaches Encountered by Windows Programmers").

6. Child Controls Have the CS_PARENTDC Style Bit Set

Windows 3.1 added some optimization code to controls in order to bring up dialogs more quickly. One of these optimizations was to set the CS_PARENTDC style bit for the styles. Using the parent DC does speed up display and creation significantly, but it also causes grief for many programs when they have overlapping child controls. Whenever you find that you are having painting problems with your child controls (such as clipping problems, and incorrect region updates), try removing the CS_PARENTDC style bit.

See Listing 1.4 for some code to superclass a list box in order to remove the CS_PARENTDC style bit and create a new style called "SuperListbox." Use "SuperListbox" wherever you would have used "ListBox" for list boxes that should not have the CS_PARENTDC style bit.

LISTING 1.4 SUPERCLASSING A LISTBOX TO REMOVE THE **CS_PARENTDC** STYLE BIT

```
// This code superclasses a listbox to remove the
// CS_PARENTDC style bit for more controlled painting
```

```
BOOL SuperClassListBox ( HANDLE hInstance )
{
  WNDCLASS    wndclass  ;

  GetClassInfo ( GetModuleHandle ("USER"), "listbox", &wndclass );

  wndclass.hInstance      = hInstance ;
  wndclass.style          &= ~(CS_GLOBALCLASS | CS_PARENTDC);
  wndclass.lpszClassName   = "SuperListBox";

  return RegisterClass (&wndclass);
}
```

By using superclassed controls without CS_PARENTDC, you can overlap them and use the **BringWindowToTop** API with the expected results. The penalty you pay is a very small increase in the amount of time it takes to bring up a dialog box. However, as Windows becomes more advanced (and Windows 95 has *really* optimized its drawing code), this should become less of an issue.

5. How to Send Keystrokes to a Windows Application the Right Way

Sending keystrokes to another application (or even your own) is achievable through a variety of ways. Almost every way has some sort of quirk in it, simply because the receiving application may check the less-considered portions of the WM_KEYDOWN/CHAR/KEYUP message. Also, the message input queue and order have something to do with the way WM_KEYDOWN/CHAR/KEYUP messages are handled.

The solution to all of this confusion is to use a Journal Playback Hook to play the information directly back into the system queue. Some aspects of this playback hook code are not too clearly documented. Check out Listing 1.5 for a completely documented and commented Journal Playback Hook DLL that can be used to send keystrokes to any program.

LISTING **1.5** FAKING KEYBOARD INPUT WITH A JOURNAL PLAYBACK HOOK

```
//==========================================================
//
// SENDKEY.H- 16 or 32 Bit Journal Playback Hook
//
//==========================================================

typedef struct tagMYKEYARRAY
  {
  WORD    wKeyCode;
  UINT    uiMsg;
  BOOL    bVirtualKey;
  }
MYKEYARRAY;

typedef MYKEYARRAY FAR * LPMYKEYARRAY;

void CALLBACK
    SENDKEY_SendKeys ( LPMYKEYARRAY lpMyKeyArray, WORD wNumKeys );


//==========================================================
//
// SENDKEY.C - A Real Sendkeys Function That Works. This is a DLL
//
//==========================================================

#include <windows.h>
#include "sendkey.h"

HANDLE          ghDLLInst;
HHOOK           ghJournalHook;
WORD            gKeyToPlace;
WORD            gwNumKeysToPlayBack;
LPMYKEYARRAY    glpMyKeyArray;

LRESULT CALLBACK
    JournalPlaybackProc ( int     iCode,
                          WPARAM  wParam,
                          LPARAM  lParam
                        );

#ifdef WIN_DOS
```

```
//*************************************************************************
//
//
//
//*************************************************************************

int FAR PASCAL LibMain(HANDLE hModule, WORD wDataSeg, WORD cbHeapSize, LPSTR
lpszCmdLine)
{
    ghDLLInst = hModule;
    return 1;
}


int FAR PASCAL WEP (BOOL bSystemExit)
{
    return(1);
}
#endif


#ifdef WIN_NT
//*************************************************************************
//
//   LibMain- Called once, when first app loads it
//
//*************************************************************************

int APIENTRY LibMain(HANDLE hinstDLL, DWORD fdwReason, LPVOID lpReserved)
{
  ghDLLInst = hinstDLL;
  return TRUE;
}
#endif


//*************************************************************************
//
// Public Exported Function
//
//*************************************************************************

void CALLBACK
    SENDKEY_SendKeys ( LPMYKEYARRAY lpMyKeyArray, WORD wNumKeys )
{
    gKeyToPlace          = 0             ;
    gwNumKeysToPlayBack  = wNumKeys      ;
    glpMyKeyArray        = lpMyKeyArray ;
```

```
        ghJournalHook = SetWindowsHookEx ( WH_JOURNALPLAYBACK,
                                           (HOOKPROC)JournalPlaybackProc,
                                           ghDLLInst,
#ifdef WIN_DOS
                                           NULL
#endif
#ifdef WIN_NT
                                           0
#endif
                                         );
}


//*************************************************************************
//
//
//
//*************************************************************************

#define FAKE_EVENT ((LPEVENTMSG)lParam)

4LRESULT CALLBACK
        JournalPlaybackProc ( int      iCode,
                              WPARAM   wParam,
                              LPARAM   lParam
                            )
{
  WORD pL;
  UINT iMsg;
  UINT uiScanCode;
  BOOL vKey;

  switch ( iCode )
    {
    case HC_SKIP:

        // This is called when the next message is to be placed
        // in the input queue. Unhooking a hook is generally
        // VERY BAD to do in the hook's callback, but special
        // provisions have been made for this hook by the
        // Windows developers in order to make this paradigm
        // work.

        gKeyToPlace++;
        if (gKeyToPlace >= gwNumKeysToPlayBack)
          {
```

```
            UnhookWindowsHookEx(ghJournalHook);
            ghJournalHook = NULL;
            }
        return 0L;

    case HC_GETNEXT:

        // This is called for each item in the stream.
        // The array of keystrokes supplied by the calling
        // application is translated into some rather nasty
        // looking bits and bytes to correctly emulate
        // a recorded journal log.

        // Step 1: Grab the raw data

        pL   = glpMyKeyArray[gKeyToPlace].wKeyCode;
        iMsg = glpMyKeyArray[gKeyToPlace].uiMsg;
        vKey = glpMyKeyArray[gKeyToPlace].bVirtualKey;

        // Step 2: Munge to a scan code

        uiScanCode = MapVirtualKey( pL , 0 );

        // Step 3: Assemble the bit patterns

        FAKE_EVENT->message = iMsg;
        FAKE_EVENT->paramL  = LOBYTE ( uiScanCode ) << 8;
        FAKE_EVENT->paramL += LOBYTE ( pL );

        if (vKey)
          FAKE_EVENT->paramH  = 0x8001;
        else
          FAKE_EVENT->paramH  = 0x0001;

        // Step 4: Add the time stamp

        FAKE_EVENT->time    = GetTickCount();

        // Step 5: Send it on its merry way!

        return CallNextHookEx ( ghJournalHook, iCode, wParam, lParam );
    }

    return 0L;
}
```

This DLL has a single function, **SENDKEY_SendKeys**, that takes an array of keystrokes. This array is defined in the structure *MYKEYARRAY*, which holds the information you would like to show up in the WM_KEY* messages. To use this function, build an array of *MYKEYARRAY* structures, and then call the function.

For example, consider a situation in which you want to play CTRL-INSERT to any application in order to suck the selection into the clipboard. The action you want would be the same as if the user presses CTRL, INSERT, and then releases INSERT and then CTRL, as follows:

```
#define DIMOF(Array) ((sizeof(Array)/sizeof(Array[0])))
const MYKEYARRAY MyKeyArray[] =

{
{VK_CONTROL, WM_KEYDOWN,  TRUE},
{VK_INSERT,  WM_KEYDOWN,  TRUE},
{VK_INSERT,  WM_KEYUP,    TRUE},
{VK_CONTROL, WM_KEYUP,    TRUE}
};

SENDKEY_SendKeys ( MyKeyArray, DIMOF(MyKeyArray) );
```

4. How to Make Your Ordinary List Box Think Like a Drop Server

Windows 95's new controls provide for easy implementations of dragging and dropping (See Chapter 11, "Windows 95 User Interface Goodies," for example implementations). However, a considerable amount of Windows 3.1 code already exists. What I am providing here a way to get that Windows 95 drag-drop look-and-feel functionality in an ordinary Windows 3.1 list box control.

As a Windows 3.1 example, File Manager allows you to drag files from one list box to another. When you are dragging over the "to drop on" list box, the item that your mouse cursor is over highlights temporarily to indicate the place you are going to drop this file. This functionality is not documented anywhere, yet can be done with a little blood, sweat, and *ownerdraw* list boxes. Listing 1.6 is a small example program that emulates this functionality in a self-contained control. The control is a list box wrapper window (called "DropListBox") that uses a couple of new messages (DLB_INITIALIZE and DLB_SHOWDROPPOINT) to handle the work.

LISTING 1.6 MAKING AN ORDINARY LISTBOX ACT AS A DROP SERVER

```
//=======================================================
//
// DROPLIST.H
//
//=======================================================


// ————- wParam Values for WM_COMMAND ——-

#define DLB_HIDEDROPPOINT    100
#define DLB_SHOWDROPPOINT    101
#define DLB_NOTIFY_DROP      200


// ———————— Structres ————-

typedef struct tagDROPNOTIFY
  {
  HWND   hWndListbox;
  WPARAM wpIndex;
  }
DROPNOTIFY;


typedef DROPNOTIFY FAR * LPDROPNOTIFY;


// ————- Extra Byte Constants ——-

#define EXTRABYTE_wDROPINDEX   0

#define EXTRABYTE_REQUIREMENTS (sizeof(WORD))

// ————- Public Function Prototypes ——-

BOOL  DROPLIST_RegisterClass ( HANDLE hInstance );
LPSTR DROPLIST_szDropListBox ( void );
```

```
//=========================================================
//
// DROPLIST.C - Source for a "DropListBox" control
//              class that lets you do some drag-drop
//              action on it easily. Shows how to
//              wrap a standard control up in a code
//              wrapper.
//
//=========================================================


//
// ——————————————————————
//
// This control will act just like a regular listbox,
// except for the following changes:
//
// The real listbox will be created with the
// LBS_OWNERDRAWFIXED style bit, and the DropListControl
// window will handle the painting.
//
// There are two new messages that can be sent to this
// DropListBox, using the WM_MYCOMMAND message:
//
// Message            Meaning
// ——————————————————————
// DLB_HIDEDROPPOINT  Remove any drop indiciations
//                    that may be present. This should
//                    be called when the user lets go
//                    of the mouse or when the mouse
//                    moves outside of the listbox's
//                    range. If the lParam parameter is
//                    a valid hWnd, a notification message
//                    is sent to indicate the item selected.
//                    See the code in BASE1.C for example.
//
// DLB_SHOWDROPPOINT  When the mouse moves over the
//                    droplistbox, send this message to
//                    the droplistbox to highlight the
//                    item. See the code in BASE1.C
//                    to see how this is done.
//
// There is a notification message sent if the DLB_HIDEDROPPOINT
// message is sent to the listbox with a valid hWnd stored
// in lParam. The WM_MYCOMMAND message is used again.
//
// Message            Meaning
// ——————————————————————
```

```
// DLB_NOTIFY_DROP     The user has elected to drop onto
//                     this list box. lParam points to
//                     a DROPNOTIFY structure that indicates
//                     the listbox and index.
//
//
// *** BE SURE TO EXPORT THE FUNCTION DROPLIST_WndProc
// *** IN YOUR DEF FILE!!!
//


#include <windows.h>
#include "basedefs.h"
#include "droplist.h"


// Private strings. Use the  DROPLIST_szDropListBox API below to
// get the contents of the clsDropListBox string.

static char clsDropListBox[] = "DropListBox";
static char clsListBox[]     = "ListBox";


static char szNullString[]   = "";

// Function Prototypes


BOOL    CreateNormalListbox  ( HWND hWndParent, LPARAM lParamCreate );
WINPROC DROPLIST_WndProc     ( WINDOWS_PARAMS );
LRESULT WM_MYCOMMAND_Handler ( HWND hWnd, WPARAM wParam, LPARAM lParam );
void    UpdateItem           ( HWND hWnd, WORD wSelection );
LPARAM  DrawItem             ( HWND hWndParent, LPARAM lParam );


//********************************************************
//
//   Register the DropListBox Class- Do this in WinMain
//
//********************************************************

BOOL  DROPLIST_RegisterClass ( HANDLE hInstance )
{
  WNDCLASS wndclass  ;

  wndclass.style        = CS_HREDRAW | CS_VREDRAW;
  wndclass.lpfnWndProc  = (WNDPROC)DROPLIST_WndProc ;
  wndclass.cbClsExtra   = 0 ;
  wndclass.cbWndExtra   = EXTRABYTE_REQUIREMENTS ;
```

```
    wndclass.hInstance    = hInstance ;
    wndclass.hIcon        = NULL;
    wndclass.hCursor      = LoadCursor (NULL, IDC_ARROW) ;
    wndclass.hbrBackground = GetStockObject ( NULL_BRUSH ) ;
    wndclass.lpszMenuName  = (LPSTR)NULL;
    wndclass.lpszClassName = clsDropListBox ;

    return RegisterClass (&wndclass);
}


//*********************************************************
//
// Returns the classname of this control so apps can
// make this control with CreateWindow
//
//*********************************************************


LPSTR DROPLIST_szDropListBox ( void )
{
    return (LPSTR)clsDropListBox;
}


//*********************************************************
//
// Wrapper Control for Listbox
//
//*********************************************************


WINPROC DROPLIST_WndProc ( WINDOWS_PARAMS )
{
    switch ( msg )
      {
      case WM_COMMAND:   // These are notification messages
                         // sent up from the real listbox.
                         // Pass them on to the real parent.

        return SendMessage ( GetParent(hWnd), msg, wParam, lParam );

      case WM_MYCOMMAND: // These are the special messages
                         // for this control.

        return WM_MYCOMMAND_Handler ( hWnd, wParam, lParam );
        break;

      case WM_CREATE:    // Create the listbox control using
```

```
                        // the style bits

        // Set the listbox to have no drop highlighting

        SetWindowWord ( hWnd, EXTRABYTE_wDROPINDEX, (WORD)-1 );

        // Create the real LB

        if (!CreateNormalListbox ( hWnd, lParam )) return -1L;
        break;

      case WM_DRAWITEM:

        // Draw the item

        return DrawItem (hWnd, lParam);

      default:      // Send the LB_* messages down to the listbox

        if (msg >= WM_USER)
          return SendDlgItemMessage ( hWnd,
                                      GetWindowWord ( hWnd, GWW_ID ),
                                      msg,
                                      wParam,
                                      lParam
                                    );
        else
          return DefWindowProc ( hWnd, msg, wParam, lParam );
        break;


    }
  return 0L;


}
//*******************************************************
//
// Process the WM_MYCOMMAND Messages for the listbox wrapper
//
//*******************************************************

LRESULT WM_MYCOMMAND_Handler ( HWND hWnd, WPARAM wParam, LPARAM lParam )
{
  WORD          wCurrentSelection, wOldSelection;
```

```
DROPNOTIFY    DropNotify;
POINT         pt;
RECT          rc;
HWND          hWndLB;

// Figure where the drop select is currently located

wOldSelection     =
wCurrentSelection = GetWindowWord ( hWnd, EXTRABYTE_wDROPINDEX );

switch ( wParam )
  {
  case DLB_HIDEDROPPOINT:

    // This means user has let go of mouse button. Check
    // To see if a notification message is needed

    if ( (WORD)-1 != wCurrentSelection )
      {
      DropNotify.hWndListbox = hWnd;
      DropNotify.wpIndex      = wCurrentSelection;

      // Invalidate this region, when the WM_PAINT
      // message comes, the selection will be turned off

      UpdateItem ( hWnd, wCurrentSelection );

      // Send the notification to the parent of the control
      // if lParam was NULL, otherwise send it to the hWnd
      // indicated by the lParam

      if (!lParam)
        SendMessage ( GetParent (hWnd),
                      WM_MYCOMMAND,
                      DLB_NOTIFY_DROP,
                      (LONG)&DropNotify
                    );
      else
        SendMessage ( (HWND)lParam,
                      WM_MYCOMMAND,
                      DLB_NOTIFY_DROP,
                      (LONG)&DropNotify
                    );

      // Turn the drop selection off
```

```
    SetWindowWord ( hWnd, EXTRABYTE_wDROPINDEX, (WORD)-1 );
    }
  break;

case DLB_SHOWDROPPOINT: // lParam = Screen pos of mouse

  pt.x = LOWORD (lParam);
  pt.y = HIWORD (lParam);
  GetWindowRect ( hWnd, &rc );

  // Get the handle to the real listbox

  hWndLB = GetDlgItem ( hWnd, GetWindowWord ( hWnd, GWW_ID ));

  if (!PtInRect ( &rc, pt))          // If outside the LB
    {
    wCurrentSelection = (WORD)-1;
    }
  else                              // Else inside the LB
    {
    ScreenToClient ( hWnd, &pt );

    // Figure the location

    wCurrentSelection =
      min (
          (
            (WORD)SendMessage ( hWndLB, LB_GETTOPINDEX, 0, 0L )
            +
            (pt.y
              /
              (WORD)SendMessage ( hWndLB, LB_GETITEMHEIGHT, 0, 0L )
            )
          ),
          ((WORD)SendMessage ( hWndLB, LB_GETCOUNT, 0, 0L ) - 1)
        );
    }

  // Only do the drawing if the selection changed, this eliminates
  // flicker

  if (wOldSelection != wCurrentSelection)
    {
    UpdateItem ( hWnd, wOldSelection     );
```

```
        SetWindowWord ( hWnd,
                        EXTRABYTE_wDROPINDEX,
                        (WORD)wCurrentSelection
                    );
        UpdateItem ( hWnd, wCurrentSelection );
        }
      break;
    }
}


//******************************************************
//
//
//
//******************************************************

void UpdateItem ( HWND hWnd, WORD wSelection )
{
  RECT rc;

  // Get the handle to the real listbox

  hWnd = GetDlgItem ( hWnd, GetWindowWord ( hWnd, GWW_ID ));

  // Get the position of the item relative to the top of the LB

  wSelection -= (WORD)SendMessage ( hWnd, LB_GETTOPINDEX, 0, 0L );

  // Calculate the rectangle's new top and bottom, use the
  // windows's right and left

  GetClientRect ( hWnd, &rc );

  rc.top    = wSelection     * (WORD)SendMessage ( hWnd,
                                                   LB_GETITEMHEIGHT,
                                                   0,
                                                   0L
                                                 );
  rc.bottom = (wSelection+1) * (WORD)SendMessage ( hWnd,
                                                   LB_GETITEMHEIGHT,
                                                   0,
                                                   0L
                                                 );
```

```
  // Cause a WM_PAINT message to force a WM_DRAWITEM message
  // later...

  RedrawWindow ( hWnd, &rc, NULL, RDW_INVALIDATE );
}


//*******************************************************
//
//   This function creates the regular listbox inside the
//   wrapper window. The listbox style bits are then stripped
//   from the wrapper window, along with the WS_TABSTOP
//   and WS_VSCROLL style bits, since this wrapper window
//   should not be doing anything.
//
//*******************************************************

#define CS ((LPCREATESTRUCT)lParamCreate)

BOOL CreateNormalListbox ( HWND hWndParent, LPARAM lParamCreate )
{
  HWND  hWndListbox;
  DWORD dwStyle;
  WORD  wBorderThicknessX;
  WORD  wBorderThicknessY;

  dwStyle = GetWindowLong ( hWndParent, GWL_STYLE );

  // Turn off the scroll bar for the wrapper window,
  // listboxes are usually created with the WS_VSCROLL style bit,
  // and those styles are now applied to our wrapper window.

  if (dwStyle & WS_VSCROLL )
    SetScrollRange ( hWndParent, SB_VERT, 0, 0, TRUE );

  // Do some sleaze to get around the WS_BORDER style bit.
  // We need to shrink the LB to fit inside the wrapper's
  // client area.

  if (dwStyle & WS_BORDER )
    {
    wBorderThicknessX = GetSystemMetrics ( SM_CXBORDER );
    wBorderThicknessY = GetSystemMetrics ( SM_CYBORDER );
    }
```

```
else
  {

 wBorderThicknessX = 0;
 wBorderThicknessY = 0;
 }


// Create the LB window using the CREATESTRUCT info
// from the creation of the wrapper window.

hWndListbox = CreateWindowEx
                (
                0,
                clsListBox,
                szNullString,
                CS->style | LBS_OWNERDRAWFIXED | LBS_HASSTRINGS,
                wBorderThicknessX,
                wBorderThicknessY,
                CS->cx - 4*wBorderThicknessX,
                CS->cy - 4*wBorderThicknessY,
                hWndParent,
                (HMENU)CS->hMenu,
                CS->hInstance,
                NULL
                );


// Remove the listbox styles and other paraphenalia
// from the wrapper control

dwStyle &= ~(WS_TABSTOP | WS_VSCROLL | WS_BORDER |
                LBS_NOTIFY              |
                LBS_SORT               |
                LBS_NOREDRAW           |
                LBS_MULTIPLESEL        |
                LBS_OWNERDRAWFIXED     |
                LBS_OWNERDRAWVARIABLE  |
                LBS_HASSTRINGS         |
                LBS_USETABSTOPS        |
                LBS_NOINTEGRALHEIGHT   |
                LBS_MULTICOLUMN        |
                LBS_WANTKEYBOARDINPUT  |
                LBS_EXTENDEDSEL        |
                LBS_DISABLENOSCROLL
                );
```

```
  SetWindowLong ( hWndParent, GWL_STYLE, dwStyle );

  return (BOOL)hWndListbox;
}


//*********************************************************
//
// Simple code to draw an item in the listbox
//
//*********************************************************

#define HWNDLISTBOX    (pDIS->hwndItem)  // handle to LB
#define PHDC           (pDIS->hDC    )   // HDC of LB
#define PRC            (pDIS->rcItem )   // Area to draw
#define MAXBUFFERSIZE (255          )    // Max string length

LPARAM DrawItem ( HWND hWndParent, LPARAM lParam )
{
  char               szColumnBuffer[MAXBUFFERSIZE];
  DRAWITEMSTRUCT FAR *pDIS;
  HFONT              hFont;
  HFONT              hOldFont;
  BOOL               bDropSelected;

  // Get the pointer to the drawitem struct for our macros

  pDIS = (DRAWITEMSTRUCT FAR *)lParam;

  // Don't bother drawing these cases— avoids flash

  if ((pDIS->itemAction) & (ODA_FOCUS))
    {
    DrawFocusRect ( PHDC, &PRC );
    return 0L;
    }

  if ((pDIS->itemState) & (ODS_FOCUS))
    return 0L;

  if (!SendMessage (HWNDLISTBOX, LB_GETCOUNT, 0, 0L ))
    return 0L;

  // If we are in "drop" mode, find out if this is the one to
```

```
// be highlighted for dropping

bDropSelected =
  (
    pDIS->itemID == GetWindowWord (
                                    hWndParent,
                                    EXTRABYTE_wDROPINDEX
                                    )
  );


// Get the font, if one is selected

hFont = SendMessage (HWNDLISTBOX, WM_GETFONT, 0, 0L );

if (hFont)
  hOldFont = SelectObject ( PHDC, hFont );


// Select the color for text and background

if ((pDIS->itemState) & (ODS_SELECTED))
  {
  SetBkColor   ( PHDC, GetSysColor ( COLOR_HIGHLIGHT     ) );
  SetTextColor ( PHDC, GetSysColor ( COLOR_HIGHLIGHTTEXT ) );
  }
else
  {
  SetBkColor   ( PHDC, GetSysColor ( COLOR_WINDOW        ) );
  SetTextColor ( PHDC, GetSysColor ( COLOR_WINDOWTEXT    ) );
  }


// Get the text

SendMessage ( HWNDLISTBOX,
              LB_GETTEXT,
              (WPARAM)pDIS->itemID,
              (LPARAM)(LPSTR)szColumnBuffer
            );


// Splat it out to the DC

ExtTextOut  (
              PHDC,
              PRC.left,
```

```
                PRC.top,
                ETO_CLIPPED | ETO_OPAQUE,
                &PRC,
                szColumnBuffer,
                lstrlen(szColumnBuffer),
                NULL
                );

    // Draw the Drop feedback if neccessary

    if (bDropSelected)
      DrawFocusRect ( PHDC, &PRC );

    // Housekeep

    if (hFont)
      SelectObject ( PHDC, hOldFont );

    return 0L;
}
```

Here's how this control does its "magic." When the mouse cursor is moved over the list box, the DLB_SHOWDROPPOINT message is sent to the list box. The list box then converts the mouse position point to the index of the item it is over. This item is then redrawn by using the **RedrawWindow** API. Since this is an owner-draw list box, the WM_DRAWITEM message is sent to the list box wrapper, where the item is then drawn. Since the list box is in "drop mode," the item is highlighted if it is the correctly indexed item in the list box. Conversely, the previously highlighted item is also drawn unhighlighted to keep only one item highlighted at a time.

3. Cool Things to Do with the File Open Common Dialog

The common dialogs in Windows make it very easy to handle routine tasks. Two less-than-obvious applications of the common dialog are discussed here.

Changing the Information in the Common Dialog Programmatically

The drive and directory, and "List Files of Type" combo box are all changeable/ selectable by the user, but no documented way exists to do this programmatically. What if you wanted to add a button to the common dialog to tell it to automatically switch to the Windows directory? Actually, the following really quick-and-dirty method works now and tomorrow:

1. Create a string that contains the drive and directory, (for example, "C:\\WINDOWS").

2. Send the WM_SETREDRAW message to the filename edit control with *wParam = FALSE*.

3. Set the text of the filename edit control to the string from Step 1.

4. Send the WM_SETREDRAW message to the filename edit control with *wParam = TRUE*.

5. Fake pressing the OK button.

The "List Files of Type" combo box is a bit easier. Just change the selection by using the CB_SETCURSEL message, and then notify the dialog with the CBN_SELCHANGE message.

It is also possible to change the actual contents of the items in this combo box. The combo box is a normal CBS_DROPDOWNLIST combo box. The strings in the combo box are added with CB_ADDSTRING, the extensions are indexed, and the indexes are stored with CB_SETITEMDATA. The index points to the start of the extension string (such as *.TXT or *.WRI) in the *lpstrFilter* field in the *OPENFILENAME* structure.

To change the contents, it is easiest to rebuild the string and refill the combo box from the start.

Listing 1.7 is a portion of the sample program that demonstrates all these features. The code is verbosely commented, with each concept isolated from the rest. The complete program is on the disk that accompanies this book. Only the code that relevant to this tip is in the listing.

LISTING 1.7 COMMON DIALOG MANIPULATION, PART 1

```
//**********************************************************
//
// This is where the techniques for using common dialogs
// are demonstrated:
//
// 1. Changing the drive/directory programatically in a
//    File open common dialog
//
// 2. Rebuilding the information in the "List Files of Type"
//    combobox.
//
// 3. Changing the selection of the "List Files of Type"
//    combobox.
//
//**********************************************************

DLGPROC COMDLG_OpenFile_WM_COMMAND ( DIALOG_PARAMS )
{
  CRACKER_VARS
  CRACK_MESSAGEsc

  switch ( CRACKER_wID )
    {
    case IDD_WINDOWS:

      // Change directories and drives to the windows dir
      {
      char szWindowsDir[256];
      GetWindowsDirectory ( szWindowsDir, sizeof(szWindowsDir));

      SendDlgItemMessage ( hDlg, edt1, WM_SETREDRAW, FALSE, OL);
      SetDlgItemText     ( hDlg, edt1, szWindowsDir            );
      SendDlgItemMessage ( hDlg, edt1, WM_SETREDRAW, TRUE,  OL);

      NOTIFYPARENT ( hDlg, IDOK, BN_CLICKED )
      }
      break;

    case IDD_TYPES:

      // Rebuild the File Type combobox
```

```
        ComDlgFormatFilterString();    // This function has been modified
                                       // to alternate between two filters.
                                       // Check out the code, it just
                                       // loads one of two strings from
                                       // the stringtable.
                                       //
                                       // Your real-life program will
                                       // probably generate this string
                                       // on-the-fly instead of loading
                                       // it from a stringtable anyway.


        RebuildCommDlgFileTypes ( hDlg, szFilenameFilter );


        // Set File Type to first item in list

        SendDlgItemMessage ( hDlg, cmb1, CB_SETCURSEL, 0, 0L);
        NOTIFYPARENT ( hDlg, cmb1, CBN_SELCHANGE )
        break;


      default:

        break;
      }
    return FALSE;
}


//*************************************************************************
//
// This function fills the "List files of Type" combobox in a dialog
// given the supplied formatting string. The formatting string is
// a list of "doublestrings", where the first string is the human
// readable string, and the second string is the machine readable string.
// There is an extra terminating zero at the end of the last string.
//
// The combobox stores the human readable string in the combobox's
// listbox, while the index to the machine readable string is stored
// in the extra item data for each listbox item.
//
// Look at this sample string. Since it is not easy to show a
// null terminator in a text file, we will substitute it with a
// vertical bar (|) for this comment example only:
//
// These numbers are a handy way to show the byte index of the string...
//
//          11111111112222222222333333333344444444445555555555566666666
```

```
// 01234567890123456789012345678901234567890123456789012345678901234567
// ————————————————————————————————————
//            a                  b                               c
// All Files|*.*|Program Files|*.EXE;*.DLL;*.COM|Settings Files|*.INI||
//
//                               ^    ^—Terminator 2 for 2nd string pair
//                               |——Terminator 1 for 2nd string pair
//
// This string would be reprsented in the combobox's listbox like this:
//
// String in Listbox        Item Data (via CB_SETITEMDATA)
// ===================================================================
// All Files                10 (a)
// Program Files            28 (b)
// Settings Files           61 (c)
//
//*********************************************************************

void RebuildCommDlgFileTypes ( HWND hDlg, LPSTR szFilenameFilter )
{
    HWND   hWndCombo;    // hWnd of the combobox in the File open dlg
    LPSTR  szStringPtr;  // Floating string pointer
    int    iLen;         // Length of string from start of szFilenameFilter
    int    iIndex;       // Index of item added to combobox
    int    iSel;         // Temporary combo selection storage variable

    // Get the combobox and its selected item
    hWndCombo = GetDlgItem ( hDlg, cmb1);
    iSel = (int)SendMessage ( hWndCombo, CB_GETCURSEL, 0, 0L );

    // Turn off painting until we are done
    SendMessage ( hWndCombo, WM_SETREDRAW, FALSE, 0L );

    // Nix the current contents
    SendMessage ( hWndCombo, CB_RESETCONTENT, 0, 0L );

    // Start at beginning of szFilenameFilter
    iLen = 0;

    // Calculate the string pointer
    szStringPtr = szFilenameFilter + iLen;

    // Loop through each set of strings
```

```
while (*szStringPtr)  // while there are strings
  {
  // Add the human-readable string to the combobox
  iIndex = (int)SendMessage ( hWndCombo,
                              CB_ADDSTRING,
                              0,
                              (LONG)(LPSTR)szStringPtr
                            );

  // Add length of current string to total length,
  // add one to skip Terminator 1
  iLen += lstrlen (szStringPtr) + 1;

  // Bump up string pointer to the machine readable string
  szStringPtr = szFilenameFilter + iLen;

  // Add that index to the combobox
  SendMessage ( hWndCombo,
                CB_SETITEMDATA,
                (WPARAM)iIndex,
                (LONG)iLen
              );

  // Add length of current string to total length,
  // add one to skip Terminator 2
  iLen += lstrlen (szStringPtr) + 1;

  // Bump up string pointer to the next string
  szStringPtr = szFilenameFilter + iLen;

  } // I'll be back!

// Turn on painting
SendMessage ( hWndCombo, WM_SETREDRAW, TRUE, 0L );

// Force repaint
InvalidateRect ( hWndCombo, NULL, TRUE );

// Restore selected item
SendMessage ( hWndCombo, CB_SETCURSEL, iSel, 0L );

}
```

Selecting a Directory

The File Open dialog can be used for selecting directories, as well. To do this, simply use a different dialog template that hides all of the file-specific controls, and then also hide them in the WM_INITDIALOG code. Along with this initial cosmetic work, you can do some extra work to ensure that the directory chosen is the one selected (that is, the highlighted selection), not the one that is actually open. This is because the user should not have to double-click on a directory to select it when the dialog box is simply a directory selection.

Listing 1.8 is a sample program that contains all the code to select a directory for a Windows 3.1 style dialog. In the hook procedure to intercept messages for the common dialog (**COMDLG_PickDirHook**), if the OK button is pressed, the act of double-clicking on the list box is first faked, and then the OK button is pressed again. This little snippet of code ensures that the user did not have to double-click on a directory in order to select it.

LISTING 1.8 COMMON DIALOG MANIPULATION, PART 2

```
// COMDLG.C—This has the Common Dialog code in it
//
// Sample code from the SDK with minimal changes
//

#include <windows.h>
#include <commdlg.h>
#include <dlgs.h>      // for fileopen.dlg
#include <direct.h>

#include "comdlg.h"    // Stuff for other apps

#include "cddemo.h"

#include "base1.h"  // This depends on your app

char szFilenameFilter    [256];
char szInitialdir        [256];
char szDefaultExtension  [4] = "*"; // Wildcard
```

```
#define PARAMETER_VALIDATION

#define DEBUGOUT(szLine)          \
  {                               \
  OutputDebugString ( szLine );  \
  OutputDebugString ( "\r\n" );  \
  }


DLGPROC COMDLG_PickDirHook ( DIALOG_PARAMS );


/****************************************************************************
*                                                                         *
*  Function:  ComDlgFormatFilterString(void)                              *
*                                                                         *
*   Purpose:  To initialize the szFilenameFilter variable with strings from *
*             the string table.  This method of initializing szInitialdir *
*             is necessary to ensure that the strings are contiguous      *
*             in memory—which is what COMMDLG.DLL requires.               *
*                                                                         *
*   Returns:  BOOL  TRUE if successful, FALSE if failure loading string   *
*                                                                         *
*  Comments:  The string loaded from the string table has some wild       *
*             character in it.  This wild character is then replaced      *
*             with NULL.  Note that the wild char can be any unique       *
*             character the developer chooses, and must be included       *
*             as the last character of the string.  A typical string      *
*             might look like "Write Files(*.WRI)|*.WRI|" where | is      *
*             the wild character in this case.  Implementing it this      *
*             way also ensures the string is doubly NULL terminated,      *
*             which is also a requirement of this lovely string.          *
*                                                                         *
*  History:   Date      Reason                                            *
*             ____  _____-                                      *
*                                                                         *
*             11/19/91  Created                                           *
*                                                                         *
****************************************************************************/
BOOL NEAR ComDlgFormatFilterString(void)
{
   WORD   wCtr, wStringLen;
   char   chWildChar;

   *szFilenameFilter=0;

   if (!(wStringLen=LoadString(ghInst, IDS_FILTERSTRING, szFilenameFilter,
                        sizeof(szFilenameFilter))))
```

```
      {
          ERROR_ReportError(IDC_LOADSTRINGFAIL);
          return(FALSE);
      }

   chWildChar = szFilenameFilter[wStringLen-1];    //Grab the wild character

   wCtr = 0;

   while (szFilenameFilter[wCtr])
      {
          if (szFilenameFilter[wCtr]==chWildChar)
              szFilenameFilter[wCtr]=0;
          wCtr++;
      }

   return(TRUE);
}


/*************************************************************************
*                                                                       *
*   Function:  InitializeStruct(WORD, LPSTR)                            *
*                                                                       *
*   Purpose:  To initialize a structure for the current common dialog.  *
*             This routine is called just before the common dialogs     *
*             API is called.                                            *
*                                                                       *
*   Returns:  void                                                      *
*                                                                       *
*   Comments:                                                           *
*                                                                       *
*   History:  Date      Reason                                          *
*             ____    _____                                   *
*                                                                       *
*             10/01/91  Created                                         *
*                                                                       *
*************************************************************************/
void NEAR InitializeStruct(WORD wCommDlgType, LPSTR lpStruct)
{

   LPFOCHUNK          lpFOChunk;
   LPFSCHUNK          lpFSChunk;

   switch (wCommDlgType)
      {
```

```
case COMDLG_ACTION_FILEPICKDIR:

  lpFOChunk = (LPFOCHUNK)lpStruct;

  *szInitialdir = 0;

  // For picking directories, this call is irrelevant.
  // But I leave it here just in case the dialog box
  // code inside COMMDLG.DLL expects something valid.

  ComDlgFormatFilterString();  //Formats szFilenameFilter with strings

  // Set up for picking a dir

  *(lpFOChunk->szFile)          = 0;
  *(lpFOChunk->szFileTitle)     = 0;
  lpFOChunk->of.lStructSize     = sizeof(OPENFILENAME);
  lpFOChunk->of.hwndOwner       = (HWND)ghWnd;
  lpFOChunk->of.hInstance       = (HANDLE)ghInst;
  lpFOChunk->of.lpstrFilter     = szFilenameFilter;
  lpFOChunk->of.lpstrCustomFilter = (LPSTR)NULL;
  lpFOChunk->of.nMaxCustFilter  = 0L;
  lpFOChunk->of.nFilterIndex    = 1L;
  lpFOChunk->of.lpstrFile       = lpFOChunk->szFile;
  lpFOChunk->of.nMaxFile        = (DWORD)sizeof(lpFOChunk->szFile);
  lpFOChunk->of.lpstrFileTitle  = lpFOChunk->szFileTitle;
  lpFOChunk->of.nMaxFileTitle   = MAXFILETITLELEN;
  lpFOChunk->of.lpstrInitialDir = szInitialdir;
  lpFOChunk->of.lpstrTitle      = (LPSTR)NULL;
  lpFOChunk->of.Flags           = OFN_HIDEREADONLY |
                                  OFN_ENABLEHOOK |
                                  OFN_ENABLETEMPLATE |
                                  OFN_NOVALIDATE ;
  lpFOChunk->of.nFileOffset     = 0;
  lpFOChunk->of.nFileExtension  = 0;
  lpFOChunk->of.lpstrDefExt     = (LPSTR)szDefaultExtension;
  lpFOChunk->of.lCustData       = 0L;
  lpFOChunk->of.lpfnHook        = (FARPROC)MakeProcInstance
                                    (COMDLG_PickDirHook, ghInst);
  lpFOChunk->of.lpTemplateName  = (LPSTR)"PICKDIR";

  break;

case COMDLG_ACTION_FILESAVEAS:
```

```
        lpFSChunk = (LPFSCHUNK)lpStruct;

        *szInitialdir = 0;

        ComDlgFormatFilterString();  //Formats szFilenameFilter with strings

        *(lpFSChunk->szFile)           = 0;
        lpFSChunk->of.lStructSize      = sizeof(OPENFILENAME);
        lpFSChunk->of.hwndOwner        = (HWND)ghWnd;
        lpFSChunk->of.hInstance        = (HANDLE)NULL;
        lpFSChunk->of.lpstrFilter      = szFilenameFilter;
        lpFSChunk->of.lpstrCustomFilter = (LPSTR)NULL;
        lpFSChunk->of.nMaxCustFilter   = 0L;
        lpFSChunk->of.nFilterIndex     = 1L;
        lpFSChunk->of.lpstrFile        = lpFSChunk->szFile;
        lpFSChunk->of.nMaxFile         = (DWORD)sizeof(lpFSChunk->szFile);
        lpFSChunk->of.lpstrFileTitle   = lpFSChunk->szFileTitle;
        lpFSChunk->of.nMaxFileTitle    = MAXFILETITLELEN;
        lpFSChunk->of.lpstrInitialDir  = szInitialdir;
        lpFSChunk->of.lpstrTitle       = (LPSTR)NULL;
        lpFSChunk->of.Flags            = OFN_OVERWRITEPROMPT;
        lpFSChunk->of.nFileOffset      = 0;
        lpFSChunk->of.nFileExtension   = 0;
        lpFSChunk->of.lpstrDefExt      = (LPSTR)szDefaultExtension;
        lpFSChunk->of.lCustData        = 0L;
        lpFOChunk->of.lpfnHook         = NULL;
        lpFSChunk->of.lpTemplateName   = (LPSTR)NULL;

        break;

    }

   return;

}

/***************************************************************************
*                                                                         *
*  Function:  AllocAndLockMem(HANDLE *, WORD)                             *
*                                                                         *
*  Purpose:  To allocate and lock a chunk of memory for the CD            *
*            structure.                                                    *
*                                                                         *
*  Returns:  LPSTR                                                        *
*                                                                         *
```

```
*   Comments:                                                          *
*                                                                      *
*    History:   Date      Reason                                       *
*              ____    _____-                                *
*                                                                      *
*              10/01/91  Created                                       *
*                                                                      *
**********************************************************************/
LPSTR NEAR AllocAndLockMem(HANDLE *hChunk, WORD wSize)
{
   LPSTR lpChunk;

   *hChunk = GlobalAlloc(GMEM_FIXED, wSize);

   if (*hChunk)
      {
         lpChunk = GlobalLock(*hChunk);
         if (!lpChunk)
            {
               GlobalFree(*hChunk);
               ERROR_ReportError(IDC_LOCKFAIL);
               lpChunk=NULL;
            }
      }
   else
      {
         ERROR_ReportError(IDC_ALLOCFAIL);
         lpChunk=NULL;
      }
   return(lpChunk);
}


/**********************************************************************
*                                                                      *
*   COMDLG_ComDlgGetFileName                                           *
*                                                                      *
*   Fills the szFileName string with whatever the user chooses from    *
*   the File Common Dialog                                             *
*                                                                      *
*   wAction    Either IDM_FILEOPEN or IDM_FILEDUPLICATE, to bring      *
*              up the "Load" or "Save As" dialog                       *
*                                                                      *
*   szFileName Points to a string buffer for the filename              *
*                                                                      *
*   Return Value:                                                      *
*                                                                      *
```

```
 *   If user pressed OK:      TRUE                                        *
 *   If user pressed Cancel: FALSE                                        *
 *                                                                        *
 ************************************************************************/

BOOL COMDLG_ComDlgGetFileName ( WORD wAction, LPSTR szFileName )
{
  LPFOCHUNK lpFOChunk;      //Pointer to File Open block
  LPFSCHUNK lpFSChunk;      //Pointer to File Save block
  HANDLE    hfoChunk;       //Handle to File Open block of memory
  HANDLE    hfsChunk;       //Handle to File Save block of memory
  WORD      wSize;
  BOOL      bReturnValue;


  static    char szDir[256];

#ifdef PARAMETER_VALIDATION

  if (IsBadWritePtr ( szFileName, 256 ))
    {
    DEBUGOUT ("COMDLG_ComDlgGetFileName: Invalid szFileName");
    return FALSE;
    }

#endif

  switch (wAction)
    {
    case COMDLG_ACTION_FILEPICKDIR:

       wSize=sizeof(FOCHUNK);

       if (!(lpFOChunk=(LPFOCHUNK)AllocAndLockMem(&hfoChunk, wSize)))
          break;

       InitializeStruct(COMDLG_ACTION_FILEPICKDIR, (LPSTR)lpFOChunk);

       bReturnValue = GetOpenFileName( &(lpFOChunk->of) ) ;

       // This hook proc instance was set inside the InitializeStruct function

       if (lpFOChunk->of.lpfnHook)
          FreeProcInstance (lpFOChunk->of.lpfnHook);
```

```
GlobalUnlock ( hfoChunk );
GlobalFree   ( hfoChunk );


// The common dialog sets the current drive/dir,
// so to find out the dir the user selected, we simply
// get the current directory.
//
// Since most Win apps are medium model, we cant pass a
// LPSTR to the C runtime call, so we use a local static
// string (this is to allow this to run in a DLL, with
// the SS != DS debacle), and then copy it to the LPSTR
// passed in by the function. All this will be much easier
// with the Win32 API.


if (bReturnValue)
  {
  _getcwd ( szDir, sizeof(szDir) );
  lstrcpy ( szFileName, szDir );
  }


return (BOOL)bReturnValue;
break;


case COMDLG_ACTION_FILESAVEAS:

wSize=sizeof(FOCHUNK);

if (!(lpFSChunk=(LPFOCHUNK)AllocAndLockMem(&hfsChunk, wSize)))
   break;

InitializeStruct(COMDLG_ACTION_FILESAVEAS, (LPSTR)lpFSChunk);

if ( GetSaveFileName( &(lpFSChunk->of) ) )
   {
   lstrcpy ( szFileName, lpFSChunk->of.lpstrFile);
   }
else
   {
   *szFileName = 0;
   ERROR_ProcessCDError(CommDlgExtendedError());
   }

GlobalUnlock ( hfsChunk );
GlobalFree   ( hfsChunk );
```

```
        return (BOOL)*szFileName ;

        break;
#ifdef PARAMETER_VALIDATION

    default:

        DEBUGOUT ("COMDLG_ComDlgGetFileName: Invalid wAction");
        return FALSE;

#endif


        }
}


//****************************************************************************
//
//  Hook proc for Common Dialog
//
//****************************************************************************

DLGPROC COMDLG_PickDirHook ( DIALOG_PARAMS )
{
  static BOOL  bAvoidRecursion;

  switch ( msg )
    {
    case WM_INITDIALOG:

      // Hide the filename-specific controls

      ShowWindow ( GetDlgItem ( hDlg, stc3), SW_HIDE );
      ShowWindow ( GetDlgItem ( hDlg, edt1), SW_HIDE );
      ShowWindow ( GetDlgItem ( hDlg, lst1), SW_HIDE );
      ShowWindow ( GetDlgItem ( hDlg, stc2), SW_HIDE );
      ShowWindow ( GetDlgItem ( hDlg, cmb1), SW_HIDE );

      bAvoidRecursion = FALSE;

      return TRUE;

    case WM_COMMAND:

#ifdef WIN_DOS
```

```
    if (( IDOK == wParam ) && (!bAvoidRecursion))
      {
      bAvoidRecursion = TRUE;
      NOTIFYPARENT     ( hDlg, lst2, LBN_DBLCLK );
      NOTIFYPARENTPOST ( hDlg, IDOK, BN_CLICKED );
      }
#endif
#ifdef WIN_NT
    if (( IDOK == LOWORD(wParam) ) && (!bAvoidRecursion))
      {
      bAvoidRecursion = TRUE;
      NOTIFYPARENT     ( hDlg, lst2, LBN_DBLCLK );
      NOTIFYPARENTPOST ( hDlg, IDOK, BN_CLICKED );
      }
#endif
    return FALSE;

  default:

    return FALSE;
    }
}
```

The *OFN_PATHMUSTEXIST* flag has been changed to *OFN_NOVALIDATE* in the **InitializeStruct** function. This allows the user to press OK or Cancel, and, in either case, close the dialog.

2. WM_PAINT and WM_TIMER Are not Like Other Messages

These two messages are very different from the rest of the messages in WindowsLand. All the other messages are placed in the queue, and they are processed in the order in which they are received. However, these two messages are different. They are actually bits that are set inside USER, and, when the message queue empties out, these bits are checked. If these bits are set, then the WM_PAINT and the WM_TIMER messages are sent.

Why is this done? The reason is speed. If a WM_PAINT message was sent every time a window was invalidated, the system would spend almost all its time painting, and quite often a region would get painted repeatedly. This valuable CPU time could be better spent processing other messages. By always emptying out the queue first, the priority of WM_PAINT and WM_TIMER drops to nothing. By keeping this priority low, the screen gets painted and the timer ticks only when there is nothing else to do.

The WM_PAINT priority setting is a good idea. It does not really take any justification to explain why the Windows programmers did this. The WM_TIMER message does require a little explanation, however. Since WM_TIMER messages are *generated* when the timer ticks, the "placement" of them in the queue is done at a regular rate. However, messages are not executed when they are placed in the queue, but rather they are executed when they are fetched from the queue. Since it is impossible to determine how much time it will take for the message to finally get its 15 microseconds of fame, the Windows programmers figured it was just as safe to place the message at the bottom of the waiting list, which lets other processes happen on time.

So, do you want to make sure the timer is accurate? There are two ways to do this, one more accurate (but expensive) than the other. For fairly good accuracy, use a timer callback procedure for the **SetTimer** API instead of sending the message to a window. You could even have the timer callback procedure use the **SendMessage** API to send (not post) a message directly to a window of your choice. This will get you your WM_TIMER messages with better regularity.

However, this approach still isn't totally accurate, since the timer callback procedure won't get called until the operating system says it is "OK." The truly accurate way to get timer notification is to use the multimedia timer services, which are more difficult and tricky to use. However, if you need an accurate time, the multimedia timers are the only way to go.

A Note About Timers in General

Only use one timer for your application. If you need three timers that fire at intervals of 50, 140, and 200 units, instead set one timer to fire at the least-common denominator (10 units). Use a timer callback procedure to count the ticks and send out its own WM_TIMER messages to the appropriate windows at appropriate times. This will conserve timer resources, which are very limited (16 timers allowed, total), and conserve CPU time, since the operating system must not handle all those extra timers.

1. The MDIClient Window Can Be Your Friend

The MDI windowing system in Windows has plenty of nice features, but it also has some limitations. The main limitation is that it is not possible to easily create an iconized or maximized MDI child window. However, it is possible to achieve the results you desire with some simple, yet non-obvious code.

If you want to create an iconized MDI child window, follow this recipe:

1. Send the WM_SETREDRAW message to the MDIClient window with *wParam = FALSE.*

2. Create the new MDI child, in the normal size.

3. Microwave on HIGH for 30 seconds, or until code is bubbling.

4. Do a **ShowWindow (hWndChild, SW_MINIMIZE)** on the MDI Child.

5. Send the WM_SETREDRAW message to the MDIClient window with *wParam = TRUE.*

6. Redraw the MDIClient window to make the icon appear, using **InvalidateRect**.

If you want to create a maximized MDI child window, follow the same steps as before, except use **SW_MAXIMIZE** in Step 4.

CHAPTER 2

Things You Might Want to Know About Windows KERNEL

Kernel handles all sorts of great things. Things like memory management, file management, and process management. While the programmers that have to worry about these low-level Kernel issues are outnumbered by user interface designers, there are still a large group that need to access some of these powerful features.

Win32 has changed an enourmous amount of Kernel. Since Win32 is fully pre-emptive and reentrant, quite a few coding conventions have changed. Additionally, when Win32 was designed, a more uniform method of accessing the powerful features was implemented (see Tips 10, 9, and 3 to see what I mean).

Brian Staples knows Kernel. He supplied me with the information to build this list; see his bio in the introduction of this book.

10. Win32 Doesn't Support Interrupts

Software interrupts are not supported by Win32 That means that all that code you wrote using int86 will only work if your app is a 16-bit app running in compatibility mode. This is certain to make life different for programmers who interface with VxD's from thier application, and for programmers who use a lot of lover-level file I/O.

Let's talk about VxD's first. It used to be that you would do an int31, function 1684 to retrive the entry point address for a virtual device's sevice functions, now you call an API to get a handle to the virtual device, and you use device I/O control to communicate with the device. So, let's look at how you get the interface to the VWIN32 (Win 32 Virtual Machine):

```
hFile = CreateFile("\\.\VWIN32",   // Name of the driver
                GENERIC_READ,    // We are going to only read a driver
                0,               // Since we are reading, no worry on sharing
                NULL,            // No security attributes
                OPEN_EXISTING,   // Open the existing file
                FILE_ATTRIBUTE_NORMAL, // Open as a normal file
                NULL);           // No template file

DeviceIoControl(hFile,           // File from above
                VWIN32_DIOC_DOS_IOCTL,  // Int21, function 44 equal
                NULL,            // No input buffer
                0,               // No input buffer
                lpOutBuffer,     // Where to put the results
                cbOutBuffer,     // Size of where to put the data
                lpBytesReturned, // Points to BYTE that returns size
                NULL);           // No overlapped function
```

This is the equivalent of doing an Int21, function 44 under DOS, or the equivalent of doing an int2F, function 1684 under Windows 3.1 to gain the entry point for calling the VMM service to perform the DO IOCTL. Win32 wraps the process of getting the entry point and making the call into the DeviceIoControl API; the above call to DeviceIoControl not only accesses the Win32 VxD, but it also makes the IOCTL call. The information returned in **lpOutBuffer** in the above sample is the device information block for the DOS device.

9. Communications Revisited

Kiss goodbye to 16-bit's OpenComm, ReadComm, and WriteComm API's, as well as the comm notification message WM_COMMNOTIFY. These have been replaced by **CreateFile**, **ReadFile**, **WriteFile**, and **WaitForCommEvent**. Just as above in tip #10, you use the "\\\\" convention to signal **CreateFile** that you are communicating with a system driver instead of a "real file." Let's look at how you would open up a comm port, spew out some bytes to it, and close it:

```
OVERLAPPED o;
DWORD      dwEventMask;

hComm = CreateFile("\\.\COM1",      // Name of the comm port (COM1)
                   GENERIC_READ |       // We are reading and writing
                   GENERIC_WRITE,       // when we deal with Comm ports
                   0,               // Since we are reading, no worry on sharing
                   NULL,            // No security attributes
                   OPEN_EXISTING,   // Open the existing "file"
                   FILE_FLAG_OVERLAPPED, // This is allows us to do
                                         // overlapped I/O on the serial port
                   NULL);           // No template file

WriteFile(hComm,            // Hande to the comm port
          lpStuffToSpew,    // Our data to write to the comm port
          cbSizeOfSpewage,  // Size of our data
          lpcbBytesSpewed,  // How much actually gets written to the
                            //   comm port gets placed here after the call
                            //   returns
          &o);              // Points to an OVERLAPPED structure

o.hEvent = CreateEvent(NULL,    // No security
                       FALSE,   // Auto reset event
                       FALSE,   // Not signalled
                       NULL);   // No name

if (WaitForCommEvent(hComm,         // Comm port to wait on event for
                     &dwEventMask,  // Filled in on return
                     &o))           // Points to our OVERLAPPED structure
  {
  if (dwEventMask & EV_DSR)
```

```
    MessageBox ( ghWnd, "Data send ready", "Sample", MB_OK );
  }

CloseFile(hComm); // Housekeep
```

8. Think, Thank, Thunks

As much as we would all like to port all of our DLL's over to 32 bits, this is not always possible. Perhaps you bought your DLL from a third party that hasn't yet ported everything to 32 bits? Or perhaps your algorithms are so 16-bitish that porting them would be just way too time consuming.

The good news is that you don't have to throw these DLL's away. The bad news is that you still have to do a bit of work to get them to work with your 32-bit code.

Microsoft has come up with a mechanism that allows function calls across different addresing modes. They have even supplied a tool called the "Thunk Compiler" that does a lot of this dirty work for you. Take a look at Chapter 8, "Migrating to Win32" for just some of the issues we face witgh 32-bit code. The thunking mechanism handles these issues, as well as the different stack architecture and pointer resolution involved with function calls.

The Thunk Compiler takes an input script and outputs an ASM file than can be added to either a 16- or 32-bit DLL; the ASM file assembles conditionally, depending on the usage of "IS_16" or "IS-32" flags. Use either -DIS_16 or -DIS_32 on the command line for the Microsoft version of the assemblers to set these flags. If you have a 16-bit app calling a 32-bit DLL, use IS_32, and vice-versa for a 32-bit app calling a 16-bit DLL. Just remember that the flag matches the addresing mode of the DLL, not the app.

Let's imagine you have this 16-bit third party DLL that has this great function in it:

```
#define MAXLIST 256
typedef struct tagBUG
```

```
  {
  int    iNumBugs;
  char  szBugList[MAXLIST];
  }
BUG, FAR * LPBUG;

BOOL FAR PASCAL
  RoachMotel_CheckIn(LPBUG  lpBug,               // Points to BUG
                     HANDLE hSomeFillerMaterial); // A handle
```

Now, we have this great function (notice there is no RoachMotel_CheckOut). It takes a pointer to a structure, and then it takes a handle. The **int iNumBugs** value in the structure must be 16 bits in 16-BitLand, and 32 bits in 32-BitLand, as also does the **hSomeFillerMaterial** parameter. So, we must create a "thunking script" (we will call this roach.thk) to pass into the think compiler:

```
// "Genericize" the basic scalars
typedef int  INT;
typedef unsigned int UINT;
typedef UINT HANDLE;
typedef int BOOL;

// "Genericize" the structure
typedef struct tagBUG
  {
  INT    iNumBugs;
  char  szBugList[256];
  }
BUG, * LPBUG;

// "Genericize" the function
BOOL RoachMotel_CheckIn(LPBUG, HANDLE)
  {}
```

To run this through the thunk compiler, use the following command line:

```
  thunk roach.thk
```

and we will get the roach.asm file in Listing 2.1.

LISTING 2.1

```
    page,132


;Thunk Compiler Version 1.01  Aug 23 1994 16:35:46
;File Compiled Sun Oct 09 21:22:44 1994


;Command Line: C:\SDK\BINW\THUNK.EXE roach.txt


    TITLE    $roach.asm


    .386
    OPTION READONLY
    OPTION OLDSTRUCTS


IFNDEF IS_16
IFNDEF IS_32
%out command line error: specify one of -DIS_16, -DIS_32
.err
ENDIF  ;IS_32
ENDIF  ;IS_16


IFDEF IS_32
IFDEF IS_16
%out command line error: you can't specify both -DIS_16 and -DIS_32
.err
ENDIF ;IS_16
;************************ START OF 32-BIT CODE *************************


    .model FLAT,STDCALL


;- Import common flat thunk routines (in k32)


externDef AllocMappedBuffer   :near32
externDef FreeMappedBuffer        :near32
externDef MapHInstLS :near32
externDef MapHInstLS_PN  :near32
externDef MapHInstSL :near32
externDef MapHInstSL_PN  :near32
externDef FT_PrologPrime :near32
externDef FT_Prolog  :near32
externDef FT_Thunk    :near32
externDef QT_Thunk    :near32
externDef QT_ThunkPrime  :near32
```

```
externDef FT_Exit0   :near32
externDef FT_Exit4   :near32
externDef FT_Exit8   :near32
externDef FT_Exit12  :near32
externDef FT_Exit16  :near32
externDef FT_Exit20  :near32
externDef FT_Exit24  :near32
externDef FT_Exit28  :near32
externDef FT_Exit32  :near32
externDef FT_Exit36  :near32
externDef FT_Exit40  :near32
externDef FT_Exit44  :near32
externDef FT_Exit48  :near32
externDef FT_Exit52  :near32
externDef FT_Exit56  :near32
externDef SMapLS :near32
externDef SUnMapLS   :near32
externDef SMapLS_IP_EBP_8:near32
externDef SUnMapLS_IP_EBP_8  :near32
externDef SMapLS_IP_EBP_12   :near32
externDef SUnMapLS_IP_EBP_12 :near32
externDef SMapLS_IP_EBP_16   :near32
externDef SUnMapLS_IP_EBP_16 :near32
externDef SMapLS_IP_EBP_20   :near32
externDef SUnMapLS_IP_EBP_20 :near32
externDef SMapLS_IP_EBP_24   :near32
externDef SUnMapLS_IP_EBP_24 :near32
externDef SMapLS_IP_EBP_28   :near32
externDef SUnMapLS_IP_EBP_28 :near32
externDef SMapLS_IP_EBP_32   :near32
externDef SUnMapLS_IP_EBP_32 :near32
externDef SMapLS_IP_EBP_36   :near32
externDef SUnMapLS_IP_EBP_36 :near32
externDef SMapLS_IP_EBP_40   :near32
externDef SUnMapLS_IP_EBP_40 :near32
MapSL   PROTO NEAR STDCALL p32:DWORD


    .code


;************************ COMMON PER-MODULE ROUTINES ************************


    .data


public b_ThunkData32 ;This symbol must be exported.
b_ThunkData32 label dword
    dd  3130534ch   ;Protocol 'LS01'
```

```
    dd   0542h   ;Checksum
    dd   0    ;Jump table address.
    dd   3130424ch    ;'LB01'
    dd   0    ;Flags
    dd   0    ;Reserved (MUST BE 0)
    dd   0    ;Reserved (MUST BE 0)
    dd   offset QT_Thunk_b - offset b_ThunkData32
    dd   offset FT_Prolog_b - offset b_ThunkData32


    .code

externDef ThunkConnect32@24:near32


public b_ThunkConnect32@16
b_ThunkConnect32@16:
    pop edx
    pushoffset b_ThkData16
    pushoffset b_ThunkData32
    pushedx
    jmp ThunkConnect32@24
b_ThkData16 label byte
    db   "b_ThunkData16",0


pfnQT_Thunk_b    dd offset QT_Thunk_b
pfnFT_Prolog_b   dd offset FT_Prolog_b
    .data
;; Initialized for BETA-1 compatibility only.
QT_Thunk_b label byte
    db   0ebh, 30
    db   30 dup(0cch) ;Patch space.
    db   0e8h,0,0,0,0 ;CALL NEAR32 $
    db   58h  ;POP EAX
    db   2dh,32+5,0,0,0    ;SUB EAX, IMM32
    db   0bah ;MOV EDX, IMM32
    dd   offset b_ThunkData32 + 8 - offset QT_Thunk_b
    db   068h ;PUSH IMM32
    dd   offset QT_ThunkPrime
    db   0c3h ;RETN


;; Initialized for BETA-1 compatibility only.
FT_Prolog_b label byte
    db   0ebh, 30
    db   30 dup(0cch) ;Patch space.
    db   0e8h,0,0,0,0 ;CALL NEAR32 $
    db   5ah  ;POP EDX
    db   81h,0eah, 32+5,0,0,0 ;SUB EDX, IMM32
```

```
        db   52h ;PUSH EDX
        db   068h;PUSH IMM32
        dd   offset b_ThunkData32 + 8 - offset FT_Prolog_b
        db   068h;PUSH IMM32
        dd   offset FT_PrologPrime
        db   0c3h;RETN


        .code

;*********************** START OF THUNK BODIES*************************


;
public RoachMotel_CheckIn@8
RoachMotel_CheckIn@8:
    mov cx, (2 SHL 10) + (0 SHL 8) + 0
; RoachMotel_CheckIn(16) = RoachMotel_CheckIn(32) {}
;
; dword ptr [ebp+8]:  param1


; dword ptr [ebp+12]:  param2
;
public IIRoachMotel_CheckIn@8
IIRoachMotel_CheckIn@8:
    calldword ptr [pfnFT_Prolog_b]
    sub esp,258
    mov esi,[ebp+8]
    or  esi,esi
    jnz L0
    pushesi
    jmp L1
L0:
    lea edi,[ebp-322]
    pushedi ;param1: lpstruct32>lpstruct16
    or  dword ptr [ebp-20],02h   ;Set flag to fixup ESP-rel argument.
    lodsd
    stosw
    mov ecx,64
    rep movsd
L1:
    pushword ptr [ebp+12]     ;param2: dword->word
    callFT_Thunk
    movsx   ebx,ax
    jmp FT_Exit8


ELSE
;*********************** START OF 16-BIT CODE *************************
```

```
     OPTION SEGMENT:USE16
     .model LARGE,PASCAL

     .code

externDef RoachMotel_CheckIn:far16

FT_bTargetTable label word
     dw  offset RoachMotel_CheckIn
     dw      seg RoachMotel_CheckIn

     .data

public b_ThunkData16 ;This symbol must be exported.
b_ThunkData16    dd  3130534ch      ;Protocol 'LS01'
     dd  0542h    ;Checksum
     dw  offset FT_bTargetTable
     dw  seg     FT_bTargetTable
     dd  0    ;First-time flag.

     .code

externDef ThunkConnect16:far16

public b_ThunkConnect16
b_ThunkConnect16:
     pop ax
     pop dx
     pushseg     b_ThunkData16
     pushoffset b_ThunkData16
     pushseg     b_ThkData32
     pushoffset b_ThkData32
     pushcs
     pushdx
     pushax
     jmp ThunkConnect16
b_ThkData32 label byte
     db   "b_ThunkData32",0

ENDIF
END
```

When an app calls the **RoachMotel_CheckIn** function, you can read through the ASM code in the listing to see how the parameters are munged at the entry point before getting routed to the actual function. Once the actual function completes, the return values (and parameters that are passes by reference) are de-munged before returning to the calling app.

The most common reason for thunk failure under Windows 95 is neglecting to mark the DLL as a 4.0 compatiable executable. This is done using the resource compiler that comes with the Windows 95 SDK (even for 16-bit DLL's!).

There are quite a few details about the Thunk Compiler that have been left out of this tip—see the documentation that comes with Windows 95 (currently named THUNKME.TXT in the BINW directory at the time of this book's writing) for a complete description.

7. Win32 Reveals All! GetSystemInfo and GlobalMemoryStatus

No longer do you have to use all those nasty DPMI calls to find out the nitty gritty details of your system's memory, processors, page size, or (isn't this great?) your OEM ID!!!! This function returns all sorts of helpful information about the hardware platform you are using. This declaration was ruthlessly stolen right from the Win32 API Help File:

```
GetSystemInfo
────────

The GetSystemInfo function returns information about the current system.

typedef struct _SYSTEM_INFO {
    DWORD  dwOemId;                       // Computer identifier that is
                                         // specific to a particular OEM
    DWORD  dwPageSize;                    // The page size and specifies the
                                         // granularity of page protection
                                         // and commitment
    LPVOID lpMinimumApplicationAddress;  // The lowest memory address
                                         // accessible to applications and
                                         // dynamic-link libraries (DLLs)
    LPVOID lpMaximumApplicationAddress;  // The highest memory address
                                         // accessible to applications
                                         // and DLLs.
```

```
2    DWORD   dwActiveProcessorMask;       // A mask representing the set of
                                          // processors configured into the
                                          // system. Bit 0 is processor 0;
                                          // bit 31 is processor 31.
     DWORD   dwNumberOfProcessors;        // Number of processors in the
                                          // system.
     DWORD   dwProcessorType;             // Type of the current processors
                                          // in the system. All processors are
                                          // assumed to be of the same type,
                                          // have the same stepping, and are
                                          // configured with the same options.
                                          // The following processor type
                                          // constants are currently defined:
                                          //    PROCESSOR_INTEL_386
                                          //    PROCESSOR_INTEL_486
                                          //    PROCESSOR_INTEL_PENTIUM
                                          //    PROCESSOR_INTEL_860
                                          //    PROCESSOR_MIPS_R2000
                                          //    PROCESSOR_MIPS_R3000
                                          //    PROCESSOR_MIPS_R4000
                                          //    PROCESSOR_ALPHA_21064
     DWORDdwAllocationGranularity;        // The allocation granularity in
                                          // which memory will be allocated on.
                                          // This value was hard coded as 64K
                                          // in the past, but other hardware
                                          // architectures may require different
                                          // values.
     dwReserved;                          // Reserved.
};
```

The GlobalMemoryStatus API returns all of that information you want to know about available physical and virtual memory; consult the Win32 API reference for the declarations (yay! No more GlobalCompact with a -1!).

6. Long Filenames Are NOT Restricted to Only 32-Bit Apps

With a little bit of work on your part, you can enable long filename support in your 16-bit applications. The first, and most important step is to make sure you have 260 byte long buffers *everywhere* in your application to store filenames. If you were a good little programmer, you used the C constant **_MAX_PATH**, which has been defined to 260 in Visual C++ 1.51, which just means you have to recompile. Here are the other steps you muct take to enable your 16-bit application to work with long filenames:

1. You need to check which version of DOS you are running on the int21, function 30h (or if you are a Windows app, use the GetVersion API). You must be running DOS 7.0 or greater.

2. Instead of using the normal DOS calls for file creation and searching, use these new ones:

TO DO THIS	INSTEAD OF	DO THIS
Open a file	int21, function 3C	int21, function 6C (Extended Open create)
Create a directory	int21, function 39	int21, function 7139 (Extended Directory create)
Find file	int21, function 4E	int21, function 714E (Extended find file)
Find next file	int21, function 4F	int 21, function 714F (Extended find next file)
GetShortPath	n/a	int 21, function (8.3 from a long file) 7160 (GetShortPath)
Determine is volume	n/a	int 21, function 71A0 is long-file enabled (Extended get volume information)

5. Use Structured Exception Handling and GetLastError

Win32 and Visual C++ 2.0 offer excellent structured exception handling (SEH). SEH is a new way of thinking about writing code—it lets you create large blocks of code that can fail at any aribitray point inside the block and provide a consistent error handler. An entire chapter can be written just on SEH, a good source of information is Chapter 10 of Jeffrey Richter's *Advanced Windows NT*, Microsoft Press.

As well as SEH, another great programming aid to catch errors more gracefully is to use the GetLastError API in Win32. This API can be used to help you determine a more exact cause of failure in your application.

These two new mechanisms of error detection make programming under Win32 much, much more predictable and stable.

4. Use Memory Mapped Files for Shared Memory Between Win32 Applications

Under Win16, sharing memory was as easy as handing a pointer or a handle to a chunk of memory to another application. Since all 16 bit apps run in the same address space, this was a non-issue. Under Win32, each program run in its own address space. This means that passing a pointer between applications (or even a handle, which is also a pointer) will cause an access violation.

There are a few mechanisms for sharing memory under Win32, but the best method is to use a memory mapped file. Essentially, a memory mapped file is treated by the program as a pointer to memory, and by the operating system as a file. When you do an operation like this with a memory mapped file:

```
lstrcpy (lpMyData, "Hi There!");
```

you are actually writing that string to a file at the offset **lpMyData**. This is great, since all of the memory pointer operations can be used to fly throughout the file. For example, you can take your code that searches a string for a word, and simply pass the pointer to the file instead.

How can this be used to share memory between application processes? Win32 provides the CreateFileMapping API to create the memory mapped file; you then use the MapViewOfFile API to map that file into your address space. Now, just use this as just another chunk of memory. If another application also uses the same filename, they will also have access to the same chunk of memory. The two applications must have some mechanism to figure out the filename to use. This can be a temporary entry in the registry, an atom, or a pre-agreed on filename. Let's look at some actual code that one of the two applications call at startup:

```
hFile = CreateFileMapping( (HANDLE)0xFFFFFFFF, // -1 means put in memory
                           NULL,               // No security
                           PAGE_READWRITE,     // Protection
                           0,                  // Max size hiorder bytes
                           4*1024,             // Max size loorder bytes
                           szPredeterminedName); // Pre-determined filename
lpMem = (LPSTR)MapViewOfFile(hFile,           // File to map
                           FILE_MAP_WRITE,    // Map reads and writes
                           0,                 // Map from start of file
                           0,                 // Map from start of file (pt 2)
                           0);                // Map entire file
```

This code opens up a memory mapped file of szPredeterminedName for reading and writing, a maximum size of 4K, and returns the pointer to this shared memory in lpMem, cast as a LPSTR. To actually use this memory in another application, use the OpenFileMapping API, and then do a MapViewOfFile just like above.

3. Disk Utilities Alert: Exclusive Volume Locking

If you are a tools programmer who writes code to do things like disk defragmentation, read on. Win32's disk I/O subsystem is completely re-entrant, and that means that you must take additional measures to lock out everyone else from the logical disk volume before you attempt to do direct low-level manipulation of the file system.

This is accomplished through DeviceIoControl (see tip #10 above). The corresponding DOS interrupt control I/O functions are int21, function 440D, minor code 4A. The volume locking is done through a locking heirarchy, with multiple step commits to the lock: You ask for one lock, wait for that, ask for a second lock, wait for that, get the third lock, wait for that, and just like in *Die Hard*, you ask for that fourth lock, and once you get that fourth lock, you're rich! Here are the four locking levels, in the order of locking:

1: Allows open files, reads and writes upon permissions.

2: You must first obtain a level 1 lock. Allows reads, but not writes.

3: You must first obain a level 2 lock. Does not permit reads or writes.

0: Excludes everyone but the lock owner. No open files allowed.

There are also corresponding locks for physical volumes, this is used when you do things like manage partition tables and perform low-level formats.

For both type of locks, there are corresponding levels of unlocks (phew!).

2. WEP for me No More, Argentina!

Win32 has a flexible entry point name for DLL's, indicated in the /ENTRY flag for the linker. However, if you use the C Run times, *be sure* to name this function **DllMain**, or else the C runtimes will handle everything for you, and your entry function will never get called.

And, instead of a WEP that gets called with the stack in a random condition, your entry point is called again, with a different **fdwReason**. Here is a tiny sample dll entry point that initializes the C runtime:

```
BOOL WINAPI _CRT_INIT(HINSTANCE,DWORD,LPVOID);

INT  APIENTRY DllMain(HANDLE hinstDLL, DWORD fdwReason, LPVOID lpReserved)
{
if (fdwReason == DLL_PROCESS_ATTACH || fdwReason == DLL_THREAD_ATTACH)
     if (!_CRT_INIT(hinstDLL, fdwReason, lpReserved))
         return(FALSE);
```

```
if (fdwReason == DLL_PROCESS_DETACH || fdwReason == DLL_THREAD_DETACH)
    if (!_CRT_INIT(hinstDLL, fdwReason, lpReserved))
        return(FALSE);

return 1;
}
```

1. ExitWindows Usurped by InitiateSystemShutdown

First, kiss **ExitWindowsExec** goodbye. That's a violation of windows security, making it too easy for viruses to install themselves at boot time. Instead, setup programs that want to install device drivers ad naseum after the system restarts must instead mark these files as "copy at bootup," however at the time of this book's writing, the exact mechanism has not been determined yet.

Second, to shut down windows, use the **InitiateSystemShutdown** API. This API can be used to warn the user that the system is about to be shutdown, and display a message such as "This machine will self-destruct in 5 seconds." The user can then either watch their machine incinerate, or if their program is smart enough, it can use the **AbortSystemShutdown API** to abort the process.

CHAPTER 3

Party Phrases to Ensure that You Maintain Your Computer Nerd Status

We all do it. Writing code 18 hours a day does strange things to your mind. We speak Nerd. Most of the parties we go to are "ship parties" or other company-sponsored events. When you finally do break from a product cycle and find yourself in the cruel world of noncomputer-jargon-parties, chances are you may want to locate someone else who speaks your language. Here are some of the more popular phrases you may hear when talking to another fellow programming pal.

10. "Process an Interrupt"

Typical usage. Person A and B are talking, and Person C really needs to butt in. Person C says: "Can you process an interrupt?"

9. "Discardable"

Meaning: As in GMEM_DISCARDABLE.

Typical usage: "Oh, I don't remember that stuff. It's in my discardable memory."

8. "Offline"

Meaning: To stop droning on about some subject.

Typical Usage: "Take this conversation offline."

7. "Edit"

Meaning: To change something.

Typical usage: "I need to edit my burger and delete the pickles."

6. "Paged out" and "Virtual"

Meaning: To be out of reach and nonexistent.

Typical usages: "Sorry, he's paged out right now. Let me get his attention." Or, "Oh, that's your virtual girlfriend." Or, "Hannah is my Virtual Cat."

5. "Pop the stack"

Meaning: To backtrack.

Typical usage: "Oh, I can figure out how to get back home. I'll just pop the stack."

4. "NOP"

Meaning: A do-nothing.

Typical usage: "That guy is a NOP."

3. "CLI/STI"

Meaning: Check your Intel manual.

Typical usage: "I'm CLI right now. Don't interrupt me… Okay, I'm STI."

2. "Star Trek"

Typical usages: "That computer does Warp 9.9." Or, "That file will be assimilated." Or, any flavor of Warp Core breach comments.

1. "GP Fault"

Typical usage: "The VCR didn't record Trek last night—it must have GP faulted."

Bonus Nerdism

You use your friends' E-mail names instead of their real names, *even if the real name is easier to pronounce.*

CHAPTER 4

Ways to Lose, Waste, Track, or Ration System Resources

Windows 3.0 (and later versions) runs in protect mode, which opens up mega-bytes and megabytes of space for your programs to use. However, (prior to the release of Windows 95 and Windows NT) because of the segmented architecture of Intel's protect mode, getting at those mondo-megabytes required the use of the **GlobalAlloc** API to get chunks of memory greater than 64K in size. A killer application may be able to allocate a meg of memory for a bitmap, but the app is still restricted by a 64K data segment that must hold global variables, the stack, and the local heap.

KERNEL, USER, and GDI are also bound by this restriction for Windows 3.0 and 3.1. (Windows 95 and Windows NT run in "a flat memory model," which means that the 64K annoyance is gone—but read on.) USER has its own local heap, as does GDI. KERNEL does not have a local heap. Because of this 64K restriction, USER and GDI try to put as much as possible outside of their local heaps.

For example, a handle to an icon is nothing more than a handle to a chunk of memory that has stuff placed in it by **GlobalAlloc**. Icons don't eat up system resources. However, there are objects that must be in the local heaps of USER and GDI, either for performance reasons, or for "near-pointers-to-this-object-are-all-over-in-the-source-code-and-these-companies have-written-their-code-to-peek-into-the-DS-so-we-have-to-support-them" reasons.

These precious system resources must be used sparingly. You cannot increase the system resources beyond the 64K limit for Windows 3.1 (although I heard of a customer was told that his computer was low on system resources and went into a computer store to buy more system resources). For Windows 95 and Windows NT, it is still a rude-dog programming policy to use more resources than you need.

The list in this chapter covers some "gotchas" that eat system resources, some invaluable techniques for conserving system resources, and some ways to track down your pesky system-resource losses.

10. Don't Create Anything on WM_CTLCOLOR

The WM_CTLCOLOR message is sent to a parent of a standard control every time that control needs to paint. For Win32, a group of CTLCOLOR messages replaces WM_CTLCOLOR. These messages have the same functionality and, therefore, the same "gotchas."

As stated previously, this message is sent *every* time a control needs to paint. That could be hundreds (or even thousands) of times for each time the dialog box is displayed. Look at the following chunk of resource-chomping code:

```
case WM_CTLCOLOR:

  if (CTLCOLOR_LISTBOX == HIWORD(lParam))
    return CreateSolidBrush ( RGB ( 255,0,0 ));
  break;
```

I wonder how long it would take to eat up all the local heap in the Win 3.1 GDI by using identical brushes. I wonder how long it would take for Windows 95 to eat up your hard disk with virtual brushes. This code should be changed to return a handle to a globally maintained brush, which is created at WM_INITDIALOG time and destroyed when the dialog is shut down. Or, if the application wishes, the brush can be left around for the lifetime of the application (see the section, "2. Keep a Global Set of Objects," later in this chapter).

9. Hiding CreateXXX Functions from DestroyXXX Functions

There is almost no reason why an object should not be created and destroyed within the same level of execution. Usually, the create and destroy should happen in the same function, although sometimes it makes more sense to have a **CreateObjects** function and a **DestroyObjects** function. In the latter case, the call to **CreateObjects** and **DestroyObjects** should be in the same function, so it is easy to track the scope of where these functions are called.

One of the biggest "gotchas" for creating objects is to create them in response to messages sent an unknown number of times. If your code creates an object in response to a WM_TIMER message, it can be very difficult to destroy every object, since the WM_TIMER message comes at practically random intervals (see Chapter 1). In this case, it is imperative to create and destroy the object within the scope of the message.

Creating an object in response to WM_COMMAND is also risky, since your application may get many more WM_COMMAND messages than you expect.

Of course, if your are programming in C++, most of these problems go away, since you can put the **CreateXXX** function in the constructor or "create function," and the **DestroyXXX** function in the destructor. By using C++, as long as the objects are declared automatically, it is impossible to mismatch the **CreateXXX** and **DestroyXXX**, as long as you don't leak your C++ objects (see Chapter 13).

8. Not Selecting DC's to Their Original, Upright Position

Every action done to a DC must be undone before you return it to the system. In the case of DCs retrieved by way of **BeginPaint** or **GetDC** (I will call these "Type 1 DCs"), be sure to completely restore them before calling **EndPaint** or **ReleaseDC**. In the case of DCs created with **CreateCompatibleDC** or **CreateDC** ("Type 2 DCs"), be sure to clean them up before calling **DeleteDC**.

For Type 1 DCs, leaving your objects selected into these DCs can be disastrous. Imagine this scenario. Your application creates a brush and selects it into a DC. You are finished with the DC, so you release it. Now, "SomeOtherApp" written by CrashSoft has code in it that checks the return value of **SelectObject**. Their application notices that there is already a non-**GetStockObject** item in the DC and they do not bother to set up their DC. Now your object is being used by two applications, and when you later try to delete that object, it could fail, since "SomeOtherApp" has a lock on it.

Of course, each new version of Windows works harder and harder to ensure that these programming issues don't hurt the operating system. Under Windows 95, not restoring a DC won't cause the previous scenario, but it is still a bad idea to make such assumptions about your operating system.

For Type 2 DCs, leaving your objects selected into these DCs can cause **DeleteObject** to fail, since these objects are locked while they are selected. Generally, Type 2 DCs are memory DCs, and selecting an object into them is the equivalent of **GlobalLock** or **LocalLock**.

7. Windows, Windows, Windows

How about a nifty form control that has 70 fields in it, one in which the user can type in information into all 70 fields? Of course, the user can only type information into one of these fields at any one time. Creating 70 edit controls to achieve this task is an extreme waste of system resources. Instead, create one edit control that floats around the window. Use static controls (or even better, paint them manually) for the remaining fields. When you press the TAB key, you will get the WM_NEXTDLGCTL if you are in a dialog box (or using **IsDialogMessage**). You can use this as a signal to move your edit control to the next place and start all over again.

Edit controls are the piggiest of the simple Windows controls, since they must store text. Combo boxes are the piggiest of all, since they usually contain an edit control and a list box. The new controls in Windows 95's COMMCTRL.H were designed from the start to use their own heaps. However, you should still try to avoid creating any more windows than you need, since there will still be users who have only 4 MB of RAM running Windows 95.

6. CreatePatternBrush

This great function creates a patterned brush by using a bitmap that you supply as the basis. Don't forget to destroy the bitmap when you are finished. Windows will not do it for you.

5. Fonts

Fonts eat up system resources. Since it is almost always desirable to cache fonts, try to avoid creating any more fonts than you need. Some very sophisticated programs actually have developed their own **TextOut** functions that take a memory DC instead of a font. This DC contains bitmap images of every character, and the **BitBlt** function is used to draw the characters. This is a bit extreme, but if your application must have a couple dozen fonts cached, this method can in an enormous savings of resources . See the section, "1. Use One Mondo Memory DC (or Use an ImageList in Windows 95)," later in this chapter for more on this idea.

4. The Object Demystifier

When you are running in DEBUG Windows (if you are not running in DEBUG Windows as a developer, then I am blushing for you), you are notified of objects that you forgot to delete upon shutdown—similar to, "GDI: Font (0x2F29) not deleted."

This information is almost useless, unless you have your program create a LOG file that notes every font created and when (see the following section, "3. Wrap Your Object Creation and Deletion"). However, log or no, it is also possible for you to still use those objects. The program OBJECT.EXE on the disk that accompanies this book will allow you to type in the "2F29" and find out just what font you forgot to delete. The visual appearance of this font should strike an alarm in your skull so that you will be able to hop right to the code that makes the blunder. OBJECT.EXE works for fonts, bitmaps, brushes, pens, and menus.

3. Wrap Your Object Creation and Deletion (for Non-C++ Programmers)

Since tracking object creation and deletion is very difficult with CodeView or other debuggers, instead wrap up your object management in functions. Take a look at the following function to wrap up **CreateBitmap**:

```
#ifdef DEBUG
#define CALLINGFUNC LPSTR szCallingFunc,
#define FUNCID(p1) p1,
#else
#define CALLINGFUNC
#define FUNCID(p1)
#endif


HBITMAP BITMAP_MakeBitmap ( CALLINGFUNC HWND hWnd, WORD x, WORD y )
{
  HDC       hDC;
  HBITMAP   hBitmap;
```

```
  hDC       = GetDC ( hWnd );
  hBitmap   = CreateCompatibleBitmap ( hDC, x, y );
  ReleaseDC ( hWnd, hDC );

  if (hBitmap)
    AddBitmapToValidList ( FUNCID(szCallingFunc) hBitmap );
  else
    OutputDebugString ( "BITMAP_MakeBitmap puked\r\n" );

  return hBitmap;
}


void BITMAP_DeleteBitmap ( HBITMAP hBitmap )
{
  if (BitmapInValidList (hBitmap))
    {
    DeleteObject ( hBitmap );
    RemoveBitmapFromValidList ( hBitmap );
    }
  else
    {
    OutputDebugString ( "Invalid hBitmap passed to BITMAP_DeleteBitmap\r\n" );
    }
}


//************** SAMPLE CALL

void MySample ( void )
{
  HBITMAP hBitmap;

  BITMAP_MakeBitmap ( FUNCID("MySample") hWnd, 100, 100 );
  /* do stuff here */
  BITMAP_DeleteBitmap ( hBitmap );
}
```

These wrapper functions encapsulate the creation and deletion functions, and, for debugging builds, it also identifies where the object was created. The programmer-supplied function **AddBitmapToValidList** adds the object to some data structure (and for debugging builds, the function name), while the **RemoveBitmapFromValidList** function does the opposite. The **BitmapInValidList** simply checks that data structure for validity.

By wrapping the base GDI functions in wrappers like this, your code can very easily track (and manage) your GDI objects. The *ValidList functions can serve as a watchdog for your code to make sure that you never have more than (*n*) objects created at any one time. Also, every addition and deletion can be logged onto disk, and you can then use this information to track down your problems.

2. Keep a Global Set of Objects

As mentioned previously, keeping duplicate copies of fonts around is unnecessary, and it is also dangerous to spread **CreateXXX** calls all over your code. Instead, architect your code so that the core objects are created in WinMain before your message loop, and destroyed after your message loop. These objects are then maintained by some very centralized code that handles these objects. This centralized code not only handles creation and deletion of these objects, but also reference.

Think about how C++ implements static data members. They are essentially encapsulated global variables. Just as the **GetStockObject** API returns an object that Windows has created and tucked away in a global variable, your application can implement its own **GetMyStockObject** API that returns handles to objects that are global in scope.

1. Use One Mondo Memory DC (or Use an ImageList in Windows 95)

Many programs do a considerable amount of off-screen drawing in memory DCs, and have many bitmaps and images to store away. Instead of creating a separate memory DC for every bitmap and image, create one all-encapsulating memory DC, and then put all your bitmaps into it. Windows does this for the bitmaps it used to show checkbox bitmaps. Just do a **LoadBitmap (NULL, OBM_CHECKBOXES)** and see how many images are crammed into the bitmap (or take a peek with **Heapwalk**).

Why do this? Because a DC takes up system resources and a bitmap does not. Using one memory DC with a large bitmap takes up no more resources than a memory DC with a small bitmap. Therefore, instead use up the global heap, of which the user's machines have plenty.

If you are writing for Windows 95, use the **ImageList** (see Chapter 11, "Windows 95 User Interface Goodies"). This **ImageList** handles almost all the dirty work for you (which makes your life easier), in addition to letting the operating system use the most efficient means possible to do the dirty work.

These are just the tip of the iceberg for system resource management. Most of the methods used to manage your resources do not involve having an intimate knowledge of Windows (besides, Windows 95 changes a lot of those rules). Instead, managing resources is more an exercise of the programmer to gain an intimate knowledge of his or her own code. Use the object demystfier, and wrap up your object creation functions. It will make your programming life much easier. But most of all, consider writing any new code in C++. The constructor/destructor idea behind an object in C++ makes the list in this chapter much, much smaller.

CHAPTER 5

Common Headaches Encountered by Windows Programmers

Programming in Windows is difficult. Luckily, using the STRICT compiler option, and the Debug kernel of Windows helps to find a large percentage of programming blunders. However, some elusive programming problems still can turn the most simple of applications into a literal roach motel. Here are some of the hair-pulling nasties Windows programmers run into.

10. Forgetting to Set the Length Field for Structures

More and more Windows structures have a length field. As an example, take a look at the following *WINDOWPLACEMENT* structure:

```
typedef struct tagWINDOWPLACEMENT
{
```

```
    UINT  length;
    UINT  flags;
    UINT  showCmd;
    POINT ptMinPosition;
    POINT ptMaxPosition;
    RECT  rcNormalPosition;
} WINDOWPLACEMENT;
```

The length field in this structure is *not* automatically set up for you, even for the "Get" functions. Your application must set this up before using any APIs that use this structure, as shown here (or else the API will fail):

```
WINDOWPLACEMENT wp;
wp.length = sizeof(WINDOWPLACEMENT);
GetWindowPlacement ( hWnd, &wp );
```

The reason for this requirement is of great value. Your code will automatically version-bind these structures. In Windows 3.1, this structure is 22 bytes long. For Windows 95, all of those *UINT* values will be 4 bytes long, so this structure will be 44 bytes long. The **sizeof** operator actually tags this structure's size, and the internal code inside of Windows can then use the correct version of the structure. If the size is 22 bytes, then Windows knows to use the old, obsolete version. If the size is 44 bytes, then Windows knows to use the new version.

Of course, you are saying, "Wait, won't the size of the length field also look different? How can Windows tell what size the first field is?" The answer to that is, "Oops!" The Windows developers probably should have used a *DWORD* for that field. Instead, their code in Windows 95 must assume either size for the first field, and, therefore, read both a *WORD* and a 32-bit *UINT*, as shown here:

```
wValue = *((LPWORD)(lpWindowPlacement));  // Windows 3.1 UINT
lValue = *((UINT *)(lpWindowPlacement));  // Windows 95's UINT
```

If the calling program was using the 16-bit Windows 3.1 version of the structure, *wValue* would have a sensible value, while *lValue* would have garbage. If the calling program was a 32-bit Windows 95 application, *wValue* would have garbage in it, and *lValue* would have a sensible value. Of course, this extra work could have been avoided if the length field of *WINDOWPLACEMENT* was declared as a type of fixed length, such as *WORD* or *DWORD*.

So far, only the 16-bit-to-32-bit migration has been used as an example of how a structure can use the length field to determine its layout. However, what if the version of Windows that comes out after Windows 95 must add a totally new field to the *WINDOWPLACEMENT* structure? The value of the length field can be used as a litmus test to see if the calling program is using the older version of the *WINDOWPLACEMENT* structure that does not have this totally new field.

If you haven't already made a mental note, this is a great coding convention to follow for your own structures. However, make sure that no two versions of your structures are the same size, or else you will fool your own code. Be sure to keep in mind that structure alignment has an effect on the **sizeof** operator. Therefore, if you change your structure alignment values in future versions, be sure to write "thunk-wannabe" functions that will map the old alignment structures to the new alignment structures.

9. Forgetting to Export Your Function in the DEF file or Through the Compiler

Okay, we all do it. It's all right to admit that you have spent an entire evening trying to figure out why all your variables are weird, or why that dialog does not initialize correctly. How do you avoid this? Use the *_export* keyword in your code, and you won't have to worry about exporting functions in your DEF file. The *CALLBACK* function type defined in WINDOWS.H automatically includes *_export*, so, if you declare your functions with *CALLBACK*, you will live happily ever after.

8. Custom Controls Keep Dialogs from Appearing

If your dialog template includes custom controls, and your dialog box refuses to pop up, look at your debugging output. Chances are you may find a line squirt out on your debugger that says something akin to, "CreateWindow failed." Sure enough, if *any* control fails to create, the *entire* dialog creation process will abort, and your call to **CreateDialog** (or other dialog API) will fail.

The reason for this is very simple. An application may depend on the existence of that suicidal control. If that control cannot create, the possibility exists that the program may get a bit loopy and pull a Wyle E. Coyote off the nearest coding cliff.

7. "hWnd Destroyed Unexpectedly by Callback"—Make it Stop!

This is one of those messages you get on your debugging terminal that often eludes explanation. When does a window expect to be destroyed? The answer is when the **DispatchMessage**() API sends a WM_CLOSE message to your window procedure from the application's message queue. If you use a **SendMessage** API to send a message to the window that instantiates a call to **DestroyWindow**, you will run into this message.

Generally, this problem arises for windows that like to terminate themselves abnormally. They do this by calling **DestroyWindow** in response to an event, such as a WM_LBUTTONUP or a WM_COMMAND message. To get rid of the debugging warning, simply use **PostMessage (hWnd, WM_CLOSE, 0, 0)**, and let Windows shut down your window normally.

6. CallNextHookEx Invalid Parameter Message (Windows 3.1)

What causes this message to show up on your debugging terminal? Check out your calls to **SendMessage**. If you pass bogus parameters to **SendMessage**, (namely, an invalid *hWnd*), this obscure error message pops up.

5. When to Send and When to Post Messages

This is the "Question Eternal." Windows programmers have been pelted with soapbox lectures about message ordering, recursion, queue size, and the posting and sending of messages. It is quite easy to find two sets of documentation that contradict each other.

The primary differences between **PostMessage** and **SendMessage** is, of course, the fact that **SendMessage** gives you a return value, and the results of **SendMessage** happen instantly. Therefore, if you need a return value, you have no choice but to use **SendMessage**. (Or do you? See the section, "Intertask Message Boxes Under Windows 3.1," later in this chapter.)

PostMessage is used when a neither a return value nor instant results are required. **PostMessage** eats up a slot on your application's message queue. This queue is, by default, eight messages big for Windows 3.1 (Windows 95 and Windows NT dynamically expand the queue for you). You can adjust that upward by using the **SetMessageQueue** API, but it is not always necessary to post messages.

Think of **SendMessage** as a function call. If you want to immediately pass control to another part of your application, have that part of your application do its thing, and then return control back to you (while in the same stack frame), then **SendMessage** is your bag.

Think of **PostMessage** as a notification of a future task to do. If you want to cause your application to do something in the future (consider "future" as any point in time after the currently dispatched message is complete), use **PostMessage**. Generally, **PostMessage** is used to fake Windows events (such as posting a WM_CLOSE as mentioned in the section, "7. 'hWnd Destroyed Unexpectedly by Callback'—Make it Stop!"), or it is used for ordering tasks. An example of ordering tasks would be if you are using messages to control program flow. If you use WM_USER+(n) messages to call up certain recalculations, drawings, communications, and so forth, then you could use **PostMessage** to issue a "batch job" to your application.

Why would an application use messages to control the flow of an application? The following three reasons come to mind:

1. The user has the choice of controlling the flow by way of menus.

2. Message-based code control lends to an artificial "thread-based" architecture.

3. Messages can be used to drive a "state machine."

Personally, I find reason 2 leads to headaches, and enormously long debugging sessions. Reasons 1 and 3 are much more realistic implementations of using **PostMessage**.

An example of reason 1 would be if your program supports a batch language (or OLE Automation). Your batch processor (or OLE Automation processor) may encounter a command to apply bold formatting to some text. This processor can most easily mimic the action of a user boldfacing text by simply posting a message to the main frame window to fake the "Bold" menu option. An example of reason 3 could be using private messages as a state machine to control a file-transfer protocol (this is an actual example of an implementation that a colleague wrote).

With Windows 95 and Windows NT, threads are for real. Use them instead. Keeping this in mind, it is much easier to decide when to use **PostMessage** and when to use **SendMessage**.

Use **SendMessage** when you need a return value, immediate execution, or when the documentations say so (they say to use **SendMessage** to communicate with a control). Also, use **SendMessage** when you are unsure if a window will be destroyed before a posted message can reach it.

Use **PostMessage** when you must have your action happen in the future, or when your action could be messed up by message ordering. If you are going to do something in response to the third of five Windows messages, assume that those five messages may end up changing order in the future, and post yourself a message. The following code is a sample of using **PostMessage** to get around message ordering:

```
case LBN_SELCHANGE:

  PostMessage ( hWnd, WM_MYGETTEXT, 0, (HWND)hWndListbox );
  break;
...
```

```
case WM_MYGETTEXT:

    wIndex = (WPARAM)SendMessage ( (HWND)lParam, LB_GETCURSEL, 0, 0L );
    SendMessage ( (HWND)lParam, LB_GETTEXT, wIndex, (LPARAM)(LPSTR)sz );
    break;
```

This code does not make the assumption that the LBN_SELCHANGE message is sent *after* the current selection has changed. In fact, with some combo boxes, code like this is required, since the combo box sends out its notification *before* changing the current selection. By posting a message to itself, this code lets Windows "do its dirty work" before checking out the data.

A Note About Dialog Boxes

As you know, the dialog box's procedure only expects one of two return values: TRUE or FALSE. If you want to send a message to a dialog box and use the return value for something important, then you will need to set the DWL_MSGRESULT extra bytes before returning.

Wrong:

```
case IDC_WANTFONT:
    return (LRESULT)hFont;
```

Right:

```
case IDC_WANTFONT:
    SetWindowLong(hDlg, DWL_MSGRESULT, (LONG)hFont);
    return TRUE;
```

The reason for this different programming practice is because the actual window procedure for a dialog box lives in USER (it's just another window class, after all). That window procedure inside USER calls your dialog procedure and expects a TRUE or FALSE return value (to determine whether to process the message). The actual return value of the window procedure inside USER depends on what is stored inside those extra bytes.

4. Backslashes

See this code?

```
hFile = OpenFile ( "C:\WINDOWS\WIN.INI", &of, OF_READ );
```

It won't work. Change it to the following:

```
hFile = OpenFile ( "C:\\WINDOWS\\WIN.INI", &of, OF_READ );
```

I know, I know, this is a cheezy tip. However, I know programmers who simply forget such simple things. Just as Einstein had his problems with simple arithmetic, many of programmers (including yours truly) forget simple C "gotchas."

3. Equal Signs

And, speaking of cheezy C tips, look at the following dangerous code:

```
if (msg == WM_MOUSEMOVE ) ...
```

Change it to:

```
if (WM_MOUSEMOVE == msg)
```

and avoid the easy mistake of using the single equal sign instead of the double equal signs. If you can ever set up a comparison where the *lValue* would evaluate to an error in the case of assignment, do it.

2. MDI Programs Gone Crazy!

A common problem programmers encounter when writing MDI programs is that they find that their MDI interfaces don't quite fit the description of what an MDI application is supposed to do. For example, their menus are either knocked all out of whack, or their menus don't change. Or, sometimes the captions don't update correctly.

Almost every problem with the MDI interface can be traced to the improper use (or lack of use) of the **DefMDIChildProc** API. This API must be called for the WM_MOVE and WM_SIZE messages, *even if you process them.* Therefore, at the end of your code block for the WM_MOVE and WM_SIZE messages, be sure to return **DefMDIChildProc**.

One other nasty MDI issue comes with "wild menus." This scenario is best described as a poltergeist that seems to magically change innocent menus into the "<n> MYDOC.DOC" stuff that is supposed to go on your "Window" menu. This is generally caused by not using a large enough value for the *idFirstChild* field in the *CLIENTCREATESTRUCT* structure. This field must be larger than any possible menu ID that your application uses. Windows is free to use the range above this value. Therefore, it makes sense to keep your menu IDs down in the four-digit categories, and then you can safely set the *idFirstChild* field to something nice and huge (like 10042).

1. Where Have All the Notifications Gone?

If you have ever used **SetParent** to move an edit control from one window to another, you may have found that your EN_CHANGE notification message did not tag along for the ride. The reason for this is because the edit control (along with almost all the other controls) cache away their parent at creation time in an internal data structure. When you change the control's parent by using **SetParent**, the internal data structure is not updated, and your notification messages still go to the original parent.

The best workaround I have found for this problem is to originally create the control parented to a "traffic cop" window. This traffic cop window will always get the notification messages for that control, even if the control is reparented. Since your program owns the code for this traffic cop window, your program can now redirect the messages, using GetParent on the control to figure out its real parents.

INTERTASK MESSAGE BOXES UNDER WINDOWS 3.1

A great way to hang a Windows 3.1 application is to have App A send a message to App B, and have App B put up a message box in response. The reason for this hang is because App B then goes into its own private message loop, and expects Windows to know that App B has been activated by the internal task scheduler. Well, App A is still the officially activated task. Windows get confused, and hangs.

However, App A usually calls on App B to put up a message box since App A wants an answer. The **ReplyMessage** API won't always work in this situation, even though the documentations say so.

A better workaround is to put App A to "sleep" and then wake up App B. This is done by posting a message to App B, and then putting App A to sleep. Allow App A to yield normally (this will happen when App A's message queue empties), and App B eventually will be awakened. App B then puts up the message box, and, when the user answers that message box, App B posts a message back to App A, which wakes up App A.

Of course, this headache goes away in Windows 95 and Windows NT (joy!).

CHAPTER 6

Very Bad Things to Do While Writing Windows Code

As newer versions of Windows come out, and as Windows NT and the Microsoft Foundation Classes (MFC) turn our GUI programming lives into multiplatforms, it becomes tougher and tougher to write that politically correct piece of code that is an easy port/update to the next platform/version of GUI. It is very easy to get into some habits while writing Windows code, or to employ some shortcuts to get results that may work today, but may certainly break tomorrow. The best way to write code with the most likely chance of working on the next version is to code using MFC. Unfortunately, the current installed code base consists of probably about 95 percent straight C code. The program managers and "mucky-mucks" or large corporations are not going to buy off on letting you ditch your complete code base and move over to MFC.

The list in this chapter has a hodgepodge of sources. Some of these bad things I have done myself and paid the price. Some of these bad things have been done by other programmers and I have had to hop on my soapbox. And some of the other items on this list I got by asking other programmers what horrid things they have heard of. Most of the items on this list deal with straight C and the Windows SDK, though tip number 4 ("To MFC or not to MFC") deals with MFC, while tip number 2 ("Make Assumptions About the Environment") deals with any programming language.

10. Rely on Message Ordering

This one is a killer. I have seen many applications that expect to see the WM_xxx message come immediately after WM_yyy, or even worse, the WM_xxx message to always come after something has happened. A very typical example of this is the CBN_SELCHANGE notification message. In my applications, I got that message before the current selection variable buried deep inside the combo boxes data structure changed. Therefore, code like the following would break:

```
case CBN_SELCHANGE:
    iSel = (int)SendMessage(hWndCombo, CB_GETCURSEL, ...)
```

This code would give me the selection of what formerly had the selection. Now, the docs have been updated to reflect this, saying, "The CBN_SELCHANGE message is sent when the selection of a combo box is about to change," making this particular message safe to rely on. However, for many other messages (namely your own private messages), the ordering or time of departure is not defined too clearly. If you have code that relies on the timing of a message, modify your code to expect that message after the action has taken place, and then post yourself a user-defined message to really take the action. For example, consider this modification to the previous code:

```
#define CBN_MYSELCHANGE  (4242)
...
case CBN_SELCHANGE:
```

```
    widCombo = LOWORD(wParam);
    PostMessage(hWnd, WM_COMMAND, MAKELONG(widCombo, CBN_MYSELCHANGE), lParam);
    break;
case CBN_MYSELCHANGE:
    iSel = (int)SendMessage(hWndCombo, CB_GETCURSEL, ...)
```

9. Use PeekMessage Loops to Fake Threads When You Don't Have To

Many applications toss this code in whenever they want to "yield" periodically:

```
while (PeekMessage(&msg, 0, 0, 0, PM_REMOVE))
    {
    TranslateMessage(&msg);
    DispatchMessage(&msg);
    }
```

This is a coding horror, sure to make you go postal. Imagine you are doing a loopy calculation inside a dialog box (a modal dialog, which means that a message loop is spinning inside USER), and inside that loop you use the previous **PeekMessage** code to "keep the flow going" (which now pushes USER's **PeekMessage** loop down one level on the call stack). Now, imagine that while the calculation is going on, you bring up a nested dialog. USER again has the **PeekMessage** loop, which freezes your calculation, and has your **PeekMessage** code also on the call stack. This situation can get very hairy, especially if you break out of the dialogs without unwinding all these nested **PeekMessage** loops.

However, this is just the tip of the iceberg. Even if you succeed in getting all that nesting of jumps in and out of USER's **PeekMessage** loop, you run into another issue: Who has control? The previous spaghetti code jumps around so much that the scope and context of variables change with enough fervor to turn your debugging brain into such a thick mush that only television shows with purple dinosaurs would look appealing.

But wait, there's more! In addition to the stacking/debugging nightmare, you also can actually break your application quite nicely. The previous

PeekMessage code is missing things like **TranslateAccelerator**, **IsDialogMessage**, ad nauseam. Therefore, during certain times of your program's execution, keyboard accelerators or MDI functionality temporarily stop working, which in turn lights up your product support lines. The only workaround to that problem is to start storing the current dialogs and states of your program in global variables, put all those extra APIs in your **PeekMessage** loop, and then pray you have a new job before you are called on to fix some "random strange focus bugs that only some customers suffer" in the shipping application.

A much more elegant solution to this problem is to use messages as a state variable, and do your calculations based on the state machine. For example, say you want to copy a hundred files. You could build a list of the files to copy, and then post yourself a custom message. This message causes your code to copy a file from the list and then advance a pointer to the next file. If the end of the list is not reached, post yourself the message again. This method allows the currently running message loop to elegantly handle your requests, while letting other normal messages (such as the user clicking on the Cancel button or pressing the ESC key) to slip in between the file copies.

8. Mix and Match Window Styles

I have seen an application use both the WS_POPUP and WS_CHILD style bits in the same window. Guess what? It broke under Windows 3.1, and it will break again under Windows 95. The docs specifically say not to do this. Trust me, even if doing a no-no works today, it may not work tomorrow.

7. Leave Files Open Between Messages

If you open a file, close it in the same message, if at all possible. This is because you may wait a really long time before getting that next message to close the file—possibly indefinitely if your application is hung, or if you suffer a system failure. Files that have been opened but not closed keep companies like Symantec in business with their disk-repair utilities. If your application needs to maintain a serial data structure between messages, consider using a memory image, and then, when the operation is complete, blast the whole thing out to a file in one swoop.

6. Count on Extra Bytes

All of the built-in controls use extra bytes to store some information. Some clever programmers have superclassed these controls and added some of their own:

```
#define MYEDITEXTRA 42
GetClassInfo (hinst, "edit", &wc);
wc.cbWndExtra += sizeof(LONG);
...
lValue = GetWindowLong (hWndEdit, MYEDITEXTRA);
```

The previous code counts on the fact that the number of extra bytes in the edit control will never change. Well, they will, especially with Win32, since things that used to be 2 bytes (*ints*) now take 4 bytes. There is a better way, though.

```
#define MYEDITEXTRA sizeof(LONG)
GetClassInfo (hinst, "edit", &wc);
gcbEditExtra = wc.cbWndExtra;
wc.cbWndExtra += MYEDITEXTRA;
...
lValue = GetWindowLong (hWndEdit, gcbEditExtra + MYEDITEXTRA);
```

The previous code determines at runtime the indices of the extra bytes you are adding onto the end. This code will work for every version of Windows, no matter what the platform.

5. Not Checking Return Values

No list of naughty programming habits would be complete without this one. 'Nuff said—do it!

117

4. To MFC or not to MFC

As we move our programs over to MFC (yay!), we find it tempting to cut and paste existing C algorithms into our code. After all, you can access any of the zillion SDK functions by simply descoping it, as shown here:

```
IconWidth = ::GetSystemMetrics(SM_CXICON);
```

Using code like this is dangerous in an MFC application because it breaks the idea of using an application framework, it binds you to an API's parameters, and it forces you rely on that API being available. These restrictions are practically unavoidable in straight C programming. With MFC, however, it is possible to completely shield yourself from the operating system's native calls. This is extremely important, since VC++ 2.0 allows you to create Macintosh applications using the same MFC code base. The catch is that your code must be completely written in "clean" MFC. A dirty MFC application, which has descoped SDK calls like the previous example, must either be translated by a software layer (speed hit), or will require a conditional compilation to make a Mac (or other non-Windows platform) version. Yech.

If you use all of MFC's functions, and avoid using any direct API, you can write code that not only ports easy to the Mac, but also will port easily to any new platform for which Microsoft decides to make MFC available. But, alas, this isn't always possible.

If you must use APIs directly in your program, be sure to abstract yourself away from them. Create an object called something like COperatingSystem that has member functions to get to the APIs you desire. That way, when you move to a new platform, you must simply change this COperatingSystem object. Be sure that you write this class to give you the information you need, versus writing just a wrapper. For example, take a look at the following two different implementations of a tiny COperatingSystem object:

Bad Way:

```
class COperatingSystem
    {
```

```
public:
    int GetSystemMetrics(int nIndex) {return ::GetSystemMetrics(nIndex); }
};
...
COpSys COperatingSystem;
iIconWidth = COpSys.GetSystemMetrics(SM_CXICON);
```

Good Way:

```
class COperatingSystem
    {
    public:
        int IconWidth() {return ::GetSystemMetrics(SM_CXICON); }
    };
...
COpSys COperatingSystem;
iIconWidth = COpSys.IconWidth();
```

The Bad Way still binds your program to the operating system. Your code still must know that it must call the **GetSystemMetrics** call, and it still must use the SM_CXICON constant. What if the **GetSystemMetrics** API didn't even exist on your new platform?

The Good Way provides the information you want—the icon width. The means of getting this width is contained completely in the COperatingSystem class.

3. Putting 1,000,000 Items in a List Box

Okay, I couldn't resist. I have, in my lifetime of being a Windows programming support person, more than once had customers who wanted to know a way to put 1,000,000 items into a list box. These customers seemed to forget that human beings use list boxes, and that no one in a sane state of mind would have the patience to press the PAGEDOWN key a hundred thousand times to search for something. I guess the purpose of this item is to make you laugh, but if you must try to get a message from this tip, how about, "remember that humans use your software."

2. Make Assumptions About the Environment

Most programs break when run on newer versions of an operating system because of assumptions made about the operating system have changed. The operating environment in which your program runs provides you with a rich set of features, and you may make assumptions about these features.

The most common assumption made about Windows programs is that they use 8.3 filenames. Now, with Windows 95 and Windows NT, you find yourself recoding your applications to accommodate the longer filenames. So, all programs that pick apart filenames based on the 8.3 construct will now end up getting a file-system overhaul. This is the most commonly made assumption, but less-than-obvious assumptions are often made by programmers.

Consider, for instance, the assumption that a toolbar always will be stuck on the top of your MFC application. Well, that's how it was for the MFC included with VC++ 1.5, but VC++ 2.0 now uses those newfangled "floating/docking/have-it-your-way" toolbars. MFC programs that assumed the toolbar always would be on the top are in for a big surprise.

Consider another assumption: negative window coordinates. Some programmers made the assumption that putting a window in negative coordinate-land would make it hidden (they did this instead of hiding the window properly, possibly to unsuccessfully try to get WM_PAINT messages). Under the current version of Windows, negative window coordinates work wonderfully for hiding windows. However, if your application is written in MFC and ported over to the Mac, you may find that those negative window coordinates will pop that hidden window over on the secondary video device attached to the Mac.

What can you do? First, try to avoid using any hard-coded constant anywhere in your program if the operating system can do it for you. A lot of code uses 32 as the width of an icon. Windows 95 now allows 48x48 and 16x16 icons, which means that all those programs that hard-coded 32 as an icon width may be in for a bit of maintenance nightmare. If the operating system provides a way to find out an attribute about itself, make sure to use that mechanism (and keep in mind tip number 4, "To MFC or not to MFC," in this chapter).

Just to be ludicrous, consider a wild assumption that virtually every program makes today: square client areas. Wild. Never mind. Some things you must assume. Well, actually, it's not that ludicrous to think of nonrectangular windows. Think about OLE, and how nice it would be to have an in-place server that was the shape of the object, instead of the bounding rectangle. You could make some very, very wicked, cool drawing programs if they could insert any OLE server object and let the user manipulate them. Actually, as of the writing of this book, nonrectangular windows were not going to happen for Windows 95, but they are a *very* requested feature, and you should expect to eventually see them.

1. Use Undocumented Anything

As helpful as they may be, using undocumented features, characteristics, APIs, messages, or anything undocumented in Windows is a surefire recipe for disaster. Not only do you run the chance of your program completely bombing in the next release of Windows, but also you run the risk of encountering, shall we say, some "legal hurdles" during your lifetime. As of the writing of this book, quite a few headlines have appeared about legal issues surrounding undocumented features. Even Microsoft takes a beating by using them—they end up making special releases of their software after every Windows release (WinWord 1.1 came out because of Windows 3.0, and WinWord 2.0b came out because of Windows 3.1, just to name a few).

CHAPTER 7

Tricks, Hints, and Techniques for Programming in Windows

Everybody who works with the Microsoft Windows operating system has a few favorite tricks. I'm going to share my ten favorites. Some of them I invented myself, others I figured out by examining other people's code, and a few I was just told about by fellow engineers.

Why do I like these tricks? First, they're easy. None of the sample programs here are monstrous, and some of them seem so obvious that you're going to say "Why didn't I write this list?" Second, they avoid anything undocumented. They contain no peeking around in private data structures, no taking advantage of broken features, and no relying on message ordering. Third, they require minimal work, and usually look really cool (although some of my favorites don't have anything to do with visuals). And finally, they are in demand. I get questions almost every day that can be answered by this list.

10. Keep Strings in a String Table and Out of Your DS

Even though Windows 95 uses a flat memory model, your program still has something like a DS. Instead of this DS being some chunk of memory that can be up to 64K in size, you are allocated an arbitrarily large chunk of memory to suit the needs of your program. However, just because you are no longer bound by a 64K DS, you cannot assume the world is your oyster and you can start devouring all of your memory. Many users out there are going to be running three or four large-scale applications simultaneously on an 8 MB machine. The less piggy your program is, the better. For ease of reading, I am still going to use the term "DS" throughout this list.

String constants are DS eaters. By moving all string constants out of your DS, you can use a larger stack while maintaining the same footprint, which means your application can have nastier recursive algorithms and deeper stack-intensive code. Keeping all of your strings in one place (the RC file) makes internationalization life easier by reducing a "scan through source code for strings" exercise to a more textbook-style "here's a list of phrases—translate them" endeavor.

The two exceptions where you would want to have strings in your DS are speed and death. Strings that are called upon frequently (such as a formatting string inside a loop) could be kept in your DS. A better method would be to cache the string into a local variable so that it only eats some stack space temporarily. Strings that may be used in a zillion places in your program (such as your application name) could be tucked away. The other reason you would want a string in your DS is for handling those cases where your program may die Real Soon Now. For example, the string "Critical Disk Failure: Shutting Down" should be in your DS, since that is guaranteed to be already loaded into memory. (**LoadString** could fail at a critical time such as this.)

Look at the following code:

```
lstrcpy ( szBuffer, Record.szFirstName );
if (Record.szMiddleName[0])
  {
```

```
  lstrcat ( szBuffer, "\r\n" );
  lstrcpy ( szBuffer, Record.szMiddleName );
  }
if (Record.szLastName[0])
  {
  lstrcat ( szBuffer, "\r\n" );
  lstrcpy ( szBuffer, Record.szLastName );
  }
```

This tiny bit of sample code wastes 6 bytes of the DS. The string *\r\n* is repeated. The following very simple change could save those bytes:

```
static const char szCrLf[] = "\r\n";
lstrcpy ( szBuffer, Record.szFirstName );
if (Record.szMiddleName[0])
  {
  lstrcat ( szBuffer, szCrLf );
  lstrcpy ( szBuffer, Record.szMiddleName );
  }
if (Record.szLastName[0])
  {
  lstrcat ( szBuffer, szCrLf );
  lstrcpy ( szBuffer, Record.szLastName );
  }
```

The "static" and "const" operators are much more important than you think in terms of DS usage and compiler optimization. Take a look at the following stinky Windows 95 code:

```
void Stinky()
{
  char szMessage[] = "This is a message that is read-only";
  printf(szMessage);
}
```

This causes the compiler to generate stinky code:

```
_DATA SEGMENT
$SG155 db "This is a message that is read-only", 0
_DATA ENDS

        sub     esp, 36
        mov     ecx, 9
        push    esi
```

```
push    edi
mov     esi, offset FLAT:$SG155
lea     edi, [esp][44]
rep     movsd
lea     eax, [esp][44]
push    eax
call    _printf
add     esp, 4
pop     edi
pop     esi
ret
```

By sticking the word "static" in front, you get less stinky code, such as

```
void LessStinky()
{
  static char szMessage[] = "This is a message that is read-only";
  printf(szMessage);
}
```

which results in the much simpler compiled code that runs faster:

```
push    offset FLAT:$SG155
call    _printf
add     esp, 4
ret
```

By adding "const," you get code like this:

```
void SmellsLikeRoses()
{
  static const char szMessage[] =
        "This is a message that is read-only";
  printf(szMessage);
}
```

The string will be placed in your RDATA segment, which will remove it completely from your DS. This is the ultimate protection, since that string will now also be marked "read-only," which will give you a nice friendly fault if you accidentally trash **szMessage**. Bonus!

Now, imagine how many extra bytes can be saved with the following declarations:

```
static const char szEdit[] = "edit";
static const char szListbox[] = "listbox";
static const char szStatic[] = "static";
static const char szButton[] = "button";
```

Every CreateWindow function call can save a few bytes here and there. And, as an added bonus, if you decide to superclass all of the controls, you can change these declarations to point to your superclass. An example of superclassing controls would be if you removed the CS_PARENTDC style bit so that your controls could overlap each other and still make sense of z-order during paints (see Chapter 1, number 6).

Now, look at the following sample code:

```
if (-1 == iIndex)
  MessageBox ( NULL, "Invalid Index found in Database!",
          "KillerApp", MB_OK );
```

This message box will eat up about 40 bytes of your DS. And your localization people are going to have a cow when you ask them to localize your program to German (or, should I say, they'll "eine Kuh haben").

Consider the following:

```
if (-1 == iIndex)
  MessageBox ( NULL, szLoadString (IDS_INVALIDINDEX),
          szAppName, MB_OK );
```

In this example, **szAppName** still lives in your DS (or in the code segment), but only once for the whole program. The **szLoadString** function loads the string from the string table resource (generated using an RC file) into a buffer and returns a pointer to the string to you (see Listing 7.1). This function either could use the DS of the application (but that still eats DS), or it could use a global chunk of memory that you manage. Even if you use the DS of your application, you will still most likely use less space. (One large application I wrote had 23K of strings, and the whole application was still minute compared to Microsoft Excel or Word for Windows.) Remember, a smaller DS means your program has a smaller working set, which means translates into better performance.

LISTING 7.1 szLOADSTRING FUNCTION

```
LPSTR szLoadString ( int iID )
{
  // These strings MUST be static so they don't live on the stack.  Since we
  // will be returning a pointer to one of these strings, we want the information
  // to be there once we exit this function
  // The number of strings in the circular buffer depends on how many times the
  // szLoadString function will be called in a single function call.  For
  // example, if you do this:
  //
  //    MessageBox ( NULL,
  //                 szLoadString(IDS_ERROR1),
  //                 szLoadString(IDS_MSGBOXTITLE),
  //                 MB_OK );
  //
  // Then you will need at least two different buffers, since both strings need
  // to be
  // loaded before the MessageBox function can be called.  I picked three for
  // this example beause that's how many cats I have.

  static int WhichString = 0;
  static char szLoadedString1[MAXSTRINGLEN];
  static char szLoadedString2[MAXSTRINGLEN];
  static char szLoadedString3[MAXSTRINGLEN];


  // These are just normal local varaibles used for looping and return values
  // and string magic

  BOOL bKeepLoading;
  int  i,j;
  char *szLoadedString;
  char szLoadBuffer[MAXSTRINGLEN];


  // This implements a circular buffer through the three strings. This means that
  // the pointer you get back from szLoadString will have the correct string in
  // it until szLoadString has been called three more times.

  switch (WhichString)
    {
    case 0: szLoadedString = szLoadedString1; break;
    case 1: szLoadedString = szLoadedString2; break;
    case 2: szLoadedString = szLoadedString3; break;
    }
```

```
WhichString++;
if (3==WhichString) WhichString=0;

// This is allows loading of strings greater than 255 characters. If the
// first character of the string is an exclamation point, this means to
// tack on the string with a value of ID+1.  This continues until
// the next string does not exist or the first character is not an
// exclamation point

szLoadedString[0] = 0;  // Init the string to emptyville.

do
  {
  bKeepLoading = FALSE;
  if (LoadString ( ghInst, iID, szLoadBuffer, sizeof(szLoadBuffer)))
    {
    if ('!' == *szLoadBuffer)   // Continuation character found. Keep the loop going
      {
      bKeepLoading = TRUE;

      // Assume next entry in string table is in numerical order
      iID++;

      lstrcat ( szLoadedString, szLoadBuffer+1 );
      }
    else
      {
      lstrcat ( szLoadedString, szLoadBuffer );
      }
    }
  }
while (bKeepLoading);

  return (LPSTR)szLoadedString;
}
```

Now, look at the following string table from an RC file:

```
STRINGTABLE
BEGIN
  IDS_ERROR,       "There was an Error"
  IDS_AREYOUSURE,  "Are you sure you want to do this?"
  IDS_OPENDOOR1,   "!Open the pod bay"
  IDS_OPENDOOR2,   "doors, Hal."
END
```

This string table uses the exclamation point (!) as a continuation character in order to load strings longer than one line of your RC file. Make sure that the value of *IDS_OPENDOOR2* is *IDS_OPENDOOR1+1*, or the scheme won't work.

This scheme will make localization of your programs much easier. Just hand your localization experts the RC file. Once they change all of the strings in the string table, menus, and dialog boxes, your application will speak a different language. Of course, there is more to localization than language (such as date and currency formats), but language is one of the more tedious and time-consuming conversions.

What if you want to cache a string in the DS for the life of the program, but still include it in the string table to keep your localizers happy? Just declare a global string buffer that can hold the string, and then fill it with the **szLoadString** function, as shown here:

```
char gszAppName[APPNAMESIZE];

    .
    .
    .

lstrcpy ( gszAppName, szLoadString(IDS_APPNAME));
```

9. Use the Nonvisible Sections of List Boxes to Hide Data Record Numbers/Invisible Static Windows

How many times have you had a list box full of data that you needed to keep associated with a database record number or a filename?

Look at the very small database sorted by name in Figure 9.1. Then look at that same group of records in a list box sorted by age in Figure 7.2. How will the program know that when the user clicks on the first item in the list box, it should bring up the information in record number 2? You have a couple ways to do this.

Name	Age	Record Number
Alayo	32	0
Edson	28	1
Foote	22	2
Scott	30	3
Woodruff	26	4

FIGURE 7.1 UNSORTED DATABASE

FIGURE 7.2 DATABASE SORTED BY AGE

One way is to use an owner-draw list box where you store the record number as a *DWORD* using *LB_SETITEMDATA*. When you process the *WM_DRAWITEM* message, you can get the record number with *LB_GETITEMDATA*, do a fetch on the database, and then display it. This is not always practical, because the database fetch may be pig-dog slow (such as on a network), so the performance of the list box will be poor.

The documentation may not directly say it, but the list box control actually allows you to store both a *DWORD* and a string. Therefore, you can use a normal, boring list box and still use *LB_SETITEMDATA* and *LB_GETITEMDATA* along with the strings added by way *LB_ADDSTRING* to achieve your results.

However, what if the record number you want to add isn't storable in a *DWORD*? For example, your record number may not be a linear number (such as a telephone number with hyphens), or it may contain alphabetic characters. Maybe your record number is a filename.

A solution is to store the record number in the list box string along with the user-readable data. Just hide it. The following code shows how you would put those strings into the list box:

```
for (i = 0; i < iNumItems; i++ )
    {

.


.    //Fetch your piece of data here
.


    wsprintf ( szBuffer, "%s\t%d\t%ld",
             (LPSTR)ChunkOData.szName,
             (LPSTR)ChunkOData.iAge,
             lRecordNumberOfMyIncrediblyComplexData);
    SendMessage ( hListBox, LB_ADDSTRING, OL,(LPARAM)szBuffer );
    }
```

Notice the tabs. By using the LBS_USETABSTOPS style bit, you can set tabs for each of the three columns. Do something like the following:

```
int iTabs[2];
iTabs[0] = 60;          // First tab at 60 dialog units
                        // (about 15 characters)
iTabs[1] = 511;         // Second tab at max position off
                        // edge of screen
SendMessage ( hListBox, LB_SETTABSTOPS, 2, (LPARAM)iTabs);
```

Now, only the first two columns will be visible and the record number will be casually tucked away in your virtual column. When you want to know the record number, simply grab the line with *LB_GETTEXT*, and parse out the record number from the end.

The sample program LONGFILE (see Listing 7.2) demonstrates this. It displays the "long filenames" of a directory of Windows 3.1 EXE files. Instead of showing the actual EXE name, the information contained in the DEF file is displayed (see Figure 7.3). The actual filename is off in virtual-column land. Here, instead of keeping track of the record numbers, I keep track of the actual filenames.

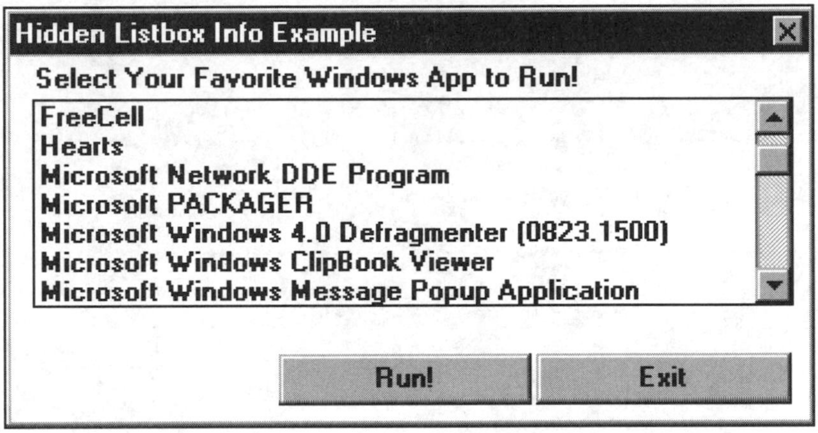

FIGURE 7.3 LONGFILE

LISTING 7.2 **LONGFILE** SAMPLE PROGRAM

```c
#include <windows.h>

#include "longfile.h"
#include "basedefs.h"

WINPROC WndProc ( WINDOWS_PARAMS );
DLGPROC DlgProc ( DIALOG_PARAMS  );
void    ExtractRealFileName ( HWND hListbox, LPSTR szFileToRun );
BOOL    CreateLongFileName ( LPSTR lpFileName, LPSTR lpLongFileName );
void    FillLBWithFileName ( HWND hListBox );

//========= These constants are used by CreateLongFileName to
//          snoop in the EXE header.
```

```
#define HDR_FTYPE          0x18
#define HDR_TYPEWINDOWS    0x40
#define HDR_NEWOFFSET      0x3C
#define HDR_NONRESIDENT    0x2C


#define MAXLEN_MODULEDESC  256


#define SEEK_SET    0
#define SEEK_CUR    1
#define SEEK_END    2

/****************************************************************
*                                                              *
*                    Global Variables                          *
*                                                              *
****************************************************************/


HANDLE ghInst;
HWND   ghWnd;
char   szAppName[] = "LONGFILE";


/****************************************************************
*                                                              *
*                       WinMain                                *
*                                                              *
****************************************************************/

int PASCAL WinMain (HANDLE hInstance,  HANDLE hPrevInstance,
                    LPSTR lpszCmdLine, int    nCmdShow        )
{
  MSG        msg      ;
  WNDCLASS   wndclass ;

  if (!hPrevInstance)
    {

    // Register Parent Window Class

    wndclass.style          = CS_HREDRAW | CS_VREDRAW | CS_BYTEALIGNCLIENT;
    wndclass.lpfnWndProc    = (WNDPROC)WndProc ;
    wndclass.cbClsExtra     = 0 ;
    wndclass.cbWndExtra     = 0 ;
    wndclass.hInstance      = hInstance ;
    wndclass.hIcon          = NULL;
```

```
    wndclass.hCursor        = LoadCursor (NULL, IDC_ARROW) ;
    wndclass.hbrBackground = GetStockObject ( GRAY_BRUSH ) ;
    wndclass.lpszMenuName  = (LPSTR)"PlainMenu" ;
    wndclass.lpszClassName = szAppName ;


    if (!RegisterClass (&wndclass))
        return FALSE;
    }


 ghInst    = hInstance;


 ghWnd =         CreateWindow (szAppName, "Hidden Listbox Info Example",
                              WS_OVERLAPPEDWINDOW,
                              GetSystemMetrics ( SM_CXSCREEN ) /4,
                              GetSystemMetrics ( SM_CYSCREEN ) /4,
                              GetSystemMetrics ( SM_CXSCREEN ) /2,
                              GetSystemMetrics ( SM_CYSCREEN ) /2,
                              NULL, NULL, hInstance, NULL) ;


 ShowWindow ( ghWnd, nCmdShow );
 UpdateWindow ( ghWnd );


 while (GetMessage((LPMSG)&msg, NULL, 0, 0))
   {
   TranslateMessage(&msg);
   DispatchMessage(&msg);
   }
}


/**********************************************************************
*                                                                   *
*              ModalDialog: Calls a Modal Dialog Box                *
*                                                                   *
**********************************************************************/

int ModalDialog ( LPSTR TemplateName, FARPROC FunctionName, LONG dwParam )
{
  FARPROC  lpDialogProc;
  int      RetVal;


  lpDialogProc = MakeProcInstance ( FunctionName, ghInst );
  RetVal       = DialogBoxParam ( ghInst, TemplateName, ghWnd,
                                  lpDialogProc, (DWORD)dwParam );
  FreeProcInstance ( lpDialogProc );
  return RetVal;
```

```
}

/************************************************************************
*                                                                      *
*                    WndProc: Main Message Translator                  *
*                                                                      *
************************************************************************/

WINPROC WndProc ( WINDOWS_PARAMS )
{
  switch ( msg )
    {
    case WM_DESTROY :

      PostQuitMessage (0) ;
      break ;

    case WM_COMMAND :

      switch ( wParam )

        {
        case IDM_MODAL :

          ModalDialog ( "MODALDIALOG", DlgProc, 0L );
          break;

        default:

          return DefWindowProc ( hWnd, msg, wParam, lParam ) ;
          break;
        }

      break;

    default :

      return DefWindowProc ( hWnd, msg, wParam, lParam );

    }
  return 0L ;
}
```

```
/**********************************************************************
*                                                                    *
*                   Vanilla Dialog Box Procedure                     *
*                                                                    *
**********************************************************************/

DLGPROC DlgProc ( DIALOG_PARAMS )
{
  char szFileToRun[144];
  int  iTab;

  switch (msg)
    {
    case WM_INITDIALOG:


      /*
       *  Here we will set the virtual column to be at position 511,
       *  and we will fill the listbox with LongFileName\tREALNAME.EXE
       *
       */

      iTab = 511;
      SendDlgItemMessage ( hDlg, IDD_LISTBOX, LB_SETTABSTOPS, 1,
                           (LONG)(LPINT)&iTab );

      FillLBWithFileName ( GetDlgItem ( hDlg, IDD_LISTBOX ));
      break;

    case WM_COMMAND:

      switch (wParam)
        {
        case IDD_LISTBOX:

          if (LBN_DBLCLK != HIWORD(lParam)) break;

          // Else FALL THROUGH to mimic the OK button

        case IDOK:

          // This function grabs all of the text in the line after the
          // last tab.

          ExtractRealFileName ( GetDlgItem ( hDlg, IDD_LISTBOX ), szFileToRun
```

```
                              );

            if (*szFileToRun)
              WinExec ( szFileToRun, SW_SHOW );
            break;


        case IDCANCEL:

            EndDialog ( hDlg, TRUE );
            return TRUE;

        default:

            return FALSE;
          }
        break;

    default:

        return FALSE;
    }

  return TRUE;
}


/********************************************************************
*                                                                  *
*                                                                  *
*                                                                  *
********************************************************************/

void ExtractRealFileName ( HWND hListbox, LPSTR szFileToRun )
{
  char szListboxLine[512];
  int  iIndex;

  // Search backwards through the string, until a tab or the beginning
  // of the line is found. Then copy that portion to the szFileToRun
  // string.  If there are no tabs found, we will just crash (just
  // kidding, I copy the entire string in that case).

  *szFileToRun = 0;
```

```
iIndex = (int)SendMessage ( hListbox, LB_GETCURSEL, 0, 0L );

if (LB_ERR != iIndex)
  {
  SendMessage ( hListbox, LB_GETTEXT, iIndex, (LONG)(LPSTR) szListboxLine );

  iIndex = lstrlen ( szListboxLine ) -1;



  while ( (iIndex) && (szListboxLine[iIndex] != '\t') ) iIndex--;



  if (szListboxLine[iIndex] != '\t')
    lstrcpy ( szFileToRun, szListboxLine+iIndex   );
  else
    lstrcpy ( szFileToRun, szListboxLine+iIndex+1 );
  }
}


/*********************************************************************
*                                                                  *
*     This function was heavily inspired by Byran Woodruff         *
*     In fact, he wrote 90% of it                                  *
*                                                                  *
*********************************************************************/

BOOL CreateLongFileName ( LPSTR lpFileName, LPSTR lpLongFileName )
{
   HFILE     hFile ;
   BYTE      bStrLen ;
   OFSTRUCT  ofFile ;
   WORD      wTemp ;
   char      szMagicHeader[3];
   int       i;

   if ((HFILE)NULL == (hFile = OpenFile( lpFileName, &ofFile, OF_READ )))
      {
      lstrcpy (lpLongFileName, lpFileName);
      lstrcat (lpLongFileName, " (Non-Windows App)");
      }

   // Check to make sure this file starts with MZ, the exe's magic word

   _lread( hFile, (LPSTR) szMagicHeader, 2 ) ;
```

```
szMagicHeader[2] = 0;
if (lstrcmp(szMagicHeader, "MZ"))
  {
  _lclose ( hFile );
  return FALSE;        // Not an EXE file
  }


// Reset the file postion to beginning of file

_llseek( hFile, 0L, 0 );


// Now do bryans magic

_llseek( hFile, (LONG) HDR_FTYPE, SEEK_SET ) ;
_lread( hFile, (LPSTR) &wTemp, 2 ) ;

if (wTemp != HDR_TYPEWINDOWS) // Yikes! A DOS App
  {
  _lclose ( hFile );
  lstrcpy (lpLongFileName, lpFileName);
  lstrcat (lpLongFileName, " (Non-Windows App)");

  return TRUE;        // An EXE file
  }
else
  {
  _llseek( hFile, (LONG) HDR_NEWOFFSET, SEEK_SET ) ;
  _lread( hFile, (LPSTR) &wTemp, 2 ) ;
  _llseek( hFile, (LONG) wTemp, SEEK_SET ) ;
  _llseek( hFile, (LONG) HDR_NONRESIDENT, SEEK_CUR ) ;
  _lread( hFile, (LPSTR) &wTemp, 2 ) ;
  _llseek( hFile, (LONG) wTemp, SEEK_SET ) ;
  _lread( hFile, (LPSTR) &bStrLen, 1 ) ;
  _lread( hFile, lpLongFileName, (WORD)bStrLen ) ;
  lpLongFileName[bStrLen] = 0 ;
  _lclose( hFile ) ;

  // Last minute paranoid check.  If any characters are > 128, then
  // We read some garbage, and this file is probably something like
  // emm386.exe or some other device driver

  for ( i = 0; i < lstrlen(lpLongFileName); i++ )
    if (
        (lpLongFileName[i] > 128) ||
```

```
        (lpLongFileName[i] < 32 )
        )
     return FALSE;


  if (!lstrlen(lpLongFileName))
    return FALSE;


  return TRUE;        // Okay, its an EXE file
  }


}


/**********************************************************************
*                                                                    *
*                                                                    *
*                                                                    *
**********************************************************************/

void FillLBWithFileName ( HWND hListbox )
{
  char  szBuffer [144];
  char  szBuffer1[512];
  int   iNumItems;
  int   iIndexFound;
  int   i, j;
  BOOL  bFoundShortName;
  BOOL  bTabFound;


  // Step 1: Get the plain file titles

  GetWindowsDirectory ( szBuffer, sizeof(szBuffer));
  lstrcat (szBuffer, "\\*.EXE");
  SendMessage (hListbox, LB_DIR, 0, (LONG)(LPSTR)szBuffer);


  iNumItems = (int)SendMessage (hListbox, LB_GETCOUNT, 0, OL );


  // Step 2: Keep going through the listbox as long as there are
  //         plain filenames. We can't just go through the list
  //         on a single pass, because the listbox is sorted,
  //         and the sort order changes every time.

  do
    {
```

```
      bFoundShortName = FALSE;

      for ( i = 0; (i < iNumItems)&&(!bFoundShortName); i++ )
        {
        SendMessage (hListbox, LB_GETTEXT, i, (LONG)(LPSTR)szBuffer);

        // Look for a tab. If we found one, this string needs no conversion.

        bTabFound      = FALSE;
        iIndexFound    = i;

        for ( j = 0; (j < lstrlen(szBuffer)) && (!bTabFound); j++)
          if ('\t' == szBuffer[j]) bTabFound = TRUE;

        if (!bTabFound) bFoundShortName = TRUE;
        }

    if (bFoundShortName)
      {
      SendMessage (hListbox, LB_DELETESTRING, iIndexFound, 0L );

      if (CreateLongFileName ( szBuffer, szBuffer1 ))
        {
        lstrcat ( szBuffer1, "\t" );
        lstrcat ( szBuffer1, szBuffer );

        SendMessage (hListbox, LB_ADDSTRING, 0, (LONG)(LPSTR)szBuffer1);
        }
      else
        {
        iNumItems--;  // Removing this nasty from the list
        }
      }
    }
  while (bFoundShortName);

}
```

The function **CreateLongFileName** takes a pointer to a buffer containing an EXE name, generates the module description, and places that into another buffer. This function is called by the **FillLBWithFileName** function, which converts the list box of plain filenames into a list box of long filenames (and hidden real filenames).

When the user clicks on the Run button (or double-clicks on the list box item), the **ExtractRealFileName** function is called. This function takes the line from the list box, does some Comp Sci 101 string parsing, and returns the actual filename.

Another place that you can hide data is in invisible static strings. Add a static text control to your dialog with x,y,cx,cy = 0,0,0,0 and presto! You have a dynamic buffer into which you can stuff information. It's considerably quicker than using extra bytes that point to buffers you must manage (referencing extra bytes when you're in a dialog box routine is sometimes undesirable) and it's easier than using dialog box properties.

Don't get too carried away, however, because this is not the most memory-friendly approach. Each static field is a window that takes up bytes in USER's heap. If you have ten different strings, then you really should store a pointer to a structure in the DWL_USER extra bytes (see Chapter 1), and reference the strings through conventional C pointer mechanisms.

8. Create Invisible Windows to Eat Input During Gigunda Tasks

Sometimes you want to prevent the user from clicking around while you are doing things. For example, you may have a dialog box displayed, and, when the user clicks a button, it does a nasty recalculation. While the recalculation is crunching away, the user may get worried that something is weird and start a clicking fit that boggles the imagination. Once the recalculation completes, all those mouse messages that queued up will get delivered, and then the application seems to have a mind of its own for a while.

There are ways to get around this. You could disable all of the buttons on the dialog, do the recalculation, and then enable them all. Sure, your dialog box may resemble a disco, but at least the user knows that clicking won't do anything. This could get tricky, though, if some buttons are supposed to be disabled at certain times, or if your dialog box is a tabbed dialog.

How about creating a little window with the style WS_EX_TRANSPARENT and no border or caption, then doing a **SetCapture** on it? Now all mouse input will go to that window instead of to your dialog box. Once your recalculation is complete, you can destroy the invisible window (remember to **ReleaseCapture** first), and merrily go on your way.

The callback function for the invisible window does nothing except call **DefWindowProc**, so your mouse and keyboard messages are deliciously eaten. Of course, you'll want to set the class cursor for that window to an hourglass, so that the user gets the idea that clicking now will do nothing. And, if you are programming in Windows 95, **SetCapture** will still let other applications run normally, as long as you did not **SetCapture** in response to a WM_LBUTTONDOWN message. This bonus functionality ensures that only *your* application is "on hold" while the gigunda task is executing.

However, this method is extremely nonmultitasking-aware for your application. Your application cannot process any mouse input during this time. If your nasty recalculation has other threads running that may appreciate user input, then you can take a slightly different approach. When you create the invisible window, make it the size of the client area of the dialog, make it a child, and don't call **SetCapture**. This way, the user will be blocked out from "click-o-mania" on your application, but can do something else on another window while yours is crunching.

Of course, if you want to completely block out the user, be sure to disable the other exposed parts of your app (that is, by way of a modal dialog) so that your user can have a total clicking fit without causing any problems anywhere else in your application. An example of where you may want to let the user click elsewhere in your app while using this trick to disable the dialog might be a spell checker—the user presses "Look up word" and you can still let the user select text elsewhere.

MOUSEEAT (see Listing 7.3) brings up a dialog box with a recalculation button. The recalculation in this case is simply a loop that waits for the number of seconds indicated in the edit control. During this loop, you can click away elsewhere in your application (or on other applications) and get something done, but you can't do anything dangerous to MOUSEEAT's dialog. Using a little **BringWindowToTop** action, I have "uncovered" the Cancel button so that the user can still cancel the recalculation. The hourglass cursor appears when you move the mouse pointer over the dialog (except the Cancel button).

LISTING 7.3 MOUSEEAT SAMPLE PROGRAM

```c
#include <windows.h>

#include "mouseeat.h"
#include "basedefs.h"

/*****************************************************************
*                                                               *
*                  Function Prototypes                          *
*                                                               *
*****************************************************************/


WINPROC WndProc ( WINDOWS_PARAMS );
WINPROC InvisoWndProc ( WINDOWS_PARAMS );
DLGPROC DlgProc ( DIALOG_PARAMS  );
HWND    hCreateInvisoWindow ( HWND hParent );


/*****************************************************************
*                                                               *
*                  Global Variables                             *
*                                                               *
*****************************************************************/


HANDLE ghInst;
HWND   ghWnd;
char   szAppName[]    = "MOUSEEAT";
char   szInvisoName[] = "INVISOWINDOW";


/*****************************************************************
*                                                               *
*                  WinMain                                      *
*                                                               *
*****************************************************************/

int PASCAL WinMain (HANDLE hInstance,  HANDLE hPrevInstance,
                    LPSTR lpszCmdLine, int    nCmdShow        )
{
  MSG        msg      ;
  WNDCLASS   wndclass ;

  if (!hPrevInstance)
    {
```

```
    // Register Parent Window

    wndclass.style        = CS_HREDRAW | CS_VREDRAW | CS_BYTEALIGNCLIENT;
    wndclass.lpfnWndProc  = (WNDPROC)WndProc ;
    wndclass.cbClsExtra   = 0 ;
    wndclass.cbWndExtra   = 0 ;
    wndclass.hInstance    = hInstance ;
    wndclass.hIcon        = NULL;
    wndclass.hCursor      = LoadCursor (NULL, IDC_ARROW) ;
    wndclass.hbrBackground = GetStockObject ( GRAY_BRUSH ) ;
    wndclass.lpszMenuName = (LPSTR)"PlainMenu" ;
    wndclass.lpszClassName = szAppName ;


    if (!RegisterClass (&wndclass))
        return FALSE;


    // Register the message eater

    wndclass.style        = 0;
    wndclass.lpfnWndProc  = (WNDPROC)InvisoWndProc ;
    wndclass.cbClsExtra   = 0 ;
    wndclass.cbWndExtra   = 0 ;
    wndclass.hInstance    = hInstance ;
    wndclass.hIcon        = NULL;
    wndclass.hCursor      = LoadCursor (NULL, IDC_WAIT) ;
    wndclass.hbrBackground = GetStockObject ( NULL_BRUSH ) ;
    wndclass.lpszMenuName = (LPSTR)NULL;
    wndclass.lpszClassName = szInvisoName ;


    if (!RegisterClass (&wndclass))
        return FALSE;
    }


  ghInst   = hInstance;


  ghWnd =        CreateWindow (szAppName, "Cheezy Mouse Eater",
                        WS_OVERLAPPEDWINDOW,
                        GetSystemMetrics ( SM_CXSCREEN ) /4,
                        GetSystemMetrics ( SM_CYSCREEN ) /4,
                        GetSystemMetrics ( SM_CXSCREEN ) /2,
                        GetSystemMetrics ( SM_CYSCREEN ) /2,
                        NULL, NULL, hInstance, NULL) ;


  ShowWindow ( ghWnd, nCmdShow );
  UpdateWindow ( ghWnd );
```

```
  while (GetMessage((LPMSG)&msg, NULL, 0, 0))
    {
    TranslateMessage(&msg);
    DispatchMessage(&msg);
    }

  return msg.wParam ;
}


/***********************************************************************
*                                                                     *
*                ModalDialog: Calls a Modal Dialog Box                *
*                                                                     *
***********************************************************************/

int ModalDialog ( LPSTR TemplateName, FARPROC FunctionName, LONG dwParam )
{
  FARPROC   lpDialogProc;
  int       RetVal;

  lpDialogProc = MakeProcInstance ( FunctionName, ghInst );
  RetVal       = DialogBoxParam ( ghInst, TemplateName, ghWnd,
                                  lpDialogProc, (DWORD)dwParam );
  FreeProcInstance ( lpDialogProc );
  return RetVal;
}


/***********************************************************************
*                                                                     *
*                WndProc: Main Message Translator                     *
*                                                                     *
***********************************************************************/

WINPROC WndProc ( WINDOWS_PARAMS )
{

  CRACKER_VARS

  switch ( msg )
    {
    case WM_DESTROY :

      PostQuitMessage (0) ;
      break ;
```

```
    case WM_COMMAND :

    CRACK_MESSAGEsc

    switch ( CRACKER_wID )
      {
      case IDM_MODAL :

          ModalDialog ( "MODALDIALOG", DlgProc, 0L );
          break;

      default:

          return DefWindowProc ( hWnd, msg, wParam, lParam ) ;
          break;
      }

      break;

    default :

      return DefWindowProc ( hWnd, msg, wParam, lParam );

    }
  return 0L ;
}
/*********************************************************************
*                                                                  *
*                    InvisoWndProc: A message eater                *
*                                                                  *
*********************************************************************/

WINPROC InvisoWndProc ( WINDOWS_PARAMS )
{
    return DefWindowProc ( hWnd, msg, wParam, lParam );
}


/*********************************************************************
*                                                                  *
*                    Vanilla Dialog Box Procedure                  *
*                                                                  *
*********************************************************************/

DLGPROC DlgProc ( DIALOG_PARAMS )
```

```
{
  static HWND    hWndInviso;      // hWnd of the message eater. Also used as a
                                  // recalc semaphore
  static int     iTimerCount;     // Number of seconds that have elapsed during
                                  // recalc
  static int     iRecalcTime;     // Number of seconds user requested

         BOOL    err;             // Used by GetDlgItemInt

  CRACKER_VARS

  switch (msg)
    {
    case WM_INITDIALOG:

        // Reset the semaphore

        hWndInviso = NULL;
        break;

    case WM_TIMER:

        // This is the cheesy recalc. Does nothing, but it takes a while.

        iTimerCount++;
        SetDlgItemInt ( hDlg, IDD_LEFT, iTimerCount, FALSE );
        if (iTimerCount >= iRecalcTime)
          {
          KillTimer ( hDlg, 1 );

          // Beep to tell the user that the recalc is done

          MessageBeep (0);

          // Reset the dialog to its original, upright position

          SetDlgItemText ( hDlg, IDD_LEFT, "" );
          SetFocus ( GetDlgItem ( hDlg, IDOK ) );

          // Kill the message eater and reset the semaphore wannabe

          DestroyWindow (hWndInviso);
          hWndInviso = NULL;
```

```
        }
    break;

case WM_COMMAND:

    CRACK_MESSAGEsc

    switch (CRACKER_wID)
      {
      case IDCANCEL:

          // Check to see if user cancelled during a recalc, if so housekeep

          if (hWndInviso)
            {
            KillTimer ( hDlg, 1 );
            DestroyWindow (hWndInviso);
            hWndInviso = NULL;
            }
          EndDialog ( hDlg, TRUE );
          return TRUE;

      case IDOK:

          if (hWndInviso) break; // In a recalc, don't start another recalc

          if (BN_CLICKED == HIWORD(lParam))
            {
            iRecalcTime = GetDlgItemInt ( hDlg, IDD_RTIME, &err, FALSE );
            iTimerCount = 0;

            SetDlgItemText ( hDlg, IDD_LEFT, "0" );
            SetTimer ( hDlg, 1, 1000, NULL );
            hWndInviso = hCreateInvisoWindow ( hDlg );
            }

          break;

      default:

          return FALSE;
      }
    break;
```

```
    default:

      return FALSE;
    }

  return TRUE;
}


/**********************************************************************
*                                                                   *
*                                                                   *
*                                                                   *
**********************************************************************/

HWND hCreateInvisoWindow ( HWND hParent )
{
  RECT r;
  HWND hWnd;

  GetClientRect ( hParent, &r );

  hWnd = CreateWindowEx
          (
          WS_EX_TRANSPARENT,
          szInvisoName,
          "",
          WS_CHILD | WS_VISIBLE,
          0, 0,
          r.right, r.bottom,
          hParent,
          (HMENU)42,
          ghInst,
          NULL
          );

  // Cover all controls with the message eater

  BringWindowToTop ( hWnd );

  // Bring the cancel button up from "below" so the user can bag the recalc

  BringWindowToTop ( GetDlgItem ( hParent, IDCANCEL) ); // Uncover the Cancel key

  // Set focus so that the hourglass appears
```

```
    SetFocus ( hWnd );

    return hWnd;
}
```

The **InvisoWndProc** function is the callback for the invisible window. It just processes all messages in a nice boring fashion, preventing the user from getting any extraneous mouse messages queued up. The **hCreateInvisoWindow** function creates the invisible window, "covers" all the controls, and then "exposes" the Cancel button. As long as your dialogs use *IDCANCEL* for the Cancel button's control ID, you can use this code unmodified for all of your dialogs.

7. Modify Messages to Suit Your Needs (Within Bounds)

How many times have you wanted to move objects around on the screen dynamically with the mouse, but the thought of doing all that painting just made you cringe? Moving an object around the screen involves repainting the object in its new location and refreshing the areas of the screen that are uncovered by the objects. That's a lot of work and it's a good thing you can have Windows do all of it for you—well, almost.

As long as your objects are rectangular, you can easily use a window for the object. Then, using a few tricks, you can let Windows do the walking when it comes to the grunt work of moving and placing and listening to mouse input. The secret is to change message values.

Changing the values of messages and using them to lie to other windows is a great way to get what you want easily. If you move your mouse over a child window, the parent of that child will not get the WM_MOUSEMOVE message. However, you can override that functionality with very little work and still stay within the bounds of Software Coolness.

PASSMSG (see Figure 7.4) puts up a child window on the screen and allows the user to move it around by using the mouse. The real trick here is in the child window's callback procedure, **FormWndProc** (see Listing 7.4).

All the important mouse messages are passed back to the parent, in parent coordinates (WM_LBUTTONDOWN, WM_LBUTTONUP, WM_MOUSEMOVE). If you were going to move an object around by using the hit-testing approach, these are the messages you would look for. However, hit-testing does nothing for you automatically.

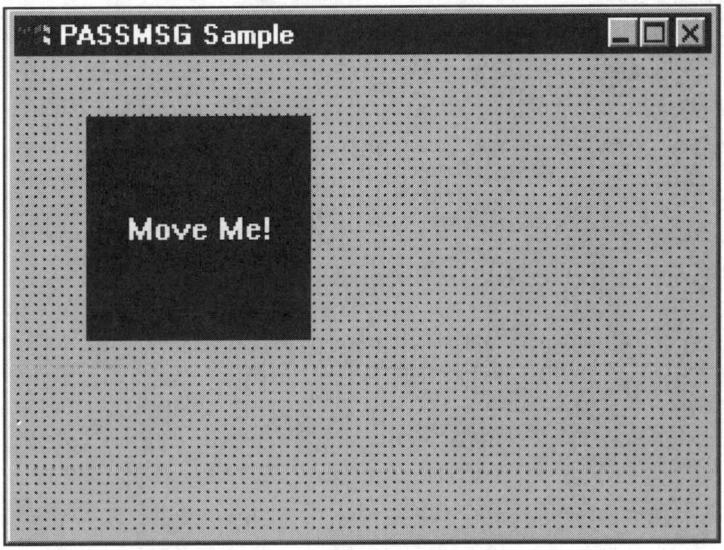

FIGURE 7.4 PASSMSG

LISTING 7.4 PASSMSG SAMPLE PROGRAM

```
#include <windows.h>

#include "basedefs.h"
#include "passmsg.h"

WINPROC WndProc     ( WINDOWS_PARAMS );
WINPROC FormWndProc ( WINDOWS_PARAMS );


/****************************************************************
```

```
*                                               *
*                Global Variables               *
*                                               *
*****************************************************************/


HANDLE    ghInst;
HWND      ghWnd;
HWND      ghWndChild;
char      szNullString[] = "";
char      szAppName[] = "BASE1";
char      szChildName[] = "Ben";
char      szMoveMe[]    = "Move Me!";


/****************************************************************
*                                                              *
*                       WinMain                                *
*                                                              *
*****************************************************************/


int PASCAL WinMain (HANDLE hInstance,  HANDLE hPrevInstance,
                    LPSTR lpszCmdLine, int    nCmdShow        )
{
  MSG        msg       ;
  WNDCLASS   wndclass  ;
  int        dx        ;
  HBRUSH     hFormBrush ;
  HBITMAP    hFormBM    ;


  dx = 24;
  while ((!SetMessageQueue(dx)) && (dx >= 8)) dx–;


  hFormBM = LoadBitmap ( hInstance, "FORM" );
  hFormBrush = CreatePatternBrush ( hFormBM );
  DeleteObject ( hFormBM );


  if (!hPrevInstance)
    {

    // Register the Parent Window

    wndclass.style          = CS_BYTEALIGNCLIENT;
    wndclass.lpfnWndProc    = (WNDPROC)WndProc ;
    wndclass.cbClsExtra     = 0 ;
    wndclass.cbWndExtra     = 0 ;
    wndclass.hInstance      = hInstance ;
```

154

```
wndclass.hIcon          = NULL;
wndclass.hCursor        = LoadCursor (NULL, IDC_ARROW) ;
wndclass.hbrBackground  = hFormBrush;
wndclass.lpszMenuName   = NULL;
wndclass.lpszClassName  = szAppName ;

if (!RegisterClass (&wndclass))
    return FALSE;


// Register the Child Window

wndclass.style          = CS_BYTEALIGNCLIENT | CS_HREDRAW | CS_VREDRAW;
wndclass.lpfnWndProc    = (WNDPROC)FormWndProc ;
wndclass.cbClsExtra     = 0 ;
wndclass.cbWndExtra     = 0 ;
wndclass.hInstance      = hInstance ;
wndclass.hIcon          = NULL;
wndclass.hCursor        = LoadCursor (hInstance, "HAND" );
wndclass.hbrBackground  = GetStockObject ( LTGRAY_BRUSH ) ;
wndclass.lpszMenuName   = (LPSTR)NULL;
wndclass.lpszClassName  = szChildName ;

if (!RegisterClass (&wndclass))
    return FALSE;
}


ghInst  = hInstance;

ghWnd =       CreateWindow (szAppName, "PASSMSG Sample",
                            WS_OVERLAPPEDWINDOW | WS_BORDER,
                            GetSystemMetrics ( SM_CXSCREEN ) /4,
                            GetSystemMetrics ( SM_CYSCREEN ) /4,
                            GetSystemMetrics ( SM_CXSCREEN ) /2,
                            GetSystemMetrics ( SM_CYSCREEN ) /2,
                            NULL, NULL, hInstance, NULL) ;


ghWndChild =  CreateWindow (szChildName, szNullString,
                            WS_CHILD | WS_VISIBLE,
                            10, 10,
                            100, 100,
                            ghWnd, NULL, hInstance, NULL) ;


ShowWindow ( ghWnd, nCmdShow );
UpdateWindow ( ghWnd );
```

```
  while (GetMessage((LPMSG)&msg, NULL, 0, 0))
    {
    TranslateMessage(&msg);
    DispatchMessage(&msg);
    }

  DeleteObject ( hFormBrush );

  return msg.wParam ;
}


/**********************************************************************
*                                                                    *
*                    WndProc: Main Message Translator                *
*                                                                    *
**********************************************************************/

WINPROC WndProc ( WINDOWS_PARAMS )
{
  static BOOL    bDragging;
  static POINT   ptLastPos;

  switch ( msg )
    {
    case WM_LBUTTONDOWN:

      ptLastPos.x = LOWORD ( lParam);
      ptLastPos.y = HIWORD ( lParam);

      ptLastPos.x = LOWORD ( lParam ) - LOWORD ( lParam )%8;
      ptLastPos.y = HIWORD ( lParam ) - HIWORD ( lParam )%8;

      if (ChildWindowFromPoint(hWnd, ptLastPos) != hWnd)  // must be the child!
        {
        SetCapture ( hWnd );
        bDragging = TRUE;
        }
      break;

    case WM_LBUTTONUP:

      if (bDragging)
        {
        InvalidateRect ( ghWndChild, NULL, TRUE );
```

```
        ReleaseCapture ( );
        bDragging = FALSE;
        }
    break;

case WM_MOUSEMOVE:

    if (bDragging)
        {
        POINT ptNew;

        ptNew.x = LOWORD ( lParam ) - LOWORD ( lParam )%8;
        ptNew.y = HIWORD ( lParam ) - HIWORD ( lParam )%8;

        if (
             ( ptNew.x != ptLastPos.x )
             ||
             ( ptNew.y != ptLastPos.y )
            )
            {
            POINT ptTopLeft;

            // Figure out current position of Child window

            ptTopLeft.x = 0; // Modify these values if you add a thick border or other
            ptTopLeft.y = 0; // adornments to reflect the client area offset

            ClientToScreen ( ghWndChild, &ptTopLeft );
            ScreenToClient ( hWnd,        &ptTopLeft );

            // Move child Window to new spot

            SetWindowPos (ghWndChild,
                          NULL,
                          ptTopLeft.x + (ptNew.x-ptLastPos.x),
                          ptTopLeft.y + (ptNew.y-ptLastPos.y),
                          0,
                          0,
                          SWP_NOSIZE | SWP_NOZORDER
                         );

            InvalidateRect (ghWndChild, NULL, TRUE );
            UpdateWindow (ghWndChild);

            ptLastPos = ptNew;
```

157

```
            }
        }

      break;

    case WM_CREATE  :

      break;

    case WM_DESTROY :

      PostQuitMessage (0) ;
      break ;

    default :

      return DefWindowProc ( hWnd, msg, wParam, lParam );


    }
  return 0L ;
}
/*********************************************************************
*                                                                  *
*                                                                  *
*                                                                  *
*********************************************************************/

WINPROC FormWndProc ( WINDOWS_PARAMS )
{
  POINT        pt;
  HDC          hDC;
  PAINTSTRUCT  ps;
  RECT         rc;

  switch ( msg )
    {
    case WM_ERASEBKGND:  // Eat this message to avoid flicker

      break;


    case WM_CREATE  :
```

```
      break;

case WM_LBUTTONDOWN:
case WM_LBUTTONUP:
case WM_MOUSEMOVE:

  // Pass all mouse messages on through to parent, in parent coordinates

  pt.x = LOWORD ( lParam );
  pt.y = HIWORD ( lParam );

  ClientToScreen ( hWnd,             &pt );
  ScreenToClient ( GetParent(hWnd), &pt );

  PostMessage ( ghWnd, msg, wParam, MAKELONG (pt.x, pt.y ));
  break;

case WM_PAINT:

  // Just draw a simple little something centered in the window with nice

  hDC = BeginPaint ( hWnd, &ps );
  GetClientRect ( hWnd, &rc );

  SetBkColor   ( hDC, RGB (   0,   0, 128 ));
  SetTextColor ( hDC, RGB ( 255, 255,   0 ));

  {
  SIZE size;

  GetTextExtentPoint ( hDC, szMoveMe, lstrlen(szMoveMe), &size);

  pt.x = (rc.right  - size.cx)/2;
  pt.y = (rc.bottom - size.cy)/2;
  }

  ExtTextOut ( hDC, pt.x, pt.y, ETO_OPAQUE, &rc, szMoveMe,
               lstrlen (szMoveMe), NULL );

  EndPaint ( hWnd, &ps );
  break;

default :
```

```
      return DefWindowProc ( hWnd, msg, wParam, lParam );

   }
  return 0L ;
}
```

In PASSMSG, the **FormWndProc** handles the sizing and painting of the child window. If this example were implemented by using hit-testing (and hence, the blue square would not be a child window, but instead some graphical object the program manages), then the program must be responsible for moving, painting, sizing, cursor maintenance, and refreshing the background of the parent window. This is an inordinate amount of work, considering that Windows can do it all for you. By converting the previous three messages into the equivalent messages for the parent, you can employ the poor man's move of a window.

Consider how these messages are handled by the parent procedure. When a WM_LBUTTONDOWN message is processed by **WndProc**, the code determines if this message was passed down by the child window. The **ChildWindowFromPoint** function returns the *hWndChild* handle if the point is inside the client area of a child. If the point is not inside any child windows, the parent window handle is returned. Therefore, for this example, if the return value is different from the parent, the program can assume that the message came from the child window. If you implement multiple child windows, you should maintain a data structure to help you determine which child window you are over. In this example, though, the program will manage only one child, so I can get away with using the *ghWndChild* variable everywhere instead of looking up the value in some data structure.

If the point is in the child window's client area, then a "semaphore-wannabe" variable, *bDragging*, is set. This puts the auto-move code under WM_MOUSEMOVE into action. The **SetCapture** function is called to make sure that the WM_LBUTTONUP message is going to happen sometime in the future. If the mouse is not captured, the user could move out of the client area of the parent, release the mouse button, and the *bDragging* "semaphore-wannabe" would not be cleared, with unpredictable and annoying results.

The auto-move code under WM_MOUSEMOVE checks the new position of the mouse against the old position of the mouse. Then, the child window's position and new position are calculated, and the child window is repositioned. The **InvalidateRect** and **UpdateWindow** functions are called to immediately redraw the child window being moved. Since the user will be staring at this child window, it is important that this window be updated immediately for a pleasing effect.

The child window has the WS_THICKFRAME style, so the user can still resize the window. The messaging protocol for sizing the child window does not get passed back to the parent because these messages are WM_NCMOUSEMOVE messages, not WM_MOUSEMOVE messages.

PASSMSG gives you the basics on implementing an active form editor. The child window has ugly sizable borders on it, but moves around really nicely. Trick 1 in this list discusses some fun games you can play with the WM_NCHITTEST message that let you get rid of the ugly sizable borders. You could combine these two sample programs to generate a very slick dialog/ form editor that's not only user-friendly, but also uses as little program code and as much operating system code as possible.

Some other neat things can be done to enhance this program. In the WM_MOUSEMOVE and WM_LBUTTONDOWN sections of code in WndProc, try rounding the coordinates to the nearest multiple of eight, as shown here:

```
case WM_LBUTTONDOWN:

    .
    .
    .



    ptLastPos.x = LOWORD (lParam) - LOWORD(lParam)%8;
    ptLastPos.y = HIWORD (lParam) - HIWORD(lParam)%8;

    .
    .
    .


case WM_MOUSEMOVE:
```

```
        .
        .
        .

ptNew.x = LOWORD (lParam) - LOWORD(lParam)%8;
ptNew.y = HIWORD (lParam) - HIWORD(lParam)%8;

        .
        .
        .
```

Now the form snaps to a grid eight pixels wide by eight pixels high. This makes it easier to line up fields, and the program only needs to repaint the window one-eighth as many times, which will improve performance considerably on slower machines.

6. ExtTextOut Is Your Fast Friend

The **ExtTextOut** function was introduced in Windows 3.0. It's used to write a character string in a rectangle, and it has more features than the **TextOut** function from Windows 2.x. However, many programmers still don't know about it, even with Windows 95. **ExtTextOut** is an easier (and sometimes faster) means of drawing text and rectangles on the screen.

Although Windows 95 has made every GDI operation as blazingly fast as possible, **ExtTextOut** is still the ultimate API in terms of convenience. A really nice feature of **ExtTextOut** is the *ETO_OPAQUE* flag. Using this flag, **ExtTextOut** can lay down a background color for a given rectangular region, and the text can then be drawn on top of it.

If your program needed to display a list of text by using **TextOut**, it might use code similar to the following:

```
SetBkColor   ( hDC, dwColorBk   );
SetTextColor ( hDC, dwColorText );

TextOut ( hDC, xPos, yPos, szText, lstrlen(szText) );
GetTextExtentPoint ( hDC, szText, lstrlen(szText), &TextSize);
r.left = xPos + TextSize.cx;
```

```
r.right = wRightEdge;  // right edge of region to paint
r.top   = yPos;
r.botom = yPos + TextSize.cy;

FillRect ( hDC, &r, hBrush );
```

This algorithm could be optimized a bit to avoid extra calculation, but you have no way around that extra call to **FillRect**.

Using **ExtTextOut**, you can replace the code with the following:

```
SetBkColor   ( hDC, dwColorBk   );
SetTextColor ( hDC, dwColorText );
GetTextExtentPoint ( hDC, szText, lstrlen(szText), &TextSize);
r.left =xPos;
r.right=wRightEdge;  // right edge of region to paint
r.top  =yPos;
r.botom=yPos+TextSize.cy;
ExtTextOut ( hDC, xPos, yPos, ETO_OPAQUE, &r, szText,
             lstrlen(szText), NULL );
```

The same results are achieved with only one call to **GetTextExtentPoint** and no call to **FillRect**. If you want to add extra space between the lines, **ExtTextOut** can accommodate that simply by changing the fields in the *r* structure.

It is also easier to use **ExtTextOut** to draw rectangles if you write a quick-and-dirty macro such as the following:

```
#define FASTRECT(hDC,x1,y1,x2,y2,dwColor)                \
{                                                        \
RECT r = {x1,y1,x2,y2};                                  \
SetBkColor(hDC,dwColor);                                 \
ExtTextOut(hDC,x1,y1,ETO_OPAQUE,&r,NULL,NULL,NULL);      \
}
```

5. Use IsDialogMessage to Fake Dialog Boxes

I have often wanted to create a window with some controls in it that act like a dialog box. But I don't want a dialog box. Usually I want a menu with accelerators, or I want the dialog box to actually be an MDI child that acts like a dialog box. The automatic focus control and accelerators provided by a dialog box sure are nice, and having an MDI child window with a bunch of controls in it would be very useful at times. And, of course, I am not programming in MFC today, so I can't just use the nifty form window that MFC supplies.

Even though the **IsDialogMessage** function has been around almost as long as Windows, it hasn't been used as much as it should. **IsDialogMessage** can be used on any window to make it behave more like a dialog box. Remember, modeless dialogs are practically the same as ordinary windows. **CreateDialogParam** does not do much more than parse out the resource file, create a bunch of children, and then give the handle to the dialog window back to you. Modal dialogs are just modeless dialogs encapsulated inside **PeekMessage** loops in the Dialog Manager (the parents are disabled to avoid confusing the user).

Many kinds of windows can become "dialog-wannabes." The PIF Editor supplied with Windows is a top-level window that acts like a dialog box. It can be minimized, it has a menu, and it allows the user to tab around fields. Its programmers simply changed the message loop to look similar to the following:

```
while (GetMessage((LPMSG)&msg, NULL, 0, 0))
  {
  if (!IsWindow(hWndDialogWannabe) ||
      (!IsDialogMessage(hWndDialogWannabe, &msg))
    {
    TranslateMessage(&msg);
    DispatchMessage(&msg);
    }
  }
```

4. Use Callbacks in a DLL.

Okay, this is not really a trick. Callback functions in DLLs are invoked by such common Windows APIs as **EnumWindows**, **EnumFonts**, and **LineDDA**. However, many people don't understand why they should use callbacks.

Here's an example. If you've written a DLL that manages application-defined records for a database management system (DBMS), you must put a compare function for sorting and searching in your application. If you want the DLL to treat each record as a black-box block of memory, then all knowledge of the layout of each of these structures must be contained in the application, not in the DLL. Consider a shell sort routine from a DBMS DLL. The data is contained in an array, and the routine sorts the information from the *wStart* array element to the *wStop* element (see Listing 7.5).

LISTING 7.5 A SHELL SORT

```
void ShellSort ( WORD wStart, WORD wStop )
{
  int offset;
  int sort_switch;
  int limit;
  int row;

  offset = wStop / 2;

  while (offset > 0)
    {
    limit = wStop - offset;

    do
      {
      sort_switch = 0;

      for (row = 1; row <= limit; row++)
        {
        if (COMPARE_GREATER == Compare(row-1,row+offset-1))
          {
          Swap (row-1, row+offset-1);
          sort_switch = row;
          }
        }
      limit = sort_switch - offset;
      }
```

```
    while (sort_switch);

    offset = offset / 2;
    }
}
```

The compare function, which lives in your DLL, looks like the following:

```
typedef WORD FAR PASCAL FNCOMPAREPROC (LPSTR,LPSTR);
typedef FNCOMPAREPROC FAR *LPFNCOMPAREPROC;

WORD Compare ( WORD Index1, WORD Index2 )
{
  LPSTR lpMem1, lpMem2;

  lpMem1 = DataArray+Index1;   // This is a pointer to a
                               // structure
  lpMem2 = DataArray+Index2;

  // Callback the COMPARE_PROC in the Application

  wRetVal = ((LPFNCOMPAREPROC)(glpfnCompare))(lpMem1,
                                              lpMem2);

  return wRetVal;
}
```

Figure 7.5 shows a *COMPARE_PROC* that compares ages and resides in your application. First, the function **SortTheData** accepts a pointer to the array of your data items and creates a procedure-instance address pointing to the routine **CompareAges**, a *COMPARE_PROC* in your application (see Listing 7.6). Next, **SortTheData** calls the **CallDLLSortRoutine** function that lives in the DLL. That function sets up any more data needed to call the **ShellSort** routine in the DLL. **ShellSort** calls **Compare**, which invokes the callback **CompareAges** to compare the two chunks of memory. This implementation allows you to keep all descriptions of the data's form in the application, while the DBMS DLL simply sorts chunks of memory blindly.

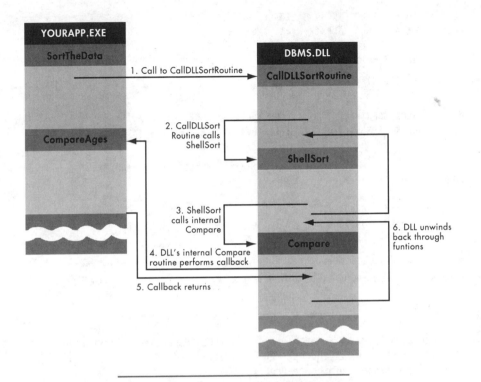

FIGURE 7.5 FLOW DIAGRAM FOR COMPARE CALLBACK

LISTING 7.6 COMPAREAGES PROCEDURE

```
typedef struct DATAtag
  {
  char    szName[30];
  int     iAge;
  }
DATARECORD;

typedef DATARECORD FAR *LPDATARECORD;
typedef WORD CALLBACK FNCOMPAREPROC (LPSTR,LPSTR);
typedef FNCOMPAREPROC FAR *LPFNCOMPAREPROC;
```

```
#define COMPARE_PROC    WORD CALLBACK
#define COMPARE_ARGS    LPSTR arg1, LPSTR arg2

#define ARG1(field) ((LPDATARECORD)arg1)->field
#define ARG2(field) ((LPDATARECORD)arg2)->field

#define CHECK_GREATER(field) if (ARG1(field) > ARG2(field)) return COMPARE_GREATER
#define CHECK_LESSER(field)  if (ARG1(field) < ARG2(field)) return COMPARE_LESSER

//******************************************************************
COMPARE_PROC CompareAges    ( COMPARE_ARGS )
{
  CHECK_GREATER(iAge);
  CHECK_LESSER (iAge);
  return COMPARE_EQUAL;
}
//******************************************************************
void SortTheData (LPDATARECORD lpDataRecords)
{
  FARPROC lpfnCompareProc;

  lpfnCompareProc = MakeProcInstance ((FARPROC)CompareAges, hInstOfApp );
  CallDLLSortRoutine (lpfnCompareProc, lpDataRecords);
  FreeProcInstance (lpfnCompareProc);
}
```

And now for something completely different. For another implementation of a callback in a DLL that implements a fancy GDI call, look at the TILEDDA.C program and CALLBACK.DLL, which draw a pattern in a box (see Figure 7.6 and Listing 7.7). Just as **LineDDA** allows you to specify the appearance of the line, TILEDDA asks the callback routine to repeatedly draw something into a tile. This way, your callback procedure can **BitBlt** a picture, draw a smiley face, or display a politically correct message.

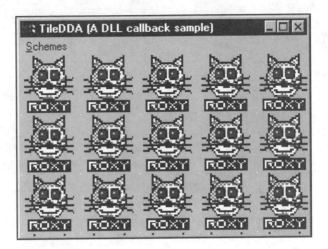

FIGURE 7.6 TILEDDA

LISTING 7.7A TILEDDA SAMPLE APPLICATION PROGRAM

```
#include <windows.h>

#include "callback.h"
#include "tiledda.h"
#include "basedefs.h"

WINPROC WndProc ( WINDOWS_PARAMS );
void FAR PASCAL CallBackProc (HDC hDC, int iXPos, int iYPos);


/***************************************************************
 *                                                             *
 *                  Global Variables                           *
 *                                                             *
 ***************************************************************/
```

```
HANDLE   ghInst;
HWND     ghWnd;
char     szAppName[] = "TILEDDA";
WORD     wMode;
int      iWidth ;
int      iHeight;
HDC      hMemDC     ;
HBITMAP  hBitmap    ;
HBITMAP  hOldBitmap ;


/****************************************************************
*                                                             *
*                      WinMain                                 *
*                                                             *
****************************************************************/

int PASCAL WinMain (HANDLE hInstance,  HANDLE hPrevInstance,
                    LPSTR lpszCmdLine, int    nCmdShow        )
{
  MSG         msg       ;
  WNDCLASS    wndclass  ;

  if (!hPrevInstance)
    {

    // Register Parent Window Class

    wndclass.style         = CS_HREDRAW | CS_VREDRAW | CS_BYTEALIGNCLIENT;
    wndclass.lpfnWndProc   = (WNDPROC)WndProc ;
    wndclass.cbClsExtra    = 0 ;
    wndclass.cbWndExtra    = 0 ;
    wndclass.hInstance     = hInstance ;
    wndclass.hIcon         = NULL;
    wndclass.hCursor       = LoadCursor (NULL, IDC_ARROW) ;
    wndclass.hbrBackground = GetStockObject ( GRAY_BRUSH ) ;
    wndclass.lpszMenuName  = (LPSTR)"PlainMenu" ;
    wndclass.lpszClassName = szAppName ;

    if (!RegisterClass (&wndclass))
        return FALSE;
    }

  ghInst  = hInstance;


  ghWnd =         CreateWindow (szAppName, "TileDDA (A DLL callback sample)",
```

```
                             WS_OVERLAPPEDWINDOW,
                             GetSystemMetrics ( SM_CXSCREEN ) /4,
                             GetSystemMetrics ( SM_CYSCREEN ) /4,
                             GetSystemMetrics ( SM_CXSCREEN ) /2,
                             GetSystemMetrics ( SM_CYSCREEN ) /2,
                             NULL, NULL, hInstance, NULL) ;


    ShowWindow ( ghWnd, nCmdShow );
    UpdateWindow ( ghWnd );


    while (GetMessage((LPMSG)&msg, NULL, 0, 0))
      {
      TranslateMessage(&msg);
      DispatchMessage(&msg);
      }
}



/***********************************************************************
*                                                                     *
*                    WndProc: Main Message Translator                 *
*                                                                     *
***********************************************************************/


WINPROC WndProc ( WINDOWS_PARAMS )
{
   FARPROC     lpfnCallBack;
   RECT        rcClient;
   PAINTSTRUCT ps;
   HDC         hDC;


   switch ( msg )
     {
     case WM_CREATE:

       wMode   = IDM_NOTHING;
       iWidth  = 64;
       iHeight = 64;


       hDC = GetDC ( NULL );
       hMemDC  = CreateCompatibleDC ( hDC );
       ReleaseDC ( NULL, hDC );
       hBitmap = LoadBitmap ( ghInst, "ROXY" );
       hOldBitmap = SelectObject ( hMemDC, hBitmap );


       break;
```

```
    case WM_DESTROY :

      SelectObject ( hMemDC, hOldBitmap );
      DeleteDC     ( hMemDC  );
      DeleteObject ( hBitmap );

      PostQuitMessage (0) ;
      break ;

    case WM_PAINT:

      GetClientRect ( hWnd, &rcClient );

      hDC = BeginPaint ( hWnd, &ps );

      lpfnCallBack = MakeProcInstance ( (FARPROC)CallBackProc , ghInst );

      TileDDA (hDC, &rcClient, iWidth, iHeight, (LPFNDRAWPROC)lpfnCallBack );

      FreeProcInstance ( lpfnCallBack );

      EndPaint ( hWnd, &ps );
      break;

    case WM_COMMAND :

      switch ( wParam )

        {
        case IDM_NOTHING   :
        case IDM_BITMAPS   :
        case IDM_SMILEYFACE:
        case IDM_PC        :

            {
            HMENU hMenu = GetMenu ( hWnd );
            CheckMenuItem ( hMenu, wMode,  MF_UNCHECKED );
            CheckMenuItem ( hMenu, wParam, MF_CHECKED   );
            }

          wMode = wParam;
```

```
            InvalidateRect ( hWnd, NULL, FALSE );
            break;

        default:

            return DefWindowProc ( hWnd, msg, wParam, lParam ) ;
            break;
        }

      break;

    default :
      return DefWindowProc ( hWnd, msg, wParam, lParam );


    }
  return 0L ;
}


/**********************************************************************
*                                                                   *
*                                                                   *
*                                                                   *
**********************************************************************/

void FAR PASCAL CallBackProc (HDC hDC, int iXPos, int iYPos)
{
  RECT    rc          ;
  RECT    rcEye        ;
  HBRUSH  hBrush       ;
  HBRUSH  hOldBrush    ;
  int     iEyeHeight   ;
  int     iEyeWidth    ;

  rc.left   = iXPos;
  rc.top    = iYPos;
  rc.right  = iXPos + iWidth ;
  rc.bottom = iYPos + iHeight;

  switch (wMode)
    {
    case IDM_NOTHING   :

      FillRect ( hDC, &rc, GetStockObject ( WHITE_BRUSH ));
```

173

```
   break;

case IDM_BITMAPS   :

   BitBlt ( hDC, rc.left, rc.top, rc.right - rc.left, rc.bottom-rc.top,
            hMemDC, 0, 0,
            SRCCOPY );

   break;

case IDM_SMILEYFACE:

   FillRect ( hDC, &rc, GetStockObject ( WHITE_BRUSH ));

   hBrush    = CreateSolidBrush ( RGB ( 255, 255, 0 ));
   hOldBrush = SelectObject ( hDC, hBrush );

   // Head

   Ellipse ( hDC,
            rc.left,
            rc.top,
            rc.right,
            rc.bottom
          );

   SelectObject ( hDC, GetStockObject ( BLACK_BRUSH ) );

   iEyeWidth  = (rc.right-rc.left)/8;
   iEyeHeight = (rc.bottom-rc.top)/8;

   // Left Eye

   rcEye.left  = rc.left    + 2*iEyeWidth;
   rcEye.right = rcEye.left + iEyeWidth;
   rcEye.top   = rc.top     + 2*iEyeHeight;
   rcEye.bottom= rcEye.top  + iEyeHeight;

   Ellipse ( hDC,
            rcEye.left,
            rcEye.top,
            rcEye.right,
            rcEye.bottom
```

```
                    );

    // RIght Eye

    rcEye.left   = rc.left    + 5*iEyeWidth;
    rcEye.right  = rcEye.left + iEyeWidth;
    rcEye.top    = rc.top     + 2*iEyeHeight;
    rcEye.bottom= rcEye.top   + iEyeHeight;


    Ellipse ( hDC,
              rcEye.left,
              rcEye.top,
              rcEye.right,
              rcEye.bottom
            );

    // Smile

    InflateRect ( &rc, -iEyeWidth, -iEyeHeight );

    Arc    ( hDC,
             rc.left,
             rc.top,
             rc.right,
             rc.bottom-iEyeWidth,
             rc.left,
             rc.bottom-2*iEyeWidth,
             rc.right,
             rc.bottom-2*iEyeWidth
           );

    SelectObject ( hDC, hOldBrush );

    DeleteObject (hBrush);

    break;

case IDM_PC        :

    ExtTextOut ( hDC,
                 iXPos,
                 iYPos,
                 ETO_OPAQUE | ETO_CLIPPED,
                 &rc,
```

```
                    "Recycle!",
                    8,
                    NULL
                );


    break;


    }
}
```

LISTING 7.7B A TileDDA's CALLBACK sample DLL

```c
#include <windows.h>
#include "callback.h"
#include "basedefs.h"


#ifdef WIN_DOS
//***************************************************************************
//
//   LibMain- Called once, when first app loads it
//
//***************************************************************************
int FAR PASCAL LibMain(HANDLE hModule, WORD wDataSeg, WORD cbHeapSize, LPSTR
lpszCmdLine)
{
  return TRUE;
}
//***************************************************************************
//
//   WEP- Called when DLL shuts down
//
//***************************************************************************
int FAR PASCAL WEP (BOOL bSystemExit)
{
    return TRUE;
}
#endif


#ifdef WIN_NT
//***************************************************************************
//
//   LibMain- Called once, when first app loads it
//
//***************************************************************************
```

```
int APIENTRY LibMain(HANDLE hinstDLL, DWORD fdwReason, LPVOID lpReserved)
{
  return TRUE;
}
#endif


//************************************************************************
//
//  The actual function
//
//************************************************************************

void FAR PASCAL TileDDA
   (
   HDC            hDC,
   LPRECT         prcPaint,
   int            ixTileSize,
   int            iyTileSize,
   LPFNDRAWPROC   lpfnDrawProc
   )
{
  int iNumTilesX;
  int iNumTilesY;
  int iRow, iCol;

  // Step 1: Figure out the number of tiles in each direction

  iNumTilesX = (prcPaint->right -prcPaint->left + ixTileSize-1)/ixTileSize;
  iNumTilesY = (prcPaint->bottom-prcPaint->top  + iyTileSize-1)/iyTileSize;

  // Step 2: Draw the tiles!

  for ( iRow = 0; iRow < iNumTilesY; iRow++ )
    for ( iCol = 0; iCol < iNumTilesX; iCol++ )
      lpfnDrawProc (hDC, iCol*ixTileSize, iRow*iyTileSize );
}
```

The function **CallBackProc** in TILEDDA.C is called by the DLL. The function **TileDDA** inside the CALLBACK.DLL invokes this callback. This example is very tiny and sort of trivial, but it demonstrates how to do all the typecasting so you don't get compiler warnings. (Besides, my cat Roxy threatened to claw up the couch if I didn't include her somewhere.)

3. Lie with Messages (WM_MYSIZE) to KEEP CODE Clean

Faking messages to reuse code can be handy. For example, suppose you want to have a toolbar stuck to the upper edge of the frame window of an MDI application. Assume that the toolbar is a child of the frame and a sibling of the MDI client window. If the user resizes the window, you will want to resize the toolbar to completely fit inside the MDI client window. Your code to resize the window may look like the following:

```
case WM_SIZE:
  rc.right = LOWORD(lParam);
  rc.bottom = HIWORD(lParam);
  rc.left = 0;
  if (toolbar is "stuck" on top)
    rc.top = Height Of toolbar;
  else
    rc.top = 0;
  SetWindowPos ( hWndClient,
                 NULL,
                 rc.left, rc.top,
                 rc.right, rc.bottom-rc.top,
                 SWP_NOZORDER);
  break;
```

If you want this toolbar to stay "stuck," space must be reserved in the frame's client for the toolbar. The MDI client window and the MDI children should not cover the button bar at any time. If you want a moveable toolbar, the MDI client area should occupy the entire client area of the frame.

If the user "tears" or "sticks" the toolbar from or to the application, this code must calculate the new size of the MDI client window. However, tearing or sticking a button bar will not cause a WM_MOVE or WM_SIZE message to be sent to the MDI client window. Sending your own WM_SIZE message is not a great idea, because the WM_SIZE message is something that Windows is supposed to send to you, not vice-versa. Also, you would be responsible for making sure that your parameters for WM_SIZE are valid.

How about faking it? Define a WM_MYSIZE message. Pick this to be WM_USER+1000. Why WM_USER+1000? Because it's recommended that you use WM_USER+x for user-defined messages. For example, the LB_GETCARET-INDEX message is defined as WM_USER+32 in 16-bit WINDOWS.H. I picked 1000 because it seemed nice and safe. Real nerds can use WM_USER+1024. Now, modify the previous code to look like the following:

```
case WM_MYSIZE:
case WM_SIZE:
  GetClientRect ( hWnd, &rc);
  if (toolbar is "stuck" on top)
    rc.top = Height Of toolbar;
  else
    rc.top = 0;
  SetWindowPos ( hWndClient,
               NULL,
               rc.left, rc.top,
               rc.right, rc.bottom-rc.top,
               SWP_NOZORDER);
  break;
```

Notice how I changed the computation of the rc structure to no longer rely on *lParam*. Now, the code to calculate the size of the window is contained inside the window's callback procedure. When I "tear" or "stick" a toolbar, I just throw in the following line of code:

```
SendMessage ( hWndApp, WM_MYSIZE, 0, 0L );
```

I am telling my application's main window to recalculate the sizes of the MDI client and repaint things as necessary. This technique shows how easy it is to encapsulate or localize sections of Windows code.

Definitely make a WM_MYCOMMAND message. You can fake menu item choices and dialog box control actions very easily this way. You can even have some special *wParam* values to do internal things.

For example, if the data in a certain window must be recalculated, you could do something like the following:

```
SendMessage ( hWnd, WM_MYCOMMAND, IMC_RECALC, 0L );
```

Here, *wParam* equals IMC_RECALC (the "IMC" is my abbreviation for "internal message control"), which tells the window to recalculate the numbers. You could use *lParam* to point to the data, but the window itself should know this information if you want to keep things as "OOPsy" as possible.

Other uses for fake messages could be telling the window to repaint a certain element of the display that only the window knows the location of (or size of), telling the window to give you some information (here you would check the return value of **SendMessage**), or telling the window that your application is in a critical section and that it needs to flush its buffers. The possibilities are endless.

2. Change a Window from a Popup to a Child Window and Back—Without Hacking

Popup windows are cool. You can put them anywhere on the screen. They stay on top of your application even if you click on windows below them. They automatically hide themselves if you minimize the parent, and they easily support menus.

Child windows are also cool. You can click on them and your parent window will not get a WM_ACTIVATE *wParam* equal to *FALSE*, which keeps the caption bar of the parent active and able to move with the parent window.

Wouldn't it be great if you could make a window that flip-flops between the two? Consider those detachable toolbars in most of Microsoft's Office Products. You can stick them to an edge or float them on top of the spreadsheet. When they are stuck to the edge, they act like a child window. When they float, they act almost like a popup window. They stay above the other windows, and you can move them out of the client area. This functionality seems to be magically changing the window from a child window to a popup window. That way, if the toolbar was "stuck" to an edge, moving Microsoft Excel carries along the toolbar. If the toolbar were floating, then moving the program would not affect the position of the toolbar.

Munging the style bits of a window from WS_POPUP to WS_CHILD and back is a really great way to generate the message, "Your DRWATSON.LOG file is getting quite large." Many of the style bits of Windows are only looked at during creation time. Changing them dynamically will either have no effect, or could cause unpredictable results.

So, do it another way. How about a nice, documented, easy-to-implement, safe, nineties-style way? Create two windows, one a popup and one a child. Both can use the same window callback function. Both have a handle to the other tucked away safely in a chunk of memory. While in the actual window procedure, your program won't care (most of the time) if it's a popup or a child window. When it does care, it can use the **IsChildWindow** or **IsPopupWindow** functions to determine which it is. Just hide the window not in use and show the window that is in use. When you convert, show the one you want to use, and then hide the one you are finished using.

POPCHILD (see Figure 7.7 and Listing 7.8) displays a little window that can be a popup or a child. Double-clicking it changes it from one to the other. POPCHILD also shows how you can make the two windows have other, different attributes—the popup has a caption and is sizable, while the child is not.

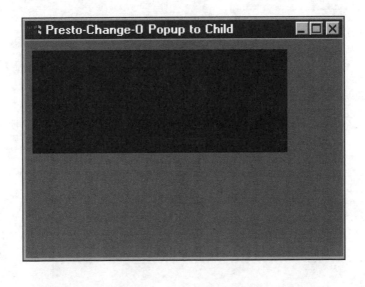

FIGURE 7.7A **POPCHILD** BEFORE DOUBLE-CLICKING ON CHILD

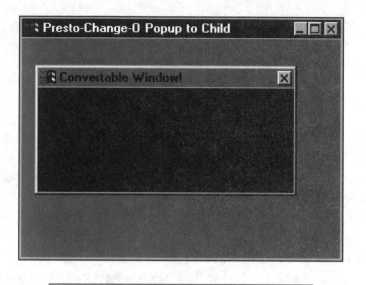

FIGURE 7.7B POPCHILD AFTER DOUBLE-CLICKING ON CHILD

LISTING 7.8 POPCHILD SAMPLE PROGRAM

```
#include <windows.h>
#include <windowsx.h>

#include "popchild.h"
#include "basedefs.h"


WINPROC WndProc                         ( WINDOWS_PARAMS );
WINPROC ConvertibleWndProc              ( WINDOWS_PARAMS );


BOOL    IsChildWindow                   ( HWND hWnd          );
BOOL    IsPopupWindow                   ( HWND hWnd          );
void    ChangeWindowFromPopupToChild    ( HWND hWndPopup );
void    ChangeWindowFromChildToPopup    ( HWND hWndChild );
void    ScreenToClientRect              ( HWND hWnd, LPRECT prRect );


/*************************************************************
*                                                           *
*                  Global Variables                         *
*                                                           *
*************************************************************/
```

182

```
HANDLE  ghInst;
HWND    ghWnd, ghWndChild;
char    szAppName[] = "BASE";
char    szConvertableClass[] = "Viper";


typedef struct CONVERTABLEDATAtag
  {
  HWND hWndChildWindow;
  HWND hWndPopupWindow;
  }
CONVERTABLEDATA;


typedef CONVERTABLEDATA FAR  *LPCONVERTABLEDATA;


/**************************************************************
*                                                           *
*                        WinMain                            *
*                                                           *
**************************************************************/


int PASCAL WinMain (HANDLE hInstance,  HANDLE hPrevInstance,
                    LPSTR lpszCmdLine, int     nCmdShow      )


{
  MSG         msg      ;
  WNDCLASS    wndclass ;

  if (!hPrevInstance)
    {

    // Register Parent Window Class

    wndclass.style         = CS_HREDRAW | CS_VREDRAW | CS_BYTEALIGNCLIENT;
    wndclass.lpfnWndProc   = (WNDPROC)WndProc ;
    wndclass.cbClsExtra    = 0 ;
    wndclass.cbWndExtra    = 0 ;
    wndclass.hInstance     = hInstance ;
    wndclass.hIcon         = NULL;
    wndclass.hCursor       = LoadCursor (NULL, IDC_ARROW) ;
    wndclass.hbrBackground = GetStockObject ( GRAY_BRUSH ) ;
    wndclass.lpszMenuName  = NULL ;
    wndclass.lpszClassName = szAppName ;


    if (!RegisterClass (&wndclass))
```

183

```
        return FALSE;

  // Convertable Window Class

  wndclass.style        = CS_HREDRAW | CS_VREDRAW | CS_BYTEALIGNCLIENT |
                          CS_DBLCLKS;
  wndclass.lpfnWndProc  = (WNDPROC)ConvertibleWndProc ;
  wndclass.cbClsExtra   = 0 ;
  wndclass.cbWndExtra   = sizeof(LONG) ;
  wndclass.hInstance    = hInstance ;
  wndclass.hIcon        = NULL;
  wndclass.hCursor      = LoadCursor (NULL, IDC_ARROW) ;
  wndclass.hbrBackground = GetStockObject ( BLACK_BRUSH ) ;
  wndclass.lpszMenuName  = (LPSTR)NULL ;
  wndclass.lpszClassName = szConvertableClass ;

  if (!RegisterClass (&wndclass))
      return FALSE;
  }

ghInst   = hInstance;



ghWnd =        CreateWindow (szAppName, "Presto-Change-O Popup to Child",
                        WS_OVERLAPPEDWINDOW,
                        GetSystemMetrics ( SM_CXSCREEN ) /4,
                        GetSystemMetrics ( SM_CYSCREEN ) /4,
                        GetSystemMetrics ( SM_CXSCREEN ) /2,
                        GetSystemMetrics ( SM_CYSCREEN ) /2,
                        NULL, NULL, hInstance, NULL) ;

ghWndChild = CreateWindow
             (
             szConvertableClass, "Convertable Window!",
             WS_CHILD | WS_BORDER | WS_VISIBLE ,
             10, 10,
             250, 100,
             ghWnd , NULL, hInstance, NULL
             );

ShowWindow ( ghWnd, nCmdShow );
UpdateWindow ( ghWnd );

while (GetMessage((LPMSG)&msg, NULL, 0, 0))
```

```
      {
   TranslateMessage(&msg);
   DispatchMessage(&msg);
      }
}


/***********************************************************************
*                                                                     *
*                    WndProc: Main Message Translator                 *
*                                                                     *
***********************************************************************/


WINPROC WndProc ( WINDOWS_PARAMS )
{
  switch ( msg )
    {
    case WM_CREATE  :

      break;

    case WM_SIZE:

      if (SIZE_MINIMIZED == wParam)
        {
        PostMessage ( ghWndChild, WM_SETREDRAW, TRUE, OL );
        }
      break;

    case WM_DESTROY :

      PostQuitMessage (0) ;
      break ;

    default :

      return DefWindowProc ( hWnd, msg, wParam, lParam );


    }
  return OL ;
}


/***********************************************************************
*                                                                     *
*                    WndProc: Main Message Translator                 *
```

```
*                                                                        *
************************************************************************/

WINPROC ConvertibleWndProc ( WINDOWS_PARAMS )
{
  LPCONVERTABLEDATA lpConvertableData;

  switch ( msg )
    {
    case WM_SETTEXT:

      // We need to mimic this function for the popup window also.  That
      // way the application only needs to set the text fo the child
      // and not worry about the popup window.


      lpConvertableData = (LPCONVERTABLEDATA)GetWindowLong ( hWnd, 0 );
      if (lpConvertableData)
        if (IsChildWindow(hWnd))
          SendMessage ( lpConvertableData->hWndPopupWindow, msg, wParam, lParam );

    break;

    case WM_CREATE:

      // Set up the extra bytes to point to the structure
      // If this is the child window (which was created first),
      // We will alloc the chunk of memory

      if (IsChildWindow(hWnd))
        {
        lpConvertableData = (LPCONVERTABLEDATA)GlobalAllocPtr (GMEM_MOVEABLE,
        sizeof(CONVERTABLEDATA));
        SetWindowLong (hWnd, 0, (LONG)(LPSTR)lpConvertableData );

        // Fill in the child window field of the structure

        lpConvertableData->hWndChildWindow = hWnd;

        // Now, create the companion popup window and fill in the field

        lpConvertableData->hWndPopupWindow = CreateWindow
                                    (
```

```
((LPCREATESTRUCT)(lParam))->lpszClass,
((LPCREATESTRUCT)(lParam))->lpszName,
WS_POPUP | WS_CAPTION | WS_SYSMENU | WS_BORDER ,
((LPCREATESTRUCT)(lParam))->x,
((LPCREATESTRUCT)(lParam))->y,
((LPCREATESTRUCT)(lParam))->cx,
((LPCREATESTRUCT)(lParam))->cy,
((LPCREATESTRUCT)(lParam))->hwndParent,
((LPCREATESTRUCT)(lParam))->hMenu,
((LPCREATESTRUCT)(lParam))->hInstance,
((LPCREATESTRUCT)(lParam))->lpCreateParams                              );
       // Set the extra bytes in the companion window to point to the same
       // strcuture

       SetWindowLong (lpConvertableData->hWndPopupWindow, 0,
                   (LONG)(LPSTR)lpConvertableData );
       }


   break;

 case WM_DESTROY:

    // Note this code. We want to free up the memory only once. Therefore,
    // make sure to check the values first, since this code will be run twice,
    // once for each window.  If you have other objects attached to this window
    // in your actual implementation, remember that you will get two
    // WM_DESTROY messages.

    lpConvertableData = (LPCONVERTABLEDATA)GetWindowLong ( hWnd, 0 );

    if (lpConvertableData)
      {
      SetWindowLong (lpConvertableData->hWndChildWindow, 0, 0L );
      SetWindowLong (lpConvertableData->hWndPopupWindow, 0, 0L );

      GlobalFreePtr (lpConvertableData);
      }
    break;

 case WM_LBUTTONDBLCLK:

    if (IsChildWindow(hWnd))
      ChangeWindowFromChildToPopup (hWnd);
    else
```

```
      ChangeWindowFromPopupToChild (hWnd);
    break;

  default :

    return DefWindowProc ( hWnd, msg, wParam, lParam );


  }
  return 0L ;
}


//*********************************************************************
//
//
//
//*********************************************************************

BOOL IsChildWindow ( HWND hWnd )
{
  DWORD dwWindowStyle;

  dwWindowStyle = GetWindowLong ( hWnd, GWL_STYLE );

  if (dwWindowStyle & WS_CHILD)
    return TRUE;
  else
    return FALSE;
}


//*********************************************************************
//
//
//
//*********************************************************************

BOOL IsPopupWindow ( HWND hWnd )
{
  DWORD dwWindowStyle;

  dwWindowStyle = GetWindowLong ( hWnd, GWL_STYLE );

  if (dwWindowStyle & WS_POPUP)
    return TRUE;
  else
```

```
    return FALSE;
}

//**********************************************************************
//
//
//
//**********************************************************************

void ChangeWindowFromChildToPopup ( HWND hWndChild )
{
  LPCONVERTABLEDATA lpConvertableData = (LPCONVERTABLEDATA)GetWindowLong (
                                        hWndChild, 0 );
  RECT              r;

  if (!IsChildWindow(hWndChild)) return;

  GetWindowRect ( hWndChild, &r );  // Get position of child window

  // Add the sizeable border

  InflateRect (&r,
            GetSystemMetrics (SM_CXFRAME)-GetSystemMetrics (SM_CXBORDER),
            GetSystemMetrics (SM_CYFRAME)-GetSystemMetrics (SM_CYBORDER)
            );

  // Account for the caption at the top

  r.top -= GetSystemMetrics ( SM_CYCAPTION );

  SetWindowPos ( lpConvertableData->hWndPopupWindow, NULL,
            r.left,
            r.top,
            r.right-r.left,
            r.bottom-r.top,
            SWP_NOZORDER );

  ShowWindow ( lpConvertableData->hWndPopupWindow, SW_SHOW );

  ShowWindow ( hWndChild, SW_HIDE );

}

//**********************************************************************
```

```
//
//
//
//*************************************************************************


void ChangeWindowFromPopupToChild ( HWND hWndPopup )
{
  LPCONVERTABLEDATA lpConvertableData = (LPCONVERTABLEDATA)GetWindowLong (
hWndPopup, 0 );
  RECT              r;

  if (!IsPopupWindow(hWndPopup)) return;

  GetWindowRect ( hWndPopup, &r );  // Get position of child window

  // remove the sizeable border

  InflateRect (&r,
               -1*(GetSystemMetrics (SM_CXFRAME)-GetSystemMetrics (SM_CXBORDER)),
               -1*(GetSystemMetrics (SM_CYFRAME)-GetSystemMetrics (SM_CYBORDER))
              );

  // Account for the caption at the top

  r.top += GetSystemMetrics ( SM_CYCAPTION );

  // Child windows are in client coordinates

  ScreenToClientRect ( GetParent(hWndPopup), &r );

  SetWindowPos ( lpConvertableData->hWndChildWindow, NULL,
                 r.left,
                 r.top,
                 r.right-r.left,
                 r.bottom-r.top,
                 SWP_NOZORDER );

  ShowWindow ( lpConvertableData->hWndChildWindow, SW_SHOW );

  ShowWindow ( hWndPopup, SW_HIDE );
}
```

```
//**********************************************************************
//
//
//
//**********************************************************************

void ScreenToClientRect ( HWND hWnd, LPRECT prRect )
{
  POINT pt;

  pt.x = prRect->left;
  pt.y = prRect->top;
  ScreenToClient ( hWnd, &pt );
  prRect->left = pt.x;
  prRect->top  = pt.y;
  pt.x = prRect->right;
  pt.y = prRect->bottom;
  ScreenToClient ( hWnd, &pt );
  prRect->right = pt.x;
  prRect->bottom  = pt.y;
}
```

The popup window and the child window both have 4 extra bytes, which contain the same values. These extra bytes form a pointer to the same structure, which is allocated by **GlobalAlloc** into a chunk of memory. The only information stored in this structure is the *hWnd* values for each window. You could store other window-specific information here. Since both windows point to the same chunk of memory, any macros or functions used to access the data in the chunk won't care for which window they are processing messages.

The **IsChildWindow** and **IsPopupWindow** functions determine the type of window style *hWnd* uses. The Windows SDK includes **IsChild**, but no **IsPopup** function. So, I supplied both as little utility functions to make the code a little easier to read. The **ScreenToClientRect** function simply converts a rectangle from screen coordinates to client coordinates.

The real fun begins at the WM_CREATE message in the **Convertable WndProc**. When this message is processed, a companion popup window is created. It uses all the same information to create the popup window, except the style bits reflect a popup window. The program checks to make sure that the window getting this message is the child window. This avoids causing an infinite loop. When the corresponding popup window is created, another WM_CREATE message is sent to the same window procedure.

This brings up an interesting point. If you want your popup window to behave differently from the child, you must use the **IsPopupWindow** and **IsChildWindow** functions.

Sometimes you will want to make sure that both windows get the message. An example is WM_SETTEXT. If you change the caption of the child, the popup also needs to get the message. It could be very tricky to try to send messages to the other window. Message traffic could be made a whole lot easier if you adopt a simple rule: Always send the messages to the same window.

For this example, all messages sent by the application are sent to the child window. The child window then sends these messages to the popup window. Your application should not send the popup window any message. This eliminates any possible infinite message loops and makes programming life easier. If you find exceptions are required, implement them carefully to avoid loops.

Now consider the functions **ChangeWindowFromPopupToChild** and **ChangeWindowFromChildToPopup**. These functions don't actually change the windows' style bits, they just hide and show the appropriate windows. A little repositioning fun is going on here. Since the child window doesn't have a caption or sizable borders, its window size is different from the popup window. However, the application wants to keep the client area of both windows the same size. The **InflateRect** and the **GetSystemMetrics** (**SM_CYCAPTION**) function calls calculate the size of the window, which is then adjusted to preserve the client size and position.

I don't cover child controls here. If your toolbar uses actual buttons on it instead of hit-testing, you can save resources by using the **SetParent** function to "move" the controls to the appropriate window. That way, you only have one set of controls for both windows, instead of duplicate sets to maintain. Put the calls to **SetParent** in the **ChangeWindowFromXXXtoYYY** functions for easiest coding bliss. Keep in mind, though, that calling **SetParent** on a control will not change where the notification messages go (see Chapter 1, "Things You Might Want to Know About Windows USER"), although in this example the edit controls can be freely parented back and forth between the child and popup windows without problems (since both the child and popup windows use the same window procedure). However, if your notification code calls the **IsChildWindow** or **IsPopupWindow** functions described previously, keep in mind that the window receiving the notification code will remain the same, regardless of whether the popup or child window is visible.

1. Fool Around with WM_NCHITTEST to Fake Sizable/Moveable Attributes

Have you ever wanted to let users size a window that does not have sizable borders? How about letting them move the window around without a caption (like the way the Clock applet does when it doesn't have a caption)?

WM_NCHITTEST is a really neat message that Windows sends your application whenever the mouse moves. This message is the way Windows asks your application, "Where is the mouse cursor right now?" If your mouse cursor is over a caption, **DefWindowProc** returns the constant *HTCAPTION* (from WINDOWS.H). If your mouse cursor is over the lower-left corner of a sizable border, **DefWindowProc** returns *HTBOTTOMLEFT*.

So, what would happen if you added processing like this to your window callback procedure?

```
case WM_NCHITTEST:
  GetClientRect ( hWnd, &rc );
  pt.x = (int) LOWORD (lParam);
  pt.y = (int) HIWORD (lParam);
  ScreenToClient ( hWnd, &pt );
  if (PtInRect (&rc, pt))
    return HTCAPTION;
  else
    return DefWindowProc ( hWnd, msg, wParam, lParam );
```

This snippet of code lies to Windows. It says, "If the cursor is over the client area, pretend that it is over the caption." This allows the user to move the window around by clicking and dragging on the client area. This is helpful for dialog editor programs that paint buttons and other controls on the screen without captions—the user can still move the controls around easily.

Consider another implementation.

```
case WM_NCHITTEST:
  GetClientRect ( hWnd, &rc );
  rc.bottom = rc.top + GetSystemMetrics (SM_CYCAPTION);
  pt.x = (int) LOWORD (lParam);
  pt.y = (int) HIWORD (lParam);
  ScreenToClient ( hWnd, &pt );
  if (PtInRect (&rc, pt))
    return HTCAPTION;
  else
    return DefWindowProc ( hWnd, msg, wParam, lParam );
```

This shrinks the structure *rc* to include the top portion of the window that is the same height as the caption. If your WM_PAINT code paints a fake-looking caption, the user wouldn't know that the caption visible is not really a caption at all. Why do all that work? Even though Windows 95 lets you create tiny-captioned windows, you may want to put that caption on a different edge than the top.

Modify the code once more.

```
case WM_NCHITTEST:
  GetClientRect ( hWnd, &rc );
  rc.right = rc.left+GetSystemMetrics(SM_CYCAPTION)/2;
  pt.x = (int) LOWORD (lParam);
  pt.y = (int) HIWORD (lParam);
  ScreenToClient ( hWnd, &pt );
  if (PtInRect (&rc, pt))
    return HTCAPTION;
  else
    return DefWindowProc ( hWnd, msg, wParam,lParam );
```

Notice how the caption is only half the standard height, and that the rectangle hit-testing fakes a caption that is on the left edge of the window. Now, look at the WM_PAINT code in Listing 7.9. It paints a caption that is half-sized, and sideways. Cool!

LISTING 7.9 PAINTING A FAKE CAPTION IN THE CLIENT AREA

```
case WM_PAINT:

  wCaptionHeight = GetSystemMetrics ( SM_CYCAPTION )/2;


  hDC = BeginPaint ( hWnd, &ps );
  hOldFont = SelectObject ( hDC, hCaptionFont );
  GetClientRect ( hWnd, &rc );


  rc.right  = wCaptionHeight;
  rc.top    = wCaptionHeight;


  GetWindowText ( hWnd, szCaption, sizeof (szCaption) );


  {
  SIZE size;
  GetTextExtentPoint ( hDC, szCaption, lstrlen(szCaption), &size);
  iWidth = size.cx;
  }


  SetBkMode ( hDC, TRANSPARENT );


  if (GetFocus() == hWnd)
    {
    hCaptionBrush = CreateSolidBrush (GetSysColor ( COLOR_ACTIVECAPTION   ));;
    SetTextColor ( hDC, GetSysColor ( COLOR_CAPTIONTEXT    ));;
    }
  else
    {
    hCaptionBrush = CreateSolidBrush (GetSysColor ( COLOR_INACTIVECAPTION   ));;
    SetTextColor ( hDC, GetSysColor ( COLOR_INACTIVECAPTIONTEXT ));;
    }


  FillRect ( hDC, &rc, hCaptionBrush );


  DeleteObject (hCaptionBrush);


  ExtTextOut ( hDC,
              rc.left,
              rc.bottom - (rc.bottom-rc.top-iWidth)/2,
```

```
                              ETO_CLIPPED,
                              &rc,
                              szCaption,
                              lstrlen (szCaption),
                              NULL );

         SelectObject ( hDC, hOldFont);

         // Draw the fake close box

         rc.right = wCaptionHeight;
         rc.left  = 0;
         rc.top   = 0;
         rc.bottom= wCaptionHeight;

         SetBkColor  ( hDC, RGB (192,192,192));
         SetBkColor  ( hDC, RGB (255,0,0));
         ExtTextOut ( hDC,
                      0,
                      0, ETO_OPAQUE|ETO_CLIPPED,
                      &rc,
                      NULL,
                      0,
                      NULL );

         MoveToEx ( hDC, (rc.right*1/5), (rc.bottom/2), NULL );
         LineTo   ( hDC, (rc.right*4/5), (rc.bottom/2) );

         EndPaint ( hWnd, &ps );
         break;
```

The sample program NCFUN (see Figure 7.8 and Listing 7.10) puts up two child windows. One employs the previous technique to create a half-sized, sideways caption and a little system menu. I used **TrackPopupMenu** to fake a system menu. The other window is an example of a control in a dialog editor. It looks like a normal button, but it is subclassed to intercept the WM_NCHITTEST message. This allows you to move the button around and resize it (as you would in a dialog editor), while letting Windows handle all of the grunt work of painting the control.

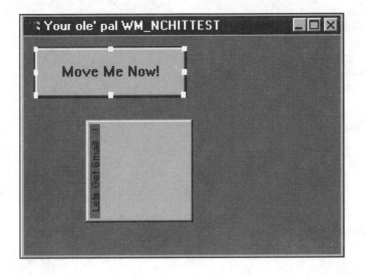

FIGURE 7.8 NCFUN

LISTING 7.10 NCFUN SAMPLE PROGRAM

```
#include <windows.h>

#include "ncfun.h"
#include "basedefs.h"

WINPROC WndProc              ( WINDOWS_PARAMS );
WINPROC HalfHeightWndProc    ( WINDOWS_PARAMS );
WINPROC ControlSubclassProc  ( WINDOWS_PARAMS );

void FigureHandleSizes ( HWND hWnd );
void ScreenToClientRect ( HWND hWnd, LPRECT prRect );


/***************************************************************
 *                                                             *
 *                   Global Variables                          *
 *                                                             *
 ***************************************************************/
```

```
HANDLE     ghInst;
HWND       ghWnd;
HWND       ghWndHalfHeight;
HWND       ghWndButton;
char       szAppName[]           = "NCFUN";
char       szHalfHeightAppName[] = "TinyTim";
FARPROC    lpprocButton;
FARPROC    lpprocButtonSubclass;
HFONT      hCaptionFont;
HMENU      hFakeSystemMenu;
HMENU      hFakeSystemPopupMenu;

typedef struct DIALOGHANDLEtag
   {
   RECT   rcArea;              // Handle's coordinates
   DWORD  dwNCHITVALUE;        // NCHITTEST return value
   }
DIALOGHANDLE;

DIALOGHANDLE DialogHandles[8]; // Handles for each area to grab


/****************************************************************
*                                                              *
*                      WinMain                                 *
*                                                              *
****************************************************************/

int PASCAL WinMain (HANDLE hInstance,  HANDLE hPrevInstance,
                 LPSTR lpszCmdLine, int    nCmdShow         )
{
  MSG         msg     ;
  WNDCLASS    wndclass ;

  if (!hPrevInstance)
    {

    // Register Parent Window Class

    wndclass.style        = CS_HREDRAW | CS_VREDRAW | CS_BYTEALIGNCLIENT;
    wndclass.lpfnWndProc  = (WNDPROC)WndProc ;
    wndclass.cbClsExtra   = 0 ;
    wndclass.cbWndExtra   = 0 ;
    wndclass.hInstance    = hInstance ;
    wndclass.hIcon        = NULL;
    wndclass.hCursor      = LoadCursor (NULL, IDC_ARROW) ;
```

```
wndclass.hbrBackground = GetStockObject ( GRAY_BRUSH ) ;
wndclass.lpszMenuName  = NULL;
wndclass.lpszClassName = szAppName ;

if (!RegisterClass (&wndclass))
    return FALSE;


// Register the Half-Height Caption Child Window Class

wndclass.style         = CS_BYTEALIGNCLIENT;
wndclass.lpfnWndProc   = (WNDPROC)HalfHeightWndProc ;
wndclass.cbClsExtra    = 0 ;
wndclass.cbWndExtra    = 0 ;
wndclass.hInstance     = hInstance ;
wndclass.hIcon         = NULL;
wndclass.hCursor       = LoadCursor (NULL, IDC_ARROW) ;
wndclass.hbrBackground = GetStockObject ( LTGRAY_BRUSH ) ;
wndclass.lpszMenuName  = NULL ;
wndclass.lpszClassName = szHalfHeightAppName ;

if (!RegisterClass (&wndclass))
    return FALSE;
}

hCaptionFont = CreateFont ( -1*(GetSystemMetrics(SM_CYCAPTION)/2),
                            0, 900, 900, 400, FALSE, FALSE, FALSE,
                            ANSI_CHARSET, OUT_CHARACTER_PRECIS,
                            CLIP_DEFAULT_PRECIS, PROOF_QUALITY,
                            VARIABLE_PITCH | FF_SWISS, (LPSTR)"Arial" );


ghInst   = hInstance;


hFakeSystemPopupMenu = LoadMenu ( ghInst,"FakeSysMenu" );


hFakeSystemMenu = GetSubMenu( hFakeSystemPopupMenu, 0 );


lpprocButtonSubclass = MakeProcInstance ( (FARPROC)ControlSubclassProc, ghInst );


ghWnd =             CreateWindow (szAppName, "Your ole' pal WM_NCHITTEST",
                            WS_OVERLAPPEDWINDOW,
                            GetSystemMetrics ( SM_CXSCREEN ) /4,
                            GetSystemMetrics ( SM_CYSCREEN ) /4,
                            GetSystemMetrics ( SM_CXSCREEN ) /2,
                            GetSystemMetrics ( SM_CYSCREEN ) /2,
```

```
                                 NULL, NULL, hInstance, NULL) ;


   ghWndHalfHeight =    CreateWindow (szHalfHeightAppName, "Lets Get Small",
                                 WS_POPUP | WS_VISIBLE | WS_THICKFRAME |
                                 WS_BORDER,
                                 200, 200,
                                 100, 100,
                                 ghWnd, NULL, hInstance, NULL) ;


   ghWndButton =        CreateWindow ("button", "Move Me Now!",
                                 WS_CHILD | WS_VISIBLE | WS_BORDER |
                                 BS_PUSHBUTTON,
                                 10, 10,
                                 150, 50,
                                 ghWnd, NULL, hInstance, NULL) ;


   lpprocButton = (FARPROC)
                 SetWindowLong(
                              ghWndButton,
                              GWL_WNDPROC,
                              (LONG)lpprocButtonSubclass
                         );
   ShowWindow ( ghWnd, nCmdShow );
   UpdateWindow ( ghWnd );

   while (GetMessage((LPMSG)&msg, NULL, 0, 0))
     {
     TranslateMessage(&msg);
     DispatchMessage(&msg);
     }

   DeleteObject ( hCaptionFont );
   DestroyMenu  ( hFakeSystemPopupMenu );
}

/*********************************************************************
 *                                                                   *
 *                 WndProc: Main Message Translator                  *
 *                                                                   *
 *********************************************************************/

WINPROC WndProc ( WINDOWS_PARAMS )
{
  switch ( msg )
    {
```

```
   case WM_DESTROY :

     PostQuitMessage (0) ;
     break ;

   default :

     return DefWindowProc ( hWnd, msg, wParam, lParam );


   }
 return OL ;
}
/**********************************************************************
*                                                                   *
*                    WndProc: Main Message Translator               *
*                                                                   *
**********************************************************************/

WINPROC HalfHeightWndProc ( WINDOWS_PARAMS )
{
   RECT          rc;
   POINT         pt;
   HDC           hDC;
   PAINTSTRUCT   ps;
   char          szCaption[128];
   int           iWidth;
   HFONT         hOldFont;
   HBRUSH        hCaptionBrush;
   WORD          wCaptionHeight;

   switch ( msg )
     {
     case WM_SIZE:

       InvalidateRect ( hWnd, NULL, FALSE );
       break;

     case WM_ACTIVATE:

       // Force a repaint of the fake caption

       GetClientRect ( hWnd, &rc );
       rc.right = rc.left + GetSystemMetrics ( SM_CYCAPTION )/2;
       InvalidateRect ( hWnd, &rc, FALSE );
```

```
        break;

    case WM_NCHITTEST:

      GetClientRect ( hWnd, &rc );

      // Figure the height of the fake caption
      rc.right = rc.left + GetSystemMetrics ( SM_CYCAPTION )/2;

      // remove out the area where the fake system menu is
      rc.top = GetSystemMetrics ( SM_CYCAPTION )/2;

      pt.x = (int) LOWORD (lParam);
      pt.y = (int) HIWORD (lParam);
      ScreenToClient ( hWnd, &pt );
      if (PtInRect (&rc, pt))
        return HTCAPTION;
      else
        return DefWindowProc ( hWnd, msg, wParam, lParam );

    case WM_LBUTTONDOWN:

      if  (
          (LOWORD (lParam) < (GetSystemMetrics ( SM_CYCAPTION )/2))
          &&
          (HIWORD (lParam) < (GetSystemMetrics ( SM_CYCAPTION )/2))
          )
          {
          pt.x = -1;
          pt.y = (GetSystemMetrics ( SM_CYCAPTION )/2)-1;
          ClientToScreen ( hWnd, &pt );
          TrackPopupMenu ( hFakeSystemMenu, 0, pt.x, pt.y, 0, hWnd, NULL );
          }
        break;

    case WM_PAINT:

      wCaptionHeight = GetSystemMetrics ( SM_CYCAPTION )/2;

      hDC = BeginPaint ( hWnd, &ps );

      hOldFont = SelectObject ( hDC, hCaptionFont );
      GetClientRect ( hWnd, &rc );
```

```
rc.right   = wCaptionHeight;
rc.top     = wCaptionHeight;


GetWindowText ( hWnd, szCaption, sizeof (szCaption) );


{
SIZE size;
GetTextExtentPoint ( hDC, szCaption, lstrlen(szCaption), &size);
iWidth = size.cx;
}


SetBkMode ( hDC, TRANSPARENT );


if (GetFocus() == hWnd)
  {
  hCaptionBrush = CreateSolidBrush (GetSysColor ( COLOR_ACTIVECAPTION  ));;
  SetTextColor ( hDC, GetSysColor ( COLOR_CAPTIONTEXT    ));;
  }
else
  {
  hCaptionBrush = CreateSolidBrush (GetSysColor ( COLOR INACTIVECAPTION
                              ));;
  SetTextColor ( hDC, GetSysColor ( COLOR_INACTIVECAPTIONTEXT ));;
  }


FillRect ( hDC, &rc, hCaptionBrush );


DeleteObject (hCaptionBrush);
ExtTextOut ( hDC,
             rc.left,
             rc.bottom - (rc.bottom-rc.top-iWidth)/2,
             ETO_CLIPPED,
             &rc,
             szCaption,
             lstrlen (szCaption),
             NULL );


SelectObject ( hDC, hOldFont);


// Draw the fake close box


rc.right = wCaptionHeight;
rc.left  = 0;
rc.top   = 0;
```

```
        rc.bottom= wCaptionHeight;

    SetBkColor   ( hDC, RGB (192,192,192));
    SetBkColor   ( hDC, RGB (255,0,0));
    ExtTextOut ( hDC,
                 0,
                 0, ETO_OPAQUE|ETO_CLIPPED,
                 &rc,
                 NULL,
                 0,
                 NULL );

    MoveToEx ( hDC, (rc.right*1/5), (rc.bottom/2), NULL );
    LineTo   ( hDC, (rc.right*4/5), (rc.bottom/2) );

    EndPaint ( hWnd, &ps );
    break;

case WM_COMMAND :

    switch ( LOWORD(wParam) )

        {
        case IDM_SYSMOVE :

            SendMessage ( hWnd, WM_SYSCOMMAND, SC_MOVE, (LPARAM)NULL );
            break;

        case IDM_SYSCLOSE:

            SendMessage ( hWnd, WM_SYSCOMMAND, SC_CLOSE, (LPARAM)NULL );
            break;

        default:

            return DefWindowProc ( hWnd, msg, wParam, lParam ) ;
            break;
        }

    break;

    default :
```

```
        return DefWindowProc ( hWnd, msg, wParam, lParam );


    }
  return 0L ;
}

/*********************************************************************
*                                                                   *
*                                                                   *
*                                                                   *
*********************************************************************/

WINPROC ControlSubclassProc ( WINDOWS_PARAMS )
{
  RECT   rc;
  POINT  pt;
  HDC    hDC;
  int    i;

  switch ( msg )
    {
    case WM_NCHITTEST:

      FigureHandleSizes ( hWnd );

      GetClientRect ( hWnd, &rc );
      pt.x = (int) LOWORD (lParam);
      pt.y = (int) HIWORD (lParam);

      // First, test for the "handles"

      for ( i = 0; i < 8; i++ )
        if (PtInRect (&(DialogHandles[i].rcArea), pt))
          return DialogHandles[i].dwNCHITVALUE;

      // Second, test for moving

      ScreenToClient ( hWnd, &pt );
      if (PtInRect (&rc, pt))
        return HTCAPTION;
      else
        return CallWindowProc( lpprocButton, hWnd, msg, wParam, lParam);
      break;
```

```
    case WM_PAINT:

      // Let the control draw itself first

      CallWindowProc( lpprocButton, hWnd, msg, wParam, lParam);

      // Draw Handles

      FigureHandleSizes ( hWnd );

      hDC = GetWindowDC ( hWnd );

      for ( i = 0; i < 8; i++ )
        {
        rc = DialogHandles[i].rcArea;

        ScreenToClientRect ( hWnd, &rc );

        FillRect (hDC, &rc, GetStockObject (WHITE_BRUSH));
        }

      ReleaseDC ( hWnd, hDC );

      return 0L;

    default:

      return CallWindowProc( lpprocButton, hWnd, msg, wParam, lParam);
    }
}

//**********************************************************************
//
//
//
//**********************************************************************

void ScreenToClientRect ( HWND hWnd, LPRECT prRect )
{
  POINT pt;

  pt.x = prRect->left;
```

```
  pt.y = prRect->top;
  ScreenToClient ( hWnd, &pt );
  prRect->left = pt.x;
  prRect->top  = pt.y;
  pt.x = prRect->right;
  pt.y = prRect->bottom;
  ScreenToClient ( hWnd, &pt );
  prRect->right = pt.x;
  prRect->bottom  = pt.y;
}


/**********************************************************************
*                                                                   *
*                                                                   *
*                                                                   *
**********************************************************************/

#define MAKEHANDLE(iIndex,x,y,dwHitValue)              \
  {                                                    \
  DialogHandles[iIndex].rcArea.left    = x;            \
  DialogHandles[iIndex].rcArea.top     = y;            \
  DialogHandles[iIndex].rcArea.right   = x+dx+1;       \
  DialogHandles[iIndex].rcArea.bottom  = y+dy+1;       \
  DialogHandles[iIndex].dwNCHITVALUE   = dwHitValue;   \
  }


/**********************************************************************
*                                                                   *
*                                                                   *
*                                                                   *
**********************************************************************/

void FigureHandleSizes ( HWND hWnd )
{
  RECT rc;
  int  dx = GetSystemMetrics ( SM_CXFRAME );
  int  dy = GetSystemMetrics ( SM_CYFRAME )+1;


  GetWindowRect ( hWnd, &rc );

  MAKEHANDLE( 0, rc.left,                 (rc.top+rc.bottom)/2-dy/2, HTLEFT      )
  MAKEHANDLE( 1, rc.right-dx,             (rc.top+rc.bottom)/2-dy/2, HTRIGHT     )
  MAKEHANDLE( 2, (rc.left+rc.right)/2-dx/2, rc.top,                 HTTOP       )
  MAKEHANDLE( 3, rc.left,                 rc.top,                   HTTOPLEFT   )
  MAKEHANDLE( 4, rc.right-dx,             rc.top,                   HTTOPRIGHT  )
```

```
    MAKEHANDLE( 5, (rc.left+rc.right)/2-dx/2, rc.bottom-dy,          HTBOTTOM        )
    MAKEHANDLE( 6, rc.left,                   rc.bottom-dy,          HTBOTTOMLEFT    )
    MAKEHANDLE( 7, rc.right-dy,               rc.bottom-dy,          HTBOTTOMRIGHT   )
}
```

The little white "handles" are drawn on top of the control in the subclass procedure. First, **CallWindowProc** lets the control paint itself. Then it splats the little handles on top of the control. The WM_NCHITTEST message is put to the test in this subclass procedure. First, the mouse cursor position is checked against all the elements of the *DialogHandles* array. If the cursor is in any of the regions defined by the array, the appropriate value is returned. If the cursor is not on any of these "handles", the mouse cursor is checked against the client area of the window. If the cursor is on the "handle," the *HTCAPTION* value is returned, which allows the user to move the button around easily. If the mouse is not in the client area, the message is passed on to **CallWindowProc**, which lets the button decide what to do with it.

Messing around with WM_NCHITTEST is one of my favorite ways to make Windows-based applications enjoy some of the cool aspects of programming life that you might have thought only the Microsoft Excel developers could do. If you have a really nifty implementation of using WM_NCHITTEST, I would really like to hear about it.

Part 2

Windows NT & Windows 95 Specialties

CHAPTER 8

Migrating to Win32

When writing applications for Microsoft Windows 3.1, Windows 95, and Windows NT operating systems, I've run into two types of issues: the obvious and the inobvious. The obvious issues include using message-cracker macros (or your own home-brew macros) to handle the differences in *wParam* and *lParam*, while the inobvious issues include such "beasties" as *int*-to-*WORD* arithmetic and differences in structure packing. This list is not a "how-to-port" list. Before doing your first port, be sure you have read the Microsoft Win32 API manuals concerning porting, as well as Scott Gellock's article, "Port Your 16-bit Applications to Windows NT Without Ripping Your Hair Out," *Microsoft Systems Journal*, August 1993. Actually, porting to Win32 is relatively easy, except for a few "beasties" I had to learn the hard way.

I use the term "Win32" fairly loosely in this list. When I talk about "Win32," I am talking about both Windows NT and Windows 95 as a whole, not necessarily the Win32 API set. Remember that Windows 95 is Win32 just as much as Windows NT is. Generally, all of these tips have the exact same ramifications for both Windows 95 and Windows NT.

Before I get into this Top Ten List, let me tell you about my BASEDEFS.H file. This is a little include file that contains several macros to help keep my code consistent and portable (see Listing 8.1). It has my home-brew version of the message crackers, and a few other goodies. Notice how I avoid using some of the predefined stuff that comes with the SDK (even the WIN32 macro definition). All of the Microsoft stuff is wrapped up in BASEDEFS.H, because there may be situations in the future when Microsoft is going to be forced to change declarations and end up hosing my source files. By keeping all of the Microsoft stuff under a wrapper, all they hose is BASEDEFS.H, which is easily "unhosable."

LISTING 8.1 BASEDEFS.H

```
//
// BASEDEFS.H: My private portability file
//

#ifdef WIN32
#define WIN_NT
#else
#define WIN_DOS
#endif


#ifdef WIN_DOS
#define WINPROC          long FAR PASCAL
#define MDIPROC          long FAR PASCAL
#define DLGPROC          BOOL FAR PASCAL
#define ENUMPROC         BOOL FAR PASCAL
#define WINDOWS_PARAMS HWND hWnd, unsigned msg, WPARAM wParam, LONG lParam
#define DIALOG_PARAMS  HWND hDlg, unsigned msg, WPARAM wParam, LONG lParam
#define ENUM_PARAMS      HWND hWnd, LPARAM lParam
#endif


#ifdef WIN_NT
#define WINPROC          long CALLBACK
#define MDIPROC          long CALLBACK
#define DLGPROC          BOOL CALLBACK
#define ENUMPROC         BOOL CALLBACK
#define WINDOWS_PARAMS HWND hWnd, UINT msg, WPARAM wParam, LPARAM lParam
#define DIALOG_PARAMS  HWND hDlg, UINT msg, WPARAM wParam, LPARAM lParam
#define ENUM_PARAMS      HWND hWnd, LPARAM lParam
#endif
```

```
#define CRACKER_VARS                    \
   HWND CRACKER_hWnd;                   \
   WORD CRACKER_wNotification;  \
   WORD CRACKER_wID;


#ifdef WIN_DOS
#define CRACK_MESSAGEsc                              \
   {                                                \
   CRACKER_wID           = wParam;                  \
   CRACKER_wNotification = HIWORD (lParam );  \
   CRACKER_hWnd          = LOWORD (lParam );  \
   }
#endif


#ifdef WIN_NT
#define CRACK_MESSAGEsc                              \
   {                                                \
   CRACKER_wID           = LOWORD (wParam );  \
   CRACKER_wNotification = HIWORD (wParam );  \
   CRACKER_hWnd          = (HWND)lParam;       \
   }
#endif


#ifdef WIN_DOS
#define HICHUNK(lParam) HIWORD(lParam)
#define LOCHUNK(lParam) LOWORD(lParam)
#define MAKECHUNKsc(lParam,lo,hi) lParam=MAKELONG(lo,hi);
#define HILOCHUNK DWORD
#define HILOCHUNKPARAM(lParam) (lParam)
#endif


#ifdef WIN_NT


typedef struct tagHILOCHUNK
   {
   LONG hi;
   LONG lo;
   }
HILOCHUNK;


typedef HILOCHUNK FAR *LPHILOCHUNK;


#define HICHUNK(lParam) (((LPHILOCHUNK)(lParam))->hi)
#define LOCHUNK(lParam) (((LPHILOCHUNK)(lParam))->lo)
#define MAKECHUNKsc(lParam,low,high)
```

```
      {lParam.lo=(LONG)(low);lParam.hi=(LONG)(high);}
#define HILOCHUNKPARAM(lParam) ((LONG)(&lParam))
#endif


// MACROS FOR VARAIBLE DECLARATIONS

#ifndef INMAIN
#define GLOBAL extern
#define GLOBALCHAR(p1,p2) char p1;
#endif
#ifdef INMAIN
#define GLOBAL
#define GLOBALCHAR(p1,p2) char p1 = p2;
#endif


// Endian Independant storage facilities

typedef struct diWORDtag
   {
   BYTE    bLo;
   BYTE    bHi;
   }
diWORD;
typedef struct diLONGtag
   {
   diWORD diwLo;
   diWORD diwHi;
   }
diLONG;


#define GETWORD(diWord) ((diWord).bHi*256+(diWord).bLo)
#define GETLONG(diLong) (MAKELONG(GETWORD(diLong.diwLo),GETWORD(diLong.diwHi)))


#define MAKEdiWORD(diWord,wWord)            \
   {                                        \
   (diWord).bHi = (wWord)/256;              \
   (diWord).bLo = (wWord)%256;              \
   }


#define MAKEdiLONG(diLong,lLong)            \
   {                                        \
   MAKEdiWORD((diLong).diwHi, HIWORD(lLong));  \
   MAKEdiWORD((diLong).diwLo, LOWORD(lLong));  \
   }
```

214

In BASEDEFS.H, BASE1.C (a do-next-to-nothing application), and the accompanying files in Listing 8.1, I've already followed my own advice for handling Win32 porting "beasties."

10. WORD Versus UINT Versus WPARAM

When do you use *WORD, UINT,* or *WPARAM? WORD* is always going to be a 16-bit value, while *UINT* and *WPARAM* will change, depending on the operating system.

Here is my method. Use *WORD* when you are storing a value that you know cannot change in the future. Examples of this include elements in your file data structure, dates, and font point sizes. Use *UINT* where you are uncertain of the range. Use *WPARAM* when you are using a value that is derived from the *WPARAM* portion of a Windows message. A major mistake made throughout a program of mine was code such as the following:

```
WORD wSel;

wSel = (WORD)SendMessage ( hWndListBox, LB_GETCURSEL, 0,
                           0L );
if (LB_ERR == wSel)
  {

.
.
.


  }
else
  {
  SendMessage ( hWndListBox, LB_GETTEXT, wSel,
          (LPARAM)(LPSTR)szLine );

.
.
.


  }
```

This code looks innocent enough, but it turns into debugging hell under Win32. *LB_ERR* is defined as –1 in WINDOWS.H. That computes into an integer, which is 32 bits for Win32. Therefore, –1 in 32 bits cannot be correctly represented in a 16-bit *WORD*. The check for *LB_ERR* always fails and you end up sending bogus numbers to the *LB_GETTEXT* code. If you have a monster list box with a zillion items, any item past the 65,536th item will not be accessible. (However, please don't put that many items in a list box. That's a user-interface blunder that could make anyone scream.)

Because you and I did not write the code behind the built-in Windows messages, we have to play by Microsoft's rules. So, change the code to look like the following:

```
WPARAM wSel;

wSel = (WPARAM)SendMessage ( hWndListBox, LB_GETCURSEL,
                             0, 0L );
if (LB_ERR = = wSel)
  {
  .
  .
  .
  }
else
  {
  SendMessage ( hWndListBox, LB_GETTEXT, wSel,
             (LPARAM)(LPSTR)szLine );
  .
  .
  .
  }
```

This code is portable, and fits the bits of the operating system.

9. Structures Are Aligned Differently for Win32

I was having severe problems getting the data files I created with the 16-bit MS-DOS-based version of my program to load on the Win32-based version, and vice versa. I compared the two files and found that the file size was larger for the Win32-based version. I figured out that the *sizeof* operator in C was giving me different results.

It turns out that the Win32-based compiler by default packs structures on 32-bit boundaries, and the MS-DOS-based compiler packs them on 16-bit boundaries. This means that if the second item in an array does not lie on an even boundary, the compiler will waste a byte or three to align it. This is a speed enhancement, since various microprocessors prefer (or require) aligned data. This difference makes sense to me now. This "beastie" is mentioned in the manual, but it still bites hard enough to get an entry on my list.

The only way to guarantee that the structures will be correctly and consistently arranged is to avoid structures in data files. Write out each individual element as a stream of bytes. Read each element of the array from the disk file, and then fill in each member of a structure.

However, this arrangement won't make life easy for all those programs that have already written out data as structures. Microsoft has included an excellent piece of code to help you through this. In the source code for the FontEdit sample application in the NT Win32 SDK, a module called TYPECVT.C includes functions to help you convert from one type to another. These functions handle structure alignment and Big Endian/Little Endian conversions. The **lCalculateStructOffsets** function builds a picture in memory of the structures to convert, while the **vPerformConversion** function does the actual grunt work. These functions will let your application convert from those unaligned structures to aligned structures.

However, you should still use data types that won't change depending on the platform. For example, the functions in TYPECVT.C are designed to align structures, but they are not designed to convert 16-bit ints to 32-bit ints, or vice-versa. Stick with *WORD*, *BYTE*, *DWORD*, and *char* variable types to ensure that your data does not gain or lose bits between platforms.

8. Int Variables Versus WORD Variables

Sometimes you should use *WORD*, other times you should use *int*, and still other times you should use *short*. I've already discussed when to use *WORD*, so consider when it's all right to use the *int* variable and when to use the *short* variable.

A *short* always will be an integer between −32768 and +32767. An *int* depends on the operating system. If you are counting on a variable falling in this range, use *short*. Also, if you plan on typecasting to a *WORD*, use *short*. However, if you are using a return value from Windows APIs, or Other People's Code, use *int* if the documentation says to. For example, the Windows API **GetDlgItemInt** returns an *int*, not a *short*, and, therefore, it makes sense to use the machine-dependent *int*.

An easy mistake to make, though, is to cast a *WORD* to an *int*, or vice versa. In 16-bit Windows, this happened seamlessly, since both are 16-bit values. However, Win32 uses a 32-bit *int* and a 16-bit *WORD*, which means that negative values do not correctly translate. In particular, −1 as an *int* does not translate to 65535 as a *WORD*, which will kill many programs that have lines of code such as the following:

```
if (-1 == (int)wValue)
  {
.
.
.
}
```

In a few places in my program I used *int* variables when I should have used a *WORD*. One particularly nasty bug was in a **GetDate** function. It took *LPINT*s as its parameters, yet the variables getting passed in were *LPWORD*s. Therefore, the code that modifies these pointers actually will trounce all over everything.

```
WORD w1, w2, w3;

void SetVars ( LPINT pi1, LPINT pi2, LPINT pi3 )
{
  *pi1 = 1;
  *pi2 = 2;
  *pi3 = 3;
}

void main ( void )
```

```
{
  SetVars ( (LPINT)&w1, (LPINT)&w2, (LPINT)&w3 );
}
```

For academic purposes, say the addresses of *w1*, *w2*, and *w3* are 0000, 0002, and 0004. However, the function **SetVars** will fill in the pointers as if they were 32-bit values (if this is Win32). Therefore, the variables will overlap each other. This code works perfectly on 16-bit systems, but not on 32-bit systems. So, in this case, the seemingly innocent casting of a smaller value to a larger value actually has disastrous consequences. That's something we all learned in college, assuming we showed up that day.

7. Typecast Expressions Involving Both WORDS and ints (Even Constants!) to WORD

The following code will give you a compile warning:

```
WORD wValue;
wValue = wValue - wDelta + 3;
```

The constant 3 in this code defaults to an integer, which then promotes the two variables in the expression at computation time to something like the following:

```
WORD wValue;
wValue = (WORD) ((int)wValue - (int)wDelta + (int)3);
```

If the *wDelta* variable is greater than *wValue*, this expression would evaluate negative, which would then incorrectly typecast to a *WORD*. Hence, the expression would evaluate wrong, and you would get a compiler warning about size mix-ups.

The fix for this is to cast the 3 to a WORD.

```
WORD wValue;
wValue = wValue - wDelta + (WORD)3;
```

This code will not give you any compiler warnings, and will evaluate as expected.

6. Uninitialized Local Variables in MS-DOS Are Often Zero, While in Win32 They Are Not

Conventional wisdom under 16-bit Windows was, "If the program worked fine in CodeView for Windows, but otherwise didn't, there must be an uninitialized local variable." This was because the CodeView debugger seemed to keep a lot of zeroes in the stack, and all my locals got initialized to zero. Well, the Win32 Windbg program won't do this for you.

My program contained a serious bug in the message switch statement of a window procedure. I never initialized the third *WORD* array element of a temporary variable before I sent the array down the food chain. Well, it turned out that under MS-DOS, I was getting zeros in there 100 percent of the time (because of previous stack overwrites), and the error was hidden.

Win32 is much better at leaving garbage on the stack. Since all parameters are aligned on 32-bit boundaries, recycled stack space maps to parameters more consistently. Therefore, uninitialized variables in Win32-based applications almost always are nonzero.

5. NULL Ain't Zero, and Handles Are Pointers

Considerable debate has centered on NULL and zero, and the fact that the Win32 version of NULL is not the same as the MS-DOS version of NULL. In MS-DOS, NULL was 0. In Win32, NULL is

```
((void *)0)
```

which causes lines like the following to give obnoxious compiler warnings:

```
SendMessage ( hWnd, WM_SETREDRAW, FALSE, NULL );
rc.left = NULL;
```

Bummer. Hence, I changed my program so that all scalar values got zero, and all handles and pointers kept NULL. (In Win32, handles are pointers.) Granted, this makes more sense, but many programs got used to using NULL to zero-out a variable. Using NULL as a scalar zero isn't a good idea anyway, but plenty of code (including some Microsoft sample code) is guilty of using NULL as zero.

Also, check out this innocent line of code:

```
hKiddieWindow = CreateWindow
        (
        szClass,
        szCaption,
        WS_CHILD,
        x, y,
        cx, cy,
        hWndParent,
        IDD_KIDDIE,      //parameter #9
        ghInst,          //#10
        NULL             //#11
        );
```

This will give you a crazy compiler warning telling you that parameter 10 (or sometimes 11) is failing. So, you look at parameter 10, 11, even 9, and they all look fine. Turns out that you get that warning if any parameter is wrong. The offending parameter in this case is parameter 9, *hMenu*. In 16-bit Windows, *HMENU* is a *WORD*. In Win32, it is a pointer. So, using a constant for a pointer confuses the compiler. To fix it, typecast everything that's suspect, as shown here:

```
hKiddieWindow = CreateWindow
        (
        szClass,
        szCaption,
        WS_CHILD,
        x, y,
        cx, cy,
        hWndParent,
        (HMENU)IDD_KIDDIE,
        ghInst,
        (LPVOID)NULL
        );
```

This little extra effort will keep those ambiguous compiler warnings quiet.

4. Porting Your Packed Parameters Practically Painlessly

In a Utopian world, everyone would have written their applications to work for Win32. Of course, that same Utopian world would contain a COBOL-to-C++ program converter. However, in this realistic world, everyone must take their once COBOL, then FORTRAN, then PASCAL, now C code and port it for the fifth time to Win32 (and then probably rewrite it all in C++). Chances are good that you will end up with a line of code like the following:

```
HDC        hDC;
HFONT      hFont;
        .
        .
        .

SendMessage (hSomeOtherWnd,
          WM_MYMESSAGE,
          IDC_MYACTION,
          MAKELONG ( hFont, hDC )
          );
```

Many programs use *MAKELONG* to pack together two values that were *WORD*s. In Win32, you may find that you now need to pack those two handles into a 32-bit value. Since handles are now 32 bits each, this can be especially challenging, and could require some serious code changes. But wait! There is a way out of this!

Instead of passing the packed value, pass a pointer to a structure that contains the values, and wrap the whole thing up in macros to make it invisible to the programmer. A macro that I include in BASEDEFS.H accommodates the old-fashioned packed messages. If your application uses a message that needs to pack two handles of information into *lParam*, it can get away with a *MAKELONG* under MS-DOS, but the Win32 version would have a fit. Using these macros for both the MS-DOS and Win32 version (in other words, a single source tree), you can do a quick-and-dirty patch that is nicely portable (see Listing 8.2).

LISTING 8.2 HICHUNK, LOCHUNK MACROS FOR PACKED PARAMETER PORTING

```
#ifdef WIN_DOS
#define HICHUNK(lParam) HIWORD(lParam)
#define LOCHUNK(lParam) LOWORD(lParam)
#define MAKECHUNKsc(lParam,lo,hi) lParam=MAKELONG(lo,hi);
#define HILOCHUNK DWORD
#define HILOCHUNKPARAM(lParam) (lParam)
#endif

#ifdef WIN_NT

typedef struct tagHILOCHUNK
  {
  LONG hi;
  LONG lo;
  }
HILOCHUNK;

typedef HILOCHUNK FAR *LPHILOCHUNK;

#define HICHUNK(lParam) (((LPHILOCHUNK)(lParam))->hi)
#define LOCHUNK(lParam) (((LPHILOCHUNK)(lParam))->lo)
#define MAKECHUNKsc(lParam,low,high) \
  {lParam.lo=(LONG)(low);lParam.hi=(LONG)(high);}
#define HILOCHUNKPARAM(lParam) ((LONG)(&lParam))
#endif
```

These macros will automatically use *MAKELONG, LOWORD,* and *HIWORD* for MS-DOS, and will use the structure for Win32. To pack two things together using these macros, change this

```
SendMessage (hSomeOtherWnd,
             WM_MYMESSAGE,
             IDC_MYACTION,
             MAKELONG ( hFont, hDC )
             );
```

to the following:

```
HILOCHUNK hilo;
MAKECHUNKsc(hilo, hDC, hFont)
```

223

```
SendMessage (hSomeOtherWnd,
            WM_MYMESSAGE,
            IDC_MYACTION,
            HILOCHUNKPARAM(hilo)
            );
```

This is minimal extra code and it lets you keep many of your algorithms intact when porting from 16-bit to 32-bit.

3. Parameters Are Aligned on 32-Bit Boundaries

Look at this call:

```
WORD w1, w2;

MyProc ( w1, w2 );
```

The parameters under MS-DOS each will use 2 bytes of stack space. In Win32, they will use 4 bytes of stack space. Even though the parameters are 16-bit values, they will be aligned on 32-bit boundaries. There will be 2 wasted bytes between each parameter. When passing parameters, keep this in mind as you figure out how much stack space you will need. However, the problem of *int* variables versus *WORD* variables is not resolved here. The declaration of *w1*, *w2*, and *w3* in the previous discussion on *int* variables versus *WORD* variables will not spread those values out over 32-bit boundaries, since they are not parameter lists.

2. One Mo' Time: File Layout

I briefly mentioned in the section, "10. WORD Versus UINT Versus WPARAM," at the beginning of this chapter what variables to use in a file structure. Well, this is actually a "beastie" of its own.

Consider the following code written for MS-DOS:

```
typedef struct tagFILEDATA
  {
```

```
    char    szName[30];
    int        iAge;
    LONG  lSSN;
    }
FILEDATA;


FILEDATA FileData;

    .
    .
    .

_lwrite ( hFile, (LPSTR)&FileData, sizeof(FileData));
```

This is code destined to crash and burn on Win32 and the Macintosh! The Mac? Even though Win32 is not currently running on the Mac, you should consider file transfers and network connectivity. Many applications now use core code technology that provides a single source tree for both Mac- and Windows-based versions. Since each of these platforms has different methods for storing numbers in memory, it is important to use a mechanism for consistent data storage so that these different platforms can communicate over the local network, Internet, and Sneakernet (floppies, that is).

The code in this example crashes for different reasons on Win32 and on the Mac. It will crash on Win32 because *iAge* is a different size and the structure will be packed on 4-byte boundaries instead of 2. It will crash on the Mac because the Mac is Big Endian while Intel is Little Endian. Therefore, the following three changes must be made to this code to ensure that the file is completely compatible between all platforms:

❖ Use data types that won't change (*WORD, short, LONG*).

❖ Explicitly define how to pack the structure (or use the TYPECVT code discussed previously in this chapter in the section, "9. Structures Are Aligned Differently for Win32").

❖ Break the multibyte data structures down to bytes.

Look at BASEDEFS.H for the *diWORD* and *diLONG* data types, as well as the macros used along with them. Now, look at a new version of this code in Listing 8.3.

LISTING 8.3 WRITING A DATA FILE ENDIAN INDEPENDENTLY

```
typedef struct tagFILEDATA
    {
    char   szName[30];
    WORD   iAge;
    LONG   lSSN;
    }
FILEDATA;
typedef struct tagFILEDATAFILE
    {
    char   szName[30];
    diWORD iAge;
    diLONG lSSN;
    }
FILEDATAFILE;


FILEDATA     FileData;
FILEDATAFILE FileDataFile;


....


// Create an Endian independant image of the data

lstrcpy ( FileDataFile.szName, FileData.szName );
MAKEdiWORD ( FileDataFile.iAge, FileData.iAge );
MAKEdiLONG ( FileDataFile.lSSN, FileData.lSSN );


// Write that to disk

_lwrite ( hFile, (LPSTR)(FileDataFile.szName), sizeof (FileDataFile.szName));
_lwrite ( hFile, (LPSTR)&(FileDataFile.iAge.bHi), sizeof (BYTE));
_lwrite ( hFile, (LPSTR)&(FileDataFile.iAge.bLo), sizeof (BYTE));
_lwrite ( hFile, (LPSTR)&(FileDataFile.lSSN.diwHi.bHi), sizeof (BYTE));
_lwrite ( hFile, (LPSTR)&(FileDataFile.lSSN.diwHi.bLo), sizeof (BYTE));
_lwrite ( hFile, (LPSTR)&(FileDataFile.lSSN.diwLo.bHi), sizeof (BYTE));
_lwrite ( hFile, (LPSTR)&(FileDataFile.lSSN.diwLo.bLo), sizeof (BYTE));


// To load the data back in and convert it to the native format, do

// something like this:

_lread ( hFile, (LPSTR)(FileDataFile.szName), sizeof (FileDataFile.szName));
```

```
_lread ( hFile, (LPSTR)&(FileDataFile.iAge.bHi), sizeof (BYTE));
_lread ( hFile, (LPSTR)&(FileDataFile.iAge.bLo), sizeof (BYTE));
_lread ( hFile, (LPSTR)&(FileDataFile.lSSN.diwHi.bHi), sizeof (BYTE));
_lread ( hFile, (LPSTR)&(FileDataFile.lSSN.diwHi.bLo), sizeof (BYTE));
_lread ( hFile, (LPSTR)&(FileDataFile.lSSN.diwLo.bHi), sizeof (BYTE));
_lread ( hFile, (LPSTR)&(FileDataFile.lSSN.diwLo.bLo), sizeof (BYTE));

lstrcpy ( FileData.szName, FileDataFile.szName );
FileData.iAge = GETWORD ( FileDataFile.iAge );
FileData.lSSN = GETLONG ( FileDataFile.lSSN );
```

This may seem like grunt work, but it will ensure that you produce Endian-independent data files that can be transported back and forth between the Mac- and the Intel-based machines. (The DEC Alpha and MIPS chips are Endian-programmable, and Windows NT currently requires Little Endian. However, this could change. Therefore, the previous Endian-independent rules may someday apply to different Windows NT platforms.)

Of course, if you are writing C++ applications in MFC, use the << operator along with the "ar" object in C++. This object will automagically do all of the endian-independant conversions for you in the serialization process, giving you plenty of time to lie in the berry patch. Yumm!

1. Keep In Mind Win32 Really Multitasks

Unlike 16-bit Windows 3.1, Windows 95 and Windows NT really multitask. This means that your application no longer rules the world. Normally, this has no effect on your programming pursuits, unless you are doing some operations that truly rely on total system control. I have two examples: **SetCapture** and screen updates.

SetCapture works very differently under Win32 than it does under 16-bit Windows. In 16-bit Windows, when you capture the mouse, you will unconditionally get capture until you call **ReleaseCapture**. Under Win32, you only get that same effect if the mouse button is down. Refer to the **SetCapture** comments in the *Win32 Guide to Programming* or in the Win32 Help File.

With screen updates, keep in mind that Windows NT 3.5 will continue to draw on windows even when the user is moving a window around. For example, run some sort of Qix-like screen-saver in the background, and then move your window around with the mouse by grabbing it by the caption. Sure enough, the background is still repainting itself. If your application assumes that the backgrounds will not repaint themselves, you should rework your code to give up that distinction.

CHAPTER 9

Questions About Win32

Win32 was designed to make it as easy as possible to move to a new 32-bit environment. In general, Microsoft succeeded very well in achieving this goal. The port to Win32 generally is a relatively painless process (see Chapter 8, "Migrating to Win32," for information specific to porting). However, some programming habits and techniques not simple ports. Some new concepts have been introduced (namely threads and separate address spaces) that make some common programming practices change.

Kyle Sparks (see the "Introduction" for his biography) has given me this list of top ten questions he receives about Win32. Tip number 3 was provided by Joe Rzepiejewski (his biography also is in the Introduction).

10. The Subclassing/Superclassing issue

First, let's talk about subclassing and superclassing, since very few official statements have been published to state just what these two Windows programming techniques are.

Subclassing a window involves taking an already existing window, and intercepting all messages going to it with a filter routine. The filter procedure looks just like a regular window callback procedure, except that, instead of calling **DefWindowProc**, the filter calls an API named **CallWindowProc**, which will then send the message back to the original window procedure. To subclass a window, you simply replace its callback procedure address by using the **SetWindowLong** API. This API returns to you the current callback procedure address, which is what you use for **CallWindowProc** (see Figure 9.1 for a diagram that puts all of this together, using an edit control as an example).

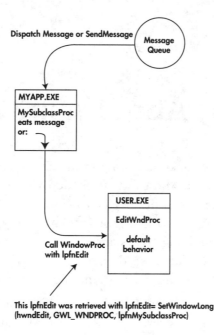

FIGURE 9.1 SUBCLASSING AN EDIT CONTROL

Superclassing a window involves cloning a current window class, with just a few DNA changes to suit your needs. Generally, you still use the same callback procedure address as the class you are cloning, you just makes some changes in the style bits or extra-byte attributes. Superclassing involves getting the

WNDCLASS structure from the clonee with the **GetClassInfo** API, changing the name of the class (and any other attributes), and the registering that new class (see Listing 9.1 for an example of removing the CS_PARENTDC style bit). You can, however, change the callback procedure address to point to your own class, but your callback procedure must then also use **CallWindowProc** to pass the message onto the clonee's original callback procedure. Otherwise, you are not really superclassing, but rather just creating a totally new class.

LISTING 9.1 SUPERCLASSING A LIST BOX TO REMOVE THE CS_PARENTDC STYLE BIT

```
// This code superclasses a listbox to remove the
// CS_PARENTDC style bit for more controlled painting

BOOL SuperClassListBox ( HANDLE hInstance )
{
  WNDCLASS    wndclass ;

  GetClassInfo ( GetModuleHandle ("USER"), "listbox", &wndclass );

  wndclass.hInstance      = hInstance ;
  wndclass.style         &= ~(CS_GLOBALCLASS | CS_PARENTDC);
  wndclass.lpszClassName  = "SuperListBox";

  return RegisterClass (&wndclass);
}
```

Applications will subclass windows when they want to intercept messages. Typically, edit controls are subclassed to look for the ENTER key getting pressed, or top-level windows are subclassed in order to let your subclass procedure have a "first strike" at getting the messages (such as WM_COMMAND).

Applications will superclass windows in order to make slight variations on a window that is not their own class (such as a control), or if they need to. A typical reason to superclass a window is to change its class style bits (such as removing the CS_PARENTDC style bit, as discussed in Chapter 1, "Things You Might Want to Know About USER,") or if the superclass filter must see messages that happen before a subclassing can occur, since a subclassing can

231

occur only after a window is created. If you wanted to get WM_NCCREATE whenever the edit control is created, you would use a different callback procedure address, which must eventually call the edit control's original address (combining Figure 9.1 and Listing 9.1 will give you an idea of this implementation).

Under Win32, the basic concept of subclassing and superclassing is exactly the same. However, you are not allowed free reign to go about merrily subclassing and superclassing anymore. Win32 introduces the following rules and restrictions:

❖ Assume the return value from **Get/SetWindowLong(hWnd, GWL_WNDPROC,xxx)** is a "black box" and don't try to use it directly. Under Win16, you could sleazily get away by type casting that return value into a window callback function and then directly calling it. Under Win32, this will break because of Unicode. Unicode? There are two types of window procedures: Unicode and not Unicode. They have different entry mechanisms, and Win32 handles this "automagically" for you. However, some of this "automagical" stuff is exposed in that **Get/SetWindowLong** return value. No longer is the return value always a procedure address. It may be a structure pointer. It may be a pointer to a pointer. It may be a collapsible baton. In any case, make no assumptions about it. You can do two, and only two things with that return value: pass it on to **CallWindowProc** (which is smart enough to handle the black box), or use it in **SetWindowLong**.

❖ You can only subclass your own process. Under Win16, you could subclass Program Manager and intercept the WM_COMMAND messages freely. Under Win32, you would not be able to do this. Program Manager (or any other process, for that matter) runs in a completely different address space than your process. Therefore, it is architecturally impossible to subclass a window in another process. There are workarounds, though. First, you could use a system-wide hook in a DLL to intercept the messages, since the hook is loaded into the address space of the calling application. Second, you could put your subclass code in a DLL and force Win32 to load that DLL into every process's address space. (For example, you could add the DLL to the \HKEY_LOCAL_MACHINE\Software\Microsoft\Windows NT\CurrentVersion\Windows\APPINIT_DLLS area of the registry, but this method is very brute force and tailored to Windows NT versus Windows 95). Or, third, you could do some nasty operations with **OpenProcess**, **WriteProcessMemory**, and **CreateRemoteThread**, which is completely discouraged and hence won't be talked about any more in this book.

❖ Global subclassing is actually recommended for Win32. The examples of subclassing discussed up to now are called *local subclassing*, since the only window that feels the effects of the subclass is the actual window modified by **SetWindowLong**. Under Win16 and Win32, you could use **SetClassLong** to globally subclass every window of that class in the current address space. Of course, under Win16, every window on the system shared the same address space, so global subclassing was very discouraged, since you would affect windows that did not belong to your application. Under Win32, your process has its own address space, and, therefore, global subclassing now changes only the behavior of every window of that class in your process (for example, you could subclass every edit control in your process, while leaving the edit controls in another process untouched).

❖ There is only one change for superclassing, and it is the same change as subclassing: You must effect windows that only live in your address space. However, since superclassing requires that you create a new window by using the new *superclassname*, this issue is a rather moot point. However, as an interesting tidbit of trivia, you can't superclass the scrollbar, since the standard window procedure for the scrollbar relies on the *classname* being called "scrollbar."

9. Hooks

Local data is often instanced, and, therefore, in a hook, you can end up getting multiple copies of local data in each process to which your hook gets attached. For instance, if you had a BOOL that indicated when a mouse click occurred, and you clicked in a button that ran another process, the BOOL would get set in the process that owned the button. However, when the other process comes up, it will DLL_PROCESS_ATTACH to your hook DLL, and a new copy of that BOOL will be created. Therefore, in the context of that new process, the BOOL will be FALSE, but in the context of the button process, it will be TRUE. This is cured by using **#pragma data_seg()** to create a separate data segment that is then marked as SHARED in your .DEF file.

8. SetCapture()

It is here that many applications are going to break. Generally, the **SetCapture** API is called in response to the user clicking down with the mouse on something, and the **ReleaseCapture** API is called when the user lets go. Dragging and dropping, as well as screen-capture programs (such as Zoomin from the SDK) all call **SetCapture** in response to the mouse button being pressed down.

However, some applications may want to set the capture when the mouse button is up. Typically, this is in response to the user choosing something from a menu. For example, the Zoomin program could have added a menu item that says "Zoom at cursor," so the user did not have to click the mouse in order to invoke the zooming process. Another example of using **SetCapture** without mouse clickage would be if the program wanted to prevent the user's mouse clicking from fitting to queue up a bunch of WM_xBUTTONx messages all over the place in a dialog—possibly during a nasty recalculation.

Well, **SetCapture** does not work the same as Win16. If you are holding the mouse button down when the **SetCapture()** is invoked, you will get all mouse messages up to and including the WM?BUTTONUP, just as you did in 16-bit-land. However, if you set capture without the mouse button down, your application will get only messages that are in your window and in the desktop. Messages for other processes still will go to those processes. What would this cause? If the Zoomin program called **SetCapture** by way of a menu choice, then the floating capture box would only work while the mouse cursor was above the Zoomin window. This would render Zoomin as a complete lemon of a program.

The workaround to this is (unfortunately) to change your code so that the mouse button is down at the time of **SetCapture**. I tried things like **SetKeyboardState** to "fake" the mouse button being down, and I even tried installing a journal playback hook to fake the WM_LBUTTONDOWN message, but NT is too smart.

7. SetKeyboardState()/GetKeyboardState()

Unlike Win16, the **SetKeyboardState** and **GetKeyboardState** are relevant only to your thread. These APIs will not affect or reflect the state of other threads. Therefore, you will want to make sure that your thread is currently receiving input before calling these APIs in order to get immediate results. If your thread is not currently receiving input, the information returned may be different than what the user is experiencing. The solution to this dilemma is to first get the current thread ID, and then **AttachThreadInput** to it to sync up the keyboard state. This will make sure that **GetSetKeyboardState** and **SetKeyboardState** act as expected.

6. Journal Playback

When you install a journal playback hook, Win32 automatically does an **AttachThreadInput** on all threads when the hook is set. This causes the keyboard state for all threads to synchronize to the state of the thread that is setting the hook. This can be *very nasty* if your keyboard is not in a normal state, such as when the keys have been "pressed" with a **SetKeyboardState** API call. The workaround is to call **GetKeyboardState** before and **SetKeyboardState** after the hook to ensure the state of the keyboard remains in its original, upright position.

5. SetActiveWindow()

In Win16, **SetActiveWindow** obediently activated any top-level window. This was handy for task-switching programs. Windows NT is a bit different, though, since each program runs with its own sets of threads and processes. To get the Win16 **SetActiveWindow** functionality, use **SetForegroundWindow()** under Win32.

4. EM_SETSEL Don't Scroll No More

Edit controls have been around ever since Windows was created, and many programs take advantage of every nook and cranny they can get to when programming. Unfortunately, a very common programming practice in Win16 does not translate to Win32. In Win16, the EM_SETSEL message used *wParam* to indicate if the selection should be scrolled into view, as shown here:

```
SendMessage (hEdit,EM_SETSEL,fScroll,MAKELPARAM (nStart, nEnd));
```

However, since this method limits the *nStart* and *nEnd* parameters to 16 bits, Win32 had to use *wParam* for *nStart* and *lParam* for *nEnd*. Unfortunately, this did not leave any room for the *fScroll* parameter. Under Win32, you must send two messages: first, the EM_SETSEL message, and second, the EM_SCROLLCARET message:

```
SendMessage (hEdit,EM_SETSEL,,nStart,nEnd);
SendMessage (hEdit,EM_SCROLLCARET,0,0);
```

3. SendMessage and Deadlock

Microsoft states that in Win32, **SendMessage** is different from Win16. It differs by the fact that one task cannot run in another thread's space. In Win16,

SendMessage is essentially a "call into" the window's procedure function. Therefore, a **SendMessage** to another thread makes the calling thread wait for the receiving thread to service the message, or "run the errand" for it.

As noted on the MSDN article "Multiple Threads in the User Interface," **SendMessages** are processed by a thread when it yields control. It yields control in the following cases: **PeekMessage**, **GetMessage**, **DialogBox**, **DialogBoxIndirect**, **DialogBoxIndrectParam**, **DialogBoxParam**, and **MessageBox**.

(It failed to mention that it will also allow messages in when you click on a menu and you are in the "menu enteridle loop.")

According to the same article, and some others describing synchronization and interprocess communication, deadlock can occur when two threads use **SendMessage** to communicate to each other. The classic example is

- ⋅⁘ Thread A does a **SendMessage** to Thread B.
- ⋅⁘ When responding to the message sent from Thread A, Thread B does a **SendMessage** to Thread A.
- ⋅⁘ The results: Deadlock!

What we may be led to believe is that sending Thread A would be blocked until the **SendMessage** was finished being processed by the receiving Thread B—when the receiving Thread B is "done with the errand." I have found that there is another place where the sending Thread A "yields" control. The sending thread will "yield" control or process a pending **SendMessage** while it is itself waiting on a **SendMessage**. Although Microsoft said it would result in deadlock, there is a little more to the story. While waiting on a "sent" message, the sending thread can "run an errand" for another thread!

Listing 9.1 provides an application that can prove this theory. This application actually tests a few cases (**SendMessage**, **SendNotifyMessage**, **PostMessage** and **PostMessage/Wait for Event**). It confirms that messages sent with **PostMessage**, **SendNotifyMessage**, and **PostAndWait** on synchronization objects will not allow a thread to process a message sent by **SendMessage**. Only a thread waiting on a **SendMessage** will process another message sent by **SendMessage**.

LISTING 9.1 TESTING FOR SENDMESSAGE, SENDNOTIFYMESSAGE, POSTMESSAGE AND
POSTMESSAGE/WAIT FOR EVENT

To test the scenario, start three instances of the application.

❖ By pressing the "Go" button in instance 1, it will be in an "infinite" loop doing a **SendMessage** to instance 2. The loop can only be broken by changing a variable to FALSE—the variable can only be set to FALSE in a response to a message from Instance 3.

❖ Instance 2 won't do anything with the message—outside of being a receiver for the **SendMessage**.

❖ Press the "Go" button in instance 3. This will then **SendMessage** to instance 1. Instance 1 will then process the message, setting the variable to FALSE, and exit the "infinite" loop.

❖ After "Go" was hit in instance 3, instance 1 would be free. **SendMessage** processed another **SendMessage**!

In case there were any doubts I also tried another scenario using the three instances of the application.

❖ By pressing the "Go" button in instance 1, it will do a **SendMessage** to instance 2.

❖ Instance 2 will then Sleep for 20 seconds. Essentially it wouldn't allow the **SendMessage** in instance 1 to continue until instance 2 was finished sleeping—20 seconds later.

❖ Press the "Go" button in instance 3. This will **SendMessage** to instance 1. When instance 1 processed the message, it would beep.

❖ While instance 1 is waiting on the **SendMessage** to instance 2, every time "Go" was hit in instance 3, instance 1 would beep. Again, **SendMessage** processed another **SendMessage**.

Note that **SendMessage** is "smart." It will not allow processing of other sent messages if the destination window handle is invalid.

Using SendNotifyMessage for Some "Real Code"

I have never seen a practical purpose for **SendNotifyMessage**, aside from the bogus (and now nonexistent) deadlock problem. Well, now I have a practical example for **SendNotifyMessage**:

Basically **SendNotifyMessage** behaves like **PostMessage** and **SendMessage**. If you are sending a message to another thread, it behaves like **PostMessage**. The message is placed into the destination thread's queue and the function returns immediately to the sending thread. It behaves in an asynchronous manner. However, if the message is sent intraprocess, within the same thread, it behaves like **SendMessage**. The message is processed immediately. The code execution in the sending routine is stopped, waiting for **SendMessage** to complete. It behaves in a synchronous manner. This is the textbook definition of **SendNotifyMessage**. Why would you want this behavior?

I want a message to be sent to another thread, but I want to wait until the message is completely processed. Because **SendMessage** allows other **SendMessages** to be serviced, I shy away from using them. Instead of using **SendMessage**, I would use **PostMessage** and **WaitOnSingleObject** **(PostAndWait)** for some event to be triggered. This way I could simulate a synchronous "**SendMessage**." There are no problems with this scheme, as long as you send messages to other threads. You do run into problems when the scheme is used in your own thread. The perfect place to make this scenario happen is by putting the sequence of code into a DLL that is used by multiple applications.

The problem is that you may wind up doing a **PostAndWait** in the same task. In this case, you would post a message to yourself, and sit and wait for the event to occur. Your task is suspended, waiting for the event to be set. But wait, you are the one who is supposed to set the event and you're stuck waiting! Since you are waiting for the event, you'll never process the message and set the event. Guess what you have? Deadlock! See Figure 9.2 for a diagram of Bad, Bad, Deadlock Brown, and the solution to fixing this junkyard dog.

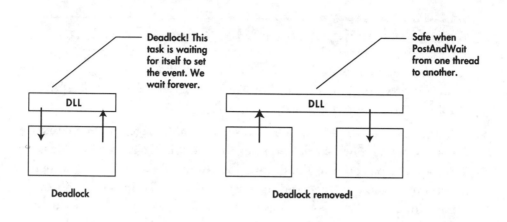

Deadlock! This task is waiting for itself to set the event. We wait forever.

Safe when PostAndWait from one thread to another.

DLL

DLL

Deadlock

Deadlock removed!

FIGURE 9.2 BAD, BAD DEADLOCK BROWN

To avoid the deadlock in Deadlock Brown, you can use **SendNotifyMessage**. Because the behavior of **SendNotifyMessage** within the same task mimics the behavior of **SendMessage**, you will handle the message synchronously. In this case you'd handle the message and set the event. So, once you returned from the **SendNotifyMessage**, the event would be set and you'd be able to continue.

This provides a quick sample of how to use **SendNotifyMessage** to avoid deadlock. This way, the DLL can service any type of request. You will not run into deadlock because of the **Wait** if the **SendNotify** is in the same task.

2. GetWindowWord()

Of course, your friendly neighborhood compiler will remind you that GWW_HINSTANCE no longer exists. Instead, use GWL_HINSTANCE. This same rule applies for all of the GWW_* values. This brings up an interesting point. Say your application stores an integer as some extra bytes in some window class. In Win16, you would use **GetWindowWord** and cast the result to an integer. You may have remembered to change the **GetWindowWord** to a **GetWindowLong**, but also remember to use the size of a Win32 integer when calculating the number of extra bytes required by a window class during registration.

Of course, the smart thing to do is to declare a structure, and then just place a pointer to that structure in the window extra bytes. This saves time when you must access multiple items from a window, since you only have to call **GetWindowLong** once to get the pointer. You can then dereference the pointer to access the individual items. By using the *sizeof* operator when declaring the extra bytes for the Window class, you can ensure that you will always correctly set up the extra bytes in your windows.

1. EXE Resources

All Win32 resources are stored in the EXE resource image in Unicode format If you go marching through resources in a Windows NT EXE, they must be dealt with in Unicode string format.

This is different with Windows 95, however. Since Windows 95 does not support Unicode, but must still support the Win32 EXE format, these resource images are munged on the fly into non-Unicode resource images in memory. Therefore, you will need conditional code in your application if you are the type that picks apart resources by way of the **FindResource/LoadResource/LockResource** method.

CHAPTER 10

Windows 95 Road Signs

Windows 95 is here! Windows 95 is here! This new, fully protected-mode operating system delivers 32 bits, multithreaded preemptive multitasking, seamless network interoperability, a great platform for communications with built-in messaging and mobile communications facilities, incredible reliability, and a new shell that will make end users cheer and die-hard programmers twitch.

Windows 95 sports a markedly new user interface, Plug and Play, long filenames, and many enhancements for us programmers. The most noticeable change is the new and improved user interface. As in OLE 2.0, users running Windows 95 no longer will think of using applications and loading files, but rather, they will think of managing documents. In fact, OLE 2.0 is the backbone of Windows 95. Documents are represented as icons that are part of an integrated manager and desktop. What this means is that a document can be sitting directly on the desktop, or it can be filed away in a folder. Dragging and dropping the objects or double-clicking them have actions associated with them. When users drag around the object, they have the ability to file away a document, or remove it from the file. If the user double-clicks an object, the object may be opened for editing. Essentially, Windows 95 electronically mimics a real desktop and file cabinet.

Of course, this new user interface requires some underlying changes to the way you program. To make these documents/objects appear in folders or on the desktop, Windows 95 implements file viewers. These viewers need a consistent way to gather information about the object. This consistent interface is achieved with the help of compound files and the OLE 2.0 registration database. Compound files, which are part of OLE 2.0, are built into Windows 95.

One of the file viewers that users will see often is the Explorer (see Figure 10.1). It offers a more graphical representation of the user's hard disk, floppy disks, CD-ROM drives, network connections, and the global network than the Windows 3.x File Manager. Incidentally, in Windows 95, these various "storage media" are considered equal. A single, unified namespace allows users to spend their time finding a file, instead of finding out on which storage medium the file is located. Notice how the Desktop root starts with My Computer and Network Neighborhood. Existing network connections are part of My Computer, while the Network tree can expand to all available network connections. This allows the user to freely browse the entire network for a computer from which to snatch files.

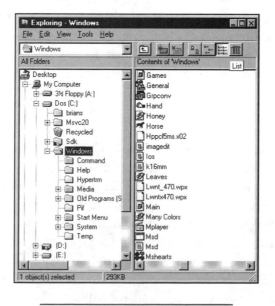

FIGURE 10.1 THE WINDOWS 95 EXPLORER

The new Windows 95 shell consists of the desktop, a "TaskBar" (a type of system toolbar along the edge of the screen that allows quick access to frequently used documents and applications), and folders. These folders contain the document icons, as well as other folder icons (one for each subdirectory of the current directory or folder). In fact, folders are simply mirror images of directories. Other big changes in the user interface include new dialogs and really nice new controls.

What I will do in this list is alert you to what you're in store for on a "marketing perspective." This list will explain what big changes are in store for you on a broader conceptual level. Chapter 11, "Windows 95 User Interface Goodies," explores the nitty-gritty programming details of the new controls.

10. Watch WM_WININICHANGED and Don't Use WIN.INI

Windows 95 is obsessed with OLE 2.0. Dragging files with the mouse can launch applications, print a file, move a file, copy a file, or link a file to where you dropped it. For example, dragging a file with the right mouse button from a folder to the desktop puts up a shortcut menu, where you're offered the choice of moving, copying, or linking the file to the desktop.

All this means that the registration database will become the standard for storing information about your application. Since the registry allows for multiple depth trees, you can set up multiple profiles, each on its own branch (see Figure 10.2). Since Windows 95 is going to be more network-aware, this approach will make it easier to deal with multi-user programs. Make it a habit to use the registration database available in Windows 3.x now to store your information (or private INI files), and stop using WIN.INI. Use the registry APIs. They already exist for both Windows 3.1 and Windows NT. Besides, the WIN.INI file is really meant for Windows, not for your applications. Using your own private INI file or registration database will make it easier to uninstall your software.

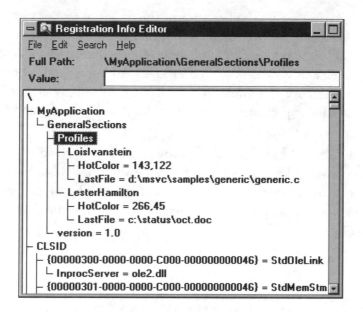

FIGURE 10.2 MULTIPLE DEPTH TREES IN THE REGISTRY FOR MULTIPLE PROFILES

However, you will want to watch the WM_WININICHANGED message very carefully. If you wish to save values from **GetSystemMetrics** for later use to eliminate system calls, reach them in response to WM_WININICHANGED.

9. Use VER.DLL

Actually, this is not unique to Windows 95. It is a universal tip that everyone should be following. Windows 95, just like any other new version of a program, contains plenty of new files. In fact, all the files will be new, since they are now 32-bit. So, you will have a new 32-bit COMDLG32.DLL, a 32-bit SHELL32.DLL, and so on. If your application installer doesn't check versions before installing, you could very easily render Windows 95 unbootable. And since Windows 95 is a new operating system that doesn't rely on MS-DOS, you could make the end user's hard disk unbootable as well.

8. Use Compound Files

Actually, compound files are part of STORAGE.DLL in OLE 2.0. This DLL is the ultimate file DLL, so you should make a switch over to this file-storage medium, even if you are not going to support OLE 2.0. This DLL essentially is a file system within a file. It allows you to create directories of files, except that the entire mess is wrapped up in a separate file. Very cool. And, when Windows 95's shell must get information about a data file, it can look for what's currently termed the "FileSummary" stream inside the data file to get information about the author, the icon to display, the file type, or a thumbnail. By moving to this system today, you will save yourself considerable trouble later, as you can just simply add a "FileSummary," for example, to your compound files as easily as you can copy a file to a directory.

Using STORAGE.DLL really has no disadvantages, except that you may find a small speed hit for file I/O, and your files may get fragmented. (However, this fragmentation is transparent to your application.). In fact, STORAGE.DLL actually uses memory as a temporary buffer, which means that writing little chunks at a time to a file will be faster than before, since STORAGE.DLL will do only one disk-write once your multiple chunk-writing frenzy is complete.

7. Think 32 Bits and Think About Compatibility

Windows 95 is a 32-bit environment. It is also a new version of Windows. Therefore, applications that peek directly into USER's DS will Hindenburg when you run them in Windows 95.

One easy way to make sure your application will run in Windows 95 is to port it to Windows NT. Once your code runs under Windows NT, you will be able to migrate it very easily to Windows 95. This is because porting an application to run under Windows NT removes your calls to undocumented features, removes funky memory addressing, and also ensures that you use the *en vogue* APIs such as **MoveToEx**.

When it comes to compatibility, think about some of the sleazy things you may have done in Windows 3.1. How about looking for windows with the class name "#32762" (icon titles). Well, you are not going to find any windows like that in Windows 95, or worse, they may be different types of windows.

Finally, be sure that you check versions correctly inside your application (as well as using VER.DLL). Check out the following self-defeating piece of code:

```
winVer = LOWORD (GetVersion());
if (HIGHBYTE(winVer) >= 10 && LOWBYTE(winVer) >= 3)

 .
 .  // run app
 .
else

 .
 .  // make app resist the temptation to run
 .
```

The high byte is checked first and, therefore, Windows 95 will fail, since the *HIGHBYTE* always returns 0. Instead, use code such as the following:

```
winVer = LOWORD(GetVersion());
winVer = (((WORD)(LOBYTE(winVer))) << 8) |
         (WORD)HIBYTE(winVer);
if (winVer >= 0x030A)  // always use a HEX value here

 .
 .  // run app
 .
else

 .
 .  // resist
 .
```

Chapter 8, "Migrating to Win32," discussed *int* versus *WORD*. As mentioned previously in this chapter, moving to Windows 95 is very similar to moving to Windows NT. In fact, if you loosely toss around *WORD*s and *ints*, you will run into the exact same problems. Since Windows 95 compiles for a 32-bit environment, *WORD*s are 16 bits long and *ints* are 32 bits long. Typecasting negative *ints* to *WORD*s (or *ints* less than 32767) will introduce all kinds of bugs with which you must deal. In fact, almost all of the Windows NT porting "beasties" apply when moving to Windows 95.

Keep in mind that if you write structures directly to disk, they will read in differently in Windows 95 (if you recompile your application for "32 bitness").

6. Be Careful About Starting Multiple Instances of an Application at a Time

Consider Homer, who just bought his computer, comes home, fires it up, and sees the Windows Program Manager screen. Homer clicks on that nifty little maximize button and now Program Manager takes up the entire screen. Homer likes that. Homer starts up Write, and starts typing a love letter to Marge. Write is not maximized, so Program Manager is still visible around the edges of Write.

While Homer is trying to compare Marge to a summer's day, he realizes that he needs to run the Calculator application still visible in Program Manager. When Homer clicks on Program Manager, Write is completely hidden by Program Manager. Homer freaks, and double-clicks on the Write icon again, to be greeted by an empty page. Homer shouts "Doh!" and starts retyping his love letter. Repeating this situation a couple more times, Homer gets very mad, calls Microsoft, and tells them that Windows keeps eating his love letters. Of course, it could be worse. Homer could run enough instances of Write that his new machine might actually crash and burn.

This scenario is just going to get worse with Windows 95 if your application doesn't change. Windows 95 makes it very easy to launch an application—the icon can be on the desktop or File Manager or in an Explorer window—and users may end up with a couple dozen copies of TETRIS running on their machines if they are not careful.

Change your applications now to act differently if a second instance is started. If your application is something trite like TETRIS, just bring up the original instance with the following simple code:

```
{
HWND hWnd, hWnd1;
// Find top-level window of prev. inst.
if (hWnd = FindWindow(szAppName, NULL))
  {
   // Find any open dialogs or msg boxes
  if (hWnd1 = GetLastActivePopup(hWnd)) hWnd = hWnd1;
  // Make it visible
  BringWindowToTop(hWnd);
  // restore prev. inst. if necess.
  if (IsIconic(hWnd))
      ShowWindow(hWnd, SW_RESTORE);
  }
return FALSE; // end this 2nd inst.
}
```

However, if your application has data files and is more complex (such as Word for Windows), you should put up a list similar to Figure 10.3 when a second instance of Word is started. This will make sure that the users really know what they are getting into, and perhaps keep the system usage optimal (and let Homer finally get that love letter off to Marge).

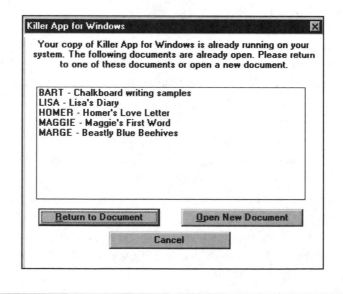

FIGURE 10.3 STARTING A SECOND INSTANCE OF A WINDOWS 95-FRIENDLY APPLICATION

5. Watch Your Stack Size

Fine-tuning your stack is also dangerous. Consider this situation. You have fine-tuned your 16-bit application's DEF file to set the *STACKSIZE* to 8472 bytes, which is exactly enough to work. Now, you run your application on Windows 95, which uses more stack space (after all, GDI is a DLL, which uses your stack). Windows 95's GDI DLL uses more stack than Windows 3.1, and, hence, you end up trashing your "DS," and getting the ultra-informative "Unknown Fault" crash log from Dr. Watson. As an easy rule of thumb, remember to add 2KB to your *STACKSIZE* and *HEAPSIZE* settings to give you that extra headroom.

Of course, in Windows 95, not having a segmented architecture means you can finally have a "DS" that is greater than 64KB, so you can be more liberal when allocating your stack. This will be necessary, since every call in 32-bit land takes the same number of bytes as a *far* call in 16-bit land. You will use more stack space to set up the code frames for each function. Parameters can be fatter, as well. If your ported applications frequently crash under Windows 95, try increasing the stack size before you start pulling out hair follicles.

4. Use Win32 Features Like Threads, Memory-Mapped Files, and Asynchronous I/O

Windows 95 is a 32-bit operating system. Windows no longer can be likened to a fancy paint job on an old MS-DOS Yugo. Because most of the operating system is freshly designed from the ground up, you now have killer features, such as threads, memory-mapped files, and asynchronous I/O.

Threads will allow your application to perform background processing easily, or take a long computation and break it down into a bunch of little tasks. Memory-mapped files will let you allocate a chunk of "memory." This chunk is actually a file. **GlobalRealloc** changes the size of the file, and if you change the contents of the chunk of "memory," you are actually updating the disk file. Imagine, to maintain a simple disk-based flat-file database, all you have to do is declare a memory-mapped file and cast it to an array of records! Asynchronous I/O will allow your applications to more easily cooperate with external data sources.

What can you do now? Work with the Windows NT samples that show these new features. You can get completely up to speed in the multithreaded, memory-mapped, asynchronous, multimodal reflection, sorting algorithm department before you have to start coding your Windows 95 application.

3. Use the New Controls and Dialogs

Windows 95 has many really sassy new controls. I will very briefly overview each one in this list. A much more detailed list explaining the programming implementation of these controls and dialogs appears in Chapter 11.

- ❖ *Slider.* The slider control is essentially a glorified scroll bar, except that the control looks just like a sliding volume control on a stereo. The Windows 3.1 Media Player uses a slider control to indicate the progress of a media file.

- ❖ *Toolbar control.* Now that everyone has finally developed custom toolbar controls, Windows 95 supplies one that is built into the system. This toolbar control will support buttons and other controls (such as a combo box) and it will support ToolTips.

- ❖ *Spin button.* This long-overdue control has the same functionality as MUSCROLL in the Windows 3.1 SDK, except that it is built into Windows 95. The control panel uses spin buttons for the Date Time dialog.

- ❖ *ListView/TreeView.* This is clearly the Mother of All Controls. Imagine a list box merged with an outline. The ListView is a more visual version of a list box (see Figure 10.4). The TreeView allows you to easily display tree structures (such as directories, registration databases, INI files—

or whatever). It automatically handles collapsing or expanding, which takes much of the burden off the programmer and provides a consistent user interface. File Manager, in Windows 3.1, uses a similar control to display directories, and the Explorer view in Windows 95 (see Figure 10.1) shows off the TreeView's capabilities.

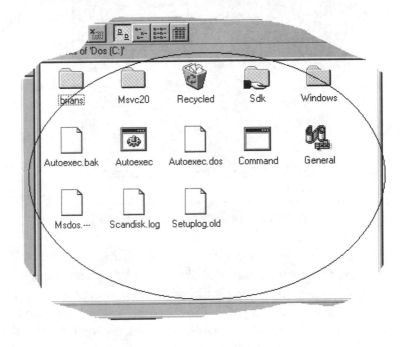

FIGURE 10.4 THE LISTVIEW CONTROL

❖ *Property sheets/tabs.* A property sheet allows for multiple "dialogs" to be displayed in the same client area, with "tabs" for each dialog. When the user clicks on a tab, that "dialog" is brought up to the top. The Desktop Properties Dialog (see Figure 10.5) currently uses an interface just like property sheets in Windows 95.

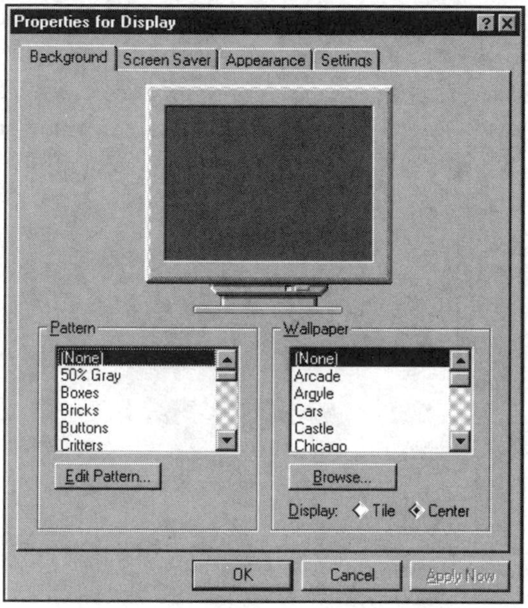

FIGURE 10.5 PROPERTY SHEET FOR THE DESKTOP

- ❖ *Progress meter.* This is a general-purpose control, commonly called a "gas gauge" (even though it looks more like a thermometer). Setup programs use it to let the user know how far along the setup has progressed. Microsoft Excel 5.0 and Word 6.0 use a segmented dashed line in the status bar to give visual feedback during lengthy file I/O.

- ❖ *Rich text edit control.* At last, rich text edit control provides an easy way to allow basic text editing and formatting. This control is discussed completely in Chapter 11.

- ❖ *Status bar.* Again, now that everyone has developed individual status bars, Windows 95 provides one for free. Every good application has a status bar along the bottom of the screen to display helpful information and that "menu help."

- ❖ *Column heading.* The column heading control is a segmented bar that can be placed along the top of a list box or another object. The user can adjust the individual columns by clicking and dragging with the mouse. Microsoft Mail uses a control like this to determine the widths of each column, and all spreadsheets have something similar along the X-axis.

❖ *Hotkey.* This is an edit control that allows the user to type in "hotkey" combinations, such as "<CTRL><F2>". Now, if you want to put up a dialog asking the user which hotkey to assign to a macro, you can just use this control and let it handle the dirty work of translating the keystrokes into human-readable text.

❖ *File Open and Save As.* This dialog looks strikingly different from the one in Windows 3.1 (see Figure 10.6). This new dialog allows much easier access to the network and the user's machine. Explorer-style visuals worked their way into this dialog. If your application is a Win16 application, the old-style Common Dialogs automatically will be used.

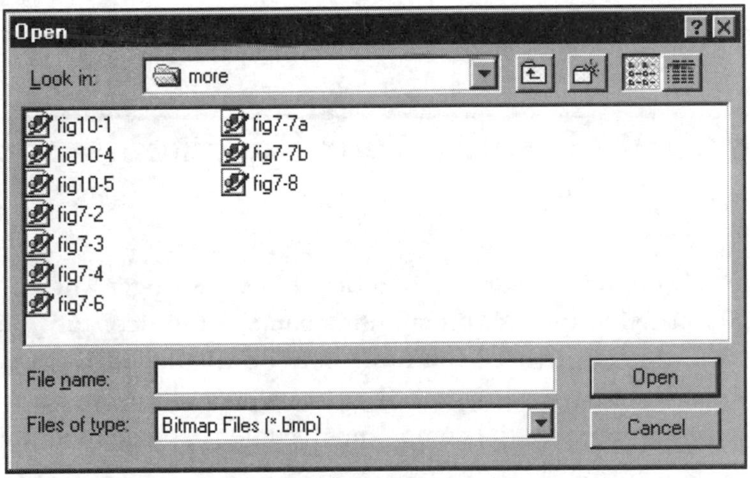

FIGURE 10.6 THE NEW FILE OPEN DIALOG

❖ *Print.* Unlike some of the other Common Dialogs, this dialog is almost identical to that in Windows 3.1. You will get some extra information about the printer to give your users that warm, fuzzy feeling, but as a programmer, if you used the original print Common Dialog, you will be fine in Windows 95.

❖ *Print Setup.* This dialog is a conformist's dream. If your application is Windows 3.1-based, this dialog will look just like the old one. If it's a Windows 95 application, this dialog will replace the Orientation and Paper regions with more information about the printer to set up.

❖ *Page Setup.* Hey, this is a new dialog! It provides a general user interface to set up a page layout. It includes orientation, paper settings, and margins. Now the Print Setup dialog will set up printers, while this dialog will set up print jobs.

❖ *Find Replace.* This feature is almost identical to Windows 3.1. Just play by the rules.

❖ *Fonts.* The only change to this dialog is that a one-line description of the selected font is displayed along the bottom of the dialog (such as, "This is a TrueType font.").

❖ *Color.* This dialog is exactly the same as the Windows 3.1 dialog (at the time this book was written).

2. Correctly Display Your Documents and Files in the Shell

Windows 95 will provide many ways to view a file. No longer will a file simply be MSQRP931.XLS. Instead, the author's name, a full descriptive title, and even a thumbnail of the document may be displayed by the viewer. ("Thumbnail" is advertising jargon for a metafile.) These properties of the file will be stored by using the compound-document storage medium.

What can you do? Be sure that you design a place to store the author's name and a descriptive title (like the way Word asks for the author name, and so on). Also, be sure that you design a way to store a thumbnail (such as a metafile) of your file. If your program is a word processor, be sure that you design a function that can make a quick little preview of the first page.

Be sure to put icons for each of your document types in your application's EXE file, and then register these types in the OLE database (see Listing 10.1). This will ensure that data files are represented with the correct icon in the shell. For example, Word could make a special RTF icon for the RTF files, and a standard Word icon for the native DOC format files. This way, the shell instantly will let the user know the type of file.

LISTING 10.1 OLE REGISTRATION SAMPLE CODE

```
//**********************************************************************
//
// This function will register an Object in the OLE 2 database to
// to associate a default icon with the object's type.
//
// Keep in mind the CLSID is a globally unique identifier (guid)
// that identifies the object to any other component object.
//
// You can generate a guid by either running the GUIDGEN app that
// comes with the OLE2 SDK (requires a netcard) or by requesting
// one from Microsoft.
//
// It is extremeley unsafe, rude, and socially unacceptable to
// use another object's class ID, just as you wouldn't use
// someone else's toothbrush.
//
//**********************************************************************

BOOL RegisterOLEIcon ( LPSTR szCLSIDObject,    // Class ID of the Object
                       LPSTR szObjectName,     // Human Readable Object Name
                       LPSTR szIconPath )      // Path and Index of Icon
                                               // i.e. "E:\\EXCEL\\EXCEL.EXE,2"
{
    HKEY hKey;
    LONG lRes = 0L;

    char lpszCLSID[]       = "CLSID";           // OLE Class ID Section of eg DB
    char lpszDefIcon[]     = "\\DefaultIcon";   // Default Icon Subkey
    char lpBuffer[64];                          // Working buffer

    // Open the reg db for the "CLSID" key, this top-level key
    // is where OLE2 and other OLE aware apps will look for
    // this information.

    lRes = RegOpenKey(HKEY_CLASSES_ROOT, lpszCLSID, &hKey);

    if (ERROR_SUCCESS != lRes)
```

```
      {
      OutputDebugString("RegOpenKey failed.\r\n");
      return FALSE;
      }

   // Register the Object

   // Set the value of the CLSID Entry to the Human Readable
   // name of the Object

   lRes = RegSetValue( hKey,
                       szCLSIDObject,
                       REG_SZ,
                       szObjectName,

                       lstrlen(szObjectName)
                     );

   if (ERROR_SUCCESS != lRes)  // bail on failure
      {
      RegCloseKey(hKey);
      return FALSE;
      }

   // Build "defaulticon" subkey string  "{ <class id> }\\DefaultIcon"
   lstrcpy (lpBuffer, szCLSIDObject);
   lstrcat (lpBuffer, lpszDefIcon);

   // Set Object's default icon entry to point to the
   // default icon for the object

   lRes = RegSetValue( hKey,
                       lpBuffer,
                       REG_SZ,
                       szIconPath,
                       lstrlen(szIconPath)
                     );

   if (ERROR_SUCCESS != lRes)  // bail on failure
      {
      RegCloseKey(hKey);
      return FALSE;
      }

   // Close the reg db
```

```
    RegCloseKey(hKey);

    return TRUE;
}


//***********************************************************************
//
// This is a little stub-o-code to demo the above function
//
//***********************************************************************

BOOL RegisterOLEIcons ( void )
{
    // This is a globally unique identifier (guid) for the FOO Object

    char lpszFooCLSID[]    = "{XXXXXXXXXX}";
    char lpszFooName[]     = "My Application's Foo Object";
    char lpszFooIconPath[] = "c:\\myapp\\myapp.exe, 0";

    // This is a globally unique identifier (guid) for the BAR Object

    char lpszBarCLSID[]    = "{YYYYYYYYYY}";
    char lpszBarName[]     = "My Application's Bar Object";
    char lpszBarIconPath[] = "c:\\myapp\\myapp.exe, 1";

    if (!RegisterOLEIcon ( lpszFooCLSID, lpszFooName, lpszFooIconPath ))
      OutputDebugString ( "Foo Object Failed to Register.\r\n" );

    if (!RegisterOLEIcon ( lpszBarCLSID, lpszBarName, lpszBarIconPath ))
      OutputDebugString ( "Bar Object Failed to Register.\r\n" );
}
```

Add data-specific commands (or "verbs," as they're called in OLE) to the OLE database for each of the document types. For example, if you add Play for sound files, the shell automatically will pick up on this and add these verbs to its own shortcut menus. The user can then select Play with the right mouse button, and, with one little twitch of the finger, can hear his or her favorite Ren and Stimpy wave file.

Your document windows should be reconfigured to display the filename and then the application name. In the old days of Windows 3.1, Paintbrush might say something like, "Paintbrush—DEDBARNY.BMP." For Windows 95, it should now say, "DEDBARNY.BMP—Paintbrush." The main reason for this is long filenames (see the following tip). If the filename is extremely long, it gets first chance to use up the space in the caption bar.

Use 16 x 16 icons, as well as the standard 32 x 32 icons, in your application. That way, shells such as the Explorer have a pretty icon to use in their small icons views. (If you don't have a 16 x 16 icon, the mighty StretchBlt will generate one for you.) Use RegisterClassEx to indicate the 16 x 16 icon for the caption.

1. Support the New File System: Think Networks

This is the most important tip of all. You can ignore all the previous tips in this chapter and chances are still fair that your application will not crash. However, ignoring this tip is a surefire recipe for a warp-core breach.

Windows 95 supports long filenames—254 characters long, to be exact. This filename is the fully qualified length, however, so you don't have to worry about a 200-character directory plus a 200-character filename. The main difference is that the filename can be longer than the 8.3 limitation. Be sure to display the filename in the title bar. Now that users can name their files with a filename long enough to forget, it is polite to make it easy for them to see how they are saving this data. The Common Dialogs are automatically designed to handle these new filenames.

Windows 95 is even more network-aware. With Windows 95, you are able to peruse freely around other people's machines and load files, without having to go through the "hoo-hah" of connecting to a drive on their machines. For example, it will be very easy to open a file called \\Ericm\Cartoons\WB\ Marvin.Martian, edit it, drop it on your desktop, and never have to worry about what drive letter is associated with \\Ericm\Cartoons\WB. This new feature is called "direct network browsing," and your applications should get used to it.

CHAPTER 11

Windows 95
User Interface Goodies

As a responsible programmer, one of the worst things you can do is spend hours or months of your life writing code for a control that Windows supplies for free. Windows 95 provides a new set of controls and tools that *really* make our lives much simpler. These controls range from RichEdit controls to software sprites. These goodies are not ordered in Coolness Factors, instead they are ordered more in a progressive fashion; you should read about goodie #10 before you read about goodie #9, and so on. I will assume that you are getting more and more comfortable by the minute as you read this list, so I will start making more assumptions about your knowledge of the "Goodie Basics" as the list progresses.

Since this chapter is so long, let's summarize the ten goodies at the top of this list:

10. Image List: This is a graphics tool that manages images for your drawing pleasure, and for some of the other goodies' pleasure. You can also use the ImageList to simulate sprites.

9. TreeView: This is a heirarchical listbox, like the left hand side of the Explorer in Windows 95.

8. RichEdit Control: This is an edit control on steroids.

7. ToolBar: You know what this is.

6. Status Bar: You also know what this is.

5. Property Sheet: This is the official name for a Tabbed Dialog.

4. Header: This is a column bar, like the row or column settings bar in spreadsheet programs.

3. ListView: This is a powerful listbox that has many views. The right hand side of the 3. Explorer uses a ListView.

2. HotKey: This is a trick little "edit control" that accepts virtual keys, such as the Control key. It would display <Ctrl> in it instead. Handy for keyboard configuration dialogs.

1. Up/Down (Spinner): This is an edit/static control that has little arrows next to it for the user to adjust with the mouse.

Goodie Basics

Set Yer Compiler Right

Before you do anything, there is something very important you must do when creating your project: Set the version. By default, Visual C++ 2.0 creates EXE images that are not marked as Windows 95 (Version 4.0). In order for the Windows 95 goodies below to work, you must mark your application as

Windows 95. To do this, select **Project... Settings** from VC++ 2.0, and choose the "Link" tab. For each target, select that target only (selecting multiple targets won't work), choose "General" in the combobox, and then modify the link line in the edit control at the bottom so that the SUBSYSTEM directive indicates Windows version 4.0. See Figure 11.1 for what you want this link line to look like.

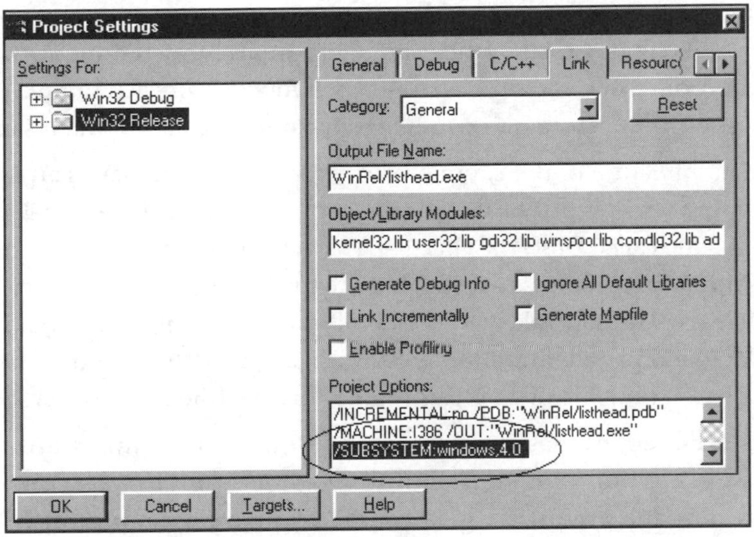

FIGURE 11.1 SETTING THE VERSION TO 4.0 IN VISUAL C++ 2.0

The Common Controls DLL

The COMCTL32.DLL file that comes with Windows 95 contains all of the code to implement the Image List and TreeView, and a lot more controls. (I used Visual C++ 2.0 along with the tools that come with the Windows 95 SDK to build all the sample code shown here.) Extra flavors of this DLL will be made available in Win32s and Win32 on Windows NT versions so that an application can run on all three platforms (Windows 95, Windows 3.1 using Win32s, and Windows NT) and take advantage of these nifty Windows doodads.

These extra flavors of the DLL should be available once the final Windows 95 product ships. To use either an Image List or TreeView, you must include COMMCTRL.H and link with the COMCTL32.LIB file.

The Microsoft Sample Framework

The Windows 95 SDK comes with a new set of sample programs not seen before. Unlike the past, all of the sample programs in the Framework follow a consistent coding style and architecture. Each function of each sample program is given its own file; these files can be easily interchanged between samples.

The architecture of the sample programs basically simulates an MFC program using straight C. All of the sample programs that are standard Windows apps have a file called DISPATCH.C that acts as the message router. Each window in the sample programs have a MSD structure: these structures act like the MFC Message Maps. Look at the GEN32 sample program included in the Framework, and pay attention to DISPATCH.C, GENERIC.C, and GLOBALS.H to get a really good feel of how this Framework Architecture works.

This architecture has its pluses and minuses. The pluses are that the code is very easy to "plug and chug" into other samples. Also, since each windows message eventually gets routed to its own unique function, the resulting programs can very easily be moved to MFC with just a little help from ClassWizard. Therefore, the Sample Framework is valuable to both straight C programmers and MFC programmers.

The disadvantage to the Framework's architecture is that it was designed to be an easy to read sample architecture; not an application development platform. The **DispMessage** function in DISPATCH.C uses a linear search loop to handle every message a window receives. In contrast, MFC uses a sophisticated hash table. As a result, message processing is less efficient in the Framework than in MFC. If you plan on using the Framework as the basis for developing your own Killer App, rewrite the **DispMessage** function to be more efficient (hint: write a hash table function, or consider sorting the MSD array so you can use a binary search).

Okay, enough prerequisites, let's check out some goodies!

10. Image Lists

An Image List is just another drawing tool, just as fonts, pens, brushes, bitmaps, regions, and palettes are today. Image Lists are essentially bitmap managers with some very sassy APIs. I like to think of an Image List as a roll of film. Each exposure on the roll of film is an image and the entire roll of film is called an Image List. Just as your typical roll of film has exposures numbered from 1 to 24, an Image List has images numbered from 0 to n–1, n being the number of images you specify (see Figure 11.2). And, as with a roll of film, each image is the same size. Certain Windows 95 controls (such as the Tree View) use this roll of film to automatically draw the images besides their items—you no longer need to implement all that owner-draw code for a control to get your graphics displayed in the list. The TreeView section of this list will explain how this is done.

FIGURE 11.2 AN IMAGE LIST AS A ROLL OF FILM

The internal means of storage used by the Image List is a bitmap. Therefore, each of your images is simply a portion of a bitmap. This bitmap can have a maximum size of 32K pixels by 32K pixels. Therefore, the maximum number of images supportable by one Image List is 32K, each image being only one pixel wide (and up to 32K pixels high). To figure out the maximum number of images your Image List can support, simply divide 32K by the width of one image. The maximum height of an image is always 32K pixels, since the Image List always stores the individual images in one row just like a roll of film does—a long strip of images.

There are two fundamental flavors of Image Lists: masked and unmasked. A masked Image List draws the image exactly like an icon is drawn today: you have two images, the real image and the mask. The mask defines transparent pixels in your image so that when your image is drawn on a DC, the background shines through (think of it as a photographic slide that you project onto the DC). The unmasked Image List just splats the entire image down like a **BitBlt(... SRCCOPY)**, obliterating all the pixels underneath it (sort of like a photographic print that you paste on top of the DC). For almost all Image Lists, expect to use the masked version.

Now since the Image List is a software object and a roll of film is not (at least not yet for most of us), there are some extra bonus features that you get with the Image List that you don't get with a roll of film, the most important being that an Image List does not have a fixed number of images. An Image List is a practically endless roll of film that grows if you add more images to it. Also, the images in an Image List can be changed whenever you want, and you can even delete or insert images. Plus, so you can pretend to be George Lucas, the Image List lets you do some special effects with the images, such as dithering.

Some of the new Windows 95 controls use Image Lists automatically: You simply provide a handle to the Image List to the control and let the control do the rest. A cornucopia of APIs for the Image List are available so that you can also use them easily in your own custom controls and applications. I will cover these APIs in varying amounts of detail here.

Creating an Image List

Before you create your Image List, as with any GDI object, you need to figure out exactly what you want. If you're going to buy a roll of film, you need to decide how many exposures (size of the Image List), what type of picture you want (prints or slides), and what format film you want to use (35mm, 6 x 7, 4 x 5, and so on). So, getting back into SDK mode, let's look at the first API, ImageList_Create:

```
HIMAGELIST ImageListCreate(int   cx,       // width of one image
                           int   cy,       // height of one image
                           BOOL  fMask,    // Masked or Unmasked
                           int   cInitial, // Number of images
                           int   cGrow );  // Growth factor
```

The **cx** and **cy** parameters specify the size of one image in the list. The **fMask** parameter specifies whether you want prints (FALSE) or slides (TRUE). The **cInitial** specifies the number of exposures in your roll of film, and the cGrow specifies the number of extra exposures to tack onto the end of the roll of film at one time if you need to add more exposures. Let's look at an example. If you specify 24 for **cInitial** and 4 for **cGrow**, when you try to add a 25th image to the Image List, your Image List will grow in size from 24 images to 28 images. Why not grow the Image List by one? Enlarging the Image List is an expensive operation on the CPUCCE (that's the CPU cycle commodity exchange). Growing an Image List involves creating new bitmaps, internal data structures, copying old data onto the new data, and freeing the old data.

If you plan on having an Image List that changes frequently, use a larger value for **cGrow** to minimize the number of times the Image List is actually grown. If you plan to have a fairly static Image List, use a smaller value for **cGrow**; this will conserve memory. The return value from this function is of type HIMAGELIST, which is how you will reference the entire Image List.

Once you have created the Image List, it is time to add images to it. There are three basic ways to add an individual image to the Image List. If you hand the Image List an icon, it will make a copy of the pixels in the icon and add them as an image. Or you can pass the Image List a pair of device-dependent bitmaps (possibly generated using **LoadBitmap**); the first bitmap is the actual image, and the second bitmap is the mask of the image (unless of course your Image List is not masked). Finally, you can give the Image List a single bitmap and specify that a certain color pixel should be considered the transparent pixel. For masked Image Lists, you would almost always use the last method, unless you have no unused colors that you can specify to be the magic transparent color. In that case, you'd have to build your mask bitmap and use the first method described to add the image (the API is called **ImageList_Add**).

Let's look at the three core APIs for adding images to the Image List (see Figure 11.3). All of these APIs will add images to the end of your Image Lists, and return the image number (exposure). The handle to the Image List and the image number are the two key pieces of information that Image List-enabled Windows 95 controls (or your custom controls) require.

```
int ImageList_Add (        HIMAGELIST  himl,        // Handle to the Image List
                           HBITMAP     hbmImage,    // Handle of bitmap
                           HBITMAP     hbmMask );   // Handle of Mask bitmap
                                                    // (NULL if not masked)

int ImageList_AddMasked (  HIMAGELIST  himl,        // Handle to the Image List
                           HBITMAP     hbmImage,    // Handle of bitmap
                           COLORREF    crMask );    // Color of "Transparent" Pixel

int ImageList_AddIcon (    HIMAGELIST  himl,        // Handle to the Image List
                           HICON       hicon);      // Handle of icon
```

FIGURE 11.3 API's FOR ADDING IMAGES

These functions copy the bitmap pixels into the private data structure of the Image List. Therefore, you need to do your own housekeeping: if you do not delete the **hbmImage** and **hbmMask** bitmaps at some point after adding them to the Image List, your system resources will drop faster than that first gut-wrenching plunge of the Coney Island Cyclone roller coaster.

One API allows you to do a wham-bam-slam initialization of an Image List (see Figure 11.4). **ImageList_LoadImage** requires you to create a little filmstrip of images using Windows Paintbrush (or some other bitmap editing facility), and then store this bitmap in your resource file. You can then use the **ImageList_LoadImage** API to load that bitmap, and let the API divvy up the filmstrip into individual frames and create the entire Image List for you. If you want to dynamically assemble Image Lists, then you need to use the above bunch of APIs.

```
HIMAGELIST ImageList_LoadImage(  HINSTANCE  hi,        // Instance handle to load bitmap
                                 LPSCTR     lpBmp,     // Points to the resource identifier
                                 int        cx,        // Width of one image
                                 int        cGrow,     // Growth factor
                                 COLORREF   crMask     // Color of "Transparent"
                                                       // pixel
                                 UINT       uType,     // Type of image we are loading
                                                       // (currently IMAGE_BITMAP)
                                 UINT       uFlags);   // Leave at 0
```

FIGURE 11.4 IMAGELIST_LOADBITMAP

Maintaining the Image List

Of course, there are some handy APIs to allow you to modify and delete the images in the Image List. All of them are self-explanatory (see Figure 11.5).

```
BOOL    ImageList_Remove(      HIMAGELIST    himl,      // Handle to the Image List
                               int           i );       // Image Number


BOOL    ImageList_Replace (    HIMAGELIST    himl,      // Handle to the Image List
                               int           i,         // Image Number to replace
                               HBITMAP       hbmImage,  // Handle of bitmap
                               HBITMAP       hbmMask ); // Handle of Mask bitmap


int     ImageList_ReplaceIcon( HIMAGELIST    himl,      // Handle to the Image List
                               int           i,         // Image number to replace
                               HICON         hicon);    // Handle of new icon
```

FIGURE 11.5 API's FOR MODIFYING AND DELETING IMAGES

Of course, just to make things fun, **ImageList_Replace** returns TRUE or FALSE, depending on success or failure, while the **ImageList_ReplaceIcon** returns the index or –1, depending on success or failure. And just as with the Add family of functions, you need to delete the **hbmImage** and **hbmMask** bitmaps after you have called these APIs to avoid leaking memory.

If you call **ImageList_Remove**, all of the images beyond the image you just removed will shift down by one. It's just as if you deleted an item from an array. Therefore, if you have the image numbers stored away in some control (such as the TreeView), you really don't want to call this function unless you are willing to update all of the items in the control(s) using this Image List.

After you have had all your fun with your Image List, use the **Image-List_Destroy** API to clean up your Image List and free up any chunks of memory associated with the Image List. Its only parameter is the handle to the Image List:

```
BOOL    ImageList_Destroy(HIMAGELIST   himl);  // Handle to the Image List
```

You can also find out just about anything you want to know about the actual images in the Image List. These APIs allow you to count the number of images in the list, determine the size of an image, determine the size of the icon inside the Image List, or get detailed information about the bitmap representation of an image inside the Image List (see Figure 11.6).

```
int     ImageList_GetImageCount(  HIMAGELIST       himl);         // Handle to the Image List

BOOL    ImageList_GetImageRect(   HIMAGELIST       himl,          // Handle to the Image List
                                  int              i,             // Image Number
                                  RECT FAR*        prcImage);     // Points to RECT
                                                                  // receiving info


BOOL    ImageList_GetIconSize(    IMAGELIST        himl,          // Handle to the Image List
                                  int FAR *        cx,            // points to cx receiving info
                                  int FAR *        cy);           // points to cy receiving info

BOOL    ImageList_GetImageInfo(   HIMAGELIST       himl,          // Handle to the Image List
                                  int              i,             // Image number
                                  IMAGEINFO FAR*   pImageInfo);   // Pointer to
                                                                  // IMAGEINFO
```

FIGURE 11.6 API's FOR GETTING IMAGE INFORMATION

The first three functions in Figure 11.6 are straightforward. The last one, **ImageList_GetImageInfo**, lets you get very detailed information about the actual bitmap used when the image is drawn. The IMAGEINFO structure contains this information, most of which is standard bitmap nomenclature (see Figure 11.7).

```
typedef struct _IMAGEINFO {
    HBITMAP  hbmImage;        // bitmap containing the images
    HBITMAP  hbmMask;         // mono bitmap containing the mask (if applicable)
    int      cPlanes;         // number of color planes in hbmImage
    int      cBitsPerPixel;   // bits per pixel in hbmImage
    RECT rcImage;             // Bounding rectangle of the image in the Image List bitmap
} IMAGEINFO;
```

FIGURE 11.7 THE **IMAGEINFO** STRUCTURE

There is also a way to actually create an icon based on the image inside an Image List. **ImageList_ExtractIcon** will create a new icon and fill it in for you.

```
HICON    ImageList_ExtractIcon(HINSTANCE  hAppInst, // Instance of app to own icon
                               HIMAGELIST himl,     // Handle to Image List
                               int        i);       // Image number
```

This is a great way to manufacture icons in a hurry (I expect to see some really sizzling icon editors show up after Windows 95 ships). One thing to remember: the icons you get are brand new icons—they are not connected in any way to the image inside the Image List.

Special Effects

The two types of special effects provided by the Image List are merging and dithering (see Figure 11.8). Merging Image Lists is like the Hollywood blue-screen matte special effect: the second image is drawn over the first image using the second image's mask, and a handle to a brand-new third Image List is returned. For example, the first Image List could have a star field, and the second list could have the Death Star. Merge the two together, and you have the Death Star floating in space. Cool.

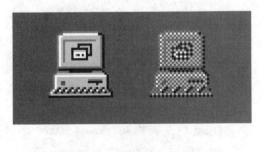

FIGURE 11.8 MERGING AND DITHERING

Dithering Image Lists involves taking an image from a source Image List, running it through a GDI blender, and then placing the dithered image in the destination Image List.

271

ImageList_Merge simply copies the image from a source Image List and places it the destination Image List for you. Three APIs are provided just to make it easier to shuffle around images (see Figure 11.9). You need the x and y offsets in these functions because the source and destination images may be of a different size. For example, the star field from above could be 100 by 100 pixels, while the Death Star may only be 40 pixels by 40 pixels. The x and y offsets can be used to correctly place the Death Star in the most threatening position on the star field.

```
HIMAGELIST   ImageList_Merge(          HIMAGELIST    himl1,     // Handle of first (background)
                                                                // Image List
                                       int           i1,        // Image number of first image
                                                                // to merge
                                       HIMAGELIST    himl2,     // Handle of second (foreground)
                                                                // Image List
                                       int           i2,        // Image number of first second
                                                                // image to merge.
                                       int           dx,        // x offset of second image
                                       int           dy);       // y offset of second image


void         ImageList_CopyDitherImage( HIMAGELIST   himlDst,   // Handle of Destination
                                        WORD         iDst,      // Image # in destination
                                        int          xDst,      // x Offset in destination
                                        int          yDst,      // y Offset in destination
                                        HIMAGELIST   himlSrc,   // Handle of source
                                        int          iSrc);     // Image # in source


int          ImageList_AddFromImageList( HIMAGELIST  himlDest,  // Handle of
                                                                // destination
                                         HIMAGELIST  himlSrc,   // Handle of
                                                                // Source
                                         int         iSrc);     // Image #
                                                                // of source
```

FIGURE 11.9 API'S FOR MOVING IMAGES

Using Image Lists in Custom Controls

If you plan on writing a custom control, or just want to use the Image List as an easy way to manage a group of bitmaps, then you will be very interested in the APIs supplied for drawing images from the Image List. There are also some helper functions for transparent drawing on backgrounds.

Before I get into how to draw an image, let's take a quick peek at how background colors are utilized by the Image List. For masked images, the background color can be set to a defined color (an RGB value) or you can choose to have no background color (the constant CLR_NONE). No background color means the image is to be drawn on top of the existing device context, leaving the pixels under the image's transparent pixels intact. You would want to use no background color if you were going to draw an image on a complex background, such as a bitmap. If you are going to draw a masked image on a solid background, it is cool to set the background color; this means better performance. Use these functions for setting/getting the background color of an Image List:

```
COLORREF    ImageList_SetBkColor(HIMAGELIST  himl,    // Handle to Image List
                                 COLORREF     clrBk);  // New background color
                                                       // or CLR_NONE (default)
COLORREF    ImageList_GetBkColor(HIMAGELIST  himl);    // Handle to Image List
```

To draw an image from the Image List, use the **ImageList_Draw** API.

```
BOOL    ImageList_Draw(HIMAGELIST  himl,     // Handle of Image List to draw from
                       int         i,        // Image number to draw
                       HDC         hdcDst,   // Device context to draw to
                       int         x,        // x position on device context
                       int         y,        // y position on device context
                       UINT        fStyle);  // ILD_* flags (see above)
```

This API requires that you specify the Image List, the image number, a device context, a location on the device context, and some flags to indicate how to draw the image. These flags let you apply some extra attributes to the image you are about to draw. One of the interesting flags is ILD_OVERLAY-MASK. This tells the **ImageList_Draw** API to first draw the image you asked it to, and then draw another masked image on top of it (see Figure 11.10). It's going to do the same thing as merging the two images, except the images are merged only at draw time, leaving the actual images inside the Image List intact. Of course, some restrictions do apply. You can't use just any image from your Image List as the overlay image; you have to specify which image to use in advance using the **ImageList_SetOverlayImage** API which I'll discuss in a moment. You can specify up to four images from your Image List to be used as overlay images (so you could use the Death Star, a TIE fighter, an X-Wing, and a Sneaker for the overlay images, and then all sorts of space backdrops for the regular images). You put both the overlay images and the backdrop images in the same Image List; you just need to tag certain images as overlay masks. Do this, with the **ImageList_SetOverlayImage** API:

```
BOOL ImageList_SetOverlayImage(HIMAGELIST   himl,        // Handle to Image List
                               int          iImage,      // Image to set as an overlay
                               int          iOverlay);   // The mask # (0, 1, 2 or 3)
```

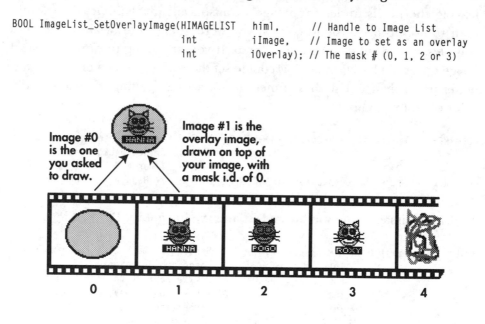

FIGURE 11.10 DRAWING AND OVERLAYING IMAGES

The **iOverlay** parameter is the most important, as it's the number you will use in COMMCTRL.H's INDEXTOOVERLAYMASK macro when you actually draw the image. Figure 11.11 shows the flags for drawing images.

ILD_NORMAL Draw the image using the background color for the image list. If the background color is CLR_NONE the image is drawn transparently using the mask.

ILD_TRANSPARENT	Draws the image transparently using the mask, regardless of the background color. This flag has no effect if the image list does not contain a mask.
ILD_SELECTED	Draws the image dithered with the system highlight color to indicate that it is selected. This flag has no effect if the image list does not contain a mask.
ILD_FOCUS	Draws the image striped with the system highlight color to indicate that it has the focus. This flag has no effect if ILD_SELECTED is not also specified or the image list does not contain a mask.
ILD_OVERLAYMASK	Draws the image and overlays it with an overlay mask. The index of the overlay mask must be combined with the ILD_OVERLAYMASK style. Also, the index must be specified by using the INDEXTOOVERLAYMASK macro.

FIGURE 11.11 IMAGE DRAWING FLAGS

As you can see, the **ImageList_Draw** API is extremely powerful and flexible. You can not only maintain images for controls, it's also a handy way to manage bitmap drawing. You can now quit doing the CreateCompatibleDC/SelectObject/BitBlt /SelectObject/DeleteDC rigmarole, and enjoy the painless functionality of the Image List.

Image List Drag-and-Drop Melancholy

As mentioned, the Image List provides the graphical grunt work for implementing drag-and-drop. Your application is still responsible for the implementation of the drag-and-drop (that is, it needs to do something once the user has dropped the object), but the Image List will handle the GUI work of moving a little graphic around the screen until the user lets go of the mouse button.

The Image List will create a fake cursor out of an indicated image, and move it around the screen until your program instructs it to stop.

There are three steps your program must take to let the Image List handle the GUI part of drag and drop.

✢ Start the drag (on WM_XBUTTONDOWN).

✢ Move the drag/drop image (on WM_MOUSEMOVE).

✢ End the drag (on WM_XBUTTONUP).

Listing 11.1 is a code fragment that shows how you'd implement these three steps in your WinProc.

For the first step, you erase the mouse cursor (since the Image List's fake cursor will be used instead of the real mouse cursor), set mouse capture (so you are guaranteed to get the WM_XBUTTONUP), call the **ImageList_SetDragCursorImage API**, and then call the ImageList_StartDrag API.

LISTING 11.1 IMAGE LIST DRAG AND DROP CODE

```
case WM_LBUTTONDOWN:

  // Get the mouse position
  pt.x      = LOWORD (lParam);
  pt.y      = HIWORD (lParam);


  // Figure the hit test region of the 32x32 image
  rc.left   = iXPos;
  rc.top    = iYPos;
  rc.right  = rc.left + 32;
  rc.bottom = rc.top + 32;


  // Figure out where in the region the user clicked,
  // and figure the hotspot offset
  dxHotspot = pt.x - iXPos;
  dyHotspot = pt.y - iYPos;


  // If the hittest passes...
  if ( hImageList && PtInRect ( &rc, pt ))
    {
    // Set drag flag
```

```
                bDragging = TRUE;

                // Hide the cursor
                ShowCursor ( FALSE );

                // Capture the mouse
                SetCapture ( hWnd );

                // Set up the drag image and the hotspot
                ImageList_SetDragCursorImage(hImageList, 0, dxHotspot, dyHotspot);

                // Call the ImageList API to start the drag process
                ImageList_StartDrag ( hImageList,   // Handle to Image list
                                      hWnd,          // hWnd of this client
                                      0,             // Image #0
                                      iXPos,         // Position of image
                                      iYPos,         // Position of image
                                      0,             // Hotspot offset
                                      0);            // Hotspot offset
            }
        break;

    case WM_MOUSEMOVE:

        if ( bDragging )
          {
          // Call the ImageList API to automatically move the image around
          ImageList_DragMove ( LOWORD (lParam),
                               HIWORD (lParam)
                             );
          }
        break;

    case WM_LBUTTONUP:

        if ( bDragging )
          {
          // Tell the ImageList to stop dragging and erase the "fake" cursor
          ImageList_EndDrag ();
          // Release mouse capture
          ReleaseCapture ();
          // Bring back the real cursor
          ShowCursor ( TRUE );
          // Calculate the image's new position
          iXPos = LOWORD (lParam) - dxHotspot;
          iYPos = HIWORD (lParam) - dyHotspot;
```

LISTING 11.1 CONTINUED

```
    // Force a repaint
    InvalidateRect ( hWnd, NULL, TRUE );
    // Clear the drag flag
    bDragging = FALSE;
    }
  break;
```

For the second step, call **ImageList_DragMove** to move the drag/drop image cursor wannabe on the screen.

And finally, for the third step, call the **ImageList_EndDrag** API to let the Image List know you are finished with it and erase the fake cursor. You also want to release capture, show the real mouse cursor again, and also take some action in response to whatever your program is supposed to do when the user drops the Death Star on top of the Borg cube.

The Image List has some extra goodies to make it really easy to do some drag-and-drop dinking around. Just to be different, let's first look at the functions involved in making this happen (see Figure 11.12).

```
BOOL       ImageList_StartDrag( HIMAGELIST  himl,       // Image list to use image from
                                HWND        hwndLock,   // Handle to draw image on.
                                                        // Use NULL for anywhere on
                                                        // the screen.
                                int         i,          // Image number to use
                                int         x,          // Where to draw (usually the
                                int         y,          // cursor position
                                int         dxHotspot,  // Hotspot (usually the same as the
                                int         dyHotspot); // cursor position)
BOOL       ImageList_DragMove(  int         x,          // Where to draw
                                int y);                 // (usually the cursor position)

HIMAGELIST ImageList_EndDrag(   VOID);                  // Do this when done
```

FIGURE 11.12 IMAGE LIST DRAG AND DROP FUNCTIONS

IMAGELST

I have tossed together a tiny little sample program that shows some of the basics of the Image List (see Figures 11.13 and Listing 11.2). The IMAGELST sample program simply creates a tiny Image List and paints an image (a TIE fighter) on the client area. The user can click and drag this TIE fighter around the screen with the mouse. That's it. Let's go.

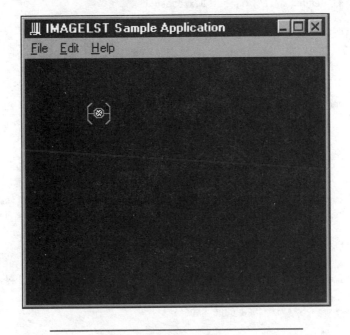

FIGURE 11.13 IMAGELST SAMPLE PROGRAM AT WORK

LISTING 11.2 **IMAGELST** SAMPLE PROGRAM

```
#include <windows.h>          // required for all Windows applications
#if !defined(_WIN32)
#include <ver.h>
#endif
#include "IMAGELST.h"          // specific to this program
```

LISTING 11.2 CONTINUED

```
//********************** NEW CODE START *******

#include "commctrl.h"              // for Image List

//********************** NEW CODE END *******

// Windows NT defines APIENTRY, but 3.x doesn't
#if !defined (APIENTRY)
#define APIENTRY far pascal
#endif

// Windows 3.x uses a FARPROC for dialogs
#if !defined(_WIN32)
#define DLGPROC FARPROC
#endif

HINSTANCE        hInst;                      // current instance
HWND             hWndClient;                 // Handle to Client Window

char szAppName[]        = "IMAGELST";        // The name of this application
char szTitle[]          = "IMAGELST Sample Application"; // The title bar text

//********************** NEW CODE START *******

char szAppNameClient[] = "ImageClient";      // The client window class

//********************** NEW CODE END *******

//
//    FUNCTION: WinMain(HINSTANCE, HINSTANCE, LPSTR, int)
//
//    PURPOSE: calls initialization function, processes message loop
//
//    COMMENTS:
//
//        Windows recognizes this function by name as the initial entry point
//        for the program.  This function calls the application initialization
//        routine, if no other instance of the program is running, and always
//        calls the instance initialization routine.  It then executes a
//        message retrieval and dispatch loop that is the top-level control
//        structure for the remainder of execution.  The loop is terminated
```

```
//      when a WM_QUIT  message is received, at which time this function
//      exits the application instance by returning the value passed by
//      PostQuitMessage().
//
//      If this function must abort before entering the message loop, it
//      returns the conventional value NULL.
//

int APIENTRY WinMain(
            HINSTANCE hInstance,
            HINSTANCE hPrevInstance,
            LPSTR lpCmdLine,
            int nCmdShow
            )
{
   MSG msg;
   HANDLE hAccelTable;

   // Other instances of app running?
   if (!hPrevInstance) {
     // Initialize shared things
     if (!InitApplication(hInstance)) {
        return (FALSE);                 // Exits if unable to initialize
     }
   }

   // Perform initializations that apply to a specific instance
   if (!InitInstance(hInstance, nCmdShow)) {
      return (FALSE);

   }   hAccelTable = LoadAccelerators (hInstance, szAppName);

   // Acquire and dispatch messages until a WM_QUIT message is received.
   while (GetMessage(&msg,    // message structure
                  NULL,    // handle of window receiving the message
                  0,       // lowest message to examine
                  0)){     // highest message to examine
       if (!TranslateAccelerator (msg.hwnd, hAccelTable, &msg)) {
         TranslateMessage(&msg);// Translates virtual key codes
         DispatchMessage(&msg); // Dispatches message to window
       }
   }

   // Returns the value from PostQuitMessage
   return (msg.wParam);
```

LISTING 11.2 CONTINUED

```
    // This will prevent 'unused formal parameter' warnings
    lpCmdLine;
}


//
//    FUNCTION: InitApplication(HINSTANCE)
//
//    PURPOSE: Initializes window data and registers window class
//
//    COMMENTS:
//
//        This function is called at initialization time only if no other
//        instances of the application are running.  This function performs
//        initialization tasks that can be done once for any number of running
//        instances.
//
//        In this case, we initialize a window class by filling out a data
//        structure of type WNDCLASS and calling the Windows RegisterClass()
//        function.  Since all instances of this application use the same
//        window class, we only need to do this when the first instance is
//        initialized.
//


BOOL InitApplication(HINSTANCE hInstance)
{
    WNDCLASS  wc;

    // Fill in window class structure with parameters that describe the
    // main window.
    wc.style         = CS_HREDRAW | CS_VREDRAW; // Class style(s).
    wc.lpfnWndProc   = (WNDPROC)WndProc;        // Window Procedure
    wc.cbClsExtra    = 0;                        // No per-class extra data.
    wc.cbWndExtra    = 0;                        // No per-window extra data.
    wc.hInstance     = hInstance;               // Owner of this class
    wc.hIcon         = LoadIcon (hInstance, szAppName);// Icon name from .RC
    wc.hCursor       = LoadCursor(NULL, IDC_ARROW); // Cursor
    wc.hbrBackground = (HBRUSH)GetStockObject (WHITE_BRUSH);// Default color
    wc.lpszMenuName  = szAppName;               // Menu name from .RC
    wc.lpszClassName = szAppName;               // Name to register as

    // Register the window class and return success/failure code.
    if (!RegisterClass(&wc)) return FALSE;
```

```
//********************** NEW CODE START *******

    // Fill in window class structure with parameters that describe the
    // client area window.

    wc.style          = CS_HREDRAW | CS_VREDRAW; // Class style(s).
    wc.lpfnWndProc    = (WNDPROC)ClientWndProc;  // Window Procedure
    wc.cbClsExtra     = 0;                       // No per-class extra data.
    wc.cbWndExtra     = 0;                       // No per-window extra data.
    wc.hInstance      = hInstance;               // Owner of this class
    wc.hIcon          = NULL;
    wc.hCursor        = LoadCursor(NULL, IDC_ARROW); // Cursor
    wc.hbrBackground  = (HBRUSH)GetStockObject (BLACK_BRUSH);// Default color
    wc.lpszMenuName   = (HMENU)NULL;             // Menu name from .RC
    wc.lpszClassName  = szAppNameClient;         // Name to register as

    // Register the window class and return success/failure code.
    return (RegisterClass(&wc));


//********************** NEW CODE END *******


}


//
//   FUNCTION:  InitInstance(HINSTANCE, int)
//
//   PURPOSE:  Saves instance handle and creates main window
//
//   COMMENTS:
//
//      This function is called at initialization time for every instance of
//      this application.  This function performs initialization tasks that
//      cannot be shared by multiple instances.
//
//      In this case, we save the instance handle in a static variable and
//      create and display the main program window.
//

BOOL InitInstance(
        HINSTANCE     hInstance,
        int           nCmdShow
        )
{
    HWND    hWnd; // Main window handle.
```

LISTING 11.2 CONTINUED

```
    // Save the instance handle in static variable, which will be used in
    // many subsequence calls from this application to Windows.

    hInst = hInstance; // Store instance handle in our global variable

    // Create a main window for this application instance.
    hWnd = CreateWindow(
        szAppName,           // See RegisterClass() call.
        szTitle,             // Text for window title bar.
        WS_OVERLAPPEDWINDOW | WS_CLIPCHILDREN,// Window style.
        CW_USEDEFAULT, 0, CW_USEDEFAULT, 0,// Use default positioning
        NULL,                // Overlapped windows have no parent.
        NULL,                // Use the window class menu.
        hInstance,           // This instance owns this window.
        NULL                 // We don't use any data in our WM_CREATE
        );

    // If window could not be created, return "failure"
    if (!hWnd)
        return (FALSE);

//*********************** NEW CODE START *******

    hWndClient = CreateWindow ( szAppNameClient,
                                "",
                                WS_CHILD | WS_VISIBLE,
                                0, 0, 0, 0,
                                hWnd,
                                (HMENU)NULL,
                                hInstance,
                                NULL
                               );

    if (!hWndClient) return FALSE;

//*********************** NEW CODE END *******

    // Make the window visible; update its client area; and return "success"
    ShowWindow(hWnd, nCmdShow); // Show the window
    UpdateWindow(hWnd);         // Sends WM_PAINT message

    return (TRUE);              // We succeeded...
```

284

```
}


//
//    FUNCTION: WndProc(HWND, UINT, WPARAM, LPARAM)
//
//    PURPOSE:  Processes messages
//
//    MESSAGES:
//
//       WM_COMMAND    - application menu (About dialog box)
//       WM_DESTROY    - destroy window
//
//    COMMENTS:
//
//       To process the IDM_ABOUT message, call MakeProcInstance() to get the
//       current instance address of the About() function.  Then call Dialog
//       box which will create the box according to the information in your
//       IMAGELST.rc file and turn control over to the About() function.  When
//       it returns, free the instance address.
//

LRESULT CALLBACK WndProc(
        HWND hWnd,          // window handle
        UINT message,       // type of message
        WPARAM uParam,      // additional information
        LPARAM lParam       // additional information
        )
{
    FARPROC lpProcAbout;    // pointer to the "About" function
    int wmId, wmEvent;

    switch (message) {

        case WM_SIZE  :

            if ( hWndClient)
                SetWindowPos ( hWndClient, NULL, 0, 0,
                        LOWORD ( lParam ),
                        HIWORD ( lParam ),
                        SWP_NOZORDER
                    );
            break;

        case WM_COMMAND:  // message: command from application menu

            // Message packing of uParam and lParam have changed for Win32,
```

LISTING 11.2 CONTINUED

```c
// let us handle the differences in a conditional compilation:
#if defined (_WIN32)
    wmId   = LOWORD(uParam);
        wmEvent = HIWORD(uParam);
#else
    wmId    = uParam;
    wmEvent = HIWORD(lParam);
#endif

switch (wmId) {
   case IDM_ABOUT:
      lpProcAbout = MakeProcInstance((FARPROC)About, hInst);

      DialogBox(hInst,                // current instance
         "AboutBox",                  // dlg resource to use
         hWnd,                        // parent handle
         (DLGPROC)lpProcAbout);       // About() instance address

      FreeProcInstance(lpProcAbout);
      break;

   case IDM_EXIT:
      DestroyWindow (hWnd);
      break;

   case IDM_HELPCONTENTS:
      if (!WinHelp (hWnd, "IMAGELST.HLP", HELP_KEY,(DWORD)(LPSTR)"CONTENTS"
               )) {
         MessageBox (GetFocus(),
            "Unable to activate help",
            szAppName, MB_SYSTEMMODAL|MB_OK|MB_ICONHAND);

      }
      break;

   case IDM_HELPSEARCH:
      if (!WinHelp(hWnd, "IMAGELST.HLP", HELP_PARTIALKEY,
               (DWORD)(LPSTR)"")) {
         MessageBox (GetFocus(),
            "Unable to activate help",
            szAppName, MB_SYSTEMMODAL|MB_OK|MB_ICONHAND);
      }
```

```
                break;

            case IDM_HELPHELP:
                if(!WinHelp(hWnd, (LPSTR)NULL, HELP_HELPONHELP, 0)) {
                    MessageBox (GetFocus(),
                        "Unable to activate help",
                        szAppName, MB_SYSTEMMODAL|MB_OK|MB_ICONHAND);
                }
                break;

            // Here are all the other possible menu options,
            // all of these are currently disabled:
            case IDM_NEW:
            case IDM_OPEN:
            case IDM_SAVE:
            case IDM_SAVEAS:
            case IDM_UNDO:
            case IDM_CUT:
            case IDM_COPY:
            case IDM_PASTE:
            case IDM_LINK:
            case IDM_LINKS:

            default:
                return (DefWindowProc(hWnd, message, uParam, lParam));
            }
            break;

        case WM_DESTROY:  // message: window being destroyed

            PostQuitMessage (0);
            break;

        default:                // Passes it on if unproccessed
            return (DefWindowProc(hWnd, message, uParam, lParam));
    }
    return (0);
}


//
//    FUNCTION: CenterWindow (HWND, HWND)
//
//    PURPOSE:  Center one window over another
//
//    COMMENTS:
```

LISTING 11.2 CONTINUED

```
//
//      Dialog boxes take on the screen position that they were designed
//      at, which is not always appropriate. Centering the dialog over a
//      particular window usually results in a better position.
//

BOOL CenterWindow (HWND hwndChild, HWND hwndParent)
{
    RECT    rChild, rParent;
    int     wChild, hChild, wParent, hParent;
    int     wScreen, hScreen, xNew, yNew;
    HDC     hdc;

    // Get the Height and Width of the child window
    GetWindowRect (hwndChild, &rChild);
    wChild = rChild.right - rChild.left;
    hChild = rChild.bottom - rChild.top;

    // Get the Height and Width of the parent window
    GetWindowRect (hwndParent, &rParent);
    wParent = rParent.right - rParent.left;
    hParent = rParent.bottom - rParent.top;

    // Get the display limits
    hdc = GetDC (hwndChild);
    wScreen = GetDeviceCaps (hdc, HORZRES);
    hScreen = GetDeviceCaps (hdc, VERTRES);
    ReleaseDC (hwndChild, hdc);

    // Calculate new X position, then adjust for screen
    xNew = rParent.left + ((wParent - wChild) /2);
    if (xNew < 0) {
        xNew = 0;
    }
    else if ((xNew+wChild) > wScreen) {
        xNew = wScreen - wChild;
    }

    // Calculate new Y position, then adjust for screen
    yNew = rParent.top  + ((hParent - hChild) /2);
    if (yNew < 0) {
        yNew = 0;
```

```
    }
    else if ((yNew+hChild) > hScreen) {
        yNew = hScreen - hChild;
    }


    // Set it, and return
    return SetWindowPos (hwndChild, NULL,
        xNew, yNew, 0, 0, SWP_NOSIZE | SWP_NOZORDER);
}


//
//    FUNCTION: About(HWND, UINT, WPARAM, LPARAM)
//
//    PURPOSE:  Processes messages for "About" dialog box
//
//    MESSAGES:
//
//        WM_INITDIALOG - initialize dialog box
//        WM_COMMAND    - Input received
//
//    COMMENTS:
//
//        Display version information from the version section of the
//        application resource.
//
//        Wait for user to click on "Ok" button, then close the dialog box.
//

LRESULT CALLBACK About(
        HWND hDlg,           // window handle of the dialog box
        UINT message,        // type of message
        WPARAM uParam,       // message-specific information
        LPARAM lParam
        )
{
    static  HFONT hfontDlg;

    switch (message) {
        case WM_INITDIALOG:  // message: initialize dialog box
            // Create a font to use
            hfontDlg = CreateFont(14, 0, 0, 0, 0, 0, 0, 0,
                0, 0, 0, 0,
                VARIABLE_PITCH | FF_SWISS, "");

            // Center the dialog over the application window
            CenterWindow (hDlg, GetWindow (hDlg, GW_OWNER));
```

LISTING 11.2 CONTINUED

```
        return (TRUE);

    case WM_COMMAND:                      // message: received a command
        if (LOWORD(uParam) == IDOK        // "OK" box selected?
           || LOWORD(uParam) == IDCANCEL) {// System menu close command?
            EndDialog(hDlg, TRUE);        // Exit the dialog
            DeleteObject (hfontDlg);
            return (TRUE);
        }
        break;
    }
    return (FALSE); // Didn't process the message


    lParam; // This will prevent 'unused formal parameter' warnings
}


//********************** NEW CODE START *******


// This window lives inside the client area — it does all the interesting
// stuff for this demo program

LRESULT CALLBACK ClientWndProc(
        HWND hWnd,         // window handle
        UINT message,      // type of message
        WPARAM uParam,     // additional information
        LPARAM lParam      // additional information
        )
{
    HDC             hDC;      // DC to draw to
    PAINTSTRUCT     ps;       // For BeginPaint/EndPaint
    RECT            rc;       // Rect of image (for hit testing)
    POINT           pt;       // Cursor pos

    // These static variables are placed here just to keep the
    // window proc and it's variables all on the same page.

    static int        dxHotspot;   // Offset of image and cursor
    static int        dyHotspot;   // Offset of image and cursor
    static BOOL       bDragging;   // If the user is dragging the image
    static HIMAGELIST hImageList;  // Image list handle
    static int        iXPos;       // X Location of image
    static int        iYPos;       // Y Location of image
```

```
switch ( message )
   {
   case WM_CREATE:

       // Load the Image List
       hImageList = ImageList_LoadImage ( hInst,
                                          "TIE",
                                          32,
                                          1,
                                          RGB (255,0,0),
                                          IMAGE_BITMAP,
                                          0
                                        );

       // Init position of image
       iXPos = iYPos = 0;
       bDragging = FALSE;
       break;

   case WM_PAINT:

       // Get the DC
       hDC = BeginPaint ( hWnd, &ps );

       // Draw the first image ( Image number 0 ) on the DC
       if ( hImageList )
          {
          ImageList_Draw ( hImageList,
                           0,
                           hDC,
                           iXPos,
                           iYPos,
                           ILD_TRANSPARENT
                         );
          }

       // Release the DC
       EndPaint ( hWnd, &ps );
       break;

   case WM_LBUTTONDOWN:

       // Get the mouse position
       pt.x      = LOWORD (lParam);
```

LISTING 11.2 CONTINUED

```
        pt.y      = HIWORD (lParam);

        // Figure the hit test region of the 32x32 image
        rc.left   = iXPos;
        rc.top    = iYPos;
        rc.right  = rc.left + 32;
        rc.bottom = rc.top + 32;

        // Figure out where in the region the user clicked,
        // and figure the hotspot offset
        dxHotspot = pt.x - iXPos;
        dyHotspot = pt.y - iYPos;

        // If the hittest passes...
        if ( hImageList && PtInRect ( &rc, pt ))
          {
          // Set drag flag
          bDragging = TRUE;

          // Hide the cursor
          ShowCursor ( FALSE );

          // Capture the mouse
          SetCapture ( hWnd );

          // Set up the drag image and the hotspot
          ImageList_SetDragCursorImage(hImageList, 0, dxHotspot, dyHotspot);

          // Call the ImageList API to start the drag process
          ImageList_StartDrag ( hImageList,  // Handle to Image list
                                hWnd,        // hWnd of this client
                                0,           // Image #0
                                iXPos,       // Position of image
                                iYPos,       // Position of image
                                0,           // Hotspot offset
                                0);          // Hotspot offset
          }
        break;

    case WM_MOUSEMOVE:

      if ( bDragging )
```

```
               {
               // Call the ImageList API to automatically move the image around
               ImageList_DragMove ( LOWORD (lParam),
                                    HIWORD (lParam)
                                  );
               }
          break;

     case WM_LBUTTONUP:

          if ( bDragging )
            {
            // Tell the ImageList to stop dragging and erase the "fake" cursor
            ImageList_EndDrag ();
            // Release mouse capture
            ReleaseCapture ();
            // Bring back the real cursor
            ShowCursor ( TRUE );
            // Calculate the image's new position
            iXPos = LOWORD (lParam) - dxHotspot;
            iYPos = HIWORD (lParam) - dyHotspot;
            // Force a repaint
            InvalidateRect ( hWnd, NULL, TRUE );
            // Clear the drag flag
            bDragging = FALSE;
            }
          break;

     case WM_DESTROY:  // message: window being destroyed

            // Housekeep
            if ( hImageList )
              {
              ImageList_Destroy ( hImageList );
              hImageList = NULL;
              }
            break;

     default:            // Passes it on if unproccessed
          return (DefWindowProc(hWnd, message, uParam, lParam));
     }
   return (0);
}


//*********************** NEW CODE END *******
```

Almost every new line of code is in a new window procedure called **ClientWndProc**. This procedure maintains a list of static variables to determine where to draw Vader's ship (**iXPos**, **iYPos**), and a few other helper variables.

When this client window is created, the code under WM_CREATE uses that **ImageList_LoadImage** API I blathered about earlier. The code under WM_DESTROY deletes the Image List with the **ImageList_Destroy** API.

The code under WM_PAINT is quite simple—it just calls the **ImageList_Draw** API to splat Darth's TIE onto the black background. Isn't this a lot easier than doing **BitBlts**?

The interesting code comes in the WM_LBUTTONDOWN/ WM_MOUSEMOVE/WM_LBUTTONUP trilogy. The code in WM_LBUT-TONDOWN follows the steps above for drag-and-drop. The only part that's a little weird is the calculation of the hotspot for the **ImageList_StartDrag** API call in WM_LBUTTONDOWN. Since the user can click on any pixel within the TIE fighter, that point must be set as the hotspot for the image being dragged. If you don't set the hotspot, the image will jump to the 0,0 position of the image's rectangle, which is ugly (to see this, just change **dxHotspot** and **dyHotspot** in the sample to 0,0). By subtracting the upper-left position of the image from the current cursor position, you can counter this jumpiness and give Darth Vader a smooth ride into space.

That covers the APIs and some general usage of the Image List. I have another sample program that will actually implement some of the functionality of the Image List, as well as implement the TreeView control (which is coming up next on your plate of Windows 95 goodies).

Even though the Image List is intended mainly for use by controls, there is no reason you cannot use it as a convenient bitmap drawing tool or even as an icon database. Many graphics editing tools will find the Image List invaluable for managing arrays of images and drawing them easily.

9. The TreeView Control

By now you're probably pretty bored of dragging and dropping Darth Vader all over your window. Let's take a look at the more common use of an Image

List: as a graphical enhancement to a control. Let's use the TreeView as the control.

There is another control called the ListView, which is used similarly to the TreeView. The ListView control provides for a group of items that are displayed as a name and/or icon that can be organized into several formats. See Goodie #3 for more on the ListView.

What is a TreeView good for? It's perfect for displaying lists of items that you want to group into different folders. These folders can have child folders, and it is possible to hide the information in a folder by collapsing it. To get a feel for how the TreeView control works, play with the left pane of Windows 95's Explorer, or play with the TREEVIEW sample program (see Figures 11.14 and Listing 11.3) from this list (you will need to be running Windows 95).

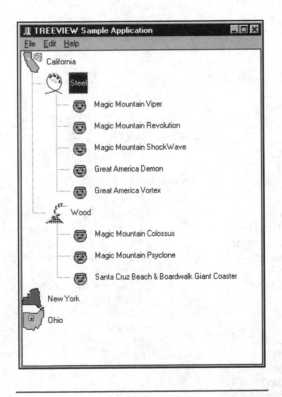

FIGURE 11.14 TREEVIEW SAMPLE PROGRAM AT WORK

LISTING 11.3 TREEVIEW SAMPLE PROGRAM

```
#include <windows.h>              // required for all Windows applications
#if !defined(_WIN32)
#include <ver.h>
#endif
#include "TREEVIEW.h"             // specific to this program


//***************** NEW CODE START *********

#include <commctrl.h>            // Common controls
#include <stdlib.h>              // for atoi


//***************** NEW CODE END *********

// Windows NT defines APIENTRY, but 3.x doesn't
#if !defined (APIENTRY)
#define APIENTRY far pascal
#endif


// Windows 3.x uses a FARPROC for dialogs
#if !defined(_WIN32)
#define DLGPROC FARPROC
#endif


HINSTANCE    hInst;                      // current instance

//******** NEW CODE START **************

HWND         ghWnd;                      // Handle of main window
HWND         hWndTreeView;               // Handle of TreeView control
HIMAGELIST   hCoasterImageList;          // Roller coaster images
int          iImageWood   ;              // Image number for the "Wood" roler
                                         // coaster
int          iImageSteel  ;              // Image number for the "Steel" roler
                                         // coaster
int          iImageCA     ;              // Images for states in open/closed...
                                         // state
int          iImageNY     ;              //
int          iImageOH     ;              //
int          iImageCA_OPEN;              //
int          iImageNY_OPEN;              //
int          iImageOH_OPEN;              //
int          iImageRider1 ;              // Image of the coaster rider when not
```

```
                                        // selected
int          iImageRider2 ;             // Image of the coaster rider when selected

// These are stored in lParam of the TV_ITEM structure, to
// help identify what type of thing the item is.

#define      ITEM_TYPE_STATE_START      0
#define      ITEM_TYPE_STATE_CA         0
#define      ITEM_TYPE_STATE_NY         1      // The Coney Island Cyclone!
#define      ITEM_TYPE_STATE_OH         2
#define      ITEM_TYPE_STATE_END        50


#define      ITEM_TYPE_COASTER_TYPE     100
#define      ITEM_TYPE_COASTER_NAME     101


void FillTreeView    ( HWND ); // Function to fill our TreeView with data
void Sample_Init     ( void ); // All added init code
void Sample_Shutdown ( void ); // All added shutdown code

//******** NEW CODE END **************

char szAppName[] = "TREEVIEW";              // The name of this application
char szTitle[]   = "TREEVIEW Sample Application"; // The title bar text


//
//    FUNCTION: WinMain(HINSTANCE, HINSTANCE, LPSTR, int)
//
//    PURPOSE: calls initialization function, processes message loop
//
//    COMMENTS:
//
//        Windows recognizes this function by name as the initial entry point
//        for the program.  This function calls the application initialization
//        routine, if no other instance of the program is running, and always
//        calls the instance initialization routine.  It then executes a
//        message retrieval and dispatch loop that is the top-level control
//        structure for the remainder of execution.  The loop is terminated
//        when a WM_QUIT  message is received, at which time this function
//        exits the application instance by returning the value passed by
//        PostQuitMessage().
//
//        If this function must abort before entering the message loop, it
//        returns the conventional value NULL.
//

int APIENTRY WinMain(
```

297

LISTING 11.3 CONTINUED

```
            HINSTANCE hInstance,
            HINSTANCE hPrevInstance,
            LPSTR lpCmdLine,
            int nCmdShow
            )
{
   MSG msg;
   HANDLE hAccelTable;

   // Other instances of app running?
   if (!hPrevInstance) {
      // Initialize shared things
      if (!InitApplication(hInstance)) {
         return (FALSE);                  // Exits if unable to initialize
      }
   }

   // Perform initializations that apply to a specific instance
   if (!InitInstance(hInstance, nCmdShow)) {
      return (FALSE);
   }

//***************** NEW CODE START *********


   Sample_Init ( );

//***************** NEW CODE END *********


   hAccelTable = LoadAccelerators (hInstance, szAppName);

   // Acquire and dispatch messages until a WM_QUIT message is received.
   while (GetMessage(&msg,    // message structure
                  NULL,    // handle of window receiving the message
                  0,       // lowest message to examine
                  0)){     // highest message to examine
      if (!TranslateAccelerator (msg.hwnd, hAccelTable, &msg)) {
         TranslateMessage(&msg);// Translates virtual key codes
         DispatchMessage(&msg); // Dispatches message to window
      }
   }

//***************** NEW CODE START *********
```

```
    Sample_Shutdown ( );

//******************* NEW CODE END *********

    // Returns the value from PostQuitMessage
    return (msg.wParam);

    // This will prevent 'unused formal parameter' warnings
    lpCmdLine;
}


//
//    FUNCTION: InitApplication(HINSTANCE)
//
//    PURPOSE: Initializes window data and registers window class
//
//    COMMENTS:
//
//        This function is called at initialization time only if no other
//        instances of the application are running.  This function performs
//        initialization tasks that can be done once for any number of running
//        instances.
//
//        In this case, we initialize a window class by filling out a data
//        structure of type WNDCLASS and calling the Windows RegisterClass()
//        function.  Since all instances of this application use the same
//        window class, we only need to do this when the first instance is
//        initialized.
//

BOOL InitApplication(HINSTANCE hInstance)
{
    WNDCLASS  wc;

    // Fill in window class structure with parameters that describe the
    // main window.
    wc.style          = CS_HREDRAW | CS_VREDRAW; // Class style(s).
    wc.lpfnWndProc    = (WNDPROC)WndProc;        // Window Procedure
    wc.cbClsExtra     = 0;                       // No per-class extra data.
    wc.cbWndExtra     = 0;                       // No per-window extra data.
    wc.hInstance      = hInstance;               // Owner of this class
    wc.hIcon          = LoadIcon (hInstance, szAppName);// Icon name from .RC
    wc.hCursor        = LoadCursor(NULL, IDC_ARROW); // Cursor
    wc.hbrBackground  = (HBRUSH)(COLOR_WINDOW+1);// Default color
    wc.lpszMenuName   = szAppName;               // Menu name from .RC
    wc.lpszClassName  = szAppName;               // Name to register as
```

LISTING 11.3 CONTINUED

```
    // Register the window class and return success/failure code.
    return (RegisterClass(&wc));
}


//
//   FUNCTION:  InitInstance(HINSTANCE, int)
//
//   PURPOSE:  Saves instance handle and creates main window
//
//   COMMENTS:
//
//       This function is called at initialization time for every instance of
//       this application.  This function performs initialization tasks that
//       cannot be shared by multiple instances.
//
//       In this case, we save the instance handle in a static variable and
//       create and display the main program window.
//

BOOL InitInstance(
        HINSTANCE       hInstance,
        int             nCmdShow
        )
{
    HWND    hWnd; // Main window handle.

    // Save the instance handle in static variable, which will be used in
    // many subsequence calls from this application to Windows.

    hInst = hInstance; // Store instance handle in our global variable

    // Create a main window for this application instance.
    hWnd = CreateWindow(
        szAppName,          // See RegisterClass() call.
        szTitle,            // Text for window title bar.
        WS_OVERLAPPEDWINDOW,// Window style.
        CW_USEDEFAULT, 0, CW_USEDEFAULT, 0,// Use default positioning
        NULL,               // Overlapped windows have no parent.
        NULL,               // Use the window class menu.
        hInstance,          // This instance owns this window.
        NULL                // We don't use any data in our WM_CREATE
        );

    // If window could not be created, return "failure"
```

```
    if (!hWnd) {
       return (FALSE);
    }


//***************** NEW CODE START *********


    ghWnd = hWnd;


//***************** NEW CODE END *********


    // Make the window visible; update its client area; and return "success"
    ShowWindow(hWnd, nCmdShow); // Show the window
    UpdateWindow(hWnd);          // Sends WM_PAINT message


    return (TRUE);               // We succeeded...
}


//***************** NEW CODE START *********


//*****************************************************


//
// Sample_Init: Creates the Image List, the TreeView, and
// calls the FillTreeView function to put some stuff into it
//
//*****************************************************


void Sample_Init ( void ) // All added init code
{
    RECT rc;

    InitCommonControls(); // This MUST be called once per instance
                          // to register the TreeView class.


    hCoasterImageList = ImageList_Create
                          (
                          32, 32,
                          TRUE,
                          5,
                          1
                          );


    iImageWood   = ImageList_AddIcon ( hCoasterImageList,
```

LISTING 11.3 CONTINUED

```
                                           LoadIcon ( hInst, "WOOD"   ));
   iImageSteel  = ImageList_AddIcon ( hCoasterImageList,
                                           LoadIcon ( hInst, "STEEL"  ));
   iImageOH     = ImageList_AddIcon ( hCoasterImageList,
                                           LoadIcon ( hInst, "OH"     ));
   iImageNY     = ImageList_AddIcon ( hCoasterImageList,
                                           LoadIcon ( hInst, "NY"     ));
   iImageCA     = ImageList_AddIcon ( hCoasterImageList,
                                           LoadIcon ( hInst, "CA"     ));
   iImageOH_OPEN= ImageList_AddIcon ( hCoasterImageList,
                                           LoadIcon ( hInst, "OH_OPEN"));
   iImageNY_OPEN= ImageList_AddIcon ( hCoasterImageList,
                                           LoadIcon ( hInst, "NY_OPEN"));
   iImageCA_OPEN= ImageList_AddIcon ( hCoasterImageList,
                                           LoadIcon ( hInst, "CA_OPEN"));


   iImageRider1 = ImageList_AddIcon ( hCoasterImageList,
                                           LoadIcon ( hInst, "RIDER1" ));
   iImageRider2 = ImageList_AddIcon ( hCoasterImageList,
                                           LoadIcon ( hInst, "RIDER2" ));


   GetClientRect ( ghWnd, &rc );


   hWndTreeView = CreateWindow ( WC_TREEVIEW,
                                 "",
                                 WS_VISIBLE | WS_CHILD | WS_BORDER |
                                 TVS_HASLINES | TVS_EDITLABELS,
                                 0, 0,
                                 rc.right, rc.bottom,
                                 ghWnd,
                                 (HMENU)NULL,
                                 hInst,
                                 NULL
                               );


   if (hWndTreeView)
     {
     TreeView_SetImageList ( hWndTreeView, hCoasterImageList, 0 );
     ImageList_SetBkColor  ( hCoasterImageList, GetSysColor ( COLOR_WINDOW ));
     FillTreeView ( hWndTreeView );
     }

//********************************************************
```

```
//
// Sample_Shutdown: Deletes the Image List
//
//*******************************************************

void Sample_Shutdown ( void ) // All added shutdown code
{
    if (hCoasterImageList) ImageList_Destroy ( hCoasterImageList );
}


//*******************************************************
//
// iNumCoasters: Returns the number of coasters in the
//               string table. The stringtable must have
//               the form where the string at the iCoasterIndex
//               is an ascii string with the number of coasters,
//               and then the strings from iCoasterIndex+1 to
//               iCoasterIndex+n+1 have the actual coasters.
//
//*******************************************************

int iNumCoasters ( int iCoasterIndex )
{
  char sz[16];

  if (LoadString ( hInst, iCoasterIndex, sz, sizeof(sz)))
    return atoi ( sz );
  else
    return 0;
}


//*******************************************************
//
// CoastersInfo: Your basic, boring string parser routine.
//               This function loads a string from the
//               string table with the format of
//               STATE,COASTER,TYPE and puts the individual
//               pieces in the pointers passed into this
//               function. Yawn.
//
//*******************************************************

BOOL CoasterInfo ( int   iCoasterIndex,
                   LPSTR szState,
                   LPSTR szCoaster,
```

LISTING 11.3 CONTINUED

```
                  LPSTR szType
               )
{
  char    szRaw[256];
  LPSTR   szPtr;
  int     i, iLen;
  int     iWZIQ = 0;


  // Get the string from the resource template

  if (!LoadString ( hInst, iCoasterIndex, szRaw, sizeof(szRaw)))
    return FALSE;


  // Change the comma delimiters to NULLs, chopping the one string
  // into a bunch of little ones

  iLen = lstrlen ( szRaw );
  for ( i = 0; i < iLen; i++ ) if ( ',' == szRaw[i] ) szRaw[i] = 0;


  // Copy the info into the parameters

  szPtr = szRaw;


  lstrcpy ( szState,   szPtr ); szPtr += lstrlen ( szPtr ) + 1;
  lstrcpy ( szCoaster, szPtr ); szPtr += lstrlen ( szPtr ) + 1;
  lstrcpy ( szType,    szPtr );


  // Success! Let's ride!


  return TRUE;
}


//*****************************************************
//
// AddTreeViewItem: This function adds an item to the
//                  TreeView control, you give it the
//                  string, images, lParam, parent,
//                  and sibling, and it fills out the
//                  data structures and makes the actual
//                  calls into the TreeView via the
//                  macros from COMMCTRL.H.
```

```
//
//********************************************************


HTREEITEM AddTreeViewItem ( HWND        hWndTV,
                            HTREEITEM   hParent,
                            HTREEITEM   hInsertAfter,
                            int         iImage,
                            int         iSelectedImage,
                            LPSTR       szText,
                            LPARAM      lParam
                          )
{
  TV_ITEM               tvItem;
  TV_INSERTSTRUCT       tvIns;

  // Set which attribytes we are going to fill out.
  tvItem.mask = TVIF_TEXT | TVIF_IMAGE | TVIF_SELECTEDIMAGE | TVIF_PARAM;


  // Set the attribytes
  tvItem.pszText        = szText;
  tvItem.iImage         = iImage;
  tvItem.iSelectedImage = iSelectedImage;
  tvItem.lParam         = lParam;


  // Fill out the TV_INSERTSTRUCT
  tvIns.hParent         = hParent;
  tvIns.hInsertAfter    = hInsertAfter;
  tvIns.item            = tvItem;


  // And insert the item, returning its handle
  return TreeView_InsertItem ( hWndTV, &tvIns );
}


//********************************************************
//
// FindOrAddTreeViewItem: This function will add an item to
//                        a TreeView in the right spot. You
//                        must specify the parent node of where
//                        this item is to be added, and then
//                        this function will check to see if a
//                        node already exists with this name.
//                        If a node with this name already
//                        exists, then its handle is returned.
//                        If the node does not exist, then the
//                        AddTreeViewItem function from
```

LISTING 11.3 CONTINUED

```
//                      above is called to add the item.
//                      See how this function is used
//                      in the FillTreeView function down
//                      below.
//
//*******************************************************

HTREEITEM FindOrAddTreeViewItem ( HWND        hWndTV,
                                  HTREEITEM   hParent,
                                  int         iImage,
                                  int         iSelectedImage,
                                  LPSTR       szText,
                                  LPARAM      lParam
                                )
{
  TV_ITEM           tvItem;       // Temporary item
  HTREEITEM         hItem;        // Handle to item
  HTREEITEM         hPrevItem;    // Handle to previous item
  char              szBuffer[256]; // Temporary buffer


  // Get the first child of the passed in parent
  hItem = TreeView_GetChild ( hWndTV, hParent );


  // Loop through all children, looking for an already existing
  // child.

  while ( hItem )
    {
    tvItem.mask       = TVIF_TEXT;       // We want the text
    tvItem.hItem      = hItem;           // Indicate the item to fetch
    tvItem.pszText    = szBuffer;        // Indicate the buffer
    tvItem.cchTextMax = sizeof(szBuffer); // Indicate buffer's size

    TreeView_GetItem ( hWndTV, &tvItem ); // Fetch, Rover!

    if (!lstrcmpi (tvItem.pszText, szText)) // Found it! Just return item
      return hItem;

    hPrevItem = hItem; // Remember the last item, since the next line
                       // of code will eventually put a NULL in the
                       // hItem variable, and we want to know the
                       // last item under the parent in case we need
```

```
                        // to add a new item.

    // Get the next sibling item in the TreeView, if any.
    hItem = TreeView_GetNextSibling ( hWndTV, hItem );
    }


  // If we made it here, then the item needs to be added
  // onto the end of the list

  return AddTreeViewItem ( hWndTV,          // Handle of TreeView
                           hParent,         // Parent item
                           hPrevItem,       // Last child in list (from above loop)
                           iImage,          // These are the parameters
                           iSelectedImage,  // passed into this
                           szText,          // function.
                           lParam           //
                         );
}


//****************************AΛ۸***************************************
//
//  This function fills the TreeView control with our coasters!
//
//*********************************************************************

#define ADDSTATEROOT(iType)                          \
  FindOrAddTreeViewItem ( hWndTV,                    \
                          TVGN_ROOT,                 \
                          I_IMAGECALLBACK,           \
                          I_IMAGECALLBACK,           \
                          szState,                   \
                          iType)


#define ADDTYPENODE(iImageType)                      \
  FindOrAddTreeViewItem ( hWndTV,                    \
                          hParent,                   \
                          iImageType,                \
                          iImageType,                \
                          szType,                    \
                          ITEM_TYPE_COASTER_TYPE)


void FillTreeView ( HWND hWndTV )
{
  int   i;     // Counter
  int   iNum;  // Number of coasters in stringtable
```

LISTING 11.3 CONTINUED

```
char szState[64];      // State coaster is in
char szCoaster[128];   // Coaster's name
char szType[64];       // Type of coaster (wood or steel)


HTREEITEM hParent;     // Parent node to add to.


iNum = iNumCoasters ( COASTERSTRING ); // Figure number of coasters


// Run through string table, adding each coaster. This algorithm
// calls the CoasterInfo function to parse the stringtable
// entry into the state, type, and coaster name. The state
// string is the topmost node, the coaster type is the secondary
// node, and the coaster name is the actual item.
// This loop first tries to find the topmost state node, and if
// it can't find it, it adds it by using the FindOrAddTreeViewItem
// function. Then, once the state node is added, the same process
// is done for the coaster type node under the appropriate state.
// Once the state node is determined, then the actual item is
// added to the TreeView in the correct place.

for ( i = 1; i <= iNum; i++ )
  {
  // Get string from stringtable and parse it
  if (CoasterInfo ( i + COASTERSTRING, szState, szCoaster, szType ))
    {
    // Add or find the state node. The ADDSTATEROOT macro defined
    // above is used for readability.

    switch (*szState)
      {
      case 'C': hParent = ADDSTATEROOT (ITEM_TYPE_STATE_CA); break;
      case 'N': hParent = ADDSTATEROOT (ITEM_TYPE_STATE_NY); break;
      case 'O': hParent = ADDSTATEROOT (ITEM_TYPE_STATE_OH); break;
      }


    // Now that we know what state node to use, add or find
    // the type of the coaster node. The ADDTYPENODE macro defined
    // above is used for readability.

    if ('W' == *szType)
      hParent = ADDTYPENODE (iImageWood);
    else
```

```
        hParent = ADDTYPENODE (iImageSteel);


    // Now that we know the parent for the actual coaster, add that
    // to the list.

    FindOrAddTreeViewItem ( hWndTV,             // TreeView control
                            hParent,            // Parent type node
                            iImageRider1,       // Placid rider
                            iImageRider2,       // Screaming rider
                            szCoaster,          // Coaster name
                            ITEM_TYPE_COASTER_NAME );

    }
  }
}


//****************** NEW CODE END *********


//
//   FUNCTION: WndProc(HWND, UINT, WPARAM, LPARAM)
//
//   PURPOSE:  Processes messages
//
//   MESSAGES:
//
//     WM_COMMAND    - application menu (About dialog box)
//     WM_DESTROY    - destroy window
//
//   COMMENTS:
//
//     To process the IDM_ABOUT message, call MakeProcInstance() to get the
//     current instance address of the About() function.  Then call Dialog
//     box which will create the box according to the information in your
//     TREEVIEW.rc file and turn control over to the About() function.  When
//     it returns, free the instance address.
//

LRESULT CALLBACK WndProc(
        HWND hWnd,         // window handle
        UINT message,      // type of message
        WPARAM uParam,     // additional information
        LPARAM lParam      // additional information
        )
{
    FARPROC lpProcAbout;  // pointer to the "About" function
    int wmId, wmEvent;
```

LISTING 11.3 CONTINUED

```
//****************** NEW CODE START *********

#define ptrNMHDR        ((LPNMHDR)lParam)
#define ptrNM_TREEVIEW ((NM_TREEVIEW *)lParam)
#define ptrTV_DISPINFO ((TV_DISPINFO *)lParam)


        RECT        rcItem;
  static HIMAGELIST hDragImage;
  static BOOL       bDragging;
  static HTREEITEM  hDragItem;


  switch (message) {

    case WM_NOTIFY: // This is a new Chicago message for control
                    // notifications

        switch (ptrNMHDR->code)
          {
          case TVN_BEGINDRAG: // Sent by TreeView when user
                              // wants to drag an item.

            // Only allow drag & drop for the actual coaster
            // items. The "itemNew" field of the NM_TREEVIEW
            // structure contains the attribytes of the item
            // we are going to drag. Therefore, since we are
            // using the lParam field to store an ITEM_TYPE_*
            // value, we check that field.

            if ( ITEM_TYPE_COASTER_NAME == ptrNM_TREEVIEW->itemNew.lParam)
              {
              // The hDragImage variable is declared static,
              // so the code in WM_LBUTTONUP can delete it when
              // the user stops dragging. Here we create a
              // drag image to use for the ImageList_StartDrag
              // API.

              hDragImage = TreeView_CreateDragImage
                      (
                      ptrNMHDR->hwndFrom,
                      ptrNM_TREEVIEW->itemNew.hItem
                      );
```

```
    // Get the location of the item rectangle's text.

    TreeView_GetItemRect
      (
      ptrNMHDR->hwndFrom,                // Handle of TreeView
      ptrNM_TREEVIEW->itemNew.hItem,     // Item in TreeView
      &rcItem,                           // RECT to store result
      TRUE                               // Rect of label text only
      );

    // Cache away the handle of the item to drag into a
    // staticly declared variable, so the code in
    // WM_LBUTTONUP can know what the user is dragging.

    hDragItem = ptrNM_TREEVIEW->itemNew.hItem;

    // Start the drag ala ImageList
    ImageList_SetDragCursorImage(hDragImage,
                                 0,
                                 ptrNM_TREEVIEW->ptDrag.x - rcItem.left,
                                 ptrNM_TREEVIFW->ptDrag.y - rcItem.top);

    ImageList_StartDrag
      (
      hDragImage,              // From TreeView_CreateDragImage
      ptrNMHDR->hwndFrom,      // Clip drag & drop to TreeView Window
      0,                       // Use first image
      ptrNM_TREEVIEW->ptDrag.x,  // Coords of image to drag
      ptrNM_TREEVIEW->ptDrag.y,
      0, // Offset hotspot
      0
      );

    // Capture the mousey to this window

    ShowCursor ( FALSE );
    SetCapture ( hWnd );

    // Set a staticly declared drag flag so the WM_MOUSEMOVE
    // and WM_LBUTTONUP messages know to take action.

    bDragging = TRUE;
    }

return 0L;  // Return value is irrelevant
```

LISTING 11.3 CONTINUED

```
case TVN_GETDISPINFO: // Sent by TreeView just before it paints
                      // an item declared with callback values.

  // Our "state" items have the I_IMAGECALLBACK value
  // used for the iImage and iSelectedImage fields. This
  // TVN_GETDISPINFO code will be called whenever the
  // item is about to be drawn. It is out responsibility
  // to add code to fill in the images. The code below
  // uses a different image depending on if the item is
  // expanded or collapsed. That attribute is in the
  // state field of the item passed in the TV_DISPINFO
  // structure.

  // Our lParam is where we store what state the item
  // represents. Therefore, we will switch on that so
  // we can indicate the correct image to use.

  if ( ptrTV_DISPINFO->item.state & TVIS_EXPANDED )
    {
    switch (ptrTV_DISPINFO->item.lParam)
      {
      case ITEM_TYPE_STATE_CA:

        ptrTV_DISPINFO->item.iImage =
        ptrTV_DISPINFO->item.iSelectedImage = iImageCA_OPEN;
        break;

      case ITEM_TYPE_STATE_NY:

        ptrTV_DISPINFO->item.iImage =
        ptrTV_DISPINFO->item.iSelectedImage = iImageNY_OPEN;
        break;

      case ITEM_TYPE_STATE_OH:

        ptrTV_DISPINFO->item.iImage =
        ptrTV_DISPINFO->item.iSelectedImage = iImageOH_OPEN;
        break;
      }
    }
  else  // Collapsed item
    {
```

```
    switch (ptrTV_DISPINFO->item.lParam)
      {
      case ITEM_TYPE_STATE_CA:

        ptrTV_DISPINFO->item.iImage =
        ptrTV_DISPINFO->item.iSelectedImage = iImageCA;
        break;

      case ITEM_TYPE_STATE_NY:

        ptrTV_DISPINFO->item.iImage =
        ptrTV_DISPINFO->item.iSelectedImage = iImageNY;
        break;

      case ITEM_TYPE_STATE_OH:

        ptrTV_DISPINFO->item.iImage =
        ptrTV_DISPINFO->item.iSelectedImage = iImageOH;
        break;
      }
    }
  return TRUE;

case TVN_BEGINLABELEDIT: // Sent by TreeView when user single
                         // clicks on an item in a TreeView
                         // that has the TVS_EDITLABELS style
                         // bit set.


  // Only allow label editing for the coaster names

  if (ITEM_TYPE_COASTER_NAME == ptrTV_DISPINFO->item.lParam)
    return 0;  // Return 0 to OK edit
  else
    return 1;  // Return non-zero to disallow edit
  break;

case TVN_ENDLABELEDIT:   // Sent by TreeView when user presses
                         // the ENTER key or ESC key, to end
                         // an in-place edit session. If the user
                         // pressed the ESC key, the pszText
                         // field of the item in the TV_DISPINFO
                         // field is NULL.


  // if user pressed ENTER to accept edits
```

LISTING 11.3 CONTINUED

```
      if ( ptrTV_DISPINFO->item.pszText)
        {
        // Set the "change mask" to indicate that the only attribute
        // we wish to change is the text field. The TV_DISPINFO
        // structure has already been filled out with the new
        // text the user typed in, we just need to pass that on
        // to the TreeView control. This is our chance to evaluate
        // the contents of this field and change it.

        ptrTV_DISPINFO->item.mask = TVIF_TEXT;

        TreeView_SetItem
          (
            ptrNMHDR->hwndFrom,        // Handle of TreeView
            &(ptrTV_DISPINFO->item)    // TV_ITEM structure w/changes
          );
        }
      break;

    }


    return (DefWindowProc(hWnd, message, uParam, lParam));

  case WM_MOUSEMOVE: // Since the mouse capture is set to this
                     // window while we do our drag & drop,
                     // we check for the drag flag and process
                     // the WM_MOUSEMOVE message.


    if (bDragging)
      {
      HTREEITEM        hTarget;  // Item under mouse
      TV_HITTESTINFO   tvht;     // Used for hit testing

      // Do standard drag drop movement

      ImageList_DragMove ( LOWORD (lParam), HIWORD (lParam));

      // Fill out hit test struct with mouse pos

      tvht.pt.x = LOWORD (lParam);
      tvht.pt.y = HIWORD (lParam);
```

```
            // Check to see if an item lives under the mouse

    if ( hTarget = TreeView_HitTest
                    (
                    hWndTreeView,    // This is the global variable
                    &tvht            // TV_HITTESTINFO struct
                    )
       )
      {
      TV_ITEM         tvi;              // Temporary Item

      tvi.mask        = TVIF_PARAM;  // We want to fetch the
                                     // lParam field.

      tvi.hItem       = hTarget;     // Set the handle of the
                                     // item to fetch.

      TreeView_GetItem ( hWndTreeView, &tvi ); // Fetch, spot!

      // Check to see if the lParam is a valid item to drop
      // onto (in this case, another roller coaster, such as
      // the Coney Island Cyclone). Skip this operation if
      // the item is already selected (to avoid flicker)

      if ( ITEM_TYPE_COASTER_NAME == tvi.lParam )
        {
        if ( hTarget != TreeView_GetDropHilight (hWndTreeView))
          {
          // Select the item
          TreeView_SelectDropTarget ( hWndTreeView, hTarget );
          }
        return OL;
        }
      }

    // If we made it here, then the user has either
    // dragged the mouse over an invalid item, or no item.
    // Hide any current drop target, this is a no-no drop

    TreeView_SelectDropTarget ( hWndTreeView, NULL );
    }
  break;

case WM_LBUTTONUP: // Since the mouse capture is set to this
                   // window while we do our drag & drop,
                   // we check for the drag flag and process
```

315

LISTING 11.3 CONTINUED

```
                    // the WM_LBUTTONUP message.

  if (bDragging)
    {
    HTREEITEM       hTarget;        // Item under mouse
    TV_ITEM         tvi;            // Temporary Item
    TV_INSERTSTRUCT tvIns;          // Insert struct
    char            szBuffer[256];  // Item text buffer

    // End the drag
    ImageList_EndDrag();
    // Bring back the cursor
    ShowCursor ( TRUE );
    // Release the mouse capture
    ReleaseCapture();
    // Clear the drag flag
    bDragging = FALSE;
    // Clean up the image list object
    ImageList_Destroy ( hDragImage );
    hDragImage = NULL;

    // First, check to see if there is a valid drop point.
    // The cheezy way to do this is to check for a highlighted
    // drop target, since the logic to validate drop points
    // is in the WM_MOUSEMOVE. Duping that code here would
    // be a headache.

    if ( hTarget = TreeView_GetDropHilight (hWndTreeView))
      {
      // If we made it here, then we need to move the item.
      // First, we will fetch it, specifying the attributes
      // we need to copy.

      tvi.mask        = TVIF_TEXT | TVIF_IMAGE | TVIF_SELECTEDIMAGE |
                        TVIF_PARAM;
      tvi.hItem       = hDragItem;
      tvi.pszText     = szBuffer;
      tvi.cchTextMax = sizeof(szBuffer);

      TreeView_GetItem ( hWndTreeView, &tvi );

      // Now, figure the new place to put it by filling out
```

```
            // the TV_INSERTSTRUCT structure, to use the drop target
            // as the sibling to insert after, and using the drop
            // target's parent as the parent to insert this one
            // after as well.

            tvIns.hParent         = TreeView_GetParent ( hWndTreeView, hTarget );
            tvIns.hInsertAfter    = hTarget;
            tvIns.item            = tvi;

            // Delete the old item

            TreeView_DeleteItem ( hWndTreeView, hDragItem );

            // And add the new item (if your app tracks the handles of
            // the items, you want to use the return value
            // of this function to update your data structure that
            // tracks the handles.

            TreeView_InsertItem ( hWndTreeView, &tvIns );
            }

        // Clear any drop highlights on the TreeView

        TreeView_SelectDropTarget ( hWndTreeView, NULL );
        }
    break;


    caseWM_SIZE:

        if ( hWndTreeView )     // Standard code to keep the TreeView
                                // sized up with the main window
        {
        SetWindowPos ( hWndTreeView,
                    NULL,
                    0, 0,
                    LOWORD (lParam),
                    HIWORD (lParam),
                    SWP_NOZORDER
                );
        }
    break;

//****************** NEW CODE END *********

    case WM_COMMAND:  // message: command from application menu
```

LISTING 11.3 CONTINUED

```
// Message packing of uParam and lParam have changed for Win32,
// let us handle the differences in a conditional compilation:
#if defined (_WIN32)
    wmId    = LOWORD(uParam);
       wmEvent = HIWORD(uParam);
#else
    wmId    = uParam;
    wmEvent = HIWORD(lParam);
#endif

switch (wmId) {
    case IDM_ABOUT:
        lpProcAbout = MakeProcInstance((FARPROC)About, hInst);

        DialogBox(hInst,              // current instance
            "AboutBox",               // dlg resource to use
            hWnd,                     // parent handle
            (DLGPROC)lpProcAbout);    // About() instance address

        FreeProcInstance(lpProcAbout);
        break;

    case IDM_EXIT:
        DestroyWindow (hWnd);
        break;

    case IDM_HELPCONTENTS:
        if (!WinHelp (hWnd, "TREEVIEW.HLP", HELP_KEY,
                    (DWORD)(LPSTR)"CONTENTS")) {
            MessageBox (GetFocus(),
                "Unable to activate help",
                szAppName, MB_SYSTEMMODAL|MB_OK|MB_ICONHAND);

        }
        break;

    case IDM_HELPSEARCH:
        if (!WinHelp(hWnd, "TREEVIEW.HLP", HELP_PARTIALKEY,
                    (DWORD)(LPSTR)"")) {
            MessageBox (GetFocus(),
                "Unable to activate help",
                szAppName, MB_SYSTEMMODAL|MB_OK|MB_ICONHAND);
```

```
                    }
                    break;

                case IDM_HELPHELP:
                    if(!WinHelp(hWnd, (LPSTR)NULL, HELP_HELPONHELP, 0)) {
                        MessageBox (GetFocus(),
                            "Unable to activate help",
                            szAppName, MB_SYSTEMMODAL|MB_OK|MB_ICONHAND);
                    }
                    break;

                // Here are all the other possible menu options,
                // all of these are currently disabled:
                case IDM_NEW:
                case IDM_OPEN:
                case IDM_SAVE:
                case IDM_SAVEAS:
                case IDM_UNDO:
                case IDM_CUT:
                case IDM_COPY:
                case IDM_PASTE:
                case IDM_LINK:
                case IDM_LINKS:

                default:
                    return (DefWindowProc(hWnd, message, uParam, lParam));
            }
            break;

        case WM_DESTROY:  // message: window being destroyed

            PostQuitMessage(0);
            break;

        default:              // Passes it on if unproccessed
            return (DefWindowProc(hWnd, message, uParam, lParam));
    }
    return (0);
}


//
//   FUNCTION: CenterWindow (HWND, HWND)
//
//   PURPOSE:  Center one window over another
//
```

LISTING 11.3 CONTINUED

```
//   COMMENTS:
//
//       Dialog boxes take on the screen position that they were designed
//       at, which is not always appropriate. Centering the dialog over a
//       particular window usually results in a better position.
//

BOOL CenterWindow (HWND hwndChild, HWND hwndParent)
{
    RECT     rChild, rParent;
    int      wChild, hChild, wParent, hParent;
    int      wScreen, hScreen, xNew, yNew;
    HDC      hdc;

    // Get the Height and Width of the child window
    GetWindowRect (hwndChild, &rChild);
    wChild = rChild.right - rChild.left;
    hChild = rChild.bottom - rChild.top;


    // Get the Height and Width of the parent window
    GetWindowRect (hwndParent, &rParent);
    wParent = rParent.right - rParent.left;
    hParent = rParent.bottom - rParent.top;


    // Get the display limits
    hdc = GetDC (hwndChild);
    wScreen = GetDeviceCaps (hdc, HORZRES);
    hScreen = GetDeviceCaps (hdc, VERTRES);
    ReleaseDC (hwndChild, hdc);

    // Calculate new X position, then adjust for screen
    xNew = rParent.left + ((wParent - wChild) /2);
    if (xNew < 0) {
        xNew = 0;
    }
    else if ((xNew+wChild) > wScreen) {
        xNew = wScreen - wChild;
    }


    // Calculate new Y position, then adjust for screen
    yNew = rParent.top  + ((hParent - hChild) /2);
    if (yNew < 0) {
        yNew = 0;
```

```
      }
   else if ((yNew+hChild) > hScreen) {
      yNew = hScreen - hChild;
   }


   // Set it, and return
   return SetWindowPos (hwndChild, NULL,
      xNew, yNew, 0, 0, SWP_NOSIZE | SWP_NOZORDER);
}


//
//    FUNCTION: About(HWND, UINT, WPARAM, LPARAM)
//
//    PURPOSE:  Processes messages for "About" dialog box
//
//    MESSAGES:
//
//       WM_INITDIALOG - initialize dialog box
//       WM_COMMAND    - Input received
//
//    COMMENTS:
//
//       Display version information from the version section of the
//       application resource.
//
//       Wait for user to click on "Ok" button, then close the dialog box.
//

LRESULT CALLBACK About(
        HWND hDlg,           // window handle of the dialog box
        UINT message,        // type of message
        WPARAM uParam,       // message-specific information
        LPARAM lParam
        )
{
   static  HFONT hfontDlg;

   switch (message) {
      case WM_INITDIALOG:  // message: initialize dialog box
         // Create a font to use
         hfontDlg = CreateFont(14, 0, 0, 0, 0, 0, 0, 0,
            0, 0, 0, 0,
            VARIABLE_PITCH | FF_SWISS, "");

         // Center the dialog over the application window
         CenterWindow (hDlg, GetWindow (hDlg, GW_OWNER));
```

LISTING 11.3 CONTINUED

```
        return (TRUE);

    case WM_COMMAND:                        // message: received a command
        if (LOWORD(uParam) == IDOK          // "OK" box selected?
            || LOWORD(uParam) == IDCANCEL) {// System menu close command?
            EndDialog(hDlg, TRUE);          // Exit the dialog
            DeleteObject (hfontDlg);
            return (TRUE);
        }
        break;
    }
    return (FALSE); // Didn't process the message

    lParam; // This will prevent 'unused formal parameter' warnings
}
```

There are many, many features available in the TreeView control. It's impossible to cover every minute detail here. I'll cover the most commonly used TreeView features: initialization and cleanup, adding items, deleting items, using an Image List, and label editing (allowing a user to change the text of an item in place). A brief discussion of drag-and-drop will also be included for your reading pleasure.

TreeView Flavors and Limitations

The TreeView control has several different appearances.

```
// TreeView window styles
#define TVS_HASBUTTONS      0x0001 // draw "plus" & "minus" sign on nodes with
                                   // children
#define TVS_HASLINES        0x0002 // draw lines between nodes
#define TVS_LINESATROOT     0x0004 // Draw the lines also at the root level
#define TVS_EDITLABELS      0x0008 // allow text edit in place
```

The two most fundamental types are those with plain text and those with Image Lists attached to them. The TreeView control can dynamically toggle between these two types. If a TreeView control is to use an Image List, then every item in the TreeView will be drawn with an image from the Image List, and every image must come from the same Image List. This means that every item in the TreeView control will have an equal-sized image tagged next to it. There is no such thing as an owner-draw TreeView control, although there is a special callback implementation that gives you a little bit of on-the-fly drawing control, but not enough to get around the equal-sized image limitation. I'll discuss how to implement this callback functionality later.

There are various styles of the TreeView control that cover the "lines" and "buttons." Lines are the connecting dotted lines from item to item in the TreeView, and buttons have plus and minus signs in them to allow the user to expand and collapse certain branches of the TreeView with a single mouse click (see Figure 11.15). Double-clicking on a node will achieve the same results.

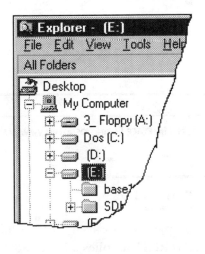

FIGURE 11.15 LINES AND BUTTONS IN A TREEVIEW

Lines have two styles: root and nodes. If you use root lines, then items at the root level will be connected. Node lines are all the lines deeper than the root level. There is only one button style: either your TreeView uses buttons or it doesn't.

Another variant of the TreeView control allows in-place editing of the TreeView text labels. When the user clicks on an already selected label in a TreeView, a little edit control pops up in-place for the user to change the value (see Figure 11.16). This feature will be discussed in more detail later.

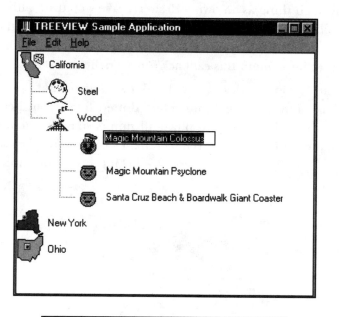

FIGURE 11.16 IN-PLACE EDITING OF A TREEVIEW LABEL

TreeView Interface Macros

The TreeView control is completely message-based; in other words there are no APIs. However, COMMCTRL.H supplies a boatload of macros, which I'll explain throughout this Goodie (and some other Goodies also use the same scheme), that make it very easy to interface to the TreeView control without dealing with message building. For this list, I will only use the macros, since they will easily recompile to different platforms. To satisfy the curious, I will put the message used in <crocodiles> after the macro:

```
TreeView_SetImageList ( hWndTV, hIml )  <TVM_SETIMAGELIST>
```

TreeView Creation and Adding Items

There are three steps to creating a TreeView control. First, you need to create the TreeView window using your old pal **CreateWindow** (the TreeView can also be part of a resource template, such as a dialog). Second, you can optionally tell the TreeView what level of indentation you want for each branch, and you can optionally tell the TreeView to use an Image List. And finally, you add your items.

A TreeView item is much more than a string. It contains the string, the image(s) from the Image List, the state (such as selected or unselected), and some user data (a DWORD, which is a handy place to put your C++ this pointer). Each item in the list box is accessible by a handle, defined as HTREEITEM in COMMCTRL.H. Unlike in a list box, you do not access an item by its index, you access it by the handle. This is very nice, since the items in a TreeView can be sorted, dragged, and dropped, yet they still keep the same handle. This makes it a lot easier for programmers to keep track of items; of course, you have to manage the handles yourself. (However, there are ways to get handle values by position.)

To add an item, you will fill out a TV_INSERTSTRUCT structure (described later) and pass it to the TreeView, which will return a handle to you. To traverse the list of items, you will communicate with the TreeView to find the first/next item in the list.

Before I get into how to get handles and traverse lists in detail, let's start from the top and look at the three steps involved with making a TreeView control. Steps 2 and 3 are optional, although if you don't do them, you will have one of the most boring TreeView programs in the known universe: an empty window. Let's look at each step in more detail.

Step 1: Create the Control

First, be sure to include COMMCTRL.H and link with COMCTL32.LIB. And, since the TreeView control is a window, you must instruct the COMCTL32.DLL to register the class. This is done with a one-time initialization call into COMCTL32.DLL:

```
InitCommonControls();  // Place this in WinMain or some other startup code
```

Now, using CreateWindow (or via a dialog template), you will want to use the class name of WC_TREEVIEW, which is currently defined as SysTreeView32 in Windows 95. This makes it easier to cross-compile for future platforms, and it lets you avoid using that string constant in a million places (which wastes memory). So, plop this in your global variable declaration:

```
char szTreeViewClass[] = WC_TREEVIEW;
```

and then use szTreeViewClass everywhere. For the style bits, use the styles in the table in Figure 11.17.

Style	Meaning
TVS_HASLINES	Show lines for the nodes
TVS_LINESATROOT	Show lines for the root items
TVS_HASBUTTONS	Show buttons for applicable items
TVS_EDITLABELS	Allow "in-place" editing of text

FIGURE 11.17 TreeView styles

Step 2: Set Optional TreeView Attributes

Once you have created the control, you may want to change the indent amount for child nodes, or you may want to use an Image List. To change the indent amount from the default (which is slightly more than the pixel width of an image if the control has an Image List, and slightly less than an icon's width if the control is plain text), use the TreeView_SetIndent <TVM_SETINDENT> macro. Likewise, you can find out the indent with the TreeView_GetIndent <TVM_GETINDENT> macro:

```
BOOL TreeView_SetIndent(HWND hWndTV,        // Handle of TreeView
                        UINT uIndent );    // Indent, in pixels

UINT TreeView_GetIndent(HWND hWndTV);      // Handle of TreeView
```

A very common attribute for the TreeView will be, of course, the Image List. The left pane of the Explorer shows how colorful graphics images can make a TreeView control take on a really vibrant appearance. To associate an Image List with a TreeView, use the TreeView_SetImageList <TVM_SETIM-AGELIST> macro, and use TreeView_GetImageList <TVM_GETIMAGELIST> to retrieve the current Image List in use by the TreeView control:

```
HIMAGELIST TreeView_SetImageList(HWND        hWndTV, // Handle of TreeView
                                 HIMAGELIST  hIml);  // Handle of Image List

HIMAGELIST TreeView_GetImageList(HWND        hWndTV); // Handle of TreeView
```

A word of caution: since an Image List is created with a default background color of transparent, you can run into some weird problems when using a default Image List with a TreeView control. Since an item in a TreeView can support one of two different images (one for a selected state and one for a nonselected state), if the actual shapes in the two images do not have the exact same size (that is, their transparent masks are not the same), then they will paint over each other as your item becomes selected or unselected. Figure 11.18 shows an item in a TreeView that has an X for the selected image and an O for the nonselected image. This item was once nonselected, and is now selected. The X was drawn right over the O, which is why both images seem to be painted in the same area. What is the solution? Since a TreeView control's background color will by default be the value returned from GetSysColor (COLOR_WINDOW), you can set the background color of the Image List to that color as well:

```
ImageList_SetBkColor (hImageList, GetSysColor ( COLOR_WINDOW ));
```

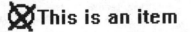

FIGURE 11.18 THE PERILS OF USING A TRANSPARENT BACKGROUND FOR DUAL IMAGES

Step 3: Add Your Items

At this point, you should have your TreeView control prepared and ready for some serious item addition action! But wait, there's more! Unlike the dinosaur list box control, adding items to the TreeView is not as simple as passing a string into the control with some Jurassic LB_ADDSTRING message. Since the TreeView control is a hierarchical list, each item must fit into some branch of the tree. Think of a TreeView as a hard disk, and each item as a file. The root directory is the equal to the root of the TreeView. The TreeView can have children (subdirectories) and those children can have children as well (more subdirectories). To make things easier, let's say that a node is an item that has children (like an MS-DOS subdirectory), and an item has no children (like a normal MS-DOS file). Remember, though, that a node and an item are both exactly the same in the eyes of the TreeView control; my terminology is just an attempt to make it easier to understand.

So when you add an item or node, you not only need to specify what it is, but where it goes. The developers of the TreeView control wisely kept these two different properties separate from each other. To specify what a TreeView item or node is, you will fill out a structure called TV_ITEM (see Figure 11.19). This structure defines the attributes of the text, images, selection state, and user-supplied data. To specify where a TreeView item or node goes, you will fill out a structure called TV_INSERTSTRUCT (see Figure 11.20). Both structures are used when you insert the item into the TreeView.

```
typedef struct _TV_ITEM
  {
  UINT      mask;           // TVIF_ flags
  HTREEITEM hItem;          // The item to be changed
  UINT      state;          // TVIS_ flags
  UINT      stateMask;      // TVIS_ flags (valid bits in state)
  LPSTR     pszText;        // The text for this item
  int       cchTextMax;     // The length of the pszText buffer
  int       iImage;         // The index of the image for this item
  int       iSelectedImage; // the index of the selected imagex
  int       cChildren;      // # of child nodes, I_CHILDRENCALLBACK for callback
```

```
    LPARAM     lParam;            // App defined data
}
TV_ITEM, FAR *LPTV_ITEM;
```

FIGURE 11.19 THE TV_ITEM STRUCTURE

```
typedef struct _TV_INSERTSTRUCT
  {
  HTREEITEM hParent;       // a valid HTREEITEM or TVI_ value
  HTREEITEM hInsertAfter;  // a valid HTREEITEM or TVI_ value
  TV_ITEM item;
  }
TV_INSERTSTRUCT, FAR *LPTV_INSERTSTRUCT;
```

FIGURE 11.20 THE TV_INSERTSTRUCT STRUCTURE

Let's first define an item. I'll start off with a plain boring text item, one that has something really boring in it (assume this TreeView control does not have an Image List attached to it):

```
TV_ITEM        tvi;
tvi.mask = TVIF_TEXT;        // This item has text
tvi.pszText = "Whitewater"; // Something really boring
```

There, that was easy. Now, I need to add this to a TreeView. To do this, I fill out a TV_INSERTSTRUCT and then call the TreeView_InsertItem <TVM_INSERTITEM> macro:

```
TV_INSERTSTRUCT tvis;
tvis.hParent= hParent;              // Set parent node
tvis.hInsertAfter= hInsertAfter;    // Indicate sibling item to add this item after
tvis.item= tvi;                     // Indicate the item (from above)
hItem =TreeView_InsertItem ( hWndTV, &tvis ); // Add the item to the TreeView,
                                              // return value is handle to item
```

If you wanted to make the above item into a node, simply add another item with **TreeView_InsertItem**, and use the above hItem return value (from the Whitewater item) as the **hParent** for your new item. This will automatically turn your Whitewater item into a node.

If your TreeView control is using an Image List, you simply need to indicate the images to use when filling out the TV_ITEM structure. Say you are using an Image List whose first image (**iFirstImage**) is a log, and the second image (**iSecondImage**) is a box of sugar-frosted milk. To add these two items to the same node in a TreeView, you would use code like Figure 11.21. Notice that both the **iImage** and **iSelected** image fields are set. That is because the TreeView will draw different images for the item depending on whether it's selected. Since this tiny sample doesn't utilize this feature, use the same value. If you only filled in the **iImage** field and used the TVIF_IMAGE style bit only, the **iSelectedImage** would default to 0, and you would find that image #0 would always be drawn on your selected item.

```
TV_ITEM          tvi;
TV_INSERTSTRUCT  tvis;
tvi.mask =       TVIF_TEXT | TVIS_IMAGE | TVIS_SELECTEDIMAGE;
                 // This item has text,
                 // and an image
tvi.pszText ="Log";      // Every kid loves Log!
tvi.iImage =
tvi.iSelectedImage =iFirstImage; // Use Log image
tvis.hParent=hParent;            // Set parent node to add this item under
tvis.hInsertAfter=hInsertAfter;  // Indicate sibling item to add this item after
tvis.item=tvi;   // Indicate the item (from above)
hItem = TreeView_InsertItem ( hWndTV, &tvis );// Add the item to the TreeView
tvi.pszText ="Sugar Frosted Milk";       // Stays crunchy in cereal!
tvi.iImage =
tvi.iSelectedImage =iSecondImage; // Use Sugar Frosted Milk Image
tvi.hInsertAfter =hItem;         // Add right after "Log"
hItem = TreeView_InsertItem ( hWndTV, &tvis );// Add the item to the TreeView
```

FIGURE 11.21 ADDING TWO ITEMS TO THE SAME NODE

See, still easy! That, actually, is basically how to add items to the TreeView. However, there is a lot of syrup to pass around the TreeView dinner table, so let's jump into some of the enhancements. These enhancements include using two images from an Image List per item/node and a snappy way of doing on-the-fly item/node drawing.

Dueling Images On "Duh" Fly With Callbacks

Sometimes you may wish to have a different image for a selected item and a non-selected item. To do this, you simply put the number of one image in the iImage field and the number of the other image in the **iSelectedImage** field of the TV_ITEM structure, and make sure to use the TVIS_IMAGE and TVIS_SELECTEDIMAGE style bits.

A more common use for two different images would be to indicate the state of a node. Say your node is a folder. If you want to draw the folder open when the node is expanded and closed when the node is collapsed, you will need to set up a callback. This callback is a different type than you're used to. Instead of calling some exported function in your program, the TreeView control will send the parent of the TreeView control a new message: WM_NOTIFY.

WM_NOTIFY

This is a new message for Windows 95, used instead of the clunky WM_COMMAND method to notify parents (which has always been a pain since menus also use WM_COMMAND).

```
// WM_NOTIFY: wParam =  id of the control, lParam points
// to a NMHDR structure.

typedef  struct tagNMHDR
  {
  HWND    hwndFrom; // Handle of control sending message
  UINT    idFrom;   // id of control sending message
  UINT    code;     // notif. code (depends on control)
  }
NMHDR;
```

The TreeView control overloads this structure by wrapping the NMHDR structure in a larger structure (making sure to keep the original NMHDR structure at the start of the new structure). So, when the TreeView sends the parent a WM_NOTIFY message, **lParam** points to a TV_DISPINFO structure:

```
typedef struct _TV_DISPINFO
  {
  NMHDR       hdr;    // from above
  TV_ITEM     item;   // Item in question
  }
TV_DISPINFO;
```

The fields in the new structure will be used differently in various scenarios. Let's look at the first scenario: On-the-fly image selection.

TVN_GETDISPINFO

If you want to determine the images or text of an item on-the-fly, use the special I_IMAGECALLBACK constant in COMMCTRL.H in place of image numbers. This will cause the TreeView control to send a callback message to the TreeView's parent.

```
tvi.iImage =
tvi.iSelectedImage = I_IMAGECALLBACK; // Use a callback
                        // to get image at Draw time
```

If you use the I_IMAGECALLBACK constant, the TVN_GETDISPINFO notification message will be sent to the parent of the TreeView control at draw time via the WM_NOTIFY message (see Figure 11.22 for a list of callbacks via WM_NOTIFY). Figure 11.23 shows what the WM_NOTIFY message will look like to your parent window. The state of the control is filled out automatically by the TreeView control. Your parent window needs to fill in the image numbers depending on the state of your item. For example, let's say you want to use the iOpenFolder and iClosedFolder images, depending on whether or not the node is collapsed or expanded. To do this, use I_IMAGECALLBACK for the iImage and iSelectedImage fields of your TV_ITEM structure, and then add WM_NOTIFY code to the parent window procedure of the TreeView control. One of the constants defined in COMMCTRL.H for the different states of an item is TVIS_EXPANDED, which indicates if the node is open or closed. Using that constant, Figure 11.24 shows a quick-and-dirty way to handle the WM_NOTIFY message. Of course, this code is for demonstration only; in your app there would most likely be many more cases of the WM_NOTIFY message (from other controls not discussed here), and you will write a WM_NOTIFY handler function.

Callback's Purpose	How to invoke it	Type of Message sent via WM_NOTIFY
Count the number of child nodes	While filling in the TV_ITEM structure, use I_CHILDRENCALLBACK for cChildren field	TVN_GETDISPINFO
Supply an Image number at draw time for an item	While filling in the TV_ITEM structure, use I_IMAGECALLBACK for iImage and/or iSelectedImage field	TVN_GETDISPINFO
Supply Label Text at draw time	While filling in the TV_ITEM structure, use LPSTR_CALLBACK for pszText field	TVN_GETDISPINFO
Allow Label Editing	Use the TVS_EDITLABELS style bit when creating the TreeView control	TVN_BEGINLABELEDIT
Accept Label Edits	Use the TVS_EDITLABELS style bit when creating the TreeView control	TVN_ENDLABELEDIT
Allow Drag and Drop	This comes for free	TVN_BEGINDRAG TVN_BEGINRDRAG
Do something in response to node Expanding or collapsing	This comes for free	TVN_ITEMEXPANDING (not covered in this list)
Do something in response to node getting deleted	This comes for free	TVN_DELETEITEM (not covered in this list)

FIGURE 11.22 TREEVIEW CALLBACK MESSAGE CODES

```
wParam = idTreeViewControl.
lParam points to a TV_DISPINFO:
    (TV_DISPINFO)lParam->hdr.hwndFrom      = hWndTV
    (TV_DISPINFO)lParam->hdr.idfrom        = idTreeViewControl
    (TV_DISPINFO)lParam->hdr.code          = TVN_GETDISPINFO
    (TV_DISPINFO)lParam->item.mask         = TVIF_IMAGE | TVIF_SELECTEDIMAGE
    (TV_DISPINFO)lParam->item.state        = (state of control)
    (TV_DISPINFO)lParam->item.lParam       = (user-defined data)
```

FIGURE 11.23 WM_NOTIFY SENT TO PARENT

```
case WM_NOTIFY:

        if (TVN_GETDISPINFO == ((LPNMHDR)lParam)->code)
          {
          if ( ((((TV_DISPINFO *)lParam)->item.state) & TVIS_EXPANDED )
            {
            ((TV_DISPINFO *)lParam)->item.iImage =
            ((TV_DISPINFO *)lParam)->item.iSelectedImage = iOpenFolder;
            }
          else
            {
            ((TV_DISPINFO *)lParam)->item.iImage =
            ((TV_DISPINFO *)lParam)->item.iSelectedImage = iClosedFolder;
            }
          return TRUE;
          }
        return (DefWindowProc(hWnd, message, uParam, lParam));
```

FIGURE 11.24 HANDLING WM_NOTIFY

Text Strings on the Fly With Callbacks

A text callback is needed if you want to determine the text for a label at draw
time. They're just like the I_IMAGECALLBACK, except that you use
LPSTR_CALLBACK for the **pszText** field of the TV_ITEM structure. Then,
when you get your TVN_GETDISPINFO message, fill in the pszText field of the
TV_DISPINFO->item field. You can use the **lParam** field of the TV_DISPINFO-

>item to access a this pointer to get your string. When you add the item to the TreeView, you can store a handle/pointer/record number/whatever in that value, and use that value now to determine the string to return.

Okay, enough on drawing the items in the TreeView. Let's move on to some more features.

In-place Label Editing

A very cool feature of the TreeView is in-place label editing. If the user clicks once on a label, a little edit control pops up for the user to change the text (refer back to Figure 11.16). You'd do this, say, if you want to rename files in the Explorer. Of course, this does not come for free. You have to do a little bit of work to get the basic functionality, and a lot of work if you want more functionality. Let's start with the basics.

There are two steps for implementing label editing. The first step is taken when the user clicks on a selected label. The TreeView's parent window is sent a TVN_BEGINLABELEDIT notification via the WM_NOTIFY message. At this point, the TreeView can do a number of things, but the most important is determining whether the label should be edited or not. For example, you may want to let the user change the labels of the child items in a TreeView, but not the root nodes. The parent window returns zero to allow editing, nonzero to abort.

The second step happens after the user completes editing (by either pressing Enter to accept or Esc to cancel). The TreeView's parent windows will get a TVN_ENDLABELEDIT notification via the WM_NOTIFY message; this is your program's chance to validate the text and update the actual label in the TreeView. The TreeView will not automatically update the label text— you must do it in response to the TVN_ENDLABELEDIT notification code.

Let's look at a simple way to do label editing. The code in Listing 11.4 will accept whatever the user types in, and will not allow editing of the root items. This code introduces two more features of the TreeView. The first is part of the query interface for the TreeView. The macro used was TreeView_GetParent <TVM_GETNEXTITEM>. This TVM_GETNEXTITEM message takes a bunch of different types of flags for wParam. I'll discuss the query interface later.

LISTING 11.4 CORE CODE FOR LABEL EDITING

```
case WM_NOTIFY:

  switch (((LPNMHDR)lParam)->code)
    {
    case TVN_BEGINLABELEDIT: // Run this code for the label edit start

      // Get the parent control using the TreeView_GetParent
      // macro <TVM_GETNEXTITEM:TVGN_PARENT>, and check to see if it
      // is the root.
      if (TVGN_ROOT != TreeView_GetParent
                        (
                          ((LPNMHDR)lParam)->hwndFrom,
                          ((TV_DISPINFO *)lParam)->item.hItem
                        )
         )
        return 0;  // Return 0 to OK edit
      else
        return 1;  // Return non-zero to disallow edit
      break;


    case TVN_ENDLABELEDIT: // Run this code when user is done

      // Check to make sure user did not cancel action.
      // If they cancelled, the string pointer is NULL.
      if ( ((TV_DISPINFO *)lParam)->item.pszText )
        {
        ((TV_DISPINFO *)lParam)->item.mask = TVIF_TEXT;
        TreeView_SetItem
          (
            ((LPNMHDR)lParam)->hwndFrom,
            &(((TV_DISPINFO *)lParam)->item)
          );
        }
      break;
    }
  return (DefWindowProc(hWnd, message, uParam, lParam));
```

The second feature is the TreeView_SetItem <TVM_SETITEM> macro, which is a way to modify items in the TreeView. I'll also discuss item maintenance features later.

Other Goodies

The above code for in-place label editing will probably be enough for 90 percent of the programs that will use the TreeView control. For programs that require more control over the label editing process, you can get the handle to that in-place edit control with the TreeView_GetEditControl <TVM_ GETEDITCONTROL> macro.

Your application should retrieve the edit control handle when it receives a TVM_BEGINLABELEDIT notification. You can then subclass this edit control, change its size, or move it as desired. But whatever you do, don't destroy it— the TreeView will do that for you. Once you get the TVM_ENDLABELEDIT message, assume that the handle to the edit control will be invalid after you return from that notification.

TreeView Drag-and-Drop

Dragging and dropping items in a TreeView is actually quite straightforward. You do this when you move files in the Explorer. There are three steps involved. The first step requires setting up the drag operation when a TVN_BEGINDRAG notification is received via WM_NOTIFY, and eventually calling the **ImageList_StartDrag** API. The second step involves calling the **ImageList_DragMove** API in response to WM_MOUSEMOVE messages captured in the TreeView's parent, and (optionally) checking for a drop target inside the TreeView control. The third step involves calling the **ImageList_EndDrag** function in response to the WM_XBUTTONUP message. Let's cover each step in more detail.

TVN_BEGINDRAG is sent via the WM_NOTIFY message to the Tree-View's parent when the user starts a drag operation. In response to this message, your program must first create a drag image. This image will look just like the item in the TreeView, but dithered. A macro called TreeView_CreateDragImage <TVM_CREATEDRAGIMAGE> will do all of this automatically, and return a handle to an Image List with the drag image already inside it. Then use the TreeView_GetItemRect <TVM_GETITEMRECT> macro to figure out where the item is positioned onscreen. Finally, call the standard **ImageList_StartDrag** and **SetCapture** code.

Make sure you cache away the handle of the item you are dragging; you will need it later when you drop the item.

A note about the WM_NOTIFY message. Instead of **lParam** pointing to a TV_DISPINFO structure, **lParam** will point to the more general-purpose NM_TREEVIEW structure. This structure is also an overloaded NMHDR structure, with different information in it:

```
typedef struct _NM_TREEVIEW
  {
  NMHDR       hdr;        // Standard NMHDR
  UINT        action;     // notif. specific action
  TV_ITEM     itemOld;    // Old item state
  TV_ITEM     itemNew;    // New item state
  POINT       ptDrag;     // Mouse cursor pos (in TV
                          // client coords)
  }
NM_TREEVIEW;
```

Using that new notification, use code like Listing 11.5a to handle Step 1.

LISTING 11.5A STEP 1 OF A TREEVIEW DRAG AND DROP

```
case WM_NOTIFY:

  switch ((((LPNMHDR)lParam)->code)
    {
    case TVN_BEGINDRAG:
      {
      RECT        rcItem;
      // hDragImage is static, so we can delete it when
```

```
// the user stops dragging. Here we create a
// drag image to use for the ImageList_StartDrag
// API.

hDragImage = TreeView_CreateDragImage
             (
             ((LPNMHDR)lParam)->hwndFrom,
             ((NM_TREEVIEW *)lParam)->itemNew.hItem
             );


// Get the location of the item rectangle

TreeView_GetItemRect
  (
  ((LPNMHDR)lParam)->hwndFrom,
  ((NM_TREEVIEW *)lParam)->itemNew.hItem,
  &rcItem,
  TRUE      // TRUE = Rect of label text only
  );


// Cache away the handle of the item to drag

hDragItem = ((NM_TREEVIEW *)lParam)->itemNew.hItem;


// Start the drag ala ImageList

ImageList_StartDrag
  (
  hDragImage,
  ((LPNMHDR)lParam)->hwndFrom,
  0,
  ((NM_TREEVIEW *)lParam)->ptDrag.x,
  ((NM_TREEVIEW *)lParam)->ptDrag.y,
  ((NM_TREEVIEW *)lParam)->ptDrag.x - rcItem.left,
  ((NM_TREEVIEW *)lParam)->ptDrag.y - rcItem.top
  );


// Capture the mousey to this window

ShowCursor ( FALSE );
SetCapture ( hWnd );


// Set a drag flag
```

LISTING 11.5A CONTINUED

```
    bDragging = TRUE;

    return 0L;  // Return value is irrelevant
    }
```

Step 2: In addition to the standard Image List drag operations, you may want to provide a touch of user feedback. When you drag the current item over another item in the TreeView, it would be really polite to highlight the drop location so the user knows he or she is dropping the item onto the correct location.

The TreeView provides a nice pair of features to make this easy. The first macro, TreeView_HitTest <TVM_HITTEST>, returns the handle to the item at a specified location. The second macro, TreeView_SelectDropTarget <TVM_SELECTDROPTARGET>, does the highlighting for you. To use TreeView_HitTest, you need to fill out a TV_HITTESTINFO structure (defined in COMMCTRL.H). See Listing 11.5b for a sample implementation.

LISTING 11.5B STEP 2 OF A TREEVIEW DRAG AND DROP

```
case WM_MOUSEMOVE:

   if (bDragging)
     {
     HTREEITEM        hTarget;   // Item under mouse
     TV_HITTESTINFO   tvht;      // Used for hit testing

     // Do standard drag drop movement

     ImageList_DragMove ( LOWORD (lParam), HIWORD (lParam));

     // Fill out hit test struct with mouse pos

     tvht.pt.x = LOWORD (lParam);
     tvht.pt.y =+ HIWORD (lParam);

     // Check to see if an item lives under the mouse
```

```
   if ( hTarget = TreeView_HitTest
                 (
                 hWndTreeView,   // This is the global variable
                 &tvht
                 )
       )
     {
     // Select the item
     TreeView_SelectDropTarget ( hWndTreeView, hTarget );
     }
   }
break;
```

Step 3: Once the user lets go of the mouse button, it is time to take two actions: clean up the drag operation and do something in response to the user dropping. Cleaning up is easy. Simply release mouse capture, call that **ImageList_EndDrag** API, and clean up the Image List. The more complex part is where your program does something with the drag-and-drop operation.

First, get the drop item using the same **TreeView_HitTest** method you used to handle the WM_MOUSEMOVE message in Step 2. Then, check to see if the handle to the drag item you cached away in Step 1 can be dropped. If so, you can do the operation. The sample code is brain-dead; it will just blindly drag and drop any item anywhere.

To move an item around, delete it and then add it back. To delete an item, use the (brace yourself) TreeView_DeleteItem <TVM_DELETEITEM> macro. To add it back, just use the **TreeView_InsertItem** macro. To automatically fill out the TV_ITEM structure, use the **TreeView_GetItem** macro. See the code in Listing 11.5c for the brain-dead drag-and-drop implementation.

LISTING 11.5C STEP 3 OF A TREEVIEW DRAG AND DROP

```
case WM_LBUTTONUP:

  if (bDragging)
    {
    HTREEITEM        hTarget;      // Item under mouse
    TV_HITTESTINFO   tvht;         // Used for hit testing
    TV_ITEM          tvi;          // Temporary Item
    TV_INSERTSTRUCT  tvIns;        // Insert struct
```

LISTING 11.5C CONTINUED

```
char            szBuffer[256]; // Item text buffer

// Clear any drop highlights on the TreeView
TreeView_SelectDropTarget ( hWndTreeView, NULL );
// End the drag
ImageList_EndDrag();
// Bring back the cursor
ShowCursor ( TRUE );
// Release the mouse capture
ReleaseCapture();
// Clear the drag flag
bDragging = FALSE;
// Clean up the image list object
ImageList_Destroy ( hDragImage );
hDragImage = NULL;


// Fill out hit test struct with mouse pos

tvht.pt.x = LOWORD (lParam);
tvht.pt.y = HIWORD (lParam);


// Check to see if an item lives under the mouse

if ( hTarget = TreeView_HitTest
            (
            hWndTreeView,  // This is the global variable
            &tvht
            )
  )
  {
  // If we made it here, then we need to move the item.
  // First, we will fetch it

  tvi.mask       = TVIF_HANDLE | TVIF_TEXT | TVIF_IMAGE | TVIF_SELECTEDIMAGE ;
  tvi.hItem      = hDragItem;
  tvi.pszText    = szBuffer;
  tvi.cchTextMax = sizeof(szBuffer);
```

```
        TreeView_GetItem ( hWndTreeView, &tvi );

        // Now, figure the new place to put it

        tvIns.hParent          = TreeView_GetParent ( hWndTreeView, hTarget );
        tvIns.hInsertAfter     = hTarget;

        // Nix the handle flag, since we will get a new handle
        // for this item

        tvi.mask               &= ~TVIF_HANDLE;

        tvIns.item             = tvi;

        // Delete old item

        TreeView_DeleteItem ( hWndTreeView, hDragItem );

        // Add new item (if your app tracks the handles of
        // the items, you want to use the return value
        // of this function).

        TreeView_InsertItem ( hWndTreeView, &tvIns );
        }

    }
break;
```

TreeView Querying

The TreeView control exposes almost every tidbit of information you can
think of. I've already used a few of them in the above samples, such as
TreeView_GetParent, **TreeView_GetEditControl**, and **TreeView_HitTest**.
Figure 11.25 lists all of the query macros with a short explanation of each.
For more information, check out the docs supplied with the Windows 95
beta SDK or look in COMMCTRL.H.

Macro	Result
TreeView_GetItemRect(hwnd, hitem, prc, code)	Gets the bounding rect in client coordinates of the item. Code is TRUE or FALSE, TRUE means the bounding rect of the item's text only. FALSE means the entire width of the TreeView control
TreeView_GetCount(hwnd)	Counts the number of items in the TreeView
TreeView_GetIndent(hwnd)	Returns the indent amount, in pixels
TreeView_GetImageList(hwnd, iImage)	Returns the handle to the current Image List
TreeView_GetNextItem(hwnd, hitem, code)	Returns the handle to an item, depending on the code. However, there are macros that eliminate the need to use this macro (such as TreeView_GetChild macro, which is actually a flavor of TreeView_GetNextItem)
TreeView_GetChild(hwnd, hitem)	Returns the handle to the first child item of a node
TreeView_GetNextSibling(hwnd, hitem)	Returns the handle to the next sibling item
TreeView_GetPrevSibling(hwnd, hitem)	Returns the handle to the previous sibling
TreeView_GetParent(hwnd, hitem)	Returns the handle to the parent node of an item
TreeView_GetFirstVisible(hwnd)	Returns the handle of the first visible item
TreeView_GetNextVisible(hwnd, hitem)	Returns the handle of the next item, if it is visible. Otherwise returns NULL
TreeView_GetPrevVisible(hwnd, hitem)	Returns the handle of the previous item, if it is visible. Otherwise returns NULL
TreeView_GetSelection(hwnd)	Returns the handle to the currently selected item
TreeView_GetDropHilight(hwnd)	Returns the handle to the currently drop-highlighted selection
TreeView_GetRoot(hwnd)	Returns the handle to the first root node
TreeView_GetItem(hwnd, pitem)	Fills a TV_ITEM structure for the TreeView, indicated by the hItem field.
TreeView_GetEditControl(hwnd)	Returns the handle to the in-place edit control during a Label Edit session
TreeView_GetVisibleCount(hwnd)	Returns the number of items that are visible
TreeView_HitTest(hwnd, lpht)	Returns the item under the coordinates specified by the TV_HITTESTINFO structure

FIGURE 11.25 TREEVIEW QUERY MACROS

Finally, every control has some oddball functions that get lumped together into a big bowl of API oatmeal. Figure 11.26 showcases these macros, and explains what they do.

Macro	Result
TreeView_Select(hwnd, hitem, code)	Selects a specified item in the TreeView.
TreeView_SelectItem(hwnd, item)	Selects the item with the caret in the TreeView.
TreeView_SortChildren(hwnd, hitem, recurse)	Sorts the items in a branch of the TreeView.
TreeView_EnsureVisible(hwnd, hitem)	Makes sure that an item is visible, by either expanding the parent node and/or scrolling the item into view.
TreeView_SortChildrenCB(hwnd, psort, recurse)	Sorts the children using a callback function. Read the docs for more information about this.
TreeView_EditLabel(hwnd, hitem)	Starts an in-place edit session on an item programatically.

FIGURE 11.26 TREEVIEW MISCELLANEOUS MACROS

The Mother of All Samples

Well, this is it. You have been reading this list for hours, days, perhaps months, and all you really wanted was just a sample program to go cut and paste from. The TREEVIEW.EXE sample program (Listing 11.3, above) builds a TreeView control that uses an Image List. The items inside the TreeView are roller coasters, such as the Coney Island Cyclone. When the sample app starts up, the TreeView is filled with a list of some of the coasters in the states of California, Ohio, and New York. You can expand or collapse the list, and pretend you are ACME Roller Coaster Relocation, Inc., and drag-and-drop the coasters from state to state. Also, the I_IMAGECALLBACK feature is used to display a different folder for the open and closed State nodes (when a state is closed, there is a little plus sign in it; when it is open, there is a piece of cheese, since this is such a cheesy example). Different images are used for the selected and non-selected coaster names. A normal coaster rider is displayed when the item is non-selected; when the coaster is selected, the rider is taking a plunge down the first gut-wrenching drop and losing their hat.

Also, label editing works, so you can change the name of a roller coaster (but not the name of a state), in case you want to rename one to "Bitchin' Camaro Cool Coaster."

So without further ado, let me explain the code. As with the Image List sample program, this TREEVIEW program is a derivative of GENERIC, with all code changes bracketed by NEW CODE START and NEW CODE END comment blocks.

The initialization of the TreeView control happens in the **Sample_Init** function. Here the **InitCommonControls** API is called to make the TreeView class available to this application. Next, the Image List for the TreeView is created from scratch, and a bunch of icons from the resource file are added. The return values from the **ImageList_AddIcon** API are stored away in global variables, since the program will use these image numbers all over the place. Then the TreeView control is created with CreateWindow, and upon success, it is filled with exciting coaster data.

The **FillTreeView** function involves a few helper functions. The **iNumCoasters** function simply grabs the string from the string table in TREEVIEW.STR and uses that number to determine how many items to add to the TreeView. Inside the loop in **FillTreeView**, the **FindOrAddTree ViewItem** function is called for each node level, starting with the root node and working deeper. This method adds new nodes as needed, always returning a handle to a node for adding the next deeper level.

The **FindOrAddTreeViewItem** function may call the **AddTreeViewItem** function, which simply fills out the appropriate structures and calls the **TreeView_InsertItem** macro. When adding items to the TreeView control, the **lParam** field of the TV_ITEM structure identifies the type of item. If this program were written in C++, I'd put the this pointer in **lParam**.

Since the topmost state nodes are created using the I_IMAGECALLBACK constants, the parent window of the TreeView will receive a WM_NOTIFY message with the TVN_GETDISPINFO message. The code to handle this lives in **WndProc**; it looks at the state of the item and fills out the appropriate images to use on-the-fly. This is how the plus sign and block of cheese images are used for the states.

Since I created the TreeView control with the TVS_EDITLABELS style bit, a WM_NOTIFY message is sent to the TreeView's parent window whenever the user clicks a selected item. The TVN_BEGINLABELEDIT code checks to see if the item the user clicked on is a coaster item. If it is, then label editing is allowed.

Once the user is finished editing the label, he or she presses **Enter** or the **Esc** key to accept or chuck edits. In both cases, you will get the WM_NOTIFY message with the TVN_ENDLABELEDIT code. If the user pressed Esc, the **pszText** pointer in the TV_DISPINFO field will be NULL; otherwise it will contain a pointer to the string the user just typed in.

Since this program blindly accepts all edits, the **TreeView_SetItem** macro is used to update the text in the item. When you receive the WM_NOTIFY:TVN_LABELEDIT message, the item field in the TV_DISPIN-FO field is already filled out with the item's attributes for you; you simply need to change the attributes you care about.

And finally, the drag-and-drop is handled in the three-step process described above. The WM_NOTIFY message is sent with the TVN_BEGINDRAG code, and the program dutifully checks to make sure the user is only moving coasters around. If this test passes, then the **TreeView_CreateDragImage** macro is called to initiate the drag-and-drop process. The rest of the code in the TVN_BEGINDRAG block is frighteningly similar to the WM_LBUTTON-DOWN code from the IMAGELST sample program.

As the user drags the object around, the WM_MOUSEMOVE code in **WndProc** checks to see if the user is dragging over a valid object. If so, the **TreeView_SelectDropTarget** macro is called to provide the user some feedback.

Finally, when the user finally drops the object, the code in WM_LBUT-TONUP does th grunt job of moving the item around by deleting it and adding it back in.

TreeView Summary

Wow, what an E-ticket ride! The TreeView control is a very powerful control that really does make it easy to accomplish many of your hierarchical list box programming goals. The new WM_NOTIFY message makes for a much more elegant way of handling the myriad of notifications associated with the TreeView control. Besides, the TreeView combined with the Image List makes for one really trick-looking user interface.

8. The RichEdit Control

The RTF edit control can format characters' fonts, sizes, subscripting/super-scripting, and color. It can format paragraph alignment. It can print. (Nope, that's not a typo. This control can actually print its contents for you.) And it provides an elegant mechanism to serialize its contents. And it is an OLE-compliant control. And it has a solution to the nation's healthcare problem. Wow, what a control!

Is this control useful? Mail programs can now have nicely formatted messages. Big monolithic corporate applications that have embedded mini text editors can now allow formatted text. The uses for this control are pretty much endless.

Throughout this list, I'll refer to the RTF Edit Control as the "RichEdit" control. That's because the control is more of a super-duper edit control than it is a full-blown RTF Edit control. RTF stands for Rich Text Format, and it is a file format designed to make it easy to interchange documents between different text editors. The RichEdit control uses a subset of RTF as its interchange format—it does not support everything that an RTF document can include. The RichEdit control can still read in any RTF document; it will simply ignore RTF formatting commands it doesn't understand. If you're interested in learning more, go to CompuServe® and download the RTF specification from the MSWORD forum, in Library 2.

You will find that the RichEdit control is contained in its own DLL. The 32-bit version is in RICHED32.DLL, and the 16-bit version is in RICHED.DLL.

There are no exported APIs in RICHED32.DLL. The control is completely message-based; your application will use the mighty **SendMessage** API to do all its communication with the RichEdit control. In fact, since there isn't a RICHED32.LIB file, your application must load it with the **LoadLibrary** API (but there is a RICHEDIT.H file). As soon as the library is loaded, the **LibMain** function inside RICHED32.DLL will automatically register the RichEdit control's window class ("RICHEDIT" for 32-bit versions, RICHED16 for 16-bit versions) for your application. So, you need to call

```
hLib = LoadLibrary ("RICHED32.DLL");
if ( !hLib )
  {
  <barf>
  }
```

to make the RichEdit control available to your application.

Once you have initialized the RichEdit control's DLL as mentioned above, you use it in pretty much the same way as you would a normal multiline edit control, except you use the window class name of "RICHEDIT" instead of "EDIT" in your CreateWindow calls and resource templates. (Or "RICHED16" for 16-bit stuff. For the rest of this list, assume I'm talking about the 32-bit version.) In fact, most of the messages you use for standard edit controls work for the RichEdit control. Figure 11.27 (which applies to the 32-bit version of the RichEdit Control) compares the standard edit control with the RichEdit control and describes the RichEdit control's new capabilities.

Message	Standard Edit Control	RTF Edit Control	wParam	lParam	Return Value	Notes
EM_CANUNDO	x	x	Zero	Zero	TRUE or False	
EM_EMPTYUNDOBUFFER	x	x	Zero	Zero	n/a	
EM_GETFIRSTVISIBLELINE	x	x	Zero	Zero	First visible Line #	
EM_GETLINE	x	x	Line #	Addr of buffer for line	# of chars copied	
EM_GETLINECOUNT	x	x	Zero	Zero	# of lines in control	

EM_GETMODIFY	x	x	Zero	Zero	TRUE if contents modified	
EM_GETRECT	x	x	Zero	LPRECT rc	n/a	
EM_GETSEL	x	x	LPDWORD lpdwStart	LPDWORD lpdwEnd	If wParam and lParam are NULL, it is MAKELONG(start, end+1)	Use EM_EXGETSEL for RTF control with > 64K text
EM_GETWORKBREAKPROC	x	x	Zero	Zero	Addr of wordwrap function	
EM_LIMITTEXT	x	x	n/a	n/a	n/a	Use EM_SETLIMITTEXT for RTF control
EM_LINEFROMCHAR	x	x	Character Index	Zero	Line # of character	Use EM_EXLINEFROMCHAR for RTF control with > 64K text
EM_LINEINDEX	x	x	Line #	Zero	Character index of line	
EM_LINELENGTH	x	x	Character Index	Zero	Length of line with character	
EM_REPLACESEL	x	x	Zero	lpszReplace	n/a	
EM_SCROLL	x	x	nScroll	Zero	MAKELONG (numlines scrolled, TRUE)	
EM_MODIFY	x	x	fModify	Zero	n/a	
EM_SETREADONLY	x	x	fReadonly	Zero	TRUE on success	
EM_SETRECT	x	x	Zero	rcRect	n/a	
EM_SETSEL	x	x	nStart	nEnd	n/a	Use EM_EXSETSEL for RTF controls with > 64K text
EM_SETWORDBREAKPROC	x	x	Zero	Addr of word break function	n/a	
EM_UNDO	x	x	Zero	Zero	TRUE on success	
WM_CHAR	x	x	Character Code	Key Data	n/a	
WM_CLEAR	x	x	Zero	Zero	n/a	
WM_COPY	x	x	Zero	Zero	n/a	
WM_CUT	x	x	Zero	Zero	n/a	
WM_GETTEXT	x	x	Num chars to copy	lpszText	Num chars copied	For RTF control, use EM_STREAM-

						OUT and EM_GETSELTEXT for better access
WM_GETTEXTLENGTH	x	x	Zero	Zero	length of text in EC	
WM_HSCROLL	x	x	Scrollcode and Pos	hWndScrollbar	n/a	
WM_KEYDOWN	x	x	Character Code	Key data	n/a	
WM_PASTE	x	x	Zero	Zero	n/a	
WM_SETFONT	x	x	hFont	fRedraw	n/a	
WM_SETTEXT	x	x	Zero	lpszText	TRUE on success	
WM_UNDO	x	x	Zero	Zero	TRUE on success	
WM_VSCROLL	x	x	Scrollcode and Pos	hWndScrollbar	n/a	
WM_CTLCOLOR	x					Obsolete for RTF Control
EM_FMTLINES	x					Obsolete for RTF Control
WM_GETFONT	x					Obsolete for RTF Control
EM_GETHANDLE	x					Obsolete for RTF Control
EM_GETPASSWORDCHAR	x					Obsolete for RTF Control
EM_SETHANDLE	x					Obsolete for RTF Control
EM_SETPASSWORDCHAR	x					Obsolete for RTF Control
EM_SETRECTNP	x					Obsolete for RTF Control
EM_SETTABSTOPS	x					Obsolete for RTF Control
EM_SETCANPASTE		x	Clipboard format to try	Zero	TRUE if pastable	Determine if the RTF control can paste from the clipboard
EM_SETCHARFROMPOS		x	Zero	LPPOINT pt	Character Pos from point (client coordinates)	Returns character position at point
WM_SETCONTEXTMENU		x	hWnd of window that got right button up	Screen coordinates of mouse via MAKELONG	n/a	Brings up a context menu for the current selection
EM_DISPLAYBAND		x	Zero	LPRECT of band to display to	TRUE if success	Must first set up RTF control with

					EM_FORMAT-RANGE
EM_EXGETSEL		x	Zero	LPCHAR-RANGE	n/a	
EM_EXLIMITTEXT		x	Zero	Max chars	n/a	
EM_EXLINEFROMCHAR		x	Zero	Character Index	Line # that has char in it	
EM_EXSETSEL		x	Zero	LPCHAR-RANGE to select	Index +1 of character selected	
EM_FINDTEXT		x	FT_MATCH-CASE or FT_WHOLE WORD	LPFINDTEXT	Char pos of next match or -1 for no match	
EM_FINDWORDBREAK		x	Word break flag	Char pos to start from	Position of Word Break	Beyond the scope of this article
EM_FORMATRANGE		x	TRUE to render text, FALSE to measure	LPFORMAT-RANGE	Format, measure, and/or draw text on a device	See Task 4 of of this article for more detail
EM_GETCHARFORMAT		x	TRUE for selection, FALSE for default	LPCHAR-FORMAT	dwMask of CHAR-FORMAT	See Task 1 of this article for more detail
EM_GETWVENTMASK		x	Zero	Zero	Event Mask	Find out what events parent will be notified about
EM_GETLIMITTEXT		x	Zero	Zero	Current text limit	
EM_GETOLEINTERFACE		x	Zero	Pointer to lRichEditOle object	TRUE on success	Beyond the scope of this article
EM_GETPARAFORMAT		x	Zero	LPPARA-FORMAT	dwMask field of PARA-FORMAT	See Task 2 of this article for more detail
EM_GTSELTEXT		x	Zero	lpszBuffer to copy to	Number of bytes copied	
EM_GETTEXTRANGE		x	Zero	LPTEXT-RANGE	Number of bytes copied	
EM_POSFROMCHAR		x	LPPOINT pos	character index	n/a	Fills in pos with window position of a character in client coordinates
EM_PASTESPECIAL		x	Clipboard format to paste	Zero	n/a	
EM_REQUESTRESIZE		x	Zero	Zero	n/a	Forces a EN_REQUEST RESIZE notification

EM_SELECTIONTYPE		x	Zero	Zero	Type of selection	
EM_SETBKGNDCOLOR		x	TRUE to use system color, FALSE to use lParam	COLOREF of background color	Old back-ground color	
EM_SETCHARFORMAT		x	SCF_SELEC-TION, SCF_WORD or both	LPCHAR-FORMAT	TRUE on success	See Task 1 of this article for more details
EM_SETEVENTMASK		x	Zero	New Event Mask	Old Event Mask	Define which events to notify parent of
EM_SETOLEINTERFACE		x	Zero	Pionter to lRichEditOle-Callback object	TRUE on success	Beyond the scope of this article
EM_SETPARAFORMAT		x	Zero	LPPARA-FORMAT	TRUE on success	See Task 2 of this article for more details
EM_SETTARGETDEVICE		x	hDC to format for	line width in the HDC	TRUE if successful	Set a target device and line width to enable WYSIWYG formatting
EM_STREAMIN		x	Format of data stream	LPEDIT-STREAM	Count of characters read	See Task 3 of this article for more details
EM_STREAMOUT		x	Format of data stream	LPEDIT-STREAM	Count of characters written	See Task 3 of this article for more details

FIGURE 11.27 RICHEDIT AND REGULAR EDIT MESSAGES

Let me explain the 64KB limit mentioned in Figure 11.27. The RichEdit control can hold more than 64KB of text. However, some of the old-style multi-line edit control messages are architected so that indexes are in WORDs, which means that these messages are only useful for getting at the first 64KB of text in a control. There are new messages that allow your program to get at all of the text, but the old style messages in Figure 11.27 have to be left alone for backwards compatibility.

Character sizes inside the edit control are measured in twips. A twip is 1/1440th of an inch. Since a point is 1/72nd of an inch, divide your twips by 20 to get the point size.

Alas, the RichEdit control is not "Microsoft Word in a box." Some restrictions do apply. Figure 11.28 explains what character formatting the RichEdit control can and cannot do. If your application needs to do formatting beyond the capabilities of the RichEdit control, consider inserting an OLE 2-enabled Word document or writing your own control.

Feature	Can the RTF Edit Control Do It?
OLE2 Client Support	Yes
Simple Bulletting	Yes
Find and Replace	Yes
Different fonts: Sizes, style, color	Yes
>64K of Text	Yes
Superscript, Subscript, Strikethrough	Yes
RTF to text to RTF conversion	Yes
Printing	Yes
Previewing	Yes
Streaming	Yes
Left, Right alignment	Yes
Full justification	No
Right and Left tabs	Yes
Ruler	No
Header/Footer Fupport	No
Decimal tabs	No
Paragraph Spacing (single, double, etc)	No
Top and Bottom margins	No
Automatic Page Numbering	No

FIGURE 11.28 RICHEDIT FORMATTING CAPABILITIES

Details, Details, Details!

Okay, enough blather. Let's take a look at how to get some very specific tasks done. Since the RichEdit control is so complex, space limitations force me to cover only the basics. These are the tasks I'll cover:

❖ Getting and applying character formatting

❖ Getting and applying paragraph formatting

❖ Serializing (loading/saving) the contents of the RichEdit control

❖ Printing and previewing data with the RichEdit control

❖ Using the RichEdit control as a RTF-to-plain-text-to-RTF converter

These five tasks should cover most uses of the RichEdit control.

Task 1: Getting and Applying Character Formatting

To get the format of characters in the RichEdit control, you send it the new EM_GETCHARFORMAT message. **wParam** indicates whether you want the formatting for the currently selected text (TRUE), or the default formatting for the control (FALSE). If no text is selected and you use TRUE for **wParam**, the character format of the text at the insertion point is retrieved. **lParam** points to a new CHARFORMAT structure—see the declaration in RICHEDIT.H (see Figure 11.29).

```
/* CHARFORMAT masks */
#define CFM_BOLD          0x00000001
#define CFM_ITALIC        0x00000002
#define CFM_UNDERLINE     0x00000004
#define CFM_STRIKEOUT     0x00000008
#define CFM_PROTECTED     0x00000010
#define CFM_SIZE          0x80000000
#define CFM_COLOR         0x40000000
#define CFM_FACE          0x20000000
#define CFM_OFFSET        0x10000000


/* CHARFORMAT effects */
#define CFE_BOLD          0x0001
#define CFE_ITALIC        0x0002
#define CFE_UNDERLINE     0x0004
#define CFE_STRIKEOUT     0x0008
#define CFE_PROTECTED     0x0010
#define CFE_AUTOCOLOR     0x40000000

typedef sta
  {
```

```
    UINT        cbSize;         // MUST be sizeof(CHARFORMAT)
    DWORD       dwMask;     // Defines which fields to use CFM_*
    DWORD       dwEffects;  // Character effects mask CFE_*
    LONG        yHeight;// Size (in twips)
    LONG        yOffset;// > 0 for superscript, < 0 for subscript
    COLORREF    crTextColor;// Color of text (unless dwEffects has CFE_AUTOCOLOR)
    BYTE        bPitchAndFamily; // Same as LOGFONT's bPitchAndFamily
    TCHAR       szFaceName[LF_FACESIZE]; // Same as LOGFONTS's szFaceName
} CHARFORMAT;
```

FIGURE 11.29 THE CHARFORMAT STRUCTURE

To get character formatting from the RichEdit control, you send the EM_GETCHARFORMAT message to the control. The **dwMask** bits are set for the fields that have the same value throughout the entire selection. For example, let's say you wanted to find out if the current text selection is underlined:

```
CHARFORMAT cf; // This is defined in RICHEDIT.H

// This line MUST be done for version control
cf.cbSize = sizeof(cf);
// Get the character formatting into the CHARFORMAT
// structure,
SendMessage(hRTFWnd, EM_GETCHARFORMAT,TRUE,(LPARAM)&cf);
if (cf.dwMask & CFM_UNDERLINE)
  {
  if (cf.dwEffects & CFE_UNDERLINE)
    MessageBox ( hWnd, "Text is underlined", "MSJ",
              MB_OK );
  else
    MessageBox ( hWnd, "Text is not underlined", "MSJ",
              MB_OK );
  }
else
  {
  MessageBox ( hWnd,
              "Text has underlined and non-underlined characters", "MSJ", MB_OK );
  }
```

If you're setting attributes, use the EM_SETCHARFORMAT message. For this message, **wParam** has slightly more depth. **wParam** can be zero to set the default formatting for newly entered text, SCF_SELECTION to apply the formatting to the selected text, SCF_WORD to apply the formatting to the word(s) containing the selection, or both SCF_SELECTION and SCF_WORD. **lParam** still points to the CHARFORMAT structure. So, to continue the above example, let's look at code that would toggle the underline attribute for a selection of text (see Figure 11.30).

```
CHARFORMAT cf; // This is defined in RICHEDIT.H

// MUST be here for version control
cf.cbSize = sizeof(cf);

// Get the character formatting into the CHARFORMAT structure,
SendMessage(hRTFWnd, EM_GETCHARFORMAT, TRUE, (LPARAM)&cf);

// Check to see if the selection is consistently underlined
if (cf.dwMask & CFM_UNDERLINE)
  {
  // Twiddle de bits, captain!
  cf.dwEffects  ^= CFE_UNDERLINE;
  }
else
  {
  // For text that has both underline and non-underline, default to set
  // all of it to underlined.
  cf.dwEffects  |= CFE_UNDERLINE;
  }

// Set the mask to tell the RTF Edit control to pay attention to
// the underline bit of the dwEffects field only.
cf.dwMask       = CFM_UNDERLINE;

// Set the new underline status to the selected text
SendMessage(hRTFWnd, EM_SETCHARFORMAT, SCF_SELECTION, (LPARAM)&cf);
```

FIGURE 11.30 TOGGLING THE UNDERLINE ATTRIBUTE IN A RICHEDIT CONTROL

These samples only illustrate changing a character's attributes. Say you want to increase the font size of a selection by 2 points. Since there are 20 twips in a point, you simply add 40 twips to the size (see Figure 11.31).

```
CHARFORMAT cf; // This is defined in RICHEDIT.H

// MUST be here for version control
cf.cbSize = sizeof(cf);

// Get the character formatting into the CHARFORMAT structure,
SendMessage(hRTFWnd, EM_GETCHARFORMAT, TRUE, (LPARAM)&cf);

if (cf.dwMask & CFM_SIZE)
  {
  // Set the mask to tell the RTF Edit control to pay attention to
  // the yHeight field only
  cf.dwMask       = CFM_SIZE;
  // Increase the font size by 40 twips (2 points)
  cf.yHeight += 40;
  // Set the new underline status to the selected text
  SendMessage(hRTFWnd, EM_SETCHARFORMAT, SCF_SELECTION, (LPARAM)&cf);
  }
else
  {
  MessageBox ( hWnd, "The text contains different sized fonts, and this program "
                     "is too brain-dead to pick it apart. Please select a range "
                     "of text that is all the same size.",
                     "MSJ", MB_OK );
  }
```

FIGURE 11.31 INCREASING THE FONT SIZE IN A RICHEDIT CONTROL

You can change the character facename via the CFM_FACE bit and **szFaceName** field, as well as its color, strikeout, and other attributes.

One fancy attribute is the "protected" attribute. If a selection of text is protected, the user will not be able to change the text. This is a handy way to make a cheezy form in an RichEdit control: protect the labels, and then let the user type in entries next to the labels.

The CFE_AUTOCOLOR attribute tells the RichEdit control to think like a chameleon and assume the default system text color for edit controls; if you remove this attribute, the text will be the color specified in the **cf.crTextColor** field. The background color defaults to the system window color; this can be changed with the EM_SETBKGNDCOLOR message (which is described in Figure 11.27, along with the other messages).

In the upcoming sample program, code will be provided to change the font size, bold, italic, underline, and face name attributes.

Task 2: Getting and Applying Paragraph Formatting

Paragraph formatting in the RichEdit control is done in one of two ways: "Window" mode, and WYSIWYG mode. By default, the RichEdit control uses Window mode. Window mode means that the right margin depends on the size of the RichEdit control window: If you resize the RichEdit control window, you will cause the word wrapping of the text to change. WYSIWYG mode means that you tell the RichEdit control how "wide" the typing field is, and the RichEdit control will word wrap to that setting, regardless of the RichEdit control window size.

To set the RichEdit control into WYSIWYG mode, you send it the EM_SETARGETDEVICE message (see Figure 11.27). For example, if you want to tell the RichEdit control that it has a piece of virtual paper 7 inches wide, you use 7*1440 for the page width.

To format a paragraph in the RichEdit control, you send it the new EM_GETPARAFORMAT message. **lParam** points to a new PARAFORMAT structure (wParam is always 0). Let's look at the declaration in RICHEDIT.H (see Figure 11.32).

Figure 11.33 shows the paragraph indent value graphically. As with character formatting, when you send the EM_GETPARAFORMAT message to the RichEdit control, the **dwMask** bits indicate which fields are consistently set throughout the selection. The code in Figure 11.34 sets a paragraph on a 7" wide sheet of paper (WYSIWYG mode) where the left margin is at 1", the right margin is at 6", the first line is indented by 1/2", and tab stops are set at 1 1/2", 2", 2 1/2", and 3".

```
{
  UINT   cbSize;        // MUST be sizeof(PARAFORMAT)
  DWORD  dwMask;        // Which fields to look at
  WORD   wNumbering;    // Either 0 or PFN_BULLET
  WORD   wReserved;     // Change this value and you may get a caning!
  LONG   dxStartIndent; // Absolute indent of the first line of the paragraph
```

```
                    (twips)
LONG  dxRightIndent;   // Size of the right indent
LONG  dxOffset;    // Relative offset of subsequent lines to the first line
WORD  wAlignment; // PFA_LEFT, PFA_RIGHT, or PFA_CENTER
SHORT cTabCount;   // Number of tab stops in the paragraph
LONG  rgxTabs[MAX_TAB_STOPS]; // Tab stop positions (twips)
} PARAFORMAT;


/* PARAFORMAT mask values */
#define PFM_STARTINDENT    0x00000001
#define PFM_RIGHTINDENT    0x00000002
#define PFM_OFFSET         0x00000004
#define PFM_ALIGNMENT      0x00000008
#define PFM_TABSTOPS       0x00000010
#define PFM_NUMBERING      0x00000020
#define PFM_OFFSETINDENT   0x80000000


/* PARAFORMAT numbering options */
#define PFN_BULLET         0x0001


/* PARAFORMAT alignment options */
#define PFA_LEFT     0x0001
#define PFA_RIGHT    0x0002
#define PFA_CENTER   0x0003
```

FIGURE 11.32 THE PARAFORMAT STRUCTURE

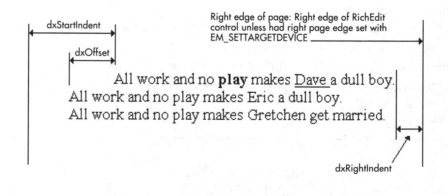

FIGURE 11.33 HOW THE RICHEDIT USES INDENTS

```
PARAFORMAT pf; // From RICHEDIT.H

// This code sets the RichEdit control to WYSIWYG mode, for a 7" wide
// piece of paper. This only needs to be called once
hDC = GetDC(hWnd);
SendMessage(hwndEdit, EM_SETTARGETDEVICE, (WPARAM)hDC, (LPARAM)(1440*7));
ReleaseDC(hWnd, hDC);

// Set the mask to tell the RTF edit control to look at these fields
pf.cbSize = sizeof(pf);

pf.dwMask = PFM_STARTINDENT | PFM_RIGHTINDENT | PFM_OFFSET | PFM_ALIGNMENT |
PFM_TABSTOPS;
pf.dxStartIndent = 2160; // 1440 twips per inch, 1.5" = 2160 twips
pf.dxOffset = -720; // rest of lines are -1/2" from the first, or at 1"
pf.dxRightIndex = 1440; // For a 7" wide sheet of paper,
                        // a 6" margin is 1" from the right edge
pf.cTabCount = 4; // 4 tabs
pf.rgxTabs[0] = 2160; // First tab at 1 1/2"
pf.rgxTabs[1] = 2880; // and each subsequent tab
pf.rgxTabs[2] = 3600; // 1/2" later
pf.rgxTabs[3] = 4320; //
// Send the EM_SETPARAFORMAT message to set the formatting
SendMessage ( hWndRTF, EM_SETPARAFORMAT, 0, (LPARAM)&pf );
```

FIGURE 11.34 SETTING PARAGRAPH MARGINS IN A RICHEDIT CONTROL

Task 3: Serializing Data

Although it'd be handy to be able to tell the RichEdit control to save its data to a file, this would limit its usefulness severely. OLE 2 embedded objects don't save to files—they save to streams. And MFC applications abstract the file I/O far away from the serialization process. For maximum flexibility, the RichEdit control "serializes" data instead of saving it, which means it takes a stream of bytes and puts it somewhere. Where that stream of bytes goes is up to the owner of the RichEdit control.

There are two types of serialization (brace yourself for the obvious): input and output. The two corresponding messages are EM_STREAMIN and

EM_STREAMOUT. These messages work a little smarter than your average message. What's so smart? The RichEdit control decides how much memory it wants to allocate for this streaming process, and passes you the information in manageable chunks. Imagine that there is 1MB of text in your control (perhaps you have the OS/2® README.TXT loaded), and you want to save that to disk. It would be a seriously blatant act of programming piggery to allocate a meg-o-memory to stream the text and then send that entire meg to the disk in one shot. Instead, the RTF control can allocate a kinder, gentler chunk of, say, 32KB and give you the text 32KB at a time, so you can then splat that bite-sized morsel to the hard disk. Keeping this approach in mind, let's go into more detail on how to get the text out of a RichEdit control.

The EM_STREAMOUT message takes the stream format in **wParam** (which can be RTF text, plain text, or RTF text excluding embedded objects), and a pointer to an EDITSTREAM structure in **lParam**. The structure looks like this:

```
typedef struct _editstream
  {
  DWORD dwCookie;          // user value passed to
                           // callback as first parameter
  DWORD dwError;           // last error
  EDITSTREAMCALLBACK pfnCallback; // Pointer to a
                                  // serialization
                                  // callback function
  }
EDITSTREAM;

typedef DWORD (CALLBACK *EDITSTREAMCALLBACK)(
  DWORD dwCookie,          // Application supplied value
  LPBYTE pbBuff,           // Pointer to the buffer with
                           // the data
  LONG cb,                 // Number of bytes in the
                           // buffer to read/write
  LONG *pcb);              // Number of bytes actually
                           // read/written
```

The callback function defined in the EDITSTREAM structure points to a callback function in your application. This callback function will be called repeatedly until the RichEdit control has completely serialized the data. Your callback function is given a pointer to a chunk of memory that contains some or all of the data, and your application then serializes that chunk. For example, if the text in the buffer is 1000 bytes, and the RichEdit control wants to write it 256 bytes at a time, your callback function gets called four times. Figure 11.35 shows what parameters are passed to your callback function for each chunk of the serialization. A very simple callback function looks like this:

```
DWORD CALLBACK RTFStreamOutCallback( DWORD   dwCookie,
                                     LPBYTE  pbBuff,
                                     LONG    cb,
                                     LONG    *pcb
{
  // For this sample, let's assume that dwCookie is a
  // file handle, and this stream code simply writes it
  // out to that file.
  cb =_lwrite( (HFILE)dwCookie, pbBuff, cb);
  *pcb = cb; // Indicate the number of bytes written to
             // the file
  return 0;  // Success!
}
```

To use this callback function, you could write a function like this:

```
void MySaveRTFFile( HWND hRTFWnd, LPSTR szFileName )
{
  HFILE       hFile;
  OFSTRUCT    of;
  EDITSTREAM  es;

  // Standard means of opening a file
  hFile = OpenFile( szFileName, &of, OF_CREATE );
  // Use the cookie for the file handle
  es.dwCookie    = (DWORD)hFile;
  // No error to start with
  es.dwError     = 0;
  // Set the callback function to the above sample
  es.pfnCallback = RTFStreamOutCallback;
  // Just do it
  SendMessage(hRTFWnd, EM_STREAMOUT, SF_RTF, (LPARAM)&es);
  // Close yer file
  _lclose ( hFile );
}
```

```
Call 1: cb = 256. Your callback procedure writes 256 bytes.
Call 2: cb = 256. Your callback procedure writes 256 bytes.
Call 3: cb = 256. Your callback procedure writes 256 bytes.
Call 4: cb = 232. Your callback procedure writes 232 bytes.
```

FIGURE 11.35 RICHEDIT SERIALIZATION CALLS, UP TO 256 BYTES AT A TIME

Loading data into the RichEdit control is done similarly, with two differences.

First, the callback function either signals the RichEdit control to continue reading by changing the ***pcb** variable to the number of bytes read, or signals the RichEdit control to stop reading by changing the ***pcb** variable to 0. The callback function returns 0 if there was no error, or a non-zero, app-defined error code if there was an error.

Second, you use the EM_STREAMIN message to stream data into the control instead of the EM_STREAMOUT message. Note that the EM_STREAMIN message by default erases the contents of whatever is in the control at the time (if you want to insert the stream at the current insertion point, logically OR SFF_SELECTION with the wParam parameter of the EM_STREAMIN message). Listing 11.6 shows code that loads a file into a RichEdit control.

LISTING 11.6 LOADING A FILE INTO A RICHEDIT CONTROL

```
DWORD CALLBACK RTFStreamInCallback( DWORD      dwCookie,
                                    LPBYTE     pbBuff,
                                    LONG       cb,
                                    LONG       *pcb
                                   )
{
  // Read in up to cb bytes
  *pcb = _lread ( (HFILE)dwCookie, pbBuff, cb);
  // Check to see if we reached the EOF or encountered an error
  if ( *pcb <= 0 )
    *pcb = 0;    // Indicate the read is complete
  return 0;
}

void MyLoadRTFFile ( HWND hRTFWnd, LPSTR szFileName )
{
  HFILE        hFile;
```

```
OFSTRUCT        of;
EDITSTREAM      es;

// Standard means of opening a file
hFile = OpenFile ( szFileName, &of, OF_READ );
// Use the cookie for the file handle
es.dwCookie    = (DWORD)hFile;
// No error to start with
es.dwError     = 0;
// Set the callback function to the above sample
es.pfnCallback = RTFStreamInCallback;
// Just do it
SendMessage(hRTFWnd, EM_STREAMIN, SF_RTF, (LPARAM)&es);
// Close yer file
_lclose ( hFile );
}
```

The samples referenced above illustrate the bare-bones way to save and load a file into the RichEdit control. If your application is an OLE server or an MFC application, set up the callbacks to serialize into whatever your data stream requires.

Task 4: Printing and Previewing with the RichEdit Control

The RichEdit control also prints and does print previews. In fact, it does it quite easily. The EM_FORMATRANGE message, in a nutshell, takes the text in the RichEdit control and draws it to a DC. The **wParam** indicates whether the RichEdit control should draw the text to the DC (TRUE), or simply measure the text and indicate how much space is required to display it (FALSE). The **lParam** either points to a FORMATRANGE structure or is NULL. If **lParam** is NULL, the RichEdit control cleans house and frees up all its internal resources needed to do the printing. An application must send a NULL **lParam** when it has completed its printing/previewing, or when the output DC changes (such as a portrait to a landscape DC). Let's look at the FORMATRANGE structure:

```
typedef struct _charrange
  {
  LONG    cpMin;    // First character of range (0 for
```

```
                         // start of doc)
  LONG     cpMax;        // Last character of range (-1 for
                         // end of doc)
  }
CHARRANGE;
typedef struct _formatrange
  {
  HDC hdc;               // Actual DC to draw on
  HDC hdcTarget;         // Target DC for determining text
                         // formatting
  RECT rc;               // Region of the DC to draw to
  RECT rcPage;           // Region of the entire DC (page
                         // size)
  CHARRANGE chrg;        // Range of text to draw (see above
                         // declaration)
  }
FORMATRANGE;
```

Now let's wrap up the EM_FORMATRANGE message to obediently display the RichEdit control's text to a given DC (see Listing 11.7). Note that this function will not provide WYSIWIG print preview. To do this, you need to set the RichEdit control to WYSIWYG mode by using the EM_FORMATRANGE message (See Task 2 above). This SplatTextToDC code assumes that the text all fits on the page; I will explain shortly how you can handle multiple pages (which will also use the currently lonely bPrinterDC parameter). Listing 11.7 isolates the RichEdit control-specific code from your application-specific code.

LISTING 11.7 USING THE RICHEDIT CONTROL TO DRAW ITS CONTENTS TO A DC

```
void SplatTextToDC ( HWNDhRTFWnd,
          HDC hDC,
          LPRECT  prcDrawTo,
          LPRECT  prcPage,
          BOOLbPrinterDC)
{
  FORMATRANGE fr;

  fr.hdc = fr.hdcTarget = hDC;   // Use the same DC for measuring and rendering
  fr.rc = *prcDrawTo;            // Indicate the area on page to draw to
  fr.rcPage = *prcPage;          // Indicate entire size of page
  fr.chrg.cpMin = 0;      // Indicate start of text through
  fr.chrg.cpMax = -1;            // end of the text
```

```
// Draw the text
SendMessage ( hRTFEnd, EM_FORMATRANGE, TRUE, (LPARAM)&fr );
// Housekeep
SendMessage ( hRTFEnd, EM_FORMATRANGE, FALSE, NULL );
}
```

Next is a simple way to put a preview of the RichEdit control text into a window's client area. Assume this code lives in the WM_PAINT section of the print preview's window procedure, and hRTFWnd is the handle to some RichEdit control.

```
case WM_PAINT:

    hDC = BeginPaint ( hWnd, &ps );    // Get a DC
    GetClientRect ( hWnd, &rcClient );// Measure the client
    SplatTextToDC ( hRTFWnd, hDC, &rcClient, &rcClient,
                    FALSE );           // Splat-o-rama!
    EndPaint ( hWnd, &ps );            // Give up the DC
    break;
```

I use **rcClient** as both the **prcDrawTo** and **prcPage** because this example uses the entire client area to preview the text. If you wanted to draw a cutesy little fake page on the screen and then put the text inside it, you would use the inside rectangle of the **CutesyPage** for **prcDrawTo**.

Now, let's look at how you'd print this to a printer. Assume that you have some WM_COMMAND processing going on and the code in Figure 11.36 is in the IDM_PRINT section. This code simply gets a printer DC, does the usual document preparation hoo-hah, calculates the twip size of the page, and calls the same **SplatTextToDC** function.

```
case IDM_PRINT:
    hDC = GetPrinterDC(); // This is some function you wrote to get a printer DC
    if ( hDC )
        {
        DOCINFO di;
        rc.left = rc.top = 0;
        // Figure width of printer area, in twips
        rc.right=(GetDeviceCaps(hDC, HORZRES)/GetDeviceCaps(hDC, LOGPIXELSX)) * 1440;
        // Figure height of printer area, in twips
```

```
        rc.bottom=(GetDeviceCaps(hDC, VERTRES)/GetDeviceCaps(hDC, LOGPIXELSY)) * 1440;
        di.cbSize = sizeof(DOCINFO);
        di.lpszDocName = "RTF Sample";
        di.lpszOutput = NULL;
        StartDoc ( hDC, &di );
        StartPage ( hDC );
        SplatTextToDC ( hRTFWnd, hDC, &rc, &rc, TRUE ); // Splat-o-rama!
        EndPage ( hDC );
        EndDoc ( hDC );
        DeleteDC ( hDC );
        }
    break;
```

FIGURE 11.36 HANDLING IDM_PRINT

For small RTF-size documents, this code works wonderfully to print out the
text, but it does not handle pagination very well. This is where the code in
Listing 11.8 can be modified to check the return value from EM_FORMAT-
TRANGE. This return value specifies the index of the first character that
would not fit on the page. Simply modify the Splat function to loop over and
over, printing as much text as possible per page. The code in Listing 11.8
checks that return value, and as long as the return value is less than the size
of the entire text, it keeps on printing.

LISTING 11.8 RICHEDIT PAGINATION

```
void SplatTextToDC ( HWND hRTFWnd,
            HDC hDC,
            LPRECT   prcDrawTo,
            LPRECT   prcPage,
            BOOL bPrinterDC)
{
  FORMATRANGE fr;
  LONG        lTextLength;
  LONG        lTextPrinted;

  fr.hdc = fr.hdcTarget = hDC;    // Use the same DC for measuring and rendering
  fr.rc = *prcDrawTo;         // Indicate the area on page to draw to
  fr.rcPage = *prcPage;       // Indicate entire size of page
  fr.chrg.cpMin = 0;      // Indicate start of text through
```

```
    fr.chrg.cpMax = -1;              // end of the text

    lTextLength = SendMessage (hRTFWnd, WM_GETTEXTLENGTH, 0, 0L );

    do
      {
      // Print the text
      lTextPrinted  = SendMessage ( hRTFEnd, EM_FORMATRANGE, TRUE, (LPARAM)&fr );
      if (bPrinterDC && (lTextPrinted < lTextLength)) // Not all printed yet!
        {
        fr.chrg.cpMin = lTextPrinted;        // Indicate start of next page
        fr.chrg.cpMax = -1;     // end of the text
        EndPage ( hDC );
        StartPage ( hDC );
        }
      }
    while (lTextPrinted < lTextLength);
    // Housekeep
    SendMessage ( hRTFEnd, EM_FORMATRANGE, FALSE, NULL );
}
```

The more adventurous could use FALSE for **wParam** to find out in advance the last character that would be printed, and then use a little app-specific logic to try and avoid "widow/orphan" lines or other word-processing subspace anomalies.

Task 5: Using the RichEdit Control as a Text Converter

This is the simplest of the tasks, mainly because I already explained how to do it. If you want to support all of the formats the RichEdit control can handle, simply modify the **MyLoadRTFFile** function to also accept the stream format:

```
void MyLoadRTFFile ( HWND hRTFWnd, LPSTR szFileName,
                     WPARAM uStreamFormat )
{
.
.
.
   // All code the same as previous MyLoadRTFFile, except
   // this line
   SendMessage(hRTFWnd, EM_STREAMIN, uStreamFormat,
```

```
                (LPARAM)&es);

   .
   .
   .
}
```

And likewise, change your MySaveRTFFile function:

```
void MySaveRTFFile ( HWND hRTFWnd, LPSTR szFileName,
                     WPARAM uStreamFormat )
{
   .
   .
   .


   // All code the same as previous MySaveRTFFile, except
   // this line
   SendMessage(hRTFWnd, EM_STREAMOUT, uStreamFormat,
               (LPARAM)&es);


   .
   .
   .
}
```

Now, to write a nifty text converter, all you need to do is stream the file into the control and then stream it back out again. Here is the world's smallest text converter function:

```
void NiftyTextConverter( HWND hAnyWnd, PSTR szInput,
                         WPARAM uInputStream,
                         PSTR szOutput,
                         WPARAM uOutputStream )
{
  HWND hRTFWnd = CreateWindow ( "RICHEDIT", "",
                                WS_CHILD,
                                0, 0, 0, 0,
                                hAnyWnd, (HMENU)0,
                                ghInst, NULL );
  MyLoadRTFFile ( hRTFWnd, szInput, uInputStream );
```

```
MySaveRTFFile ( hRTFWnd, szOutput, uOutputStream );
DestroyWindow ( hRTFWnd );
}
```

RichEdit Control Miscellany

The tasks described in the previous sections will probably handle 99 percent of your needs. But wait, there's more! In addition, the RichEdit control is also a great OLE 2 client because it allows other objects to be inserted directly into the stream of characters.

Also, the RichEdit control provides the "amazing growing edit control" feature. This allows it to send an EN_REQUESTRESIZE notification (via WM_NOTIFY, explained in Goodie #2) to its parent. In response, the parent window can resize the RichEdit control to make sure that all of the text is visible on the screen. Think of it as a bottomless edit control. For more information, refer to the RICHEDIT.H file and look for the REQRESIZE structure. Figure 11.37 shows all of the different notifications that the RichEdit control can send to its parent via WM_NOTIFY. It is important to know that the RichEdit control only sends the WM_NOTIFY notification messages if the application instructs it to do so with the EM_SETEVENTMASK message. For this message, **lParam** is a bitfield mask that indicates which types of notifications to send to the application.

Notification Message	When sent to the RTF Edit Control's Parent	Mask value required in EM_SETEVENTMASK
WM_NOTIFY:EN_DROPFILES	Sent when control receives a WM_DROPFILES message	ENM_DROPFILES
WM_NOTIFY:EN_PROTECTED	Sent when user tries to change protected text	ENM_PROTECTED
WM_NOTIFY:EN_REQUESTRESIZE	Sent when the contents of the edit control become larger or smaller than the current window size	ENM_REQUESTRESIZE

WM_NOTIFY:EN_SELCHANGE	Sent whenever the insertion point moves or the selection changes	ENM_SELCHANGE
WM_NOTIFY:EN_MSGFILTER	Sent on key and mouse events	ENM_KEYEVENTS and/or ENM_MOUSEEVENTS
WM_NOTIFY:EN_CORRECTTEXT	Sent on the SYV_CORRECT pen gesture (beyond the scope of this article)	ENM_CORRECTTEXT
WM_COMMAND:EN_CHANGE	Sent when the text changes in the edit control, after painting	ENM_CHANGE
WM_COMMAND:EN_HSCROLL and WM_COMMAND:EN_VSCROLL	Sent when the edit control scrolls	ENM_SCROLL
WM_COMMAND:EN_UPDATE	Sent when the text changes in the edit control, before painting	ENM_UPDATE

FIGURE 11.37 RICHEDIT NOTIFICATIONS

RTFSAMP

My first sample program, RTFSAMP, is simply Notepad with a new face. (The source code is on the enclosed disk. I didn't list it here because my second sample program, RTFSAMP2, contains all the code of RTFSAMP plus more.) Instead of creating a vanilla edit control, the RichEdit control is used. The Edit menu choices allow the user to apply bold, italic, and underline formatting, as well as choose the font's point size and face name. In addition, the program loads, saves, and prints the contents of the RichEdit control. The Common Dialogs handle the filename grabbing and printer DC nabbing. Right now, I'll focus on the RichEdit control code, putting some of the above sample code to use.

The base program for this sample is GENERIC again; all of the new code is in NEW CODE START to NEW CODE END comment blocks.

The **InitInstance** function adds the lines of code to load the RichEdit control DLL (which registers the classname), creates the RichEdit control window, and places the handle to the DLL and RichEdit controls in the respective global variables **hRTFLib** and **hRTFWnd**. The control is sized to fit in the client area of the parent frame window; this "size to fit" code is in the WM_SIZE case statement in the **WndProc**. The EM_SETEVENTMASK message is sent to the RichEdit control to instruct it to send the WM_NOTIFY:EN_SELCHANGE message (by default, no notifications are sent, except for EN_ERRSPACE and EN_MAXTEXT, which are holdouts from the multi-line edit control days).

Let's first look at the character formatting part of the sample program. In response to the user choosing the Bold, Italic, or Underline menu options, the **RTF_ChangeCharAttribute** function is called, using the CFM_XXX and CFE_XXX masks from RICHEDIT.H. The code inside this function is just like the character-formatting code shown above.

In response to the user choosing the Increase Font Size or Decrease Font Size menu options, the **RTF_ChangeSizeAttribute** function is called. This function is very similar to **RTF_ChangeCharAttribute**, except that the field in the CHARFORMAT structure that the code pays attention to is **yHeight**. Since the RichEdit control talks twippily, the point size delta passed in is converted to twips by multiplying it by 20.

The **RTF_ChangeFont** function is called in response to the user choosing the Fonts menu option. This function uses the font Common Dialog. The information in the CHARFORMAT structure is converted into the LOGFONT structure required by the Common Dialog, the dialog is displayed, and then the LOGFONT information is converted back to the CHARFORMAT information.

All of these functions use the EM_GETCHARFORMAT message to find out information about the selected characters. Next the function parties on the CHARFORMAT structure, and then the function uses the EM_SETCHARFORMAT to coerce the selected text into the new look.

Now, let's look at how the file I/O is taken care of. In response to the user selecting the Open menu option, the **RTF_Open** function is called. This function first gets a filename using the File Open Common Dialog, and then sets up an EM_STREAMIN callback function as described above. The **dwCookie** field of the EDITSTREAM structure contains the file handle to read from, and the **OpenCallback** function reads in as much information as the RichEdit control requests.

The **RTF_Save** function is called in response to the user selecting the Save menu option. This function is just like the **RTF_Open** function, except that the **SaveCallback** function writes the information instead of reading it.

Both of the above functions follow the same theme: get a filename, open a file, set up an EDITSTREAM callback function, stream the data, and then close the file.

For printing, I literally cut and pasted the code in Listing 11.7 into the **RTF_Print** function, and added some Common Dialog code to get the printer DC. This implementation only prints to a 6" by 9" area on the page.

The **RTF_UpdateMenuState** function checks the current selection of the RichEdit control and checks or unchecks the appropriate attributes on the Edit menu (Bold, Italic, Underline). This function is called after applying any formatting to the selection (in IDM_BOLD, and so on). The WM_NOTIFY message code looks for the EN_SELCHANGE notification message, where the **RTF_UpdateMenuState** function is also called. By calling this function in response to the EN_SELCHANGE notification, the menus dynamically update as the insertion point moves around.

That's it! In little more than a thousand lines of code, I have a relatively feature-full word processor wannabe. In the next section, I'll spruce up the sample program by adding a toolbar and a status line to make it a cool mini-word processor! That second sample is RTFSAMP2 (Listing 11.10, at the end of the next goodie).

7. The Toolbar Control

The toolbar control is part of the Common Controls DLL. As with any toolbar, little buttons on the control mimic menu actions. If you add a button for File Open to the toolbar, you give the button the same ID as the File Open menu item in your main application. Clicking on the toolbar button sends the identical WM_COMMAND message to your application.

In addition to the standard push buttons, the toolbar control also supports check buttons and radio buttons. Check buttons stick down when you press them the first time, and pop back up the second time you press them, just like check boxes. Radio buttons are grouped together, and only one can be pressed at a time. You can also add your own controls (such as a combo box) to the toolbar.

For all types of controls that can be added to the toolbar, ToolTips make it easier for the user to know what they do. A ToolTip window appears by the button if you hover your mouse over the control for more than a couple seconds (see Figure 11.38). The text for this button is determined on the fly via a WM_NOTIFY:TTN_NEEDTEXT message (which will be discussed later).

FIGURE 11.38 A TOOLTIP WINDOW

So, after a brief message overview, let's modify RTFSAMP to sport a flashy ToolTipped toolbar.

How the Toolbar Manages Buttons

The different buttons on a toolbar control are all actually pieces of one big bitmap. Each button has a bitmap index, which indicates which little piece of the bitmap to use for the button face. Sound familiar? Think back to the Image List from Goodie #1—the concept is the same. The toolbar control gets one long bitmap (the "Image List"), and each button uses an image from it (see Figure 11.39). Therefore, for each button on the toolbar, not only the WM_COMMAND ID value must be stored, but also the bitmap index. The toolbar can also place text strings underneath each button (as the toolbar buttons in Microsoft Mail do); this is optional. If you want strings underneath the bitmaps in the toolbar buttons, you supply a stringtable to the toolbar with the TB_ADDSTRING message. **wParam** is always 0, and **lParam** points to a character array of consecutive NULL-terminated strings, with the last string doubly NULL-terminated. Each string in this character array is indexed sequentially by the toolbar, the first string having an index of 0. I will show how to access these strings in the actual buttons below.

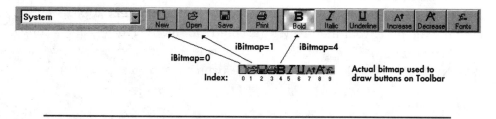

FIGURE 11.39 HOW THE TOOLBAR BITMAP FACES ARE INDEX TO THE BUTTONS ON A TOOLBAR

There are also some other values that must be stored for each button. All of these values, including the WM_COMMAND ID and the bitmap index, are accessible via the TBBUTTON structure:

```
typedef struct _TBBUTTON
  {
  int iBitmap;     /* index into bitmap of this button's
                      picture */
  int idCommand;   /* WM_COMMAND menu ID that this button
                      sends */
  BYTE fsState;    /* button's state          */
  BYTE fsStyle;    /* button's style          */
  DWORD dwData;    /* app defined data        */
  int iString;     /* index into string list */
  } TBBUTTON;
```

The **iBitmap** field specifies the bitmap image I talked about earlier (0 is the first image), and **idCommand** specifies the WM_COMMAND value that the parent application can expect when the user presses the toolbar button. The **fsState** and **fsStyle** fields indicate the appearance and capabilities of the button (see Figure 11.40). **dwData** is a free-for-all DWORD given to your application for storage of something like a C++ this pointer, and **iString** is an index into the stringtable. For example, if you want your first button on the toolbar to use the first string from the stringtable, **iString** should be zero.

The sample program at the end of the Status Bar Goodie uses a stringtable for all the buttons.

State	Description
TBSTATE_CHECKED	Checkbox type button is checked
TBSTATE_PRESSED	Push button is pressed
TBSTATE_ENABLED	Button is enabled
TBSTATE_HIDDEN	Button is hidden
TBSTATE_INDETERMINATE	Checkbox type button is neither checked or unchecked
Style	Description
TBSTYLE_BUTTON	Regular pushbutton
TBSTYLE_SEP	Separator
TBSTYLE_CHECK	Checkbox style button (two or three state)
TBSTYLE_GROUP	Part of a group (like a radio button)
TBSTYLE_CHECKGROUP	Both check and group

FIGURE 11.40 TOOLBAR BUTTON CAPABILITIES

Creating a Toolbar

Before creating a toolbar, you must make sure that the **InitCommonControls** API has been called (as with any control from the Common Controls DLL), and that your program has linked with COMCTL32.LIB. Once this has been done, there are two ways to create a toolbar. The first method involves using the **CreateToolbarEx** API. This API is a wrapper around the **CreateWindow** API, which is the second method for creating a toolbar. The **CreateToolbarEx** method of making a toolbar window involves setting up an array of TBBUTTON structures, one for each button, and then passing that array to **CreateToolbarEx**, along with a bunch of other parameters. The code in Listing 11.9 creates a tiny toolbar with just open and save buttons.

LISTING 11.9 CREATING A TOOLBAR WITH BUTTONS

```
// Declare an array of two buttons
TBBUTTON Buttons[2];
Buttons[0].iBitmap = 0;        // Use first bitmap image
Buttons[0].idCommand = IDM_OPEN; // "Menu" ID
Buttons[0].fsState = TBSTATE_ENABLED;     // Enabled button
Buttons[0].fsStyle = TBSTYLE_BUTTON;      // Normal button
Buttons[0].dwData = 0L;        // Not used
Buttons[0].iString = 0;        // Not used


Buttons[1].iBitmap = 1;        // Use first bitmap image
Buttons[1].idCommand = IDM_SAVE; // "Menu" ID
Buttons[1].fsState = TBSTATE_ENABLED;     // Enabled button
Buttons[1].fsStyle = TBSTYLE_BUTTON;      // Normal button
Buttons[1].dwData = 0L;        // Not used
Buttons[1].iString = 0;        // Not used


ws = WS_VISIBLE | WS_CHILD | WS_BORDER;// Window Style
wID = ID_TOOLBAR;              // ID of the toolbar
nBitmaps = 2;                  // Number of bitmap images
hBMInst = NULL;          // See comments below in call
wBMID = (HBITMAP)hToolbarBitmap; // Handle to bitmap to use for button faces
iNumButtons = 2;         // Number of buttons (size of array above)
dxButton = 22;               // 22 x24 button (pixels)
dyButtons = 24;
dxBitmap = 16;               // 16x18 bitmap image (pixels)
dyBitmap = 18;


hWndTB=CreateToolbarEx(  hWnd,            // Parent of toolbar
            ws,      // Window style (usually WS_CHILD)
            wID,     // ID of toolbar window (not the buttons)
            nBitmaps,    // Number of bitmap images
            hBMInst, // HINSTANCE of resource where the
                     //   bitmap for the buttons live. If NULL,
                     //   then the next parameter is the HBITMAP.
            wBMID,        // The resource ID if hBMInst is non-NULL,
                     //   otherwise HBITMAP to a bitmap.
            Buttons, // Pointer to array of TBBUTTONs
            iNumButtons, // Size of array
            dxButton,    // Width of button
            dyButton,    // Height of button
            dxBitmap,    // Width of bitmap image
            dyBitmap,    // Height of bitmap image
            sizeof(TBBUTTON) // Version control
        );
```

This code declares a tiny array of two buttons, and then calls the **CreateToolbarEx** API with the rest of the necessary parameters. For most uses, this code will work splendidly without any modifications (except you may find it useful to add more than two buttons). If you don't want to create your toolbar with a standard array of buttons, you can use the second method of creating a toolbar, via **CreateWindow**. This implementation is used in the sample program at the end of this goodie, and will be explained there.

Positioning the Toolbar

Toolbars by default stick to the top of the client area of a window. The toolbar control automatically resizes and repositions itself to stick to the top of your parent window provided you relay the WM_SIZE message to the toolbar from the parent. All that is required is that you send the WM_SIZE message on to the toolbar:

```
// (Parent window procedure code)
case WM_SIZE:
  SendMessage( hTBWnd, msg, wParam, lParam );
  break;
```

Presto! The toolbar control will automatically reposition itself. If you need to recalculate the remaining client area (which is where you may place an MDI client control for example), you can call **GetClientRect** on the toolbar window after sending it the WM_SIZE message. For example, if you wanted to resize something like, say, a RichEdit control to fill in the rest of the client area, you could modify the above code to look like this:

```
// (Parent window procedure code)
case WM_SIZE:

  SendMessage( hTBWnd, msg, wParam, lParam );
  GetClientRect( hTBWnd, &rc );
  MoveWindow( hRTFWnd, 0, rc.bottom, (LOWORD)lParam,
              (HIWORD)lParam - rc.bottom );
  break;
```

ToolTips

ToolTips come almost for free using the toolbar control. All you have to do is specify TBSTYLE_TOOLTIPS in the style field of **CreateToolbarEx** (or along with the style bits in CreateWindow), and then add some WM_NOTIFY code. The WM_NOTIFY message will be sent to the parent of the toolbar with the TTN_NEEDTEXT notification code. **lParam** will point to a TOOLTIPTEXT structure:

```
typedef struct
  {
  NMHDR hdr;              // Standard WM_NOTIFY header
  LPSTR lpszText;         // pointer to text to display
  char szText[80];        // Can use this as the buffer if
                          // desired
  HINSTANCE hinst;        // If non-NULL, lpszText has
                          // resource ID
  }
TOOLTIPTEXT;
```

The above notification is sent to your application right before the ToolTip is displayed. Your application must fill in the structure to display text. Of course, you need to know what button the text is for; this button is in the **hdr.idFrom** field. There are three ways of filling in this structure with the ToolTip text. The first method involves pointing the **lpszText** to some string that lives in your application:

```
lpToolTipText->lpszText = "Hi There!";// Point to
                                  // external buffer
                                  //(in this case, a constant)
lpToolTipText->hinst = NULL;      // Ignore this field
```

The second method involves using the temporary buffer provided in the notification message:

```
// Point to own buffer
lpToolTipText->lpszText = lpToolTipText->szText;
// Fill in buffer
wsprintf( lpToolTipText->szText,
        "Shields at %d Percent", iShieldStrength );

lpToolTipText->hinst = NULL;
```

The third method involves putting information into the structure to instruct the toolbar control to load the information from a stringtable. In this chunk of code, the stringtable has strings that share the same ID as the WM_COMMAND ID:

```
lpToolTipText->lpszText = lpToolTipText->hdr.idFrom;
                // Resource string in stringtable
                // has same ID as the wID value of
                // button.
lpToolTipText->hinst = hAppInst;
                // This app owns the stringtable
```

For all three methods, your code simply needs to trap the WM_NOTI-FY:TTN_NEEDTEXT message, fill out the structure, and then return any value (although returning 0 is politically correct).

Toolbar Messages

The toolbar control, like the TreeView control, uses messages as a means for program control. Figure 11.41 lists all the messages that can be sent to the toolbar control and how they are used.

Message	wParam	lParam	Return Value	Description
TB_ADDBITMAP32	Number of buttons	LPTBADDBIT MAP	LOWORD has index for first new button	Indicates the bitmap to use for button pictures
TB_ADDBUTTONS	Number of buttons to add	LPTBBUTTON array	n/a	Adds buttons to the toolbar
TB_ADDSTRING	Zero if lParam is a string pointer, non-zero if wParam is an instance of a resource	If wParam is zero: LPSTR to a string table. If wParam is non-zero: Resource ID to load from a RC file	LOWORD of first new string	Sets the text to draw underneath the buttons on the toolbar (see the text of this article for detail)
TB_BUTTONCOUNT	Zero	Zero	Number of buttons on toolbar	Counts the buttons on the toolbar
TB_BUTTONSTRUCTSIZE	sizeof(TBBUT TON	Zero	n/a	Version initial-izes the toolbar. MUST be sent immediately

				after creation (unless you used CreateToolbarEx).
TB_CHECKBUTTON	Button ID	LOWORD TRUE to check, FALSE to uncheck	n/a	Checks/Unchecks a button
TB_COMMANDTOINDEX	Button ID	Zero	Logical position of button	Returns the placement of a button
TB_DELETEBUTTON	Button ID	Zero	n/a	Deletes a button
TB_ENABLEBUTTON	Button ID	LOWORD: TRUE to enable FALSE to disable	n/a	Enables/Disables a button
TB_GETBUTTON	Button ID	LPTBBUTTON	n/a	Fills in a TBBUTTON structure with the gory details of the button
TB_GETFONT	Zero	Zero	HFONT to use	Gets a font from the toolbar to draw things like comboboxes
TB_GETITEMRECT	Button ID	LPRECT	TRUE on success	Fills the RECT structure with the coordinates of the toolbar
TB_GETSTATE	Button ID	Zero	LOWORD has state bits	Gets the state of a button
TB_GETTOOLTIPS	Zero	Zero	HWND of ToolTip window	Gets the handle to the ToolTips window (beyond the scope of this article)
TB_HIDEBUTTON	Button ID	LOWORD: TRUE to hide, FALSE to show	n/a	Hides or Shows a button
TB_INDETERMINATE	Button ID	LOWORD: TRUE for indeterminate, FALSE for non-indeterminate	n/a	Sets/Clears the Indeterminate state of a button
TB_INSERTBUTTON	Button Index to insert before (use the TB_COMMANDTO-INDEX message to get the index)	LPTBUTTON	n/a	Inserts a button
TB_ISBUTTONCHECKED	Button ID	Zero	LOWORD: TRUE if	Checks to see if a button

			checked	is checked
TB_ISBUTTONENABLED	Button ID	Zero	LOWORD: TRUE if enabled	Checks to see if a button is enabled
TB_ISBUTTONHIDDEN	Button ID	Zero	LOWORD: TRUE if hidden	Checks to see if a button is hidden
TB_ISBUTTONINDETER MINATE	Button ID	Zero	LOWORD: TRUE if indeterminate	Checks to see if a button is indeterminate
TB_ISBUTTONPRESSED	Button ID	Zero	LOWORD: TRUE if pressed	Checks to see if a button is pressed
TB_PRESSBUTTON	Button ID	LOWORD: TRUE to press	n/a	Presses a button
TB_SAVERESTORE	TRUE to save, FALSE to load	Array of LPSTRS, first is INI section name, second is INI file name	n/a	Saves or restores the toolbar to an INI file (beyond the scope of this article)
TB_SETBITMAPSIZE	Zero	MAKELONG (dx,dy)	n/a	Indicates the size of one bitmap image for a button (must be done before adding the bitmap)
TB_SETBUTTONSIZE	Zero	MAKELONG (dx,dy)	n/a	Indicates the size of the button to draw (must be done before adding buttons)
TB_SETSTATE	Button ID	LOWORD: State bits	n/a	Sets the state of a button
TB_SETTOOLTIPS	hWnd of ToolTips window	Zero	n/a	Sets the handle to a ToolTips control window (beyond the scope of this article)

FIGURE 11.41 TOOLBAR MESSAGES

The sample program at the end of this goodie uses the TB_INSERTBUT-TON message to insert buttons, the TB_BUTTONSTRUCTSIZE message for version control, and the TB_ADDBITMAP32 message to tell the toolbar which button to use for the button faces.

383

Adding Controls to the Toolbar

The toolbar lets you add its own type of push buttons with the TB_INSERT-BUTTON message, but you may wish to add a more powerful control, such as a combo box or edit control. You have to do most of the work here. In fact, the only help you get from the toolbar is that you can instruct it to reserve a space on itself for your control. This is done by adding a separator to the toolbar with the TB_ INSERTBUTTON message. For the **fsStyle** field of the TBBUTTON structure, use TBSTYLE_SEP, and for the **iBitmap** field, use the width of the separator in pixels. Using a value of zero defaults the separator to a "nice" width.

Once you have reserved the space on the toolbar, you can create your control, "parent" it to the toolbar, and use **MoveWindow** to position it on the toolbar. The TB_GETITEMRECT message can be used to figure out the coordinates of the placeholder separator; you can use those coordinates for your **MoveWindow** call.

A little known "feature" of Windows controls is that they cache away the parent upon creation. This means that if you create an edit control with **hWndParent** as the parent, the **hWndParent** will continue to receive the EN_XXX notification messages *even if you reparent the edit control* (See Chapter 5: "Common Headaches Encountered by Windows Programmers"). This behavior is consistent across all of the controls. Normally, this little known "feature" is a pain in the neck, but here is a case where it is actually a great help. By initially creating the control with the main window as the parent, and then reparenting it to the toolbar, your main window can get the notification messages instead of the toolbar window. This is helpful, since the window procedure for the toolbar window lives inside COMCTL32.DLL, and you would have to subclass the window to intercept messages.

Take a look at the sample program RTFSAMP2 see Listing 11.10 at the end of the Status Bar goodie; it uses a combo box on the toolbar to indicate the current font of the text, and lets the user change the font via the combo box.

6. The Status Bar

The status bar is also part of the Common Controls DLL family, which once again means you will have to use the **InitCommonControls** API and link with COMCTL32.LIB.

The status bar provides a means to display information in little panes inside its client area (see Figure 11.42). The default height of the panes is determined by the height of the status bar (although these values can be changed), and the width of the panes is determined by the application via a message (described later). Each panel can sport "innie" or "outie" indentation, or no indentation.

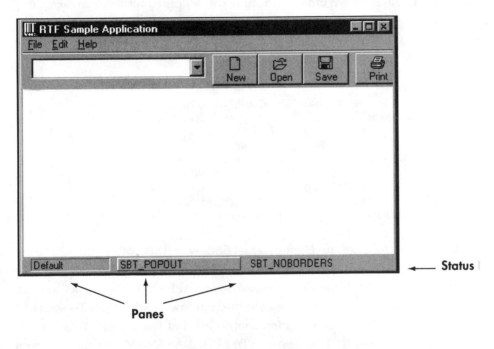

FIGURE 11.42 A STATUS BAR

In addition to displaying handy information along the bottom of the screen, the status bar also has a special simple mode. Simple mode means the status bar displays only one special pane. This simple mode is normally used when the user is flipping through the menus, and some more verbose information is getting displayed inside the status bar. When simple mode is turned off, the normal panes pop back into view.

Creating the Status Bar

First, use **InitCommonControls** and link with COMCTL32.LIB. As with the toolbar, there are two ways to create a status bar. The first method involves using the **CreateStatusWindow** API, and the second method involves using **CreateWindow** with the status bar's classname. The sample program at the end of this Goodie will use the first method; the second method, using **CreateWindow**, looks something like this:

```
                                // in COMMCTRL.H
hWndStatusBar = CreateWindow(STATUSCLASSNAME,
            "caption text",     // Pane 0 text
            WS_CHILD | WS_VISIBLE,// Style bits
            0, 0, 0, 0,         // WM_SIZE
                                // handles size
            hWndParent,         // Parent hWnd
            (HMENU)idStatus,    // Status ID
            hInst,              // Instance handle
            NULL );             // Always NULL
```

Unlike the toolbar, the **CreateStatusWindow** method offers no advantage over the **CreateWindow** method except that your code does not need to specify a classname, and the **CreateStatusWindow** API is a little bit easier to read. Another advantage that the **CreateStatusWindow** (and **CreateToolbarEx**) method has over the **CreateWindow** method is that the classname is hidden from the application. The above STATUSCLASSNAME constant from COMMCTRL.H is defined as **msctls_statusbar**. If you use the **CreateWindow** method, then you are binding your program to always using that classname. However, if your program uses the **CreateStatusWindow** API, then the Common Controls DLL manages the classname, and frees your program of one more operating system dependency.

Managing Panes

Each pane in the status bar is in numerical order from the left, starting at Pane 0. There are two types of pane sizes: fixed and springy. A fixed pane will take on an absolute width. Examples of panes that may have a fixed width include the INS/OVR panes (to toggle the insert/overwrite state of the editor), or, say, a pane with the time of day in it. These panes have a very definite width, and therefore do not need any more width than your program gives them. Springy panes have minimum sizes, but if there is any leftover space on the status bar after all the panes have been added, that extra space is given to the springy panes as a sort of "congratulations for being springy" bonus. For panes that would have a variable-length string in them, it makes sense to make the pane springy to maximize your pane's perimeter potential.

There are two steps to managing the panes in a status bar. The first involves deciding the widths for each pane (or minimum widths for springy panes). This is done by defining an array of integers, and sending that array to the status bar with the SB_SETPARTS message. Each element in the integer array defines the right-hand side of each pane (see Figure 11.43). If the value of –1 is used for a pane's right hand side, the status bar will extend that pane to the right edge of the status bar (obviously, if you do this, there will not be any bonus room for your springy panes, so using –1 in conjunction with springy panes is a self-canceling effect, much like mixing time and antitime). Likewise, the SB_GETPARTS message retrieves the current pane locations.

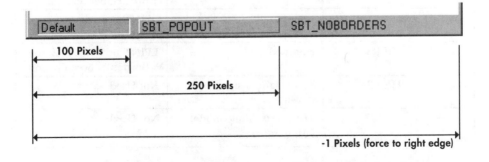

FIGURE 11.43 INDICATING THE PANE WIDTH IN A STATUS BAR

The second step in managing status bar panes involves setting the text of each pane along with its style. As mentioned above, the style of each pane determines if the pane has innie, outie, or no borders, as well as if the pane is a springy pane. In addition, the pane can be owner draw, which will cause the classic WM_DRAWITEM message to be sent to the status bar's parent.

To set the text and style bits of a pane, use the SB_SETTEXT message. For **wParam**, logically OR the style bits along with the pane number. For **lParam**, use a pointer to the string unless you are setting this pane to owner draw; then use whatever you like for **lParam**, because it will come back to you in the WM_DRAWITEM message. For example, say we wanted to set the text of Pane 2 to "Belly Button", and give it an outie look and feel:

```
4SendMessage( hStatusWnd, SB_SETTEXT, SBT_POPOUT | 2,
          (LPARAM)"Belly Button" );
```

For a complete table of the status bar style bits and messages, see Figure 11.44.

msg	wParam	lParam
SB_GETTEXT*	Pane Number	sztext
SB_GETTEXTLENGTH*	Pane Number	Not Used
SB_SETTEXT	Pane Number OR's with Style Bits	szText or NULL
SB_SETPARTS	Number of Panes	LPINT pane points
SB_SETBORDERS	Not Used	LPINT to 3 ints: X Border, Y Border, between panes
SB_GETPARTS	size of array	LPINT to Pane Array to be filled
SB_GETBORDERS	Not used	LPINT to 3 ints: X Border, Y Border, between panes
SB_SETMINHEIGHT	Min height of status bar drawing area	Not Used
SB_SIMPLE	TRUE sets simple mode, FALSE unsets	Not Used

*Returns MAKELONG(Text Len, Pane Style Bits)

Style	Meaning
SBT_OWNERDRAW	lParam of SB_SETTEXT will be returned in DRAWITEM-STRUCT.itemData
SBT_NOBORDERS	No border will be drawn for this pane
SBT_POPOUT	Draw an "outie" instead of an "innie"
SBT_SPRING	The pane will be "springy," which means it can grow to fir the text if needed

FIGURE 11.44 STATUS BAR STYLES AND MESSAGES

Handling Menu Browsing

One of the most common tasks for a status bar is menu help, where a short description of the currently selected menu item appears at the bottom of the screen. The WM_MENUSELECT message is sent to the window that owns the menu the user is scanning. Once your application has successfully picked apart this message, it can then instruct the status bar to display the menu help. As I mentioned, it is a good idea to set the status bar into simple mode so that the entire status bar is dedicated to displaying the menu help. Take a look at this sample function:

```
void DisplayStatusMenuHelp(HWND hStatusWnd, UINT idMsg)
{
  char sz[128];
  if ( -1 != idMsg )
    {
    SendMessage( hStatusWnd, SB_SIMPLE, TRUE, 0 );
    if (0 != idMsg)
      {
      LoadString(hInst, idMsg, sz, sizeof(sz));
      SendMessage( hStatusWnd, SB_SETTEXT, 255,
              (LPARAM)sz );
      }
    }
  else
    {
    SendMessage ( hStatusWnd, SB_SIMPLE, FALSE, 0 );
```

```
    }
}
```

As long as the ID of the message to display is not –1, this function will set the status bar to simple using the SB_SIMPLE:TRUE message, load a string from the application's stringtable (the ID of the string in the stringtable corresponds to the ID of the menu item), and display that string in the status bar using the SB_SETTEXT message. If the ID is –1, the status bar is set back to normal mode using the SB_SIMPLE:FALSE message. Notice how the **wParam** of the SB_SETTEXT message is 255. When the status bar is in simple mode, the pane number your program uses is always 255; this allows the information in the normal panes to be left alone.

This function is called in response to your everyday WM_MENUSELECT message (the sample program at the end of this Goodie contains an implementation of the WM_MENUSELECT message handler); it handles the dirty work of managing the status bar.

Tinkering With the Status Bar

The status bar control uses a default spacing between, above, and below the panes. The default values used depend on the display driver; the status bar figures out the most reasonable spacing parameters. If you want to change these values, you can use the SB_SETBORDERS message to change the spacing variables. **lParam** points to an array of three integers. The first element specifies the spacing from the left edge of the status bar to the first pane (and also the spacing from the right border of the status bar to the last pane). The second element specifies the top and bottom spacing, and the third element specifies the spacing between panes. All measurements are in pixels. Likewise, the SB_GETBORDERS message retrieves the current settings for the status bar's borders.

The Sample Program

The sample program, RTFSAMP2, is a mini word processor with less than 1500 lines of C code (see Listing 11.10). It's an improved version of RTF-

SAMP with the toolbar and status bar controls. All new code added to the original RTFSAMP program is marked in those "NEW CODE START" and "NEW CODE END" comment blocks.

LISTING 11.10 RTFSAMP2 SAMPLE PROGRAM

```
#include <windows.h>                 // required for all Windows applications
#if !defined(_WIN32)
#include <ver.h>
#endif
#include "RTFSAMP2.h"                 // specific to this program


// Windows NT defines APIENTRY, but 3.x doesn't
#if !defined (APIENTRY)
#define APIENTRY far pascal
#endif


// Windows 3.x uses a FARPROC for dialogs
#if !defined(_WIN32)
#define DLGPROC FARPROC

#endif

7HINSTANCE hInst;                    // current instance


char szAppName[] = "RTFSAMP2";        // The name of this application
char szTitle[]   = "RTF Sample Application"; // The title bar text


//********************** NEW CODE START *******************

#include <commctrl.h>

#define TBADDBITMAP32 TBADDBITMAP
#define TB_ADDBITMAP32 TB_ADDBITMAP

void TOOLTIP_GetText ( LPTOOLTIPTEXT lpttt );
void STATUS_DisplayStatusMenuHelp ( HWND hStatusWnd, UINT idMsg );
void STATUS_DisplayStatusInformation ( HWND hRTFWnd, HWND hStatusWnd );


//********************** NEW CODE END *******************

#include <richedit.h>
```

LISTING 11.10 CONTINUED

```c
int  RTF_GetCharAttribute ( HWND hRTFWnd, DWORD dwMask, DWORD dwEffects );
void RTF_ChangeCharAttribute ( HWND hRTFWnd, DWORD dwMask, DWORD dwEffects );
void RTF_ChangeSizeAttribute ( HWND hRTFWnd, int iPointChange );
void RTF_ChangeFont ( HWND hWnd, HWND hRTFWnd );
BOOL RTF_Open ( HWND hWnd, HWND hRTFWnd );
BOOL RTF_Save ( HWND hWnd, HWND hRTFWnd );
BOOL RTF_CheckForDirtyContents ( HWND hWnd, HWND hRTFWnd );
BOOL SelectPrinter ( LPSTR szPrinter,
                     HWND  hWndParent,
                     UINT  FAR *pdmDriverExtra );
HDC  GetPrinterDC ( LPSTR szPrinter,
                    UINT  dmDriverExtra,
                    HWND  hWndParent );
void RTF_Print ( HWND hWnd, HWND hRTFWnd );
void RTF_UpdateMenuState ( HWND hWndRTF, HWND hWnd );
void RTF_GetCurrentFont ( HWND hRTFWnd, LPSTR szFont );
void RTF_SetCurrentFont ( HWND hRTFWnd, LPSTR szFont );


UINT    dmDriverExtra;      // Used for GetPrinterDC
TCHAR   szPrinter[256];     // Used for GetPrinterDC
HANDLE  hRTFLib;            // Handle to RICHED32.DLL
HWND    hRTFWnd;            // Handle to RTF Edit Control
TCHAR   szFileName[256];    // Name of currently open file


//********************* NEW CODE START ********************


HWND    hTBWnd;            // Handle of Toolbar Window
HWND    hStatusWnd;        // Handle of Status Bar Window
HWND    hComboBox;         // Handle of Combobox on toolbar
HBITMAP hTBBmp;            // Bitmap to use for Toolbar

void Handle_WM_MENSELECT ( HWND hStatusWnd, UINT message, WPARAM uParam, LPARAM
lParam );


//********************* NEW CODE END ********************


// These are app-specific codes to determine the state of text.
// YES means the text has the attribute requested. No means it
// doesn't. WAFFLE means it is neither yes or no (has characters
// with and without the attribute requested).

#define CHAR_ATTRIB_YES    0
```

```
#define CHAR_ATTRIB_NO       1
#define CHAR_ATTRIB_WAFFLE 2


//
//    FUNCTION: WinMain(HINSTANCE, HINSTANCE, LPSTR, int)
//
//    PURPOSE: calls initialization function, processes message loop
//
//    COMMENTS:
//
//        Windows recognizes this function by name as the initial entry point
//        for the program.  This function calls the application initialization
//        routine, if no other instance of the program is running, and always
//        calls the instance initialization routine.  It then executes a
//        message retrieval and dispatch loop that is the top-level control
//        structure for the remainder of execution.  The loop is terminated
//        when a WM_QUIT   message is received, at which time this function
//        exits the application instance by returning the value passed by
//        PostQuitMessage().
//
//        If this function must abort before entering the message loop, it
//        returns the conventional value NULL.
//

int APIENTRY WinMain(
                HINSTANCE hInstance,
                HINSTANCE hPrevInstance,
                LPSTR lpCmdLine,
                int nCmdShow
                )
{
    MSG msg;
    HANDLE hAccelTable;

    // Other instances of app running?
    if (!hPrevInstance) {
        // Initialize shared things
        if (!InitApplication(hInstance)) {
            return (FALSE);                   // Exits if unable to initialize
        }
    }

    // Perform initializations that apply to a specific instance
    if (!InitInstance(hInstance, nCmdShow)) {
        return (FALSE);
    }
```

LISTING 11.10 CONTINUED

```
    hAccelTable = LoadAccelerators (hInstance, szAppName);


    // Acquire and dispatch messages until a WM_QUIT message is received.
    while (GetMessage(&msg,    // message structure
                    NULL,    // handle of window receiving the message
                    0,       // lowest message to examine
                    0)){     // highest message to examine
        if (!TranslateAccelerator (msg.hwnd, hAccelTable, &msg)) {
            TranslateMessage(&msg);// Translates virtual key codes
            DispatchMessage(&msg); // Dispatches message to window
        }
    }


    // Free RICHED32.DLL at shutdown

    if (hRTFLib)
      {
      FreeLibrary (hRTFLib);
      hRTFLib = NULL;
      }


    // Returns the value from PostQuitMessage
    return (msg.wParam);

    // This will prevent 'unused formal parameter' warnings
    lpCmdLine;
}


//
//   FUNCTION: InitApplication(HINSTANCE)
//
//   PURPOSE: Initializes window data and registers window class
//
//   COMMENTS:
//
//      This function is called at initialization time only if no other
//      instances of the application are running.  This function performs
//      initialization tasks that can be done once for any number of running
//      instances.
//
//      In this case, we initialize a window class by filling out a data
//      structure of type WNDCLASS and calling the Windows RegisterClass()
```

```
//      function.  Since all instances of this application use the same
//      window class, we only need to do this when the first instance is
//      initialized.
//

BOOL InitApplication(HINSTANCE hInstance)
{
    WNDCLASS  wc;

    // Fill in window class structure with parameters that describe the
    // main window.
    wc.style         = CS_HREDRAW | CS_VREDRAW; // Class style(s).
    wc.lpfnWndProc   = (WNDPROC)WndProc;        // Window Procedure
    wc.cbClsExtra    = 0;                        // No per-class extra data.
    wc.cbWndExtra    = 0;                        // No per-window extra data.
    wc.hInstance     = hInstance;               // Owner of this class
    wc.hIcon         = LoadIcon (hInstance, szAppName);// Icon name from .RC
    wc.hCursor       = LoadCursor(NULL, IDC_ARROW); // Cursor
    wc.hbrBackground = (HBRUSH)(COLOR_WINDOW+1);// Default color
    wc.lpszMenuName  = szAppName;               // Menu name from .RC
    wc.lpszClassName = szAppName;               // Name to register as


    // Register the window class and return success/failure code.
    return (RegisterClass(&wc));
}


//*********************** NEW CODE START ********************


// These macros add buttons/separators to the toolbar

#define ADDBUTTON( id, btntype, bmpos )                        \
{                                                              \
    tbb.fsStyle   = btntype;                                   \
    tbb.idCommand = id;                                        \
    tbb.iBitmap   = bmpos;                                     \
    tbb.iString   = bmpos;                                     \
    SendMessage ( hTBWnd, TB_INSERTBUTTON, 99, (LPARAM)&tbb ); \
}


#define ADDSEP( width )                                        \
{                                                              \
    tbb.fsStyle   = TBSTYLE_SEP;                               \
    tbb.idCommand = 0;                                         \
    tbb.iBitmap   = width;                                     \
    tbb.iString   = 0;                                         \
```

395

LISTING 11.10 CONTINUED

```
    SendMessage ( hTBWnd, TB_INSERTBUTTON, 99, (LPARAM)&tbb ); \
}


//***********************************************************
//
//  This procedure is called by the EnumFontFamilies
//  call. It fills the combobox with the font facename
//
//***********************************************************


int CALLBACK FillFontProc ( LPLOGFONT    lplf,
                            LPTEXTMETRIC lptm,
                            int          iFontType,
                            LPARAM       lParam
                          )
{

  // Only add the facename if the facename is not
  // in the combobox

  if (CB_ERR ==
      (WPARAM)SendMessage ( (HWND)lParam,
                            CB_FINDSTRING,
                            (WPARAM)-1,
                            (LPARAM)(lplf->lfFaceName)
                          )
     )
    SendMessage ( (HWND)lParam,
                  CB_ADDSTRING,
                  (WPARAM)0,
                  (LPARAM)(lplf->lfFaceName)
                );
  return TRUE;
}


//***********************************************************
//
// TOOLBAR_MakeMeAToolbar: This code creates a toolbar and
//                         sticks buttons on it
//
//***********************************************************


HWND TOOLBAR_MakeMeAToolbar ( HWND hWndParent )
```

```
{
    TBADDBITMAP32 tbadbm;    // For adding the bitmap
    TBBUTTON      tbb;       // For adding buttons
    HWND          hTBWnd;    // Handle of toolbar window
    HDC           hDC;       // a DC


    // Create the toolbar window with CreateWindow

    hTBWnd = CreateWindow(
        TOOLBARCLASSNAME,        // Classname of toolbar
        "",                      // No text
        WS_CHILD | WS_VISIBLE |
            TBSTYLE_TOOLTIPS,    // Style of toolbar
        0, 0, 0, 0,              // Will size to fit in parent's WM_SIZE code
        hWndParent,              // Use main window as parent
        NULL,                    // Don't worry about the ID
        hInst,                   // This instance owns this window.
        NULL                     // Always NULL for RTF Edit windows
        );
    if (!hTBWnd) return NULL;


    // This is version control- by sending the size of the TBBUTTON
    // structure, the toolbar knows what version of the toolbar the program
    // expects to be talking to
    SendMessage ( hTBWnd, TB_BUTTONSTRUCTSIZE, sizeof(TBBUTTON), 0 );


    // Let's use 32x32 buttons
    SendMessage ( hTBWnd, TB_SETBUTTONSIZE, 0, MAKELONG(32,32));


    // Grab the toolbar bitmap from the resources
    hTBBmp = LoadBitmap ( hInst, "TB" );


    // And instruct the toolbar to use it
    tbadbm.hInst = NULL;
    tbadbm.nID   = (UINT)hTBBmp;
    SendMessage ( hTBWnd, TB_ADDBITMAP32, 10, (LPARAM)&tbadbm );


    // Add a combobox to the toolbar. This involves three steps:
    //
    // 1. Create the combobox, using the main window as a parent
    // 2. Changing the parent to the toolbar
    // 3. Sizing the control
    //
    // The reason the parent must originally be the main window
    // is so we can get the CBN_SELCHANGE messages. Controls
```

LISTING 11.10 CONTINUED

```
// cache away their parent upon creation. Therefore, even though
// we have re-parented the combobox to the toolbar, the CBN_*
// messages still go to the original parent. This allows us to
// avoid subclassing the toolbar to look for the CBN_* messages.

hComboBox = CreateWindow ( "combobox",
                           "",
                           WS_CHILD | WS_VISIBLE | CBS_SORT |
                           CBS_DROPDOWNLIST | WS_VSCROLL,
                           0, 0, 0, 0,
                           hWndParent,
                           (HMENU)ID_COMBOBOX,
                           hInst,
                           NULL
                         );

// Fill the combobox with fonts

hDC = GetDC ( hWndParent );
EnumFontFamilies ( hDC, NULL, FillFontProc, (LPARAM)hComboBox );
ReleaseDC ( hWndParent, hDC );

// Parent the combobox to the toolbar, and make it 200 pixels wide

SetParent (hComboBox, hTBWnd );
MoveWindow ( hComboBox, 10, 5, 200, 100, FALSE );

// Set up the fields of the TBBUTTON structure that all the buttons
// will have in common. The ADDBUTTON macro fills in the fields
// that vary from button to button.
tbb.fsState   = TBSTATE_ENABLED;
tbb.dwData    = 0;

// First, add a separator that is 210 pixels wide, the combobox
// will occupy that space. The ADDSEP macro adds a button with
// TBSTYLE_SEP for the style, and the width goes in iBitmap.

ADDSEP( 210 );

// Add the buttons to the toolbar. The first parameter to the
// ADDBUTTON macro indicates the ID, the second parameter indicates
```

```
    // the type of button, and the third indicates which part of the
    // bitmap to use.

    ADDBUTTON( IDM_NEW,  TBSTYLE_BUTTON, 0 )
    ADDBUTTON( IDM_OPEN, TBSTYLE_BUTTON, 1 )
    ADDBUTTON( IDM_SAVE, TBSTYLE_BUTTON, 2 )

    ADDSEP( 0 ); // Add a "nice" width separator

    ADDBUTTON( IDM_PRINT, TBSTYLE_BUTTON, 3 )

    ADDSEP( 0 ); // Add a "nice" width separator

    ADDBUTTON( IDM_BOLD,      TBSTYLE_CHECK, 4 )
    ADDBUTTON( IDM_ITALIC,    TBSTYLE_CHECK, 5 )
    ADDBUTTON( IDM_UNDERLINE, TBSTYLE_CHECK, 6 )

    ADDSEP( 0 ); // Add a "nice" width separator

    ADDBUTTON( IDM_INCREASE_FONT, TBSTYLE_BUTTON, 7 )
    ADDBUTTON( IDM_DECREASE_FONT, TBSTYLE_BUTTON, 8 )
    ADDBUTTON( IDM_FONTDIALOG,    TBSTYLE_BUTTON, 9 )

    // Add the stringtable. The indexes of the strings for this example
    // mirror the indexes of the bitmaps, but that is specific to this
    // example program. Your program can use any index it wishes that
    // exists in the stringtable.

    SendMessage ( hTBWnd, TB_ADDSTRING, 0,
                (LPARAM)"New\0Open\0Save\0Print\0Bold\0Italic"
                "\0Underline\0Increase\0Decrease\0Fonts\0" );

    return hTBWnd;
}


//************************************************************
//
// STATUS_MakeMeAStatusLine: This code creates a status line and
//                           sticks panes on it.
//
//************************************************************

HWND STATUS_MakeMeAStatusLine ( HWND hWndParent )
```

LISTING 11.10 CONTINUED

```
{
  HWND hStatusWnd;

  // This array identifies the pane positions. The first pane
  // goes from 0 to 100, the second pane goes from a little bit
  // past the first pane to the right edge of the status line.

  int iPanesPosition[2] = { 100, -1 };

  // Create the status bar window using the nifty CreateStatusWindow
  // function (you could also just use CreateWindow, but I thought
  // I would show you an alternate method.
  hStatusWnd = CreateStatusWindow
                ( WS_CHILD | WS_VISIBLE, // Window style.
                  "Ready",                // Pane 0 text
                  hWndParent,             // Parent Window
                  4242                    // Some ID
                );

  // Tell the status bar that there are two panes, and give the
  // array from above to indicate the pane sizes.
  SendMessage ( hStatusWnd, SB_SETPARTS, 2, (LPARAM)iPanesPosition );

  // Call the function that fills in the second pane with the
  // line # of the caret in the RTF edit control. This is so the user
  // gets the feedback immediately at startup.
  STATUS_DisplayStatusInformation ( hRTFWnd, hStatusWnd);

  return hStatusWnd;
}


//*********************** NEW CODE END *******************

//
//   FUNCTION:  InitInstance(HINSTANCE, int)
//
//   PURPOSE:  Saves instance handle and creates main window
//
//   COMMENTS:
//
//       This function is called at initialization time for every instance of
```

```
//      this application.  This function performs initialization tasks that
//      cannot be shared by multiple instances.
//
//      In this case, we save the instance handle in a static variable and
//      create and display the main program window.


//
BOOL InitInstance(
        HINSTANCE      hInstance,
        int            nCmdShow
        )
{
   HWND    hWnd; // Main window handle.

   // Save the instance handle in static variable, which will be used in
   // many subsequence calls from this application to Windows.

   hInst = hInstance; // Store instance handle in our global variable

   // Create a main window for this application instance.
   hWnd = CreateWindow(
      szAppName,          // See RegisterClass() call.
      szTitle,            // Text for window title bar.
      WS_OVERLAPPEDWINDOW,// Window style.
      CW_USEDEFAULT, 0, CW_USEDEFAULT, 0,// Use default positioning
      NULL,               // Overlapped windows have no parent.
      NULL,               // Use the window class menu.
      hInstance,          // This instance owns this window.
      NULL                // We don't use any data in our WM_CREATE
      );

   // If window could not be created, return "failure"
   if (!hWnd) {
      return (FALSE);
   }


   // The call to LoadLibrary automatically registers
   // the classname of the RTF Edit control
   hRTFLib = LoadLibrary ( "RICHED32.DLL" );
   if (!hRTFLib)
     {
     MessageBox ( NULL, "LoadLibrary on RICHED32.DLL Failed", "MSJ", MB_OK );
     return FALSE;
     }
```

LISTING 11.10 CONTINUED

```
   // Create the child RTF Edit Control
   hRTFWnd = CreateWindow(
       "RICHEDIT",              // Classname of RTF Edit Control
       "",                      // Text for edit control
       WS_CHILD | WS_VISIBLE | ES_MULTILINE,// Window style.
       0, 0, 0, 0,              // Will size to fit in parent's WM_SIZE code
       hWnd,                    // Use main window as parent
       NULL,                    // Don't worry about the ID
       hInstance,               // This instance owns this window.
       NULL                     // Always NULL for RTF Edit windows
       );

   // Instruct the RTF Edit control to notify the parent whenever
   // the selection in the RTF Edit control changes. This will cause
   // the WM_NOTIFY:EN_SELCHANGE message to be sent to the parent.
   SendMessage (hRTFWnd, EM_SETEVENTMASK, 0, ENM_SELCHANGE );

//********************** NEW CODE START *******************

   // Must be called to register the classes in COMCTL32.DLL
   InitCommonControls();

   // Build the toolbar and status bar
   hTBWnd     = TOOLBAR_MakeMeAToolbar ( hWnd );
   hStatusWnd = STATUS_MakeMeAStatusLine ( hWnd );

//********************** NEW CODE END *******************

   // Make the window visible; update its client area; and return "success"
   ShowWindow(hWnd, nCmdShow); // Show the window
   UpdateWindow(hWnd);         // Sends WM_PAINT message

   return (TRUE);              // We succeeded...
}


//
//   FUNCTION: WndProc(HWND, UINT, WPARAM, LPARAM)
//
//   PURPOSE:  Processes messages
//
//   MESSAGES:
//
```

```
//      WM_COMMAND     - application menu (About dialog box)
//      WM_DESTROY     - destroy window
//
//   COMMENTS:
//
//      To process the IDM_ABOUT message, call MakeProcInstance() to get the
//      current instance address of the About() function.  Then call Dialog
//      box which will create the box according to the information in your
//      RTFSAMP2.rc file and turn control over to the About() function.  When
//      it returns, free the instance address.
//


#define ptrNMHDR         ((LPNMHDR)lParam)
#define ptrSELCHANGE     ((SELCHANGE *)lParam)


LRESULT CALLBACK WndProc(
      HWND hWnd,          // window handle
      UINT message,       // type of message
      WPARAM uParam,      // additional information
      LPARAM lParam       // additional information
      )
{
    FARPROC lpProcAbout;  // pointer to the "About" function
    int wmId, wmEvent;


    switch (message) {


//*********************** NEW CODE START *******************

      case WM_MENUSELECT:

            // Call the function to update the status bar
            Handle_WM_MENSELECT ( hStatusWnd, message, uParam, lParam );
            break;


      case WM_SIZE:
            // Sending the WM_SIZE message to the toolbar and status
            // bar makes them size themselves to appropriately fit in
            // the client area of the parent.

            if ( hRTFWnd && hTBWnd && hStatusWnd)
              {
              RECT rcTB;
              RECT rcSB;
```

LISTING 11.10 CONTINUED

```
            // Force TB and SB to resize themselves
            SendMessage ( hTBWnd,     message, uParam, lParam );
            SendMessage ( hStatusWnd, message, uParam, lParam );


            // Figure out the rectangle region to put the RTF Edit control
            // in by subtracting out the toolbar and status bar
            GetWindowRect ( hTBWnd,     &rcTB );
            GetWindowRect ( hStatusWnd, &rcSB );
            MoveWindow ( hRTFWnd, 0, rcTB.bottom-rcTB.top,
                        LOWORD (lParam),
                        (HIWORD (lParam) -
                        ((rcTB.bottom-rcTB.top) +
                        (rcSB.bottom-rcSB.top))
                        ), TRUE);
        }
    break;

case WM_NOTIFY:

    switch (ptrNMHDR->code)
        {
        case EN_SELCHANGE:

            // Call our function to check/uncheck the menu
            // items corresponding to the bold, italic, and
            // underline states of the selected text.
            RTF_UpdateMenuState ( hRTFWnd, hWnd );



            // Call our function to display the row and column
            // in the status bar.
            STATUS_DisplayStatusInformation ( hRTFWnd, hStatusWnd);
            break;


        case TTN_NEEDTEXT:

            // This message is sent when the toolbar needs
            // tooltip text.
            TOOLTIP_GetText ( (LPTOOLTIPTEXT)lParam );
            break;


        default:
```

```
            return (DefWindowProc(hWnd, message, uParam, lParam));
        } // End Switch
    break;


//********************** NEW CODE END *******************

    case WM_COMMAND:  // message: command from application menu

        // Message packing of uParam and lParam have changed for Win32,
        // let us handle the differences in a conditional compilation:
        #if defined (_WIN32)
            wmId    = LOWORD(uParam);
            wmEvent = HIWORD(uParam);
        #else
            wmId    = uParam;
            wmEvent = HIWORD(lParam);
        #endif


        switch (wmId) {


//************************* NEW CODE START ************************

        // This is sent when the user changes the selection in the
        // combobox on the toolbar

        case ID_COMBOBOX:

            if ( CBN_SELCHANGE == wmEvent )
              {
              // Get the facename from the combobox
              char szFont[LF_FACESIZE];
              GetWindowText ( hComboBox, szFont, sizeof(szFont));
              // Set the new font in the RTF edit control
              RTF_SetCurrentFont ( hRTFWnd, szFont );
              }
            break;


//************************* NEW CODE END ************************

        case IDM_ABOUT:
            lpProcAbout = MakeProcInstance((FARPROC)About, hInst);

            DialogBox(hInst,                // current instance
                "AboutBox",                 // dlg resource to use
```

LISTING 11.10 CONTINUED

```
                hWnd,                    // parent handle
                (DLGPROC)lpProcAbout);   // About() instance address

        FreeProcInstance(lpProcAbout);
        break;

    case IDM_EXIT:
        DestroyWindow (hWnd);
        break;

    case IDM_HELPCONTENTS:
        if (!WinHelp (hWnd, "RTFSAMP2.HLP", HELP_KEY,
            (DWORD)(LPSTR)"CONTENTS")) {
            MessageBox (GetFocus(),
                "Unable to activate help",
                szAppName, MB_SYSTEMMODAL|MB_OK|MB_ICONHAND);

        }
        break;

    case IDM_HELPSEARCH:
        if (!WinHelp(hWnd, "RTFSAMP2.HLP", HELP_PARTIALKEY,
            (DWORD)(LPSTR)"")) {
            MessageBox (GetFocus(),
                "Unable to activate help",
                szAppName, MB_SYSTEMMODAL|MB_OK|MB_ICONHAND);
        }
        break;

    case IDM_HELPHELP:
        if(!WinHelp(hWnd, (LPSTR)NULL, HELP_HELPONHELP, 0)) {
            MessageBox (GetFocus(),
                "Unable to activate help",
                szAppName, MB_SYSTEMMODAL|MB_OK|MB_ICONHAND);
        }
        break;

    // For the BOLD, ITALIC, and UNDERLINE menu options,
    // we change the character attribytes with our function,
    // and then update the menu to reflect the new state
    // of the current text.

    case IDM_BOLD:
```

```
        RTF_ChangeCharAttribute ( hRTFWnd, CFM_BOLD, CFE_BOLD );
        RTF_UpdateMenuState ( hRTFWnd, hWnd );
        break;

case IDM_ITALIC:

        RTF_ChangeCharAttribute ( hRTFWnd, CFM_ITALIC, CFE_ITALIC );
        RTF_UpdateMenuState ( hRTFWnd, hWnd );
        break;

case IDM_UNDERLINE:

        RTF_ChangeCharAttribute ( hRTFWnd, CFM_UNDERLINE, CFE_UNDERLINE );
        RTF_UpdateMenuState ( hRTFWnd, hWnd );
        break;

case IDM_INCREASE_FONT:

        // Increase the font size by 2 points
        RTF_ChangeSizeAttribute ( hRTFWnd, 2 );
        break;

case IDM_DECREASE_FONT:

        // Decrease the font size by 2 points
        RTF_ChangeSizeAttribute ( hRTFWnd, -2 );
        break;

case IDM_FONTDIALOG:

        // Bring up the Font Common Dialog and apply that new
        // font to the selected text.
        RTF_ChangeFont ( hWnd, hRTFWnd );
        // Update the menu state to reflect the new font.
        RTF_UpdateMenuState ( hRTFWnd, hWnd );
        break;

case IDM_NEW:

        // We check to see if the contents of the edit
        // control need to be saved with the RTF_CheckForDirtyContents
        // function. After that function has returned an acceptable
        // value, we will clear the contents of the edit control
```

LISTING 11.10 CONTINUED

```
                    // by selecting the entire range and replacing it with an
                    // empty string.

                    if (RTF_CheckForDirtyContents ( hWnd, hRTFWnd ))
                      {
                      CHARRANGE cr;

                      // Reset the global filename to an empty string
                      *szFileName = 0;

                      // Set the character range to go from start to end.
                      cr.cpMin = 0;
                      cr.cpMax = -1;

                      // The WM_SETREDRAW game keeps screen flicker down.
                      SendMessage ( hRTFWnd, WM_SETREDRAW, FALSE, 0 );
                      SendMessage ( hRTFWnd, EM_EXSETSEL,   0, (LPARAM)&cr );
                      SendMessage ( hRTFWnd, WM_SETREDRAW, TRUE, 0 );
                      SendMessage ( hRTFWnd, EM_REPLACESEL, 0, (LPARAM)"" );

                      // Clear the dirty bit
                      SendMessage ( hRTFWnd, EM_SETMODIFY, FALSE, 0 );
                      }
                    STATUS_DisplayStatusInformation ( hRTFWnd, hStatusWnd);
                    break;

                case IDM_OPEN:

                    // We check to see if the contents of the edit
                    // control need to be saved with the RTF_CheckForDirtyContents
                    // function. After that function has returned an acceptable
                    // value, we will load a file and stream it into the
                    // RTF Edit control.

                    if (RTF_CheckForDirtyContents ( hWnd, hRTFWnd ))
                      {
                      // Stream in the new file
                      RTF_Open ( hWnd, hRTFWnd );
                      // Clear the dirty bit
                      SendMessage ( hRTFWnd, EM_SETMODIFY, FALSE, 0 );
                      // Update the status bar
                      STATUS_DisplayStatusInformation ( hRTFWnd, hStatusWnd);
```

```
        }
      break;

    case IDM_SAVE:

      // Stream out the new file
      if (RTF_Save ( hWnd, hRTFWnd ))
        {
        // Clear the dirsty bit if save happened
        SendMessage ( hRTFWnd, EM_SETMODIFY, FALSE, 0 );
        }
      break;

    case IDM_SAVEAS:

      *szFileName = 0; // Forces Save As dialog to pop up
      // Stream out the new file
      if (RTF_Save ( hWnd, hRTFWnd ))
        {
        // Clear the dirsty bit if save happened
        SendMessage ( hRTFWnd, EM_SETMODIFY, FALSE, 0 );
        }
      break;

    case IDM_PRINTSETUP:

      // Standard common dialog fun
      SelectPrinter ( szPrinter, hWnd, &dmDriverExtra );
      break;

    case IDM_PRINT:

      // Print the contents of the RTF Edit Control
      RTF_Print ( hWnd, hRTFWnd );
      break;

    default:
      return (DefWindowProc(hWnd, message, uParam, lParam));

    }
  break;

case WM_SETFOCUS:

  // When the frame gets focus, set focus to the RTF Edit control
```

LISTING 11.10 CONTINUED

```
            SetFocus ( hRTFWnd );
            break;

        case WM_CLOSE:

            // We check to see if the contents of the edit
            // control need to be saved with the RTF_CheckForDirtyContents
            // function. After that function has returned an acceptable
            // value, we shut down this app.

            if (RTF_CheckForDirtyContents ( hWnd, hRTFWnd ))
                DestroyWindow ( hWnd );
            break;

        case WM_DESTROY:  // message: window being destroyed

            DestroyWindow ( hTBWnd );
            DeleteObject ( hTBBmp );
            PostQuitMessage(0);
            break;

        default:            // Passes it on if unproccessed
            return (DefWindowProc(hWnd, message, uParam, lParam));
    }
    return (0);
}


//
//   FUNCTION: CenterWindow (HWND, HWND)
//
//   PURPOSE:  Center one window over another
//
//   COMMENTS:
//
//      Dialog boxes take on the screen position that they were designed
//      at, which is not always appropriate. Centering the dialog over a
//      particular window usually results in a better position.
//

BOOL CenterWindow (HWND hwndChild, HWND hwndParent)
{
```

```
RECT    rChild, rParent;
int     wChild, hChild, wParent, hParent;
int     wScreen, hScreen, xNew, yNew;
HDC     hdc;

// Get the Height and Width of the child window
GetWindowRect (hwndChild, &rChild);
wChild = rChild.right - rChild.left;
hChild = rChild.bottom - rChild.top;

// Get the Height and Width of the parent window
GetWindowRect (hwndParent, &rParent);
wParent = rParent.right - rParent.left;
hParent = rParent.bottom - rParent.top;

// Get the display limits
hdc = GetDC (hwndChild);
wScreen = GetDeviceCaps (hdc, HORZRES);
hScreen = GetDeviceCaps (hdc, VERTRES);
ReleaseDC (hwndChild, hdc);

// Calculate new X position, then adjust for screen
xNew = rParent.left + ((wParent - wChild) /2);
if (xNew < 0) {
   xNew = 0;
}
else if ((xNew+wChild) > wScreen) {
   xNew = wScreen - wChild;
}

// Calculate new Y position, then adjust for screen
yNew = rParent.top  + ((hParent - hChild) /2);
if (yNew < 0) {
   yNew = 0;
}
else if ((yNew+hChild) > hScreen) {
   yNew = hScreen - hChild;
}

// Set it, and return
return SetWindowPos (hwndChild, NULL,
   xNew, yNew, 0, 0, SWP_NOSIZE | SWP_NOZORDER);
}

//
```

LISTING **11.10** CONTINUED

```
//   FUNCTION: About(HWND, UINT, WPARAM, LPARAM)
//
//   PURPOSE:  Processes messages for "About" dialog box
//
//   MESSAGES:
//
//     WM_INITDIALOG - initialize dialog box
//     WM_COMMAND    - Input received
//
//   COMMENTS:
//
//     Display version information from the version section of the
//     application resource.
//
//     Wait for user to click on "Ok" button, then close the dialog box.
//

LRESULT CALLBACK About(
        HWND hDlg,              // window handle of the dialog box
        UINT message,           // type of message
        WPARAM uParam,          // message-specific information
        LPARAM lParam
        )
{
    static  HFONT hfontDlg;

    switch (message) {
       case WM_CTLCOLORBTN:

           MessageBeep (0);
           SetBkColor( (HDC)uParam, RGB(128,128,128));
           return (LRESULT)GetStockObject ( WHITE_BRUSH );

       case WM_INITDIALOG:  // message: initialize dialog box
           // Create a font to use
           hfontDlg = CreateFont(14, 0, 0, 0, 0, 0, 0, 0,
              0, 0, 0, 0,
              VARIABLE_PITCH | FF_SWISS, "");

           // Center the dialog over the application window
           CenterWindow (hDlg, GetWindow (hDlg, GW_OWNER));

           return (TRUE);
```

412

```
        case WM_COMMAND:                        // message: received a command
            if (LOWORD(uParam) == IDOK          // "OK" box selected?
               || LOWORD(uParam) == IDCANCEL) {// System menu close command?
                EndDialog(hDlg, TRUE);          // Exit the dialog
                DeleteObject (hfontDlg);
                return (TRUE);
            }
            break;
    }
    return (FALSE); // Didn't process the message

    lParam; // This will prevent 'unused formal parameter' warnings
}


/************************************************************************

    The RTF_ChangeCharAttribute function will apply the character
    attributes to the selected text. The attributes used in this sample
    program are CFE_ITALIC, CFE_BOLD, and CFE_UNDERLINE. The mask
    corresponds to the attribute.

 ************************************************************************/

void RTF_ChangeCharAttribute ( HWND hRTFWnd, DWORD dwMask, DWORD dwEffects )
{
    CHARFORMAT cf; // This is defined in RICHEDIT.H

    cf.cbSize = sizeof(cf);

    // Get the current status of the text into the CHARFORMAT structure,
    // use the selected text. wParam is TRUE to indicate the
    // selected text, FALSE for the first character in the
    // RTF Edit control.
    SendMessage(hRTFWnd, EM_GETCHARFORMAT, TRUE, (LPARAM)&cf);

    // Set the mask to tell the RTF Edit control to pay attention to
    // the appropriate bit of the dwEffects field.
    cf.dwMask      = dwMask;
    // Twiddle de bits, captain!
    cf.dwEffects  ^= dwEffects;

    // Set the new underline status to the selected text
    SendMessage(hRTFWnd, EM_SETCHARFORMAT, SCF_SELECTION, (LPARAM)&cf);
}
```

413

LISTING 11.10 CONTINUED

```
/**************************************************************************

    The RTF_GetCharAttribute function will indicate whether a selection
    of text has an attribute. The text can either have the attribute (YES),
    not have it (NO), or have some with it and some without it (WAFFLE).

**************************************************************************/

int RTF_GetCharAttribute ( HWND hRTFWnd, DWORD dwMask, DWORD dwEffects )
{
    CHARFORMAT cf; // This is defined in RICHEDIT.H

    cf.cbSize = sizeof(cf);

    // Get the current status of the text into the CHARFORMAT structure,
    // use the selected text. wParam is TRUE to indicate the
    // selected text, FALSE for the first character in the
    // RTF Edit control.
    SendMessage(hRTFWnd, EM_GETCHARFORMAT, TRUE, (LPARAM)&cf);

    if (cf.dwMask & dwMask)
      {
      if (cf.dwEffects & dwEffects)
        return CHAR_ATTRIB_YES;
      else
        return CHAR_ATTRIB_NO;
      }
    else
      {
      return CHAR_ATTRIB_WAFFLE;
      }
}


/**************************************************************************

    The RTF_ChangeSizeAttribute function will change the size of the selected
    text by the iPointChange value.

**************************************************************************/

void RTF_ChangeSizeAttribute ( HWND hRTFWnd, int iPointChange )
```

```
{
    CHARFORMAT cf; // This is defined in RICHEDIT.H

    cf.cbSize = sizeof(cf);

    // Get the current status of the text into the CHARFORMAT structure,
    // use the selected text. wParam is TRUE to indicate the
    // selected text, FALSE for the first character in the
    // RTF Edit control.
    SendMessage(hRTFWnd, EM_GETCHARFORMAT, TRUE, (LPARAM)&cf);

    // Set the mask to tell the RTF Edit control to pay attention to
    // the size bit of the dwEffects field.
    cf.dwMask      = CFM_SIZE;
    // Increase or decrease the font size, keeping it between 6 and 128 points
    if (
        ((cf.yHeight + 20*iPointChange) <= (128*20))
        &&
        ((cf.yHeight + 20*iPointChange) >= (6*20))
       )
      cf.yHeight += 20*iPointChange;

    // Set the new underline status to the selected text
    SendMessage(hRTFWnd, EM_SETCHARFORMAT, SCF_SELECTION, (LPARAM)&cf);
}


/**************************************************************************

    The RTF_ChangeFont function will use the font common dialog
    to change the font in the selected text.

**************************************************************************/

void RTF_ChangeFont ( HWND hWnd, HWND hRTFWnd )
{
    CHARFORMAT cf;                 // This is defined in RICHEDIT.H
    CHOOSEFONT ChooseFontStruct;   // Common Dialog fun
    LOGFONT    lf;                 // Log font information
    HDC        hDC;

    cf.cbSize = sizeof(cf);

    // Get the font formatting status into the CHARFORMAT structure,
    // use the selected text. wParam is TRUE to indicate the
```

LISTING 11.10 CONTINUED

```
// selected text, FALSE for the first character in the
// RTF Edit control.
SendMessage(hRTFWnd, EM_GETCHARFORMAT, TRUE, (LPARAM)&cf);


// Fill in the font info for the font common dialog

memset (&ChooseFontStruct, 0, sizeof(CHOOSEFONT));
memset (&lf, 0, sizeof(LOGFONT));


hDC = GetDC(hWnd); // Need a screen DC, use the parent's DC


// The RTF Edit control measures in twips. Each point is
// 20 twips.


lf.lfHeight = cf.yHeight / -20;


// Set up the rest of the logfont structure according to the
// information retrieved from the EM_GETCHARFORMAT message


if (cf.dwEffects & CFE_BOLD)
    lf.lfWeight = FW_BOLD;
else
    lf.lfWeight = FW_NORMAL;
lf.lfItalic = (BOOL)(cf.dwEffects & CFE_ITALIC);
lf.lfUnderline = (BOOL)(cf.dwEffects & CFE_UNDERLINE);
lf.lfCharSet = DEFAULT_CHARSET;
lf.lfQuality = DEFAULT_QUALITY;
lf.lfPitchAndFamily = cf.bPitchAndFamily;
lstrcpy(lf.lfFaceName, cf.szFaceName);


// Fire up the common dialog.

ChooseFontStruct.lStructSize = sizeof(ChooseFontStruct);
ChooseFontStruct.hwndOwner = hWnd;
ChooseFontStruct.hDC = hDC;
ChooseFontStruct.lpLogFont = &lf;
ChooseFontStruct.Flags = CF_SCREENFONTS | CF_INITTOLOGFONTSTRUCT;
ChooseFontStruct.rgbColors = RGB(0,0,0);
ChooseFontStruct.nFontType = SCREEN_FONTTYPE;


if (ChooseFont(&ChooseFontStruct))
```

416

```
    {
        // Set the mask to tell the RTF Edit control to pay attention to
        // the font formatting bits.
        cf.dwMask       = CFM_BOLD | CFM_FACE | CFM_ITALIC |
                          CFM_OFFSET | CFM_SIZE | CFM_UNDERLINE;

        //  Undo the equation from above.

        cf.yHeight = lf.lfHeight * -20;

        // Fill in the rest of the character formatting

        cf.dwEffects = 0;
        if (FW_BOLD == lf.lfWeight)
            cf.dwEffects |= CFE_BOLD;
        if (lf.lfItalic)
            cf.dwEffects |= CFE_ITALIC;

        if (lf.lfUnderline)
            cf.dwEffects |= CFE_UNDERLINE;

        cf.bPitchAndFamily = lf.lfPitchAndFamily;

        lstrcpy (cf.szFaceName, lf.lfFaceName);

        // Set the new formatting to the selected text
        SendMessage(hRTFWnd, EM_SETCHARFORMAT, SCF_SELECTION, (LPARAM)&cf);
    }

    // Don't forget this!
    ReleaseDC(hWnd, hDC);
}


/*************************************************************************


    Quick and dirty function to get a filename. bOpen decides whether
    to use a File Open or a File Save As dialog.


*************************************************************************/

BOOL GetFileName ( HWND hWnd, LPSTR szFileName, BOOL bOpen )
{
  OPENFILENAME of;
```

LISTING 11.10 CONTINUED

```
of.lStructSize        = sizeof(OPENFILENAME);
of.hwndOwner          = (HWND)hWnd;
of.hInstance          = (HANDLE)NULL;
of.lpstrFilter        = "RTF Files (*.RTF)\0*.RTF\0";
of.lpstrCustomFilter  = (LPSTR)NULL;
of.nMaxCustFilter     = 0L;
of.nFilterIndex       = 1L;
of.lpstrFile          = szFileName;
of.nMaxFile           = 256;
of.lpstrFileTitle     = NULL;
of.nMaxFileTitle      = 0;
of.lpstrInitialDir    = NULL;
of.lpstrTitle         = (LPSTR)NULL;
of.Flags              = OFN_HIDEREADONLY |
                        OFN_PATHMUSTEXIST ;
of.nFileOffset        = 0;
of.nFileExtension     = 0;
of.lpstrDefExt        = (LPSTR)"RTF";
of.lCustData          = 0L;
of.lpfnHook           = 0L;  // Zero eliminates compiler warnings
of.lpTemplateName     = (LPSTR)NULL;

if ( bOpen )
  return GetOpenFileName ( &of );
else
  return GetSaveFileName ( &of );
}


/***************************************************************************

  This is the callback stream used by the RTF Edit controls
  EM_STREAMOUT message. It is called repeatedly until the RTF Edit
  control has streamed all of the information.

***************************************************************************/

DWORD CALLBACK SaveCallback ( DWORD    dwCookie, // App supplied value
                              LPBYTE   pbBuff,   // Pointer to data
                              LONG     cb,       // size of data
                              LONG     *pcb      // Not used in streamout
                            )
{
```

```
    // Write the data to the disk for our example. dwCookie is used as a file
    // handle for our example.
    cb = _lwrite ( (HFILE)dwCookie, pbBuff, cb);
    *pcb = cb; // Indicate the number of bytes written to the file
    return 0;
}


/************************************************************************


    The RTF_Save function uses the EM_STREAMOUT message to invoke
    a callback function (above) to stream the data. Our example
    simply writes the stream to a file, your code could do whatever it
    wanted to.


************************************************************************/

BOOL RTF_Save ( HWND hWnd, HWND hRTFWnd )
{
    HFILE        hFile; // File handle
    OFSTRUCT     of;    // open file structure
    EDITSTREAM   es;    // The EDITSTREAM structure

    // Call the file save as dialog only if the szFileName is empty,
    // otherwise szFileName already has a valid filename in it.

    if (*szFileName || GetFileName ( hWnd, szFileName, FALSE ))
        {
        // Open the file, erasing previous contents
        hFile = OpenFile ( szFileName, &of, OF_CREATE );

        // Set up the EDITSTREAM structure
        es.dwCookie     = (DWORD)hFile;   // our file handle
        es.dwError      = 0;              // No error
        es.pfnCallback  = SaveCallback;   // Use above callback

        // Engage!
        SendMessage(hRTFWnd, EM_STREAMOUT, SF_RTF, (LPARAM)&es);

        // Close the file
        _lclose ( hFile );

        return TRUE;
        }
```

LISTING 11.10 CONTINUED

```
  return FALSE;
}


/**************************************************************************


   This is the callback stream used by the RTF Edit controls
   EM_STREAMIN message. It is called repeatedly until the application
   has supplied all of the information.


**************************************************************************/


DWORD CALLBACK OpenCallback ( DWORD    dwCookie,
                              LPBYTE   pbBuff,
                              LONG     cb,
                              LONG     *pcb
                            )
{
  // Read as much data as allowed in the cb variable
  *pcb = _lread ( (HFILE)dwCookie, pbBuff, cb);
  if ( *pcb <= 0 ) // EOF?
    *pcb = 0;    // Indicate the read is complete
  return 0;
}


/**************************************************************************


   The RTF_open function uses the EM_STREAMIN message to invoke
   a callback function (above) to stream the data. Our example
   simply reads the stream from a file, your code could do whatever it
   wanted to.


**************************************************************************/


BOOL RTF_Open ( HWND hWnd, HWND hRTFWnd )
{
  HFILE         hFile;  // File handle
  OFSTRUCT      of;     // open file structure
  EDITSTREAM    es;     // The EDITSTREAM structure

  // Get a filename to load from
```

```
  if (GetFileName ( hWnd, szFileName, TRUE ))
    {
    // Open the file for reading
    hFile = OpenFile ( szFileName, &of, OF_READ );

    if (hFile)
      {
      // Set up the EDITSTREAM structure
      es.dwCookie   = (DWORD)hFile; // our file handle
      es.dwError    = 0;            // No error
      es.pfnCallback = OpenCallback; // Use above callback

      // Make it so!
      SendMessage(hRTFWnd, EM_STREAMIN, SF_RTF, (LPARAM)&es);

      // Close the file
      _lclose ( hFile );
      }

    return TRUE;
    }

  return FALSE;
}


/*************************************************************************

   The RTF_CheckForDirtyContents function checks to see if the dirty
   bit has been set for the edit control. If so, the user is offered
   a chance to save their file.

 *************************************************************************/

BOOL RTF_CheckForDirtyContents ( HWND hWnd, HWND hRTFWnd )
{
  char szMsg[512];
  int  iRetVal;

  // Check dirty bit
  if (SendMessage ( hRTFWnd, EM_GETMODIFY, 0, OL ))
    {
    if (*szFileName)
      wsprintf ( szMsg,
```

421

LISTING 11.10 CONTINUED

```
                      "Do you wish to save the current file \"%s\"?",
                      szFileName
                   );
        else
          lstrcpy ( szMsg, "Do you wish to save the current untitled file?" );

        // Get their response
        iRetVal = MessageBox ( hWnd,
                               szMsg,
                               "MSJ",
                               MB_YESNOCANCEL | MB_ICONQUESTION );

        switch ( iRetVal )
          {
          case IDYES:

            RTF_Save ( hWnd, hRTFWnd );
            return TRUE;

          case IDNO:

            return TRUE;

          case IDCANCEL:

            return FALSE;


          }
        }
      else
        {
        return TRUE;
        }
}


/***********************************************************************

  The SelectPrinter function simply uses the common dialog to
  get the parameters needed to satisfy the GetPrinterDC function.

***********************************************************************/
```

```
BOOL  SelectPrinter ( LPSTR szPrinter,
                      HWND  hWndParent,
                      UINT  FAR *pdmDriverExtra )
{
  PRINTDLG    pd;          // From commdlg.h
  LPDEVMODE   lpDevMode;   // From print.h
  HANDLE      hDevMode;
  LPSTR       szMem;
  int         i;

  szMem = (LPSTR)&pd;
  for ( i = 0; i < sizeof(pd); i++ ) szMem[i] = 0;

  /* Initialize the necessary pd structure members. */

  pd.lStructSize = sizeof(PRINTDLG);
  pd.hwndOwner   = hWndParent;
  pd.Flags       = PD_PRINTSETUP;

  /* Get the info we need */

  if (!PrintDlg(&pd)) return 0;

  hDevMode = pd.hDevMode;

  if (hDevMode)
    {
    lpDevMode = (LPDEVMODE)GlobalLock ( hDevMode );

    *pdmDriverExtra = lpDevMode->dmDriverExtra;

    lstrcpy ( szPrinter, lpDevMode->dmDeviceName);

    GlobalUnlock ( hDevMode );
    GlobalFree ( hDevMode );

    return TRUE;
    }
  else
    {
    *pdmDriverExtra = 0;
    return FALSE;
    }
}
```

LISTING 11.10 CONTINUED

```
/*****************************************************************

    The GetDCHook function is the dialog procedure for the
    print common dialog. This function's sole purpose in life is
    to press the OK button instantly. This causes the dialog to never
    appear, yet we can get a printer DC back from it.

*****************************************************************/

BOOL CALLBACK GetDCHook ( HWND hDlg, UINT msg, WPARAM wParam, LPARAM lParam )
{
  switch ( msg )
    {
    case WM_INITDIALOG:

      PostMessage ( hDlg, WM_COMMAND, IDOK, OL );
      return FALSE;

    default:

      return FALSE;
    }
}


/*****************************************************************

    This GetPrinterDC function calls the print common dialog
    and uses the above hook to instantly press the OK button,
    which ensures the dialog never appears. By using the PD_RETURNDC
    flag, we can get back a printer DC for whatever print the user
    selected without having to do any gross stuff.

*****************************************************************/

HDC GetPrinterDC ( LPSTR szPrinter,
                   UINT  dmDriverExtra,
                   HWND  hWndParent )
{
  PRINTDLG  pd;            // From commdlg.h
  LPDEVMODE lpDevMode;     // From print.h
  HANDLE    hDevMode;
```

424

```
    LPSTR       szMem;
    int         i;


    hDevMode = GlobalAlloc ( GHND, sizeof(DEVMODE)+(LONG)dmDriverExtra);
    if (!hDevMode) return (HDC)0;


    lpDevMode = (LPDEVMODE)GlobalLock ( hDevMode );


    lstrcpy ( lpDevMode->dmDeviceName, szPrinter);
    lpDevMode->dmSize       = sizeof(DEVMODE);
    lpDevMode->dmSpecVersion = 0x030A;
    lpDevMode->dmDriverExtra = dmDriverExtra;


    GlobalUnlock ( hDevMode );


    szMem = (LPSTR)&pd;
    for ( i = 0; i < sizeof(pd); i++ ) szMem[i] = 0;


    /* Initialize the necessary pd structure members. */


    pd.lStructSize  = sizeof(PRINTDLG);
    pd.hwndOwner    = hWndParent;
    pd.Flags        = PD_RETURNDC | PD_ENABLEPRINTHOOK;
    pd.hDevMode     = hDevMode;
    pd.lpfnPrintHook= GetDCHook;


    if (!PrintDlg(&pd)) return 0;


    GlobalFree ( hDevMode );


    return pd.hDC;
}


/**********************************************************

  The RTF_Print function gets a printer DC and then prints one
  page at a time.

***********************************************************/

void RTF_Print ( HWND hWnd, HWND hRTFWnd )
{
  HDC          hPrinterDC;
```

LISTING 11.10 CONTINUED

```
FORMATRANGE   fr;
DOCINFO       di;
LONG          lTextLength, lTextPrinted;

// Get a printer DC
if (*szPrinter || SelectPrinter ( szPrinter, hWnd, &dmDriverExtra ))
  {
  hPrinterDC = GetPrinterDC ( szPrinter, dmDriverExtra, hWnd );
  if (!hPrinterDC)
    {
    MessageBox ( hWnd, "CreateDC Failed", "RTF", MB_OK );
    return;
    }
  }
else
  {
  MessageBox ( hWnd, "No printer selected", "RTF", MB_OK );
  return;
  }


// At this point, we have a printer DC

// Step 1: Identify the page size

// Rendering to the same DC we are measuring
fr.hdc = fr.hdcTarget = hPrinterDC;

// Set up a 6x9" printing area
fr.rc.left    = fr.rc.top = 0;
fr.rc.right   = 6*1440;  // 6" wide
fr.rc.bottom  = 9*1440; // 9" down
fr.rcPage     = fr.rc;

// Default the range of text to print as the entire document
fr.chrg.cpMin = 0;
fr.chrg.cpMax = -1;

// Set up the print job (standard printing stuff here)
di.cbSize = sizeof ( DOCINFO );
if (*szFileName)
  di.lpszDocName = szFileName;
else
```

```
    di.lpszDocName = "(Untitled)";
  di.lpszOutput = NULL;


  // Ensure the printer DC is in MM_TEXT mode
  SetMapMode ( hPrinterDC, MM_TEXT );


  StartDoc ( hPrinterDC, &di );
  StartPage ( hPrinterDC );


  // Find out real size of document in characters
  lTextLength = SendMessage ( hRTFWnd, WM_GETTEXTLENGTH, 0, 0 );

  do
    {
    // Print as mush as will fit on a page. The return value
    // is the index of the first character on the next page.
    lTextPrinted = SendMessage ( hRTFWnd, EM_FORMATRANGE, TRUE, (LPARAM)&fr );


    // If there is more text to print, spit this page from the printer
    // and start another one.
    if (lTextPrinted < lTextLength)
      {
      EndPage ( hPrinterDC );
      StartPage ( hPrinterDC );


      // Adjust the range of characters to print to start at the
      // character of the next page
      fr.chrg.cpMin = lTextPrinted;
      fr.chrg.cpMax = -1;
      }
    }
  while (lTextPrinted < lTextLength);


  // Restore the RTF Edit control to its original, upright position
  SendMessage ( hRTFWnd, EM_FORMATRANGE, TRUE, (LPARAM)NULL );


  // Spit out last page
  EndPage ( hPrinterDC );
  EndDoc ( hPrinterDC );
  // Remove that pesky DC
  DeleteDC ( hPrinterDC );
}


//************************ NEW CODE START ************************
```

LISTING 11.10 CONTINUED

```
/*******************************************************************

   The TOOLBAR_DetermineToolbarButtonState function will
   check/uncheck/waffle a toolbar button.

*******************************************************************/

void TOOLBAR_DetermineToolbarButtonState (HWND hTBWnd, UINT iID, UINT iState)
{
  switch ( iState )
    {
    // For YES or NO values, remove the waffle (INDETERMINATE) style
    // from the button, and then check or uncheck it.
    case CHAR_ATTRIB_YES:
    case CHAR_ATTRIB_NO :

      SendMessage (hTBWnd, TB_INDETERMINATE, iID, MAKELONG(FALSE,0) );
      SendMessage (hTBWnd, TB_CHECKBUTTON, iID,
                   MAKELONG((CHAR_ATTRIB_YES==iState),0) );
      break;

    // Otherwise, set the waffle (INDETERMINATE) style
    default: // CHAR_ATTRIB_WAFFLE

      SendMessage (hTBWnd, TB_INDETERMINATE, iID, MAKELONG(TRUE,0) );
      break;
    }
}


/*******************************************************************

   The RTF_GetCurrentFont function filled in the szFont string with
   the facename of the current selection in the RTF Edit control.

*******************************************************************/

void RTF_GetCurrentFont ( HWND hRTFWnd, LPSTR szFont )
{
    CHARFORMAT cf;                  // This is defined in RICHEDIT.H

    cf.cbSize = sizeof(cf);
```

```
    // Get the font formatting status into the CHARFORMAT structure,
    // use the selected text. wParam is TRUE to indicate the
    // selected text, FALSE for the first character in the
    // RTF Edit control.
    SendMessage(hRTFWnd, EM_GETCHARFORMAT, TRUE, (LPARAM)&cf);

    if (cf.dwMask & CFM_FACE)
      lstrcpy ( szFont, cf.szFaceName );
    else
      *szFont = 0;


}


/******************************************************************

  The RTF_SetCurrentFont function sets the font of the current
  selection of the RTF Edit control to the font pointed to by
  the szFont string.

******************************************************************/

void RTF_SetCurrentFont ( HWND hRTFWnd, LPSTR szFont )
{
    CHARFORMAT cf;                    // This is defined in RICHEDIT.H

    cf.cbSize = sizeof(cf);

    // Get the font formatting status into the CHARFORMAT structure,
    // use the selected text. wParam is TRUE to indicate the
    // selected text, FALSE for the first character in the
    // RTF Edit control.
    SendMessage(hRTFWnd, EM_GETCHARFORMAT, TRUE, (LPARAM)&cf);

    cf.dwMask = CFM_FACE;

    lstrcpy ( cf.szFaceName, szFont );

    SendMessage(hRTFWnd, EM_SETCHARFORMAT, SCF_SELECTION, (LPARAM)&cf);
}


/**********************************************************

  The RTF_UpdateMenuState function will check/uncheck the
```

LISTING 11.10 CONTINUED

Bold, italic, and Underline menu options if the current text
selections have those attributes. It will also update the
toolbar.

```
***************************************************************/

void RTF_UpdateMenuState ( HWND hWndRTF, HWND hWnd )
{
  // Values of CHAR_ATTRIB_YES, CHAR_ATTRIB_NO, or CHAR_ATTRIB_WAFFLE
  int       iBold, iItalic, iUnderline;

  HMENU     hMenu;                // Menu to munge
  char      szFont[LF_FACESIZE]; // Current font facename
  WPARAM    wFontIndex;          // Index into combobox


  // Get the attributes for each type of attrib
  iBold = RTF_GetCharAttribute ( hRTFWnd,
                                 CFM_BOLD, CFE_BOLD );
  iItalic = RTF_GetCharAttribute ( hRTFWnd,
                                   CFM_ITALIC, CFE_ITALIC );
  iUnderline = RTF_GetCharAttribute ( hRTFWnd,
                                      CFM_UNDERLINE, CFE_UNDERLINE );
  // And check/uncheck the menus
  hMenu = GetMenu ( hWnd );
  CheckMenuItem (hMenu, IDM_BOLD,      MF_BYCOMMAND |
                CHAR_ATTRIB_YES==iBold     ? MF_CHECKED : MF_UNCHECKED );
  CheckMenuItem (hMenu, IDM_ITALIC,    MF_BYCOMMAND |
                CHAR_ATTRIB_YES==iItalic    ? MF_CHECKED : MF_UNCHECKED );
  CheckMenuItem (hMenu, IDM_UNDERLINE, MF_BYCOMMAND |
                CHAR_ATTRIB_YES==iUnderline ? MF_CHECKED : MF_UNCHECKED );

  // And check/uncheck/waffle the toolbar buttons
  TOOLBAR_DetermineToolbarButtonState (hTBWnd, IDM_BOLD,      iBold     );
  TOOLBAR_DetermineToolbarButtonState (hTBWnd, IDM_ITALIC,    iItalic   );
  TOOLBAR_DetermineToolbarButtonState (hTBWnd, IDM_UNDERLINE, iUnderline);

  // Get the facename of the current font
  RTF_GetCurrentFont ( hRTFWnd, szFont );

  // Find and select it in the toolbar
  wFontIndex = (WPARAM)SendMessage ( hComboBox, CB_FINDSTRING, (WPARAM)-1,
```

```
(LPARAM)szFont );
   SendMessage ( hComboBox, CB_SETCURSEL, wFontIndex, 0L );
}


/**********************************************************

   The TOOLTIP_GetText function is called in response to the
   WM_NOTIFY:TTN_NEEDTEXT message. We need to fill in lpszText to
   point to a string to display in the tooltip.

   **********************************************************/


void  TOOLTIP_GetText ( LPTOOLTIPTEXT lpttt )
{
   static char  szText[128];

   lpttt->lpszText = szText; // Point to a buffer

   // Grab a string from the stringtable. The
   // lpttt->hdr.idFrom field contains the ID of the button
   // that needs text. The TOOLTIPOFFSET is a constant that
   // is used in the stringtable in this program's RC file.

   LoadString(hInst,
             lpttt->hdr.idFrom + TOOLTIPOFFSET,
             szText,
             sizeof(szText));
}


/**********************************************************

   This function is called from the Handle_WM_MENSELECT function
   below. If idMsg is not -1, the status bar is set to simple
   mode and the text from the string table with that id is displayed
   in it. if idMsg is -1, the status bar is returned back to
   normal mode.

   **********************************************************/


void STATUS_DisplayStatusMenuHelp ( HWND hStatusWnd, UINT idMsg )
{
   char sz[128];

   if ( -1 != idMsg )
```

LISTING 11.10 CONTINUED

```
      {
      // Set status bar to simple mode
      SendMessage ( hStatusWnd, SB_SIMPLE, TRUE, 0 );

      if (0 != idMsg)
         {
         // Get the string from the stringtable
         LoadString(hInst, idMsg, sz, sizeof(sz));
         // Set the text
         SendMessage ( hStatusWnd, SB_SETTEXT, 255, (LPARAM)sz );
         }
      }
   else
      {
      // Set the status bar back to normal mode
      SendMessage ( hStatusWnd, SB_SIMPLE, FALSE, 0 );
      }

}


/***********************************************************

  The STATUS_DisplayStatusInformation fills in the pane
  of the status bar that indicates the row and column of the

  caret inside the RTF edit control

***********************************************************/

void STATUS_DisplayStatusInformation ( HWND hRTFWnd, HWND hStatusWnd )
{
   char      sz[256];
   int       iRow, iCol;
   CHARRANGE cr;

   // Find out the position of the caret (if a selection is set,
   // use the endpoint of the selection).
   SendMessage ( hRTFWnd, EM_EXGETSEL, 0, (LPARAM)&cr );

   // Figure the row and column
   iRow = (int)SendMessage ( hRTFWnd, EM_EXLINEFROMCHAR, 0, (LPARAM)(cr.cpMax) );
   iCol = (int)
```

```
                (
                cr.cpMax - (int)SendMessage ( hRTFWnd, EM_LINEINDEX, iRow, 0 )
                );

    // Format the string
    wsprintf ( sz, "Ln %d     Col %d", iRow+1, iCol+1 );

    // Set the text in the second pane (Pane #1)
    SendMessage ( hStatusWnd, SB_SETTEXT, 1, (LPARAM)sz );
}

#define GET_WM_MENUSELECT_FLAGS(uParam, lParam) ((UINT)HIWORD(uParam))
#define GET_WM_MENUSELECT_CMD(uParam, lParam)   ((UINT)LOWORD(uParam))
#define GET_WM_MENUSELECT_HMENU(uParam, lParam) ((HMENU)lParam)


/************************************************************

    The Handle_WM_MENSELECT function below is a pared down
    cheezy sample to figure out the ID of the currently selected
    menu. It returns 0 if a popup menu is selected, -1 of no menu
    is selected (i.e. closed), and a positive nonzero value
    if a menu item is selected.


*************************************************************/

void Handle_WM_MENSELECT ( HWND hStatusWnd, UINT message, WPARAM uParam, LPARAM
lParam )
{
    static char szBuffer[128];
    UINT   nStringID = 0;

    UINT   fuFlags = GET_WM_MENUSELECT_FLAGS(uParam, lParam) & 0xffff;
    UINT   uCmd    = GET_WM_MENUSELECT_CMD(uParam, lParam);
    HMENU  hMenu   = GET_WM_MENUSELECT_HMENU(uParam, lParam);

    szBuffer[0] = 0;                            // First reset the buffer

    nStringID = 0;

    if (fuFlags == 0xffff && hMenu == NULL)     // Menu has been closed
        nStringID = (UINT)-1;

    else if (fuFlags & MFT_SEPARATOR)           // Ignore separators
        nStringID = 0;
```

433

LISTING 11.10 CONTINUED

```
    else if (fuFlags & MF_POPUP)                // Popup menu
        {
        if (fuFlags & MF_SYSMENU)               // System menu
            nStringID = 0;
        } // for MF_POPUP
    else                                        // Must be a command item
        {
        nStringID = uCmd;                // String ID == Command ID
        }

    // Update the status bar
    STATUS_DisplayStatusMenuHelp ( hStatusWnd, nStringID );
}


//*********************** NEW CODE END *******************
```

The functions TOOLBAR_MakeMeAToolbar and STATUS_MakeMeA StatusLine create the toolbar and status bar controls. TOOLBAR_MakeMeA Toolbar uses the **CreateWindow** API with TOOLBARCLASSNAME. After creating this toolbar, the TB_BUTTONSTRUCTSIZE message is sent to the toolbar to "version enable" it. A combo box control is created (with the main window as a parent), filled with fonts, parented to the toolbar, and sized to look nice. A separator large enough to reserve space for the combo box is added to the start of the toolbar. A bitmap is then loaded from the resource file and attached to the toolbar using the TB_ADDBITMAP32 message. Next, each button is added by filling in the TBBUTTON structure and using the ADDBUTTON macro (defined right above the TOOLBAR_MakeMeAToolbar function) to add the buttons to the toolbar. Finally a string-table is attached to the toolbar to cause it to draw text underneath each button's picture.

STATUS_MakeMeAStatusLine creates the status bar window using the **CreateStatusWindow** API, which takes the style bits, the caption (which is really the default text for Pane 0), the parent, and an ID value for the status bar. Then the SB_SETPARTS message partitions the status bar into two panes, and finally calls the STATUS_DisplayStatusInformation function to set the text inside the status bar along with the style bits. STATUS_DisplayStatusInformation assumes that the RichEdit control has already been created.

STATUS_DisplayStatusInformation figures out the row and column position of the insertion point using the EM_EXGETSEL, EM_EXLINEFROMCHAR, and EM_LINEINDEX messages, formats this into a human-readable format, and sets the second pane (Pane 1) to this new text.

The Handle_WM_MENUSELECT code is your standard WM_MENUSE-LECT parse-o-rama; it eventually ends up calling the STATUS_Display-StatusMenuHelp function, which expects the handle to the status bar along with a string ID. If the ID is –1, the user has closed up the menu and the status bar is changed back to normal mode from simple mode. If the ID is 0, the user is over a separator or on a pop-up menu, and no string should be displayed; all other values of the ID signal the STATUS_DisplayStatusMenuHelp function to set the status bar into simple mode and display a string from the stringtable with the indicated ID.

In addition to the TOOLBAR_MakeMeAToolbar function, there is also WM_NOTIFY code added to the main window procedure to look for TTN_NEEDTEXT. The TOOLTIP_GetText function is called, which takes the ID of the button and uses it as a reference to look up the string in the resource stringtable and point the **lpszText** field of the TOOLTIPTEXT structure to the character buffer used in **LoadString**. The TOOLBAR-_DetermineToolbarButtonState function checks to see if the current selection in the RichEdit control has character formatting, and then checks/unchecks/ makes indeterminate the button corresponding to the formatting with the TB_INDETERMINATE and TB_CHECKBUTTON messages.

The code to update the information in the combo box is called from RTF_UpdateMenuState, then the current font is retrieved and updated in the combo box. The CBN_SELCHANGE notification message goes to the main window procedure (since that is the biological parent of the combo box), and code in that main window procedure calls RTF_SetCurrentFont to change the selected font to reflect the new combo box selection.

That's all that was added to the original RTFSAMP program! Now you have a very sassy little Windows 95-based text editor. Moreover, you should be able to cut and paste individual functions from this sample and splat them into your new and upcoming Windows 95 programs with ease.

5. Property Sheets

In this Goodie, I'll cover one of the most coveted features in today's software: tabbed dialogs. As an added bonus, I will talk briefly about the implementation of tabbed dialogs in MFC 3.0 (which comes with Visual C++ 2.0) so you can see how these two implementations will eventually merge.

Tabbed Dialogs: A Vocabulary Primer

The entire non-Microsoft world calls this feature *tabbed dialogs*, but in the Windows 95 SDK and MFC 3.0, Microsoft calls them *property sheets*. This is because the most common application of a tabbed dialog is to allow the user to set multiple attributes or properties for an object. For example, the desktop property sheet in Figure 11.45 contains four different pages (I only show two of them here to get the point across). Each page has a completely separate set of attributes from those of any other page. Perhaps the reason for calling this a property sheet is to discourage you from using it merely as an excuse to get more controls into a single dialog by arbitrarily splitting them up between pages.

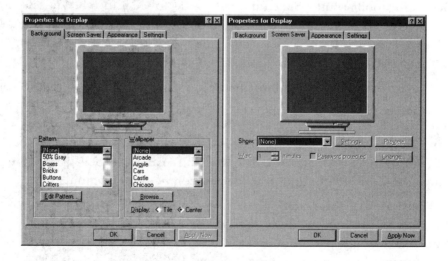

FIGURE 11.45 TABBED DIALOG PAGES

Meet the Sheets: An Introduction

Judging by the amount of calls I get from customers, I would say that writing code to manage a property sheet is a most disgruntling experience. So, before you become a disgruntled postal employee (go postal from hereon) trying to write your own, consider taking one of two avenues. If you are writing straight C SDK code, use the property sheet APIs included with the common controls DLL (COMCTL32.DLL)—see the section on SDK property sheets. Unlike the other common controls, the property sheet currently has its own include file (PRSHT.H), although this may get folded into COMMCTRL.H by the time Windows 95 is released. For a complete discussion on the common controls DLL, see Part I of this series.

If you are writing MFC code, use the **CPropertySheet** object as supplied with MFC 3.0. Even though MFC 3.0's current implementation doesn't use one iota of Windows 95 SDK code, I will show you how both implementations have very similar interfaces; the next version of MFC will just map itself to the SDK APIs. (The current version of MFC was written long before Windows 95's property sheets were stable enough to rely on; that's why it was written all from scratch.)

A property sheet is a collection of modal dialogs; each dialog is a page. Each page's dialog has its own resource template and its own dialog procedure (although I will show how to use one dialog procedure for multiple pages later in this Goodie). For the most part, the code you use for each of these pages will exactly resemble a typical dialog box procedure. The two major differences are the lack of OK and Cancel buttons in the template, and the lack of the **EndDialog** API call in your dialog procedure.

There are two approaches to building and displaying a property sheet. The first involves planning everything in advance: your program will set up a "storyboard" of all of the pages in the property sheet, indicating such information as the page's dialog resource template, dialog procedure, icons, and attributes. Once you have set up all the important information, you then splat the entire behemoth on the screen and let the user skim through the pages.

The second approach involves building a property sheet on-the-fly. In this implementation you create a "base" property sheet using techniques from the first approach, and then add pages dynamically to it as you see fit. This is fairly unconventional; users would probably hiccup if they saw an extra page suddenly appear on their property sheet, unless it happened, say, in response to some dynamic event such as a Plug and Play notification.

A property sheet must have at least one page; if you try to create a property sheet with no pages, or if you dynamically remove all the pages, Windows 95 will close the property sheet. If you have only one page and you wish to replace it with another, add the second page before removing the first.

Programming Pages in Your Property Sheet

I have two new sample programs. The first, PROPC (Listing 11.14), will be written in straight C, using the Windows 95 property sheet APIs from the common controls DLL. The second, smaller sample, PROPMFC (Listing 11.15), will be a quick and dirty implementation of MFC's property sheets.

PROPC brings up three property sheets. The first uses the approach of laying out everything in advance; the second uses the approach of building sheets on the fly; and the third is like the first property sheet, except in it I use the same dialog procedure for all the pages in the sheet.

PROPMFC just brings up one property sheet; it is built the conventional MFC way. I will compare PROPMFC to PROPC during PROPMFC's construction, so you can see the similarities and differences.

SDK Property Sheets

Okay, let's first focus on the property sheets in Windows 95. There are only three APIs for property sheets:

```
int PropertySheet ( LPCPROPSHEETHEADER lppsph);
HPROPSHEETPAGE CreatePropertySheetPage (LPCPROPSHEETPAGE lppsp);
BOOL DestroyPropertySheetPage( HPROPSHEETPAGE hPage);
```

The **Create** and **Destroy** functions do just that; they create and destroy pages. I'll return to the **CreatePropertySheetPage** function later.

The **PropertySheet** API most closely resembles the **DialogBox** API that we've all grown to love over the years. The **lppsph** parameter points to a property sheet header (PROPSHEETHEADER) structure; this structure defines the, er, properties of the property sheet and indicates an array of pages to populate the property sheet with. Some of the fields in the PROPSHEETHEADER depend on the individual page types (the PROPSHEETPAGE structure), so first take a look at the page structure in Figure 11.46.

```
typedef struct _PROPSHEETPAGE
  {
  DWORD       dwSize;        // Size of this structure (including extra data)
  DWORD       dwFlags;       // PSP_* bits define the use and meaning of fields
  HINSTANCE   hInstance;     // Where to load the resources from
  union
    {
    LPCSTR            pszTemplate; // If dwFlags don't have PSP_DLGINDIRECT:
                                   // Template to use
    LPCDLGTEMPLATE  pResource;   // If dwFlags have PSP_DLGINDIRECT: pointer to
                                 // resource
                                 //    in memory
    };
  union
    {
    HICON             hIcon;   // If dwFlags have PSP_USEICON: hIcon to use
    LPCSTR            pszIcon; // If dwFlags have PSP_USEICONID: Icon name string
                              // or id
    };
  LPCSTR      pszTitle;    // Name to override the template title or string id
  DLGPROC     pfnDlgProc;  // Page's Dialog procedure
  LPARAM      lParam;      // User-defined data
  LPFNRELEASEPROPSHEETPAGE pfnCallback; // PSP_USERELEASEFUNC: function will be
                                        // called
                                        // before HPROPSHEETPAGE is destroyed
  UINT FAR * pcRefParent;  // PSP_USERREFPARENT: pointer to ref count variable
  } PROPSHEETPAGE, FAR *LPPROPSHEETPAGE;

typedef const PROPSHEETPAGE FAR *LPCPROPSHEETPAGE;
```

FIGURE 11.46 THE PROPSHEETPAGE STRUCTURE

There is an interesting note to keep in mind about the **dwSize** field. Just as you overload the NMHDR structure for notifications (See the NMHDR in the TreeView Goodie #2), you can overload this structure as well. This is most commonly achieved by declaring a wrapper structure with the extra data tagged at the end. **dwSize** then is the size of the overloaded structure. In my example, I will tag on the window handle and the page number to the end of the structure:

```
typedef struct _MYPAGE
  {
  PROPSHEETPAGE psp;      // The original structure
  HWND          hDlg;     // Handle to the dialog
  int           iPageNum; // Page index
  }
MYPAGE, *LPMYPAGE;
```

I'll fill out the MYPAGE structure and explain how to get at it a little later, so just hang on.

The **dwFlags** and **hInstance** fields are straightforward; after that it gets a little more complex. Figure 11.47 shows all the possible values for dwFlags. The first union of the PROPSHEETPAGE structure provides two ways to indicate which dialog template to use for a property sheet page: either instruct Windows to look for the template in an application's RC file, or build the dialog template yourself and then pass the pointer to that template directly. If you simply want to tell Windows where to go to get the template, make sure you have the hInstance field indicating where to get the template, and then fill in the pszTemplate field with the name or MAKEINTRE-SOURCE value of your template. If you want to build your own homebrew dialog template on the fly and pass that pointer, make sure the dwFlags field has the PSP_DLGINDIRECT bit set, and then place the pointer to the resource in the pResource field.

PSP_DEFAULT	Use the default meaning for all structure members.
PSP_DLGINDIRECT	Use pResource instead of pszTemplate for the page.
PSP_USEHICON	Use the hIcon field to assign a tab icon.
PSP_USEICONID	Use the pszIcon field to assign a tab icon.
PSP_USETITLE	Use the pszTitle field for the tab text (otherwise use the caption).
PSP_USERELEASEFUNC	Call the function specified by pfnCallback when destroying the property sheet page.
PSP_USEREFPARENT	Maintain a reference count for this page, updating the pcRefParent pointer.

FIGURE 11.47 DWFLAGS POSSIBILITIES

The next union, unlike the first, contains purely optional attributes. Each page has a corresponding tab at the top of the property sheet page, and you can put optional mini-icons on these tabs. If you want a mini-icon on the tab, either specify the PSP_USEHICON bit in **dwFlags** and fill in the **hIcon** field with the handle to your mini-icon, or specify the PSP_USEICONID bit and fill in the **pszIcon** with the name or MAKEINTRESOURCE value of the mini-icon in the module whose instance handle is indicated in the hInstance field.

```
psp[0].dwSize       = sizeof(PROPSHEETPAGE);
psp[0].dwFlags      = PSP_USEICONID | PSP_USETITLE;
psp[0].hInstance    = hInst;
psp[0].pszTemplate  = MAKEINTRESOURCE(dlgbackcolor);
// IDI_BACKCOLOR points to icon in RC file
psp[0].pszIcon      = MAKEINTRESOURCE(IDI_BACKCOLOR);
psp[0].pfnDlgProc   = BackgrndDialogProc;
psp[0].pszTitle     = "Background Color";
psp[0].lParam       = 0;
```

If you do not specify either of these flags, just put NULL in **hIcon**, grab a soda pop, and deal with just plain tabs.

The next field, **pszTitle**, allows you to specify the text that goes on the tabs, provided you set the PSP_USETITLE bit in the **dwFlags** field. If you do not specify this bit, use NULL for this field, and the caption from the dialog template will be used as the tab text. Next, the **pfnDlgProc** field is your basic, sans-**EndDialog** callback procedure. And, in keeping with the tradition of letting us programmers squeak in a this pointer, the **lParam** field is our extra pocket of information.

The **pfnCallback** field points to a program-defined callback function that is called at certain times. One of those times is just before a property sheet page is about to be destroyed. This allows your application to clean up any resources, free any memory objects, and take care of any other bloody gloves. This function will be called if the PSP_USERELEASEFUNC bit is set in the **dwFlags** field. The callback function looks like this:

```
UINT CALLBACK RemoveBloodyGloveProc (HWND hWndPage, UINT uMSG, LPPROPSHEETPAGE lppsp)
{
  if (PSPCB_RELEASE == uMSG)
    {
    /* perform cleanup here */
    }
}
```

It is called before the page is destroyed, which means that if you wanted to keep your code somewhat coherent, you could have this function simply send a message to the dialog procedure to clean up after itself. Of course, the first contrived example thing that pops into mind is "how does the callback function know how to send a message to another window to get permission to shut down?" This is where the overloaded PROPSHEETPAGE structure comes into play. The MYPAGE structure includes hPermissionWnd, which will get the handle of the window that gives permission; this structure can be filled in at WM_INITDIALOG time, since the **lParam** points to a copy of the MYPAGE structure (again, very shortly I will explain how you fill out MYPAGE):

```
. 
. /* In dialog procedure */
```

```
case WM_INITDIALOG:
  // Store away the pointer to MYPAGE
  SetWindowLong ( hDlg, DWL_USER, (LONG)lParam );
  // Set the hPermissionWnd field in the MYPAGE dialog
  ((LPMYPAGE)lParam)->hPermissionWnd = hPermissionWnd; // Contrived, contrived!
break;
```

That's enough about the structure. Now take a look at Listing 11.11 to see how you would set up a really basic page in your killer app. Though this page is indeed very basic, it will fill the needs of many applications: it has a nice little icon on the tab, along with the tab text "Schmidt" (the name of the dog belonging to a very good friend of mine), it uses the **MyDialogProc** procedure, and the WM_INITDIALOG code in the above code snippet initializes the **hPermissionWnd** parameter to a valid window handle. This is how you generate instance data for each page.

LISTING 11.11 SETTING UP A PAGE IN THE PROPERTY SHEET

```
// Declare some tiny structure that has all sorts of information in it
// Declare a page
MYPAGE MyPage;
// Fill out the page
MyPage.psp.dwSize     = sizeof(MYPAGE);                      // Includes our extra data
MyPage.psp.dwFlags    = PSP_USEICONID | PSP_USETITLE;        // Tab has icon,
                                                            // use pszTitle field
MyPage.psp.hInstance  = ghInst;                             // Instance where
resources
                                                            // live
MyPage.psp.pszTemplate= MAKEINTRESOURCE(IDD_MYDIALOGPAGE); // Dialog's ID
MyPage.psp.pszIcon    = MAKEINTRESOURCE(IDI_MYDIALOGPAGE); // Icon's ID
MyPage.psp.pfnDlgproc = MyDialogProc;                       // Dialog procedure
MyPage.psp.pszTitle   = "Schmidt";                          // Tab text (my
                                                            // friend's dog's name)
MyPage.psp.lParam     = 0L;                                 // Not used this example
MyPage.hPermission    = NULL;                               // Set to uninitialized
MyPage.iPageNum       = 1;                                  // We'll call this page 1
```

Now, looking back at that release function; I could have indicated one in the code in Listing 11.11 that might've looked like this:

```
UINT CALLBACK RemoveBloodyGloveProc (HWND hWndPage, UINT uMSG, LPPROPSHEETPAGE
lppsp)
{
  if (PSPCB_RELEASE == uMSG)
    {
    if (SendMessage (((LPMYPAGE)lppsp)->hPermissionWnd,
                      WM_CANPAGECLOSE,
                      0,
                      (LPARAM)hWndPage
                     ))
      {
      /* do clean up here */
      }
    }
}
```

That code would send the dialog procedure a WM_MYCLOSE message (an app-defined message) and politely put the pointer to the MYPAGE structure in **lParam** just so the dialog procedure could skip calling **GetWindowLong-(hDlg, DWL_USER)** to retrieve the pointer to this structure.

Once the above structure is filled out, there are two routes you can take. You can either fill out a PROPSHEETHEADER structure (which I'll show you how to do in just a moment) and indicate this page in the structure, or you can call the **CreatePropertySheetPage** API to get back a handle to a property sheet page (note: this is not the window handle of the dialog; this is an HPROPSHEETPAGE handle, which is a handle to an undocumented structure inside COMCTL32.DLL). If you plan on adding pages dynamically, you would use the second method to get a handle to the page, and then send that handle to the property sheet via the PSM_ADDPAGE message (a more complete discussion of adding pages dynamically comes after I finish the discussion on building preplanned property sheets).

Now that you have a basic understanding of a property sheet page, look at Figure 11.48 to see the PROPSHEETHEADER structure in all its glory. The **dwSize** field of this structure works more like you'd expect: here it's for version control. The **dwFlags** field is where you specify the PSH_* flags (see Figure 11.49), which indicate which fields of the structure to pay attention to.

```
typedef struct _PROPSHEETHEADER
  {
  DWORD        dwSize;        // size of this structure (version control)
  DWORD        dwFlags;       // PSH_* flags
  HWND         hwndParent;    // Parent of the property sheet
  HINSTANCE    hInstance;     // Where to load icon or caption string from
  union
    {
    HICON      hIcon;         // if dwFlags have PSH_USEHICON: hIcon to use
    LPCSTR     pszIcon;       // if dwFlags have PSH_USEICONID: or icon name string
                             // or icon id
    };
  LPCSTR       pszCaption;    // if dwFlags have PSH_PROPTITLE: Use this string in
                             //   "Properties for %s" formatting, otherwise
                             //    use only this string. Could be MAKEINTRESOURCE()
  UINT         nPages;        // # of HPROPSHEETPAGE (or PROPSHEETPAGE) elements in
                             // phpage
  UINT         nStartPage;    // Initial page to be shown (zero based)
  union
    {
    LPCPROPSHEETPAGE ppsp;            // if dwFlags have PSH_PROPSHEETPAGE: Array of
                                      //    Property sheet pages
    HPROPSHEETPAGE FAR *phpage;       // if dwFlags doesn't have PSH_PROPSHEETPAGE:
                                      //    Array of handles to property sheet pages
    };
  } PROPSHEETHEADER, FAR *LPPROPSHEETHEADER;
typedef const PROPSHEETHEADER FAR *LPCPROPSHEETHEADER;
```

FIGURE 11.48 THE PROPSHEETHEADER STRUCTURE

```
PSH_DEFAULT          Use the default meaning for every field
PSH_PROPTITLE        Preface pszCaption text with "Properties for"
PSH_USEHICON         Use the hIcon field to indicate a mini icon for the sheet
PSH_USEICONID        Use the pszIcon field to indicate a mini icon for the sheet
PSH_PROPSHEETPAGE    Use the ppsp field to look at an array of possibly
                     overloaded PROPSHEETPAGE structures instead of an array
                     of handles to property sheets.
```

FIGURE 11.49 PSH FLAGS

As with a normal dialog, **hwndParent** indicates the parent window of the property sheet (each individual page is a child of the property sheet). The **hInstance** field indicates where to load the little icon that goes in the top left corner of the property sheet from, or where to load the stringtable text for the property sheet caption from. The icon is optional; however, if you need to use it, you should use the PSH_USEHICON or PSH_USEICONID flag along with **hIcon** and **pszIcon** in the same way you did for property sheet pages.

The **pszCaption** is used in one of two ways. If you do not specify the PSH_PROPTITLE flag in the **dwFlags** field, then the exact text of this string will be used in the property sheet. If you do use PSH_PROPTITLE, the words "Properties for" (depending on the international language, of course) will preface your text; for example, if you indicate "Sale" in **pszCaption**, you get "Properties for Sale" displayed.

The **nPages** field is used to indicate the initial number of pages you are going to display in the property sheet; you can dynamically add or remove pages later on. You must specify at least one page. The **nStartPage** indicates which one of the pages to select at startup.

The final union fields contain either an array of property sheet pages or an array of handles to property sheet pages. Once all the fields of this structure have been correctly filled out, you simply call the **PropertySheet** API. See Listing 11.12 for a small chunk of sample code that defines two pages and then creates a property sheet. This sample is tiny and doesn't overload the structure with extra stuff, but it does get the general idea across. The PROPC sample, discussed later, will have a full implementation of the concepts described in this Goodie.

LISTING 11.12 SETTING UP PAGES IN A PROPERTY SHEET

```
int DoPropertySheet(HWND hwndOwner)
{
    PROPSHEETPAGE psp[2];
    PROPSHEETHEADER psh;

    psp[0].dwSize    = sizeof(PROPSHEETPAGE);
    psp[0].dwFlags   = PSP_USEICONID | PSP_USETITLE;
```

```
    psp[0].hInstance    = g_hInst;
    psp[0].pszTemplate  = MAKEINTRESOURCE(dlgbackcolor);
    psp[0].pszIcon      = MAKEINTRESOURCE(IDI_BACKCOLOR);
    psp[0].pfnDlgProc   = BackgrndDialogProc;
    psp[0].pszTitle     = "Background Color";
    psp[0].lParam       = 0;


    psp[1].dwSize       = sizeof(PROPSHEETPAGE);
    psp[1].dwFlags      = PSP_USEICONID | PSP_USETITLE;
    psp[1].hInstance    = g_hInst;
    psp[1].pszTemplate  = MAKEINTRESOURCE(dlgrectcolor);
    psp[1].pszIcon      = MAKEINTRESOURCE(IDI_SHAPES);
    psp[1].pfnDlgProc   = RectangleDialogProc;
    psp[1].pszTitle     = "Client Area Shape";
    psp[1].lParam       = 0;


    psh.dwSize          = sizeof(PROPSHEETHEADER);
    psh.dwFlags         = PSH_USEICONID | PSH_PROPSHEETPAGE | PSH_PROPTITLE;
    psh.hwndParent      = hwndOwner;
    psh.hInstance       = g_hInst;
    psh.pszIcon         = MAKEINTRESOURCE(IDI_CELL_PROPERTIES);
    psh.pszCaption      = (LPSTR)"MSJ Sample";
    psh.nPages          = sizeof(psp) / sizeof(PROPSHEETPAGE);
    psh.ppsp            = (LPCPROPSHEETPAGE) &psp;


    return PropertySheet(&psh);
}
```

Now let's take a look at how you can create a property sheet and add pages to it on-the-fly (but please keep in mind that it is a user-interface blunder to add pages to a property sheet unless you have a very special reason for doing so). I'll start with the above sample code from the first page, except that I'm going to add the second page (Client Area Shape) dynamically. So first let's create the one-page property sheet shown in Figure 11.50. Next, since the **PropertySheet** function does not return until the user dismisses the dialog, you need to find another way to add the second page. Advanced Windows 95 hacks can spin off a thread before calling **PropertySheet** and add the second page in that thread, but for simplicity's sake I will just show you how to add the second page to the property sheet in response to the user clicking on some button (IDD_SOMEBUTTON) in the first page.

```
int DoPropertySheet(HWND hwndOwner)
{
    PROPSHEETPAGE psp[1];
    PROPSHEETHEADER psh;

    psp[0].dwSize       = sizeof(PROPSHEETPAGE);
    psp[0].dwFlags      = PSP_USEICONID | PSP_USETITLE;
    psp[0].hInstance    = g_hInst;
    psp[0].pszTemplate  = MAKEINTRESOURCE(dlgbackcolor);
    psp[0].pszIcon      = MAKEINTRESOURCE(IDI_BACKCOLOR);
    psp[0].pfnDlgProc   = BackgrndDialogProc;
    psp[0].pszTitle     = "Background Color";
    psp[0].lParam       = 0;


    psh.dwSize          = sizeof(PROPSHEETHEADER);
    psh.dwFlags         = PSH_USEICONID | PSH_PROPSHEETPAGE | PSH_PROPTITLE;
    psh.hwndParent      = hwndOwner;
    psh.hInstance       = g_hInst;
    psh.pszIcon         = MAKEINTRESOURCE(IDI_CELL_PROPERTIES);
    psh.pszCaption      = (LPSTR)"MSJ Sample";
    psh.nPages          = sizeof(psp) / sizeof(PROPSHEETPAGE);
    psh.ppsp            = (LPCPROPSHEETPAGE) &psp;


    return PropertySheet(&psh);
}
```

FIGURE 11.50 A ONE-PAGE PROPERTY SHEET

It is safe to assume that the parent window of a property sheet page is the property sheet dialog, so you can use our ol' pal **GetParent** for sending messages. Take a look at Listing 11.13 for some code that would be inside the dialog procedure for the first Background Color page. This code uses the macro **PropSheet_AddPage** to send the PSM_ADDPAGE message to the property sheet window. The PSM_ADDPAGE message adds the new page to the end of the property sheet. See Figure 11.51 for a list of macros and the messages they send to the main property sheet dialog. To remove a page from the property sheet, use the **PropSheet_RemovePage (PSM_REM OVEPAGE)** macro. It takes three parameters: **hWndPropSheet**, the zero-based index of the page to delete, and the handle of the page to delete. Only one of the last two parameters need be valid for this function to work.

Msg	wParam	lParam	Retval	Macro	Action/Notes
PSM_SETCURSEL	index	hPage	n/a	PropSheet_SetCurSel(hSheet, hPage, index)	Activates a page.
PSM_REMOVEPAGE	index	hPage	n/a	PropSheet_RemovePage(hSheet, index, hPage)	Removes a page.
PSM_ADDPAGE	0	hPage	n/a	PropSheet_AddPage(hDlg, hPage)	Adds a page.
PSM_CHANGED	hPageWnd	0	n/a	PropSheet_Changed(hDlg, hPageWnd)	Tell the Property Sheet that the page changed and "Apply Now" should be enabled.
PSM_UNCHANGED	hPageWnd	0	n/a	PropSheet_UnChanged(hDlg, hPageWnd)	Tell the Property Sheet that the page has unchanged and "Apply Now" should be disabled.
PSM_RESTARTWINDOWS	0	0	n/a	PropSheet_RestartWindows(hDlg)	Tell the Property Sheet that we need to restart windows due to a change made, so the restart windows dialog will be presented when closing the property sheet.
PSM_REBOOTSYSTEM	0	0	n/a	PropSheet_RebootSystem(hDlg)	Tell the Property Sheet that we need to reboot the system due to a change made, so the reboot windows dialog will be presented when closing the property sheet.
PSM_CANCELTOCLOSE	0	0	n/a	PropSheet_CancelToClose(hDlg)	Change the OK button to Close and disable cancel. This indicates a non cancelable change has been made.
PSM_QUERYSIBLINGS	User Param1	User Param2	See "Action"	PropSheet_QuerySiblings(hDlg, wPar, lParam)	Have the Property Sheet forward this query to each initialized hwnd until a non-zero value is returned. This value is returned to the caller.
PSM_APPLY	0	0	n/a	PropSheet_Apply(hDlg)	Programatically press the "Apply Now" button.
PSM_SETTLE	Style	szText	n/a	PropSheet_SetTitle(hDlg, wStyle, lpszText)	Sets the title of the Property Sheet. iStyle can be PSH_PROPTITLE or PSH_DEFAULT. lpszText can be a string or an rcid.

| PSM_SETWIZBUTTONS | 0 | dwFlags | n/a | PropSheet_SetWizButtons(hDlg, dwFlags) | Tell the Property Sheet which wizard buttons to enable. Can be any combination of: PSWIZB_BACK, PSWIZB_NEXT, PSWIZB_FINISH. |
| PSM_PRESSBUTTON | idButton | 0 | n/a | PropSheet_PressButton(hDlg, idButton) | Programatically press a button. idButton can be one of: PSBTN_BACK, PSBTN_NEXT, PSBTN_FINISH, PSBTN_OK, PSBTN_APPLY-NOW, PSBTN_CANCEL, or PSBTN_HELP. |

FIGURE 11.51 MACROS AND MESSAGES SENT TO THE MAIN PROPERTY SHEET DIALOG

LISTING 11.13 ADDING A PAGE TO THE PROPERTY SHEET

```
...
case IDD_SOMEBUTTON:

    psp.dwSize      = sizeof(PROPSHEETPAGE);
    psp.dwFlags     = PSP_USEICONID | PSP_USETITLE;
    psp.hInstance   = g_hInst;
    psp.pszTemplate = MAKEINTRESOURCE(dlgrectcolor);
    psp.pszIcon     = MAKEINTRESOURCE(IDI_SHAPES);
    psp.pfnDlgProc  = RectangleDialogProc;
    psp.pszTitle    = "Client Area Shape";
    psp.lParam      = 0;
    hRectPage = CreatePropertySheetPage ( &psp );
    PropSheet_AddPage ( GetParent(hDlg), hRectPage );
    break;
```

That covers the basics of creating, adding, and removing property sheets using the Windows 95 SDK. Still, there are quite a few more bits of information I need to go over including enumerations and notifications.

Communicating with Other Pages in a Property Sheet

Pages in a property sheet may find reason to talk to each other. The most common example of this is when a page needs to know if another page in the dialog has had its information changed. Take, for example, the display properties dialog from Figure 11.45. The Background tab and the Appearance tab are slightly interrelated. If the user changes the desktop bitmap in the Background tab and he or she also changes the color of the desktop in the Appearance tab, then pressing the Apply Now button will cause two separate changes to the desktop. If the current tab selection is Background, that tab's dialog procedure may want to ask the other tabs if something else has changed. If the user also changed the desktop color, then the Appearance tab would respond, "Yes! I have changed," and then the code would know to handle the dual changes. There is a macro called **PropSheet_QuerySiblings (PSM_QUERYSIBLINGS)** that will send the PSM_QUERYSIBLINGS message to every page in the property sheet, provided each page in the property sheet returns a nonzero value in response to PSM_QUERYSIBLINGS.

Of course some restrictions do apply regarding this macro: namely, the fact that the dialog window for a page is not created until the user actually selects that page. (Can you say speed enhancement?) This means that when a property sheet initially comes up, there is only one child dialog window actually created. As the user starts flipping around through the pages, more and more of the dialogs are created until the user has finally navigated through all the different pages. The PSM_QUERYSIBLINGS message is only sent by the property sheet windows to existing pages, therefore this message is useful only if you want to talk to pages that the user has accessed. I will discuss a way to "preload" pages in the next section.

Enumerating Property Sheets

There is no **EnumPropertySheetPages** API to run through the pages, but it is possible to write a poor man's version using the PSM_QUERYSIBLINGS message. As mentioned above, this message is only sent to initialized property sheet pages, but there is a way to get around this by forcing a "preload" of all pages. In the WM_INITDIALOG code of your first page in your property sheet, add some code like that in Figure 11.52. This code will force every page in the property sheet to briefly get activated, which will in turn create the dialog. The reason you cannot set the zero page as the current selection is that the WM_INITDIALOG code occurs too early in the game for this message to be sent (just as you can't display a message box in response to WM_INIT-DIALOG, you can't set the selection to yourself in WM_INITDIALOG).

```
case WM_INITDIALOG:

  // Activate all the other pages to create the dialog windows
  for ( i = 1; i < iNumPagesInSheet; i++ )
    PropSheet_SetCurSel ( GetParent(hDlg), NULL, i );
  // POST a message to reactive ourselves
  PostMessage ( hDlg, WM_MYINITDIALOG, 0, 0 );
  break;


case WM_MYINITDIALOG:

  // Activate ourselves.
  PropSheet_SetCurSel ( GetParent(hDlg), NULL, 0 );
  break;
```

FIGURE 11.52 FORCING A PRELOAD OF ALL PAGES IN A PROPERTY SHEET

Now when the PSM_QUERYSIBLINGS message is sent, every single page in your property sheet will get the message, since they are all loaded into memory. Next let's say you want to write an **EnumProc** that looks like this:

```
BOOL MyPropSheetPageEnumProc ( HWND hDlgPage,
                               LPMYPAGE lpMyPage,
                               WPARAM param1,
                               LPARAM Param1 )
{
  return TRUE; // TRUE Keeps enumerating
}
```

The way to achieve this would be to add code like this into every page's dialog procedure:

```
case PSM_QUERYSIBLINGS:

    return (!MyPropSheetPageEnumProc(hDlg,
                    (LPMYPAGE)GetWindowLong(hDlg,
                    DWL_USER), wParam, lParam)));
```

This code will call the **MyPropSheetEnumProc** as each page receives this message, and the **MyPropSheetEnumProc** function returns TRUE to continue. The extra bytes stored in DWL_USER point to the MYPAGE structure, set in the WM_INITDIALOG code I showed you earlier. This enumeration procedure does not do anything, though. I'm going to have it simply count the number of pages in the property sheet by passing the address of a counter variable in one of the parameters. So, to dynamically add a page, the code above could first count the pages and make sure that there is only one page. Keep in mind that your code should find a better way to count the pages—this is just a cheezy example. See Figure 11.53 for the modified code snippets to achieve a poor man's page enumeration.

```
BOOL MyPropSheetPageEnumProc ( HWND hDlgPage, LPMYPAGE lpMyPage,
                               WPARAM param1, LPARAM Param1 )
{
  (*((LPINT)param1))++;
  return TRUE; // TRUE Keeps enumerating
}

case IDD_SOMEBUTTON:

    iCount = 0; // Init
    PropSheet_QuerySiblings ( GetParent(hDlg), &iCount, 0 );
    if (iCount < 2)
      {
      psp.dwSize      = sizeof(PROPSHEETPAGE);
      psp.dwFlags     = PSP_USEICONID | PSP_USETITLE;
      psp.hInstance   = g_hInst;
      psp.pszTemplate = MAKEINTRESOURCE(dlgrectcolor);
      psp.pszIcon     = MAKEINTRESOURCE(IDI_SHAPES);
```

```
    psp.pfnDlgProc  = RectangleDialogProc;
    psp.pszTitle    = "Client Area Shape";
    psp.lParam      = 0;
    hRectPage = CreatePropertySheetPage ( &psp );
    PropSheet_AddPage ( GetParent(hDlg), hRectPage );
    }
else
    {
    MessageBox ( hDlg, "Is this trip really necessary?", "MSJ", MB_OK );
    }

break;
```

FIGURE 11.53 A POOR MAN'S ENUMPAGES

Property Sheet Notifications and Messages

There are six types of notifications that a property sheet page can receive (see Figure 11.54 for a list of the notifications). Since dialog procedures return TRUE or FALSE, you must use the **SetDlgMsgResult** macro (found in WINDOWSX.H) to set the actual return value.

Property Sheet Notifications via WM_NOTIFY. These are sent to the property sheet page.

NOTE: RESULTS MUST BE RETURNED BY USING SetWindowLong(hdlg, DWL_MSGRESULT, result)

PSN_SETACTIVE	Page is being activated
PSN_KILLACTIVE	Page is being deactivated
PSN_APPLY	OK or Apply Now button pressed. Return TRUE to allow, or PSNRET_VALID to abort.
PSN_RESET	Cancel button has been pressed.
PSN_HASHELP	Sent to the page to ask if the Help button should be enabled. Return TRUE or FALSE.

PSN_HELP	Help Button has been pressed
PSN_WIZBACK	Back button has been pressed (Wizards only)
PSN_WIZNEXT	Next button has been pressed (Wizards only)
PSN_WIZFINISH	Finish button has been pressed (Wizards only)
PSN_QUERYCANCEL	Cancel button is being pressed, return TRUE to reject cancel

FIGURE 11.54 PROPERTY SHEET NOTIFICATIONS

The notification you can count on using most is PSN_APPLY. This notification comes whenever your user presses the Apply Now button in the property sheet dialog. This is your chance to take all of that valuable information in the dialog and apply it to whatever attribute that drives your program. Of course in order to get the Apply Now button, you will need to tell the property sheet that the user has changed something in the dialog. This can be done by calling the **PropSheet_Changed(PSM_CHANGED)** macro:

```
PropSheet_Changed( hPropSheet, hPage );
// Activates the Apply Now button
```

As an added bonus, the **PropSheet_UnChanged(PSM_UNCHANGED)** macro does the opposite, graying out the Apply Now button.

Likewise, if users get completely fubar while filling in the multitudes of fields in all the different pages of your dialog, they may choose the ejector seat and press the Cancel button. In this case, you will get the PSN_RESET notification, which gives your program a chance to restore your data structures and attributes back to their original upright position.

Two other related notifications are PSN_SETACTIVE and PSN_KILLACTIVE. These notifications are closest in resemblance to the WM_ACTIVATE message, yet they have a little more functionality. The most important feature of the PSN_KILLACTIVE notification is that not only does it come before the page is deactivated, but also that your application can abort the deactivation. If the page's dialog procedure returns TRUE (via **SetDlgMsgResult**) in response to the PSN_KILLACTIVE notification, the page will not be allowed to lose activation.

```
case PSN_KILLACTIVE:
  SetDlgMsgResult(hDlg, PSN_KILLACTIVE, TRUE);
  return TRUE;
```

If you prevent a page from losing focus, it is your responsibility to notify users that they are not playing by the rules by putting up a message box stating the errors of their ways.

The two other notification messages that you'll be interested in are PSN_HASHELP and PSN_HELP. If your procedure sets the return value to TRUE in response to the PSN_HASHELP notification message, the Help button on the property sheet will snap to life and ungray. Once the Help button is activated, pressing it will generate the PSN_HELP notification, where your application can then fire up the help system.

Property Sheet Odds and Ends

Well, that covers the mechanics of property sheets. Before I get into the PROPC sample program, there are a few other bits of information about property sheets that you should know.

First off, the common dialogs are not going to be usable as property sheet pages. (Of course common dialogs are in Windows 95 in the COMDLG32.DLL.) If you want to use a font dialog or a file dialog as a page in your property sheet, you will just have to write it yourself. Second, be sure that you use the WS_CHILD style instead of WS_POPUP for your dialog templates. This prevents some funny-looking activation issues while using the property sheets, namely losing the active border for the property sheet when clicking on a page. Third, make sure that all of your pages are the same size. If you use a bunch of differently sized property sheet pages, you will find interesting clipping and painting issues to contend with. Fourth, don't put OK, Cancel, Apply Now, or Help buttons in your dialog templates—let the property sheet do this for you. Fifth, don't call **EndDialog**. You will shut down the entire property sheet faster than a speeding Bronco if you do.

If you plan on having controls that stay consistent between pages (such as having an edit control at the top of every page with some text in it), then you would be best off using a single dialog procedure for all pages. This way you can cache away the values from one page and put them into another by using a static variable:

```
static char szText[MAXFIELDLEN];
      .
      .
      .
case PSN_KILLACTIVE:
   SetWindowLong ( hDlg, DWL_MSGRESULT, 0 );
   GetDlgItemText ( hDlg, IDD_EDITTEXT, szText,
                    sizeof(szText));
   break;

case PSN_SETACTIVE:
   SetWindowLong ( hDlg, DWL_MSGRESULT, 0 );
   SetDlgItemText ( hDlg, IDD_EDITTEXT, szText );
   break;
```

Note how the edit control on every page must have the same ID for this approach to work, or else you would have to maintain a list of IDs for each page. Another important thing to keep in mind if you have a control span across pages: keep it in the exact same location. The user certainly doesn't want to have to play hide-and-seek looking for a roaming edit control.

The Sample: PROPC

The first sample program, PROPC (see Listing 11.14), is based on the GENERIC sample included in the Windows 95 SDK. All new code has been bracketed with "New Code Start" and "New Code End" comment blocks. The program has three menu choices added to the File menu: Pre-Planned, Dynamic, and Single Procedure.

LISTING 11.14 PROPC SAMPLE PROGRAM

```
#include <windows.h>          // required for all Windows applications
#if !defined(_WIN32)
```

LISTING 11.14 CONTINUED

```
#include <ver.h>
#endif
#include "generic.h"              // specific to this program
#include "resource.h"
#include <commctrl.h>             // Common controls
#include <stdio.h>                // for atoi

// Windows NT defines APIENTRY, but 3.x doesn't
#if !defined (APIENTRY)
#define APIENTRY far pascal
#endif

// Windows 3.x uses a FARPROC for dialogs
#if !defined(_WIN32)
#define DLGPROC FARPROC
#endif

HINSTANCE   hInst;                       // current instance
HWND        ghWnd;                          // Main window handle.

char szAppName[] = "Generic";        // The name of this application
char szTitle[]   = "Generic Sample Application"; // The title bar text

//************** NEW CODE START *********

COLORREF    crColorWindow = RGB(255,0,0); // Color of client area
int         iPattern = IDD_NONE;          // Pattern of client area

VOID PrePlannedPropertySheet(HWND);  // Test functions for
VOID DynamicPropertySheet    (HWND); // each type of property
VOID SingleProcPropertySheet(HWND);  // sheet

// This is an app-defined message to make this sample
// small enough to fit in a magazine article.

#define WM_MYCHANGESETTINGS (WM_USER+1000)  // Send to ghWnd to indicate
                                            // the color/pattern has changed

//************** NEW CODE END *********

//
```

```
//   FUNCTION: WinMain(HINSTANCE, HINSTANCE, LPSTR, int)
//
//   PURPOSE: calls initialization function, processes message loop
//
//   COMMENTS:
//
//      Windows recognizes this function by name as the initial entry point
//      for the program.  This function calls the application initialization
//      routine, if no other instance of the program is running, and always
//      calls the instance initialization routine.  It then executes a
//      message retrieval and dispatch loop that is the top-level control
//      structure for the remainder of execution.  The loop is terminated
//      when a WM_QUIT  message is received, at which time this function
//      exits the application instance by returning the value passed by
//      PostQuitMessage().
//
//      If this function must abort before entering the message loop, it
//      returns the conventional value NULL.
//


int APIENTRY WinMain(
            HINSTANCE hInstance,
            HINSTANCE hPrevInstance,
            LPSTR lpCmdLine,
            int nCmdShow
            )
{
    MSG msg;
    HANDLE hAccelTable;

    // Other instances of app running?
    if (!hPrevInstance) {
        // Initialize shared things
        if (!InitApplication(hInstance)) {
            return (FALSE);                 // Exits if unable to initialize
        }
    }

    // Perform initializations that apply to a specific instance
    if (!InitInstance(hInstance, nCmdShow)) {
        return (FALSE);
    }

    hAccelTable = LoadAccelerators (hInstance, szAppName);

    // Acquire and dispatch messages until a WM_QUIT message is received.
```

LISTING 11.14 CONTINUED

```c
    while (GetMessage(&msg,    // message structure
                      NULL,    // handle of window receiving the message
                      0,       // lowest message to examine
                      0)){     // highest message to examine
        if (!TranslateAccelerator (msg.hwnd, hAccelTable, &msg)) {
          TranslateMessage(&msg);// Translates virtual key codes
          DispatchMessage(&msg); // Dispatches message to window
        }
    }


    // Returns the value from PostQuitMessage
    return (msg.wParam);


    // This will prevent 'unused formal parameter' warnings
    lpCmdLine;
}


//
//   FUNCTION: InitApplication(HINSTANCE)
//
//   PURPOSE: Initializes window data and registers window class
//
//   COMMENTS:
//
//     This function is called at initialization time only if no other
//     instances of the application are running.  This function performs
//     initialization tasks that can be done once for any number of running
//     instances.
//
//     In this case, we initialize a window class by filling out a data
//     structure of type WNDCLASS and calling the Windows RegisterClass()
//     function.  Since all instances of this application use the same
//     window class, we only need to do this when the first instance is
//     initialized.
//

BOOL InitApplication(HINSTANCE hInstance)
{
    WNDCLASS  wc;

    // Fill in window class structure with parameters that describe the
    // main window.
```

```
    wc.style          = CS_HREDRAW | CS_VREDRAW; // Class style(s).
    wc.lpfnWndProc    = (WNDPROC)WndProc;         // Window Procedure
    wc.cbClsExtra     = 0;                         // No per-class extra data.
    wc.cbWndExtra     = 0;                         // No per-window extra data.
    wc.hInstance      = hInstance;                 // Owner of this class
    wc.hIcon          = LoadIcon (hInstance, szAppName);// Icon name from .RC
    wc.hCursor        = LoadCursor(NULL, IDC_ARROW); // Cursor
    wc.hbrBackground  = (HBRUSH)(COLOR_WINDOW+1);// Default color
    wc.lpszMenuName   = szAppName;                 // Menu name from .RC
    wc.lpszClassName  = szAppName;                 // Name to register as


    // Register the window class and return success/failure code.
    return (RegisterClass(&wc));
}


//
//    FUNCTION:  InitInstance(HINSTANCE, int)
//
//    PURPOSE:  Saves instance handle and creates main window
//
//    COMMENTS:
//
//      This function is called at initialization time for every instance of
//      this application.  This function performs initialization tasks that
//      cannot be shared by multiple instances.
//
//      In this case, we save the instance handle in a static variable and
//      create and display the main program window.
//


BOOL InitInstance(
        HINSTANCE      hInstance,
        int            nCmdShow
        )
{

    // Save the instance handle in static variable, which will be used in
    // many subsequence calls from this application to Windows.

    hInst = hInstance; // Store instance handle in our global variable

    // Create a main window for this application instance.
    ghWnd = CreateWindow(
        szAppName,         // See RegisterClass() call.
        szTitle,            // Text for window title bar.
```

LISTING 11.14 CONTINUED

```
        WS_OVERLAPPEDWINDOW,// Window style.
        CW_USEDEFAULT, 0, CW_USEDEFAULT, 0,// Use default positioning
        NULL,                  // Overlapped windows have no parent.
        NULL,                  // Use the window class menu.
        hInstance,          // This instance owns this window.
        NULL                   // We don't use any data in our WM_CREATE
        );

    // If window could not be created, return "failure"
    if (!ghWnd) {
        return (FALSE);
    }


//************** NEW CODE START *********

    InitCommonControls();  // This MUST be called once per instance
                           // to register the common controls

//************** NEW CODE END *********

    // Make the window visible; update its client area; and return "success"
    ShowWindow(ghWnd, nCmdShow); // Show the window
    UpdateWindow(ghWnd);         // Sends WM_PAINT message

    return (TRUE);               // We succeeded...

}


//
//   FUNCTION: WndProc(HWND, UINT, WPARAM, LPARAM)
//
//   PURPOSE:  Processes messages
//
//   MESSAGES:
//
//      WM_COMMAND    - application menu (About dialog box)
//      WM_DESTROY    - destroy window
//
//   COMMENTS:
//
//      To process the IDM_ABOUT message, call MakeProcInstance() to get the
```

```
//      current instance address of the About() function.  Then call Dialog
//      box which will create the box according to the information in your
//      generic.rc file and turn control over to the About() function.  When
//      it returns, free the instance address.
//

LRESULT CALLBACK WndProc(
     HWND hWnd,          // window handle
     UINT message,       // type of message
     WPARAM uParam,      // additional information
     LPARAM lParam       // additional information
     )
{
   FARPROC lpProcAbout;  // pointer to the "About" function
   int wmId, wmEvent;
   HDC hDC;
   PAINTSTRUCT ps;
   RECT rc;
   HBRUSH hBrush;
   int  x, y;

   switch (message) {

//************** NEW CODE START *********

     case WM_PAINT:

        // Get the client area size
        GetClientRect ( hWnd, &rc );

        // Get a DC to paint to
        hDC = BeginPaint ( hWnd, &ps );

        // Use ExtTextOut as a fast way to fill the rect with color
        SetBkColor ( hDC, crColorWindow);
        ExtTextOut ( hDC, 0, 0, ETO_OPAQUE, &rc, NULL, 0, NULL );

        // Draw the pattern
        switch (iPattern)
          {
          case IDD_CIRCLES:

             // Hollow circles
             hBrush = SelectObject ( hDC, GetStockObject ( NULL_BRUSH ));
```

LISTING 11.14 CONTINUED

```
                // Basic loop to draw circles
                for ( x = 0; x < ((rc.right+31)/32); x++ )
                  for ( y = 0; y < ((rc.bottom+31)/32); y++ )
                    {
                    Ellipse ( hDC, x*32, y*32, (x+1)*32, (y+1)*32 );
                    }

                // Miss Manners sez clean up
                SelectObject ( hDC, hBrush );
                break;

            case IDD_SQUARES:

                // Hollow squares
                hBrush = SelectObject ( hDC, GetStockObject ( NULL_BRUSH ));

                // Basic loop to draw squares
                for ( x = 0; x < ((rc.right+31)/32); x++ )
                  for ( y = 0; y < ((rc.bottom+31)/32); y++ )
                    {
                    Rectangle ( hDC, x*32, y*32, (x+1)*32, (y+1)*32 );
                    }

                // Get rid of that evidence
                SelectObject ( hDC, hBrush );
                break;

            }

        // Release the DC
        EndPaint ( hWnd, &ps );
        break;

    case WM_MYCHANGESETTINGS:

        // This message is sent by the property sheet page
        // for color and pattern. If the user clicks the
        // Apply button, the associated dialog procedure for
        // that page sends the WM_MYCHANGESETTINGS message here
        // to instantly update the client area.

        switch ( uParam )
```

```
            {
            case IDD_RED:   crColorWindow = RGB ( 255,    0,    0 ); break;
            case IDD_GREEN: crColorWindow = RGB (   0, 255,    0 ); break;
            case IDD_BLUE:  crColorWindow = RGB (   0,    0, 255 ); break;
            case IDD_CIRCLES:
            case IDD_SQUARES:
            case IDD_NONE:  iPattern = uParam; break;
            }


            // Force the repaint
            InvalidateRect ( hWnd, NULL, FALSE );
            break;


//************** NEW CODE END *********

        case WM_COMMAND:  // message: command from application menu

            // Message packing of uParam and lParam have changed for Win32,
            // let us handle the differences in a conditional compilation:
            #if defined (_WIN32)
                wmId    = LOWORD(uParam);
                    wmEvent = HIWORD(uParam);
            #else
                wmId    = uParam;
                wmEvent = HIWORD(lParam);
            #endif

            switch (wmId) {
                case IDM_ABOUT:
                    lpProcAbout = MakeProcInstance((FARPROC)About, hInst);

                    DialogBox(hInst,            // current instance
                        "AboutBox",             // dlg resource to use
                        hWnd,                   // parent handle
                        (DLGPROC)lpProcAbout);  // About() instance address
                    FreeProcInstance(lpProcAbout);
                    break;
                case IDM_EXIT:
                    DestroyWindow (hWnd);
                    break;

                case IDM_HELPCONTENTS:
                    if (!WinHelp (hWnd, "GENERIC.HLP", HELP_KEY,
                                (DWORD)(LPSTR)"CONTENTS")) {
                        MessageBox (GetFocus(),
```

LISTING 11.14 CONTINUED

```
                    "Unable to activate help",
                    szAppName, MB_SYSTEMMODAL|MB_OK|MB_ICONHAND);

        }
        break;

    case IDM_HELPSEARCH:
        if (!WinHelp(hWnd, "GENERIC.HLP", HELP_PARTIALKEY,
                    (DWORD)(LPSTR)"")) {
            MessageBox (GetFocus(),
                "Unable to activate help",
                szAppName, MB_SYSTEMMODAL|MB_OK|MB_ICONHAND);
        }
        break;

    case IDM_HELPHELP:
        if(!WinHelp(hWnd, (LPSTR)NULL, HELP_HELPONHELP, 0)) {
            MessageBox (GetFocus(),
                "Unable to activate help",
                szAppName, MB_SYSTEMMODAL|MB_OK|MB_ICONHAND);
        }
        break;

//************** NEW CODE START *********

        // Call the three test functions

    case IDM_PREPLANNED:

        PrePlannedPropertySheet(hWnd);
        break;

    case IDM_DYNAMIC:

        DynamicPropertySheet(hWnd);
        break;

    case IDM_SINGLEPROC:
        SingleProcPropertySheet(hWnd);
        break;

//************** NEW CODE END *********
```

```
            // Here are all the other possible menu options,
            // all of these are currently disabled:
             case IDM_NEW:
            case IDM_OPEN:
            case IDM_SAVE:
            case IDM_SAVEAS:
            case IDM_UNDO:
            case IDM_CUT:
            case IDM_COPY:
            case IDM_PASTE:
            case IDM_LINK:
            case IDM_LINKS:

            default:
                return (DefWindowProc(hWnd, message, uParam, lParam));
        }
        break;

    case WM_DESTROY:  // message: window being destroyed

        PostQuitMessage(0);
        break;

    default:            // Passes it on if unproccessed
        return (DefWindowProc(hWnd, message, uParam, lParam));
    }
    return (0);
}


//
//   FUNCTION: CenterWindow (HWND, HWND)
//
//   PURPOSE:  Center one window over another
//
//   COMMENTS:
//
//      Dialog boxes take on the screen position that they were designed
//      at, which is not always appropriate. Centering the dialog over a
//      particular window usually results in a better position.
//

BOOL CenterWindow (HWND hwndChild, HWND hwndParent)
{
    RECT    rChild, rParent;
    int     wChild, hChild, wParent, hParent;
    int     wScreen, hScreen, xNew, yNew;
```

LISTING 11.14 CONTINUED

```
    HDC     hdc;

    // Get the Height and Width of the child window
    GetWindowRect (hwndChild, &rChild);
    wChild = rChild.right - rChild.left;
    hChild = rChild.bottom - rChild.top;

    // Get the Height and Width of the parent window
    GetWindowRect (hwndParent, &rParent);
    wParent = rParent.right - rParent.left;
    hParent = rParent.bottom - rParent.top;

    // Get the display limits
    hdc = GetDC (hwndChild);
    wScreen = GetDeviceCaps (hdc, HORZRES);
    hScreen = GetDeviceCaps (hdc, VERTRES);
    ReleaseDC (hwndChild, hdc);

    // Calculate new X position, then adjust for screen
    xNew = rParent.left + ((wParent - wChild) /2);
    if (xNew < 0) {
       xNew = 0;
    }
    else if ((xNew+wChild) > wScreen) {
       xNew = wScreen - wChild;
    }

    // Calculate new Y position, then adjust for screen
    yNew = rParent.top  + ((hParent - hChild) /2);
    if (yNew < 0) {
       yNew = 0;
    }
    else if ((yNew+hChild) > hScreen) {
       yNew = hScreen - hChild;
    }

    // Set it, and return
    return SetWindowPos (hwndChild, NULL,
       xNew, yNew, 0, 0, SWP_NOSIZE | SWP_NOZORDER);
}

//
```

```
//    FUNCTION: About(HWND, UINT, WPARAM, LPARAM)
//
//    PURPOSE:  Processes messages for "About" dialog box
//
//    MESSAGES:
//
//        WM_INITDIALOG - initialize dialog box
//        WM_COMMAND    - Input received
//
//    COMMENTS:
//
//        Display version information from the version section of the
//        application resource.
//
//        Wait for user to click on "Ok" button, then close the dialog box.
//


LRESULT CALLBACK About(
        HWND hDlg,            // window handle of the dialog box
        UINT message,         // type of message
        WPARAM uParam,        // message-specific information
        LPARAM lParam
        )
{
    static  HFONT hfontDlg;

    switch (message) {
        case WM_INITDIALOG:  // message: initialize dialog box
            // Create a font to use
            hfontDlg = CreateFont(14, 0, 0, 0, 0, 0, 0, 0,
                0, 0, 0, 0,
                VARIABLE_PITCH | FF_SWISS, "");


            // Center the dialog over the application window
            CenterWindow (hDlg, GetWindow (hDlg, GW_OWNER));


            return (TRUE);


        case WM_COMMAND:                            // message: received a command
            if (LOWORD(uParam) == IDOK              // "OK" box selected?
                || LOWORD(uParam) == IDCANCEL) {// System menu close command?
                EndDialog(hDlg, TRUE);              // Exit the dialog
                DeleteObject (hfontDlg);
                return (TRUE);
            }
            break;
```

LISTING **11.14** CONTINUED

```
    }
    return (FALSE); // Didn't process the message

    lParam; // This will prevent 'unused formal parameter' warnings
}


//************** NEW CODE START *********

// MyPropSheetPageEnumProc is called by each property sheet
// page receiving the PSM_QUERYSIBLINGS message. In this
// ultra cheezy example, param1 is a pointer to an integer,
// and we simply increment the value pointed to by the
// pointer.

BOOL MyPropSheetPageEnumProc( HWND hDlgPage, WPARAM param1 )
{
  (*((LPINT)param1))++;
  return TRUE;
}


// The SingleProcDialogProc is the dialog procedure for
// both the "Gender" and "Age" pages in the SingleProcPropertySheet
// example function.

LRESULT CALLBACK SingleProcDialogProc(HWND hDlg,
                        UINT uMessage,
                        WPARAM uParam,
                        LPARAM lParam)
{
  static char szName[32]; // Static buffer to hold name between
                          // page transitions. Must be static to
                          // hold contents between PSN_KILLACTIVE
                          // and PSN_SETACTIVE messages.

  switch ( uMessage )
    {
    case WM_INITDIALOG:

      // If this is the first WM_INITDIALOG, page #0 (stored in lParam of
      // the PROPSHEETPAGE structure, then clear the static text
```

```
        if (!((LPCPROPSHEETPAGE)lParam)->lParam) *szName = 0;


        // Cache away the pointer to this pages PROPSHEETPAGE struct so
        // we can tell in the future what page we are in if we desire.

        SetWindowLong ( hDlg, DWL_USER, (LONG)lParam );
        break;

    case WM_NOTIFY:

      switch (((LPNMHDR)lParam)->code)
        {
        // When a page loses focus, store away the contents of the
        // edit control into the static variable.

        case PSN_KILLACTIVE:

          SetWindowLong ( hDlg, DWL_MSGRESULT, 0 );
          GetDlgItemText ( hDlg, IDD_NAME, szName, sizeof(szName));
          return TRUE;


        // When a page gains focus, set the contents of the
        // edit control from the static variable.

        case PSN_SETACTIVE:

          SetWindowLong ( hDlg, DWL_MSGRESULT, 0 );
          SetDlgItemText ( hDlg, IDD_NAME, szName);
          return TRUE;


        default:

          return FALSE;
        }
      break;

    default:

      break;
    }
    return FALSE;
}
```

LISTING 11.14 CONTINUED

```
// The PatternPageDialogProc is the dialog procedure for
// the "Pattern" pages in the PrePlannedPropertySheet and
// DynamicPropertySheet sample functions.

LRESULT CALLBACK PatternPageDialogProc(HWND hDlg,
                                       UINT uMessage,
                                       WPARAM uParam,
                                       LPARAM lParam)
{
    int wmId, wmEvent;

    switch ( uMessage )
     {
     // This is our Poor Man's enum child pages procedure.
     // If we receive this message, call the MyPropSheetPageEnumProc
     // function.

     case PSM_QUERYSIBLINGS:

       return (!MyPropSheetPageEnumProc( hDlg, uParam ));

     case WM_NOTIFY:

       switch ((((LPNMHDR)lParam)->code)
         {
         case PSN_APPLY: // User pressed the Apply button

           // Send the appropriate WM_MYCHANGESETTINGS message
           // back to the top level main window.

           if (IsDlgButtonChecked(hDlg, IDD_NONE))
             SendMessage (ghWnd, WM_MYCHANGESETTINGS, IDD_NONE, OL );
           if (IsDlgButtonChecked(hDlg, IDD_CIRCLES))
             SendMessage (ghWnd, WM_MYCHANGESETTINGS, IDD_CIRCLES, OL );
           if (IsDlgButtonChecked(hDlg, IDD_SQUARES))
             SendMessage (ghWnd, WM_MYCHANGESETTINGS, IDD_SQUARES, OL );
           return TRUE;

         default:

           return FALSE;
```

```
         }
      break;

   case WM_COMMAND:

      // Message packing of uParam and lParam have changed for Win32,
      // let us handle the differences in a conditional compilation:
      #if defined (_WIN32)
         wmId    = LOWORD(uParam);
         wmEvent = HIWORD(uParam);
      #else
         wmId    = uParam;
         wmEvent = HIWORD(lParam);
      #endif
      switch (wmEvent)
        {
        case BN_CLICKED:

           // If the user clicks on a radio button, enable
           // the Apply button.

           PropSheet_Changed(GetParent(hDlg), hDlg);
           break;
        }
      break;

   default:

      break;
   }
  return FALSE;
}


// The ColorPageDialogProc is the dialog procedure for
// the "Pattern" pages in the PrePlannedPropertySheet and
// DynamicPropertySheet sample functions.

LRESULT CALLBACK ColorPageDialogProc(HWND hDlg,
                           UINT uMessage,
                           WPARAM uParam,
                           LPARAM lParam)
{
   int wmId, wmEvent;
   int iCount;
```

LISTING 11.14 CONTINUED

```
switch ( uMessage )
 {
 // This is our Poor Man's enum child pages procedure.
 // If we receive this message, call the MyPropSheetPageEnumProc
 // function.

 case PSM_QUERYSIBLINGS:

   return (!MyPropSheetPageEnumProc( hDlg, uParam ));

 case WM_NOTIFY:

   switch (((LPNMHDR)lParam)->code)
     {
     case PSN_APPLY: // User pressed the Apply button

       // Send the appropriate WM_MYCHANGESETTINGS message
       // back to the top level main window.

       if (IsDlgButtonChecked(hDlg, IDD_RED))
         SendMessage (ghWnd, WM_MYCHANGESETTINGS, IDD_RED, OL );
       if (IsDlgButtonChecked(hDlg, IDD_GREEN))
         SendMessage (ghWnd, WM_MYCHANGESETTINGS, IDD_GREEN, OL );
       if (IsDlgButtonChecked(hDlg, IDD_BLUE))
         SendMessage (ghWnd, WM_MYCHANGESETTINGS, IDD_BLUE, OL );
       return TRUE;


     default:

       return FALSE;
     }
   break;


 case WM_COMMAND:

   // Message packing of uParam and lParam have changed for Win32,
   // let us handle the differences in a conditional compilation:
   #if defined (_WIN32)
      wmId    = LOWORD(uParam);
      wmEvent = HIWORD(uParam);
   #else
```

```
    wmId     = uParam;
    wmEvent = HIWORD(lParam);
#endif
switch (wmEvent)
   {
   case BN_CLICKED:

     switch ( wmId )
        {
        case IDD_SOMEBUTTON: // Add a new page if allowed

           // First, let's count the number of buttons

           // Reset counter
           iCount = 0;

           // Invoke the poor man's version of enumerating pages
           PropSheet_QuerySiblings ( GetParent(hDlg), (WPARAM)(&iCount), 0 );

           // Only add a page if we have less than two pages
           if ( iCount < 2 )
              {
              HPROPSHEETPAGE hPage;
              PROPSHEETPAGE psp;

              // Fill out the "Pattern" page structure
              psp.dwSize     = sizeof(PROPSHEETPAGE);
              psp.dwFlags    = PSP_USETITLE;
              psp.hInstance  = hInst;
              psp.pszTemplate = "PATTERNPAGE";
              psp.pfnDlgProc = PatternPageDialogProc;
              psp.pszTitle   = "Pattern";
              psp.lParam     = 0;

              // Create a page, get back a handle
              hPage = CreatePropertySheetPage ( &psp );

              // Add the page to the property sheet
              PropSheet_AddPage ( GetParent (hDlg), hPage);

              // Select that new page (this insures the dialog
              // window for that page is created, and the
              // Poor Man's enum pages idea from above works.
              // Since this is the second page, it has the index
```

LISTING 11.14 CONTINUED

```
                        // of 1.
                        PropSheet_SetCurSel ( GetParent(hDlg), NULL, 1 );
                        }
                    else
                        {
                        // Kibosh!
                        MessageBox ( hDlg, "Is this trip really necessary?", "MSJ",
                                MB_OK );
                        }
                    break;

                default: // Must be one of the radio buttons

                    // If the user clicks on a radio button, enable
                    // the Apply button.

                    PropSheet_Changed(GetParent(hDlg), hDlg);
                    break;
                } /* end switch wmID */
            break;
        } /* end switch wmEvent */
      break;

    default:

      break;
    } /* end switch uMessage */
  return FALSE;
}


// The PrePlannedPropertySheet sample function
// creates a property sheet with two pages, the
// "Color" page and the "Pattern" page. Each page
// has it's own dialog procedure and dialog template.

VOID PrePlannedPropertySheet(HWND hWndParent)
{
    PROPSHEETPAGE psp[2];
    PROPSHEETHEADER psh;

    // First, initialize the array of pages to
```

```
    // indicate each page.

    psp[0].dwSize       = sizeof(PROPSHEETPAGE);
    psp[0].dwFlags      = PSP_USETITLE;
    psp[0].hInstance    = hInst;
    psp[0].pszTemplate  = "COLORPAGE";
    psp[0].pfnDlgProc   = ColorPageDialogProc;
    psp[0].pszTitle     = "Color";
    psp[0].lParam       = 0;


    psp[1].dwSize       = sizeof(PROPSHEETPAGE);
    psp[1].dwFlags      = PSP_USETITLE;
    psp[1].hInstance    = hInst;
    psp[1].pszTemplate  = "PATTERNPAGE";
    psp[1].pfnDlgProc   = PatternPageDialogProc;
    psp[1].pszTitle     = "Pattern";
    psp[1].lParam       = 0;


    // Now, initialize the property sheet structure
    // to use these two pages and parent it to the
    // main window.

    psh.dwSize          = sizeof(PROPSHEETHEADER);
    psh.dwFlags         = PSH_PROPSHEETPAGE | PSH_PROPTITLE;
    psh.hwndParent      = hWndParent;
    psh.hInstance       = hInst;
    psh.pszIcon         = NULL;
    psh.pszCaption      = (LPSTR)"Client Area";
    psh.nPages          = sizeof(psp) / sizeof(PROPSHEETPAGE);
    psh.ppsp            = (LPCPROPSHEETPAGE) &psp;


    // And finally, display the property sheet.

    PropertySheet(&psh);

    return;
}


// The DynamicPropertySheet is exactly like the
// PrePlannedPropertySheet function, except that it
// only adds the first page, and uses a slightly different
// template for that first page (this template has an
// "Add Page" button on it.

VOID DynamicPropertySheet(HWND hWndParent)
```

LISTING 11.14 CONTINUED

```
{
    // Still use an array because this is cut & paste code
    PROPSHEETPAGE    psp[2];
    PROPSHEETHEADER psh;

    // First, initialize the (small) array of pages to
    // indicate each page.

    psp[0].dwSize      = sizeof(PROPSHEETPAGE);
    psp[0].dwFlags     = PSP_USETITLE;
    psp[0].hInstance   = hInst;
    psp[0].pszTemplate = "COLORPAGEDYNO";
    psp[0].pfnDlgProc  = ColorPageDialogProc;
    psp[0].pszTitle    = "Color";
    psp[0].lParam      = 0;

    // Now, initialize the property sheet structure
    // to use the page and parent it to the
    // main window.

    psh.dwSize         = sizeof(PROPSHEETHEADER);
    psh.dwFlags        = PSH_PROPSHEETPAGE | PSH_PROPTITLE;
    psh.hwndParent     = hWndParent;
    psh.hInstance      = hInst;
    psh.pszIcon        = NULL;
    psh.pszCaption     = (LPSTR)"Client Area";
    psh.nPages         = sizeof(psp) / sizeof(PROPSHEETPAGE);
    psh.ppsp           = (LPCPROPSHEETPAGE) &psp;

    // And finally, display the property sheet.

    PropertySheet(&psh);

    return;
}


// The SingleProcPropertySheet sample function
// creates a property sheet with two pages, the
// "Gender" page and the "Age" page. Each page
// uses the same dialog procedure, but each page
// uses a different dialog template. Controls that
// are shred between pages (such as the edit control
```

```
// in this sample) are placed at the same coordinates, and
// use the same ID. In addition, the lParam field of
// the PROPSHEETPAGE structure is used to indicate the page.
// The dialog procedure can access the instance-specific
// PROPSHEETPAGE structure for each page, and the lParam
// can then be referenced.

VOID SingleProcPropertySheet(HWND hWndParent)
{
    PROPSHEETPAGE psp[2];
    PROPSHEETHEADER psh;

    // First, initialize the array of pages to
    // indicate each page.

    psp[0].dwSize      = sizeof(PROPSHEETPAGE);
    psp[0].dwFlags     = PSP_USETITLE;
    psp[0].hInstance   = hInst;
    psp[0].pszTemplate = "PAGE0SINGLEPROC";
    psp[0].pfnDlgProc  = SingleProcDialogProc;
    psp[0].pszTitle    = "Gender";
    psp[0].lParam      = 0; // Page number


    psp[1].dwSize      = sizeof(PROPSHEETPAGE);
    psp[1].dwFlags     = PSP_USETITLE;
    psp[1].hInstance   = hInst;
    psp[1].pszTemplate = "PAGE1SINGLEPROC";
    psp[1].pfnDlgProc  = SingleProcDialogProc;
    psp[1].pszTitle    = "Age";
    psp[1].lParam      = 1; // Page number


    // Now, initialize the property sheet structure
    // to use these two pages and parent it to the
    // main window.

    psh.dwSize      = sizeof(PROPSHEETHEADER);
    psh.dwFlags     = PSH_PROPSHEETPAGE | PSH_PROPTITLE;
    psh.hwndParent  = hWndParent;
    psh.hInstance   = hInst;
    psh.pszIcon     = NULL;
    psh.pszCaption  = (LPSTR)"Carbon Based Unit";
    psh.nPages      = sizeof(psp) / sizeof(PROPSHEETPAGE);
    psh.ppsp        = (LPCPROPSHEETPAGE) &psp;


    // And finally, display the property sheet.
```

LISTING 11.14 CONTINUED

```
    PropertySheet(&psh);

    return;
}


//************** NEW CODE END *********
```

As with all other programs in this series, you call the **InitCommon Controls** API inside the **InitInstance** function. This registers the common controls, which in this case allows access to the property sheet control.

The **WndProc** function has been modified to accept the new menu choices, as well as paint its client area with a color and a pattern, depending on the global variables **crColorWindow** and **iPattern**.

The first sample function, **PrePlannedPropertySheet**, sets up an array of two PROPSHEETPAGE structures and creates the property sheet (see Figure 11.55). The second sample function, **DynamicPropertySheet**, creates one page on a property sheet (color) and also uses a different dialog template for the color page (the new template has an Add Page button on it).

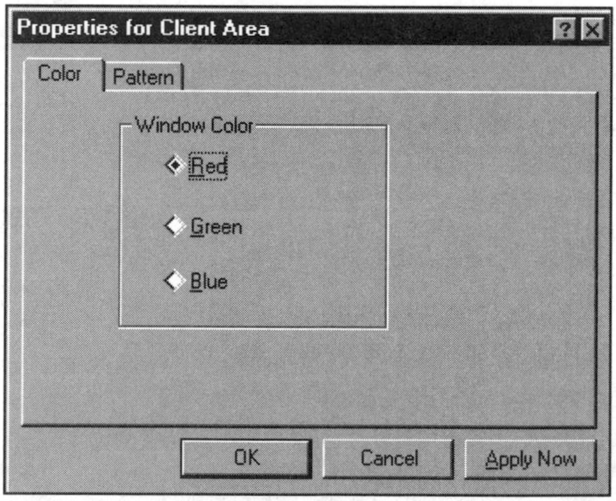

FIGURE 11.55 A PRE-PLANNED PROPERTY SHEET

The sample functions are used by two dialog procedures: **ColorPageDialogProc** and **PatternPageDialogProc**. **ColorPageDialogProc** looks for three events: receiving a PSM_QUERYSIBLINGS message, receiving a PSN_APPLY notification message, and receiving a WM_COMMAND:IDD_ _SOMEBUTTON message. The code for the PSM_QUERYSIBLINGS calls the **MyPropSheetEnumPageProc**, passing only the first parameter (which is the pointer to the iCount variable, described later). This code is almost exactly like the code discussed earlier in the "Enumerating Property Sheets" section of this Goodie.

The code for the PSN_APPLY notification takes a look and sees which radio button is checked, and sends the appropriate user-defined WM_ MYCHANGESETTINGS message back to the main parent window (which will then repaint itself to reflect the changes).

The WM_COMMAND code in **ColorPageDialogProc** does one of two things. If the user clicks the IDD_SOMEBUTTON button, then you need to count the pages using the **PropSheet_QuerySiblings** macro, which passes the pointer to the **iCount** variable as **param1** (**param1** is passed in via **uParam** in the PSM_QUERYSIBLINGS message). Provided the user has not already added the new page, a new PROPSHEETPAGE structure is filled out and a handle to a page is created with the **CreatePropertySheetPage** API. This page is then added to the property sheet and activated. This activation is important: by activating this page with the **PropSheet_SetCurSel** macro, the page's dialog window is actually created. This will allow subsequent calls to the **PropSheet_QuerySiblings** macro to hit the new page.

If the WM_COMMAND message is not for IDD_SOMEBUTTON, then you assume the user clicked on one of the radio buttons and you call the **Prop-Sheet_Changed(PSM_CHANGED)** macro to enable the Apply Now button.

The **PatternPageDialogProc** is exactly like the **ColorPageDialogProc**, except that it has the different radio button IDs for the patterns and it does not have code to look for the IDD_SOMEBUTTON button.

Now let's look at the third sample function, in PROPC's GENERIC.C **SingleProcPropertySheet**. This, like the first function, creates a predefined property sheet with two pages. In this case, however, both pages share the same dialog procedure, **SingleProcDialogProc**. And the dialog templates both have the IDD_NAME edit control in the exact same location, using the same ID. I have also used the **lParam** field of the PROPSHEETPAGE structure to identify the different pages, using 0 for the first page and 1 for the second.

The WM_INITDIALOG code for the **SingleProcDialogProc** code does two things. First, it checks to see if the page being created is the first page. If so, the static buffer that holds text is cleared. The reason for this check is that the second page's dialog won't be created until the user selects the tab (or unless the application code "preloaded" all the pages briefly as discussed earlier). Because of this behavior, you will get the second page's WM_INIT-DIALOG message after the first page calls **GetDlgItemText** in response to the PSN_KILLACTIVE notification. This then causes the contents of the static variable to be erased between pages. (Speaking of PSN_KILLACTIVE, the remainder of the **SingleProcDialogProc** function utilizes the methods just described to transfer the text between the two edit controls on each page.)

Property Sheets in MFC

Okay, you should now have enough information about the common controls implementation of property sheets to keep you out of the sunlight for a little while. However, Visual C++ 2.0's MFC 3.0 prerelease for the Windows 95 beta contains a very elegant implementation of property sheets as well. Application programmers who are writing their programs using the application framework will not have to wait for their turn.

In fact, the implementation of MFC's property sheets pretty much maps directly to the common controls implementation. The advantage of using the MFC implementation is that you can slap together a property sheet in less time than it would take to read the above documentation, and also that you have significantly more flexibility.

The property sheets in MFC have no code in common with the common controls DLL. In fact, in keeping with the tradition of C++, the complete source code can be found in the MFC\SRC directory, in the DLGPROP.CPP file.

So keep in mind all the vernacular from above, and I'll take you on a whirlwind tour of how you would implement a property sheet in MFC and then fly into a tiny sample. First, you need to fire up the resource editor of

Visual C++ 2.0 and create a dialog template or two. Make sure all the templates are the same size, use WS_CHILD, and have the Thin border (so far this is exactly like the SDK implementation). Next, turn on the titlebar and disabled check boxes (this step is a little different than the SDK method since the MFC classes rely on these styles to manage the pages). Finally, set the caption text to what you want to see in the tab, just as you would for the SDK implementation.

Okay, now it is time to create the classes for the dialog template(s). Using ClassWizard, create a new class and derive it from **CPropertyPage** instead of **CDialog**. Create the class and its variables in the same way you would for a regular dialog (after all, a property page really is just a dialog). Say for this example that you have created two classes, **CMSJPage** and **CTabloidPage**; each would have its own dialog template.

Now, create a property sheet by declaring an object of the type **CPropertySheet**. The only required parameter to fill in is the caption (see the MFC documentation for the optional parameters):

```
CPropertySheet MyPropSheet("MSJ MFC OLE CHZ GUI TLA!");
                              // Acronym Overload!
```

Before bringing up the property sheet, you need to create a page for each of your classes:

```
CMSJPage MyMSJPage;
CTabloidPage MyTabloidPage;
```

Add these new pages to the **MyPropSheet** object:

```
MyPropSheet.AddPage(&MyMSJPage);
MyPropSheet.AddPage(&MyTabloidPage);
```

And finally, bring up this property sheet with the **DoModal** member function:

```
ReturnValue = MyPropSheet.DoModal();
```

Unlike the SDK implementation, you can get a modeless property sheet the same way you make modeless dialogs, by using the **Create** member function instead of the **DoModal** member function. All of the rules you learned for **CDialog** objects apply here.

Just as you would call the **PropSheet_Changed** macro in the SDK to enable the Apply Now button, in MFC you would call the page's **SetModified** member function:

```
// This code is in a page class
SetModified(TRUE); // Enable the Apply Now button
```

Here is where things get a little different. Unlike the SDK property sheet, you now need to do a little work to handle the Apply Now button. You can either override the **CPropertySheet**'s **OnOK** function (which requires you to pass pointers around a bit to get to the information you need), or you can derive a new class from **CPropertySheet**, where you just handle the BN_CLICKED:ID_APPLY_NOW as usual. This can be found in Listing 11.15 in the **CMyPropSheet::OnApplyNow** function in MYPROPSH.CPP. In any case, be sure to call the Page's **SetModified** member function with FALSE to gray out the Apply Now button once you have responded to the user pressing the Apply Now button. My PROPMFC sample program (see Listing 11.15) takes the second approach since this also allows you to change other attributes of the property sheet, such as adding new controls. (To add your own controls to the property sheet, you will need to override the **CPropertySheet::CreateStandardButtons** and **CPropertySheet::RecalcLayout** member functions.)

LISTING 11.15 PROPMFC SAMPLE PROGRAM

```
//*****************************************************
// msjpage.cpp : implementation file
//*****************************************************

#include "stdafx.h"
#include "propmfc.h"
#include "msjpage.h"

#ifdef _DEBUG
#undef THIS_FILE
static char BASED_CODE THIS_FILE[] = __FILE__;
```

```
#endif

/////////////////////////////////////////////////////////////////////////
// CMSJPage property page. Based on the CPropertyPage object

CMSJPage::CMSJPage() : CPropertyPage(CMSJPage::IDD)
{
    //{{AFX_DATA_INIT(CMSJPage)
        // NOTE: the ClassWizard will add member initialization here
    //}}AFX_DATA_INIT
}


void CMSJPage::DoDataExchange(CDataExchange* pDX)
{
    CPropertyPage::DoDataExchange(pDX);
    //{{AFX_DATA_MAP(CMSJPage)
        // NOTE: the ClassWizard will add DDX and DDV calls here
    //}}AFX_DATA_MAP
}


BEGIN_MESSAGE_MAP(CMSJPage, CPropertyPage)
    //{{AFX_MSG_MAP(CMSJPage)
    ON_BN_CLICKED(IDC_CSDK, OnCsdk)
    ON_BN_CLICKED(IDC_MFC, OnMfc)
    ON_BN_CLICKED(IDC_VB, OnVb)
    //}}AFX_MSG_MAP
END_MESSAGE_MAP()


/////////////////////////////////////////////////////////////////////////
// CMSJPage message handlers
//
// For all three of these functions, if the user clicks on of the
// radio buttons on the MSJ Property Sheet Page, we want to set
// the modified state of the page to TRUE, which will enable the
// Apply Now button.

void CMSJPage::OnCsdk()
{
    SetModified(TRUE);


}


void CMSJPage::OnMfc()
{
    SetModified(TRUE);
```

LISTING 11.15 CONTINUED

```
}

void CMSJPage::OnVb()
{
    SetModified(TRUE);
}


//*****************************************************
// mypropsh.cpp : implementation file
//*****************************************************
//
// This is the CMypropSheet object, which is derived from the
// CPropertySheet object. This derived class adds the message
// map ID_APPLY_NOW button entry so that we can do something
// when the user presses the Apply Now button

#include "stdafx.h"
#include "propmfc.h"
#include "mypropsh.h"

#ifdef _DEBUG
#undef THIS_FILE
static char BASED_CODE THIS_FILE[] = __FILE__;
#endif


/////////////////////////////////////////////////////////////////////////////
// CMyPropSheet

CMyPropSheet::CMyPropSheet(LPCSTR pszCaption):CPropertySheet(pszCaption)
{
}

CMyPropSheet::~CMyPropSheet()
{
}

BEGIN_MESSAGE_MAP(CMyPropSheet, CPropertySheet)
    //{{AFX_MSG_MAP(CMyPropSheet)
    ON_COMMAND(ID_APPLY_NOW, OnApplyNow)
    //}}AFX_MSG_MAP
END_MESSAGE_MAP()
```

```
/////////////////////////////////////////////////////////////////////////
// CMyPropSheet message handlers

void CMyPropSheet::OnApplyNow()
{
  // Do something really pedestrian when the user presses
  // the Apply Now button.
  AfxMessageBox("Apply Button Pressed!");

  // Reset that page's modified state back to false
  // to turn off the Apply now button. m_nCurPage is a
  // member variable of the CPropertySheet object, and
  // GetPage is a member function that returns a pointer
  // to the CPropertyPage object.
  GetPage(m_nCurPage)->SetModified(FALSE);
}


//********************************************************
// propmvw.cpp : implementation of the CPropmfcView class
//********************************************************

#include "stdafx.h"
#include "propmfc.h"

#include "propmdoc.h"
#include "propmvw.h"
#include "msjpage.h"
#include "tabloidp.h"
#include "mypropsh.h"

#ifdef _DEBUG
#undef THIS_FILE
static char BASED_CODE THIS_FILE[] = __FILE__;
#endif


/////////////////////////////////////////////////////////////////////////
// CPropmfcView

IMPLEMENT_DYNCREATE(CPropmfcView, CView)

BEGIN_MESSAGE_MAP(CPropmfcView, CView)
    //{{AFX_MSG_MAP(CPropmfcView)
    ON_WM_LBUTTONUP()
    //}}AFX_MSG_MAP
```

LISTING 11.15 CONTINUED

```
    // Standard printing commands
    ON_COMMAND(ID_FILE_PRINT, CView::OnFilePrint)
    ON_COMMAND(ID_FILE_PRINT_PREVIEW, CView::OnFilePrintPreview)
END_MESSAGE_MAP()

/////////////////////////////////////////////////////////////////////////////
// CPropmfcView construction/destruction

CPropmfcView::CPropmfcView()
{
    // TODO: add construction code here

}


CPropmfcView::~CPropmfcView()
{
}


/////////////////////////////////////////////////////////////////////////////
// CPropmfcView drawing

void CPropmfcView::OnDraw(CDC* pDC)
{
    CPropmfcDoc* pDoc = GetDocument();
    ASSERT_VALID(pDoc);

    // TODO: add draw code for native data here
}


/////////////////////////////////////////////////////////////////////////////
// CPropmfcView printing

BOOL CPropmfcView::OnPreparePrinting(CPrintInfo* pInfo)
{
    // default preparation
    return DoPreparePrinting(pInfo);
}


void CPropmfcView::OnBeginPrinting(CDC* /*pDC*/, CPrintInfo* /*pInfo*/)
{
    // TODO: add extra initialization before printing
```

```
}

void CPropmfcView::OnEndPrinting(CDC* /*pDC*/, CPrintInfo* /*pInfo*/)
{
    // TODO: add cleanup after printing
}


/////////////////////////////////////////////////////////////////////////
// CPropmfcView diagnostics

#ifdef _DEBUG
void CPropmfcView::AssertValid() const
{
    CView::AssertValid();
}


void CPropmfcView::Dump(CDumpContext& dc) const
{
    CView::Dump(dc);
}


CPropmfcDoc* CPropmfcView::GetDocument() // non-debug version is inline
{
    ASSERT(m_pDocument->IsKindOf(RUNTIME_CLASS(CPropmfcDoc)));
    return (CPropmfcDoc*)m_pDocument;
}
#endif //_DEBUG


/////////////////////////////////////////////////////////////////////////
// CPropmfcView message handlers

void CPropmfcView::OnLButtonUp(UINT nFlags, CPoint point)
{
    // Declare a CMyPropSheet object, which is derived from the
    // CPropertySheet object. Use "MSJ Sample" as the title.
    CMyPropSheet    MyPropSheet("MSJ Sample");

    // Declare the two pages, these pages are derived from the
    // CPropertyPage object.
    CMSJPage        MyMSJPage;
    CTabloidPage    MyTabloidPage;

    // Add the two pages to the property sheet
    MyPropSheet.AddPage(&MyMSJPage);
```

LISTING 11.15 CONTINUED

```
    MyPropSheet.AddPage(&MyTabloidPage);

    // Presto-matic! Bring up the property sheet just like a modal dialog
    MyPropSheet.DoModal();
}


//*******************************************************
// tabloidp.cpp : implementation file
//*******************************************************


#include "stdafx.h"
#include "propmfc.h"
#include "tabloidp.h"


#ifdef _DEBUG
#undef THIS_FILE
static char BASED_CODE THIS_FILE[] = __FILE__;
#endif


/////////////////////////////////////////////////////////////////////////////
// CTabloidPage property page

CTabloidPage::CTabloidPage() : CPropertyPage(CTabloidPage::IDD)
{
    //{{AFX_DATA_INIT(CTabloidPage)
        // NOTE: the ClassWizard will add member initialization here
    //}}AFX_DATA_INIT
}


void CTabloidPage::DoDataExchange(CDataExchange* pDX)
{
    CPropertyPage::DoDataExchange(pDX);
    //{{AFX_DATA_MAP(CTabloidPage)
        // NOTE: the ClassWizard will add DDX and DDV calls here
    //}}AFX_DATA_MAP
}


BEGIN_MESSAGE_MAP(CTabloidPage, CPropertyPage)
    //{{AFX_MSG_MAP(CTabloidPage)
    ON_BN_CLICKED(IDC_BRONCOS, OnBroncos)
    ON_BN_CLICKED(IDC_ICESKATE, OnIceskate)
    ON_BN_CLICKED(IDC_CANING, OnCaning)
```

490

```
    //}}AFX_MSG_MAP
END_MESSAGE_MAP()


/////////////////////////////////////////////////////////////////////////
// CTabloidPage message handlers
//
// For all of the radio buttons on the CTabliodPage, set the
// modified state of the page to TRUE, causing the Apply Now
// button to spring to life.

void CTabloidPage::OnBroncos()
{
    SetModified(TRUE);
}


void CTabloidPage::OnIceskate()
{
    SetModified(TRUE);
}


void CTabloidPage::OnCaning()
{
    SetModified(TRUE);
}
```

The MFC Sample: PROPMFC

Okay, that was a very short dissertation on the MFC implementation of property sheets. Now let's take a second look at my tiny sample program, PROPMFC. The first thing I did was use AppWizard to create the most blasé sample: I just used the defaults. Elapsed time, 30 seconds. Second, I used the resource editor to make the MSJ and Tabloid pages. Elapsed time, 5 minutes. Third, I ran ClassWizard on these new dialogs and created my two new classes. Elapsed time, 1 minute. Next I added an **OnLButtonUp** member function to the View class using ClassWizard so I could bring up my dialog; this took another 30 seconds. It took me at least 2 minutes to edit the **OnLButtonUp** code to look like this:

```
void CPropmfcView::OnLButtonUp(UINT nFlags,
                               CPoint point)
```

```
{
    CPropertySheet    MyPropSheet("MSJ Sample");
    CMSJPage          MyMSJPage;
    CTabloidPage      MyTabloidPage;

    MyPropSheet.AddPage(&MyMSJPage);
    MyPropSheet.AddPage(&MyTabloidPage);

    MyPropSheet.DoModal();
}
```

Another microsecond to compile, and presto! I had property sheets up and kinda working!

In order to make that Apply Now button work, I added some member functions behind the radio buttons in the pages. This was just a simple, ClassWizard exercise to look for the BN_CLICKED notifications. In each of the member functions, I simply called **SetModified** (TRUE) to enable the Apply Now button.

Next I needed to intercept that Apply Now button. I created a new class based on **CPropertySheet** called **CMyPropSheet**, which has the **OnApplyNow** member function. The **OnApplyNow** member function calls the page's **SetModified** member function with FALSE to disable the Apply Now button until the user changes the information. Again, see the MYPROPSH.CPP file for the nitty-gritty details.

There. In less than 20 minutes I was able to make a property sheet, enable the Apply Now button, react to the Apply Now button, and basically have a properly programmed property sheet. The most difficult part was coming up with the tabloid stories.

Writing Wild Wizards Within Windows

The final topic of this series is the wizard control. When you install the second beta release of Windows 95, you will notice that there's a Setup wizard. If you have been using any of Microsoft's application products in the past year or so, you will have seen wizards there too. When I first saw a wizard in Windows 95, I thought, "Hey, that looks just like a property sheet without the tabs!" Well, that's exactly what it is.

If you want to write a wizard, follow the same process as if you were creating a property sheet, with the following differences:

- ❖ Use the PSH_WIZARD style bit in the **dwFlags** field of the PROP-SHEETHEADER.

- ❖ Look for the PSN_WIZBACK, PSN_WIZNEXT, and PSN_WIZFINISH notifications instead of PSN_APPLY.

- ❖ Use the **PropSheet_SetWizButtons(PSM_SETWIZBUTTONS)** macro to tell the property sheet which wizard buttons to enable. The flags are PSWIZB_BACK, PSWIZB_NEXT, and PSWIZB_FINISH. See COMMCTRL.H for the exact declarations.

- ❖ Use the WIZ_CXDLG and WIZ_CYDLG constants in COMMCTRL.H for the sizes of the pages in your wizard. This way you will conform to the New World Order and look like every other cool wizard the user may encounter.

That's it! These are the only programmatic differences between a wizard and a property sheet. Unfortunately, I do not see a **CWizard** class in MFC 3.0, so if you want to write wizards, you will either have to use the SDK or write your own classes in MFC to take advantage of the property sheets in the SDK.

4. The Header Control

The Header control is a horizontal segmented bar that allows the user to change the widths of the segments with the mouse (see Figure 11.56). In almost every case, the Header control is used to allow the user to adjust columns. And, in almost every case of columns, the ListView control (coming next) will suffice. Because of that, I am going to give a more terse than normal discussion about the Header control.

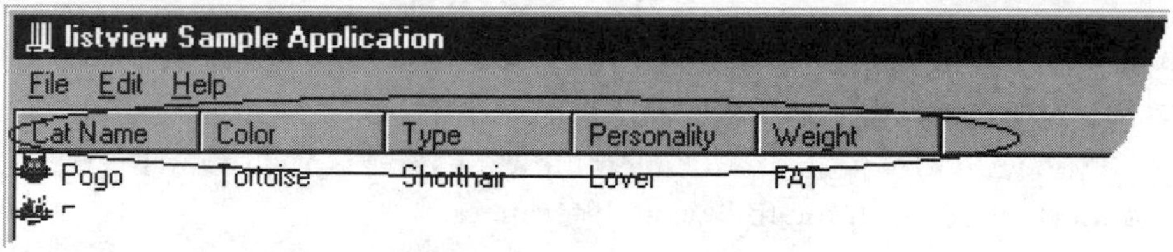

FIGURE 11.56 THE HEADER CONTROL

Creating and Initializing the Header

To create a Header control, use **CreateWindow** with WC_HEADER as the window class. You use the HDS_HORZ style bit (which happens to be 0) to indicate that this header is a horizontal header control. The HDS_BUTTONS style bit allows each segment of the Header control to act as a button—think of how Microsoft Mail lets you sort the mailbox by clicking on its column header bar.

Each segment of a Header control is an "item". Adding items to the header control is achieved by filling out an HD_ITEM structure in Figure 11.57. Once you have filled out this structure, you then use the **Header_InsertItem <HDM_INSERTITEM>** macro to add each item to the header:

```
iIndex = Header_InsertItem(hWndHeader, int iIndex, &hd_item);
```

where the return value indicates the index of where the item actually ended up. If you want to add the item to the end of the Header, simply use an iIndex value greater than or equal to the number of items in the Header. Listing 11.16 is some sample code to create a Header control that has three segments in it.

```
typedef struct _HD_ITEM
  {
  UINT    mask;                 // Indicates which fields matter
                                //    HDI_WIDTH
                                //    HDI_TEXT
                                //    HDI_FORMAT
                                //    HDI_LPARAM
                                //    HDI_BITMAP
  int     cxy;                  // width of item in pixels
  LPSTR   pszText;              // Text for header
  HBITMAP hbm;                  // Bitmap to use (implies HDF_BITMAP, see below)
  int     cchTextMax;           // For GetItem: contains size of buffer
  int     fmt;                  // HDF_* value:
                                //    HDF_LEFT        Left Justified
                                //    HDF_RIGHT       Right Justified
                                //    HDF_CENTER      Centered
                                //    HDF_OWNERDRAW   Ownerdraw
                                //    HDF_STRING      Use psztext field
                                //    HDF_BITMAP      Use hBM field
  LPARAM  lParam;               // App-defined value
  }
HD_ITEM;
```

FIGURE 11.57 THE HD_ITEM STRUCTURE

LISTING 11.16 CREATING A HEADER CONTROL

```
HD_ITEM hdItem;

hWndHD = CreateWindow ( WC_HEADER,        // Class of Header control
                        NULL,             // No text
                        WS_CHILD,         // a child window
                        x, y, dx, dy,     // pos and size
                        hWndParent,       // parent
                        (HMENU)IDD_HEADER, // ID
                        hInstApp,         // Instance
                        NULL);            // No extra goodies
```

LISTING 11.16 CONTINUED

```
// For the first segment, we will use the label "Name",
// left aligned
// Indicate the fields that matter
hdItem.mask     = HDI_WIDTH | HDI_TEXT | HDI_FORMAT;
// Set the width to 120 pixels wide
hdItem.cxy      = 120;
// Indicate the text (in your real code, don't use hard coded
// string constants, see Chapter 1 for reasons why)
hdItem.psztext  = "Name";
// Set the alignment to left
hdItem.fmt      = HDF_LEFT;
// Add the item using the Header_InsertItem macro,
// to position #0
iIndex = Header_InsertItem(hWndHD, 0, &hdItem);

// For our second segment, we will use the same values
// for everything, except we will change the label
// and alignment.
hdItem.psztext  = "Age";
hdItem.fmt      = HDF_RIGHT;
// Insert at segment position #1
iIndex = Header_InsertItem(hWndHD, 1, &hdItem);

// For our third segment, we will use the same values
// from the second segment, except we will change the label.
hdItem.psztext  = "Brain Cell Count";
// Insert at position #2
iIndex = Header_InsertItem(hWndHD, 2, &hdItem);
```

Header Notifications

When the user clicks on the Header control segments, or they resize the Header, there are a number of notifications that are sent to the parent. Figure 11.58 is a table of each notification and what causes it.

Notification (via WM_NOTIFY)	Cause
HDN_ITEMCHANGING	Segment (item) in the Header is getting changed via the Header_SetItem <HDM_SETITEM> macro.
HDN_ITEMCHANGED	Segment in the Header has been changed via the Header_SetItem macro.
HDN_ITEMCLICK	Segment has been clicked by the user (Header must have the HDS_BUTTONS style).
HDN_ITEMDBLCLK	Segment has been double clicked by the user (Header must have the HDS_BUTTONS style).
HDN_DIVIDERDBLCLICK	The divider area between the segments has been double clicked.
HDN_BEGINTRACK	User clicked down on a divider area, which means they are starting to adjust a segment width- this is the equal of WM_LBUTTONDOWN on the Header.
HDN_ENDTRACK	User finished adjusting the width, equal to WM_LBUTTONUP on the Header.
HDN_TRACK	User is currently adjusting the width, equal to WM_MOUSEMOVE on the Header. This is a good place to draw any visual feedback that the header is changing.

FIGURE 11.58 HEADER NOTIFICATIONS

Header Miscellany

In addition to the creation functions and the above notifications, the Header control also allows you to delete and modify the individual segments using the **Header_DeleteItem <HDM_DELETEITEM>** and **Header_SetItem**

<HDM_SETITEM> macros. You can also interrogate the Header item with the **Header_GetItem <HDM_GETITEM>** macro.

What If I Want a Header on a ListBox?

If you want to use the Header control to allow the user to adjust columns in a listbox, then you should really use the ListView control in the "Report View" mode. That way you don't have to do anything with the Header control at all (except indicate your segment labels). Read on to learn about the ListView control.

3. The ListView Control

A Killer Listbox. The ListView control follows many of the same concepts as the TreeView control (Goodie #9) when it comes to adding and removing items. That's nice. But the ListView control differs significantly in appearance. Unlike the TreeView, the ListView supports four different "Views". Each view is completely different from the others.

The first view is called the Report View. This view most closely resembles a listbox with column support and a nice column header bar (Goodie #4) above the items. The user can adjust the widths of each column using the Header bar, and the program can manage the list in a very similar fashion as the TreeView.

The second view is called the Icon View. This view most closely resembles a group from that old Windows Program Manager. Full size icons are displayed with a caption underneath them. The icons can either "snap" to a grid, or they can float free form.

The third view is called the Small Icon view. This view is like the Icon View except the icons are those little dinky 16x16 icons. To see this view, choose "Small Icons" from the right hand side of the Explorer.

The final view is called the List View. This view is like a normal listbox that optionally uses an image list. The default configuration for the right hand side of the Explorer is the List View.

See Figures 11.59a through 11.59d for each of the four views in our sample program LISTVIEW that I will explain shortly.

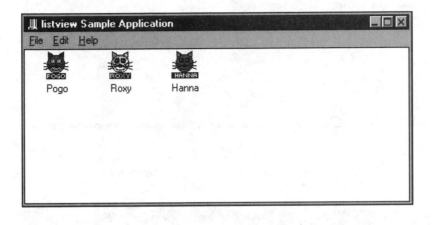

FIGURE 11.59A THE ICON VIEW OF A LISTVIEW

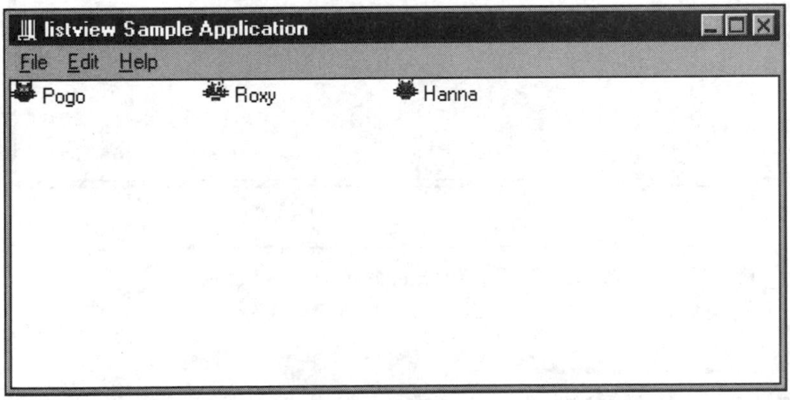

FIGURE 11.59B THE SMALL ICON VIEW OF A LISTVIEW

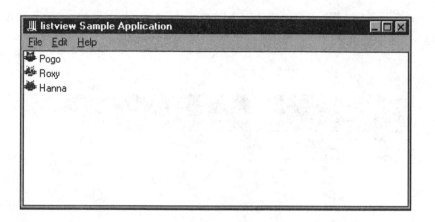

FIGURE 11.59C THE LIST VIEW OF A LISTVIEW

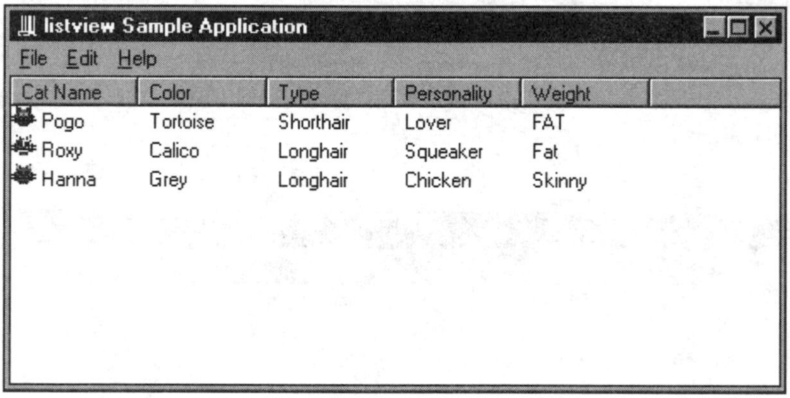

FIGURE 11.59D THE REPORT VIEW OF A LISTVIEW

Items in a ListView

Each item in a ListView control occupies one "slot" in the view. This slot would be an icon in one of the icon views, or it would be a row of information in the report and the list views. Each item, however, can have multiple pieces of text associated with it. There are two types of text pieces associated with each item: The "Label" and the "SubLabels". The Label of an item is the primary tag of text to identify the item. If the view is Icon or Small Icon, this is the only information you see painted along with the icon. If you are using the Report View or the List View, the subitems are displayed as additional columns.

Adding an item into the listview is a process that involves one mandatory step, and an indefinite number of optional additional steps. The first mandatory step involves defining the main item, which indicates its Image List images (just like the TreeView), the Label text, and an additional parameter (for things like a this pointer). The optional addition steps involve adding SubLabels to the item. For example, if you wanted to mimic the right hand side of the Explorer, you would for each file do the following steps:

1. Create an item, which would include the file's icons, and filename.

2. Add a subitem to that item to indicate the file's extension

3. Add another subitem to that item to indicate the file's date/time/ size information

When using the Icon View or the Small Icon View, you would only see the icon and the filename. When using the Report View or the List View, you would also see the additional giblets of information concerning the file extension and date/time/size information.

So, let's define a nice array of stuff to display. We want to create a table of my cats (who else?) like Figure 11.60. So, let's be naughty and hard-code this as in Figure 11.61. Now we have this array of stuff. Now, if we wanted to add these items to the ListView, we follow these steps:

1. Declare an LV_ITEM structure (see Figure 11.62) and fill out the parameters.

2. Use the ListView_InsertItem <LVM_INSERTITEM> macro to insert that item.

3. Use the ListView_SetItemText <LVM_SETITEMITEM> macro to add additional text SubLabels. Notice how the SubLabels start at index 1, index 0 is actually the main Label.

Cat's Name	Color	Type	Personality	Weight
Pogo	Tortoise	Shorthair	Lover	FAT
Roxy	Calico	Longhair	Squeaker	Fat
Hannah	Grey	Longhair	Chicken	Skinny

FIGURE 11.60 TABLE OF CATS

```
// Header labels
const static LPSTR pszHeaderLabels[NUMHEADERLABELS] =
  { "Cat Name", "Color", "Type", "Personality", "Weight" };

typedef struct tagITEMLIST
  {
  int    iImageBig;
  int    iImageSmall;
  LPSTR  szLabel;
  LPSTR  szSubLabel[NUMSUBITEMSPERITEM];
  }
ITEMLIST, FAR * LPITEMLIST;

ITEMLIST ItemList[NUMITEMS] =

//  This is the hard-coded data for our example
//
//  iBig iSmall Label    Sub1         Sub2         Sub3      Sub4
//                       (color)      (type)       (pers)    (weight)
//  ─────────────────────────────────
{
  { 0,   0,     "Pogo",  {"Tortoise", "Shorthair", "Lover",    "FAT"   },
  { 1,   1,     "Roxy",  {"Calico",   "Longhair",  "Squeaker", "Fat"   },
  { 2,   2,     "Hanna", {"Grey",     "Longhair",  "Chicken",  "Skinny" }
};
```

FIGURE 11.61 NAUGHTY HARD-CODED TABLE OF CATS

```
typedef struct _LV_ITEM
  {
  UINT mask;          // LVIF_ flags- which fields matter
```

```
    int iItem;         // App-defined index of the item
    int iSubItem;      // App defined sub-index of the item
    UINT state;        // LVIS_ flags
    UINT stateMask;    // LVIS_ flags (valid bits in state)
    LPSTR pszText;     // Points to text of label
    int cchTextMax;    // Used for getting text- size of pszText
    int iImage;        // Image # to use for icon views
    LPARAM lParam;     // App-defined value
}
LV_ITEM;
```

FIGURE 11.62 THE LV_ITEM STRUCTURE

Take a look at some sample code in Figure 11.63 to illustrate. That code works fine, except that as a side effect, an extra copy of the data is made for the ListView's internal code to manage. That means that you have to go in and manually change the label text in the ListView if your data structure changes. Another approach would be to use a LPSTR_CALLBACK method, just like we did with the TreeView sample program a hundred or two pages ago. If we used this LPSTR_CALLBACK method, we would simply be adding a bunch of sublabel placeholders to each label; our callback routine would actually be responsible for filling in the data. Let's look at how we would modify the above code to achieve this. The most important yet subtle change is the usage of the **lParam** field— we store a pointer to the ITEMLIST array element in it. See Listing 11.17 for the final code to fill the ListView with data.

```
    LV_ITEM lvi;    // Declare the item
    int iItem;      // Outer Loop counter for each item and Label
    int iSubItem;   // Inner Loop counter for each item and SubLabel

    // Set the fields to some standard values
    lvi.mask       = LVIF_TEXT | LVIF_IMAGE | LVIF_PARAM | LVIF_STATE;
    lvi.state      = 0;
    lvi.stateMask  = 0;
    lvi.lParam     = 0; // Not used in this sample text

    // For each item, add it to the list
    for (iItem = 0; iItem < iNumItems; iItem++)
      {
```

```
    lvi.iItem      = iItem;
    lvi.iSubItem   = 0;
    lvi.pszText    = ItemList.szLabel;
    lvi.cchTextMax = 0; // Ignored for Set
    lvi.iImage     = iItem; // use sequential numbers for imagelist


    if (ListView_InsertItem(hWndListView, &lvi) == -1)
       return FALSE;


    // For each sublabel, add it to the item. The iItem field above
    // is used to determine which item to add these SubLabels to.
    for (iSubItem = 0; iSubItem < iNumSubsPerItem; iSubItem++)
      {
      ListView_SetItemText(hWndListView,
                           iItem,
                           iSubItem+1,
                           ItemList.szSubLabel[iSubItem]
                           );
      }
    }
```

FIGURE 11.63 FILLING UP A LISTVIEW CONTROL

LISTING 11.17 FILLING THE LISTVIEW CONTROL WITH DYNAMIC CALLBACK "STRINGS"

```
BOOL FillListViewWithData( HWND          hWndListView,
                           int           iNumItems,
                           int           iNumSubsPerItem,
                           LPITEMLIST    lpItems)
{
  LV_ITEM lvi;
  int iItem;
  int iSubItem;

  // We are adding text, an image, and an lParam
  lvi.mask       = LVIF_TEXT | LVIF_IMAGE | LVIF_PARAM | LVIF_STATE;
  lvi.state      = 0;
  lvi.stateMask  = 0;

  // Loop through each item
  for (iItem = 0; iItem < iNumItems; iItem++)
    {
```

```
lvi.iItem      = iItem;              // Identify this item's index
lvi.iSubItem   = 0;                  // No sub item here
lvi.pszText    = LPSTR_TEXTCALLBACK; // Callback function for string
lvi.cchTextMax = 0;                  // Ignored for Set
lvi.iImage     = iItem;              // An image
lvi.lParam     = (LPARAM) &lpItems[iItem]; // Point to the ITEMLIST
                                           // element which has strings


    if (ListView_InsertItem(hWndListView, &lvi) == -1)
       return FALSE;


    // For each sublabel, add it to the item. The iItem field above
    // is used to determine which item to add these SubLabels to.
    for (iSubItem = 1; iSubItem < iNumSubsPerItem; iSubItem++)
       {
       ListView_SetItemText(hWndListView,
                          iItem,
                          iSubItem,
                          LPSTR_TEXTCALLBACK);

       }
    }


    return TRUE;
}
```

The second example looks almost exactly like the first example, except that the second example will cause the WM_NOTIFY message to get sent to the parent window of the listview control whenever the listview wants to know the strings associated with labels and sublabels. See Listing 11.18 for the implementation of the WM_NOTIFY processing. This callback method is generally more flexible, since your program can dynamically update the information in the ITEMLIST array and simply invalidate the ListView control to reflect the changes.

LISTING 11.18 HANDLING DYNAMIC "STRINGS" VIA WM_NOTIFY

```
// This code is in your window procedure
case WM_NOTIFY:

    switch (((LPNMHDR)lParam)->code)
       {
```

LISTING **11.18** CONTINUED

```
    case LVN_GETDISPINFO:


        // Supply the text for the individual labels
        HandleListViewDispInfo ( (LV_DISPINFO *)lParam );
        break;
    }
  return (DefWindowProc(hWnd, message, uParam, lParam));

// This code is the function to supply the text strings
void HandleListViewDispInfo ( LV_DISPINFO * lpLVDispInfo )
{
  // Since we used lParam to point to the ITEMLIST element,
  // let's get that information into an LPITEMLIST pointer
  LPITEMLIST lpItem    = (LPITEMLIST)(lpLVDispInfo->item.lParam);

  // Return different strings for each label/sublabel
  switch (lpLVDispInfo->item.iSubItem)
    {
    case 0: // Main item label

      lpLVDispInfo->item.pszText = lpItem->szLabel;
      break;

    default: // Subitem label. Index 1 is first item, so we subtract 1
            // from our array index
      lpLVDispInfo->item.pszText =
        lpItem->szSubLabel[lpLVDispInfo->item.iSubItem-1];
      break;
    }
}
```

Image Lists in a ListView

Unlike the TreeView control, the ListView control uses two separate Image
Lists. The small icon view has its image list, and the large icon view has its
image list. The **ListView_SetImageList <LVM_SETIMAGELIST>** macro is
just like the **TreeView_SetImageList** macro from Goodie #9, with the addition
of an additional parameter to indicate if this is the Image List for the small

or large icons:

```
ListView_SetImageList(hWndListView, hListViewSmallIcons, LVSIL_SMALL);
ListView_SetImageList(hWndListView, hListViewLargeIcons, LVSIL_NORMAL);
```

Changing Views in a ListView

Since the ListView control has those four different views, your program will most likely want to let the user change the view at their wish. To change the view in a ListView, you need to change the ListView's view style bits. These bits are erasable with the LVS_TYPEMASK constant, and then the appropriate new style can be set. It is *critical* that your application is marked as a Windows 4.0 executable (See "Set Yer Compiler Right" at the top of this list), or else this won't work. The reason it won't work is because the ListView control counts on getting the new WM_STYLECHANGED message to signal the ListView control to update itself. This message is sent when the SetWindowLong (... GWL_STYLE ...) API is called *if* the application is a Windows 4.0 app.

ListView Drag and Drop Melancholy and Other Similarities

Dragging and dropping in a ListView control, as well as almost all of the other cool operations you can do with the ListView are done in an identical fashion as the TreeView control. Instead of me rehashing all of that drivel, please take a look at COMMCTRL.H and see how the drag, drop, and miscellaneous functions of the ListView match up with the functionality of the TreeView control.

A ListView Sample

Ah, what would life be without a sample? The LISTVIEW sample program (Listing 11.19) is very small; it creates a listview control, fills it with the cat data from above (using the LPSTR_CALLBACK method), uses a couple

Image Lists, and lets the user change the view. Nothing too complex, but it does provide you with some cut & paste code to use in your application if you desire.

LISTING 11.19 LISTVIEW SAMPLE PROGRAM

```
#include <windows.h>              // required for all Windows applications
#if !defined(_WIN32)
#include <ver.h>
#endif
#include "listview.h"             // specific to this program
#include <commctrl.h>             // Common controls
#include <stdio.h>                // for atoi


// Windows NT defines APIENTRY, but 3.x doesn't
#if !defined (APIENTRY)
#define APIENTRY far pascal
#endif


// Windows 3.x uses a FARPROC for dialogs
#if !defined(_WIN32)
#define DLGPROC FARPROC
#endif


HINSTANCE   hInst;                      // current instance


HWND        hWndListView; // Listview control
HWND        hWndHeader;   // Header control


// Table of constants for each item

#define NUMITEMS                3
#define NUMSUBITEMSPERITEM      4
#define NUMHEADERLABELS         (NUMSUBITEMSPERITEM+1)


HIMAGELIST  hListViewSmallIcons;
HIMAGELIST  hListViewLargeIcons;


typedef struct tagITEMLIST
  {
  int    iImageBig;
  int    iImageSmall;
```

508

```
    LPSTR   szLabel;
    LPSTR   szSubLabel[NUMSUBITEMSPERITEM];
    }
ITEMLIST, FAR * LPITEMLIST;


// Header labels
const static LPSTR pszHeaderLabels[NUMHEADERLABELS] =
  { "Cat Name", "Color", "Type", "Personality", "Weight" };


ITEMLIST ItemList[NUMITEMS] =


//  This is the hard-coded data for our example
//
//  iBig  iSmall Label     Sub1            Sub2            Sub3       Sub4
//                         (color)         (type)          (pers)     (weight)
//  ───────────────────────────────────────────────-
{
  { 0,    0,     "Pogo",  {"Tortoise",   "Shorthair",   "Lover",    "FAT"    }},
  { 1,    1,     "Roxy",  {"Calico",     "Longhair",    "Squeaker", "Fat"    }},
  { 2,    2,     "Hanna", {"Grey",       "Longhair",    "Chicken",  "Skinny" }}
};


char szAppName[] = "listview";          // The name of this application
char szTitle[]   = "listview Sample Application"; // The title bar text


#define LPLPSTR LPSTR FAR *
BOOL SetListViewHeader( HWND     hWndListView,
                        int      iNumLabels,
                        const LPLPSTR szLabels);


BOOL FillListViewWithData( HWND         hWndListView,
                           int          iNumItems,
                           int          iNumSubsPerItem,
                           LPITEMLIST   lpItems);


void HandleListViewDispInfo ( LV_DISPINFO * lpLVDispInfo );


BOOL CreateListViewImageLists ( HIMAGELIST *lphimlSmall,
                                HIMAGELIST *lphimlLarge);


//
//   FUNCTION: WinMain(HINSTANCE, HINSTANCE, LPSTR, int)
//
//   PURPOSE: calls initialization function, processes message loop
```

LISTING 11.19 CONTINUED

```
//
//    COMMENTS:
//
//        Windows recognizes this function by name as the initial entry point
//        for the program.  This function calls the application initialization
//        routine, if no other instance of the program is running, and always
//        calls the instance initialization routine.  It then executes a
//        message retrieval and dispatch loop that is the top-level control
//        structure for the remainder of execution.  The loop is terminated
//        when a WM_QUIT  message is received, at which time this function
//        exits the application instance by returning the value passed by
//        PostQuitMessage().
//
//        If this function must abort before entering the message loop, it
//        returns the conventional value NULL.
//

int APIENTRY WinMain(
                HINSTANCE hInstance,
                HINSTANCE hPrevInstance,
                LPSTR lpCmdLine,
                int nCmdShow
                )
{
   MSG msg;
   HANDLE hAccelTable;

   // Other instances of app running?
   if (!hPrevInstance) {
     // Initialize shared things
     if (!InitApplication(hInstance)) {
        return (FALSE);                 // Exits if unable to initialize
     }
   }

   // Perform initializations that apply to a specific instance
   if (!InitInstance(hInstance, nCmdShow)) {
     return (FALSE);
   }

   hAccelTable = LoadAccelerators (hInstance, szAppName);

   // Acquire and dispatch messages until a WM_QUIT message is received.
```

```
    while (GetMessage(&msg,     // message structure
                      NULL,     // handle of window receiving the message
                      0,        // lowest message to examine
                      0)){      // highest message to examine
        if (!TranslateAccelerator (msg.hwnd, hAccelTable, &msg)) {
          TranslateMessage(&msg);// Translates virtual key codes
          DispatchMessage(&msg); // Dispatches message to window
        }
    }


    if (hListViewSmallIcons)
      ImageList_Destroy(hListViewSmallIcons);
    if (hListViewLargeIcons)
      ImageList_Destroy(hListViewLargeIcons);


    // Returns the value from PostQuitMessage
    return (msg.wParam);


    // This will prevent 'unused formal parameter' warnings
    lpCmdLine;
}


//
//    FUNCTION: InitApplication(HINSTANCE)
//
//    PURPOSE: Initializes window data and registers window class
//
//    COMMENTS:
//
//        This function is called at initialization time only if no other
//        instances of the application are running.  This function performs
//        initialization tasks that can be done once for any number of running
//        instances.
//
//        In this case, we initialize a window class by filling out a data
//        structure of type WNDCLASS and calling the Windows RegisterClass()
//        function.  Since all instances of this application use the same
//        window class, we only need to do this when the first instance is
//        initialized.
//


BOOL InitApplication(HINSTANCE hInstance)
{
    WNDCLASS  wc;

    // Fill in window class structure with parameters that describe the
```

LISTING 11.19 CONTINUED

```
    // main window.
    wc.style         = CS_HREDRAW | CS_VREDRAW; // Class style(s).
    wc.lpfnWndProc   = (WNDPROC)WndProc;        // Window Procedure
    wc.cbClsExtra    = 0;                       // No per-class extra data.
    wc.cbWndExtra    = 0;                       // No per-window extra data.
    wc.hInstance     = hInstance;               // Owner of this class
    wc.hIcon         = LoadIcon (hInstance, szAppName);// Icon name from .RC
    wc.hCursor       = LoadCursor(NULL, IDC_ARROW); // Cursor
    wc.hbrBackground = (HBRUSH)(COLOR_WINDOW+1);// Default color
    wc.lpszMenuName  = szAppName;               // Menu name from .RC
    wc.lpszClassName = szAppName;               // Name to register as


    // Register the window class and return success/failure code.
    return (RegisterClass(&wc));
}


//
//    FUNCTION:  InitInstance(HINSTANCE, int)
//
//    PURPOSE:  Saves instance handle and creates main window
//
//    COMMENTS:
//
//      This function is called at initialization time for every instance of
//      this application.  This function performs initialization tasks that
//      cannot be shared by multiple instances.
//
//      In this case, we save the instance handle in a static variable and
//      create and display the main program window.
//


BOOL InitInstance(
        HINSTANCE    hInstance,
        int          nCmdShow
        )
{
   HWND    hWnd; // Main window handle.

   // Save the instance handle in static variable, which will be used in
   // many subsequence calls from this application to Windows.

   hInst = hInstance; // Store instance handle in our global variable
```

```
// Create a main window for this application instance.
hWnd = CreateWindow(
    szAppName,           // See RegisterClass() call.
    szTitle,             // Text for window title bar.
    WS_OVERLAPPEDWINDOW,// Window style.
    CW_USEDEFAULT, 0, CW_USEDEFAULT, 0,// Use default positioning
    NULL,                // Overlapped windows have no parent.
    NULL,                // Use the window class menu.
    hInstance,           // This instance owns this window.
    NULL                 // We don't use any data in our WM_CREATE
    );

// If window could not be created, return "failure"
if (!hWnd) {
    return (FALSE);
}


InitCommonControls();   // This MUST be called once per instance
                        // to register the common controls


CreateListViewImageLists ( &hListViewSmallIcons, &hListViewLargeIcons);


// Make the listview control here
hWndListView = CreateWindow(WC_LISTVIEW, "",
                            WS_VISIBLE | WS_CHILD | WS_BORDER |
                            LVS_REPORT | LVS_AUTOARRANGE,
                            0, 0,
                            0, 0,
                            hWnd,
                            (HMENU)42,
                            hInst,
                            NULL);


ListView_SetImageList(hWndListView, hListViewSmallIcons, LVSIL_SMALL);
ListView_SetImageList(hWndListView, hListViewLargeIcons, LVSIL_NORMAL);

if (!hWndListView)
  {
  DestroyWindow(hWnd);
  return FALSE;
  }

// Set up the header for the report view
SetListViewHeader(hWndListView, NUMHEADERLABELS, pszHeaderLabels);
```

LISTING 11.19 CONTINUED

```
    // Jam some data in there!
    FillListViewWithData (hWndListView,
                          NUMITEMS,
                          NUMSUBITEMSPERITEM,
                          &(ItemList[0]));

    // Make the window visible; update its client area; and return "success"
    ShowWindow(hWnd, nCmdShow); // Show the window
    UpdateWindow(hWnd);         // Sends WM_PAINT message

    return (TRUE);              // We succeeded...
}


//
//   FUNCTION: WndProc(HWND, UINT, WPARAM, LPARAM)
//
//   PURPOSE:  Processes messages
//
//   MESSAGES:
//
//       WM_COMMAND    - application menu (About dialog box)
//       WM_DESTROY    - destroy window
//
//   COMMENTS:
//
//       To process the IDM_ABOUT message, call MakeProcInstance() to get the
//       current instance address of the About() function.  Then call Dialog
//       box which will create the box according to the information in your
//       listview.rc file and turn control over to the About() function.  When
//       it returns, free the instance address.
//

LRESULT CALLBACK WndProc(
    HWND hWnd,           // window handle
    UINT message,        // type of message
    WPARAM uParam,       // additional information
    LPARAM lParam        // additional information
    )
{
    FARPROC lpProcAbout; // pointer to the "About" function
    int wmId, wmEvent;
    DWORD dwStyle;

    switch (message) {
```

```
case WM_NOTIFY:


    switch (((LPNMHDR)lParam)->code)
      {
      case LVN_GETDISPINFO:


        // Supply the text for the individual labels
        HandleListViewDispInfo ( (LV_DISPINFO *)lParam );
        break;


      }
    return (DefWindowProc(hWnd, message, uParam, lParam));


case WM_SIZE:

    if (hWndListView)
      {
      MoveWindow (hWndListView,
                  0, 0,
                  LOWORD(lParam), HIWORD(lParam), FALSE);
      InvalidateRect(hWndListView, NULL, FALSE);
      }
    break;

case WM_COMMAND:  // message: command from application menu

    // Message packing of uParam and lParam have changed for Win32,
    // let us handle the differences in a conditional compilation:
    #if defined (_WIN32)
        wmId    = LOWORD(uParam);
          wmEvent = HIWORD(uParam);
    #else
        wmId    = uParam;
        wmEvent = HIWORD(lParam);
    #endif


    switch (wmId) {
        case IDM_ABOUT:
            lpProcAbout = MakeProcInstance((FARPROC)About, hInst);


            DialogBox(hInst,         // current instance
               "AboutBox",           // dlg resource to use
               hWnd,                 // parent handle
```

LISTING 11.19 CONTINUED

```
                    (DLGPROC)lpProcAbout);   // About() instance address

                FreeProcInstance(lpProcAbout);
                break;

            case IDM_EXIT:
                DestroyWindow (hWnd);
                break;

            case IDM_HELPCONTENTS:
                if (!WinHelp (hWnd, "listview.HLP", HELP_KEY,
                    (DWORD)(LPSTR)"CONTENTS")) {
                    MessageBox (GetFocus(),
                        "Unable to activate help",
                        szAppName, MB_SYSTEMMODAL|MB_OK|MB_ICONHAND);

                }
                break;

            case IDM_HELPSEARCH:
                if (!WinHelp(hWnd, "listview.HLP", HELP_PARTIALKEY,
(DWORD)(LPSTR)"")) {
                    MessageBox (GetFocus(),
                        "Unable to activate help",
                        szAppName, MB_SYSTEMMODAL|MB_OK|MB_ICONHAND);
                }
                break;

            case IDM_HELPHELP:
                if(!WinHelp(hWnd, (LPSTR)NULL, HELP_HELPONHELP, 0)) {
                    MessageBox (GetFocus(),
                        "Unable to activate help",
                        szAppName, MB_SYSTEMMODAL|MB_OK|MB_ICONHAND);
                }
                break;

            case IDM_ICONFORMAT     :

                dwStyle = GetWindowLong(hWndListView, GWL_STYLE);
                dwStyle &= ~(LVS_TYPEMASK);
                dwStyle |= LVS_ICON;
                SetWindowLong(hWndListView, GWL_STYLE, dwStyle);
```

```
            break;

        case IDM_SMALLICONFORMAT:

            dwStyle = GetWindowLong(hWndListView, GWL_STYLE);
            dwStyle &= ~(LVS_TYPEMASK);
            dwStyle |= LVS_SMALLICON;
            SetWindowLong(hWndListView, GWL_STYLE, dwStyle);
            break;

        case IDM_LISTFORMAT      :

            dwStyle = GetWindowLong(hWndListView, GWL_STYLE);
            dwStyle &= ~(LVS_TYPEMASK);
            dwStyle |= LVS_LIST;
            SetWindowLong(hWndListView, GWL_STYLE, dwStyle);
            break;

        case IDM_REPORTFORMAT    :

            dwStyle = GetWindowLong(hWndListView, GWL_STYLE);
            dwStyle &= ~(LVS_TYPEMASK);
            dwStyle |= LVS_REPORT;
            SetWindowLong(hWndListView, GWL_STYLE, dwStyle);
            break;

        // Here are all the other possible menu options,
        // all of these are currently disabled:
        case IDM_NEW:
        case IDM_OPEN:
        case IDM_SAVE:
        case IDM_SAVEAS:
        case IDM_UNDO:
        case IDM_CUT:
        case IDM_COPY:
        case IDM_PASTE:
        case IDM_LINK:
        case IDM_LINKS:

        default:
            return (DefWindowProc(hWnd, message, uParam, lParam));
    }
    break;

case WM_DESTROY:  // message: window being destroyed
```

LISTING 11.19 CONTINUED

```
            PostQuitMessage(0);
            break;

        default:            // Passes it on if unproccessed
            return (DefWindowProc(hWnd, message, uParam, lParam));
    }
    return (0);
}


//
//   FUNCTION: CenterWindow (HWND, HWND)
//
//   PURPOSE:  Center one window over another
//
//   COMMENTS:
//
//      Dialog boxes take on the screen position that they were designed
//      at, which is not always appropriate. Centering the dialog over a
//      particular window usually results in a better position.
//

BOOL CenterWindow (HWND hwndChild, HWND hwndParent)
{
    RECT    rChild, rParent;
    int     wChild, hChild, wParent, hParent;
    int     wScreen, hScreen, xNew, yNew;
    HDC     hdc;

    // Get the Height and Width of the child window
    GetWindowRect (hwndChild, &rChild);
    wChild = rChild.right - rChild.left;
    hChild = rChild.bottom - rChild.top;

    // Get the Height and Width of the parent window
    GetWindowRect (hwndParent, &rParent);
    wParent = rParent.right - rParent.left;
    hParent = rParent.bottom - rParent.top;

    // Get the display limits
    hdc = GetDC (hwndChild);
    wScreen = GetDeviceCaps (hdc, HORZRES);
    hScreen = GetDeviceCaps (hdc, VERTRES);
```

```
   ReleaseDC (hwndChild, hdc);


   // Calculate new X position, then adjust for screen
   xNew = rParent.left + ((wParent - wChild) /2);
   if (xNew < 0) {
      xNew = 0;
   }
   else if ((xNew+wChild) > wScreen) {
      xNew = wScreen - wChild;
   }


   // Calculate new Y position, then adjust for screen
   yNew = rParent.top  + ((hParent - hChild) /2);
   if (yNew < 0) {
      yNew = 0;
   }
   else if ((yNew+hChild) > hScreen) {
      yNew = hScreen - hChild;
   }


   // Set it, and return
   return SetWindowPos (hwndChild, NULL,
      xNew, yNew, 0, 0, SWP_NOSIZE | SWP_NOZORDER);
}


//
//    FUNCTION: About(HWND, UINT, WPARAM, LPARAM)
//
//    PURPOSE:  Processes messages for "About" dialog box
//
//    MESSAGES:
//
//       WM_INITDIALOG - initialize dialog box
//       WM_COMMAND    - Input received
//
//    COMMENTS:
//
//       Display version information from the version section of the
//       application resource.
//
//       Wait for user to click on "Ok" button, then close the dialog box.
//

LRESULT CALLBACK About(
      HWND hDlg,          // window handle of the dialog box
      UINT message,       // type of message
```

LISTING 11.19 CONTINUED

```
        WPARAM uParam,          // message-specific information
        LPARAM lParam
        )
{
    static  HFONT hfontDlg;

    switch (message) {
        case WM_INITDIALOG:  // message: initialize dialog box
            // Create a font to use
            hfontDlg = CreateFont(14, 0, 0, 0, 0, 0, 0, 0,
                0, 0, 0, 0,
                VARIABLE_PITCH | FF_SWISS, "");

            // Center the dialog over the application window
            CenterWindow (hDlg, GetWindow (hDlg, GW_OWNER));

            return (TRUE);


        case WM_COMMAND:                        // message: received a command
            if (LOWORD(uParam) == IDOK          // "OK" box selected?
               || LOWORD(uParam) == IDCANCEL) {// System menu close command?
               EndDialog(hDlg, TRUE);           // Exit the dialog
               DeleteObject (hfontDlg);
               return (TRUE);
            }
            break;
    }
    return (FALSE); // Didn't process the message

    lParam; // This will prevent 'unused formal parameter' warnings
}

//
//   FUNCTION: SetListViewHeader(HWND, int, LPLPSTR)
//
//   PURPOSE:  Set the header text for a ListView
//

BOOL SetListViewHeader( HWND          hWndListView,
                        int           iNumLabels,
                        const LPLPSTR szLabels)
{
```

```
    LV_COLUMN lvc;
    int       iCol;


    // Initialize the LV_COLUMN structure.


    lvc.mask     = LVCF_FMT | LVCF_WIDTH | LVCF_TEXT | LVCF_SUBITEM;
    lvc.fmt      = LVCFMT_LEFT;
    lvc.cx       = 75;



    // Add the columns.


    for (iCol = 0; iCol < iNumLabels; iCol++)
      {
      lvc.iSubItem = iCol;
      lvc.pszText  = szLabels[iCol];
      if (-1 == ListView_InsertColumn(hWndListView, iCol, &lvc))
        return FALSE;
      }


    return TRUE;
}


//
//    FUNCTION: FillListViewWithData(HWND, int, int, LPITEMLIST)
//
//    PURPOSE:  Fill the ListView control with data, using pointers
//              to the lpItems array as the lParam.
//


BOOL FillListViewWithData( HWND               hWndListView,
                           int                iNumItems,
                           int                iNumSubsPerItem,
                           LPITEMLIST         lpItems)
{
  LV_ITEM lvi;
  int iItem;
  int iSubItem;


  lvi.mask       = LVIF_TEXT | LVIF_IMAGE | LVIF_PARAM | LVIF_STATE;
  lvi.state      = 0;
  lvi.stateMask  = 0;


  for (iItem = 0; iItem < iNumItems; iItem++)
```

LISTING 11.19 CONTINUED

```
      {
      lvi.iItem        = iItem;
      lvi.iSubItem     = 0;
      lvi.pszText      = LPSTR_TEXTCALLBACK;
      lvi.cchTextMax   = 0; // Ignored for Set
      lvi.iImage       = iItem;
      lvi.lParam       = (LPARAM) &lpItems[iItem];


      if (ListView_InsertItem(hWndListView, &lvi) == -1)
        return FALSE;



      for (iSubItem = 1; iSubItem < iNumSubsPerItem; iSubItem++)
        {
        ListView_SetItemText(hWndListView,
                             iItem,
                             iSubItem,
                             LPSTR_TEXTCALLBACK);
        }
      }

  return TRUE;
}


//
//   FUNCTION: HandleListViewDispInfo( LVDISPINFO * )
//
//   PURPOSE:  Called in response to the WM_NOTIFY
//             message sent by the listview for LVN_GETDISPINFO
//

void HandleListViewDispInfo( LV_DISPINFO * lpLVDispInfo )
{
  LPITEMLIST lpItem    = (LPITEMLIST)(lpLVDispInfo->item.lParam);

  switch (lpLVDispInfo->item.iSubItem)
    {
    case 0: // Main item

      lpLVDispInfo->item.pszText = lpItem->szLabel;
      break;
```

```
    default: // Subitem. Index 1 is first item

      lpLVDispInfo->item.pszText =
          lpItem->szSubLabel[lpLVDispInfo->item.iSubItem-1];
      break;
    }
}


//
//   FUNCTION: CreateListViewImageLists ( HIMAGELIST *,
//                                        HIMAGELIST * )
//
//   PURPOSE:  Create the lareg and small image lists to be used
//             by the LIstView control
//


BOOL CreateListViewImageLists ( HIMAGELIST *lphimlSmall,
                                HIMAGELIST *lphimlLarge)
{
  HIMAGELIST hSmall, hLarge;

  hSmall = ImageList_Create(16,16, TRUE, NUMITEMS, 1);
  if (!hSmall) return FALSE;
  hLarge = ImageList_Create(32,32, TRUE, NUMITEMS, 1);
  if (!hLarge)
    {
    ImageList_Destroy(hSmall);
    return FALSE;
    }

  ImageList_AddMasked (hSmall, LoadBitmap(hInst, "POGO16"),   RGB(255,0,255));
  ImageList_AddMasked (hSmall, LoadBitmap(hInst, "ROXY16"),   RGB(255,0,255));
  ImageList_AddMasked (hSmall, LoadBitmap(hInst, "HANNAH16"), RGB(255,0,255));

  ImageList_AddIcon   (hLarge, LoadIcon(hInst, "POGO32"));
  ImageList_AddIcon   (hLarge, LoadIcon(hInst, "ROXY32"));
  ImageList_AddIcon   (hLarge, LoadIcon(hInst, "HANNAH32"));

  *lphimlSmall = hSmall;
  *lphimlLarge = hLarge;

  return TRUE;
}
```

2. The Hotkey Control

The Hotkey control makes it very easy for you to get key combinations from the user. If the user has focus set to the hotkey control, and they type <Ctrl>+G, instead of a beep, the Hotkey control will (if allowed) display the string "Ctrl + G". When I mean "allowed," I mean that the program can set up rules for the hotkey to follow. These rules tell the Hotkey control which key combinations are valid, and what to do with them.

A hotkey value is a WORD, the lobyte is the virtual key code (such as VK_DELETE, or an ASCII value for normal letters), and the hibyte is the "modifier" status of the key, which can be any combination of the values HOTKEYF_SHIFT, HOTKEYF_CONTROL, HOTKEYF_ALT, and HOTKEYF_EXT.

Creating, Initializing, and Querying the Hotkey Control

To create a hotkey control, just use **CreateWindow** with the HOTKEY _CLASS classname (or you can put it in your dialog template). Nothing else special is required.

To set a value in the hotkey control, you send it the HKM_SETHOTKEY message, passing the hotkey value in **wParam** and passing 0 in **lParam**. For example, to set a Ctrl+C, you would use code like this:

```
#define MAKEHOTKEYVALUE(keycode,modifier) \
  (WPARAM) ( ((BYTE)keycode) + ((WORD)modifier << 8) )

SendMessage ( hWndHotkey,
              HKM_SETHOTKEY,
              MAKEHOTKEYVALUE('C', HOTKEYF_CONTROL),
              0L );
```

Likewise, to get the current value of a hotkey, you can use the HKM_GETHOTKEY message, looking at the return value:

```
wResult = (WORD)SendMessage( hWndHotkey, HKM_GETHOTKEY, 0, 0L );
```

```
cbCode = LOBYTE (wResult);
cbModifier = HIBYTE(wResult);
```

Setting Hotkey Rules

The hotkey control by default allows any combination of the Control, Alt, and Shift keys. You can set up some rules to only allow certain keys. The HKM_SETRULES message uses **wParam** to define "invalid" modifier keys, and **lParam** as instructions as to what to do with the invalid modifier. Think of the **wParam** and **lParam** as "if the user presses **wParam**, convert it to **lParam**". As an example, let's say we only want to look at hotkeys that are Control-key combinations; we don't give a hoot about the Alt key or the Shift key. We would then indicate that the Alt and the Shift keys are invalid, and we want to convert them to the Control key:

```
SendMessage ( hWndHotkey,          // Handle of control
            HKM_SETRULES,          // Set rules message
            HKCOMB_SA | HKCOMB_A | HKCOMB_S,  // We don't allow
                                         // Shift+Alt, Shift, or Alt
            HOTKEYF_CONTROL);  // And we convert those invalid modifiers to
                               // a control key
```

For **wParam**, the key combinations defined in COMMCTRL.H are:

```
HKCOMB_NONE      no modifiers
HKCOMB_S         only shift
HKCOMB_C         only control
HKCOMB_A         only alt
HKCOMB_SC        shift+control
HKCOMB_SA        shift+alt
HKCOMB_CA        control+alt
HKCOMB_SCA       shift+control+alt
```

For **lParam**, the modifier constants defined in COMMCTRL.H are:

```
HOTKEYF_SHIFT        Shift Key
HOTKEYF_CONTROL      Control Key
HOTKEYF_ALT          Alt key
HOTKEYF_EXT          Keyboard extended key bit
```

Itsy Bitsy Sample Program

The sample program HOTSPIN (See Listing 11.20) adds the Hotkey and the Spinner Controls (see the next goodie).

LISTING 11.20 HOTSPIN SAMPLE PROGRAM

```
#include <windows.h>              // required for all Windows applications
#if !defined(_WIN32)
#include <ver.h>
#endif
#include "hotspin.h"             // specific to this program
#include <commctrl.h>            // Common controls
#include <stdio.h>               // for atoi


// Windows NT defines APIENTRY, but 3.x doesn't
#if !defined (APIENTRY)
#define APIENTRY far pascal
#endif


// Windows 3.x uses a FARPROC for dialogs
#if !defined(_WIN32)
#define DLGPROC FARPROC
#endif


HINSTANCE    hInst;                       // current instance

void Stub ( HWND );


char szAppName[] = "hotspin";        // The name of this application
char szCatIcon[] = "CatIcon";        // Our special cat icon class
char szTitle[]   = "hotspin Sample Application"; // The title bar text

LRESULT CALLBACK CatIconWndProc(
     HWND hWnd,          // window handle
     UINT message,       // type of message
     WPARAM uParam,      // additional information
     LPARAM lParam       // additional information
     );

//
```

```
//   FUNCTION: WinMain(HINSTANCE, HINSTANCE, LPSTR, int)
//
//   PURPOSE: calls initialization function, processes message loop
//
//   COMMENTS:
//
//       Windows recognizes this function by name as the initial entry point
//       for the program.  This function calls the application initialization
//       routine, if no other instance of the program is running, and always
//       calls the instance initialization routine.  It then executes a
//       message retrieval and dispatch loop that is the top-level control
//       structure for the remainder of execution.  The loop is terminated
//       when a WM_QUIT   message is received, at which time this function
//       exits the application instance by returning the value passed by
//       PostQuitMessage().
//
//       If this function must abort before entering the message loop, it
//       returns the conventional value NULL.
//

int APIENTRY WinMain(
            HINSTANCE hInstance,
            HINSTANCE hPrevInstance,
            LPSTR lpCmdLine,
            int nCmdShow
            )
{
    MSG msg;
    HANDLE hAccelTable;

    // Other instances of app running?
    if (!hPrevInstance) {
        // Initialize shared things
        if (!InitApplication(hInstance)) {
            return (FALSE);              // Exits if unable to initialize
        }
    }

    // Perform initializations that apply to a specific instance
    if (!InitInstance(hInstance, nCmdShow)) {
        return (FALSE);
    }

    hAccelTable = LoadAccelerators (hInstance, szAppName);
```

LISTING 11.20 CONTINUED

```
    // Acquire and dispatch messages until a WM_QUIT message is received.
    while (GetMessage(&msg,    // message structure
                     NULL,     // handle of window receiving the message
                     0,        // lowest message to examine
                     0)){      // highest message to examine
        if (!TranslateAccelerator (msg.hwnd, hAccelTable, &msg)) {
            TranslateMessage(&msg);// Translates virtual key codes
            DispatchMessage(&msg); // Dispatches message to window
        }
    }


    // Returns the value from PostQuitMessage
    return (msg.wParam);


    // This will prevent 'unused formal parameter' warnings
    lpCmdLine;
}


//
//   FUNCTION: InitApplication(HINSTANCE)
//
//   PURPOSE: Initializes window data and registers window class
//
//   COMMENTS:
//
//       This function is called at initialization time only if no other
//       instances of the application are running.  This function performs
//       initialization tasks that can be done once for any number of running
//       instances.
//
//       In this case, we initialize a window class by filling out a data
//       structure of type WNDCLASS and calling the Windows RegisterClass()
//       function.  Since all instances of this application use the same
//       window class, we only need to do this when the first instance is
//       initialized.
//


BOOL InitApplication(HINSTANCE hInstance)
{
    WNDCLASS  wc;

    // Fill in window class structure with parameters that describe the
    // main window.
```

```
    wc.style          = CS_HREDRAW | CS_VREDRAW; // Class style(s).
    wc.lpfnWndProc    = (WNDPROC)WndProc;        // Window Procedure
    wc.cbClsExtra     = 0;                       // No per-class extra data.
    wc.cbWndExtra     = 0;                       // No per-window extra data.
    wc.hInstance      = hInstance;               // Owner of this class
    wc.hIcon          = LoadIcon (hInstance, szAppName);// Icon name from .RC
    wc.hCursor        = LoadCursor(NULL, IDC_ARROW); // Cursor
    wc.hbrBackground  = (HBRUSH)(COLOR_WINDOW+1);// Default color
    wc.lpszMenuName   = szAppName;               // Menu name from .RC
    wc.lpszClassName  = szAppName;               // Name to register as

    if (!RegisterClass(&wc)) return FALSE;

    // Fill in window class structure with parameters that describe the
    // CatIcon window.
    wc.style          = CS_HREDRAW | CS_VREDRAW; // Class style(s).
    wc.lpfnWndProc    = (WNDPROC)CatIconWndProc; // Window Procedure
    wc.cbClsExtra     = 0;                       // No per-class extra data.
    wc.cbWndExtra     = 0;                       // No per-window extra data.
    wc.hInstance      = hInstance;               // Owner of this class
    wc.hIcon          = NULL;                    // Icon name from .RC
    wc.hCursor        = LoadCursor(NULL, IDC_ARROW); // Cursor
    wc.hbrBackground  = (HBRUSH)(COLOR_WINDOW+1);// Default color
    wc.lpszMenuName   = NULL;                    // Menu name from .RC
    wc.lpszClassName  = szCatIcon;               // Name to register as

    // Register the window class and return success/failure code.
    return (RegisterClass(&wc));
}


//
//   FUNCTION:  InitInstance(HINSTANCE, int)
//
//   PURPOSE:  Saves instance handle and creates main window
//
//   COMMENTS:
//
//      This function is called at initialization time for every instance of
//      this application.  This function performs initialization tasks that
//      cannot be shared by multiple instances.
//
//      In this case, we save the instance handle in a static variable and
//      create and display the main program window.
//

BOOL InitInstance(
```

LISTING 11.20 CONTINUED

```
        HINSTANCE     hInstance,
        int           nCmdShow
        )
{
   HWND    hWnd; // Main window handle.


   // Save the instance handle in static variable, which will be used in
   // many subsequence calls from this application to Windows.


   hInst = hInstance; // Store instance handle in our global variable


   // Create a main window for this application instance.
   hWnd = CreateWindow(
      szAppName,          // See RegisterClass() call.
      szTitle,            // Text for window title bar.
      WS_OVERLAPPEDWINDOW,// Window style.
      CW_USEDEFAULT, 0, CW_USEDEFAULT, 0,// Use default positioning
      NULL,               // Overlapped windows have no parent.
      NULL,               // Use the window class menu.
      hInstance,          // This instance owns this window.
      NULL                // We don't use any data in our WM_CREATE
      );


   // If window could not be created, return "failure"
   if (!hWnd) {
      return (FALSE);
   }


   InitCommonControls();  // This MUST be called once per instance
                          // to register the common controls


   // Make the window visible; update its client area; and return "success"
   ShowWindow(hWnd, nCmdShow); // Show the window
   UpdateWindow(hWnd);         // Sends WM_PAINT message


   return (TRUE);              // We succeeded...
}


//
//   FUNCTION: WndProc(HWND, UINT, WPARAM, LPARAM)
//
```

```
//    PURPOSE:  Processes messages
//
//    MESSAGES:
//
//       WM_COMMAND    - application menu (About dialog box)
//       WM_DESTROY    - destroy window
//
//    COMMENTS:
//
//       To process the IDM_ABOUT message, call MakeProcInstance() to get the
//       current instance address of the About() function.  Then call Dialog
//       box which will create the box according to the information in your
//       hotspin.rc file and turn control over to the About() function.  When
//       it returns, free the instance address.
//


LRESULT CALLBACK WndProc(
        HWND hWnd,         // window handle
        UINT message,      // type of message
        WPARAM uParam,     // additional information
        LPARAM lParam      // additional information
        )
{
    FARPROC lpProcAbout;   // pointer to the "About" function
    Int wmId, wmEvent;

    switch (message) {

      case WM_COMMAND:   // message: command from application menu

          // Message packing of uParam and lParam have changed for Win32,
          // let us handle the differences in a conditional compilation:
          #if defined (_WIN32)
              wmId    = LOWORD(uParam);
                 wmEvent = HIWORD(uParam);
          #else
              wmId    = uParam;
              wmEvent = HIWORD(lParam);
          #endif

          switch (wmId) {
             case IDM_ABOUT:
                 lpProcAbout = MakeProcInstance((FARPROC)About, hInst);

                 DialogBox(hInst,              // current instance
```

LISTING 11.20 CONTINUED

```
            "AboutBox",            // dlg resource to use
            hWnd,                  // parent handle
            (DLGPROC)lpProcAbout); // About() instance address

        FreeProcInstance(lpProcAbout);
        break;

    case IDM_EXIT:
        DestroyWindow (hWnd);
        break;

    case IDM_HELPCONTENTS:
        if (!WinHelp (hWnd, "hotspin.HLP", HELP_KEY,
            (DWORD)(LPSTR)"CONTENTS")) {
            MessageBox (GetFocus(),
                "Unable to activate help",
                szAppName, MB_SYSTEMMODAL|MB_OK|MB_ICONHAND);

        }
        break;

    case IDM_HELPSEARCH:
        if (!WinHelp(hWnd, "hotspin.HLP", HELP_PARTIALKEY,
            (DWORD)(LPSTR)"")) {
            MessageBox (GetFocus(),
                "Unable to activate help",
                szAppName, MB_SYSTEMMODAL|MB_OK|MB_ICONHAND);
        }
        break;

    case IDM_HELPHELP:
        if(!WinHelp(hWnd, (LPSTR)NULL, HELP_HELPONHELP, 0)) {
            MessageBox (GetFocus(),
                "Unable to activate help",
                szAppName, MB_SYSTEMMODAL|MB_OK|MB_ICONHAND);
        }
        break;

    // Here are all the other possible menu options,
    // all of these are currently disabled:
    case IDM_NEW:
    case IDM_OPEN:
```

```
            case IDM_SAVE:
            case IDM_SAVEAS:
            case IDM_UNDO:
            case IDM_CUT:
            case IDM_COPY:
            case IDM_PASTE:
            case IDM_LINK:
            case IDM_LINKS:

            default:
                return (DefWindowProc(hWnd, message, uParam, lParam));
        }
        break;

    case WM_DESTROY:   // message: window being destroyed

        PostQuitMessage(0);
        break;

    default:                   // Passes it on if unproccessed
        return (DefWindowProc(hWnd, message, uParam, lParam));
    }
    return (0);
}


//
//   FUNCTION: CenterWindow (HWND, HWND)
//
//   PURPOSE:  Center one window over another
//
//   COMMENTS:
//
//      Dialog boxes take on the screen position that they were designed
//      at, which is not always appropriate. Centering the dialog over a
//      particular window usually results in a better position.
//

BOOL CenterWindow (HWND hwndChild, HWND hwndParent)
{
    RECT    rChild, rParent;
    int     wChild, hChild, wParent, hParent;
    int     wScreen, hScreen, xNew, yNew;
    HDC     hdc;

    // Get the Height and Width of the child window
```

533

LISTING 11.20 CONTINUED

```
    GetWindowRect (hwndChild, &rChild);
    wChild = rChild.right - rChild.left;
    hChild = rChild.bottom - rChild.top;

    // Get the Height and Width of the parent window
    GetWindowRect (hwndParent, &rParent);
    wParent = rParent.right - rParent.left;
    hParent = rParent.bottom - rParent.top;

    // Get the display limits
    hdc = GetDC (hwndChild);
    wScreen = GetDeviceCaps (hdc, HORZRES);
    hScreen = GetDeviceCaps (hdc, VERTRES);
    ReleaseDC (hwndChild, hdc);

    // Calculate new X position, then adjust for screen
    xNew = rParent.left + ((wParent - wChild) /2);
    if (xNew < 0) {
        xNew = 0;
    }
    else if ((xNew+wChild) > wScreen) {
        xNew = wScreen - wChild;
    }

    // Calculate new Y position, then adjust for screen
    yNew = rParent.top  + ((hParent - hChild) /2);
    if (yNew < 0) {
        yNew = 0;
    }
    else if ((yNew+hChild) > hScreen) {
        yNew = hScreen - hChild;
    }

    // Set it, and return
    return SetWindowPos (hwndChild, NULL,
        xNew, yNew, 0, 0, SWP_NOSIZE | SWP_NOZORDER);
}


//
//   FUNCTION: About(HWND, UINT, WPARAM, LPARAM)
//
//   PURPOSE:  Processes messages for "About" dialog box
```

534

```
//
//    MESSAGES:
//
//        WM_INITDIALOG - initialize dialog box
//        WM_COMMAND    - Input received
//
//    COMMENTS:
//
//        Display version information from the version section of the
//        application resource.
//
//        Wait for user to click on "Ok" button, then close the dialog box.
//

LRESULT CALLBACK About(
        HWND hDlg,              // window handle of the dialog box
        UINT message,          // type of message
        WPARAM uParam,         // message-specific information
        LPARAM lParam
        )
{
    switch (message) {
        case WM_INITDIALOG:  // message: initialize dialog box


            // Center the dialog over the application window
            CenterWindow (hDlg, GetWindow (hDlg, GW_OWNER));

            // Hotkey control #1 has no rules, so we don't have to send it any
            // rules message

            // Hotkey #2 only takes the control key, so we filter out the
            // shift and the alt, changing then into control keys
            SendDlgItemMessage ( hDlg,
                                 IDD_HOTKEY2,
                                 HKM_SETRULES,
                                 (WPARAM)(HKCOMB_SA | HKCOMB_S | HKCOMB_A),
                                 (LPARAM)HOTKEYF_CONTROL
                               );

            // Hotkey #3 won't take the alt key, so we filter out the alt
            // key, and turn it into a control key
            SendDlgItemMessage ( hDlg,
                                 IDD_HOTKEY3,
                                 HKM_SETRULES,
```

535

LISTING 11.20 CONTINUED

```
                                    (WPARAM)(HKCOMB_A | HKCOMB_SA | HKCOMB_CA),
                                    (LPARAM)HOTKEYF_CONTROL
                            );

            // Set the Spinner #1 range from 1-10
            SendDlgItemMessage ( hDlg,
                            IDD_SPINNER1,
                            UDM_SETRANGE,
                            (WPARAM)0,
                            MAKELPARAM(10,1)
                            );

            // Set the Spinner #2 range from 1-3
            SendDlgItemMessage ( hDlg,
                            IDD_SPINNER2,
                            UDM_SETRANGE,
                            (WPARAM)0,
                            MAKELPARAM(3,1)
                            );

            // Buddy it up to the cat control
            SendDlgItemMessage ( hDlg,
                            IDD_SPINNER2,
                            UDM_SETBUDDY,
                            (WPARAM)GetDlgItem(hDlg,IDD_SPINNERBUD2),
                            0
                            );


        return (TRUE);

    case WM_COMMAND:                        // message: received a command
        if (LOWORD(uParam) == IDOK          // "OK" box selected?
          || LOWORD(uParam) == IDCANCEL) {// System menu close command?
          EndDialog(hDlg, TRUE);            // Exit the dialog
          return (TRUE);
        }
        break;
    }
    return (FALSE); // Didn't process the message

    lParam; // This will prevent 'unused formal parameter' warnings
}
```

```
//
//   FUNCTION: CatIconWndProc(HWND, UINT, WPARAM, LPARAM)
//
//   PURPOSE:  Processes messages
//
//   MESSAGES:
//
//      WM_PAINT      - Paint the icon
//      WM_SETTEXT    - Force a repaint
//

LRESULT CALLBACK CatIconWndProc(
        HWND hWnd,          // window handle
        UINT message,       // type of message
        WPARAM uParam,      // additional information
        LPARAM lParam       // additional information
        )
{
    PAINTSTRUCT ps;
    HDC         hDC;
    char        szCaption[5];

    switch (message) {

        case WM_PAINT:  // message: window being destroyed

            hDC = BeginPaint ( hWnd, &ps);

            GetWindowText ( hWnd, szCaption, sizeof (szCaption));
            switch ( *szCaption )
              {
              default:
              case '1': DrawIcon ( hDC, 0, 0, LoadIcon(hInst, "Pogo")); break;
              case '2': DrawIcon ( hDC, 0, 0, LoadIcon(hInst, "Roxy")); break;
              case '3': DrawIcon ( hDC, 0, 0, LoadIcon(hInst, "Hannah")); break;
              }

            EndPaint ( hWnd, &ps);

            break;

        case WM_SETTEXT:

            InvalidateRect ( hWnd, NULL, FALSE );
```

537

LISTING 11.20 CONTINUED

```
        return (DefWindowProc(hWnd, message, uParam, lParam));

    default:          // Passes it on if unproccessed
        return (DefWindowProc(hWnd, message, uParam, lParam));
  }
  return (0);
}
```

1. The Up/Down (Spinner) Control

The spinner control has been around in some shape or form since Windows 3.0 was released. Back in those days, it was Kraig Brockschmidt's MUSCROLL.DLL sample program included with the Windows SDK (and that sample lived on until Windows 95).

As with the other controls, the spinner control can be created with Create-Window, using the class UPDOWN_CLASS. The actual spinner control consists only of the two buttons; either an up and down arrow button, or a left and right arrow button; this depends on if you use the UDS_HORZ style bit or not.

The spinner control has a scalar "value", this value falls into a "range." See the "ranges" section below for more detail on this, but for right now, think of the spinner control as nothing more than a scrollbar with an attitude.

Buddies

Since the Spinner control only consists of the arrow buttons, your code will almost surely want to attach it to an edit control so the user can see the value of the control. This edit control (actually, it does not have to be an edit control, but for all of my examples, it will be) is called the Spinner's "Buddy". A Spinner control has a special relationship with it's buddy.

First off, when you tell a Spinner that it has a buddy, the Spinner will attach itself to the right side of the buddy control (if you specify the UDS_ALIGNRIGHT style bit). So, if you are using an edit control as the buddy, the Spinner will attach to the right edge of the edit control, or the left side if you use UDS_ALIGNLEFT.

Second, the UDS_SETBUDDYINT style bit will cause the Spinner to automatically update the buddy's text as the user updates the Spinner's arrows (via **SetWindowText**, provided you are not a listbox). If you use a private window class instead of an edit control, you can look at the numeric value in your caption and display a choice other than the numeric value (such as a bitmap, color, or word). I will demonstrate this in the HOTSPIN sample program.

Third, this buddy-repositioning-attachment doohickey only happens once: when you send the UDM_SETBUDDY message to the Spinner control. If you move your buddy, you will need to send this UDM_SETBUDDY message again. The UDS_AUTOBUDDY style bit simply means that the Spinner control will buddy up to the previous Z-order window *at creation time, but won't resize itself* (since you are creating the control, you can figure out the size). Even Spinners with UDS_AUTOBUDDY will need to get the UDM_SETBUDDY message when their buddies move.

Ranges

Just like a scrollbar, the Spinner control has a range. And, just like a scrollbar, if you set the upper and lower ranges to the same value, the Spinner control will disable itself.

Unlike the scrollbar, if you set the lower range to be higher than the upper range, the Spinner will work backwards; pressing the up arrow will decrease the number, and vice-versa.

To set a Spinner's range, use the UDM_SETRANGE message. See the HOTSPIN sample program for an implementation.

Spinner Miscellany

The Spinner control works in bases other than Base 10. If you want to use Hex, you can set the base of the Spinner control to Base 16 by using the

UDM_SETBASE message. Also, you can tell the Spinner button to accelerate the scrolling through the numbers if the user presses and holds the mouse button by using the UDM_SETACCEL message. See the docs for more on these extra rare features.

HOTSPIN Sample Program

The HOTSPIN sample is (once again) GENERIC with a new face (See Listing 11.20). All of the new code is in the About box (which now has three Hotkey controls, and two Spinner controls in it). The Hotkey controls allow different types of input (See Goodie #2 above for a detailed discussion about the Hotkey control).

The first Spinner control in the About dialog is your basic Spinner buddied up with an edit control, the range is from 1 to 10. I used the UDS_AUTO-BUDDY style bit in the dialog template, therefore I was required to specify the exact size of the Spinner control in the dialog template. The second Spinner control is buddied up in WM_INITDIALOG with a private window class that draws an icon depending on the caption. The Spinner's range is from 1-3, and the style UDS_WRAP is used to allow the Spinner to "roll over" back to 1 if the user tries to move past 3.

The Mother of all Summaries

Wow. That was a big list. In fact, about a third of this entire book is this list alone. However, you should now have a solid background on how to use the basic (and sometimes advanced) features of the Common Controls DLL and the RichEdit control. These controls will allow your application to share the same look and feel as all of the other Windows 95 programs, and they should save you an enormous amount of time.

I'm sure that by the time Windows 95 ships, some of the API's for these goodies will change. However, this book was sent to bed at M7 time, and that milestone is generally considered to be the "code complete" milestone for

Windows 95. If you find that your program doesn't compile, or a feature no longer works right, take a gander at the shrink-wrap manuals or help files—the answer may lie in there.

An extra special thanks goes to Chris Guzak—without your extreme patience during my dumb questions, this list would never have happened.

CHAPTER 12

Names of Pets Owned by Windows Programmers

Okay, my cat names are Pogo, Roxy, Hanna, and the Late Lucy. So, I don't qualify for naming my animals after weird computer terms. However, I stand rather alone on this one, so read on…

10. BitBlt

9. Pixel

8. Worf

7. Rastero

6. Twip

5. Lisa (think real hard about this one)

4. CDog or CCat

3. Thunkie

2. Bill

1. GeePeeFault

Bob Schmidt bonus name: Tilda

Part 3

MFC

CHAPTER 13

MFC Gotchas

The Microsoft Foundation Classes (MFC) included with Visual C++ (and licensed from a few other compiler companies, such as Symantec) open up a huge box of goodies for the typical Windows programmer. By sticking within the MFC Application Framework, you can get free toolbars, status bars, printing, print preview, MFC, OLE 2.0, File I/O, all while keeping the code reusable. It's the way of the future. However, the quarter of a million C/SDK programmers have been joined by another quarter of a million C++/MFC newcomers, and now about half a million Windows programmers have the daunting task of learning C++ and MFC simultaneously (and most likely while under a deadline).

Those programmers in that the half million who have made it over the Hump of MFC Knowledge probably won't find anything revolutionary in this chapter. However, those who are still climbing that proverbial curve of learning may find that not every feature of MFC is spelled out clearly in the "Scribble" tutorial, and you may run into some small snags during your development cycle.

The ideas for the following list of MFC gotchas came from Brian Scott (see his biography in the "Introduction").

10. Be Aware of the Difference Between the Frame, Document, and View Objects

Frames and documents and views, oh my! This is a concept of MFC programming that must sink in early, or else you will end up spending a lot of time getting angry.

A *frame window* in MFC is the equivalent of a typical window in your regular SDK application. An SDI application usually has only one frame window: the top-level window that has the caption, menu, toolbar, and status bar. An MDI application has multiple frame windows: the main frame window (which is the top-level window that contains the caption, menu, toolbar, status bar, and MDI client window) and the child frame windows (which are the MDI child windows). For OLE2 applications, a third type of frame window is the OLE2 in-place frame window where everything from the object sits (similar to an SDI main frame window without conventional sizing borders, and with the captions, toolbars, and other gadgets placed in the OLE2 container's main frame window). One thing that all frame windows have in common is that they literally frame the objects inside them. For SDI applications, the frame defines the outside edges of the application. For MDI applications, the main frame defines the outside edges of the main applications, and the child frames define the edges of each individual view into a document.

A *document* in MFC is an object that provides access to the actual data you are managing, along with methods to manage that data. These methods usually are one of two types: commands or member functions. A *command* is nothing more than a *member function* that is enacted by a command message sent to the object. A member function is one that is made public for direct manipulation by code outside of the object.

An example of a document's member function made public for direct manipulation in the "Scribble" tutorial is the **DeleteContents** member function. To call this member function, you simply use code such as

```
pDoc->DeleteContents();
```

An example of a member function enacted by a command would be the **OnEditClearAll** member function. This function is not made public. Instead it is typically called upon by the *message map* feature of MFC. The message map is accessed instead by the application framework (usually a toolbar button or menu click) by way of ON_COMMAND, and then routed to the protected member function. Therefore, you would not generally use code like CMyDoc.OnEditClearAll(). Instead, the user must do an action that the framework will recognize in the message map and route accordingly (in this case, selecting "Clear All" from the "Edit" menu).

Even though the document object has a message map, it does not have a window. You cannot use **SendMessage** to send a WM_COMMAND message to the document, since there is no window. You cannot get a screen DC from the document, since there is no window. For document objects, command messages in MFC are not the same as messages in the Windows SDK. Command messages in MFC are sent across objects, not just windows. This is because the document object is not a window. Therefore, the message map paradigm you see implemented in a document's message map are rerouted Windows WM_COMMAND messages. The application framework gets those Windows WM_COMMAND messages at the frame level, and then routes them through the message maps down through the object hierarchy until the destination object responds to the message.

The WM_COMMAND message is unique in this design. Other Windows messages go directly to the window associated to them (for example, WM_MOUSEMOVE messages go to the window with focus, and that window has an **OnMouseMove** handler). However, WM_COMMAND messages are rerouted, since the main frame window that gets the messages does not care about the message. Instead, some object somewhere along the object highway does. Generally, the destination object is a document object, but in certain cases command messages get routed to other objects. An example is provided in the "quickie summary" at the end of this gotcha.

A *view* in MFC is a peek into a document. A document can have as many views as it wishes (an example of a document with multiple views is a splitter window). For each view, there is a window associated. Let's expound on that for a moment.

A document object in MFC contains the actual object being manipulated. Returning to the sample program, Scribble, consider the responsibility of the view window. The view window provides a user interface for the document object. A user interface really can be broken down into two objectives: (1) displaying the data in human-readable form, and (2) translating human actions into commands the object can understand in order to cook the data to a nice golden brown.

To achieve the first objective, the view window would interrogate the document for its data, and then display that data in human-readable forms in the view's client area. That is generally what the **OnDraw** member function of a view is supposed to do. To achieve the second goal, the view must know to look for direct user actions (such as mouse movement or keystrokes) and translate them into commands that the document object can understand.

As mentioned previously, command actions (such as a menu selection or toolbar button click) generally are handled by the document object. The view window(s) generally are contained inside the client area of a frame window. Since a single document can have multiple views on it, the document maintains a list of the different views currently looking into it—automatically.

The following is a quick summary look at what the responsibilities are for a frame, a document, and a view in SDK programming terms:

- A frame is responsible for containing either a view or views (SDI), or several frames (MDI). For both MDI and SDI, the frame is responsible for the toolbar, status bar, menu, and other "decorations."

- A document is responsible for maintaining the data of the object, to provide a WM_COMMAND equivalent (message maps), and a programmatic means for manipulating the data by way of public member functions.

- A view is responsible for painting the object in human-readable form, for providing a WM_PAINT equivalent (**OnDraw**), and for translating direct user input (such as mouse movement and keyboard input) into calls to a document's public member functions for data manipulation or interrogation. This is where you handle the

WM_LBUTTONDOWN equivalent (**OnLButtonDown**) if your application requires an action for the user clicking the mouse on the view. In some cases, a view might be interested in a rerouted command message. A very common case is if your menu has a "Zoom" menu item on it. The document object manages data, not how the data is presented. Therefore, if the user chooses a menu item that says "Zoom to fit Page," the view window is the object that should process that message, since the view window is the object that controls how the document is displayed.

9. Don't Use Control Variables in the Dialog Before the Dialog Is Up

MFC does dialogs right. A dialog box in MFC is treated as an object. For modal dialogs, you declare the object, fill in some starting values, display the dialog with **DoModal**, and then retrieve your values (see Listing 13.1 for a sample from Scribble). MFC provides a layer called the *data exchange* that simplifies the tedious task of setting/getting/verifying values to and from the dialog box. In Listing 13.1, the data exchange is responsible for initially filling out the fields in the dialog with *dlg.m_nThinWidth* and *dlg.m_nThickWidth,* and is also responsible for getting valid values from the dialog box back into *dlg.m_nThinWidth* and *dlg.m_nThickWidth* after the user presses the OK button.

LISTING 13.1 A SAMPLE OF DOING MODAL DIALOG BOXES IN MFC

```
void CScribDoc::OnPenWidths()
{       CPenWidthsDlg dlg;
        // Initialize dialog data
        dlg.m_nThinWidth = m_nThinWidth;
        dlg.m_nThickWidth = m_nThickWidth;
        // Invoke the dialog box
        if (dlg.DoModal() == IDOK)
            {
            // retrieve the dialog data
            m_nThinWidth =
```

```
        dlg.m_nThinWidth;
        m_nThickWidth = dlg.m_nThickWidth; }
```

This data-exchange medium is designed to let the calling object get relevant information about the dialog object, not the actual dialog. However, the control variables in a dialog are not valid until after a dialog is displayed. A *control variable* is actually an object inside the dialog class that is associated with the control.

Consider the sample CSampleDlg class in Listing 13.2. The *m_ListBox* control variable is associated with a list box control. Now, take a look at the code in Listing 13.3. This code tries to add a bunch of strings to the list box before calling **DoModal**(). The problem is that since the dialog has not been created yet by way of **DoModal**(), the list box window has not yet been created either. Therefore, the call to *m_ListBox.AddString* will fail, since there is no valid window handle to which to send the LB_ADDSTRING message.

LISTING 13.2 A DIALOG CLASS WITH THE LIST BOX CONTROL VARIABLE

```
// sampledl.h : header file
// ///////////////////////////////////////////////////////////////////////////
// CSampleDlg dialog
class CSampleDlg : public CDialog
{
// Construction
public:
    CSampleDlg(CWnd* pParent = NULL);   // standard constructor
// Dialog Data
    //{{AFX_DATA(CSampleDlg)
    enum { IDD = IDD_DIALOG1 };
    CListBox    m_ListBox;
    //}}AFX_DATA
// Implementation
protected:
    virtual void DoDataExchange(CDataExchange* pDX);   // DDX/DDV support
    // Generated message map functions
    //{{AFX_MSG(CSampleDlg)
// NOTE: the ClassWizard will add member functions here
    //}}AFX_MSG
    DECLARE_MESSAGE_MAP()
};
```

LISTING **13.3** USING **MFC** DIALOG CONTROL VARIABLES INCORRECTLY

```
// This function lives in the document class
void CMyDoc::OnDoSample()
{
    CSampleDlg dlg;
    // Initialize dialog data
    dlg.m_ListBox.AddString ("Coney Island Cyclone");
    dlg.m_ListBox.AddString ("Magic Mountain Viper");
    dlg.m_ListBox.AddString ("Space Mountain");
    dlg.m_ListBox.AddString ("Batman the Ride");
    // Invoke the dialog box
    if (dlg.DoModal() == IDOK)
        {
        // Party on the dlg structure here.
        }
}
```

What to do? You want to keep the initialization code to fill the list box inside the CMyDoc class, but since this dialog is a modal dialog, you pass control to the Cdialog class code until the user presses the OK button. One solution is to add a member variable to the CSampleDlg that contains a pointer to the CMyDoc class, and then override the **OnInitDialog** member function of CSampleDlg to call the init code inside CMyDoc. See Listing 13.4 for this implementation.

LISTING **13.4** USING **MFC** DIALOG CONTROLS CORRECTLY

```
// sampledl.h : header file
class CSampleDlg : public CDialog
{
// Construction
public:
CSampleDlg(CWnd* pParent = NULL);    // standard constructor
// Pointer to the CMyDoc object (where the listbox fill code lives) CMyDoc*
m_pCMyDoc;
// Dialog Data
        //{{AFX_DATA(CSampleDlg)
        enum { IDD = IDD_DIALOG1 };
        CListBox      m_ListBox;
        //}}AFX_DATA
// Implementation
```

```
protected:
        virtual void DoDataExchange(CDataExchange* pDX);      // DDX/DDV support
        // Generated message map functions
        //{{AFX_MSG(CSampleDlg)
        virtual BOOL OnInitDialog();
        //}}AFX_MSG
        DECLARE_MESSAGE_MAP()
};
// In the implementation of CSampleDlg...
BOOL CSampleDlg::OnInitDialog()
{
        CDialog::OnInitDialog();
        // Call the CMyDoc class function to fill in the listbox
        m_pCMyDoc->InitDialog(this);
        return TRUE;   // return TRUE  unless you set the focus to a control
}
// This is the member function of the CMyDoc to fill in the listbox
void CMyDoc::InitDialog ( CSampleDlg* pDlg )
{
        pDlg->m_ListBox.AddString ("Coney Island Cyclone");
        pDlg->m_ListBox.AddString ("Magic Mountain Viper");
        pDlg->m_ListBox.AddString ("Space Mountain");
        pDlg->m_ListBox.AddString ("Batman the Ride");
}
// And modify the OnDoSample() function from Listing 13.2
void CMyDoc::OnDoSample()
{
            CSampleDlg dlg;
// Initialize the dialog data so that it can call back to this
// object to fill in the listbox after creation
            dlg.m_pCMyDoc = this;
            // Invoke the dialog box
            if (dlg.DoModal() == IDOK)
                {
                // Party on the dlg structure here.
}
}
```

8. Be Sure to Put a CWinApp Object in _USRDLL DLLs

The CWinApp object really should have been called the CWinCore object. That's because this object handles the core functionality of a Windows executable file or a DLL. Because it is named CWinApp, many developers do not include it in their MFC DLLs.

Take a look at the WINMAIN.CPP file (in the MFC source directory) to see how a WinMain or LibMain/WEP function is declared, depending if _USRDLL is defined. Notice how both have calls to **AfxGetApp()->InitInstance()** and **AfxGetApp()->ExitInstance()**. If you take a look at the help file, you find that the **AfxGetApp()** function returns a pointer to the CWinApp object for the application. Therefore, MFC considers a DLL to also be an application, since the calls to **InitInstance** and **ExitInstance** are also done for DLLs using the _USRDLL convention.

This brings up a very easy way to add initialization and shutdown code to your DLLs. Simply overload the **InitInstance** and/or **ExitInstance** and put in your init/shutdown code. Make sure whatever you put in ExitInstance uses very little or no stack space. In Windows 3.1, this code is executed from the WEP, which is riding on a temporary stack provided by KERNEL. Therefore, try to keep your code restricted to things like **DeleteObject** or other cleanup code. Don't even think of putting a message box in **InitInstance**. You will most certainly crash.

For you 16-bit programmers, you should also know a couple little giblets of information about these _USRDLL DLLs. First, declare the WEP in your DEF file, as shown here:

```
EXPORTS
    WEP @1 RESIDENTNAME
```

Second, make sure you link with the MFC Class library and the C runtime library before you link with other LIB files from other DLLs. This will ensure that you don't use their WEP instead of the ones in the MFC class library and C runtime.

7. When Iterating a List, Remember the Position

One of the collection classes in MFC that is quite handy is the CObList class. This class lets you use the **GetNext** and **GetPrev** member functions to iterate the list. Keep in mind that the *POSITION* variable is passed by reference, and it will change to point to the next or previous item in the list before returning from the **GetNext** or **GetPrev** function. Therefore, the code in Listing 13.5 won't pass the right position to the **DummyFunction**. If you want to keep the *POSITION* of the item around for future use, store it away before calling **GetNext**. See Listing 13.6 for a correct implementation.

LISTING 13.5 PASSING THE WRONG POSITION

```
...
POSITION pos;
pos = MyObject.GetHeadPosition();
while ( NULL != pos)
        {
        thing = MyObject.GetNext(pos);
        DummyFunction (pos);
        }
```

LISTING 13.6 PASSING THE RIGHT POSITION

```
...
POSITION pos, curpos;
pos = MyObject.GetHeadPosition();
while ( NULL != pos )
        {
        curpos = pos;
        thing = MyObject.GetNext(pos);
        DummyFunction (curpos);
        }
```

6. Leaky Memory, Part 1

As beautiful as MFC is for declaring objects and housekeeping, it is still possible to accidentally create extra objects and leak memory. This is done by declaring pointers to classes and calling the new operator more than once for a pointer without calling the delete operator first. See Listing 13.7 for some ultra-brain-dead code that leaks memory.

LISTING 13.7 BRAIN-DEAD C++ CODE

```
CDoubleAgentObject * pObject = new CDoubleAgentObject; // Allocates memory (add
                                                       //some innocent code here)
CDoubleAgentObject * pObject = new CDoubleAgentObject; // Allocates memory
                                                       //(again),
                                                       // first object leaked
```

The memory leak in Listing 13.7 is compounded further if the constructor for the object creates other objects, especially GDI objects. Can you imagine if the constructor for CDoubleAgentObject had three **CreateSolidBrush** calls in it? Every time the brain-dead code leaked an object, GDI's heap would be chipped away. Therefore, it is a good idea to restrict the constructor code of an object to safer operations (such as initializing member variables), especially if you are going to have other (possibly less-than qualified) programmers use your code.

5. GP Faults Galore: Using C++ Member Functions as Callbacks.

Let's put an SDK hat on for a moment. A callback function is any function in your application that is called by a DLL (including Windows' built-in DLLs, such as KERNEL, USER, and GDI). Other than Window procedures, though, there are other type of callbacks. Think back to that **EnumFonts API**:

```
int EnumFonts(  HDC            hdc,
                LPSTR          lpszFace,
                FONTENUMPROC   fntenmprc,
                LPARAM         lParam);
```

This API takes a FONTENUMPROC, which is a placeholder for some application-defined callback in your program. Your may supply a function like this:

```
int CALLBACK MyEnumFontsProc(  LPLOGFONT        lplf,
                               LPNEWTEXTMETRIC  lpntm,
```

```
              int              FontType,
              LPARAM           lpData);
```

This function is called once for each font supportable by the hdc enumerated. Easy enough. Let's call this method of callbacks "Type 1".

"Type 2" callbacks are slightly different. Take a look at the **SetTimer API**:

```
UINT SetTimer(  HWND       hwnd,
                UINT       idTimer,
                UINT       uTimeout,
                TIMERPROC  tmprc);
```

Unlike Type 1 callbacks, this callback happens continuously until the timer is stopped. It cannot be contained in a tight little chunk of code like the Type 1 callback. Your program theoretically never knows when this callback function will be put to use. These types of callbacks are generally tied to an event, versus a being tied to a call to an **EnumXXX** function.

Both of these types of callback functions, however, have a few things in common. They are called by a DLL back to your application, you can specify where the callback procedure lives, and they pass some information back to the callback procedure.

Now, here is where it gets interesting. Suppose you place a Type 1 callback function in your view object—say it was CMyView::**MyEnumFontsProc** so you can look at the previous example and see the parameter list. Now, consider having two views open at the same time.

The code for the object only lives once. It would make no sense at all to duplicate the bytes necessary for the code for each view object. Therefore, for both view objects, the address of CMyView::**MyEnumFontsProc** is identical. When the **EnumFonts** function is called, there is only one address to call back, no matter which object invoked the callback. So, where does the data for the object live?

It lives in one of three places: the object's static data area (for member variables declared static), the stack, or on the heap. Static member variables are not instance-specific. All objects declared from that class will access the same memory address for static member variables. If one object changes a static member variable, all objects of the same class feel the change. All the member variables declared in a class that are not static live either on the stack (for those declared without the new operator), in the program's static data area (for those objects declared globally, but a separate memory address for each object's nonstatic member variables), or in the heap (for those objects declared by pointer and then created with the new operator).

For all objects, no matter how they were created, however, the nonstatic member variables live in a chunk of memory somewhere. That chunk of memory has a pointer to it, and in C++ that pointer is known as the *this* pointer. When your C++ programs are compiled, the *this* pointer is quietly tacked onto the end of the parameter list of every function. The compiler then uses the *this* pointer to access member functions. Take a look at a tiny function as viewed by humans and by the compiler:

By humans:

```
CMyObject::MyFunction ( int iParam1, int iParam2 )
{
     m_iVal1 = iParam1;
     m_iVal2 = iParam2;
}
```

By the compiler:

```
CMyObject::MyFunction ( int iParam1, int iParam2, CMyObject* this ) {
     this->m_iVal1 = iParam1;
     this->m_iVal2 = iParam2;
}
```

The stowing away of the *this* pointer works wonderfully when compiling C++ programs as long as the compiler also gets to compile all of the code that makes the function calls (so that it can also pass the *this* pointer at the end of the parameter list). Here is where the fly in the ointment shows up for DLL callbacks.

When you call **EnumFonts**, the callback was initiated in Windows' GDI module. Well, your application certainly didn't compile GDI, and therefore the double secret probation *this* pointer didn't get tacked onto the end of the parameter list when calling your callback function. However, since your callback function was compiled in MFC, it expects to get that hidden *this* pointer. The results are globalthermonuclear. The callback function will grab the expected *this* pointer from the stack where it thought it was going to be, and then still use the "By the compiler" code. Since that *this* pointer is whatever happened to be on the stack at the time, the previous code uses a very bogus pointer and a very realistic GP fault happens.

Another fly in the ointment is that since the current ANSI C++ standard does not specify stack frames and parameter passing (and probably never will), it would be very unsafe to assume the *this* pointer always will be tacked on the end.

How do you get around this? Luckily, most of the callback functions supplied with Windows are Type 1 callbacks. If you look at the callback functions, they all take that extra parameter *lParam*, which is defined in the docs as "an application-supplied value." For C++ programs, you want to put your *this* pointer in that parameter when calling the function that will invoke the callback. In your callback function, you want to fake the previous "By the compiler" code. Here is how you would call **EnumFonts** from MFC:

```
hdc.EnumFonts(NULL, MyFontEnumProc, (LPARAM)this);
```

Your **MyFontEnumProc** function would be modified to look like this:

```
CMyObject::MyFontEnumProc (    LPLOGFONT            lplf,
                               LPNEWTEXTMETRIC      lpntm,
                               int                  FontType,
                               LPARAM               PassedThis)
{
((CMyObject *)PassedThis)->m_FontType = FontType;
        /* ad nauseum */
}
```

This coding method will make sure to access the data for the same object that called **EnumFonts**, since the *this* pointer was hidden away in that extra parameter. Just to make your code more bulletproof, declare the previous function static as well. Static member functions don't pass a *this* pointer, and, therefore, you won't be able to access this specific information without utilizing the previous **PassedThis** method.

For Type 2 callbacks, if you have a place to store that 32-bit value, then use the exact method you did for the previous examples. However, the **SetTimer** callback function is a bit trickier. The timer callback function does not provide a place to hide the *this* pointer, as shown here:

```
void CALLBACK TimerProc( HWND hwnd, UINT msg, UINT idTimer, DWORD dwTime)
```

However, there still is something unique about the callback: idTimer. With a little gruntwork, you can use idTimer to get around this missing *this* problem. Your object must maintain a list of *this* pointers, using the CDWordArray collection object. Make sure the array is declared static in your class—that ensures that all of your objects declared with this class can get to that array (and hence, there is no need for a *this* pointer to access the static data member variables). Now, when you call **SetTimer**, first add the *this* pointer to the CDWordArray object, and then use the *POSITION* of the *this* pointer as the idTimer. Then your timer callback routine can access the *this* pointer by looking at the static array and using the idTimer as the *POSITION*. By the way, if you are using a Type 1 callback that does not provide a 32-bit parameter, you can use this method as well.

This brings up one more point: What about callback functions from DLLs that are by third parties (such as yourself, or from a tools vendor). If you wrote the code, just make sure that you mimic the Windows **EnumXXX** callbacks, and include an *lParam* sized application-supplied value to all your callback designs. That will enable programmers who use your callbacks to easily follow the same coding conventions as they do for the SDK callback functions.

If you are forced to use a five-year-old DLL that doesn't provide any way to hide the *this* pointer, then you will have no choice but to put the *this* pointer in a static member variable before calling the function that invokes the callback, and then referring to it. This technique is extremely undesirable, since it is not re-entrant, and hence, you cannot have more than one callback going on at one time. Since Windows 95 and NT both support multiple threads, the chances of re-entrant situations will go up in the future as your program becomes multithreaded. So, instead of using that five-year-old DLL, write a new one (or force tools vendors to modify theirs for you to include that *lParam* parameter).

4. OnInitialUpdate Can Be Called More than Once in SDI Applications

MDI applications have an MDI child per document. When you close a document, the MDI child window(s) associated with that document are destroyed, which will cause the view object(s) associated that MDI child window also to be destroyed. Opening a new document involves creating a new MDI child, which causes creation of a new view window. The **OnInitialUpdate** member function of a CView object is called when the MDI child is ready to display the view for the first time.

SDI applications are a little bit different, though. Unlike an MDI application where the view is created and destroyed synchronously with document creation and deletion, the view and document are created only once at startup, and files are shuffled through these objects. Upon a user closing a document, the application frameworks simply will call CDocument::**DeleteContents()** instead of deleting the document and view object. The most likely action, however, is when the user loads in a new document over an older one. The application frameworks will call CDocument::**DeleteContents**() for the old file, load in the new data into the document, and then send the WM_INITIAL-UPDATE message to the view window again. This will cause the CView:**OnInitialUpdate**() member function to be called again for the already existing view.

So, why should you care? If your view does some one-time initialization (such as creating pens, allocating memory, or playing a .WAV file of a sheep baahing), you do not want to place this code in the **OnInitialUpdate** member function of your view with unconditional code. However, placing it in the constructor for the view would not be the wisest idea either (see number 6 in this chapter), and it may also make perfect sense in your design to put your code in **OnInitialUpdate**.

An easy solution that would make your code also quite easier to MDI-ize would be to add an *m_bAlreadyInitialized* member variable. Set this variable to TRUE the first time your OnInitialUpdate (or OnCreate if you desire) member function is called. That way, subsequent calls to this member function will let your code smartly skip over the one-time initialization. This method makes it easy to move your object over to an MDI atmosphere, since the **OnInitialUpdate/OnCreate** member function will act identically for both MDI and SDI applications.

3. Hey! My Status Bar Has a Mind of its Own!

In MFC, the status bar's pane 0 is automatically updated by the MFC framework whenever the message loop is idle to the string defined as AFX_IDS_IDLEMESSAGE in your application's resource template. This is easy to change if you want a static string during idle time (the default string is "Ready").

However, your sophisticated application may want to put a dynamic string into the status bar, though, such as the time of day, or the state of your application (that is, "Edit Mode", "View Mode", and so on) in this status bar. If you try to set something into pane 0, it will be wiped out very quickly when the message queue goes empty and your application becomes idle. See the "Use the Source, Luke!" sidebar in this chapter for an explanation of why.

2. Oncommand Handlers for Commands Sent by Dialog Bars Need to Be in the Object in the Command Routing, andnot in the CDialogBar Class

Just like a toolbar or menu, the CDialogBar is a command message-generating machine. And just like the toolbar or menu, your code to handle the command message lives in the object that wants to receive the message, not in the CDialogBar itself.

Take a look at your ole' pal Scribble. The message map for the CScribDoc object looks like that in Listing 13.8. Notice how the document object handles the ON_COMMAND and ON_UPDATE_COMMAND_UI messages, not the toolbar or the menu.

LISTING 13.8 COMMAND MESSAGE MAP FOR THE SCRIBBLE DOCUMENT

```
BEGIN_MESSAGE_MAP(CScribDoc, COleServerDoc)
    //{{AFX_MSG_MAP(CScribDoc)
        // NOTE - the ClassWizard will add and remove mapping macros here.
        //      DO NOT EDIT what you see in these blocks of generated code !
    ON_COMMAND(ID_EDIT_CLEAR_ALL, OnEditClearAll)
    ON_UPDATE_COMMAND_UI(ID_EDIT_CLEAR_ALL, OnUpdateEditClearAll)
    ON_COMMAND(ID_PEN_THICK_OR_THIN, OnPenThickOrThin)
    ON_UPDATE_COMMAND_UI(ID_PEN_THICK_OR_THIN, OnUpdatePenThickOrThin)
    ON_COMMAND(ID_PEN_WIDTHS, OnPenWidths)
    ON_COMMAND(ID_EDIT_COPY, OnEditCopy)
    //}}AFX_MSG_MAP
END_MESSAGE_MAP()
```

This ideology is kept consistent with the CDialogBar class, and, therefore, you must make sure to provide the command handlers for the buttons in the CDialogBar as well. If you don't, expect to have the same results as if you removed to command handlers for a menu or a toolbar button: The menu item or toolbar button will be grayed out.

1. Leaky Memory, Part 2

The archive object will create a new object for you automatically when you extract from it. Therefore, if you declare a pointer to an object, don't allocate the actual object with the new operator, or else you will double-allocate your object, and the first one will be lost to the great bit-bucket of the sky. Except in this case, you could be getting into mondo trouble if the constructor for this object of yours happens to have a GDI or USER object created (see number 6, "Leaky Memory, Part 1"). Those objects will hang around even after your application terminates. See Listing 13.9 for incorrect and correct implementations.

LISTING 13.9 SIX MONTHS IN A LEAKY MFC APP

Bad:

```
CMyObject* pObject = new CMyObject;      // Allocates memory
myArchive >> pObject;    // Allocates memory (again)
```

Good:

```
CMyObject* pObject;      // Declares pointer
myArchive >> pObject;    // Allocates memory
```

"USE THE SOURCE, LUKE"

The single best tool to understanding how MFC works, and why your program may not be behaving the way you would like, is right in front of you: the MFC source code. If you want to see how something works, or see how something does not work, simply use the debugger to trace into the MFC source code (sometimes many levels deep), and eventually you will find the familiar Windows SDK APIs. Which brings us to a very important revelation: MFC is nothing new. It is just a whole bunch of code already written for us in C++ so that we don't have to waste our time writing grunty old menu, dialog, and MDI code ad nauseum. Deep down in the bowels of MFC, you will find that the code is eventually written using the exact same APIs that your already existing plain C programs are using.

If you don't know how to write applications without using MFC, you are in for a very rough ride. If you just got back from your local software store with your copy of Visual C++ 2.0, ripped off the shrink-wrap so fast that the static cling makes it stick to your cat, installed it on your machine, ran AppWizard to generate an OLE2 Container-Server, and then found yourself saying "What is the difference between a modal and modeless dialog?", then you need to take a step back.

How big of a step? Well, first off, go back to your local software store and get Charles Petzold's *Programming Windows* book and read it. Then read my first book, *Writing Windows Applications from Start to Finish*. Now you have dabbled enough with straight C that you can graduate up to MFC and C++. The "behind the scenes" knowledge you will gain from writing at least one straight C application will be invaluable to you when you find that you need to enhance the classes supplied with MFC.

Here is an example of how the sources were used to figure out what was going on. Refer back to number 3, "Hey! My Status Bar has a Mind of its Own!" There you find that the status bar changes pane 0 as soon as the program enters an idle state. First, put your SDK hat on, and remember what your main message loop looks like this:

```
while (GetMessage((LPMSG)&msg, NULL, 0, 0))
    {
    if ( !TranslateAccelerator (ghWnd, hAccel, &msg))
        {
        TranslateMessage(&msg);
        DispatchMessage(&msg);
        }
    }'
```

This SDK code yields to other applications at **GetMessage** if there are no messages in the program's queue, but never exits the loop while the program is "alive," since **GetMessage** will always return TRUE until the WM_QUIT message is retrieved. Therefore, if the application is idle, this loop is where program control would be. Since you are looking to see why the status bar pane is changed when the program goes idle, you just need to find the equivalent of the previous code inside MFC.

I grabbed Scribble, and added a member function to the CMainFrame class that is based off a message (such as WM_MENUSELECT). I then set a breakpoint on that member function, and ran Scribble. Once I hit that, I looked at the Call Stack in VC++'s debugger, and found that there is a function called

PumpMessage. Going to that function, I found that it was called by the **Run** member function. Here is an abbreviated version of that **Run** function:

```
/ Main running routine until application exits
int CWinApp::Run()
{
    /* Code removed for readability */
    // Acquire and dispatch messages until a WM_QUIT message is received.
    for (; ;)
    {
        LONG lIdleCount = 0;
        // check to see if we can do idle work
        while (!::PeekMessage(&m_msgCur, NULL, NULL, NULL, PM_NOREMOVE)
            &&
            OnIdle(lIdleCount++))
        {
            // more work to do
        }
        // either we have a message, or OnIdle returned false
if (!PumpMessage())
            break;
    }
    return ExitInstance();
}
```

There I found that **OnIdle** was getting called if the **PeekMessage** call returned false (which means the message queue is empty).

So, I now knew to look for the **OnIdle** member function. I found that in the same class, and found that it sent the WM_IDLEUPDATECMDUI message to its descendants. So, off I go to the CFrameWnd class and I find the following lines of code in WINFRM.CPP's CFrameWnd::**OnIdleUpdateCmdUI** member function:

```
    // set the current message string if necessary
if (m_nIDTracking != m_nIDLastMessage) {
        SendMessage(WM_SETMESSAGESTRING, (WPARAM)m_nIDTracking);
        ASSERT(m_nIDTracking == m_nIDLastMessage);
    }
```

Now I see that the WM_SETMESSAGESTRING message is sent when the program goes idle, which explains problem number 3. Look at the **OnSetMessageString** member function in WINFRM.CPP:

```
LRESULT CFrameWnd::OnSetMessageString(WPARAM wParam, LPARAM lParam)
{
CWnd* pMessageBar = GetMessageBar(); if (pMessageBar != NULL)
    {
        LPCSTR lpsz = NULL;
        char szBuffer[256];
        // set the message bar text
        if (lParam != NULL)
            {
ASSERT(wParam == 0);     // can't have both an ID and a string
                        // set an explicit string
                lpsz = (LPCSTR)lParam;
}
        else if (wParam != 0)
            {
// use the wParam as a string ID
if (_AfxLoadString(wParam, szBuffer) != 0)
                    lpsz = szBuffer;
                else
TRACE1("Warning: no message line prompt for ID 0x%04X\n", (UINT)wParam);
            }
        pMessageBar->SetWindowText(lpsz);
    }
    UINT nIDLast = m_nIDLastMessage;
    m_nIDLastMessage = (UINT)wParam;      // new ID (or 0)
    m_nIDTracking = (UINT)wParam;         // so F1 on toolbar buttons work
    return nIDLast;
}
```

There is a public member variable in CFrameWnd called *m_nIdleFlags* (look in AFXWIN.H to see it) that is nonzero if the application is idle. Therefore, you can do one of two things, both involve overriding the previous **OnSetMessageString** function:

First, you could set the redraw state of the status bar to FALSE, call the previous base class function, set the redraw state of the status bar back to TRUE, and then you could draw what you wanted in the status bar. Of course, you only do all this hoo-hah if the *m_nIdleFlags* variable is nonzero, otherwise just call the base class and call it a day.

Second, you could copy the previous code from WINFRM.CPP, paste it into your overridden function, and modify it as needed. I like the first method better, since it leaves the base class code in the MFC implementation, and your special code in your overridden class (which means you won't hose yourself when you recompile with the new class libraries that come out the day after your application ships):

```
LRESULT CMyFrame::OnSetMessageString(WPARAM wParam, LPARAM lParam)
{
    LRESULT lRetVal;
    CWnd* pMessageBar = GetMessageBar();
    if (m_nIdleFlags)
        {
        if (pMessageBar != NULL) pMessageBar->SetRedraw(FALSE);
        }
lRetVal = CFrameWnd::OnSetMessageString(wParam, lParam);
    if (m_nIdleFlags)
        {
        if (pMessageBar != NULL)
            {
            pMessageBar->SetRedraw(TRUE);
            pMessageBar->SetWindowText ( pszTheTextYouWant );
            }
        }
    return lRetVal;
}
```

This example required only two things: You had to know how the SDK stuff works, and then you had to go hunting through the sources (and editor with GREP built in is most excellent) to find out where the magic happens.

As an additional note, look into the .H and .INL files in the MFC\INCLUDE directory. There you will find inline functions and macros.

CHAPTER 14

Cool MFC Ideas

The previous list was aimed at solving pressing issues that may completely halt program development. They are the types of questions that programmers want answered at 3 o'clock in the morning. This list is of the same flavor, except the items of this list aren't "gotcha's," they are "solutions." None of the solutions in this list are going to get you out of a programming bind at 3am, but they could make your program just a bit sassier, and your programmers will find that these solutions open up a bit more flexibility to their MFC programs.

As with the last list, I got these ideas from Brian Scott, please see his biography in the Introduction of this book.

10. Easier Access to Your Main Application Objects

If you take a look in the sources to MFC, you will notice that the **AfxGetApp()** function is used an awful lot. This function returns a pointer to the main application object (the **CWinApp class**), which contains the special information pertaining to the current instance of your MFC program. For example, the **m_hInstance** member variable lives in this class.

There are undoubtedly going to be variables that you care about as well for your application on a global sense. These variables could be declared globally, but the whole idea of objects is to associate all of your data with some class somewhere. Since your applications always derive a class from **CWinApp** to place your **InitInstance** code in, this is also a great place to put your application-scope member variables. In the Scribble program, the new class defined in SCRIBBLE.H is called **CScribbleApp**.

MFC provides a mechanism to get at the base **CWinApp** object that your **CScribbleApp** is derived from; this lets you get at the member variables of the **CWinApp** base class. This mechanism is the global function **AfxGetApp**, which returns a pointer to the **CWinApp** object. However, if you add member variables to your app's derived object (**CScribbleApp**), you would end up casting every time you wanted to access that member variable:

```
((CScribbleApp*)AfxGetApp())->m_myVariable
```

However, by writing just one global function, you can make all of the member variables in the **CScribbleApp** cla*ss and* the **CWinApp** class easily accessible throughout your program; instead of declaring all of them global, or instead of accessing them via typecasting or scope resolution pointers:

```
CScribbleApp* GetMyApp() { return (CScribbleApp*)AfxGetApp();}
```

This way, you could access the **m_hInstance** member variable of your derived **CWinApp** the exact same way as your **m_myVariable** member variable from **CScribbleApp**:

```
GetMyApp()->m_hInstance
GetMyApp()->m_myVariable
```

9. A New View on New Views

Raise your hand if you like Figure 14.1.

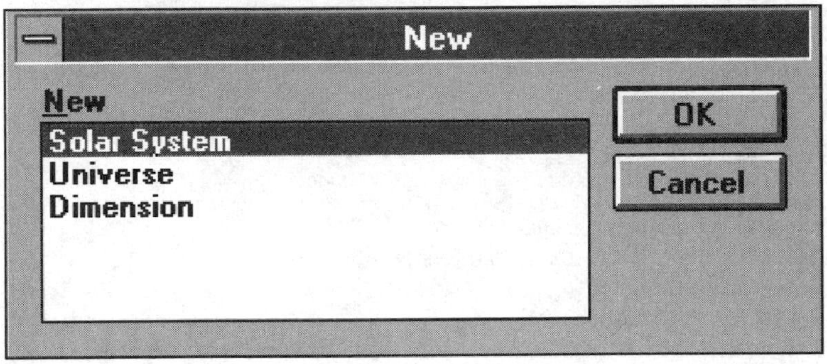

FIGURE 14.1 A "NEW" DIALOG BOX

Okay, for those of you with your hands down, let's think about how we may improve on the way MFC handles the "New" menu item from the File menu. For example, let's say our application was something tiny, like, Gigunda for Windows, and it had "New Solar System," "New Universe," and "New Dimension" on it's File menu. Instead of that really ugly dialog in Figure 14.1, these three menu options would instantly bring up the new document pertaining to Solar Systems, Universes, or Dimensions. Doing this is actually quite straightforward. Take a look at the code in your standard AppWhiz outta the box gigunda.cpp modified to handle three different documents and views:

```
// Register the application's document templates.  Document templates
//  serve as the connection between documents, frame windows and views.

CMultiDocTemplate* pSolarSysDocTemplate;
pSolarSysDocTemplate = new CMultiDocTemplate(
    IDR_SOLARSYSTYPE,
    RUNTIME_CLASS(CSolarSystemDoc),
    RUNTIME_CLASS(CMDIChildWnd),          // standard MDI child frame
    RUNTIME_CLASS(CSolarSystemView)
    );
AddDocTemplate(pSolarSysDocTemplate);


CMultiDocTemplate* pUniverseDocTemplate;
pUniverseDocTemplate = new CMultiDocTemplate(
```

```
    IDR_UNIVERSETYPE,
    RUNTIME_CLASS(CUniverseDoc),
    RUNTIME_CLASS(CMDIChildWnd),        // standard MDI child frame
    RUNTIME_CLASS(CUniverseView)
    );
AddDocTemplate(pUniverseDocTemplate);


CMultiDocTemplate* pDimensionDocTemplate;
pDimensionDocTemplate = new CMultiDocTemplate(
    IDR_DIMENSIATYPE,
    RUNTIME_CLASS(CDimensionDoc),
    RUNTIME_CLASS(CMDIChildWnd),        // standard MDI child frame
    RUNTIME_CLASS(CDimensionView)
    );
AddDocTemplate(pDimensionDocTemplate);
```

The idea is to go ahead and create those document templates, but don't call the **CWinApp::AddDocTemplate** function. Instead, save these away in member variables (of type **CMuliDocTemplate**), then replace the "New" item on the File menu with your three choices: "New Solar System", "New Universe", and "New Dimension".

Once you have your resources taken care of above, add message handlers in the **CWinApp** class for those menu items, such as:

```
CMyWinApp::OnNewSolarSystem ( ... )
{
  // NULL means open a new document
  m_pSolarSystemDocTemplate->OpenDocumentFile(NULL);
}
```

8. Dialog Boxes and Message Loops

If you go digging down in the MFC source code for **CDialog::DoModal**, you will eventually end up calling the SDK API **DialogBox**. This API keeps the message loop deep down inside USER (See Chapter 1, tip #9). So, just as you had to worry about losing control of your message loop in SDK Land, you also have to worry about it in MFC Land.

So, what do you lose by having USER do the message looping in MFC? Well, MFC does quite a bit in its main message loop. In particular, it does some idle background processing. The background processing handles things such as object cleanup, calling **PreTranslateMessage** (which handles accelerators), and updating user interface gadgets such as the status bar. To see what I mean, run your favorite MFC app, open the about box, and start banging away on the **CAPS LOCK** key. You will notice that the little light on your keyboard comes on, but the status bar on the main frame does not update. This is because the status bar is updated during idle processing (See Chapter 13's sidebar on using the source for an in-depth look at the status bar updates).

If you need the MFC main message loop to be active during a modal dialog, use a modeless dialog, and disable the parent. Just like in SDK land.

7. Leave My Captions Alone!

MFC by default handles the text in your captions. But what if your app had a really slick name like "My Really Slick App?" You certainly wouldn't want MFC to tack on the filename to the end of that already long title. So, here is a way to take control of that feature of MFC.

Remove FWS_ADDTOTITLE (casting it to a long for you 16-bit programmers) from the main frame window or MDI child windows to prevent MFC from changing the window captions. Do this in **PreCreateWindow**. Therefore, you have them manually change them, most likely when you change views. So, add code like this to each view object:

```
CMyView::OnActivateView( BOOL bActivate... )
{
  // It is your option to use bActivate for whatever...

  // This is how you change the Main frame's app
  AfxGetMainWnd()->SetWindowText("blah blah blah parent sez blah");

  // Only do this if you are an MDI application
  // This is how you change the MDI child's caption
```

```
GetParentFrame()->SetWindowText( "blah blah blah child blah");
  ...
}
```

6. Dare to Be Different-Custom Icons and Backgrounds

Not every application wants to look like AppWizard residue. Register a new AFX window class to get a custom icon or cursor or background color for your window. Use **AfxRegisterWndClass** in **PreCreateWindow**:

```
CMyFrameWnd::PreCreateWindow ( CREATESTRUCT& cs )
{
  // Call base class to fill this thing out however it feels like doing
  BOOL bResult = CFrameWnd::PreCreateWindow ( cs );

  // Call AfxRegisterWndClass to make yer own special class
  cs.lpszClass =
      AfxRegisterWndClass( CS_DBLCLKS,                    // we want double clicks
                           LoadCursor(IDC_DEADBARNEY), // An American Icon
                                                       //   is dead
                           GetStockObject(BLACK_BRUSH),// Black brush for
                                                       //   Dead Barneys!
                           LoadIcon(IDI_EYE)           // Some nice eyecon
                         );
  // return the base class' result
  return bResult;
}
```

5. Handling Different MDI Children

When you switch between MDI child windows (which usually means you are switching to a view of a potentially different document type), it is often nice to make some changes to the ornamentation of your frame window. You may want to change the toolbar, or update the menu dynamically.

To achieve this, override **OnMDIActivate** to do something every time an MDI child window is activated. Since the normal **OnMDIActivate** function does a lot of important things, you would think that calling the base class is a good idea. However, one of those important things the base class does is the call to **DrawMenuBar()**. To avoid having the base class draw the menu bar, and then have your class draw the menu bar (which results in a disco show), do the ole' "copy and paste the code from the MFC sources" game. What follows is the exact function from the MFC sources. I leave it as an exercise to the reader to have your fun with this function (such as changing out the toolbar):

```
CMyMDIClass:: OnMDIActivate( BOOL bActivate, CWnd* pActivateWnd,
                             CWnd* pDeactivateWnd )
{
    m_bPseudoInactive = FALSE;  // must be happening for real

    // make sure MDI client window has correct client edge
    UpdateClientEdge();

    // send deactivate notification to active view
    CView* pActiveView = GetActiveView();
    if (!bActivate && pActiveView != NULL)
        pActiveView->OnActivateView(FALSE, pActiveView, pActiveView);


    // allow hook to short circuit normal activation
    BOOL bHooked = FALSE;
#ifndef _AFX_NO_OLE_SUPPORT
    if (m_pNotifyHook != NULL && m_pNotifyHook->OnDocActivate(bActivate))
        bHooked = TRUE;
#endif

    // update titles (don't AddToTitle if deactivate last)
    if (!bHooked)
        OnUpdateFrameTitle(bActivate || (pActivateWnd != NULL));

    // re-activate the appropriate view
    if (bActivate)
    {
        if (pActiveView != NULL && GetMDIFrame() == GetActiveWindow())
            pActiveView->OnActivateView(TRUE, pActiveView, pActiveView);
    }

    // update menus
```

```
    if (!bHooked)
    {
        OnUpdateFrameMenu(bActivate, pActivateWnd, NULL);
        GetMDIFrame()->DrawMenuBar();
    }
}
```

4. Sizing a FormView Window Using the Dialog Template's Dimensions

The form view window is nice, but one of the major beefs programmers have about it is the fact that the window is sizeable, and it always comes up to the wrong size to start with. You would be much happier if this window would be created the same size as the dialog template implied while you were creating it in AppStudio.

For SDI applications, this is done by calling the **RecalcLayout** and **ResizeParentToFit** functions:

```
void CMyFormView::OnInitialUpdate()
{
  CFormView::OnInitialUpdate();
  GetParentFrame()->RecalcLayout();
  ResizeParentToFit();
  ResizeParentToFit(); // bShrink = TRUE
}
```

Why the **ResizeParentToFit** call twice?. MFC will on occasion create the view with negative coordinates. The **ResizeParentToFit** function will spend its first call fixing this, and the second call actually sizing the form to fit.

Word of warning: Design your forms on a VGA screen. This method, coupled with removing the sizing borders on the MDI child (via overriding the **PreCreateWindow** member function), will make it impossible for the user to size the form view (and create scrollbars if needed). If your dialog is too big on a VGA screen, your users will barf.

For MDI applications, you don't need to call **RecalcLayout()**, so your **OnInitialUpdate** function is even simpler:

```
void CMyMDIFormView::OnInitialUpdate()
{
  CFormView::OnInitialUpdate();
  ResizeParentToFit();
  ResizeParentToFit(); // bShrink = TRUE
}
```

3. Switching Views Programatically

Since each document can have multiple views, a programming issue that comes up often is the desire to let the user flip between multiple views of a document without switching windows. An example of this may be if you want to switch your slide presentation from Outline View to Slide Sorter view. To switch views within a frame window (such as an MDI child) without changing windows, you must take some additional steps.

Let's look at how you would do this for an SDI application (I won't cover MDI applications, since MDI apps generally create new windows for new views). First, let's assume you have two views. We will have CView1 and CView2. By default, CView1 comes up; it is the one defined in the **CDocumentTemplate**. However, the user can switch between CView1 and CView2 from some mechanism (like the menu). Here's what you do:

1. Create your CView2 view and attach it to the document. Here is some sample code you would use in the InitInstance() member for the CWinApp object. Remember, in this example, both views are created at startup, and persist thought the lifetime of the application. You could do this dynamically if you want.

```
#include "afxpriv.h"  // required for some private functions
CMyWinApp::InitInstance (...)
```

```
{
   ...
   OnFileNew();   // This code is already here from AppWizard, add the code below

   // Get the currently active view (CView1) and store it in your
   // new member variable m_pView1.
   CView* pActiveView = ((CFrameWnd*) m_pMainWnd)->GetActiveView();
   m_pView1 = pActiveView;

   // Now, create the secondary view, and store it in your new member variable
   // m_pView2
   m_pView2 = (CView*) new CView2;

   // Get the document object pointer
   CDocument* pCurrentDoc = ((CFrameWnd*) m_pMainWnd)->GetActiveDocument();

   // Initialize a CCreateContext to point to the active document.
   // With this context, the Cview2 is also added to the document
   // when the view is created in CView::OnCreate().
   CCreateContext newContext;
   newContext.m_pNewViewClass = NULL;
   newContext.m_pNewDocTemplate = NULL;
   newContext.m_pLastView = NULL;
   newContext.m_pCurrentFrame = NULL;
   newContext.m_pCurrentDoc = pCurrentDoc;

   // The ID of the initial active view is AFX_IDW_PANE_FIRST.
   // Incrementing this value by one for additional views works
   // in the standard document/view case but the technique cannot
   // be extended for the CSplitterWnd case.
   UINT viewID = AFX_IDW_PANE_FIRST + 1;
   CRect rect(0, 0, 0, 0); // gets resized later

   // Create the new view. In this example, the view persists for
   // the life of the application. The application automatically
   // deletes the view when the application is closed.
   m_pView2->Create(NULL,
                    "PogoRoxyHannah",  // arbitrary name
                    WS_CHILD,
                    rect,
                    m_pMainWnd, viewID, &newContext);

   // When a document template creates a view, the WM_INITIALUPDATE
```

```
// message is sent automatically. However, this code must
// explicitly send the message, as follows.
m_pView2->SendMessage(WM_INITIALUPDATE, 0, 0);
...
}
```

If you create the view class in ClassWizard, you must modify the code to change the access specifier for the constructor, destructor, and **OnInitialUpdate()** function from protected to public.

N O T E

2. Add code like the following to switch views. This code is called in response to whatever your user does to switch views (such as choosing a menu item).

```
CView* CMyWinApp::SwitchView(CView* pNewView)
{
    // Get the current view (could be either CView1 or CView2
    CView* pActiveView = ((CFrameWnd*) m_pMainWnd)->GetActiveView();

    // exchange view window ID's so RecalcLayout() works
    UINT temp = ::GetWindowWord(pActiveView->m_hWnd, GWW_ID);
    ::SetWindowWord(pActiveView->m_hWnd, GWW_ID,
                ::GetWindowWord(pNewView->m_hWnd, GWW_ID));
    ::SetWindowWord(pNewView->m_hWnd, GWW_ID, temp);

    // Show the new view, hide the old view
    pActiveView->ShowWindow(SW_HIDE);
    pNewView->ShowWindow(SW_SHOW);

    // Set the active view, housekeep, and repaint
    ((CFrameWnd*) m_pMainWnd)->SetActiveView(pNewView);
    ((CFrameWnd*) m_pMainWnd)->RecalcLayout();
    pNewView->Invalidate();

    // Return a pointer to the old view in case program wants to destroy it
    // (after calling CDocument::RemoveView(), of course)
    return pActiveView;
}
```

2. Subclassing, SDK Style in MFC

Normally, you don't have to subclass windows (SDK Style, See Chapter 9 for more detailed information) in MFC. That's because you can simply derive a new class, and add the additional filtering you need. For example, if you want an Edit control to only take alphanumeric characters, you would derive a class from CEdit and filter out everything you didn't want with an **OnChar** member function.

However, what if the edit control was not created with the **CEdit::Create** member function? Such as an edit control in a dialog box template? This edit control was created by USER when the dialog box was created, you would normally **Attach()** to that edit control. However, subclassing the edit control is a little different. When you Attach a window to a window object, you simply associate the member functions of that window object to the window handle. This causes member functions like **SetWindowText** and **GetWindowText** to work nicely. However, the messages sent to that edit control are not going to be intercepted by MFC and routed through the message maps. In order for this to happen, MFC needs to trap those messages. When you use the **Create** member function of a CEdit object, this trapping mechanism is instantiated. The **SubclassDlgItem** member function will attach and instantiate the message trapping mechanism. This allows you to add message handlers to this CEdit object in the exact same way as you would for windows objects created with the **Create** member function. Here's how you do it:

1. Derive a class from CEdit, modify the message map to do whatever you want.

2. Add a data membber of that type to your **CDialog** class.

3. In **OnInitDialog**, call the **SubClassDlgItem** with the ID of the item you want to subclass:

```
m_myNiftynewEdit.SubclassDlgItem ( IDC_EDIT_TO_SUBCLASS, this );
```

1. Subclassing the MDI Client Window

First, let me explain what the MDI client window is. In an MDI application, you have the frame window, the ornaments, the MDI client, and the MDI children. The ornaments are the toolbar, status bar, and any other indicator gadgets you want to stick to the frame. The remaining client area of the main frame is occupied by the MDI Client window. This special window is responsible for containing all of the MDI children (which contain views), handling the little icons when you minimize the MDI children, and for handling mundane tasks such as tiling, cascading, ad naseum. Generally, the MDI client window acts silently and magically, doing all the grunt work of an MDI application for you without one iota of your intervention.

However, you could subclass the MDI client window to do things like paint a nice background. But wait! There is no CMIDClientWindow! We must dig a little deeper. CMDIFrameWnd has the m_hWndMDIClient member variable that you can get to. So, we take a similar approach that we did above in tip #2. Except, since there is no CMDIClientWindow defined, we need to make one:

1. Derive a class from **CWnd** (call it something like **CMDIClientWindow**) that will be your MDI client window, and add a member variable for it in your **CFrameWnd** object (let's call it **m_myClientWnd**).

2. In your main frames' **OnCreate** member function, use code like this:

```
CMyMDIFrame::OnCreate ( LPCREATESTRUCT lpCreateStruct )
{
  // Call the base class first so that the MDI client window gets created
  int iResult = CMDIFrame::OnCreate ( lpCreateStruct );

  // Now, subclass it on success (return value is 0)
  if (!i) m_myClientWnd.SubClassWindow(m_hWndMDIClient);

  // Return the right value
  return iResult;
}
```

CHAPTER 15

Pre-IBM PC Trivia

You young whippersnappers! This is such a weird industry. I've been part of this computer revolution since 1978 when I got my first computer, the Ohio Scientific Superboard II. Things have changed. For you freshies to the industry who have grown up with the IBM PC, here's a little grouping of totally random tidbits from the pre-IBM-dominated world of personal computing. For your "old-timers," well, maybe you will recognize a couple of these (and no, I don't like "Matlock").

10. Ohio Scientific (OSI)

Of course, my first trip down memory lane must start with my first computer. The Ohio Scientific Superboard II was the same as their Challenger 1P, except that I had to build the case, add a power supply, and provide all connectors to the "devices"—devices such as a little black-and-white TV. The OSI had a

25x25 character display (actually, it was 32x32, but only 25x25 was visible). The BACKSPACE key did not back up the cursor (unless you spent $120 to buy this ROM chip from a third-party vendor). Instead it printed an underscore character after the character you wanted to delete. For example, if you typed the word DOG, but hit the keys D, I, BACKSPACE, O, and G, your display would look like this:

```
DI_OG
```

If this text was part of a line of code, it would correctly list as DOG when you printed it out (or relisted it at the prompt).

My computer came with 1K of RAM, but it was quickly upgraded to 8K by my dad (hey, I was only 13 at the time). It had BASIC-In-ROM, written by Microsoft! I wouldn't be surprised if Bill Gates wrote it himself. The OSI used a 6502 microprocessor. I learned assembly language because BASIC was too slow to write a good clone of "Space Invaders" on.

9. Core Memory

Really—my OSI computer used static RAM, but it wasn't that long ago that computers used magnetic core memory to store information. Of course, core memory was way expensive and bulky and hot, but at least it remembered the information after the power was shut off.

8. TRS-80

The "Trash-80" was the second computer I owned. "TRS" stood for "Tandy-Radio Shack," and the 80 stood for the Zilog Z-80 microprocessor inside. Of course, Zilog is based in Nampa, Idaho, which was about 10 miles from my house. So, as a 13-year-old, I thought that the entire computer industry was central to Nampa, Idaho.

Of course, by the time I bought a TRS-80, it was their Color Computer, and it used a 6809 microprocessor, which still is a really, really cool chip.

Programming the 6809 was a dream for a 14-year-old kid who had been fighting the OSI's 6502 for a year.

7. Kilobyte

No one talks "kilobytes" anymore. They all talk "megs." The smallest K size mentioned in casual computer nerd conversation is 64K, and with Windows 95, even that will go bye-bye.

6. Pet

Remember this computer? Remember how it was a huge hit, and how it put Commodore (Rest in Peace) on the map? Remember that three-line program you could type in that would make it catch fire? I always remembered the store salesman saying that "nothing you can type into a computer can hurt it," and I always thought back to that three-line program that would cause a Pet computer to burst into flames.

I'm stretching my memory here, but I think it went something like this (kids, don't try this at home):

```
10 MOTOR 1
20 MOTOR 0
30 GOTO 10
```

5. D/C/W/M?

Ah, a quiz. On the Ohio Scientific computers, this was your boot screen. When you reset your computer (which you had to do even when you powered up), you got this simple little prompt. Pressing D accessed the floppy disk drive (if you were lucky enough to have one). Pressing C caused a cold boot, which would put you into BASIC. Pressing W did a warm boot, which never worked, so you ended up cold booting. Pressing M put you into this weird little machine-code memory display, which would let you change the byte locations of any address.

4. Cassette Tapes for Mass Storage

I hate floppy disks. They are slow, bulky, fragile, and, quite honestly, they don't taste very good. This was not the case when I was 13 years old. The old TRS-80s, the Pets, the OSIs, and even the cheap Apples used a cassette tape to store the information. Basically, you sent your program out through a serial RS-232 port, and you recorded the static (just like if you were a wiretapper recording a modem conversation). Then, to load your program back in, you had to do the opposite. Of course, the quality of the tape, as well as the recording volume and tone, all mattered. My tape player (a Radio Shack special) had the volume and tone knobs glued into place once I got it right. And I had to use Maxell tapes to guarantee my program would save right.

3. Pretzeland Software/Aardvark Software

They were the first software houses I had heard of, and I tip my hat to them for selling some of my early programs. They taught me at a very early age that there is money to be made with computers.

2. CompuServe—"The Nighttime Utility"

Remember when CompuServe was only running at night? That's because H&R Block, the company that owns CIS, used the computers during the day to run their business. Some inventive programmers thought up the service in their spare time, and H&R Block figured out that they could make a lot of money by charging people to use their computer. Eventually, H&R Block made enough money to dedicate CIS to a 24-hour-a-day machine.

1. Osborne

Heavy. Luggable. Bankrupt. 'Nuff said. I've seen one. Okay, it's post IBM-PC, but not by much.

CHAPTER 16

MFC Programming Checklist

Designing an application in MFC is considerably different than designing one using the Windows SDK. When you write an SDK app, you generally start from scratch, using only the built-in features of the operating system. If you want to print, you either start from scratch, buy a DLL that prints for you, or you start with a code library. When it comes to designing the user interface, you have to start from scratch, or possibly you have some souped-up GENERIC.EXE program that you begin with. Of course, as you start to add more and more functionality to your code, your program becomes a very unique entity, with less and less reusable code becoming available, and more and more time being spent figuring out what makes it tick.

MFC changes that. Your friend AppWizard builds up a nice skeleton to start with, much like starting with that GENERIC.EXE program from above. However, if you look at the GENERIC.EXE from SDK-Land and compare it with the hot-off-the-AppWizard starter program, you immediately notice a startling difference: The MFC app is a true skeleton. Not a single line of code in the AppWiz starter program is that cut-and-paste-from-GENERIC junk. All of it is either code specific to your application (such as the name of the document objects, view objects, and files), or it is hollow code functions that you must fill in. All of that underlying code to handle the drudgery of **DefWindowProc**, **BeginPaint**, **EndPaint** ad naseum is hidden away in the MFC libraries.

This has good and bad ramifications. The good part is that the code in your app is all *about* your app, not about the underlying way that a Windows app works. This means that an app written in pure MFC will be very easy to port to a non-Windows platform, such as the Mac. Let me describe "pure MFC." Pure MFC means you do not use any ::SDK ::API's because they ::make ::your ::code ::hard ::to ::read, hard to port, and hard to fold into the MFC Framework. The MFC framework is designed to completely hide the windowing part of the operating system, and provide you with the platform independant Document-View paradigm of programming. So that's the good part. The bad part is that since the way the MFC framework functions is still largely unknown by many, it is very easy to make bad decisions during the design process simply because the programmers were not given any documentation about how the MFC framework is designed. This list does not attempt to dissect the MFC Framework. No, that is best done by Mary Kirtland's book, *MFC Internals* (Addison-Wesley). This list instead offers advice based on the framework, along with explanations as to why you should take this advice. If you are a program manager, addressing these considerations before you write a single line of code (or click a single AppWizard button) can help you produce the app you want the first time.

10. Dueling TLA's: VBX's vs OCX's

At the time this book was written, Visual Basic Controls (VBX's) were all the rage. You could pick up a copy of any techno-nerd magazine and find dozens of ads for cool VBX's that ranged from spreadsheet controls to multimedia display controls to Orwellian "watch every keystroke to measure the worker" controls. Visual C++ Versions 1.0 and 1.5 supported these VBX's painlessly—well kind of painlessly.

Also at the time this book was written, Visual C++ 2.0 was just released, and it includes the next generation of controls: OLE Controls (sometimes called OCXs). These controls are actually very similar to an OLE server, except that they don't have all of the confinements of an OLE in-place server. Namely, they act like controls, not another program. This is the future of computing. Repeat: *The Future*. Not the present. Currently, at the time of this book's writing, there are no OCX controls on the market. If you bought my book right when it came out, you may find a handful of OCXs available that hopefully will suit your needs. If you are at the half price bookstore right now standing in the clearance isle, there are probably a lot of OCX controls available.

So, which one, if either to use? If you have to cater to 32-bit audiences (which includes Windows 95 and Windows NT, which should mean everybody), then you need to use OCXs. The architecture of a VBX is so oriented towards 16-bitness that you probably won't ever see 32-bit VBXs. That's right. All those companies that are making their bread and butter selling VBXs are frantically reworking their code to become OCXs (or maybe they are just taking their millions of dollars and moving to Hawaii). If you are stuck in the world of 16 bits (say, perhaps, that you work for the government), then you could find that the vast library of VBXs is instantly available to you at very economical prices.

9. Decide If You Want to Use the Document/View Architecture

The document/view architecture is the backbone of MFC. If you are not using this paradigm, you will be fighting MFC every step of the way (unless you are writing a very specific program that does not work with documents and views, such as, perhaps, a program without an interface). AppWizard generates a doc/view architecture skeleton program for you.

Besides the fact that MFC is really designed around the doc/view architecture, there are other reasons you should use it for applications that view/manipulate data. The first reason is OLE. If you follow the doc/view architecture, and if you clicked the right buttons in AppWizard, you will start off with a most excellent OLE ready program. Sure, you still are going to have to do some extra work, but you will be saved from writing thousands and thousands of lines of code to deal with the OLE interfae.

The second reason is portability. Not only between platforms (you are supposed to be able to take a pure MFC program and simply recompile it for the Mac), but between versions of MFC. If you wrote a pure MFC program using Visual C++ 1.5, you will be able to simply recompile that program for Visual C++ 2.0 in 32 bits, and the only issues you will need to worry about are the sizes of scalar data items such as integers (see Chapter 8: Porting Beasties).

The third reason for using the doc/view architecture is your users. They are going to get severely used to running programs that were concieved with AppWizard, and if you don't subscribe to this New World Order, your program will never feel like a broken in baseball mitt to the typical end user.

Now, you may think that your program can't subscribe to this Doc/View architecture. Think again. Almost any program can be implemented as a doc/view architecture. If your program has to load anything, change it, and then save it, that's an obvious candidate for Doc/View. Lets look at a program that manages stuff in an INI file (or the Registry, or whatever). The view is the front end, and the document is the INI file. You just simply override the Serialize member functions to read/write the INI file instead of sending it to the **CArchive** object.

Now, let's look at a program that does not have any data file, but would greatly be improved if it was written with the doc/view architecture: Chat. You know, that cool little program that lets you have a CB style conversation over the net with someone else? Imagine if the document object for this program linked up with the Net DDE (or RPC) and managed the conversation, while the view displayed the data? Now you could make WinChat an OLE Server object. Which means you could put it in your compound document with some caption like "double click this to chat me." Yeah, very very cool. An electronic RSVP.

Of course, there are some programs that don't need the dov/view architecture. Namely programs that would be usless as OLE servers, and really don't have any data of their own to manage. Some games would fall into this category.

Other programs that may not need to be doc/view are tiny little programs that basically splat up a dialog box, let the user change a flag or two, and then close down. The MFC Trace options program is an example of a program that would be slight overkill if you implemented a full doc/view architecture around it.

8. Decide on Your Method of Archiving Information

Almost every program in the world opens a file, messes with it, and saves the messed-with file back out to the archive. This archive may be a disk-based file, it may be a stream in a compound file, or it may be an embedded object in some other app.

Archiving data is done via a multitude of ways in the SDK. There are low-level File I/O functions such as **_lread** and **_lwrite**, and there are the Compound Document API's from STORAGE.DLL. All of these mechanisms are also available in MFC, but there is an easier way. MFC provides "serialization," which is another term for moving your data into or out of some archive. If you use MFC's serialization features, you do not need to worry about disk I/O, disk problems (such as the disk is full, write-protected, or locked). You do not need to worry about saving the data into an OLE container's data stream. You do not need to worry about converting little-Endian to big-Endian across platforms. The **CArchive** object in MFC handles all of these issues for you. The price you pay, of course, is backwards compatibility.

If you are writing a program to handle .BMP files, you are going to need to care about the exact layout of the bytes in the file. If you use the **CArchive** object, you have no control over the ordering of the bytes in the file. Even if the current version of MFC simply places the bytes in the file in the same order as the **CArchive** object receives them, this is no guarantee that the **CArchive** object will act this way in the future. Therefore, if you deeply care about the exact ordering of the bytes in the file (such as for that .BMP file, or for your previous file formats), you will still end up using the old-fashioned **_lread** and **_lwrite** algorithms.

If your application is a document-based application that would greatly benefit from the **CArchive** object, build a converter for the old file formats. Simply open the old file with the conventional SDK API's and then serialize them into a new object using the **CArchive**. This will then bring your file formats up to date, and let you take advantage of the very powerful and versitile serialization features of MFC.

7. DLL's in MFC

In SDK-Land, we wrote DLL's not only as toolboxes, but as ways to share memory and information, or to house some low-level "stuff." Well, MFC lets us avoid that low-level "stuff," and makes it easy to share information with OLE. So why write DLL's anymore? Consistency, size, and the entire object-oriented paradigm.

DLL's written in MFC (these are the AFX DLL's, not the _USR DLL's) are pretty much exactly like an application written in MFC. You don't have that sort of "client-server" relationship that SDK apps did with their DLL's. Taking user-interface components of your MFC application and moving them to MFC DLL's allows you to use the same user-interface tools for multiple applications. Take a look at the **CToolBar** class thatcomes with MFC. Well, if you use the MFC30.DLL instead of linking with the static MFC libaries, your code works exactly the same. Except for the fact that it is significantly smaller, and will even load faster if the MFC DLL is already in use by another application. Since your application is an MFC application, and the DLL is an MFC DLL, the two modules fit together like Yin and Yang. All of the inheritance rules and other C++ programming goodies work like a champ.

Therefore, think about what parts of your MFC application may be shared across your suite of software. Write these parts as an MFC AFX DLL, make them flexible enough to suit the needs of all your applications, and then sit back as your applications load faster, have a smaller footprint and working set, and share a consistent whever-it-is-you-put-in-the-DLL. If you put your user interface stuff in the DLL, you could simply update the single DLL to change the user interface of your entire application suite. Just as OLE servers and OLE controls are individual components of a much larger application, your MFC DLL's can also become little components to make putting together one of your apps an even easier experience.

Of course, a restriction does apply. Namely that your applications and your DLL's all must be written in MFC, using the AFX DLL model, and you must all be using the same version of MFC. But that's easy.

6. If U Can Make Do With the UI, say "I Do"

Okay, so the **CToolbar** class in Visual C++ 1.5 wouldn't float and dock. It does in Visual C++ 2.0. So what? Well, MFC supplies you with lots and lots of user interface gadgets. VC++ 2.0 has added things like those floating toolbars and property sheets. Use them. If you find that a user interface gadget supplied in MFC does 95% of your job, seriously try to compromise your program to fit the UI model. That is, leave things on the "File" menu that belong there, and don't spin your wheels fighting the MFC UI features. If you fight MFC's UI features, you will spend a lot of time writing your own code and tweaking other parts of the MFC framework to cooperate with your code. And, when the next version of MFC comes out, you will have to re-write your interfaces to catch up. By simply focusing your energy on the specific things your application is supposed to do that are *unique* to your application, and letting the MFC developers focus on things like toolbars, status bars, and property sheets, you will ship a product that is not only easier to maintain, but easier for your users to relate to (after all, they have probably had the MFC user interface literally bludgeoned into them by dozens of other programs they are using).

5. Construction versus Creation of Objects

Take a look at the **CWnd** object's constructor from VC++ 1.5:

```
CWnd::CWnd()
{
    m_hWnd = NULL;
```

```
    m_hWndOwner = NULL;
    m_pDropTarget = NULL;
}


CWnd::CWnd(HWND hWnd)
{
    m_hWnd = hWnd;
    m_hWndOwner = NULL;
    m_pDropTarget = NULL;
}
```

Now, take a look at the **CWnd** object's Create member function:

```
BOOL CWnd::CreateEx(DWORD dwExStyle, LPCSTR lpszClassName,
        LPCSTR lpszWindowName, DWORD dwStyle,
        int x, int y, int nWidth, int nHeight,
        HWND hWndParent, HMENU nIDorHMenu, LPSTR lpParam /* = NULL*/)
{
    // allow modification of several common create parameters
    CREATESTRUCT cs;
    cs.dwExStyle = dwExStyle;
    cs.lpszClass = lpszClassName;
    cs.lpszName = lpszWindowName;
    cs.style = dwStyle;
    cs.x = x;
    cs.y = y;
    cs.cx = nWidth;
    cs.cy = nHeight;
    cs.hwndParent = hWndParent;
    cs.hMenu = nIDorHMenu;
    cs.hInstance = AfxGetInstanceHandle();
    cs.lpCreateParams = lpParam;

    if (!PreCreateWindow(cs))
    {
        PostNcDestroy();
        return FALSE;
    }


    _AfxHookWindowCreate(this);
    HWND hWnd = ::CreateWindowEx(cs.dwExStyle, cs.lpszClass,
            cs.lpszName, cs.style, cs.x, cs.y, cs.cx, cs.cy,
            cs.hwndParent, cs.hMenu, cs.hInstance, cs.lpCreateParams);
    if (!_AfxUnhookWindowCreate())
```

```
      PostNcDestroy();          // cleanup if CreateWindowEx fails too soon

   if (hWnd == NULL)
      return FALSE;
   ASSERT(hWnd == m_hWnd); // should have been set in send msg hook
   return TRUE;
}

BOOL CWnd::Create(LPCSTR lpszClassName,
   LPCSTR lpszWindowName, DWORD dwStyle,
   const RECT& rect,
   CWnd* pParentWnd, UINT nID,
   CCreateContext* pContext /* = NULL */)
{
   // can't use for desktop or pop-up windows (use CreateEx instead)
   ASSERT(pParentWnd != NULL);
   ASSERT((dwStyle & WS_POPUP) == 0);

   return CreateEx(0, lpszClassName, lpszWindowName,
      dwStyle | WS_CHILD,
      rect.left, rect.top, rect.right - rect.left, rect.bottom - rect.top,
      pParentWnd->GetSafeHwnd(), (HMENU)nID, (LPSTR)pContext);
}
```

The real work of the **CWnd** object is done when the application calls the **Create** or **CreateEx** member functions, not when the object is actually constructed. The reason for the above **CWnd**'s method is twofold.

First, C++ objects are referred to by a this pointer. Windows are referred to by a handle. All of the **CWnd**'s member functions need this window handle. However, there are cases where you may not want to have the constructor of the **CWnd** object actually create a window and get this handle. What if your application uses a third-party DLL that is not written in MFC? That DLL may return to you a window handle. Your application may want to write a class that uses that window handle. The **Attach** member function is used for this purpose. By breaking the construction of the object and the creation of the actual window into two steps, you give the application more freedom to use the **CWnd** object as an interface to the window instead of the actual window. Likewise, the **Detach** member function allows the window to be dissasociated with the **CWnd** object so that the window is not destroyed when the **CWnd** object is deleted.

Second, the time a **CWnd** object is constructed may not necessarily be the time the window is to be created. Think about this code:

```
CMyApp::SomeFunction ()

{
// m_pSomeWnd is a member function defined in the MYAPP.H file
m_pSomeWnd = new CWnd; // Object gets contructed here
CreateTheWindow ( m_pSomeWnd ); // And created here
}


CSomeOtherObject::CreateTheWindow ( CWnd * pSomeWnd )
{
  int nResult = AfxMessageBox("Wanna Make it Sizeable?", MB_YESNO);
  pSomeWnd->Create ( (LPCSTR)"SomeClass", (LPCSTR)"Some Title",
                 (IDYES == nResult) ?
                     WS_CHILD | WS_BORDER | WS_THICKFRAME :
                     WS_CHILD | WS_BORDER,
                 CRect(0,0,100,100),
                 m_toplevelwnd, // some window to use as a parent
                 42 );
}
```

Let's pretend the **CWnd** constructor could have taken all of those **Create** parameters and the window could have been created when the **CWnd** object was declared:

```
CMyApp::SomeFunction ()

{

int nResult = AfxMessageBox("Wanna Make it Sizeable?", MB_YESNO);
m_pSomeWnd = new CWnd ((LPCSTR)"SomeClass", (LPCSTR)"Some Title",
                 (IDYES == nResult) ?
                     WS_CHILD | WS_BORDER | WS_THICKFRAME :
                     WS_CHILD | WS_BORDER,
                 CRect(0,0,100,100),
                 m_toplevelwnd,
                 42 );
}
```

This would work in the above situation, but what if the message box code needed to live in a DLL and the **CWnd** object needed to live in the app? Then

600

the two lines of code above would need to be split up between two functions. But the logic of asking the user a question about the window and acting on that logic should both be in the same object, as in the previous code sample. Splitting up the question from the action goes against the paradigm of object oriented programming. And in the case of the **CWnd** object, there may be only one **CWnd** object, but that **CWnd** object can have many flavors.

So what should you do when designing objects? Think about flavors. If you have objects that can be created with a common interface, but different flavors, consider including a **Create** member function to handle the actual object's creation. A good example would be for an SQL database. Your **CSQL** object's constructor simply initializes its member variables and allocates any memory it needs. The **CSQL** object's **Create** member function takes the name of the table, and actually opens it up for queries.

A totally different, yet even stronger reason to split up the construct and create actions is because of the symmetry between C++ and Windows (or whatever your object emcompasses). When an object is constructed in C++, the out of memory and other reasons for failure are handled gracefully by the operating system and also through structured exception handling. When a Windows object is created, you have a different set of rules to play by concerning success or failure. Just because the new **CWnd** statement succeeded, it does not mean that the **CWnd->Create(...)** will. C++ does a great job constructing and destructing its own inherent C++ objects. Windows does a great job of creating and destroying windows. Keep them separate. If your database module or other module already has tested robust creation/destruction code, keep the symmetry.

And even if the windows objects are guaranteed to create, you still want to keep the create functions separate from the constructors for *yet another* reason. There are going to be times when the operating system creates windows for you that you don't have **CWnd** objects for. Such as in dialog boxes. When you create a **CDialog** object, you don't have to declare member variables for every control. These controls are created by USER in response to the **DialogBoxParam** code buried deep in MFC. If you want to acess the listbox only temporarily, you can just declare a **CListBox** on the stack, use **Attach**() to hook it up to the listbox in the dialog box (retrieved by using **GetDlgItem**), party on the listbox, use **Detach**() to dissassociate yourself from the listbox, and then let C++ cleanup the **CListBox** object for you when the function exits. In this example, the window was already created, our code simply creates a temporary **CListBox** object so we can access it using MFC conventions.

On the same flavor, think about Windows Sockets. Your constructor should not create one, since your MFC app may interact with a Non-MFC app that just hands you the handle to a Socket as a DWORD. Your **CMyWinSocket** object could write its own **Attach** member function to let you work with that Socket in the same way you work with your other MFC objects.

4. Design Your Code to be Debugged

From the very start, design your MFC applications for easy debugging. MFC supplies some very handy tools for writing more bullet-proof code: ASSERT and TRACE. These tools quietly vanish in the retail builds of your product, yet they work in full force in the debug builds of your product. Your EXE's won't fatten up in retail builds, not matter how many ASSERTs and TRACEs you put in. And, by using these debugging tools from the start, your programmers won't have that daunting task of adding a bunch of ASSERTS and TRACES to a broken program in a last minute grope to find a bug.

Keep in mind that your objects are going to be abused. People will derive new classes from your classes and change member functions, and they will also try to just plug your class into a spot where their class was. An example that I ran into is the **CScrollView** class. It has this cool ASSERT in it:

```
void CScrollView::OnPrepareDC(CDC* pDC, CPrintInfo* pInfo)
{
    ASSERT_VALID(pDC);

#ifdef _DEBUG
    if (m_nMapMode == MM_NONE)
    {
        TRACE0("Error: must call SetScrollSizes() or SetScaleToFitSize()"
            " before painting scroll view\n");
        ASSERT(FALSE);
        return;
```

```
    }
#endif //_DEBUG
...
```

This code ensures that the user has set up a scroll range. Why is this check here? Because the programmer may have been using **CView** as the base class before, and they may have just quickly changed the base class to **CScrollView**. Forgetting, of course, to set the scroll range. Which would cause the **CScrollView** to act exactly like the **CView** if it was not for the above ASSERT. So the above ASSERT code ensures that the programmer has correctly set up the **CScrollView** before using it and prevents the programmer from spending hours trying to figure out why that damn **CScrollView** won't scroll.

Also, use the MFC diagnostic features such as **CMemoryState** and DEBUG_NEW to check for memory leaks and clean-up problems. By adding this debug code to your objects during design time versus during debug time, you will be able to enjoy more robust, correctly used code during your entire coding cycle. After all, wouldn't it suck to find that the night before you have to ship your Killer App you discover you are using a class totally wrong?

3. Design Your Class Interaction Well

For each new class that you design think about what classes it will need to interact with. Usually your document objects and your View objects are closely tied together. Think long and hard about what member variables need to be in which object. And expose those variables with member functions that are consistent across different flavors of the object. For example, if you have two different types of document objects, but both of them have a title, use a member function like **GetTitle** for both of them. If you can provide a completely consistent interface for all of the data in the documents, you can use the same view for both types of documents. This works the other way, also, in that you can have two different views on the same object, provided the view objects provide congruent interfaces for the document object.

Keep in mind that there is going to be the need for some app-wide global variable wannabes. These could be member variables in your **CWinApp** object. MFC has some global functions like **AfxGetApp()** that can make it very easy and quick to get at the **CWinApp** object. See Chapter 14 for more about AfxGetApp().

2. Put the Right Code in the Right Place

MFC's architecture makes it really easy to write code quickly. But don't write it too quickly. Think about where you want to place your code. Some member functions are called more often than others, and if you place code in the wrong place, you can write inefficient programs, or even worse, programs that puke. Let's take a look at one such poorly written program. How about one from the SAMPLES directory in Visual C++ 1.5:VBCHART.

In the CHARTVW.CPP file, we find that the **OnDraw** member function eventually ends up calling one of the **PlotXXXChart** member functions. In each of these member functions, the **GetChartMetrics** member function is called. The **GetChartMetrics** member function calculates the size of the chart so that the remaining code can then draw the chart.

Every time the **CChartView** object repaints, the **OnDraw** member function is called. Every time the **CChartView** object repaints, the size of this chart is calculated, *even if the chart has not changed.* Calling the **GetChartMetrics** member function in response to **OnDraw** is wasting CPU cycles. The only time the chart's size needs to be recalculated is when the chart's size is going to change. That would be when the chart's data changes, or possibly if the view is resized.

So far, I am only whining about the innefiiciency of the above sample. However, let's cause this poor design to crash. Change the base class of the **CChartView** class from **CView** to **CScrollView**. Add the **SetScrollSizes** member function to the **CChartView**'s constructor to avoid the ASSERT mentioned in tip #4 above, and recompile. So far, everything works fine, and your program looks exactly the same.

Now, let's set the scroll range for the **CChartView** to fit whatever chart we come up with. Let's modify the **CChartView**'s **GetChartMetrics** member function to set the scroll range after recalculating the size of the chart. The code in boldface is new:

```
int CChartView::GetChartMetrics(CDC* pDC, int nHDiv, int nVDiv,
    CSize& sizeGraph, CSize& sizePixelsPerTick, CPoint& ptOrigin)
{
    CSize sizeText = pDC->GetTextExtent("0", 1);

    // Determine minimum size for graph
    sizeGraph = sizeText;

    // Minimum size of a Division == 5 chars
    // Allow 5 chars for Vertical Captions and 2.5 chars on each side of chart

    sizeGraph.cx *= (5 * nHDiv) + 10;
    sizeGraph.cy *= nVDiv + 3;

    // Grow size if permitted by display area
    CRect rect = GetDisplayRect(pDC);
    if (rect.Width() > sizeGraph.cx)
        sizeGraph.cx = rect.Width();
    if (rect.Height() > sizeGraph.cy)
        sizeGraph.cy = rect.Height();

    SetScrollSizes (MM_TEXT, CSize(sizeGraph.cx, sizeGraph.cy));
    sizePixelsPerTick.cx = (sizeGraph.cx - 10 * sizeText.cx) / nHDiv;
    sizePixelsPerTick.cy = (sizeGraph.cy -  3 * sizeText.cy) / nVDiv;

    ptOrigin.x = sizeText.cx * 15 / 2;
    ptOrigin.y = sizePixelsPerTick.cy * nVDiv + sizeText.cy * 3 / 2;

    return sizeText.cy;
}
```

The above code should readjust the scrolling range of the view whenever the graph's size changes, right? Exactly. Unfortunately, this sample was architected with the belief that the graph's size changes every single time the view paints (after all, did call **GetChartMetrics** in response to **OnDraw**, didn't they?). So now we end up calling **SetScrollSizes** every time we repaint. Problem. **SetScrollSizes** causes the view to repaint. That causes **GetChartMetrics** to get called, which then calls **SetScrollSizes**, which then...

Eventually your wild elephant code from above will run out of stack space for this recursive nightmare and crash. Of course, in the meantime, you get a really cool 70's disco light show.

The fix for VBCHART, unfortunatley is quite complex, given the fact that this is supposed to be a tiny little sample program. You need to move the call to **GetChartMetrics** to the **OnUpdate** member function (after all, **OnUpdate** is called when the data changes, not when the view repaints), and cache away those values into some member variables for the **CChartView** object. Now, you need to change all of the **PlotXXXChart** member functions to look at those member variables instead of calling **GetChartMetrics**. That's a lot of changes for a tiny program. Imagine if this was your MondoProgram just about to ship?

So, when designing your MFC applications, be sure to review each and every member function's role. Know when it is called, and how often. Don't get lazy and just toss it where it does not belong in order to avoid adding yet another member function and recompile your entire app.

1. Use OLE

I would dare to say that 99% of programs written today can be OLE enabled. You may someday want to insert a TETRIS object into your Games document. Really. On a more serious side, though, you should really think hard about what you want your OLE app to do. Think about the interfaces you wish to expose. Think about OLE automation. Design and organize your data so that it lends itself well to OLE. Decide if you want to have your program run standalone, or only as an OLE server, or if you want your application to also be an OLE container. Think about these things *before* you design anything else.

A great start is to read *Inside OLE2* by Kraig Brockschmidt (Microsoft Press). By the time you finish that book, you will know enough about OLE to at least design yours right from the start.

DON'T RUN APPWIZARD UNTIL YOU KNOW YOUR CLASS NAMES AND FUNCTIONS

Running AppWizard is *not* a way to design your application. Before you run this program, decide the following:

- What classes you will want

- What classes interact with other classes

- What OLE features you want to support

- What the names of your classes will be

If you do not think about these far in advance, you will run AppWizard, generate all of your base program, and then be stuck using that **CWordDocument** object name for life. Imagine if you realized afterwards that you really aren't working with a **CWordDocument**, but actually you were working with a report? Changing **CWordDocument** to **CReportDocument** throughout your code would be a mega-pain in the programming butt.

This brings up another interesting point: Most good MFC programmers will have the courage to throw away a complete program or design if they realize it was flawed in the first place. You may actually find yourself saving time by tossing out the stinky garbage and starting over again with new code.

Part 4

Programming à la C

Bob Schmidt's Dedication

I dedicate this work to Debra Ann Schmidt and Daniel I.L. Saks, respectively, the most significant personal and professional influences resulting in this book. Without them, I would have lacked the knowledge and faith to create what you are about to read.

Acknowledgments from Bob Schmidt

Since I may never win an Oscar, I'll practice my short acceptance speech here. I thank Deb Schmidt for enduring my time hibernating in our home office as I wrote this, Dan Saks for taking me on as acolyte all these years, Eric Flo for helping me get my old life back, Lisa Everett for helping me get my new life started, David Long for letting us take over his home for three months, Sabina Nawaz for believing in me enough to give me a second chance, and Doug Payne for no reason in particular, other than to get his name in print.

Dave Edson gets some credit, for agreeing to let me actually write on this one. Kate Edson gets credit for living with Dave.

I thank my parents for deciding to have children. And I suppose I should also thank a couple anonymous profs from Wright State University, whose Organic Chemistry and Vertebrate Biology classes persuaded me to change majors to Computer Science. Finally, to help comfort those of you far from the technical vanguard, know that I wrote this book entirely with Microsoft's PWB, and checked my spelling with Microsoft's DOS Word 4.0, all on my rip-roarin' state-of-the-art (1989) Toshiba T5100. The age of miracles is indeed still with us.

P.S. Dave and I really are buddies, all my barbs aside. I just haven't forgiven him for that Rolling Stones concert in Vancouver five years ago.

Biography

Bob Schmidt was born in Huber Heights, OH, but has called Sedona, AZ, North Ryde, NSW, Australia, Limestone, NY, and (most recently) Redmond, WA, home. His past occupations include newspaper carrier, wild-animal caretaker, store clerk, planetarium and observatory operator, radio DJ, security guard, private investigator, warehouse truck loader, pool hall overseer, and teacher of students ages 5 through adult. Currently, when not writing, he earns most of his keep as a computer programmer.

The only cars he's ever owned are '71 and '73 Mustangs, his lowest bowling score is 17, his favorite color is indigo. He's seen all the Messier objects, and he shares space with cats named Artemis and John Lodge. His next major life goal is becoming ensconced in a small college town near the sea, teaching and studying something right-brained for a change. He can be reached via Internet e-mail as *rschmidt@netcom.com.*

INTRODUCTION

Originally, I was not going to write for this book. I had worked as technical editor with Dave on his previous effort, and reckoned that would be my role this go-around. As we got into the project, though, I came up with ideas and recommendations that didn't quite jibe with Dave's Windows-centric material. Over time, we agreed these more generic topics would help balance the book, and decided they were better suited to my knowledge and interest. Ultimately, I signed on to contribute material directly to what is ostensibly Dave's book.

To that end, I'm presenting a collage of programming ideas I've developed over the years. Some are specific to C, or relate to C++ as an extension of C, while others are independent of a particular language. Some of these ideas I'm putting down on virtual paper for the first time. Some date back to my undergraduate days. My primary audience is C programmers looking to add to their craft, possibly by migrating to C++. A secondary audience is those working in any language, who want to make their coding life easier.

"Easier," here, is relative, of course. I define it to include portability (among platforms or languages), maintainability, and intent ("what you get is what you expected"). If, along the way of reading this book, you learn and have fun, I've done my job. As my father is fond of saying, this stuff is not brain surgery or rocket science. It's more applying some of the common-sense approaches taken to other life aspects, and mapping them to the world of programming.

Assumptions

As Dave's text requires C and C++ acumen, I choose these as my primary languages. However, this is not a C or C++ primer. The topics I cover (and the weight I give them) almost certainly do not match those of a more standard text. Given this, I make zero attempt to teach C or C++ in these passages, but rather assume you have at least phrase-book fluency in these languages. I also makes occasional lapses into other languages, but these are, for the most part, incidental. You can probably guess their meanings even if you don't know the languages (much as a Spanish reader can pick through Italian or Portuguese).

Conversely, unlike Dave, I don't assume much Windows knowledge. While I cite Windows on occasion, this is only to make certain concepts concrete, or to offer specific examples of real-life lessons. I figure that I should adopt a common frame of reference. Given the overall nature of this book, Windows seems the smartest choice. However, in principle, you need never have touched the Windows SDK to make sense of most of this section.

Although I generally eschew Windows, most of my code samples are developed with Microsoft compilers. I make no guarantees they will even compile with Brands B or S or W, let alone the various flavors of Brand U. My experience with C and C++ has been almost exclusively with Microsoft's compilers, starting with version 4. Possible reasons for this brand loyalty, given where I live today, are left as an exercise for the reader.

Some C++ features—notably templates and exceptions—will not be available from Microsoft until MSVC 2.0 or C 9 (just released as I write). Code using these features, as well as code in all other languages, is compiled by using ocular regression (that is, by eye). Please don't panic if those samples generate syntax errors in the real world.

Administrivia

Chapters 17 through 19 detail underused, misused, and misunderstood aspects of ANSI C. Chapters 20 and 21 show where C++ and other languages do and do not intersect. Chapter 22 is an apparent heresy, supporting the notion that not all programs or programmers should move from C to C++.

Quicky Glossary

K&R C, a.k.a. classic C The C language as documented in the first edition of Kernighan and Ritchie's classic tome "The C Programming Language."

ANSI C, a.k.a. standard C The C language as originally standardized by the ANSI X3J11 committee in 1989.

ANSI C++ The emerging C++ standard upon which ANSI X3J16 are cogitating. This standard may be released before the Jupiter 2 launches. Just think, the Robot may be programmed in pre-ANSI C++. No wonder they were lost.

MSVC Microsoft Visual C/C++, version 1.0 (also called C version 8), unless otherwise specified.

Windows 16-bit Windows, unless otherwise noted, although in practice this should make little difference.

Bob Schmidt
September 1994

CHAPTER 17

Hints for Better Living Under ANSI C

Like other languages (FORTRAN springs to mind immediately), the single language called "C" has actually been several different languages over its life-time. The two incarnations most known are K&R C and ANSI C. Oddly, even though ANSI first blessed it's standard five years ago, many programmers continue to use the language as if it were little more than K&R C with prototypes. In truth, ANSI C added several new features, and tightened the meanings of several old ones.

These hints explore using ANSI C in ways you may not have thought to. Some hints are specific to ANSI C. Others are general to programming, using C as their expressive medium. I suppose, in some cases, I could add an 11th hint, "use C++." This list is for those who can't, or won't, switch languages.

10. Use Enumerations

Among students of C, a common early Satori is that, unlike Pascal and its brethren, C has no concept of symbolic constants. That is, you cannot write a C equivalent of the following Pascal code:

```
const
    PRISONER = 6;
    SCARLET = 'A';
    AVAGADRO = 6.02 * 10**23;
    EDSON_EFFECT = -1 div 0;
```

C can approximate constants by way of preprocessor macros. While preferable to magic values, macros suffer from several limitations, including

* Tricky syntax resolution
* No scope
* Symbols not known to the debugger
* No inherent relationship within a sequence of symbols

All these problems are resolved by enumerated types, which is one of the least-used gifts of ANSI C. Sometimes I think I'm the only person outside academia who uses enumerations, and I'm not sure why. I can only reckon that C programmers weaned on K&R C (or assembly) never learned the true power of enumerations.

This is particularly bothersome in Windows. Microsoft's WINDOWS.H file defines a seemingly infinite number of macro symbols. In addition, Windows programmers often define their own private message symbols. Most of these symbols are defined successive values. Many of them would be useful if displayed in a CodeView watch window.

To illustrate, assume you have a series of the following private messages:

```
#define WM_BOGUS   (-1)
#define WM_FAUX     0
#define WM_ERSATZ   1
#define WM_FAKE     2
```

You can replace this with the following enumeration:

```
enum
    {
    WM_BOGUS = -1,
    WM_FAUX,
    WM_ERSATZ,
    WM_FAKE,
    };
```

Now, assume you want to insert **WM_SPURIOUS** ahead of **WM_FAUX**. In the first method, you would have to manually rewrite most of the macro definitions to get

```
#define WM_BOGUS     (-1)
#define WM_SPURIOUS  0 /* new */
#define WM_FAUX      1 /* changed */
#define WM_ERSATZ    2 /* changed */
#define WM_FAKE      3 /* changed */
```

While in the second method, you only need insert only one line, as shown here:

```
enum
    {
    WM_BOGUS = -1,
    WM_SPURIOUS,   /* new */
    WM_FAUX,
    WM_ERSATZ,
    WM_FAKE,
    };
```

Because the enumeration constant names are in the compiler's symbol table, they are often available to the debugger. Contrast this to preprocessor symbols, which are stripped (actually, expanded) before the symbol table is built. Such constant names are especially useful if the enumerated type defines a type name, as in

```
typedef enum PRIVATE_MESSAGE
    {
    WM_BOGUS = -1,
```

619

```
    WM_SPURIOUS,
    WM_FAUX,
    WM_ERSATZ,
    WM_FAKE,
    }
PRIVATE_MESSAGE;

PRIVATE_MESSAGE Message;
```

Now, instead of a debugger's watch window showing a variable like

```
int Message = 2
```

the debugger, knowing the true type of *Message*, can show the more meaningful

```
PRIVATE_MESSAGE Message = WM_ERSATZ
```

In the case of MSVC and CodeView, we get half a loaf—C enumerators manifest as integral values, while C++ enumerators actually show up as their symbolic names. In fact, if a C++ enumeration object contains an out-of-bounds value, CodeView shows an error.

Finally, because they are scoped, enumeration constants can be easily reused, as in

```
enum {MAX = 10};
char String[MAX];

void func(void)
    {
    enum {MAX = 200};
    int Array[MAX];
    /*...*/
    }
```

In fairness, macro constant symbols are useful in some contexts where enumerations are not. In particular, enumerations cannot be used in conditional compilation directives. So, the line

```
#if SYMBOL > 0
```

is legal if SYMBOL is a macro, but not if SYMBOL is an enumeration constant.

Other limitations of enumerations include

- ❖ *Cannot represent floating-point numbers.* Enumeration constants assigned floating-point values truncate the value to the integer portion.

- ❖ *Cannot represent pointers, including character strings.*

- ❖ *Signed.* This means that they may not compare to unsigned *ints* in the expected way.

- ❖ *No guarantee of size.* In implementations where enumerated types are *int* and *sizeof(long) > sizeof(int),* *long* constants cannot be represented as enumerations. This affects 16-bit Windows, where some *#defines* in WINDOWS.H are 32-bit, while enumerations are 16-bit.

9. Avoid Cut-and-Paste Code

Programmers learn early on to package similar (or identical) code into functions. However, in some contexts, functions are either impossible or unwieldy. In those cases, C programmers often turn to the C preprocessor.

A common preprocessor idiom is a pseudo-inline function like

```
#define square(x) x * x
```

Such definitions are so common, in fact, that many programmers know the previous macro is more properly written as

```
#define square(x) ((x) * (x))
```

to avoid operator-precedence surprises. These same programmers probably also know such definitions can hide side effects. For example,

```
square(i++)
```

expands to

```
((i++) * (i++))
```

incrementing *i* twice, which is probably not the intended effect. As another example, the standard library function **getchar** is typically implemented as a macro, suffering the same side-effect liability.

An alternative solution is to create a template. To illustrate, consider transforming the code

```
#define abs(a) ((a) > 0 ? (a) : (-(a)))

void main(void)
    {
    int i = abs(1848);
    float f = abs(3.14F);
    long l = abs(-12L);
    }
```

so that **abs** no longer has side effects. At first, you may believe **abs** can be replaced with a single function, given that the logic of absolute value is the same regardless of argument type. However, because **abs** is invoked here three times with differently typed arguments, and C (unlike C++) does not support overloaded functions, you actually need three different **abs** clones, such as:

```
int abs_int(int);
```

```
float abs_float(float);
```

```
long abs_long(long);
```

This does not mean, however, that you must cut-and-paste the same code into all three function definitions. Macros are brilliant for encapsulating repeated code. In this case, the common aspects among all three functions are

‡ Number of arguments (one)

‡ Arguments never modified

❖ Function name systematically derived from argument's type name

❖ Logic to decide and return the absolute value

Incorporating these common aspects into a template (or pattern) yields the following macro:

```
#define template_abs(type)\
    type abs_##type(const type a)\
        {\
        return (a > 0 ? a : -a);\
        }
```

The macro invocation

```
template_abs(int)
```

expands into the following function definition:

```
int abs_int(const int a)
    {
    return (a > 0 > a : -a);
    }
```

The same pattern applies to the other types—every invocation of *template_abs* with a new type creates the definition of a uniquely named function. The complete example becomes

```
#define abs(type, value) abs_##type(value)

#define template_abs(type)\
    type abs_##type(const type value)\
        {\
        return (value > 0 ? value : -value);\
        }

template_abs(int)
template_abs(float)
template_abs(long)

void main(void)
```

623

```
    {
    int i = abs(int, 1848);
    float f = abs(float, 3.14F);
    long l = abs(long, -12L);
    }
```

which yields, after macro expansion,

```
int abs_int(const int value)
    {
    return (value > 0 ? value : -value);
    }


float abs_float(const float value)
    {
    return (value > 0 ? value : -value);
    }


long abs_long(const long value)
    {
    return (value > 0 ? value : -value);
    }


void main(void)
    {
    int i = abs_int(1848);
    float f = abs_float(3.14F);
    long l = abs_long(-12L);
    }
```

Templates use what are called "parameterized types." That is, a type name (*int, float, long*) is a parameter to the macro. True C functions cannot accept types as parameters. Templates can be implemented only as macros. Note that the ANSI C++ committee has added templates as an intrinsic part of that language. I don't expect the ANSI C committee ever to make such an addition.

The example shown here is a bit contrived, but does represent the potential and power of such templates. You can extend this concept to subfunctions, data structures, and whole source modules.

I close out my discussion of collapsing redundant code with the following sequence I once found in a colleague's C source code:

```
s->m2 = (WORD) (f((WORD) s->m2, s->m1, s->m0) - n);
s->m3 = (WORD) (f((WORD) s->m3, s->m1, s->m0) - n);
s->m4 = (WORD) (f((WORD) s->m4, s->m1, s->m0) - n);
s->m5 = (WORD) (f((WORD) s->m5, s->m1, s->m0) - n);
```

Code like this is pleading to be encapsulated in a macro, such as

```
#define Chimera(x)\
    (s->m##x = (WORD) (f((WORD) s->m##x, s->m1, s->m0) - n))


Chimera(2);
Chimera(3);
Chimera(4);
Chimera(5);
```

Note that, in this context, *Chimera* cannot be a function—the arguments 2, 3, and so on, are not values, but literal characters lexically expanded into the code. Thus, you could not replace this code with

```
int i;

for (i = 2; i <= 5; i++)
    Chimera(i); /* tempting but wrong */
```

8. Practice Safe Types

One of the more religious debates within programming circles is the question of "permissive" versus "puritanical" languages, especially with respect to type checking. Die-hard assembler and K&R C programmers feel that data types are a semantic nuisance, or worse, a form of software totalitarianism. Those coming from a Pascal or an Ada background feel that anything short of strict type checking is chaos, danger waiting to happen. I'm certain that, collectively, billions of dollars have been spent forwarding Usenet traffic that counts the angels on this pinhead.

I am of the puritanical camp (after all, I did work a while in the Ada Joint Project Office). When I first came to classic C, I found the lack of type control unsettling. The ANSI C committee helped some. Unfortunately, that august body has as its Prime Directive the noninterference in the lives of primitive C code. That is, wherever practical, ANSI C does not "break" existing K&R code. Fortunately, the committee found ways to extend the type safety that did not violate this directive.

Probably the biggest type-checking boon to come from ANSI C is function prototyping (an idea borrowed from C++). Having used prototypes for years now, I find it almost impossible to believe C programmers could write reliable code without them. Note that ANSI C does not require prototypes. If you use a function without prototyping it, ANSI C will synthesize a prototype based on how the function is first called. I've heard this called the Miranda Rule, which I believe was first coined by P.J. Plauger in ANSI C committee meetings, although I have only apocryphal evidence. The rule states

- ❖ You have a right to remain silent about your arguments.
- ❖ You have the right to a prototype.
- ❖ If you cannot afford a prototype, one will be appointed for you.

Those favoring less type checking often point to the wonderful hardware-level representations expressible in C, or the vaunted ability to "get close to the machine." Put another way, such C programs strip away the abstracted model reality, and reveal/betray the physical reality beneath. I will not debate that this ability renders C more suitable than other high-level languages for some system-level programming. Such programming includes device drivers, code generators, and OS kernels—software that must be cognizant of the underlying hardware environment.

What I will debate is the necessity to operate at such an unprotected and atomic level all the time. This is especially abhorrent while programming for Windows in C. Beyond the stupifying plethora of APIs, the Windows SDK defines many types that are not meant to be mixed. Although they may be implemented identically, they are conceptually distinct. However, in C, *typedefs* do not introduce new types, but rather simply create aliases for existing types. Thus, while a sequence such as

```
typedef HBRUSH int;
typedef HWND   int;
```

would look to render invalid

```
HBRUSH Brush;
HWND Wnd = Brush;
```

this code is, in fact, valid C (and C++) code. I cannot begin to tell you how many errors I've seen in Windows code from this lack of type distinction. Thankfully, Microsoft fixed this in Windows 3.10 and later by way of the *STRICT* symbol. This trick takes advantage of the one way in C to create distinct types—through type aggregation (in this case, *struct*s).

In this scheme, when *STRICT* is defined, the previous definitions become (in essence)

```
typedef struct HBRUSH
    {
    int unnamed;
    }
HBRUSH;

typedef struct HWND
    {
    int unnamed;
    }
HWND;
```

Now, attempts such as

```
HBRUSH Brush;
HWND Wnd = Brush;
```

to assign across types will generate a compile-time error.

All of this type checking can be rendered impotent under the spell of casts. Every language I've used (even Ada, amazingly enough) has some way to bypass type security. Only C legalizes and endorses such lapses. Type casts make data types like traffic lights—they have no real power if you choose not to obey them. They are to data sanity what *gotos* are to code sanity—robbers of predictability.

With casts, any variable can be made to appear to be of any type. Every appearance of a cast in your code is one less place the compiler can call your bluff. Here again, Windows encourages bad practice. A typical Windows callback function accepts parameters of integral types that, in reality, either contain pointer values, or pack shorter integral values into a single, longer integral value. Depending on the value of the function's message parameter, these integral values are interpreted in different ways. The result is many casts and shifts of these extra parameters into their "real" types.

As with *STRICT*, Windows 3.10 introduced macros (so-called message crackers) to hide this casting and decomposition. The real reason for this was portability to future Windows platforms, since the size and layout of these integral parameters would change. However, the macros also nicely package away the details of converting these "generic" parameters into their target types.

Every time I use a cast in my code, I feel like I'm driving without a seatbelt. I strongly recommend that you use as few casts as possible, and that you document all casts. This may seem Draconian, but I believe that stronger typing improves your program's conformance to your intent (that is, it's more likely to do what you think it does). Besides, if you start documenting all casts, you may well find alternative methods that are more type safe.

A huge exception to the "no casting" rule comes with untyped arguments. A common example is the **printf** family of functions. The statements

```
void *WhereProhibited;
long AndWindingRoad;
union LABEL LookFor;


printf("%c%c%c", WhereProhibited, AndWindingRoad, LookFor);
```

will generate no complaints from the compiler. Only the first argument (the format string) of **printf** is prototyped. The rest are unchecked, requiring the programmer to "play compiler" and ensure that the arguments match the formats. I recommend you explicitly cast all arguments to these types of functions, forcing the arguments to match the format strings. Thus, the previous example would be recoded as:

```
printf("%c%c%c", (char) WhereProhibited, (char) AndWindingRoad,
       (char) LookFor);
```

Note that, while this may not give a very useful result, it does match the argument types with what **printf** expects as it parses through the argument list.

A more meaningful example is:

```
int Count;

printf("Count = %d\n", Count);
```

If *Count* is ever changed to a *long,* the **printf** statement will suffer undefined runtime behavior. Solutions include:

```
int Count;

printf("Count = %d\n", (int) Count);
```

or better,

```
int Count;

printf("Count = %ld\n", (long) Count);
```

which will work regardless of *Count*'s size (at least until ANSI C specifies a *long long* type).

Finally, even if you never use a cast, C will still, in effect, use them for you, in the form of implicit conversions. C allows you to liberally mix built-in types by silently transforming variables of different types into some common type. Even experienced C programmers stumble here, especially when porting code across platforms.

I discuss this notion at greater length in Chapter 18, "Things not to Assume About Your C Environment."

7. Heed Compiler Warnings

In college, I volunteered for the university's radio station. A high school buddy and I hosted a classical music show together, driving in his Fiat to the station two nights a week. Almost without fail, the little red lamp under his gas gauge would glow, telling him the gas was just about gone. I can probably count on one hand the number of times he actually stopped to get gas when that low-fuel indicator went on.

My father calls such indicators "idiot lights." Warnings are a compiler's idiot lights. (I suppose, then, that errors are a compiler's flat tire, and fatal internal compiler errors are a broken timing chain.) You should never ignore a warning. Further, you should compile at the highest warning level available. The compiler knows more about the language than you do, and errors are cheaper to find at compile time than at runtime.

Warnings are often caused by type violations. Such warnings are easily chased away by type casting. However, type casting here is like drinking espresso when you're tired—it alleviates symptoms, but not the underlying causes.

Some warnings are legitimate. Examples include unsized array members ending structures (a commonly used non-ANSI C extension) and unused parameters (a frequent problem in Windows callbacks). Fortunately, many compilers today allow warnings to be selectively turned off. However, this still cures symptoms, not causes, even if those causes are deemed benign.

If you must disable warnings, localize the region of the disabling. For example, if you define a structure with an unsized array, use a construct such as

```
#pragma warnings(off)

struct WillRobinson
    {
    /*...*/
    int Disarray[];
    };

#pragma warnings(on)
```

That is, treat warning-disabled code like critical sections. Keep warnings off as little as possible.

I recommend documenting all disabled warnings. If your compiler does not let you disable warnings, then document all warnings the compiler generates. In these cases, you can simulate warning-disabling yourself. A common technique is to "turn off" warnings about unused parameters with the following code:

```
void Func(int UnusedParam)
    {
    (void) UnusedParam; /* no-op, but makes warning go away */
    /*...*/
    }
```

Lack of this trick can become quite annoying in Windows, which requires all callbacks of the same type to sport the same prototype, even if some of the parameters are not used in a particular instance.

Many programmers package this trick into an UNUSED macro. In the following example, assume *Broiled* and *Change* are required by the function prototype, but are not referenced in the function body (for example, the code may still be under development):

```
#define UNUSED(Parameter) ((void) Parameter)

void Funk(char Broiled, long Suffering, short Change)
    {
    UNUSED(Broiled);
    UNUSED(Change);
    /*...*/
    }
```

Be sure to document all such tricks.

6. Use Const Liberally and Honestly

Like enumerations, *const* is a sorely underused aspect of ANSI C. Unfortunately, the committee only went halfway with *const*. It introduced the notion into the language, but did not tighten the type checking enough to make sure *const* really means the same thing in all contexts.

Most C programmers write statements like

```
char *Name = "Ishmael";
```

with little thought. Because C allows this, *Ishmael* cannot be safely stored in ROM. *Name* is not *const*, so the string it points to can be legally written to without a cast.

If *Ishmael* is used as a constant string, this definition is more properly

```
const char *Name = "Ishmael";
```

Now, *Name* cannot be written to without a cast, so *Ishmael* can be stored in ROM.

I would prefer that literal strings be implicitly *const*, rendering the first example illegal without a cast. In reality, that statement is legal even in C++. I suspect the rationale is to avoid breaking existing code.

Were the definition changed to

```
char Name[] = "Ishmael";
```

or

```
const char Name[] = "Ishmael";
```

then *Ishmael* could be in ROM. *Name* is an array, not a pointer, and has its own copy of the string.

Altering the example to

```
extern void Func(char *);

void main(void)
    {
    char *Name = "Ishmael";
    Func(Name);
    }
```

632

is still all right in both C and C++. However, changing the type of *Name* as in

```
extern void Func(char *);

void main(void)
    {
    const char *Name = "Ishmael";
    Func(Name);
    }
```

yields an error in C++ (you cannot pass a *const* argument into a non-*const* parameter), but at best a warning in C. The most type-safe solution, of course, is

```
extern void Func(const char *);
```

which accepts all strings, *const* and non-*const*.

For a more concrete example, look at one of the standard library headers, say STRING.H. There you'll find prototypes such as the following:

```
char *strncpy(char *s1, const char *s2, size_t length);
```

This tells the caller that the string referenced by *s2* won't be changed. Since this string is the source in *strncpy*, this makes sense. That *s1* is not *const* also makes sense, given *strncpy*'s job is to modify s1.

The presence of *const* here does not actually guarantee the string won't be changed. The implementation of *strncpy* may, for some nefarious reason, intentionally cast *s2* to non-*const*, although this could be fatal if *s2* really were a ROM-based object. To be safe, you should always treat *const* variables and parameters as if they were in ROM. Don't cast away *const*-ness. Treat the presence of *const* in a parameter list as a contract to the caller, promising that the corresponding object will not change.

Note the difference between

```
const char *s;
```

and

```
char * const s;
```

The former says, "the pointer can change, but whatever string it points to cannot be modified," while the latter says, "the pointer cannot change, but the string it points to can be modified." Also, in the former, *const* is a type qualifier, while in the latter *const* is an object qualifier.

As an example, in the declaration

```
const char *s, *t, *u;
```

all three objects (variables) *s*, *t*, and *u* are of type const *char *.* The *const* type qualifier propogates across the entire declaration. Contrast this to

```
char * const s, *t, *u;
```

where all variables are of type *char *,* and the *const* only qualifies *s*.

As an aside, note that *const char * * and *char const * * are synonymous. I prefer the first form, since I find it shows the type qualifier and propogation nature of *const* more clearly.

These uses of *const* can be combined into

```
const char * const s;
```

A seriously read-only *strncpy* would then be prototyped

```
char *strncpy(char * const s1, const char * const s2,
     const size_t length);
```

protecting both the caller and the implementor. *strncpy* internally cannot accidentally move the pointers, or change the length (this technique is analogous to Ada's *in* mode).

5. Keep Each Variable in a Well-Defined State

C programmers move variables through state transitions, often unconsciously. To demonstrate, consider the following simple example:

```
int i;

/*...*/

for (i = 0; i < MAX; i++)
    {
    /*...*/
    }

/*...*/
```

The variable *i* undergoes the following three states:

- ❖ Uninitialized/random
- ❖ Well-defined, when taking on values from 0 to (MAX - 1), inclusive
- ❖ Out-of-bounds, when taking on value MAX

I would generalize these states, in decreasing order of desirability, to be

- ❖ Defined and valid
- ❖ Defined but invalid
- ❖ Undefined and invalid

Only within the loop is *i* defined and valid. Before the loop, *i* contains random values (undefined). After the loop, *i* is out-of-bounds (defined/known value, but invalid). Assuming this loop is contained in a significantly larger code piece, and assuming that *i* is not supposed to be used again, *i* actually spends most of its life invalid.

In my experience, there is a strong correlation between these so-called "domains of exception" (variables in undefined/invalid states) and buggy code, for the following two fundamental reasons:

- ❖ For those reading or maintaining such code, exceptions defeat the reader's assumptions about the meaning of a variable over its lifetime.
- ❖ Variables accidentally used outside their valid domains have unpredictable (or predictable, but incorrect) results.

635

You should prefer keeping variables well-defined and valid. When that is not a choice, keep variables at least well-defined. This becomes especially crucial with pointers.

In general, pointers always should point to one of the following two things:

+ A valid memory address
+ NULL

Thus, when you define a pointer, the definition should look like either:

```
char *Pointer = malloc(10);
```

or

```
char *Pointer = NULL;
```

Similarly, free a chunk of memory by

```
free(Pointer);
Pointer = NULL;
```

to keep *Pointer* in a well-defined state.

Dangling pointers occur when a pointer references memory that is no longer valid. In the sequence

```
char *p = malloc(10);
free(p);
```

p is a dangling pointer. The address that it contains references invalid memory. Dangling pointers are usually not so blatant. More often, they come from multiple pointers aliasing the same memory, as in

```
char *p;
char *String = malloc(100);

strcpy(String, "Yo ho, yo ho, a pirate's life for me!");
for (p = String; *p != '\0'; p++)
```

```
     {
     /*...*/
     }
free(String);
```

p still points into what was *String*. Attempts to dereference *p* are undefined. In a protected environment like Windows, *free* may mark the memory as unreadable, so that any appearance of **p* could generate a protection violation. Alternatively, immediately following the *free* call, the operating system may switch to another task blocked on some resource allocation request, giving the freed memory to that task. *p* would then reference memory belonging to another process.

In any event, accidental references through *p* may produce bugs quite difficult to isolate or understand, since the value of *p* will vary, as will the meaning of memory at the address referenced by *p*. Such dangling pointers appear to observe Heisenberg's Uncertainty Principle (especially with regard to debuggers): The presence of the debugger moves the memory allocated to *p*, changing the symptoms. Anyone who has loaded CodeView in Windows, only to watch a bug "disappear," knows exactly what I mean.

The real fix, of course, is not to dereference dangling pointers. However, before you can effect the fix, the dangling pointers must betray themselves. One of the easier ways to achieve this is to simply set pointers to NULL when they are no longer needed. In this context, NULL is defined, but invalid. In fact, NULL is the one pointer value guaranteed by C to be always defined and always invalid. Many operating systems know this. They have special detection for NULL dereferences, and handle them in a consistent manner. That manner may not be elegant, but it will be predictable.

You could buy (or write) memory-management libraries to enhance or replace *malloc* and *free*. One possible extension is to disallow memory to be freed if some pointer references it. That is, in the code

```
     /*
          * "Smart" dynamic memory allocation. Records the address
          * of it's returned pointer value.
          */
     extern void *SmartMalloc(const size_t Size);
```

```
/*
 * "Smart" free that return success flag, and changes
 * its pointer argument to NULL when its memory is freed.
 */
extern int SmartFree(void **Pointer);

/*
 * Assign one pointer to another's value.
 * Allows the value of Source to be recorded.
 * Returns Source.
 */
extern void *SmartAssign(void **Target, const void *Source);

char *p1, *p2;
p1 = SmartMalloc(10); SmartAssign(&p2, p1);

/*...*/

SmartFree(&p1);
```

the **SmartFree** call would fail, since *p2*, having been recorded by **SmartAssign**, still references the memory. Such a scheme really forces one to set unused pointers to NULL by way of a "smart" assignment function like

```
extern void *SmartAssign(void **Target, const void *Source); SmartAssign(p2, NULL);
```

to avoid memory leaks.

An even more intelligent memory manager would detect multiple references to the same object, even when those references are to different addresses, such as

```
extern void *SmartCalloc(size_t Count, size_t Size);

int *Element, *Vector;

Vector = SmartCalloc(100, sizeof(*Vector));
SmartAssign(&Element, &Vector[20]);

/*...*/

SmartFree(&Vector);
```

Vector points to a collection (in this case, array) of *int*, while *Element* points to one *int* of that collection. When *Vector* is freed, ostensibly no other pointer will reference the whole collection. However, the memory manager still can detect a reference to some part of the whole object (that is, that some pointer holds the address of one of the 200 integers of the array).

NOTE These are examples where C++ is clearly superior to C. Properly overriding *new*, *delete*, the = and * operators, and the copy constructor can yield the same or better results, while retaining normal C++ syntax. Indeed, so-called "smart" pointer classes are common in C++ programs.)

These techniques trap instances where a programmer accidentally uses a variable outside of its intended context. An alternative trick is to define automatic variables within a block scope. When the block ends, so do the lifetimes of the variables. This is really a generalization of what every C programmer does when defining automatic variables local to a function. For example,

```
/*...*/
{
    char *p = malloc(...);
    /*...*/
    free(p);
}
/* p no longer exists */
```

This trick is also handy for creating *for*-loop indices that will only be used within the loop, as in

```
{
    int i;
    for (i = 0; i < 10; i++)
        {
        /*...*/
        }
}
/* i no longer exists */
{
    int i; /* different from i above */
    for (i = 0; i < 20; i++)
        {
```

```
    /*...*/
    }
}
```

This mimics Ada's scoped loop parameter.

I would argue that each loop has a conceptually unique and independent iterator, and that, in this case, happens to be implemented with the same-named *int* variable. A scheme like the previous one not only better maps the spirit of the program, it also prevents *i* from being accidentally reused later.

4. Encapsulate Code by Way of Source Modules

Computerdom has long sung the praises of modular design and encapsulation. In such a design, each module is a "black box" with a well-defined interface (encapsulation barrier) between it and the rest of the world. In fact, outside the module's implementation, the module is synonymous with its interface.

A common example of this design in action is Windows, where each device (for example, screen, printer, or keyboard) has a standard interface. Programs communicate with a Windows device independently of how that device actually is implemented. When a hardware vendor comes out with a new "giga-pixel" display, that vendor implements a new video driver to support that particular hardware. From the point of view of every other program in Windows, the interface stays the same.

(Well, all right, so maybe Windows isn't totally device-independent—as anyone who's written dialog boxes for both EGA and VGA can attest—but the principle is there.)

C does not directly support modules at the source level (that is, distinct compilation units with separate interfaces and implementations). Compare this to languages such as Modula-2, Ada, and C++. In fact, until ANSI C (and prototypes), C didn't even support the interface/implementation model within a single function. Applying some conventions, however, you can simulate modules in C fairly well.

Over the years, I have evolved a style in C to support modules that, at its core, creates a mutual one-to-one correspondence between an .H file and a .C file. Everything known to the outside world about the module should be defined (types and constants) or declared (variables and functions) in the corresponding .H file. This .H file becomes the module's public interface. Every declaration in the .H file has a corresponding definition (implementation) in the .C file. This is analogous to public members in C++.

By implication, everything not defined/declared in the .H file is private to the .C file. This is analogous to private members in C++. Put another way, anything not needed by the outside world stays out of the .H file.

The following example demonstrates encapsulation construction, not encapsulation design. What you'll see is far from a paragon of module design.

```
/*
 *  Example interface MODULE.H
 */

    #if !defined(MODULE_H_)
        #define   MODULE_H_

    #include <stdio.h>

    typedef union
        {
        int x;
        }
    ALLATROPY;

    extern int Array[];

    extern void Func1(int, const FILE *);
    extern int Func2(ALLATROPY *);

    #endif /* !defined(MODULE_H_) */

/*
 *  Example implementation MODULE.C
 */

    #include "module.h"
```

```
enum
    {
    MAX_HEADROOM = 10,
    };

int Array[MAX_HEADROOM];

static void *Phlogiston = NULL;

void Func1(int n, const FILE *f)
    {
    /*...*/
    }

int Func2(ALLATROPY *a)
    {
    /*...*/
    }

static void Func3(void)
    {
    /*...*/
    }
```

In the following discussion, "public" refers to identifiers appearing in both MODULE.H and MODULE.C (and thus visible to the outside world), while "private" refers to identifiers appearing in only MODULE.C.

The MODULE.C file includes MODULE.H. In this instance, MODULE.H is needed for MODULE.C to see the type definition of *ALLATROPY*. However, even if MODULE.C did not need any definition from MODULE.H, the header should still be included in the implementation. This ensures that, at compile time, MODULE.H and MODULE.C jibe.

The MODULE.H file is wrapped in conditional-compilation to prevent multiple inclusion. This is a common technique. Just make sure you pick a method and standardize on it. Also, I recommend #*if defined* over the older (and less-versatile) #*ifdef.*

The variable *Array* is public. However, the dimension of *Array* (*MAX_HEADROOM*) is private, since it is only needed in the implementation's *Array* definition. If you wanted to take the *sizeof(Array)* outside the module, *MAX_HEADROOM* should be public.

The public function **Func1** takes a parameter of type *FILE **. This type is defined in the standard header file STDIO.H. Hence, STDIO.H is included in MODULE.H. In general, an interface should be complete, including all other interfaces it needs. In this case, MODULE.H needs the interface to the standard C stream I/O library.

Another public function, **Func2**, takes a parameter of type *ALLATROPY*. Since this type is used by a function seen by the outside world, the definition of *ALLATROPY* must appear in the interface. If **Func2** were private, *ALLATROPY* would also be private.

Private function **Func3** and private variable *Phlogiston* are defined *static*. This prevents them from being accessed even accidentally outside this module. In general, all private definitions should be static. A caveat here is that symbolic diagnostic tools (such as Microsoft's Dr. Watson, and debug Windows FatalExit stack traces) are often only aware of public symbols (symbols known to the linker). One solution is

```
#if defined DEBUG
    #define static
#endif
```

which will "turn off" the *static* keyword when DEBUG is set, so that all symbols become public. This technique may have problems, though, if the same *static* (but now temporarily public) symbol is used in multiple source files. The linker may complain if it sees multiple definitions for the same symbol.

In some contexts, the interface/implementation model doesn't make sense. Not all header files have an implementation behind them. They exist simply to provide universal constant and type definitions. The Standard C header file LIMITS.H is such a file, although I suppose it can be considered an "interface" to the compiler's built-in types.

Also, the one-to-one correspondence of interface to implementation may not map to a one-to-one correspondence between .H and .C files. Especially lengthy implementations may be more manageable if they are split among several physical .C files. That is, a large file MONDO.C may be broken into smaller files MONDO_1.C, MONDO_2.C, MONDO_3.C, and so on. The multiple physical files still are conceptually a single logical module (with a single logical interface) and appear that way to the outside world.

In such a scheme, you could have a monolithic MONDO.H included by all the MONDO_X.C files. Alternatively, each MONDO_X.C file could have its own .H file, with all those .H files in turn included in MONDO.H. Such file-splitting techniques don't just foster source file management. They also make for more precise object libraries, as only the parts of the module actually called are linked in. However, these techniques also have several drawbacks, including file name-space pollution, and arbitration of global variable storage across multiple files.

3. Program Defensively

In high school, I was drilled on the notion of "defensive driving." That is, never assume the rest of the world behaves the way I want it to. C programmers should adopt a similar attitude of "defensive programming," especially when interfacing with other code. Rules of defensive programming include

- Every encapsulated programming entity (function, module, program) must be able to tell the outside world its state.
- All code interfacing to those entities must query the state before assuming the state is valid.
- That same code must take some action upon discovering an error state. This can be summarized as error reporting, detection, and recovery.

Consider the statement

```
free(p);
```

free has no return value. Thus, the caller has no way to know if **free** succeeded or failed. In practice, programmers typically assume that **free** works, and carry on. Because it returns nothing, **free** thwarts even the most defensive programmers.

Contrast this with the equivalent Windows API **GlobalFree**, which returns zero to indicate failure, and nonzero to indicate success. Because it does report errors, **GlobalFree** allows callers the option of error detection and recovery.

Unfortunately, all the error reporting in the world does no good if no one reads the reports. At some point, we all run across code such as

```
char *p = malloc(10);
strcpy(p, "12345");
```

or, worse,

```
strcpy(malloc(10), "12345");
```

that assumes **malloc** succeeds. Checking error codes is annoying, and many programmers blithely assume (especially in these days of seemingly limitless virtual memory) that small allocations just never fail.

Styles such as these become lethal in the realm of Windows APIs. Just about every API, it seems, returns some sort of code. These codes are far too often ignored in the rush to generate reams of Windows C code. Windows maintains so many internal states that ignoring return codes eventually will kill your program.

Truly attentive (retentive?) Windows code will be peppered with lines such as

```
Brush = GetStockObject(...);
if (Brush == 0)
   /*...*/

/*...*/

Handle = GlobalAlloc(...);



if (Handle == 0)
    /*...*/

/*...*/

Key = RegCreateKey(...);
```

```
if (Key != ERROR_SUCCESS)
    /*...*/
```

The Windows API, like the Standard C runtime, generally has settled on return codes as an error-notification mechanism. Other methods include setting a global state variable (much like the C runtime's *errno*), generating an exception (by way of *longjmp*), or providing a status-query function.

However, detecting these errors is not enough. I once inherited code littered with statements such as

```
Handle = GlobalAlloc(...);
if (Handle == 0)
    MessageBox(..., "GlobalAlloc failed", ...);
/*
 *  now carry on as if GlobalAlloc succeeded
 */
Pointer = GlobalLock(Handle);
/*...*/
```

The code correctly noted that **GlobalAlloc** failed, but did nothing to recover from this error. In this particular case, I replaced the **MessageBox** call with a **FatalAppExit** call, since the program in question could not easily recover from failed allocations.

(Windows purists will note a more robust solution would return to the main message loop, free up all application resources, and exit. Given that this program was designed to be the only application running and was an internal test tool, terminating the application and rerunning Windows was not a terrible choice.)

Techniques such as the previous one cover errors reported by other code to you. You also must also design the converse—reporting errors to others. I demarcate such error-checking into the following categories:

- ❖ Bugs in your code
- ❖ The caller passing invalid arguments to you
- ❖ Exceptional (but legal) conditions

Most C programmers are aware of the standard C idiom *assert* to detect the first category of errors. Unfortunately, assertions are typically activated in only the debug prerelease versions of programs, under the rationale that such diagnostic code is too big and too slow for a retail release. At the very least, such asserts should be active for all internal and beta-site testing. If benchmarks show that some asserts can reasonably stay in the retail code, then leave them in.

Windows DLLs and drivers (or any code called by programs other than yours) should have precondition checks. You cannot guarantee that other programs actually will call you with valid arguments. You could adopt an attitude of "caveat emptor," saying it's the caller's obligation to call you right, and that you make no promise about what otherwise happens. Windows once had that attitude, until too many Windows developers moaned. For Windows 3.10, Microsoft added parameter-validation to the APIs, and there was much rejoicing. At the very least, such validation preserves the internal sanity of Windows, so it benefits Windows itself as much as it does other programs.

The final category contains all the miscellaneous things that you hope never happen, but eventually will anyway. I don't consider assertions appropriate here, since these conditions don't indicate an error so much as an annoyance for which you must compensate. Also, the typical assertion method of saying "you have a bug in this file at this line" really does little good to the user of your word processor who runs out of file handles.

Often, you can group these errors into classes (for example, out of global memory, out of local memory, out of some system resource such as DCs), and package the relevant APIs into your own functions that contain error checking. So, for example, in the example cited previously (**GlobalAlloc** failing), I could replace the code with

```
void *GlobalAllocAndLock(...)
    {
    HGLOBAL Handle;
    void *Pointer;

    Handle = GlobalAlloc(...);
    if (Handle == 0)
```

```
        FatalAppExit(...);
    Pointer = GlobalLock(Handle);
    if (Pointer == 0)
        {
        GlobalFree(Handle);
        FatalAppExit(...);
        }
    return Pointer;
    }


/*...*/

void Pointer = GlobalAllocAndLock(...);
```

2. Write Code that Will Work the Same in Both C and C++

I have more to say on this in Chapter 20, "Ways C++ is not C," but the subject bears a short mention here.

Regardless of your thoughts on its merit, C++ is the future. Given that the ANSI C++ committee X3J16 should spew forth a standard by the end of 1996, most new coding currently done in C will, by decade's end, be done in C++.

Like its ANSI C counterpart, X3J16 has the explicit goal of not breaking existing code. In this case, existing code essentially means ANSI C. However, because of prevailing conventions in older (late-1980s) C++ code, and requirements to support non-C features, some C code will either not compile in C++, or will compile but behave differently.

Given that most programming groups will migrate existing code to C++ (rather than rewriting it all from scratch), these incompatibilities might seem to be a roadblock. The reality is, though, that you can fairly easily write code that will behave identically in either environment, without hopelessly compromising your C style.

Further, because C++ enforces stronger type checking than does C, you can use a C++ compiler as a lint to catch problems a C compiler can't or won't. So, if possible, compile all your code through both C and C++ compilers.

You win in the short term (with more robust code) and in the long term (with easy migration to C++).

Beyond code-level compatibility, you should consider design-level compatibility. As you probably know, C++ encourages object-oriented programming (OOP). In fact, while it may not encourage OOP, C does at least tolerate OOP in a limited sense. Some of these OOP aspects, and examples of each, are

- Encapsulation (see the discussion of modules elsewhere in this list)
- Data abstraction (*void **, encompassing *structs*, **get/put** functions)
- Overloading (STDIO.H functions **printf, sprintf, fprintf**)
- Polymorphism (Windows messages, discriminated unions)
- Object instances (many Windows APIs)

However, C cannot even remotely fake inheritance, which precludes C from being a true OOP language. Even the OOP aspects enumerated previously are not expressly supported in C. Rather, they are not expressly prohibited. You must contrive conventions and techniques to simulate these OOP concepts in C, concepts that C++ supports directly.

When writing new C code, then, the code should not only compile as C++, but also the code should be designed around those C++ OOP concepts that C can fudge. This is not, strictly speaking, a migration requirement, as is the code-level compatibility discussed previously. Once in C++, you will almost certainly start designing object-oriented programs. If your existing C code is already quasi-OOP, you will find it works better with (and migrates more easily to) C++.

1. Pick an Aesthetic Style and Stick with It

I won't even enter the religious fray over naming conventions, or indentation width, or declaration ordering, or "where the braces go," or the myriad of other ponderings that turn programmers into gladiators (other than to say my programming examples, here and in other chapters, should betray many of my own prejudices).

Programmers apparently sometimes suffer amnesia, and attempt to define styles for all members of their groups, with mixed results. I have yet to see a style that enough people like to willingly adopt. Such programming styles remind me of Ada—attempts to define an end-all be-all that satisfies almost no one.

Whether you pick your own style or someone else picks it for you, is ultimately irrelevant. The important thing is to apply a style uniformly. In the end, it doesn't matter whether you use 2 or 4 or 40 spaces per indent. Just don't use 2 and 4 and 40 in the same code.

Write all code as if someone else (in addition to you) must understand it. Many of the suggestions made in this chapter distill down to the single concept, "make your programs predictable" (or, "bring forth order from chaos"). A style applied consistently keeps a reader from having to guess your intent. Don't see style conventions as artistic straightjackets. They actually free you and your readers to concentrate on the salient (and creative) aspects of your code.

Compare this to reading any book. When the author's organization is haphazard, or word choice obscure, you lose the flow, and are pulled out of the context of being "in the book." You become consciously aware of the act of reading. Consistent styles help keep the readers within the point of view of your program. Put another way, the code is the medium, the program is the message. You and your readers want to know the message. The code is just a means to that end.

CHAPTER 18

Things not to Assume About Your C Environment

In the world of logic, assumptions constrain truth. The more things you assume or expect, the fewer things that can satisfy those assumptions or expectations. This notion is captured in Occam's Razor, which teaches to favor the path making the fewest assumptions. However, implicit assumptions are an unconscious part of everyday life. Conversations and relationships would be tedious and mechanistic if you did not assume certain attributes of your partners, and believe that they assume certain attributes about you.

Contexts do exist in which implicit assumptions are inappropriate. For example, legal or diplomatic proceedings often are tortuous exercises in making assumptions explicit. Software, in its scientific and engineering aspect, is another such context, although many programmers hide assumptions without knowing it. As mentioned previously, assumptions constrain truth—they narrow the true (correct) domain of your program's context. Put another way, the more assumptions your code makes, the less freedom it has when moving to another environment.

I counter this notion of few assumptions with the "real world" truth that some things must be assumed, lest software remain in the realm of vapor. The trick is finding the balance, between few assumptions and a product that meets the project goals.

10. Operating Environment

This may be the most difficult assumption to overcome, especially in these days of multithreaded GUI monstrosities. You may think the ascendancy of such programs would simplify porting. After all, most of these systems use similar object and event models. In practice, though, these systems are different enough that migration becomes a Gordian Knot, requiring armies of consultants and libraries to unravel.

It turns out that the real portability seems to lie at the other end of the spectrum, with the lowly single-task console (text-based) applications, as championed by Unix and, later, MS-DOS. These programs have remained essentially unchanged for a generation. They can generally run in a "DOS box" under Windows, OS/2, and Windows NT. In fact, with the proper libraries, they even can be recompiled to become true native Windows applications.

When OS/2 first came out, Microsoft had APIs (the **VIO** subset) for old-timers who couldn't give up console applications. However, Microsoft clearly expected their GUI Presentation Manager to be the future rave, and removed the **VIO** APIs in later OS/2 versions. I haven't used OS/2 since IBM inherited it, so I don't know if those APIs are back. I have used Windows NT, and find it instructive that operating system has a new robust set of console APIs.

The moral is if you are looking to make money, you probably want a GUI application. If you are looking for portability, you may want to reconsider text-based applications. Who knows how the Mac would have fared had it supported text applications?

If you are fated to stay in the GUI world, you have some choices. You can craft or buy a library that insulates you from your system's implementation. Know that such a Lowest Common Denominator among the systems may come at the cost of system-specific functionality, possibly turning a implementation-bound useful system into a portable less-useful system.

If you settle on Windows, you have more liberty, finally. In the past, Microsoft seemed unconcerned about portability. They acted as if you would program in ASCII 16-bit real mode on Intel processors until the sun went nova. Windows has undergone enough migrations that Microsoft has borne the pain of their own shortsightedness.

Today, MSVC has class wrappers (MFC) around the Windows APIs and Windows types, making migration almost automatic. If you choose to stay in the C world, your road will be more treacherous, but not impassable. Microsoft seems to have placed their bets on the happy marriage of Windows and objects, as given witness by OLE's Component Object Model, and the future Cairo release of Windows NT. "Objectification" will become increasingly ingrained into the consciousness of Windows programmers.

At its heart, Windows always has supported object-oriented programming (OOP). Unfortunately, programming for Windows in C has often been like reading a newspaper with a magnifying glass—the OOP notions got lost in the detail. Certain OOPisms (such as subclassing, messaging, and per-instance data) were apparent. However, the overriding Windows programming paradigm seemed to discourage global OOP design, in favor of Frankenstein programs cobbled together from a dozen cut-and-pasted textbook examples.

The bottom line on all this is that if you want to insulate yourself from the operating system, go with objects, while knowing even then that your programs can never be completely ignorant of their environments.

9. File System

Amazingly enough to some people, ANSI C does not require the presence of a file system. You may wonder, "What about include files?" Surely the presence of:

```
#include <stddef.h>
```

implies the existence of a real file called STDDEF.H.

The fact is, included "files" don't have to actually exist as files. The compiler must only act in such a way that the definitions and declarations are made available in the way you expect.

The compiler may textually insert the file into your code, or it may just add appropriate symbol table entries (as is commonly done with so-called "precompiled headers"). Your code cannot assume a real file is there, and, in practice, this is not a problem. C programs don't really care how included files are implemented.

This all seems to bring up another apparent conflict. If ANSI C does not require a file system, how can functions such as **printf** be considered part of the standard library? Wouldn't **printf** imply that a file system exists? And don't all ANSI C conforming implementations have **printf**?

No, ANSI C distinguishes between freestanding and hosted environments. In this parlance, a "hosted environment" requires a file system and other pieces of an OS beneath it, while a "freestanding environment" does not. PCs are probably the most familiar example of hosted environments, while embedded systems—such as the microchip smarts in automobiles or microwave ovens—are common examples of freestanding environments. Most programmers I know unconsciously assume a hosted environment, but that may not always be a true assumption.

In freestanding environments, only the headers FLOAT.H, LIMITS.H, STDARG.H, and STDDEF.H need to be present. Dissecting these headers, you'll note they only contain definitions for macros and types. They contain no external declarations requiring external files for resolution.

I have actually adopted code written for embedded systems for use on a PC. The code was originally written for an electronic scale, running on an Intel 8051. Because testing directly on the scale was so tedious, I wrote a test harness on the PC, emulating much of the scale's hardware. Other than this harness, most of source was shared between the scale and the PC.

If you decide your code must assume a hosted environment, watch out for assumptions about that environment's file system. For example, a common include statement on UNIX systems is

```
#include <sys/stat.h>
```

This statement assumes

- ⁜ The character "/" demarcates subdirectories.
- ⁜ The file STAT.H is subordinate to some directory called SYS.

The former is not necessarily true on MS-DOS and its progeny (OS/2, Windows, Windows NT). Nonetheless, Microsoft's compilers have long recognized either

```
#include <sys/stat.h>
```

or

```
#include <sys\stat.h>
```

in source files (although, inconsistently, their command-line interpreters only recognize "/"). This "/" versus "\" confusion betrays the origins of MS-DOS as an amalgam of CP/M and UNIX.

Interestingly, MSVC accepts

```
#include "sys/stat.h"
```

and

```
#include "sys\stat.h"
```

and even

```
#include "sys\\stat.h"
```

equally. Apparently, the parsing mechanism used on other C string literals is not used by the preprocessor.

Another common file-system assumption is the length of filenames. For more than a decade, MS-DOS users have labored under the familiar tyranny of 8.3-style names (another CP/M legacy), but now Windows NT rescues us with long filenames. To maintain backward compatibility with older applications,

Windows NT essentially maintains 2 names for every file, the long name and an 8.3 alias.

If you want to write a program designed to run on all flavors of Windows, what do you do? Prudence says you assume 8.3 names only, to work on all systems. Tragically, however, it's possible to "break" the long filenames this way. If your 8.3-aware program opens a file with a long filename, Windows NT will present to your program an 8.3 name instead. If you manipulate the file by that name, and copy it or otherwise hand it off to another party, the file may "forget" the long name it had.

The safest bet, then, is to query the system, find out what type of file names it supports, then manipulate the files in the native tongue. As with all interaction, human or machine, don't assume—ask first.

8. Compiler

Stick to ANSI-compliant features whenever possible. The truth is, though, that commercial compiler vendors are similar to Sirens, luring programmers to crash on the rocks of vendor-specific **#pragma**'s, keywords, and libraries.

Extensions are the lawless Wild West territory of programming. They are not portable across compilers, and there's no guarantee that different vendors won't use the same extension for different purposes—or, alternately, that the same vendor won't use different extensions for the same purpose. For example, Microsoft has, at various times, used the keywords *huge*, *_huge*, and *__huge* for the same extension.

Try to isolate compiler-specific features into a small set of source files. Some integrated development environments fight this, insisting on makefiles that apply the same compiler options to all files. In such cases, try using ANSI compliance by default, and turn on compiler-specific features by way of **#pragma**, or possibly a hand-tuned makefile.

C++ is a wildcard here, since it has no ANSI standard. The safest bet is to assume ANSI C compliance will put you close to eventual ANSI C++ compliance.

7. Processor

This assumption can be deadly in these days of multiplatform systems such as Windows NT. Programmers who are porting Intel code from 16-bits (which is obscenely aware of Intel's much-beloved segment:offset architecture) to 32-bits are currently learning the joy of this assumption. Happily, these dependencies often can be hidden by a header file.

Many compilers sport inline assembler by way of *asm* or some similar keyword (ANSI C++ is considering making *asm* part of the language). Such code is, of course, not portable across processor architectures, nor indeed within the same architecture in different modes (16-bit versus 32-bit Intel).

6. Structure Member Ordering and Alignment

C guarantees the order of members within a structure. In the definition

```
typedef struct QUANDRY
    {
    int Chicken;
    int Egg;
    }
QUANDRY;
```

you can assume that *Chicken* comes before *Egg*. Thus, marching through the structure by way of

```
QUANDRY Quandry;

int *Pointer = (int *) &Quandry;

*Pointer++ = ChickenData; /* Pointer == &Quandry.Chicken */
*Pointer   = EggData;      /* Pointer == &Quandry.Egg */
```

is valid from that standpoint.

However, you cannot assume the alignment between those members. The previous structure could be implemented internally as the equivalent of

```
/* assume sizeof(int) == 2 */

typedef struct QUANDRY
    {
    int Chicken; /* 2 bytes */
    int padding; /* 2 bytes */
    int Egg;     /* 2 bytes */
    int padding; /* 2 bytes */
    }
QUANDRY;
```

if the implementation aligns all structure members on 4-byte boundaries. Thus, the previous code

```
QUANDRY Quandry;

int *Pointer = (int *) &Quandry;

*Pointer++ = ChickenData; /* OK * /
*Pointer   = EggData;     /* Wrong; Pointer references the
                             padding between members */
```

will be invalid.

If you write such a structure in binary form, then read it on a system using a different alignment or ordering method, the structure will not be what you expect. Clearly, then, structure I/O across implementations is not guaranteed portable.

Indeed, because most compilers allow you to choose the alignment, passing binary structures among programs on the same platform (or even functions within the same program) may not be guaranteed safe.

Wherever possible, choose the machine's most "natural" structure alignment, typically the same as **sizeof(int)**. Otherwise, you may suffer space/performance penalties.

ANSI solves the dilemma of locating members within a structure by way of the *offsetof* macro. This macro is the only portable way to find a member's offset. Accept no substitutes.

5. Bit Field Ordering

Little is guaranteed about bit fields. You cannot assume

- *sizeof* bit fields
- The number of bit fields that can appear in a single structure
- The order of bit fields within an integral unit
- The alignment of bit fields within an integral unit

You also cannot take the address of a bit field, since the bit field may not align on a machine-addressable boundary.

For all practical purposes, bit fields are completely nonportable. To use bit fields, you really must have intimate knowledge of their implementations. As they are typically used for a hardware-specific application (for example, reading a status register), this is usually not a portability hardship.

4. Byte Ordering

One little, two little, three Little Endians—or Big Endians, depending on architecture.

This dependency is fairly easy to isolate. Pick a standard portable byte order, and create a package of macros or functions that convert between your local byte order and this portable order. Never read/write binary data without filtering through this package.

Another possibilty (especially for small files) is to perform all I/O as text, and convert to/from binary by way of **scanf** and **printf**, as in

```
/* program A */

void Writer(const QUANDRY *Quandry)
    {
    printf("%d %d", (int) Quandry->Chicken, (int) Quandry->Egg);
    }
```

```
/* program B */

void Reader(QUANDRY *Quandry)
    {
scanf("%d %d", &Quandry->Chicken, &Quandry->Egg); }
```

There are still some implementation dependencies here. For example, **sizeof(int)** for *Reader* must be less than or equal to **sizeof(int)** for *Writer*, or *Reader* will lose data. In general, however, this technique is portable, and masks many implementation vagaries.

Before rejecting this solution as "too slow," run some benchmarks. You may find the free portability and simpler code outweigh any performance penalties, or indeed that the performance penalties are trivial, or even nonexistent.

3. Size of Types

Don't assume the sizes of built-in types. Use **sizeof** instead.

This restriction applies to user-defined types as well, especially structures and unions. As discussed previously, because of alignment differences, structure sizes are never certain, even on the same platform.

Unfortunately, **sizeof** can't be used in conditional-compilation directives. In those instances, use the symbols in LIMITS.H and FLOAT.H. So, instead of the illegal construct

```
#if sizeof(int) == sizeof(short)

      /* ints are shorts */

#elif sizeof(int) == sizeof(long)

      /* ints are longs */

#endif
```

use:

```
#include <limits.h>

#if INT_MAX == SHRT_MAX

    /* ints are shorts */

#elif INT_MAX == LONG_MAX

    /* ints are longs */

#endif
```

2. Sign of char

Experienced C programmers still either forget, or never knew, that characters have no sign guarantee. This business of mixing *char* and *int* so freely in C, and of treating *char* as "*tiny int*," is a major abomination of the language. It results in programs that manipulate characters at inconsistent levels of abstraction—sometimes as text, sometimes as underlying text encoding, sometimes as machine bytes. C programmers often unconsciously equate an abstract "character" to its machine representation. I much prefer Ada's notion that characters are a built-in enumerated type.

As it is, you should not assume the sign of *char*. If you must know the sign of *char*, use the previously introduced convention of

```
#include <limits.h>

#if CHAR_MAX == SCHAR_MAX

    /* char is signed */

#else
```

```
    /* char is unsigned */

#endif
```

Better still, avoid using signless *chars* altogether, and make *typedefs* for explicitly *signed char* and *unsigned char*, such as:

```
typedef   signed char schar;
typedef unsigned char uchar;
```

Declare variables of these types. Manipulate *char* only for compatibility with library functions.

This question of sign can give surprising results. The output of:

```
const char c1 = '\x7F';
const char c2 = '\x80';

if (c1 < c2)
    printf("c1 < c2\n");
else if (c1 > c2)
    printf("c1 > c2\n");
```

and

```
char c = '\xFF';

printf("%d\n", (int) c);
```

varies, depending on the sign of *char*.

1. Expression Evaluation Order

ANSI C has well-defined places (called "sequence points") at which all proceeding expressions are guaranteed to be evaluated. Between sequence points, you cannot assume the order of expression evaluation. In particular, you cannot assume the order of side effects. This includes statements such as:

```
int a = 0;
int a = a++ + ++a; /* what is the final value of a? */
```

(which no competent C programmer would write, anyway), as well as more subtle statements such as:

```
z[n] = ++n; /* which comes first, indexing or incrementing? */
```

and

```
func(10, x, 1, x++); /* in which order are arguments evaluated? */
```

With this last example, note that Windows programs often force you to be aware of function-call evaluation order. Sixteen-bit Windows differentiates *pascal* calling convention (arguments evaluated left-to-right) from *cdecl* calling convention (arguments evaluated right-to-left). Almost all Windows APIs are declared as *pascal*. Moreover, callback functions you provide for Windows must also be declared *pascal*.

Finally, remember that the sequence points && and || are short-circuiting. This means that, in C and C++, the statement:

```
if (a == b || a == c)
```

will first evaluate *a == b*. If that expression is true, the *if* statement exits, and *a == c* is not evaluated. Compare this to Pascal, where in:

```
if a = b or a = c then
```

both *a = b* and *a = c* are always evaluated. As a side note, Ada supports both forms, with:

```
if a = b or a = c then
```

acting as in Pascal, and:

```
if a = b or else a = c then
```

being short-circuited.

Because of this short-circuiting, C statements with side effects such as:

```
if (*p == 'a' && *(++p) == 'z')
```

may not work as you expect. Here, *p* will be incremented if (and only if) *p* == '*a*' is true.

CHAPTER 19

ANSI C Features that Might not Work the Way You Expect

In a way, it's unfortunate that C of all languages became so popular. I believe it's easier to introduce bugs with C (and C++) than it is with most other languages—not bugs so much based on design errors (although those certainly come up), but more bugs based on the language not doing what you think it does. That is, your design and intent may be correct, but the language doesn't behave the way you expect.

From what I can tell, C was never designed as the be-all end-all language it's become. As a result, some of C's greatest strengths (expressiveness, operator richness, low-level capability, alleged portability) are also, in other contexts, it's greatest weaknesses. Further, because K&R C was so popular, yet so incomplete, and because so many people were using it in ways for which it was not suited, the ANSI folks expanded the language's original charter.

The resulting language is still not complete, but it certainly is more complicated (although ANSI C is downright libertarian compared to the forthcoming ANSI C++). Like lawyers making laws, it seems the more language designers attempt to plug all the holes, the more new leaks spring up. What follows is a potpourri of features showing how inconsistent, incomplete, or unintuitive some aspects of C can be.

10. Negative Numbers Are not Always Negative

At first blush, this hint's title may seem ridiculous, or self-contradictory. The statement seems to counter the logical notion, "for all A, A is A," or more succinctly put in algebra's reflexive axiom

```
a = a
```

where here *a* is replaced with the notion of "being negative." Surely, you learned that negative numbers are always less than zero, and that, as an example, the statement

```
-1 < 0
```

is always true.

But I maintain my list heading is still valid. Perhaps there's something a bit more Zen going on here. Maybe the two uses of the word "negative" don't mean the same things at all.

To begin this mental rumination, consider the following Pascal expression:

```
-1 < 0
```

What is the result? I would expect any Pascal programmer to look at this and almost instinctively claim "true." Here, mathematical sense jibes with Pascal's, and integers behave the way you expect.

Mathematically, integers are boundless, while in Pascal they have some implementation-defined limits. Put another way, Pascal maps some finite number of abstract mathematical integers to its machine integers. This mapping defines the domain of integers Pascal "knows." From Pascal's point of view, these are the only integers existing in its universe.

On a number line, this can be represented as

```
<=== ... -n-2 -n-1 -n -n+1 ... -2 -1 0 1 2 ... n-1 n n+1 ... ===>
            |—— range of Pascal integers ————|
```

where n is the largest number in Pascal's reality and *-n-1* the smallest. All Pascal integers are inclusive within this domain. Of course, the domain of true mathematical integers extends infinitely away from these limits.

Now, interpret the expression as C, where

```
-1 < 0
```

is implicitly

```
(signed int) -1 < (signed int) 0
```

As with the Pascal example, most C programmers would quickly say the expression is true.

In this expression, C *ints* map, as do Pascal *integers*:

```
<=== ... -n-2 -n-1 -n -n+1 ... -2 -1 0 1 2 ... n-1 n n+1 ... ===>
            |—–- range of C signed int ————|
```

Unfortunately, C does not always preserve our intuitive sense of integers this way. Like Pascal, C has a finite mapping of abstract mathematical integers to machine integers. Unlike Pascal, C can choose which portion of the integer continuum to map. Sometimes the compiler must resolve conflicts between what makes sense mathematically, and what is credible for the machine representation.

To see this, change the previous expression to

```
-1L > 0
```

or its equivalent

```
(signed long) -1 > (signed int) 0
```

Assuming *sizeof(long) > sizeof(int)*, C's reality shifts. The domain of integers expands, encompassing more of the mathematical integer world. A new number line for this is

```
<=== ... -N-1 ... -n-1 ... -2 -1 0 1 2 ... n ... N ... ===>
              |- range of C signed int -|
       |----- range of C signed long ----------|
```

where *-N-1* and *N* now represent the *signed long* bounds. Because the *int* reality is wholly contained within the *long* reality, *signed* 0 maps directly to *long* 0, and the result is still true.

Changing the statement once more to

```
-1 < 0U
```

or alternately

```
(signed int) -1 < (unsigned int) 0
```

we have a contradiction. *unsigned int*s are, by C's definition, non-negative; *-1* is, by mathematical definition, negative. In our number-line representation, this becomes

```
                   |-- unsigned int --|
<=== ... -n-1 ... -2 -1 0 1 2 ... n ... 2n+1 ... ===>
         |----- signed int ---------|
```

where *signed* -1 is not within the same domain as *unsigned* 0. A conflict, which can only be resolved by either mapping *signed* -1 into the u*nsigned* domain, or mapping *unsigned* 0 to the *signed* domain. C chooses the former, so the condition is treated as

```
(unsigned int) -1 < (unsigned int) 0
```

The size of these domains is the same; only their values differ. C's effective mapping of each *signed* int into *unsigned int* is

```
signed int  maps to  unsigned int
----------           ------------
-n-1                 n+1
```

```
-n-2                    n+2
 .                       .
 .                       .
 .                       .
-2                      2n
-1                      2n+1
 0                       0
 1                       1
 .                       .
 .                       .
 .                       .
n-1                     n-1
n                       n
```

Thus, *signed* -1 is translated to the largest *unsigned* integer. The expression effectively becomes

```
UINT_MAX < 0U
```

which is false. The net result, then, is that in the original expression, the apparently negative -1 is greater than zero.

Finally, combine the previous scenarios in

```
-1L < 0U
```

or, equivalently,

```
(signed long) -1 < (unsigned int) 0
```

Is this true or false? The answer, perhaps surprisingly, depends on *sizeof(long)* and *sizeof(unsigned)*.

If s*izeof(long)* > *sizeof(unsigned)*, the domains are

```
                  |—- unsigned int —-|
<=== ... -N-1 ...  -2 -1 0 1 2 ... n ... 2n+1 ... N ... ===>
        |——— signed long ———-|
```

Because the *signed long* domain contains every element in the *unsigned int* domain, C converts the *unsigned int* to *signed long*. The expression then becomes

```
(signed long) -1 < (signed long) 0
```

which is true.

However, if *sizeof(long)* == *sizeof(unsigned)*, the domains are

```
                       |-- unsigned int ------|
<=== ... -N-1 ...   -2 -1 0 1 2 ... N ... 2N+1 ... ===>
        |--- signed long -----------|
```

This time, not all *unsigned ints* are contained in the *signed long* domain. C reacts by converting both operands to *unsigned long*, yielding an effective expression of:

```
(unsigned long) -1 < (unsigned long) 0
```

As with the earlier example, -1 is translated to the largest *unsigned long* positive value, and the expression is false.

The upshot for Windows programmers is that, on 16-bit platforms, the expression is true, while on 32-bit platforms, it is false. Thus, a seemingly innocuous expression such as:

```
-1L < 0U
```

is a chameleon, changing truth depending on its context.

The seeming contradiction in this list's title really betrays ambiguity in the notion of "negative." Don't let C's notation and rules fool you. The language has its own algebra, which may not always match yours.

9. Prototypes Do not Provide Type-Safe Linkage

Assume the following two source modules:

```
/*
 *   nematode.c
 */

void Nematode(int)
    {
    /*   ... */
```

```
    }
```

and

```
/*
 *  main.c
 */

void Nematode(int);

/* ... */

void main(void)
    {
    Nematode(); /* error */
    }
```

The latter will generate a compiler error, since the use of *Nematode* contradicts the prototype. Suppose that, in fixing the error, you change the module to:

```
/*
 *  main.c
 */

void Nematode(void);

/* ... */

void main(void)
    {
    Nematode();
    }
```

This makes the compiler happy—the prototype and use agree. You can even link the two modules to produce an executable. However, this program is incorrect, and will suffer undefined and possibly fatal runtime behavior. This is because C only checks types within a single translation unit. NEMATODE.C prototypes *Nematode* as

```
void Nematode(int);
```

while MAIN.C prototypes it as

```
void Nematode(void);
```

Because the use is consistent within each module, C believes there are no errors. If the compiler could somehow look across multiple source files, to be sure the prototypes are consistent, this error would be caught before the program was linked, let alone run.

But C does not type-check across modules, either at compile time or at link time. The safest way to avoid this problem is to prototype each function only once, in a header file, and include that header everywhere the prototype is needed (see Chapter 20, "Top Ten Hints for Better Living Under ANSI C," for more).

C++, like C, does not check this at compile time. The previous code will compile cleanly in C++. However, at link time, C++ will detect the mismatch. More accurately, C++ "mangles" names, effectively embedding prototype information in the symbols seen by the linker.

In MSVC, C++ mangles the fully qualified prototypes

```
void __far __cdecl Nematode(int);
```

and

```
void __far __cdecl Nematode(void);
```

into

```
?Nematode@@ZAXH@Z
```

and

```
?Nematode@@ZAXXZ
```

respectively. Module *main* references *?Nematode@@ZAXXZ*, but the linker cannot find that symbol. The reference is unresolved, and the linker reports an error.

672

Finally, note that Ada is smarter still, and ensures consistent prototypes across files at compile time. While providing greater type safety, this checking does come at the cost of longer compile times and more complicated compilers.

8. NULL Might not Be Implemented as a Machine Zero

In the old pre-ANSI days, I'd see code such as

```
char *p;
/* ... */
if (p)
```

implicitly comparing a pointer to integer 0, and I'd cringe. Coming from a Pascal and Ada background, this implied *p* was of some Boolean type. I was somewhat mollified by *if (p == 0)* although, to me, this was a violation of type compatibility, comparing pointer apples and integer oranges. Better was

```
if (p == NULL)
```

Even though I knew NULL was just #*defined* to be 0, mentally I considered it to be of some typeless pointer. Unfortunately, such a NULL definition required me to enforce the pseudo-type checking, since definitions such as

```
float f = NULL; /* OK; really float f = 0; */
```

would elicit nary a peep from the compiler.

Once ANSI introduced true typeless pointers by way of *void **, many compiler vendors defined NULL as *((void *) 0)*. This prevented statements such as the aforementioned

```
float f = NULL; /* error; really float f = ((void *) 0); */
```

Once again, all was right with the world.

Interestingly, C++ throws a curveball here. Unlike C, C++ does not consider *void* * assignment compatible to all pointers. The statement

```
int *p = NULL; // error; really int p = ((void *) 0);
```

generates an error in C++. Here, the cast

```
int *p = (int *) NULL;
```

is absolutely required.

Knowing this, C++ vendors typically define NULL as in the old days, to be plain 0. Microsoft's STDDEF.H covers both forms with

```
#ifndef NULL
    #ifdef __cplusplus
        #define NULL 0
    #else
        #define NULL ((void *)0)
    #endif
#endif
```

Thus, in what is supposedly a more strongly typed language, C++ permits

```
float f = NULL;
```

while C does not. In fact, many C++ authors now dispense with the symbol NULL altogether, preferring to use the symbol 0 to represent the NULL pointer. What goes around comes around.

In all these cases, the value of NULL ultimately distills down to the symbol 0 of some type. The symbol 0 is sacred to C—the only value guaranteed to be (1) assignable to all pointers, and (2) an invalid address, not representing real storage.

Unfortunately, 0 is also the symbol used to represent integer zero. It's tempting—and wrong—to assume the NULL pointer represented by 0 is, at the machine level, identical to the integer zero represented by 0. If I could wave a magic wand, I would give C a keyword analogous to Pascal's *nil*, or make NULL itself a keyword, representing the NULL pointer value.

It's entirely possible (and legal) for an implementation to transform 0 used as a NULL pointer into something other than machine zero. Indeed, NULL pointers assigned to different pointer types may even be different from one another. Consider an Intel medium-model program. Not all pointers are the same size, implying the same NULL pointer machine value cannot be used for all those pointers.

In practice, most every machine you are likely to see represents the NULL pointer with a machine zero. I've read about architectures that don't (for example, some Honeywell-Bull mainframes), but never have actually used them. Regardless, in most contexts, you will never know, or have to know, your machine's representation—most contexts, but not all.

As a counterpoint, consider the calls

```
char **p = calloc(100, sizeof(char *));
```

or, in Windows,

```
char **p = GlobalAllocPtr(GMEM_ZFROINIT, sizeof(char *) * 100);
```

Each call returns a pointer to an array of 100 character pointers. The array is filled with machine zeroes (implicitly in *calloc*, explicitly in **GlobalAllocPtr**). The intent is to fill the array with NULL pointers. However, if the NULL character pointer is implemented as something other than machine zero, these pointer values are not NULL.

7. for Loop Logistics

When learning C, many of us read something to the effect that a *for* statement like:

```
for (i = 0; i < 10; i++)
    {
    /* ... */
    }
```

is equivalent to the *while* loop:

```
i = 0;
while (i < 10)
    {
    /* ... */
    i++;
    }
```

Many of us also learned that *continue* is really the dreaded *goto* with an implied label. That is,

```
while (!Bankrupt)
    {
    if (Doubles)
        continue;
    /* ... */
    }
```

can be alternately written as:

```
while (!Bankrupt)
    {
    if (Doubles)
        goto Roll;
    /* ... */
    Roll:;
    }
```

Given that, what is the expected behavior of:

```
for (i = 0; i < 10; i++)
    {
    /* #1 */
    continue;
    /* #2 */
    }
```

Mapping *for* and continue to their *while* and *goto* equivalents apparently results in:

```
i = 0;
```

```
while (i < 10)
    {
    /* #1 */
    goto CONTINUE;
    /* #2 */
    i++;
    CONTINUE:;
    }
```

However, this would yield in an infinite loop, since *i* never changes. In truth, the loop is not infinite, and:

```
for (i = 0; i < 10; i++)
    {
    /* #1 */
    continue;
    /* #2 */
    }
```

behaves identically to:

```
for (i = 0; i < 10; i++)
    {
    /* #1 */
    }
```

Perhaps, then, *for* and *continue* are implemented as:

```
i = 0;
while (i < 10)
    {
    /* #1 */
    goto CONTINUE;
    /* #2 */
    CONTINUE:;
    i++;
    }
```

This supports the observed behavior, but it also violates the equivalence relationship between *for* and *while*, since a real *while* loop of:

```
i = 0;
while (i < 10)
```

```
{
/* #1 */
continue;
/* #2 */
i++;
}
```

does, in fact, loop forever.

So, it seems that *continue* alters normal *for* loop behavior. Use caution when mixing these two. Their communal behavior may not match your expectations.

6. Arrays and Pointers Are not Always Synonymous

Consider the following Pascal sequence:

```
var
     a : ^integer;
begin
new(a);
a[4] = 42; { error }
end.
```

The compiler complains that *a* is a pointer to a single integer, not an array of integers. Change the definition of *a* as in

```
var
     a : ^array[1..10] of integer;

begin
new(a);
a[4] = 42; { error }
end.
```

so that *a* points to an array, and the compiler still whines. What it's looking for is:

```
var
    a : ^array[1..10] of integer;

begin
new(a);
a^[4] = 42; { OK }
end.
```

a is of type pointer to integer array; *a* ^ is of type integer array, and can by subscripted.

This all seems subterfuge to C programmers, who unconsciously exploit the alter egos of arrays and pointers. The C equivalent of the previous Pascal code is:

```
int *a = malloc(10);
a[3] = 42; /* 0-based a[3] analogue of Pascal's 1-based a[4] */
```

Even though *a* is defined as a pointer to a single integer, this works—the compiler performs one of its famous silent conversions, turning:

```
a[3]
```

into:

```
*(a + 3)
```

In most contexts, C will transform any array construct:

```
a[n]
```

into:

```
*(a + n)
```

This leads to the arcane notation of 3[a], derived by:

```
a[3] == *(a + 3) == *(3 + a) == 3[a]
```

I encourage the doubters among you to try compiling:

```
char a[10];
3[a] = 'x';
```

What I don't encourage is that you actually use this, although it is fun to throw at C novices. A special case of this array/pointer identity is:

```
a[0] == *(a + 0)
```

Taking the address of each side gives:

```
&a[0] == a + 0
```

or

```
&a[0] == a
```

That is, the name of an array is synonymous with the address of its first element. As with prototypes, this equivalence only applies within a given translation unit. Failure to observe this can lead to strange consequences. Several years ago, a colleague was asked to figure out a customer's C programming problem. The customer in question had two C modules conceptually like:

```
/*
 *  module Scylla
 */

int Peril[4] = {0, 1, 2, 3};

/*
 *  module Charybdis
 */

extern int *Peril;

void main(void)
    {
    int i;
```

```
for (i = 0; i < 4; i++)
    printf("%d\n", Peril[i]);
}
```

The customer was trying to use the array/pointer equivalence, and felt safe referencing *Peril* as a pointer, even though it was defined as a true array. What he expected module *Charybdis* to print was:

```
0
1
2
3
```

What he actually got was random behavior.

Assume a 16-bit far-data model Windows program. Further assume that *Peril* is stored starting at absolute address 100. *Peril* would then be laid out as:

```
address     storage    meaning
_____ -   _____ -  _____ -
            +---+
100         | 0 |       Peril[0]
            +---+
102         | 1 |       Peril[1]
            +---+
104         | 2 |       Peril[2]
            +---+
106         | 3 |       Peril[3]
            +---+
```

However, module *Charybdis* expects *Peril* to be stored as a pointer like

```
address     storage    meaning
_____ -   _____ -  _____ -
            +---+
100         | 0 |       offset  of pointer Peril
            +---+
102         | 1 |       segment of pointer Peril
            +---+
104         | 2 |       ignored
            +---+
106         | 3 |       ignored
            +---+
```

Thus, *Charybdis* interprets the 4 bytes addressed by *Peril* as a far pointer, in this case 1:0. The subsequent **printf** will attempt to access whatever happens to be at that address. The easiest and best solution, of course, is to make the prototype match the definition, changing *Charybdis* to:

```
extern int Peril[];

void main(void)
    {
    int i;
    for (i = 0; i < 4; i++)
        printf("%d\n", Peril[i]);
    }
```

Now *Charybdis* interprets *Peril* correctly.

Consider a cumbersome, but perhaps more educational, solution, recalling the identities:

```
a[n] == *(a + n)

a    == &a[0]
```

from which we can derive:

```
a[n] == *(&a[0] + n)
```

This identity is implicit for arrays. We know from *Scylla* that *Peril* is really stored as an array. However, the compiler sees *Charybdis* treating *Peril* as a pointer, so it does not know to honor this identity. If we make explicit what the compiler cannot assume, by way of:

```
extern int *Peril;

void main(void)
    {
    int i;
    for (i = 0; i < 4; i++)
        printf("%d\n", *((int *) &Peril + i));
    }
```

the code works.

5. getchar Does not Get a char

Then why is it called *getchar*? There are historical reasons behind this, which distill down to the UNIX community's desire for a platform-independent representation of end-of-file. Rather than usurping a valid character, *getchar* returns *EOF*, defined as some negative integer (usually -1). This requires that *getchar* have an effective prototype of

```
int getchar(void);
```

Even so, the compiler, eternally helpful, well happily let you write

```
char c = getchar();
```

without flagging an error (MSVC generates a warning). With this definition, depending on your platform, there is an excellent chance that c == EOF will never be true and the loop

```
while ((c = getchar()) == EOF)
    {
    /* ... */
    }
```

will not terminate correctly.

4. Operator Interpretation

Compiler writers must despise C, since there are so many places the compiler cannot unambiguously divine a program's intent. For openers, consider the following statements:

```
int i;
int j;
int k;

i = j&&&k;
```

What does this mean? The compiler really doesn't know, so it falls back on a "greedy" algorithm. That is, given a choice, the compiler considers a character part of its current token, rather than starting a new token. With this heuristic, the compiler interprets the previous statement as:

```
i = j && &k;
```

which is valid.

Now try

```
int y;
int x = y*z;
```

The answer changes, depending on the type of z. If the full construct is:

```
int z;
int y;
int x = y*z;
```

* is the binary multiplication operator, and the code compiles. On the other hand, if the full construct is:

```
int *z;
int y;
int x = y*z;
```

* is the unary pointer dereference operator, and the assignment statement is invalid. Finally ponder:

```
int a;
int b;
int c;

a = b+++c;
```

I leave it as an exercise for the reader to find all possible permutations, including the compiler's actual interpretation.

Beyond these lexical curiosities, C and C++ operators form an imposing bureaucracy. C has 47 operators grouped into 15 levels of hierarchy. C++ adds five operators and two levels. This sometimes bewildering array of operators, and operator interaction, can lead to some fairly opaque expressions.

I would hope that most C programmers have an innate feel for the precedence in constructs such as:

```
y = -d + f(x) * a[n]
```

```
!x < y || y && z
```

```
p == q ? c = d, d = 0 : c += d
```

More problematic are less frequently used operators, or common operators close in precedence. Examples include:

```
if (c = getchar() == EOF)
```

```
*a[n]++
```

```
++s->m = &a++
```

```
if (w0 == w1 & 0xFF00 >> 8)
```

These are equivalent to the explicitly parenthesized constructs:

```
if (c = ((getchar()) == EOF))
```

```
*((a[n])++)
```

```
(++(s->m)) = (&(a++))
```

```
if ((w0 == w1) & (0xFF00 >> 8))
```

some of which may not match your intuition or guesses. If you aren't instantly sure of precedence, odds are others reading your code won't be either. Don't be afraid to use parenthesis to make certain your intent, if not to the compiler, than at least to yourself and them.

3. Trigraphs

For many (most?) of us, our canonical "first C program" is:

```
void main(void)
    {
    printf("Hello world\n");
    }
```

I remember, when first coming to C, how awkward-looking I found that \n. Now my brain parses it without skipping a beat.

Those backslashes are tricky. As Dave mentions elsewhere, a statement such as:

```
printf("c:\windows\system\vga.drv");
```

which really prints:

```
c:windowssystemvga.drv
```

occasionally fools us all.

For something a little trickier, guess the results of:

```
printf("Halt, who goes there??!\n");
```

The answer is:

```
Halt, who goes there|
```

For explanation, we must segue to the ANSI committee, and their desire to include non-U.S. character sets into the language.

We in the U.S. take the ASCII character set for granted, as a universal standard. As with so many things American, this supposed "universal" standard is not universal at all. In particular, some European countries use computing equipment that does not support all the ASCII characters traditionally used in C programs.

To remedy this, the committee devised lexical alternates for these symbols. These symbols had to be unambiguous, so the compiler would not accidentally scan them as something else. The committee chose the sequence ?? to start these symbols, since that sequence does not otherwise appear in the language.

As these symbols consist of three characters—?? followed immediately by some other character—they are collectively called *trigraphs*. As an example, the construct:

```
void main(void)
    ??<
    /* ... */
    ??>
```

contains two trigraphs. These are lexically replaced by the compiler to form:

```
void main(void)
    {
    /* ... */
    }
```

This syntax is stone ugly, and will probably be replaced with keywords in an addenda to the C standard, and possibly in the emerging C++ standard. For the time being, it exists as a curiosity that may catch you unaware.

Reconsider the original statement

```
printf("Halt, who goes there??!\n");
```

The string literal contains the valid trigraph sequence ??!. This is lexically replaced by the compiler with |, converting the statement effectively to:

```
printf("Halt, who goes there|\n");
```

To print the intended statement, use:

```
printf("Halt, who goes there\?\?!\n");
```

2. typedef Does not Create a New Type

In the code

```
typedef union Jack
    {
    long UK;
    }
JohnBull;
```

what new types are defined? Note that this definition is shorthand for:

```
union Jack
    {
    long UK;
    };

typedef union Jack JohnBull;
```

The answer is *union Jack*. What about *JohnBull?*

Contrary to the name, **typedef** does not define a new type. Rather, it defines a new alias to an existing type (maybe the keyword should be something baroque like *typealiasdef*). In the previous construct, *JohnBull* is just an alias for *union Jack*. This is illustrated by

```
typedef union Jack
    {
    long UK;
    }
JohnBull;

JohnBull Tory;
union Jack Royalist;

Tory = Royalist;
```

This compiles because *Tory* and *Royalist* are of the same data type. Change the code to:

```
typedef union Jack
    {
    long UK;
    };

typedef union
    {
    long UK;
    }

JohnBull;
JohnBull Tory;
union Jack Royalist;

Tory = Royalist;
```

Now *JohnBull* is a type alias for an unnamed union. Even though that union and *union Jack* have the same layout, they are considered distinct types, and the assignment is invalid.

The moral, then, is that you cannot rely on **typedef** as a vehicle to generate distinct types. In this regard, **typedef** is really much like a scoped **#define**.

1. Comments Do not Nest

Suppose your code contains

```
char *gnirts; /* reversed string */
```

At some point, you decide to temporarily hide this definition by commenting out the line with:

```
/*

char *gnirts; /* reversed string */

*/
```

Sadly, this refuses to compile. The compiler sees an unmatched */. The culprit is the already-present comment:

```
/* reversed string */
```

where */ inadvertently terminates the outer comment.

If your C compiler supports them, or if you are compiling C++, you could consider using inline comments. Then, an encompassing comment such as:

```
/*

char *gnirts; // reversed string

*/
```

will work.

The best solution is to comment-out code by way of:

```
#if 0

char *gnirts; /* reversed string */

#endif
```

Such conditional statements nest, and allow any comment style you choose. They also lend themselves to more sophisticated comment-out schemes such as:

```
#if defined(DEBUG)

char *gnirts; /* reversed string */

#endif
```

CHAPTER 20

Ways C++ is not C

At its heart, C++ is C with classes, which in turn are C structures with two key differences:

- ⊹ Members can be functions.
- ⊹ Members can be hidden.

Looked at another way, C structures are a limited instance of classes, with all members data, and all members visible ("public" in C++ parlance).

Had C++ stayed "C with classes," giving us modules ala Modula 2 or Ada, the language syntax and semantics would have changed relatively little. However, neither the language nor the language's Founding Fathers (and Mothers) stayed so modest.

Classes as modules are nice, but classes as object types are nicer still. With more language twiddling, object types could look built-in. This requires yet more language features (such as operator overloading, references, constructors, and destructors).

If you're doing classes and objects, make the language truly OOPS by allowing class reuse through inheritance. But why stop at single inheritance, when you can so easily extend to multiple inheritance?

Now that the language can let you build types that look built-in, make that runtime library truly usable by adding all the types and routines everyone ends up creating from scratch anyway.

Finally, tidy up some of the sloppy type checking and other loose ends from C that make language purists wince.

In this rush to craft the Perfect Language, you must never forget your cherished and venerable C roots. All this object stuff must still allow you to write code that looks and walks and quacks like C. Among the ANSI folks' years of deliberations, compiler vendors' years of upgrades, and all programmers' years of coding, a C legacy has been created that is not easily ignored. For C++ to "break" this code, would be C sacrilege, a blasphemy not likely tolerated amongst the programming masses.

Sadly, as with so many human endeavors, you find yourself wanting two pretty much mutually exclusive things simultaneously, to wit:

- ⁙ OOPS language features freed of C's constraints and assumptions, requiring extending C's syntax and semantics
- ⁙ 100 percent unambiguous C compatibility

I call this "P and not P," from my predicate calculus days. A common trap people find themselves in, believing "P and not P" leads to any arbitrary conclusion "Q." For the curious, one possible derivation is

1. P   Premise
2. ~P   Premise
3. P v Q   1 Addition
4. Q   3,2 Disjunctive Syllogism

So, believing C++ can be all things to all people allows you to logically conclude anything under the sun. Pretty heady stuff.

What this distills down to, of course, is that C code compiled as C++ will not always work as it does under C. In general, the changes are small—small, but not zero. Many of them tighten C loopholes, enforcing standards that are good practice in both C and C++. Others are a consequence of C++-specific features. The C code masquerading as C++ doesn't use these features explicitly, but the language still must accommodate them. Finally, some appear, to me anyway, as arbitrary sadistic changes meant to break code making the wrong assumptions.

What follows is far from exhaustive. The actual number of changes numbers in the dozens. I've selected here a representative list, to give you a flavor of the changes so you can plan your migrations accordingly.

10. void *

ANSI needed to represent several models of "nothingness" not covered by K&R. As a solution, they created the keyword *void*, overloaded to mean

- Generic typeless pointer
- Empty parameter list
- Function returning nothing

C does not allow you to define objects of type *void*, thus avoiding an interesting philosophical consequence. What would an object of type *void* mean? An empty object? And object of size zero? And what would an array of such objects mean?

You can't create an object of type *void*, yet you can point to one of these nonexistent objects. But what does it mean to point to ("remember") a *void* object, especially when no such object exists (the set of *void* objects being void)?

In fact, pointers to *void* objects are unique, in that they must, in reality, reference something other than what their data type implies. *void** can never reference a *void*. Every other pointer type, barring type conversion, points to what its type says it does.

693

In C, pointers to *void* are truly generic. They can be freely transmuted to and from pointers of any other type without a cast, as in:

```
IMMATURE *Caterpillar;
void *Cocoon = Caterpillar;
ADULT *Moth = Cocoon;
```

The real use of this is in functions like the C runtime's memory allocation and manipulation. In classic C, for example, *malloc* was prototyped as:

```
char *malloc();
```

Note the return type. *char** commonly meant "generic pointer" in the *void*less days. Fact is, given C's type checking then, a prototype of:

```
int *malloc();
```

or even

```
unsigned long *malloc();
```

would have worked as well. Compare this to the classic C function:

```
char *strcpy();
```

which really truly returned a *char **. You needed some ulterior knowledge of the library to know when *char ** meant *char **.

ANSI rescues us with tighter type checking and true generic pointers. Today's new and improved *malloc* prototypes as:

```
void *malloc(size_t);
```

The understanding here is that you implicitly convert the *void** to the correct object type before using the memory. That is, constructs like:

```
void *v = malloc(10);
*v = 17;
```

are not allowed. *v references a void object, which, as already discussed, cannot exist. Why this anomaly? Principally because the compiler cannot know the size and alignment of a *void* object, precluding pointer dereference. *void* is a placeholder—you must fill in the real type. A more usual construct is:

```
int *i = malloc(10);
```

allocating (in this instance) an array of integers. Note that you do not need:

```
int *i = (int *) malloc(10);
```

as the compiler converts the types for you. Compare this to:

```
char *s;
char *t;

int *i = strcpy(t, s); /* error - mismatched pointer types */
```

which requires a cast, as in:

```
int *i = (int *) strcpy(t, s); /* dubious but legal */
```

This business of assigning *malloc* return values to non-*void* pointers is among the most common C idioms—and one of the constructs that breaks under C++.

Compiled as C++, the code:

```
int *i = malloc(10); // error - mismatched pointer types
```

fails. *void** loses its magic powers of automatic silent conversion. In C++, you must cast, as in:

```
int *i = (int *) malloc(10);
```

However, perhaps unexpectedly, C++ allows implicit conversion to *void*, so that:

```
void *v = strcpy(t, s);
```

is valid. What's the story?

The rationale is type safety. C++ allows you to go from a more strict type (say *char **) to a less strict type (*void**), but not the other way. The change to *void** causes loss of type information; C++ will not assume that information later when you decide to "uncast" from *void** back to some other type. You must explicitly tell the language the new type. In effect, you are reapplying the type-safety.

(Note that, in practice, C++ programmers don't use *malloc* much anyway, preferring *new* instead.)

This anomaly pops up somewhat unexpectedly in the construct:

```
char *c = NULL;
```

surely one of the more benign assignments in C. Here NULL is a Trojan Horse, for after preprocessing, the statement quite often is actually

```
char *c = ((void *) 0);
```

which is legal C, but illegal C++. Only a C++ usage such as

```
void *and = NULL;
```

is not null and void.

I mention this in Chapter 19, "ANSI C Features that Might not Work the Way You Expect," so I won't belabor it here. Current C++ practice is to move away from NULL toward a stark 0 anyway. In net effect, defining NULL as a *void** really buys little in C, and less in C++.

The silent conversion from strict non-*void* type to loose *void* type speaks up when *const* and *volatile* are thrown into the mix. C++ uniformly disallows implicit conversion from *const* to non-*const*, or from *volatile* to non-*volatile*. So, while:

```
char *c = 0;
void *v = c;
```

is okay, the statements:

```
const char *c = 0;
void *v = c;
```

and

```
volatile char *c = 0;
void *v = c;
```

are not. As before, the rationale is type safety, only of a different sort. Before the problem was loss of type size and alignment, while here the problem is loss of type attribute.

9. Pointer Conversions in General

The previous discussion generalizes nicely into a discussion of pointer types. C's legacy as a high-level assembler shows in its treatment of pointers as machine addresses with syntactic sugar. The actual pointer data types are almost an afterthought.

As mentioned previously, conversions to and from *void ** warrant nary a peep from the compiler. Conversions among non-*void* pointers may rouse the compiler enough to produce warnings, but even those go away if you set your warning level threshold high enough. For any types *APPLE* and *ORANGE* in standard C, the assignment:

```
APPLE *a;
ORANGE *o = a;
```

never generates an error. In fact, you get more grief from MSVC for mixing different data pointers sizes than you do for mixing different data pointer types. That is, the statements:

```
__far char *f;
__near char *n = f;
```

generates a warning at level 4, while

```
int *i;
char *c = i;
```

does not.

C++, predictably, tightens all these rules. Other than the implicit coercion to *void* * mentioned previously, C++ does not let you intermingle pointer types. So, unless they happen to alias to the same type, or *ORANGE* is really *void*, the earlier statement:

```
APPLE *a;
ORANGE *o = a;
```

is invalid. Note that this applies to C-compatible constructs only, and does not include C++-specific behavior (such as pointer-to-derived converting to pointer-to-base).

C's freewheeling pointer conversions are land mines for those porting to C++. If you migrate a nontrivial C program to C++, you will almost certainly run into such type violations. Resist the temptation to treat these errors like demons, casting them away (so to speak). If you find your former C code rife with pointer-conversion errors in C++, consider those errors Distant Early Warnings that your design is vulnerable.

8. main Is not a Normal Function

main's claim to fame (in Spain on the plain) is as the standard program entry point. Otherwise, **main** has no intrinsic magic properties. In fact, in every environment I've seen, **main** is not even the true entry point. Typically, that honor belongs to some low-level routine in the C runtime (for example, *_astart* in Microsoft C). This routine sets up the runtime context, establishes *argc* and *argv*, and calls or jumps to **main**.

Once entered, **main** behaves as any function. Returning from main actually returns to the aforementioned runtime code, which cleans up the context and exits, returning a result code to the caller.

There is nothing to keep you from taking the address of **main**, as in:

```
void *m = &main;
```

This implies calling **main**—although questionable—is perfectly legal.

C++ regards **main** differently, preserving C's **main** syntax as an illusion for compatibility. In reality, C++'s **main** is not a "normal" function, and indeed may not be implemented as a function at all. Thus, in C++, you cannot take the address of **main**, nor can you call **main**.

As an aside, note that C++ giveth, and C++ taketh away. While taking the address of **main** in C++ is illegal, taking the address of a *register* variable, as in:

```
register int x;

int *i = &x;
```

is now legal.

7. Scope

"Identifier scope" is a hazy notion to many C programmers. Indeed, until I wrote a compiler as an undergraduate independent project, I really hadn't appreciated the trouble languages (and compiler writers) went through to permit and enforce scope.

C has the following three scopes:

- ❖ File scope
- ❖ Function scope
- ❖ Block scope

File scope is often called "global" scope, although that term is ambiguous. File scope identifiers appear outside any function body, and are known to the entire translation unit from point-of-declaration onward. They typically appear before any function definitions, either as express declarations, or in header files (see Chapter 20, "Top Ten Hints for Better Living Under ANSI C").

Function scope applies to labels. In the function:

```
void f(void)
   {
```

```
goto LABEL;
while (some_condition)
    if (some_other_condition)
        LABEL:
        ;
goto LABEL;
}
```

LABEL is known throughout the entire function. Unlike file-scoped or block-scoped identifiers, labels can be referenced before they are "seen."

Many C programmers believe function parameters are at function scope, while in fact they are a special (and common) case of *block scope.* That is, in:

```
int main(int argc, char **argv)
    {
    /* ... */
    }
```

argc and *argv* generally have the same scope as if they appeared as:

```
int main(void)
    {
    int argc;
    char **argv;
    /* ... */
    }
```

with the big difference, of course, that the parameters are initialized.
    Continuing this example,

```
extern void *argc;

int main(int argc, char **argv)
    {
    /*
     * in this block — the function body —
     * the global argc is not visible
     */
    if (argc == 1)
        {
        long argc;
        /*
         * here the parameter argc is not visible
```

```
        */
    }
/*
 * here argc refers to the parameter
 */
}
```

shows that block scope identifiers "trump" the same identifier used at an outer scope. Looked at another way, when resolving an identifier, the language looks from the most local scope outward, all the way to file scope.

Now consider the nested blocks in the following:

```
struct S1
    {
    struct S2
        {
        int i;
        } s;
    };

struct S2 x;
```

The definition of *x* appears invalid. No declaration of *struct S2* appears visible. And yet, disturbingly, C allows this. More precisely, in C, the name of a nested structure or union is at the same scope as the enclosing structure or union. For this example, it's as if the code were:

```
struct S2
    {
    int i;
    };

struct S1
    {
    struct S2 s;
    };

struct S2 x;
```

C++ changes this by introducing *class scope*, analogous to block scope. In the original example, when interpreted as C++, *S2* exists only within the scope of *S1*. No *S2* is available at the scope of *x*, and the definition of *x* fails.

Class scope may sound like an obvious and logical extension to C, but it comes at great cost to C++. To accommodate nested classes, the ANSI C++ committee has changed rules governing identifier lookup in general, affecting such seemingly unrelated concepts as inlining and friend functions. These changes took the committee three years of wrangling to produce.

6. Type Name Spaces

In C, type names have the following two name spaces at a given scope:

- ❖ Tag name space (the identifier following keyword *enum, struct,* or *union*)
- ❖ Normal name space (everything else)

This means the same type name can appear in both name spaces simultaneously. So the construct:

```
struct Yin
    {
    int y;
    };

struct Yang /* OK - puts Yang in tag name space */
    {
    int y;
    };

typedef struct Yin Yang; /* OK - puts Yang in normal name space */
```

is legal C—the two definitions of *Yang* are in mutually exclusive name spaces.

In many of Microsoft's header files, a common idiom is

```
typedef struct tagSTRUCTURE
    {
    /* ... */
    } STRUCTURE;
```

where the structure name (existing in the tag name space) is different from the **typedef**ed name. I've never reckoned this, since it doesn't buy anything that I can fathom. The tag name cannot clash with the normal name. I see more sense in a definition such as the following:

```
typedef struct STRUCTURE
    {
    /* ... */
    } STRUCTURE;
```

which is equivalent to:

```
struct STRUCTURE
    {
    /* ... */
    };

typedef struct STRUCTURE STRUCTURE;
```

C++ provides this **typedef** for you automatically. That is, the C++ definition:

```
struct STRUCTURE
    {
    /* ... */
    };
```

immediately allows declarations such as:

```
STRUCTURE s;
```

without the intervening **typedef**. If you provide the **typedef** as shown previously, C++ will accept and ignore it for backward compatibility with C.

This all comes about because C++, unlike C, places tag names in the same name space as other identifiers in the same scope. This strikes me as much more consistent and simple. Certainly I've never figured out the rationale behind C having separate name spaces for these identifiers. I also suspect many C programmers are unaware that these separate name spaces even exist.

Because of this implicit **typedef**ing, and the removal of a separate tag name space, the earlier example:

```
struct Yin
    {
    int y;
    };

struct Yang // OK - puts Yang in normal name space
    {
    int y;
    };

typedef struct Yin Yang; // error - Yang already declared
```

breaks in C++, since all type identifiers at the same scope exist in the same name space.

5. Enumerations

Chapter 17, "Hints for Better Living Under ANSI C," extolled the virtues of enumerations. Enumerations are arguably more beneficial under C++, but that benefit comes at some cost to C compatibility.

For example, the C statements:

```
enum cranial
    {
    olfactory = 1,
    optic,
    oculomotor,
    trochlear,
    trigeminal,
    abducens,
    facial,
    vestibulocochlear,
    glossopharyngeal,
    vagus,
    accessory,
    hypoglossal,
    };
```

```
enum cranial viva_las = vagus;
viva_las++; /* == accessory */
viva_las *= 2; /* == ? */
```

are perfectly legal. In C, enumerations are implicitly of some implementation-defined integral type, so arithmetic operations like ++ are legal. Further, C is silent about out-of-bounds enumerators, so the statement:

```
viva_las *= 2;
```

even though it results in an undefined enumerator mapping, is valid. In this instance, *viva_las* acts like a variable of some "normal" integral type. C, then, does not hold a clear distinction between the "meaning" or symbolism of enumerators and their integral implementation. C programmers often treat enumerators as synonyms for their integral representations, in the same way they treat characters.

In C, enumerations are really some sort of integer that have symbolic names for some values. Integral types always have symbolic values, such as 0, 42L, or -32768. The enumerators are just alternate spellings for those built-in symbols.

Compile this same code in C++, and reality shifts. C++ treats enumerations as distinct types, just as if you had defined a new class. One concession to C practice is that enumerators automatically convert to integral types. They just don't convert from integrals. This is much like pointers automatically converting to *void **, but not the other way around. In both cases, C++ allows conversion from stronger to looser typing.

As you might imagine, then, enumeration types do not automatically support the arithmetic operators. If you want

```
viva_las++;
```

in C++, you need to roll your own ++ operator:

```
cranial operator++(cranial &, int);
```

where the presence of the *int* parameter is a syntactic artifice telling C++ this is the post-increment, not pre-increment, operator.

Alternately, you can cast enumerations to some other type that supports those operators. So, to achieve:

```
viva_las *= 2;
```

you could try casting, as in

```
(int) viva_las *= 2;
```

except C++ doesn't allow it. The cast creates an r-value, while *= demands an l-value. You need an intermediary l-value, such as:

```
int i = viva_las;
i *= 2;
viva_las = (cranial) i;
```

But this puts the enumerator mapping of *viva_las* outside the range of *cranial* enumerators. You are effectively referencing a 20th cranial nerve, which does not exist (much to the relief of nursing students, who have enough trouble conjuring mnemonics to cover 12).

While C silently allows this out-of-bounds condition, C++ renders such behavior undefined—you have no guarantee of what will happen. Even if your compiler allows this, another may not. It's entirely possible the final ANSI C++ standard will define a standard exception to be thrown in this circumstance.

Finally, my admonishment to use anonymous C enumerations as true symbolic constants does not apply so much to C++, which has true PASCAL-like constants. That is, statements such as

```
const int DIMENSION = 10;
```

```
char String[DIMENSION];
```

are now legal, and preferred.

C++ *enum* types are truer to the spirit of enumerations, as a collection of some related symbolic values that, as a secondary effect, map to integral values. In principle, your code should not care to what integral values your enumerators map, or even in what order they appear. If you later resequence or remap your enumerators, and your code suffers ill effects, you may well have questionable assumptions in your code.

Certainly there are some enumerators that have an inherent order (for example, the ubiquitous days of the week), or that must map to some well-defined numeric value (such as bit masks). I posit that those are the exceptions rather than the rule. Take some time to analyze what your enumerations are abstracting, and try to ferret out as much implementation (enumeration-to-integral mapping) dependencies as possible. Your maintainers will thank you.

4. Default Global Constant Linkage

Just this week, I watched this one baffle a colleague. Assume two C files, the first containing

```
char global = 'A'; /* at file scope */
```

and the second:

```
extern char global;

void main(void)
    {
    char local = global;
    }
```

Most C programmers know that the file scope declaration:

```
char global = 'A';
```

is tantamount to:

```
extern char global = 'A';
```

That is, the symbol *global* has external linkage. It is known to the linker, and can be referenced in other translation units. The previous C code compiles and links as you'd expect. If you interpret the code as C++, it still builds and runs correctly.

Now, change the declarations slightly, adding the keyword *const*, so the files are:

```
const char global = 'A'; /* added const keyword */
```

and

```
extern const char global; /* added const keyword */

void main(void)
    {
    char local = global;
    }
```

In C, this first is equivalent to:

```
extern const char c = 'A';
```

and all works as before. But in C++, the link fails. Why?

Turns out that, in C++, *const* names at file scope default to internal linkage. That is, it's as if the first file contained

```
static const char global = 'A';
```

and not

```
extern const char global = 'A';
```

as in C. Thus, there was no *global* to which the second file could link. For this to work in C++, the definition must be explicitly *extern*.

To be honest, I don't know the precise motivation for this one, but I certainly applaud the decision. Personally, I would prefer that all file scope objects—*const* and otherwise—default to internal linkage as a matter of improved encapsulation. Certainly, my coding style discourages public data, whether they be true *public* class members or global variables like these.

In a job I held several years ago, one of my first C maintenance tasks was to track down all *extern* variables that were not supposed to be referenced outside their defining modules, converting those variables to *static.* By the time I finished, I had reduced the linker's symbol table by about one-third, and with it many opportunities for accidental use of symbols across module boundaries.

3. Functions Prototypes and Headings

In C, a function prototype of

```
long DuckDong();
```

says to the compiler "I'm giving you no clue what my parameters are, so just assume whatever usage you first see." That is, the code:

```
long DuckDong();
```

```
/* ... */
```

```
DuckDong(16, "candles");
```

tells the compiler to assume the prototype is really:

```
long DuckDong(int, char *);
```

This is a holdover from the K&R days, when functions had no prototypes (another remnant of C's high-level assembler origin).

In C++, the same function prototype tells the compiler "this function takes no parameters," as if it had been written:

```
long DuckDong(void);
```

Thus, the valid C sequence:

```
long DuckDong();
```

```
/* ... */

DuckDong(16, "candles");
```

generates a compiler error in C++. In C, empty () cannot be interpreted this way. C++ is not beholden to this legacy, and interprets () as other languages do.

In a similar severing of ties to the past, C++ does not allow K&R-vintage function headings. The legal—if obsolescent—C construct:

```
long DuckDong(age, cake_ornament)
    int age;
    char *cake_ornament;
    {
    /* ... */
    }
```

is a no-no in C++.

2. Length of Initialized Character String

Consider the C definition:

```
char array[4] = "1234";
```

This compiles fine, but probably does not yield the desired result, as the string does not have room for the null terminator. Possible corrections are:

```
char array[4] = "123"; /* 1, 2, 3, and null terminator */

char array[5] = "1234"; /* room for 4 digits + null */

char array[] = "1234"; /* automatically sized */
```

In C++, the original definition:

```
char array[4] = "1234";
```

generates a compiler error. The language insists the length of the initializing string, including the null terminator, not exceed the array size.

This prevents a class of off-by-one error all too common in C. Such errors love to manifest as protection violations in Windows. A pointer marching through the string runs off the end (finding no null), into uncharted and eventually enemy territory.

1. Type of Character Literals

Simply put, in C, character literals are of type *int*, implying:

```
sizeof('A') == sizeof(int)
```

In C++, character literals are of type *char*, meaning:

```
sizeof('A') == sizeof(char)
```

In practice, this will have little or no effect on ported C code. The real effect comes in how C++ chooses among overloaded functions. For example, if you have functions declared:

```
void Overload(char); // version 1
```

```
void Overload(int); // version 2
```

the statement:

```
Overload('A');
```

will call version 1.

This is especially important in the stream I/O operators. As C++ is defined, the statement

```
cout << 'A';
```

prints

A

as expected. If character literals were actually of type *int*, the statement would instead somewhat unintuitively print

65

which is the ASCII numeric code for the letter "A." The sequence:

```
cout << 'A' << " " << (int) 'A';
```

shows this.

CHAPTER 21

Features of C++ Shared by Other Common Procedural Languages

I have been a "food weenie" since Day One. If everyone has an Achilles heel, fear of trying new food is surely one of mine. This condition is exacerbated by food zealots, would be Sams-I-Am who swear their particular culinary nostrum will revitalize my palate and banish my taste-test trepidation. Compared to my ancestral Ohio home, these enthusiasts seem more concentrated in Seattle, maybe because food preparation is often done indoors, out of the rain.

This business of being food-challenged reached its zenith while I was living in Sydney, Australia. There I found principally three kinds of restaurants: American fast food, fish and chips, and little ethnic Mom-and-Pop (or there, I suppose, Mum-and-Dad) shops, often run by Asian or European immigrants.

One can only eat so much fast-food mystery meat, or even fresh John Dory, so, over time I ventured into the smaller shops—and beheld a wonder of gastronomical proportions. I discovered that much of this formerly scary food, some of which I couldn't even pronounce, was actually not dangerous at all.

The moral here, then, is that some fears are just irrational and are based less on experience, and more on superstition. As with me and food, for some bizarre reason, C++ scares a fair number of C "linguaphobes." These same programmers, when pressed, may mumble something about "deep call stacks," "weird syntax," "device drivers don't need objects," or maybe even "job security."

C++ is really a Frankenstein's monster, with the ideas of other languages sewn into C's body. I'd like to demystify the language, showing that C++ contains not brand-new ideas, but more a unique combination and expression of ideas learned elsewhere (much like Dave's portion of this book).

10. Default Arguments

C++ example:

```
float CoinValue(unsigned Year = 1804, float Denomination = 1.00);
```

Ada example:

```
function coin_value(year : natural := 1804;
     denomination : float := 1.00) return real;
```

Notes

Don't get carried away with default arguments. Careless callers may inadvertently forget arguments with no complaint from the compiler. This is especially a problem for functions sporting long or convoluted arguments sequences.

Also, remember that constructors with all default arguments act as default constructors, which may not be your intent.

Default arguments are probably best used when those arguments are truly the most natural or common, as in

```
void GetLine(char *Line, char LineTerminator = '\n');
```

9. Modules

C++ example:

```
class Pedantic
    {
    public:
        static unsigned Count;
        static char GetChar(void);
        // ...
    private:
        static int Current;
        // ...
    };
```

Modula 2 example:

```
(*
 * public
 *)

DEFINITION MODULE pedantic;

VAR
    count : CARDINAL;

PROCEDURE get_char : CHAR;

(* ... *)

(*
 * private
 *)
```

```
IMPLEMENTATION MODULE pedantic;

VAR
    current : INTEGER;


(* ... *)
```

Notes

Modules provide encapsulation, and as such, form a necessary (but not suffi-
cient) condition to provide Object Oriented Programming (OOP). In C++, a
module is essentially a class with all static members and no inheritance. This
implies that a module defines not a new type so much as a collection of related
definitions and declarations. You declare objects of a type. You use objects
already declared within a module.

With some programmer discipline, encapsulation is possible in nonmodular
languages. For more information on this, see Chapter 17.

8. Templates

C++ example:

```
//
//  interface and implementation
//
template <class t>
    t BobAndDoug(t Value)
        {
        return Value * 2 + 30;
        }


//
//  instantiation and use
//
int    Coarse = BobAndDoug(20);
```

```
float Fine   = BobAndDoug(19.81);
```

Ada example:

```
--
--  interface
--
generic
    type t is private;
    function bob_and_doug(value : t) return t;


--
--  implementation
--
function bob_and_doug(value : t) return t is
    begin
    return value * 2 + 30;
    end bob_and_doug;


--
--  instantiation
--
function fahrenheit is new bob_and_doug(integer);
function fahrenheit is new bob_ nd_doug(float);


--
--  use
--
coarse : integer := fahrenheit(20);
fine   : float   := fahrenheit(19.81);
```

Notes

Seemingly every major feature added to ANSI C++ wrestles with scope or type ambiguities. Templates are certainly no exception. Judging from the missives on *comp.std.c++*, many programmers are wandering lost in the template desert.

As an example, consider

```
template <class t>
    class Quanta
```

```
    {
    void Reality(long z);
    void Reality(t z);
    };
```

If *t* is instantiated to *long* by way of

```
    Quanta<long> DocBrown;
```

the class instance, in effect, becomes

```
class Quanta
    {
    void Reality(long z);
    void Reality(long z); // t instantiated to long
    };
```

Which *Reality* does *DocBrown* use?

Templates are relatively new to C++, and are not yet widely implemented. MSVC 1.x does not directly support templates. It does have a pseudo-template mechanism by way of macros, using techniques much like those described in Chapter 17. MSVC 2.0 will support templates directly (although certain template-like features, such as RTTI, will be unavailable).

7. Constants

C++ example:

```
const int CONCERT_A = 440;
```

Pascal example:

```
const
    concert_a = 440;
```

Notes

See the discussion on enumerations in Chapter 17 for the rationale supporting true compile-time symbolic constants.

In C++, symbolic constants can be used in almost every context supporting literal constants. The glaring exceptions are preprocessor directives, especially conditional compilation. Otherwise, symbolic constants obviate the need for "magic numbers" and macro pseudo-constants.

In fact, a growing sentiment within the C++ community (and within the ANSI C++ committee) is that the preprocessor is Evil Incarnate. I wouldn't be terribly surprised if, by the time a standard spews forth, the preprocessor is mostly or completely replaced by C++ language constructs.

6. Function and Operator Overloading

C++ example:

```
struct Thingo
    {
    //
    // ...
    //
    };

void Put(int i);
void Put(Thingo t);

Thingo operator +(Thingo t, int i);

void Test(Thingo t)
    {
    Put(t + 3); // alternative is Put(operator +(t, 3));
    }
```

Ada example:

```
type thingo is
   record
      _
      _...
      _
   end record;

procedure put(i : integer);
procedure put(t : thingo);

procedure "+"(t : thingo; i : integer) return thingo;

procedure test(t : thingo) is
   begin
   put(t + 3);—alternative is put("+"(t, 3));
   end test;
```

Notes

Operator overloading may be the single feature most seductive to C programmers new to C++. I've heard that C++ is a lens, making good programmers look better and bad programmers look worse. Use of operator overloading certainly supports this maxim. I discuss this again in Chapter 22, "Reasons not to Migrate from C to C++."

5. Pass by Reference

C++ example:

```
void PhilosophersStone(Element Lead, Element &Gold);
```

Pascal example:

```
procedure philosophers_stone(lead : element; var gold : element);
```

Notes

The route you take to reach C++ heavily influences your attitude toward reference parameters. Programmers steeped in the lore of Pascal and its progeny find references natural. Conversely, C programmers find references confusing, since the C statement

```
PhilosophersStone(Lead, Gold);
```

does not return a changed value of *Gold*. The C paradigm, of course, is

```
PhilosophersStone(Lead, &Gold);
```

calling a function prototyped

```
PhilosophersStone(Element, Element *);
```

If *Element* is some large data structure, performance-minded C programmers would opt for

```
PhilosophersStone(&Lead, &Gold);
```

calling

```
PhilosophersStone(Element *, Element *);
```

Drawbacks of this pointer mechanism include

- ❖ *PhilosophersStone* implementation and callers must use syntactically messier pointer notation.
- ❖ Pointer implementation is betrayed to all callers, subverting abstraction.
- ❖ *Elements* always must be passed by address. If *PhilosophersStone* later changes to pass Elements by value or reference, all code calling *PhilosophersStone,* and the *PhilosophersStone* implementation itself, must be rewritten.

Corresponding benefits of references include

- ❖ *PhilosophersStone* implementation and callers use cleaner by-value notation.

- ❖ *PhilosophersStone* implementation uses *Elements* within the problem domain, not within the solution domain. That is, *Elements* are accessed as their abstract values, not by way of their pointer mechanics.

- ❖ Callers do not always know (or care) that *Elements* are passed by reference. From the caller's point of view, all *Elements* appear to be passed by value. If any of them later changes from reference to value (or visa versa), only the function prototype changes. This lets the *PhilosophersStone* implementor decide on the best passing mechanism without affecting other code.

Here we have one of those places where C++ simply is not C, and should not be held hostage to C's legacy. Other than the confusion instilled in C programmers, reference parameters afford too many advantages over pointer parameters. On the whole, I find the scales tip in favor of references.

This generality is not without exception. In particular, C programmers new to C++, and C++ programmers writing code to be read by C programmers, may want to favor pointers over references.

C++ contains many places where the assumptions and conventions of C programs and programmers are obsolete. I devote an entire list to this subject in Chapter 20, "Ways C++ is not C."

4. Exceptions

C++ example:

```
void ExceptionDemo()
    {
    enum Exception
        {
        GAME_OVER_MAN,
```

```
        HAIL_MARY,
        };
    try
        {
        if (AliensRunningAmuck)
            throw GAME_OVER_MAN;
        else if (FourthAndLong)
            throw HAIL_MARY;
        else
            {
            // ...
            }
        }
    catch (Exception Code)
        {
        switch (Code)
            {
            case GAME_OVER_MAN:
                // ...
                break;
            case HAIL_MARY:
                // ...
                break;
            default:
                // ...
                break;
            }
        }
    }
```

Ada example:

```
procedure exception_demo is
    begin
    game_over_man, hail_mary : exception;
    if aliens_running_amuck then
        raise game_over_man
    elsif fourth_and_long
        raise hail_mary
    else
        -...
    end if;
    exception
        when game_over_man =>
            -...
        when hail_mary =>
```

```
        -...
    when others =>
        -...
end exception_demo;
```

Notes

Exceptions are still evolving. That there will be terminating exceptions in
C++ is almost assured, as is their mechanism. Finer points (for example,
behavior within constructors/destructors or a set of predefined exceptions)
are still in limbo.

MSVC 1.0 tries to fake exceptions with macros, but the result is little better
than *setjmp* and *longjmp*. In particular, these macros don't invoke destructors as
they unwind through the call stack. They also require MFC.

MSVC 2.0 implements exceptions according to the emerging ANSI C++
standard.

3. String Type

C++ example:

```
//
// type definition
//
class String
    {
    public:
        friend String operator+(const String&, const String&);
        String(const String&);
        String(const char *);
        // ...
    };


//
// object declaration and use
//
String a ("Marco");
String b ("Polo");
```

```
String c (a + " " + b);
```

BASIC example:

```
REM
REM      type definition implicit in language
REM
REM      object declaration implicit with first use
REM

A$ = "Marco"
B$ = "Polo"
C$ = A$ + " " + B
```

Notes

As much as "real" programmers may pooh-pooh it, BASIC actually runs rings around C in the world of string handling. C has no notion of an innate string type or string operations. Library functions such as **strcat** are poor substitutes.

Interestingly, where it is weak with strings of characters, C is actually quite capable with characters themselves, permitting freedom I haven't found in other languages. Sometimes that freedom can be misapplied (see Chapter 18, "Things not to Assume About Your C Environment"). However, that freedom also lets C distinguish the compile-time character set from the runtime character set. Thus, programs written in single-byte ASCII characters can manipulate wide or multibyte characters.

Unfortunately, many C programmers have a hard-coded notion of what constitutes a character string, confusing the abstract notion of a string with the traditional physical implementation (a zero-terminated array of single bytes). The standard library assumes this, but there's no organic reason why strings cannot, for example, be implemented with an encoded length, or with multibyte characters.

C++ improves on C dramatically here, by allowing for string classes that can look built-in. Such classes permit silent migration among different physical implementations, often with an escape valve to transmogrify abstract strings

725

to/from C's notion of strings. This satisfies the C++ longhairs, who want to view strings as closer to their natural-language abstraction, and the C crowd who see *string* and subconsciously think *char **.

2. Complex Type

C++ example:

```
//
//  type definition
//
class Complex
    {
    public:
        friend Complex operator+(const Complex&, const Complex&);
        Complex(const Complex&);
        Complex(float, float);
        // ...
    };


//
//  object declaration and use
//
Complex a (-1., 0.);
Complex b (3.1416, 2.7183);
Complex c (a + b);
```

FORTRAN example:

```
C
C    TYPE DEFINITION IMPLICIT IN LANGUAGE
C
C    OBJECT DECLARATION
C
     COMPLEX A, B, C
C
C    OBJECT USE
C
     A = (-1., 0.)
     B = (3.1416, 2.7183)
     C = A + B
```

Notes

A friend of mine worked as an engineer for the government. Many of his colleagues programmed in FORTRAN, even when C became a superior tool for their jobs. Their rationale was that C lacked a built-in complex data type. Add-on libraries with functions such as **complex_add** and so on just didn't appease them. I will have to ask him what these same people would say to a C++ complex class that looks completely built-in.

A beauty of classes is the ability to let C++ adopt cherished features of other languages. More than syntactic sugar, more than a glorified runtime library, a class such as *complex* makes the language truly extensible. In almost every sense, it is as if C++ can understand complex numbers as viscerally as it does integers.

(Note that as this is written, the ANSI C++ committee have just added type *complex* to their proposed standard library.)

1. Loop-Scope Variables

C++ example:

```
for (unsigned i = 0; i < 10; i++)
    {
    //
    //  i is available here
    //
    }

//
//  i is not available here
//

for (int i = 100; i > 0; i-)
    {
    //
    //  i is distinct from i in loop above
    //
    }
```

Ada example:

```
for i in 0..9 loop
   --
   -- i is available here
   --
   end loop;


--
-- i is not available here
--

for i in reverse 100..1 loop
   --
   -- i is distinct from i in loop above
   --
   end loop;
```

Notes

More properly, this feature allows object declarations within the controlling condition of

- *for*
- *if*
- *switch*
- *while*

and scopes those objects to the statement controlled by the condition. This permits constructs such as

```
switch (char c = getchar())
    {
    // can use c here
    }
// can't use c here
```

A long-overdue enhancement to C++, condition-scope variables were recently added to ANSI C++. They are not supported in MSVC 1.0, and may not be in MSVC 2.0.

The previous *for*-loop example is functionally equivalent to

```
{
unsigned i;
for (i = 0; i < 10; i++)
    {
    // ...
    }
}


{
int i;
for (i = 100; i > 0; i-)
    {
    // ...
    }
}
```

as discussed in Chapter 17.

Chapter 22

Reasons not to Migrate from C to C++

C++ is not absolutely, self-evidently, the one true way in all contexts. Indeed, the emerging ANSI C++ has detractors even amongst its creators. Karmic winds blow upon C++ as surely as they blow upon C, sometimes even more strongly. The language, while certainly solving many of C's limitations and ambiguities, does create problems of its own, problems any serious adopter must consider.

10. No Standard

C++ is a beta language. If any vendor in the world today implements ANSI C++, it's complete serendipity, for that language does not exist. The moment a vendor introduces a compiler, that compiler is guaranteed to be, in part, obsolete, for the language will have changed before the compiler can reach market. Compilers do not sprout from Zeus' forehead fully mature. Any serious C++ compiler is years in gestation.

Every vendor, then, implements a language that I call C± (read "C plus or minus"). C± is not a subset of C++, since each vendor undoubtedly has features that won't appear in the final language. When you select an implementation, you are really selecting that implementation's variation of C±. You risk breaking your code when porting it to another implementation.

This porting hazard is certainly true even in C, where implementation-defined behavior is rampant. However, at least the parts of the C language deigned immutable are the same for all vendors. No such pact exists in C++, and each vendor is free to predict what it believes the final language will be.

If the ANSI C process is any indication, the language will largely stabilize before the standard is actually published. Until then, I recommend you consider the Annotated Reference Manual (ARM) and the ANSI C standard as your guides. If you are serious about porting, I also recommend you keep abreast of the changes in the ANSI Working Paper.

For now, take a union of the ARM and the ANSI C standard to create a prototype ANSI C++ language standard. If you are more adventuresome, I further recommend you study the writings of ANSI committee members, both official (the Working Paper) and unofficial (for example, articles in *The Journal of C Language Translation*).

Fortunately, the pace of C++ language change has slowed, so that a reasonable set of language features almost certain to make the final cut are now implemented by all the major vendors.

9. Fewer Vendors

I suspect one reason C became the dominant programming language in the 1980s is that enough credible C compiler vendors ported C from UNIX to MS-DOS—so many, in fact, that for a time I expected to start finding C compiler disks given away in cereal boxes. Perusal of any programming magazine back then yielded a glut of C compilers for MS-DOS. Those compilers—their vendors perhaps inspired by Borland's Turbo PASCAL from years before—were both cheap and powerful, enough for any C-literate programmer to churn out shareware, or for a startup to fill in some niche in the software ecosystem.

Such a compiler plethora does not exist today. Compared to C, C++ is a much more difficult language for compiler vendors to implement. It's not a language easily knocked off in someone's spare time, or as a graduate project. C++ compilers are expensive to produce, test, and support, so the number of serious vendors is small (about half a dozen for MS-DOS).

Unlike the pre-ANSI days of C, there is no *de facto* "standard" library universally supported by pre-ANSI C++ vendors. In the old days, C impelementors provided a variant of the UNIX C libraries. Today, most all C++ vendors typically support the ANSI C libraries, plus some *iostream* class. Beyond that, you must use a particular vendor's class library. If you try to port your C++ code to another implementation, you face a possible major code rewrite.

8. Doesn't Do Windows

Windows was created long ago, when C ruled the roost. This heritage sometimes renders C++ code frustrating for Windows programmers, and is most apparent in exported functions.

Windows does not provide a *this* pointer when invoking user-defined callback functions. Thus, such exported functions must be defined as static members, limiting their utility. Further, C++ functions are often represented to the linker in "mangled" form, so that what looks like f in C++ source appears as something like *?f@@ZAXXZ* when exported by the linker. Exporting this name as something friendly, like the desired *f*, requires surgery with .MAP and .DEF files.

Some C++ programmers throw in the towel here, and wrap these functions in:

```
extern "C"
    {
// C++ function here
    }
```

so the function is defined as if it were written in C. Such functions gain ease of Windows use at the cost of class membership and other C++ niceties.

Windows is also not designed to export objects and classes. This precludes DLLs acting as true runtime objects. Microsoft recognizes this limitation. Microsoft's Component Object Model (COM) largely fixes this, expanding C++'s static typing within a single runtime unit to COM dynamic typing within multiple runtime units. C++ actually maps much better to COM than does C. As Microsoft pushes COM as its new standard interface (and MFC as it's standard implementation), I expect C++ to replace C as the Windows language of choice.

7. Fewer Programmers

There are many C programmers in the world, and I'd reckon many of them have no current plans to learn C++. Before you can stage a play, you'd best be certain you can cast actors to fill the roles. Similarly, before embarking on a C++ migration, make sure that you can find programmers willing and able to make that migration along with your code.

ANSI or near-ANSI C compilers have existed on MS-DOS for almost a decade now, and along with them a mature C programmer community. C++ is young, and introduces new concepts. It will be some years before the C++ community reaches the levels the general C community occupies today.

Part of that lag comes from "programmer inertia." Many programmers wear C like an old pair of jeans—the fit may be tight in some places, loose in others, there may be inconvenient or embarrassing holes, there are some wrinkles that never come out. Overall, however, the jeans are familiar and comfortable, their weaknesses known and accommodated, even loved. Programmers are loathe to discard these C jeans for what they see as a C++ leisure suit, theoretically more versatile but stylistically an abomination.

Most programmers I know are less inclined (than is the general population) to adopt a new way simply because someone tells them it's better. Certainly, an OOPS zealot, eager to show all backward C programmers the proverbial C++ light, are among the worst to persuade die-hard C programmers to join the fold.

So many C programmers have become ensconced in the "C way" that they are reluctant to plunge into the C++ depths, lest they suffer the programming analogue of nitrogen narcosis. I submit the way to coax C programmers into the C++ realm is not through the OOPS hard sell. In fact, I'd recommend keeping your OOPS denizens far away from C programmers making first steps toward C++.

6. Less Help

Even if you overcome the technology and talent shortage, you are still left with a dearth of help, to wit:

- Check out your local software book seller, and compare the number of C titles to C++ titles, for both books and periodicals.
- Call your vendor's technical support line, and compare the levels of C and C++ programming support. Because each C++ implementation is quite vendor-specific, and because third parties have not filled the void, you will unfortunately be relying more on your vendor for advice in areas it may be less equipped to understand.
- Compare Usenet newsgroups like *comp.lang.c* to *comp.lang.c++*, and see which offers more answers than questions.

Although the C++ community is growing, there remain many more acolytes than masters. My feeling is that most true masters live amongst the ANSI committee denizens, although even they do not always agree on what the language is, let alone what it should or will be.

5. Fodder for Language Lawyers

Speaking of Usenet, another unfortunate effect is that the programming newsgroups brings the C++ language lawyers out of hiding. *comp.std.c++* in particular is rife with C++ fundamentalists, quoting chapter and verse from the ARM. This often shows little compelling about the language, and more about the inconsistencies and ambiguities in the ARM.

Other frequent Usenet flyers are C++ Sherlocks, looking for clues by comparing different vendor's behavior compiling and running the most arcane and useless C++ code. These discussions have an amazingly high noise-to-signal ratio, often only stopping when one of the Founders steps in to proclaim a Truth, quieting the masses for a time.

If you are unfamiliar with C++, I urge you not to evaluate the language based on these postings. These people often pontificate on the language fringes, areas that are often either known to be perilous, or require an obtuse design that no sane program could pass through a code inspection anyway.

4. Possible Error Explosion

The relative merits of C and C++ change when migrating existing code, as compared to writing a project from scratch. What is perfectly legal C may explode with errors when ported to C++. Much of this comes from the tightened type safety, especially regarding pointers and *const*.

You may find that the headache of intelligently redesigning around the errors, and then avoiding more errors as the code is transformed to classes, trumps the gain of migrating existing C code to C++. Indeed, even something as simple as adding a few *consts* within an existing C++ project can cause this explosion.

3. C++ Wolf in C's Sheep Clothing

As expounded upon in Chapter 20, "Ways C++ Is not C," that a C++ compiler can ingest C code is, in some sense, an illusion. The compiler doesn't understand C, but rather a C++ subset that happens to also compile as C. The temptation to evaluate all C++ code that "looks like C" as if it were C can lead to unpleasant surprises.

Seasoned C programmers are familiar enough with the C language that they abstract away language details and make sweeping assumptions when reading and evaluating code. These same heuristics can lead to incorrect conclusions when applied to C++, especially for code that varies subtly from C. Put another way, not all code that looks like C acts like C.

Consider the following C code:

```
struct S
    {
    int i;
    };

void f(void)
    {
    struct S s;
    }
```

MSVC, compiling the function as C, generates code such as:

```
; void f(void)
;     {
_f:
    mov     ax,ss
    push    bp
    mov     bp,sp
    sub     sp,OFFSET L00104
    push    si
    push    di
    push    ds
    mov     ds,ax
; s = fffc
;     struct S s;
;     }
    pop     ds
    pop     di
    pop     si
    mov     sp,bp
    pop     bp
    ret     OFFSET 0
; Local Size: 4
```

where the only effect of the declaration:

```
struct S s;
```

is to reserve space on the stack frame for *s*. Experienced C programmers know this, and expect the only side effect of defining a automatic variable is that the compiler reserves space for it. Indeed, with optimization (turned off for this example), that space may not even be reserved, if the variable (as in this case) is not actually used.

Compiling this code as C++ yields essentially the same result. In either case, typically the definition of *struct S* would be on a header file, which doesn't affect the generated code.

Now assume this code is, in fact, ported to C++, and that at some future time the *struct S* definition requires a default constructor and destructor different from that provided by the library. The header would then be:

```
struct S
    {
    int i;
    S();
    ~S();
    };
```

while the function:

```
void f(void)
    {
    struct S s;
    }
```

stays the same. A C programmer, looking only at the function, may not be aware anything has changed. Indeed, in C, the only effect changing *struct S* can have on *f* is to change the stack space reserved for *s* in the generated code. Making this same assumption for C++ would be disastrous, for the actual code generated is now:

```
; void f(void)
;     {
?f@@ZAXXZ:
    mov     ax,ss
    push    bp
    mov     bp,sp
    sub     sp,OFFSET L00351
    push    si
    push    di
```

```
    push    ds
    mov     ds,ax
; s = fffc
;     struct S s;
    lea     ax,WORD PTR -4[bp]
    mov     dx,ss
    push    dx
    push    ax
    call    FAR PTR ??0S@@REC@XZ
;     }
    lea     ax,WORD PTR -4[bp]
    mov     dx,ss
    push    dx
    push    ax
    call    FAR PTR ??1S[BULLET]REC@XZ
    jmp     L00349
;
    pop     ds
    pop     di
    pop     si
    mov     sp,bp
    pop     bp
    ret     OFFSET 0
; Local Size: 4
```

What had been a simple stack frame adjustment now blooms to include two function calls (constructor and destructor), complete with pushed parameters (the C++ *this* pointer). Further, each of those functions may in turn implicitly call other constructors and destructors, resulting in more nested function calls.

In fact, within complex class hierarchies and aggregations, the opening { in a constructor can result in a torrent of function calls, as each member object, and some base objects, are themselves constructed. Even such innocent statements as:

```
a = b + c;
```

can result in several function calls, including construction and destruction of temporary objects. This again is not necessarily obvious to even experienced C programmers.

Here C++ has become a victim of C's success. C programmers look at C source, and often subconsciously see the generated machine code. They expect that certain C constructs behave predictably in all contexts, and extrapolate that expectation to another language that happens to look the same. Some days I think C++ would be better off if it were syntactically disjoint from C, so that no C program would compile as C++. At least then C programmers would start from zero, rather than sometimes starting from negative as then unlearn their C wisdom.

2. Concepts that Tempt and Overwhelm the Novice

C++ is a complex tool, and like any such tool, requires that newcomers start slowly, working with simple and safe features until acquiring enough mastery to move on to more challenging and potentially hazardous aspects. Without this discipline, it becomes tempting to see every programming problem as an OOPs nail requiring full-on C++ hammering.

C programmers new to C++ often hear C++'s Siren call, luring them to crash upon the programmatic rocks of over-engineered and inefficient code. These Sirens include

- Implicit conversions
- Operator overloading
- Templates
- Inheritance (especially multiple inheritance).

While these concepts most certainly have their uses, they are foreign to C, and require thinking and design often outside the bounds inhabited by C programmers. It's a not a matter of C programmers not being "smart" enough to write in C++. Every C++ programmer I know (myself included) learned C first, years ago. It's more realizing that C++ is powerful, much more so than C, and therefore requires a measure of respect. When applied deliberately and intentionally, that power can create elegant and maintainable solutions impossible in C. Misapplied, that same power can render code useless, riddled with near-invisible bugs, subtle yet systemic design flaws, and great inefficiency.

1. C++ May Be too Much Fun

If you are a programming ascetic, then don't migrate to C++—you might have too much fun, and risk karmic ruination.

After returning to the United States from Australia, I spent most of a year on "sabbatical" (read "unemployed") while sorting out some personal details. The prospect of resuming a programming career seemed offputting somehow, and I toyed seriously with a change in career path. Ultimately, my then-wife's desire to finish school—requiring a somewhat predictable income—compelled me to re-enlist as a programmer.

At the time, I expected to be writing in C. My first assignment, however, was a C++ project. During the first couple months of learning the language and the project, I found my programming fires rekindled by the expressive possibilities of this new language. I have since found others sharing this experience, discovering that, at its root, C++ is often just plain more fun than C ever was.

I'm not sure why this is, although I have suspicions. Most experienced programmers I know harbor the notion of creating their own language, or at least modifying an existing language. C++ all but allows this. Through classes and operators, you can extend the language in ways that look almost built-in.

I also believe OOPs, in general, maps to both our external physical world experiences, and internal imaginations, much more closely than does C, so much that the veil between the problem domain (what we are trying to model) and the solution domain (how we model it in a program) is often quite thin.

Finally, for those of us who nursemaid projects over years, and watch contractors working on those projects come and go, it's warming to have a software technology that encourages code maintenance. This is a realization I came to fairly late in the game, that C++ code that serves short-term goals often serves long-term maintenance goals as well.

INDEX

About the Disk

The disk in the back of the book contains the listings for all of the major programming listings in the book. To unzip the file and preserve the directory structure that the file was created with, use the PKUNZIP program with the -d switch:

PKUNZIP -d TOPTEN.ZIP

This switch will preserve the directory structure and make the appropriate subdirectories where necessary.